Alan Rogers

CW01658792

Alan Rogers

France

Quality camping & caravanning sites

INSPECTED & SELECTED CAMPSITES

Compiled by: Alan Rogers Guides Ltd

Designed by: Paul Effenberg, Vine Design Ltd

Maps created by Customised Mapping (01769 560101)
contain background data provided by GisDATA Ltd

Published by: Alan Rogers Guides Ltd,
Spelmonden Old Oast, Goudhurst, Kent TN17 1HE
www.alanrogers.com Tel: 01580 214000

British Library Cataloguing-in-Publication Data:
A catalogue record for this book is available from the British Library.

ISBN: 0-9545271-2-7

Printed in Great Britain by J H Haynes & Co Ltd

CONTENTS

the Alan Rogers approach

IT IS NEARLY 40 YEARS SINCE ALAN ROGERS PUBLISHED THE FIRST CAMPSITE GUIDE THAT BORE HIS NAME. SINCE THEN THE RANGE HAS EXPANDED TO SIX TITLES WITH GUIDES TO ITALY AND SPAIN & PORTUGAL ADDED IN 2004, AND A NEW GUIDE TO CENTRAL EUROPE AND CROATIA FOR THIS YEAR. WHAT'S MORE, ALAN ROGERS GUIDES HAVE BECOME ESTABLISHED IN HOLLAND TOO: ALL SIX TITLES ARE ALSO AVAILABLE IN THE NETHERLANDS, STOCKED BY WELL OVER 90% OF ALL DUTCH BOOKSHOPS.

There are over 11,000 campsites in France of varying quality: this guide contains impartially written reports on over 580, including some of the very finest, each being individually inspected and selected. All the usual maps and indexes are also included, designed to help you find the choice of campsite that's right for you. We hope you enjoy some happy and safe travels – and some pleasurable 'armchair touring' in the meantime!

INDEPENDENT AND HONEST

Whilst the content and scope of the Alan Rogers guides have expanded considerably since the early editions, our selection of campsites still employs exactly the same philosophy and criteria as defined by Alan Rogers in 1968.

'warts and all'

Firstly, and most importantly, our selection is based entirely on our own rigorous and independent inspection and selection process. Campsites cannot buy their way into our guides – indeed the extensive Site Report which is written by us, not by the site owner, is provided free of charge so we are free to say what we think and to provide an honest, 'warts and all' description. This is written in plain English and without the use of confusing icons or symbols.

" ...the campsites included in this book have been chosen entirely on merit, and no payment of any sort is made by them for their inclusion."

Alan Rogers, 1968

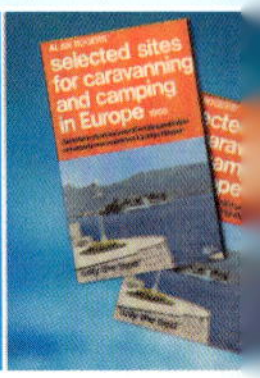

INSPECTED SINCE 1968 & SELECTED

A question of quality

The criteria we use when inspecting and selecting sites are numerous, but the most important by far is the question of good quality. People want different things from their choice of campsite so we try to include a range of campsite 'styles' to cater for a wide variety of preferences: from those seeking a small peaceful campsite in the heart of the countryside, to visitors looking for an 'all singing, all dancing' site in a popular seaside resort. Those with more specific interests, such as sporting facilities, cultural events or historical attractions, are also catered for.

The size of the site, whether it's part of a campsite chain or privately owned, makes no difference in terms of it being required to meet our exacting standards in respect of its quality and it being 'fit for purpose'. In other words, irrespective of the size of the site, or the number of facilities it offers, the essentials (the welcome, the pitches, the sanitary facilities, the cleanliness and the general maintenance) must all be of a high standard.

Expert opinions

We rely on our dedicated team of Site Assessors, all of whom are experienced campers, caravanners or motorcaravanners, to visit and recommend sites. Each year they travel some 100,000 miles around Europe inspecting new campsites and re-inspecting the older ones. Our thanks are due to them for their enthusiastic efforts, their diligence and integrity and their commitment to the philosophy of the Alan Rogers Guides.

We also appreciate the feedback we receive from many of our readers and we always make a point of following up complaints, suggestions or recommendations for possible new sites. Of course we get a few grumbles too – but it really is a few, and those we do receive usually arrive at the end of the high season and relate mainly to overcrowding or to poor maintenance during the peak school holiday period.

Please bear in mind that although we are interested to hear about any complaints we have no contractual relationship with the campsites featured in our guides and are therefore not in a position to intervene in any dispute between a reader and a campsite. If you have a complaint about a campsite featured in our guides the first step should be to take the matter up with the site owner or manager whilst on the campsite.

Widely regarded as the 'Bible' by site owners and readers alike, there is no better guide when it comes to forming an independent view of a campsite's quality. When you need to be confident in your choice of campsite, you need the Alan Rogers Guide.

- ✔ Sites only included on merit
- ✔ Sites cannot pay to be included
- ✔ Independently inspected, rigorously assessed
- ✔ Impartial reviews
- ✔ 36 years of expertise

INSPECTED & SELECTED CAMPSITES

Being written in plain English, our guides are exceptionally easy to use, but a few words of explanation regarding the layout and content may be helpful. Regular readers will see that our site reports are grouped into 19 'tourist regions' and then by the various départements in each of these regions in numerical order.

Regions and départements

For administrative purposes France is actually divided into 23 official regions covering the 95 départements (similar to our counties). However, these do not always coincide with the needs of tourists. For example the area we think of as the Dordogne is split between two of the official regions. We have, therefore, opted to feature our campsites within unofficial 'tourist regions', and the relevant départements are stated in our introduction to each region with their official number (eg. the département of Manche is number 50) included. We use these département numbers as the first two digits of our campsite numbers, so any campsite in the Manche département will start with the number 50.

Indexes

Our three indexes allow you to find sites by site number and name, by region and site name or by the town or village where the site is situated.

Campsite Maps

The maps relate to our tourist regions and will help you to identify the approximate position of each campsite.

Region

The Site Reports – *Example of an entry*

Site no Site name

Postal Address (including département)

A description of the site in which we try to give an idea of its general features – its size, its situation, its strengths and its weaknesses. This column should provide a picture of the site itself with reference to the facilities that are provided and if they impact on its appearance or character. We include details on pitch numbers, electricity (with amperage), hardstandings etc. in this section as pitch design, planning and terracing affects the site's overall appearance. Similarly we continue to include reference to pitches used for caravan holiday homes, chalets, and the like. Importantly at the end of this column we indicate if there are any restrictions, e.g. no tents, naturist sites.

Facilities

Lists more specific information on the site's facilities, as well as certain off site attractions and activities.

At a glance

Welcome & Ambience	✓✓✓✓	Location	✓✓✓✓✓
Quality of Pitches	✓✓✓✓✓	Range of Facilities	✓✓✓✓

Our inspectors grade each site out of five, giving a unique indication of certain key criteria that may be important when making your decision.

Directions

Separated from the main text in order that they may be read and assimilated more easily by a navigator en-route. Bear in mind that road improvement schemes can result in some road numbers being altered. Websites like **www.mappy.com** and others give detailed route plans.

Charges 2005

Reservations

including contact details

Open

Site opening dates.

Facilities

Toilet blocks: We assume that toilet blocks will be equipped with at least some British style WCs, washbasins with hot and cold water and hot showers with dividers or curtains, and will have all necessary shelves, hooks, plugs and mirrors. We also assume that there will be an identified chemical toilet disposal point, and that the campsite will provide water and waste water points and bin areas. If not the case, we comment. We continue to mention certain features that some readers find important: washbasins in cubicles, facilities for babies, facilities for those with disabilities and motorcaravan service points. Readers with disabilities are advised to contact the site of their choice to ensure that facilities are appropriate to their needs.

Shop: Basic or fully supplied, and opening dates.

Bars, restaurants, takeaway facilities and entertainment: We try hard to supply opening and closing dates (if other than the campsite opening dates) and to identify if there are discos or other noisy entertainment.

Children's play areas: Fenced and with safety surface (e.g. sand, bark or pea-gravel).

Swimming pools: If particularly special, we cover in detail in the first column but reference is always included in the second column. Opening dates, charges and levels of supervision are provided where we have been notified. There is a regulation whereby Bermuda shorts may not be worn in swimming pools (for health reasons). It is worth ensuring that you do take 'proper' swimming trunks with you.

Leisure facilities: E.g. playing fields, bicycle hire, organised activities and entertainment.

Dogs: If dogs are not accepted or restrictions apply, we state it here. Check the quick reference list at the back of the guide.

Off site: This briefly covers leisure facilities, tourist attractions, restaurants etc nearby. Geographical tourist information is more likely to be in the first column.

At a glance: All Alan Rogers sites have been inspected and selected – they must meet stringent quality criteria. A campsite may have all the boxes ticked when it comes to listing facilities but if it's not inherently a 'good site' then it will not be in the guide.

These 'at a glance' ratings are a unique indication of certain key criteria that may be important when making your decision. Quite deliberately they are subjective and, modesty aside, are based on our inspectors' own expert opinions at the time of their inspection.

Charges: These are the latest provided by the parks. In those few cases where 2004 or 2005 prices are not given, we try to give a general guide.

Telephone numbers: All numbers assume that you are phoning from within France. To phone France from outside that country, prefix the number shown with the relevant International Code (00 33) and drop the first 0, shown as (0) in the numbers indicated.

Opening dates: Are those advised to us during the early autumn of the previous year – sites can, and sometimes do, alter these dates before the start of the following season, often for good reasons. If you intend to visit shortly after a published opening date, or shortly before the closing date, it is wise to check that it will actually be open at the time required. Similarly some parks operate a restricted service during the low season, only opening some of their facilities (e.g. swimming pools) during the main season; where we know about this, and have the relevant dates, we indicate it – again if you are at all doubtful it is wise to check.

Reservations: Necessary for high season (roughly mid-July to mid-August) in popular holiday areas (ie beach resorts). You can reserve via our own Alan Rogers Travel Service or through tour operators. Or be wholly independent and contact the campsite(s) of your choice direct, using the phone or e-mail numbers shown in the site reports, but please bear in mind that many sites are closed all winter.

Our Accommodation Section

Over recent years, more and more campsites have added high quality mobile home and chalet accommodation. In response to feedback from many of our readers, and to reflect this evolution in campsites, we have now decided to include a separate section on mobile homes and chalets.

We have chosen a number of sites offering some of the best accommodation available and have included full details of one or two accommodation types at these sites. Please note however that many other campsites listed in this guide may also have a selection of accommodation for rent.

Points to bear in mind

Some French site owners are very laid back when it comes to opening and closing dates. They may not be fully ready by their stated opening date – grass and hedges may not all be cut or perhaps only limited sanitary facilities open. At the end of the season they also tend to close down some facilities and generally wind down prior to the closing date. Bear this in mind if you are travelling early or late in the season – it is worth phoning ahead.

The Camping Cheque low season touring system goes some way to addressing this in that participating campsites are encouraged to have all facilities open and running by the opening date and to remain fully operational until the closing date.

Whether you're an 'old hand' in terms of camping and caravanning or are contemplating your first trip, a regular reader of our Guides or a new 'convert', we wish you well in your travels and hope we have been able to help in some way. We are, of course, also out and about ourselves, visiting sites, talking to owners and readers, and generally checking on standards and new developments.

We wish all our readers thoroughly enjoyable Camping and Caravanning in 2005 – favoured by good weather of course! **The Alan Rogers Team**

VALUE, VALUE, VALUE

service and value

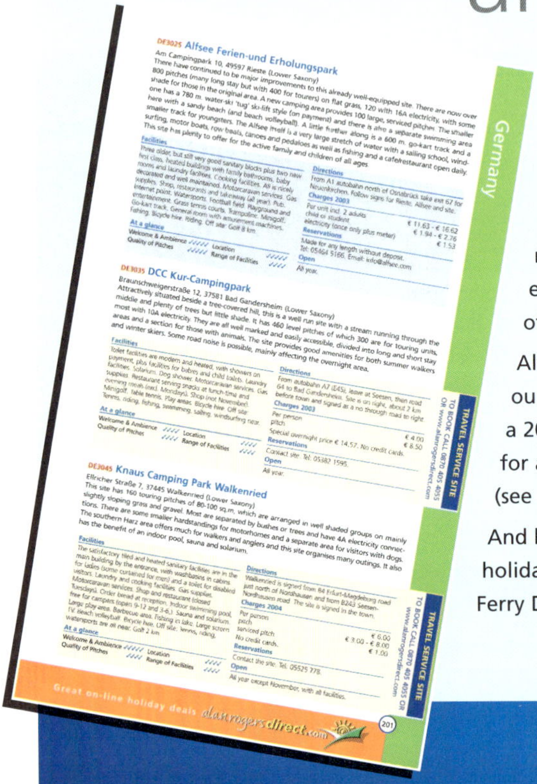
DE3025 Alfsee Ferien-und Erholungspark

Am Campingpark 10, 49597 Rieste (Lower Saxony)

There have continued to be major improvements to this already well-equipped site. There are now over 800 pitches (many long stay but with 400 for tourers) on flat grass, 120 with 16A electricity, with some shade for those in the original area. A new camping area provides 100 large, serviced pitches. The smaller one has a 780 m. water-ski 'tug' ski-lift style (on payment) and there is also a separate swimming area here with a sandy beach (and beach volleyball). A little further along is a 600 m. go-kart track and a smaller track for youngsters. The Alfsee itself is a very large stretch of water with a sailing school, wind-surfing, motor boats, row boats, canoes and pedaloes as well as fishing and a cafe/restaurant open daily. This site has plenty to offer for the active family and children of all ages.

Facilities

Three older, but still very good sanitary blocks plus two new first class, heated buildings with family bathrooms, baby rooms and laundry facilities. Cooking facilities. All is nicely decorated and well maintained. Motorcaravan services. Gas supplies. Shop, restaurants and takeaway (all year). Pub. Internet point. Watersports. Football field. Playground and entertainment. Grass tennis courts. Trampoline. Minigolf. Go-kart track. General room with amusement machines. Fishing. Bicycle hire. Riding. Off site: Golf 8 km.

At a glance

Welcome & Ambience ✓✓✓✓✓ Location ✓✓✓✓✓
Quality of Pitches ✓✓✓✓✓ Range of Facilities ✓✓✓✓

Directions

From A1 autobahn north of Osnabrück take exit 67 for Neuenkirchen. Follow signs for Rieste, Alfsee and site.

Charges 2003

Per unit incl. 2 adults	€ 11.63 - € 16.62
child or student	€ 1.94 - € 2.76
electricity (once only plus meter)	€ 1.53

Reservations

Made for any length without deposit. Tel: 05464 5166. Email: info@alfsee.com

Open

All year.

DE3035 DCC Kur-Campingpark

Braunschweigerstraße 12, 37581 Bad Gandersheim (Lower Saxony)

Attractively situated beside a tree-covered hill, this is a well run site with a stream running through the middle and plenty of trees but little shade. It has 460 level pitches of which 300 are for touring units, most with 10A electricity. They are all well marked and easily accessible, divided into long and short stay areas and a section for those with animals. The site provides good amenities for both summer walkers and winter skiers. Some road noise is possible, mainly affecting the overnight area.

Facilities

Toilet facilities are modern and heated, with showers on payment, plus facilities for babies and child toilets. Laundry facilities. Solarium. Dog shower. Motorcaravan services. Gas supplies. Restaurant serving snacks at lunch-time and evening meals (excl. Mondays). Shop (not November). Minigolf. Table tennis. Play areas. Bicycle hire. Off site: Tennis, riding, fishing, swimming, sailing, windsurfing near.

At a glance

Welcome & Ambience ✓✓✓✓ Location ✓✓✓✓
Quality of Pitches ✓✓✓✓ Range of Facilities ✓✓✓✓

Directions

From autobahn A7 (E45), leave at Seesen, then road 64 to Bad Gandersheim. Site is on right, about 2 km before town and signed as a no through road to right.

Charges 2003

Per person	€ 4.00
pitch	€ 8.50

Special overnight price € 14.57. No credit cards.

Reservations

Contact site. Tel: 05382 1595.

Open

All year.

DE3045 Knaus Camping Park Walkenried

Ellricher Straße 7, 37445 Walkenried (Lower Saxony)

This site has 160 touring pitches of 80-100 sq.m, which are arranged in well shaded groups on mainly slightly sloping grass and gravel. Most are separated by bushes or trees and have 4A electricity connections. There are some smaller hardstandings for motorhomes and a separate area for visitors with dogs. The southern Harz area offers much for walkers and anglers and this site organises many outings. It also has the benefit of an indoor pool, sauna and solarium.

Facilities

The satisfactory tiled and heated sanitary facilities are in the main building by the entrance, with washbasins in cabins for ladies (some curtained for men) and a toilet for disabled visitors. Laundry and cooking facilities. Gas supplies. Motorcaravan services. Shop and restaurant (closed Tuesdays). Order bread at reception. Indoor swimming pool, free for campers (open 9-12 and 3-6.). Sauna and solarium. Large play area. Barbecue area. Fishing in lake. Large screen TV. Beach volleyball. Bicycle hire. Off site: Tennis, riding, watersports are all near. Golf 2 km.

At a glance

Welcome & Ambience ✓✓✓✓✓ Location ✓✓✓✓
Quality of Pitches ✓✓✓✓ Range of Facilities ✓✓✓✓

Directions

Walkenried is signed from B4 Erfurt-Magdeburg road just north of Nordhausen and from B243 Seesen-Nordhausen road. The site is signed in the town.

Charges 2004

Per person	€ 6.00
pitch	€ 3.00 - € 8.00
serviced pitch	€ 1.00

No credit cards.

Reservations

Contact the site. Tel. 05525 778.

Open

All year except November, with all facilities.

Germany

TRAVEL SERVICE SITE
TO BOOK CALL 0870 405 4055 OR www.alanrogersdirect.com

Great on-line holiday deals alanrogersdirect.com

201

The Alan Rogers Travel Service was set up to provide a low cost booking service for readers. We can tailor-make a holiday to suit your requirements, giving you maximum choice and flexibility: exactly what we have been offering for some 5 years now.

Alternatively you can opt for one of our new Value+ holidays, pocketing a 20% saving off base price in return for accepting various restrictions (see opposite).

And because we organise so many holidays we can offer outstanding Ferry Deals too!

Unbeatable Ferry Deals

WE ARE ALWAYS NEGOTIATING NEW OFFERS ON CHANNEL CROSSINGS. MAKE SURE YOU ASK US ABOUT OUR FAMOUS DEALS!

- ✓ CARAVANS GO **FREE**
- ✓ TRAILERS GO **FREE**
- ✓ MOTORHOMES PRICED AS CARS

SEE PAGES 15-16

At the Alan Rogers Travel Service we're always keen to find the best deals and keenest prices. There are always great savings on offer, and we're constantly negotiating new ferry rates and money-saving offers, so just call us on

0870 405 4055

and ask about the latest deals.

or visit

www.alanrogersdirect.com

THE AIMS OF THE TRAVEL SERVICE ARE SIMPLE.

- To provide convenience - when booking a campsite yourself can be anything but convenient.
- To provide peace of mind - when you need it most.
- To provide a friendly, knowledgeable, efficient service - when this can be hard to find.
- To provide a low cost means of organising your holiday – when prices can be so complicated.

HOW IT WORKS

1 Choose your campsite(s)

2 Choose your dates

3 Choose your ferry crossing

Then just call us for an instant quote

0870 405 4055

or visit

www.alanrogersdirect.com

LET US BOOK YOUR PITCH AND FERRY FOR YOU

For full details see our FREE 2005 brochure

0870 405 4055

Ask about our incredible Ferry Deals:

- ✓ Caravans GO **FREE**
- ✓ Motorhomes Priced as Cars

NEW Value+ Holidays SAVE 20%

We can book many campsites for you, with complete flexibility: any dates, any duration, any arrival/departure day, any ferry and so on.

But some readers do not necessarily need such choice and would prefer 'off the shelf' convenience and even lower prices. So for 2005 we are introducing our new **Value+** holidays where, in return for meeting certain conditions, we can reduce your base price by a massive 20%.

We can offer **Value+** holidays at over 50 campsites within our 2005 programme. To qualify for huge savings please understand that your holiday must be...

+ Ferry-inclusive
+ Single site only – no overnight campsite stops
+ Minimum of 7 nights
+ Either 7, 14 or 21 nights duration
+ Booked at least 30 days in advance of travel
+ Subject to availability on each site

See our new 2005 brochure for details or call us today for a no-obligation quote.

0870 405 4055

PRICING YOUR HOLIDAY

WE ACT AS AGENTS FOR ALL THE CAMPSITES AND FERRY OPERATORS FEATURED IN THE TRAVEL SERVICE. AS SUCH, WE CAN BOOK ALL YOUR TRAVEL ARRANGEMENTS WITH THE MINIMUM OF FUSS AND AT THE BEST POSSIBLE PRICES. THE BASE PRICES BELOW INCLUDE 14 NIGHTS PITCH FEES AND RETURN FERRY CROSSING.

	Base Price 2 adults + car 14 nights		Extra adult		Child	Extra/fewer nights	
First night on site	Tailormade	Value+	Tailormade	Value+	(0-13)	Tailormade	Value+
Before 17 May	**£318**	**£254.40**	**£25**	**£20**	**FREE**	**£12**	**£9.60**
17/5 - 17/6	**£338**	**£270.40**	**£25**	**£20**	**FREE**	**£12**	**£9.60**
18/6 - 1/7	**£369**	**£295.20**	**£25**	**£20**	**FREE**	**£12**	**£9.60**
2/7 - 12/8	**£439**	**£351.20**	**£25**	**£20**	**FREE**	**£12**	**£9.60**
13/8 - 22/8	**£399**	**£319.20**	**£25**	**£20**	**FREE**	**£12**	**£9.60**
From 23/8	**£338**	**£270.40**	**£25**	**£20**	**FREE**	**£12**	**£9.60**

The base price of your holiday includes 14 nights pitch fees and a mid-week return ferry crossing from Dover to Calais with P&O Ferries for a car and 5 passengers (outward sailing times must be between 14:01 and 06:59. Inward sailing times must be between 20:01 and 14:59). Additional supplements are payable for caravans, trailers and motorhomes at many times and for cars at weekends and times outside those given above. There will also usually be a campsite supplement payable (see opposite). Call us on **0870 405 4055** for details and a quote.

If your holiday is longer or shorter than 14 nights, simply add or subtract the extra/fewer night rate. Tailor-made holidays must be for a minimum of 3 nights, with ferry (many sites have a minimum stay requirement). For holidays longer than 21 nights please call for a quotation. You may stay on as many sites as you wish, subject to individual site requirements, with a one-off £10 multi-site fee. Value+ holidays are subject to various restrictions. Please see page 9 for details.

LOW £100 DEPOSIT

A special low deposit of just £100 secures your holiday

(full payment is required at the time of booking for travel within 10 weeks)

14 nights pitch fees + ferry for car and passengers	from **£324** DOVER - CALAIS
14 nights pitch fees + ferry for motorhome and passengers	from **£346** PORTSMOUTH - LE HAVRE
14 nights pitch fees + ferry for car and caravan and passengers	from **£324** DOVER - CALAIS

Sample Value+ holiday at Camping Jarny Ocean, Vendée in May.

Motorhomes
Priced
as Cars

Caravans
and Trailers
GO FREE

Site Supplements

All sites operate their own independent pricing structure, and in order to reflect the differences in cost from one site to another, a nightly 'site supplement' needs to be added to the Base Prices indicated above.

All supplements are given in our 2005 brochure. Additional supplements can often apply for electricity, water and drainage or special pitches.

The simplest next step is to request a brochure or just call us for an immediate price quotation for your chosen site and all the available options, as well as any other important information, such as any minimum stay requirements.

CALL US NOW 0870 405 4055 FOR AN INSTANT QUOTE
OR VISIT www.alanrogersdirect.com

Leave The Hassle To Us

- **All site fees paid in advance – you won't need to take extra currency with you.**
- **Your pitch is reserved for you – travel with peace of mind.**
- **No endless overseas phone calls or correspondence with foreign site owners.**
- **No need to pay foreign currency deposits and booking fees.**
- **Take advantage of our expert advice and experience of camping in Europe.**

Already Booked Your Ferry?

We're confident that our ferry inclusive booking service offers unbeatable value. However, if you have already booked your ferry then we can still make a pitch-only reservation for you. Your booking must be for a minimum of 10 nights, and since our prices are based on our ferry inclusive service, you need to be aware that a non-ferry booking will always result in somewhat higher prices than if you were to book direct with the site.

You still benefit from:

- **Hassle-free booking with no booking fees and foreign currency deposits.**
- **Comprehensive Travel Pack.**
- **Peace of mind: site fees paid in advance, with your pitch reserved for you.**

FULL DETAILS IN OUR 64 PAGE 2005 COLOUR BROCHURE CALL
0870 405 4055

book on-line and save money

www.alanrogersdirect.com is a website designed to give you everything you need to know when it comes to booking your Alan Rogers inspected and selected campsite, and your low cost ferry.

Our glossy brochure gives you all the info you need but it is only printed once a year. And our friendly, expert reservations team is always happy to help on **0870 405 4055** – but they do go home sometimes!

Visit www.alanrogersdirect.com and you'll find constantly updated information, latest ferry deals, special offers from campsites and much more. And you can visit it at any time of day or night!

alan rogers **direct**.com

book on-line and save

Campsite Information

- ✓ Details of all Travel Service campsites - **instantly**
- ✓ Find latest special offers on campsites - **instantly**
- ✓ Check campsite availability - **instantly**

Ferry Information

- ✓ Check ferry availability - **instantly**
- ✓ Find latest ferry deals - **instantly**
- ✓ Book your ferry online - **instantly**
- ✓ Save money - **instantly**

Save Money!

BOOK YOUR CAMPSITE AND FERRY - INSTANTLY

Perfect Match

Find the campsite that's right for you

With so many sites to choose from it can be difficult to find a short-list. With the unique Alan Rogers Perfect Match system you can quickly find a campsite that meets your requirements. This powerful and searchable database of top campsites, all Alan Rogers inspected and selected, means you can quickly find an ideal site, book it on-line and relax in the knowledge that your holiday is safely reserved.

have you visited www.alanrogers.com yet?

INSPECTED CAMPSITES & SELECTED

Thousands have already, researching their holiday and catching up with the latest news and special offers.

Launched in January 2004 it has fast become the first-stop for countless caravanners, motorhome owners and campers all wanting reliable, impartial and detailed information for their next trip.

It features a fully searchable database of the best campsites in the UK & Ireland, and the rest of Europe: over 2,000 campsites in 26 countries. All are Alan Rogers inspected and selected, allowing you to find the site that's perfect for you, with the reassurance of knowing we've been there first.

And now it has been re-launched for the 2005 season, with more than ever before.

Crossing the Channel

One of the great advantages of booking with the Alan Rogers Travel Service is the tremendous value we offer. Our money-saving Ferry Deals have become legendary: see below. As agents for all the cross-Channel operators we can book all your travel arrangements with the minimum of fuss and at the best possible rates.

Just call us for an instant quote

0870 405 4055

or visit

www.alanrogersdirect.com

Book on-line AND SAVE

Short Sea Routes

Hop across the Channel in the shortest possible time and you can be on your way. We offer all main routes at great prices (when you book a pitch + ferry 'package' through us). And why not take advantage of our Ferry Deals? Caravans and trailers can go **FREE** on Dover – Calais with P&O Ferries.

SEAFRANCE DOVER-CALAIS FERRIES

P&O Ferries
Dover - Calais

hoverspeed
Dover – Calais
Newhaven - Dieppe

EURO TUNNEL
Folkestone – Calais

Stena Line
Harwich – Hook of Holland

Short Sea Routes **SPECIAL OFFERS**

Caravans **Go FREE** - Trailers **Go FREE** - Motorhomes **Priced as Cars**

SEAFRANCE DOVER-CALAIS FERRIES P&O Ferries Dover – Calais

Caravans Go FREE*

Available all year between 1 May 2005 – 31 Oct 2005 excluding high season weekends.

Motorhomes Priced as Cars*

Available between 1 May 2005 – 31 Oct 2005 on midweek, low season sailings and apply at all times of the day.

High season is 26-28 May and 15/7-31/8 outward and 4-5 June and 23/7-4/9 inward. Weekends are Fri/Sat outward, Sat/Sun inward.

* Applies to certain sailings only. Over-length supplements may apply. Please ask for details.

EURO TUNNEL **Folkestone – Calais/Coquelles**

FREE Caravans between midnight and 06:00.
Low caravan supplements on off peak crossings.

Don't delay – this offer is strictly subject to availability and will be first come, first served.

Just call us for an instant quote **0870 405 4055**
or visit **www.alanrogersdirect.com** BOOK ON-LINE AND SAVE

Longer Routes

Sometimes it pays to take a longer crossing: a more leisurely journey perhaps. Or a chance to enjoy dinner on board ship, followed by a night in a comfortable cabin, awaking refreshed and ready for the onward drive. Either way there are still savings to be had with our super Ferry Deals (when you book a pitch and ferry 'package' through us).

Brittany Ferries

Portsmouth – St Malo/
Caen/Cherbourg
Plymouth – Roscoff/Santander
Poole – Cherbourg
Portsmouth – Le Havre

P&O Ferries

Portsmouth – Bilbao
Hull – Rotterdam/Zeebrugge

Condorferries

Poole – St Malo
Weymouth – St Malo

Longer Routes SPECIAL OFFERS

Motorhomes Priced as Cars - Caravans FROM JUST £13 each way

Brittany Ferries Portsmouth – Le Havre**

Motorhomes Priced as Cars* on 'special sailings' from Portsmouth in low season (midweek AND weekend). Le Havre is now just £4 each way supplement over Dover-Calais on lead-in sailings for cars. Caravan supplement starts at just £13 each way on Portsmouth - Le Havre.

Many supplements for high season have reduced – **call us for an instant quote.**

Condorferries Poole/Weymouth – St Malo

Motorhomes Priced as Cars on all crossings direct to St Malo and via the Channel Islands. Travel must be on a Tuesday or Wednesday (either direction). Offer excludes high season (27/5-29/5 and 15/7-24/8 out, 3/6-5/6 and 22/7-4/9 in).

* Applies to certain sailings only. Over-length supplements may apply. Please ask for details.
** At the time going to press Portsmouth – Le Havre crossings are operated by P&O Ferries. This route may, in time, be operated by Brittany Ferries, subject to the outcome of negotiations.

1st time abroad?

PREPARATIONS FOR THAT FIRST TRIP CAN BE DAUNTING. BUT DON'T WORRY - WE'RE WITH YOU ALL THE WAY.

Don't delay – this offer is strictly subject to availability and will be first come, first served.

Just call us for an instant quote **0870 405 4055**
or visit **www.alanrogersdirect.com** BOOK ON-LINE AND SAVE

Brittany

Map 1

Rolling sandy beaches, hidden coves, pretty villages and a picturesque coastline all combine to make Brittany a very popular holiday destination. Full of Celtic culture steeped in myths and legends, Brittany is one of the most distinctive regions of France.

Départements: 22 Côtes d'Armor, 29 Finistère, 35 Ille-et-Vilaine, 56 Morbihan, 44 Loire Atlantique

Major cities: Rennes and Brest

Brittany offers 800 miles of rocky coastline with numerous bays, busy little fishing villages and broad sandy beaches dotted with charming seaside resorts. The coastline to the north of Brittany is rugged with a maze of rocky coves, while to the south, the shore is flatter with long sandy beaches. Inland you'll find wooded valleys, rolling fields, moors and giant granite boulders, but most impressive is the wealth of prehistoric sites, notably the Carnac standing stones.

Breton culture offers a rich history of menhirs, dolmens, crosses, cathedrals and castles. Strong Celtic roots provide this region with its own distinctive traditions, evident in the local Breton costume and music, the traditional religious festivals and the cuisine, featuring crêpes and cider. Many castles and manor houses, countless chapels and old towns and villages provide evidence of Brittany's eventful history and wealth of traditions. The abbey fortress of Mont-St-Michel on the north coast should not be missed and Concarneau in the south is a lovely walled town enclosed by granite rocks.

Cuisine of the region

Fish and shellfish are commonplace; traditional *crêperies* abound and welcome visitors with a cup of local cider

Agneau de pré-salé: leg of lamb from animals pastured in the salt marshes and meadows

Beurre blanc: sauce for fish dishes made with shallots, wine vinegar and butter

Cotriade: fish soup with potatoes, onions, garlic and butter

Crêpes Bretonnes: the thinnest of pancakes with a variety of sweet fillings

Galette: can be a biscuit, cake or pancake; with sweet or savoury fillings

Gâteau Breton: rich cake

Poulet blanc Breton: free-range, quality, white Breton chicken

Places of interest

Cancale: small fishing port famous for oysters

Carnac: 3,000 standing stones (menhirs)

Concarneau: fishing port, old walled town

Dinan: historical walled town

La Baule: resort with lovely, sandy bay and beach

Le Croisic: fishing port, Naval museum

Guérande: historic walled town

Perros-Guirec: leading resort of the 'Pink Granite Coast'

Quiberon: boat service to three islands: Belle Ile (largest of the Breton islands), Houat, Hoedic

Rennes: capital of Brittany, medieval streets, half timbered houses; Brittany Museum

St Malo: historical walled city, fishing port

Alan Rogers **tip**

FOR A TASTE OF LOCAL CULTURE THE INTER-CELTIC FESTIVAL IN LORIENT, HELD IN AUGUST, IS A CELEBRATION OF TRADIONAL BRETON MUSIC, POETRY AND DANCE.

FR22050 Camping Le Vieux Moulin

14 rue des Moulins, 22430 Erquy (Côtes d'Armor)

Le Vieux Moulin is a well established and busy site, open from 1 May and which becomes full with much activity in July and August. It is situated about one kilometre from a beach of sand and shingle, accessed by an unmade track which can get dusty. There is, however, a good pool complex on site with a paddling pool and water slides. There are 173 pitches, of which 150 have electricity and 30 have electricity, water and waste water. A further newer section of 39 pitches is arranged around a pond. Most pitches are of a fair size in square boxes with trees giving shade. Discos are arranged in high season which finish at midnight so expect some noise. This is a good site for children of all ages. About 60 tour operator pitches add to the busy atmosphere.

Facilities

Two good quality toilet blocks have mostly British style toilets and plenty of individual washbasins, facilities for disabled people and for babies. A further small block provides toilets and dishwashing only. Washing machines and dryer. Motorcaravan service point. Shop. Smart pizzeria and takeaway. Attractive bar and terrace overlooking the heated pool complex. Two play areas with carousel roundabout. Free tennis, free fitness gym. TV room (with satellite) and games room with table tennis. Electric barbecues are not permitted. Off site: Bicycle hire 1 km. Fishing 1.2 km. Golf 7 km. Riding 9 km.

At a glance

Welcome & Ambience	✓✓✓✓	Location	✓✓✓✓
Quality of Pitches	✓✓✓✓	Range of Facilities	✓✓✓✓✓

Directions

Site is 2 km. east of Erquy. Take minor road towards Les Hôpitaux and site is signed from junction of D786 and D34 roads

Charges 2005

Per person	€ 4,50 - € 5,50
child (under 7 yrs)	€ 3,20 - € 4,00
pitch	€ 10,00 - € 13,00
vehicle	€ 4,00 - € 5,00
electricity (6-9A)	€ 4,50 - € 5,00
dog	€ 3,00 - € 4,00

Reservations

Made for min. 1 week. Tel: 02 96 72 34 23.
E-mail: camp.vieux.moulin@wanadoo.fr

Open

30 April - 10 September.

FR22060 Camping Municipal La Hallerais

6 Bourg de Taden, 22100 Taden (Côtes d'Armor)

As well as being an attractive old medieval town, Dinan is quite a short run from the resorts of the Côte d'Armor. This useful municipal site, open for a long season, is just outside Dinan, beyond and above the little harbour on the Rance estuary. There is a pleasant riverside walk where the site slopes down towards the Rance. The 226 pitches, all with electricity (6A) and most with water and drainaway, are mainly on level, shallow terraces connected by tarmac roads, with trees and hedges giving a park-like atmosphere. This is a clean efficiently run and well organised site.

Facilities

Three traditional toilet blocks, of good quality and heated in cool weather, have some private cabins with shower and washbasin. Unit for disabled people. Laundry room. Shop. Attractive bar/restaurant with outside terrace and takeaway (all season). Swimming pool and paddling pool (20/5-15/9). Tennis courts, minigolf, games room with table tennis and TV room. Playground. Fishing. Chalets for disabled visitors. Off site: Riding 2 km. Boating 15 km. Beach 12 km.

Open

15 March - 31 October.

At a glance

Welcome & Ambience	✓✓✓✓	Location	✓✓✓✓
Quality of Pitches	✓✓✓✓	Range of Facilities	✓✓✓✓

Directions

Taden is northeast of Dinan. On leaving Dinan on D766, turn right to Taden and site before reaching large bridge and N176 junction. From N176 take Taden/Dinan exit and follow Taden signs to pick up signs for site.

Charges 2004

Per person	€ 3,10 - € 3,70
child (under 7 yrs)	€ 1,30 - € 1,60
pitch incl. electricity	€ 6,75 - € 11,55

Reservations

Made for high season only (min. 1 week) with deposit. Tel: 02 96 39 15 93.
E-mail: camping.la.hallerais@wanadoo.fr

FR22200 Camping Au Bocage Du Lac

Rue du Bocage, 22270 Jugon-les Lacs (Côtes d'Armor)

This well kept former municipal site has been updated over the past few years by the current owners M. and Mme. Riviere. It is on the edge of the village beside a lake, 25 km. from the sea. It offers 181 good size pitches, all with electrical connections, set on gently sloping grass and divided by shrubs and bushes, with mature trees providing shade. Some 40 wooden chalets and mobile homes are intermingled with the touring pitches. On-site facilities include a good pool with children's section and sunbathing patio.

Facilities

Two main sanitary blocks include facilities for disabled visitors, British and Turkish style WCs and some washbasins in cabins. Washing machine. Small shop (1/4-;31/10). Bar (1/4-31/10). Swimming pool (15/6-;10/9). Table tennis, tennis, football. Play area. Activity programmes July/Aug. Fishing. Bicycle hire. Off site: Supermarket in village (1 km). River 1 km.

Open

1 April - 31 October.

At a glance

Welcome & Ambience	✓✓✓✓✓	Location	✓✓✓✓
Quality of Pitches	✓✓✓✓	Range of Facilities	✓✓✓✓

Directions

From N176 (E401) Lamballe - Dinan road, approx. 15 km. from Lamballe take turning for Jugon-les-Lacs. Site is signed shortly after.

Charges 2004

Per person	€ 3,00 - € 3,60
child (under 7 yrs)	€ 1,70 - € 2,15
pitch	€ 5,00 - € 6,00
electricity (5A)	€ 2,80

Reservations

Contact site. Tel: 02 96 31 60 16.
E-mail: camping-le-bocage@wanadoo.fr

FR22090 Castel Camping Le Château de Galinée

La Galinée, 22380 St Cast-le-Guildo (Côtes d'Armor)

Situated a few kilometers back from St Cast and owned and managed by the Vervel family, Galinée is in a parkland setting on level grass with numerous and varied mature trees. It has 273 pitches, all with electricity, water and drainage and separated by many mature shrubs and bushes. The top section is mostly for mobile homes. An attractive pool complex has swimming and paddling pools, two new pools with a water slide and a 'magic stream'. Entertainment is organised during peak season featuring traditional Breton music at times or weekly discos. The gate is locked 23.00-07.00 hrs.

Facilities

The main tiled, modern sanitary block includes washbasins in private cabins, facilities for babies and a good unit for disabled people. Dishwashing under cover. Laundry room. Shop for basics, bar and excellent takeaway menu (both 1/7-30/8). Attractive, heated pool complex (26/5-2/9) with swimming and paddling pools. Three tennis courts. Fishing. Play area and field for ball games. Off site: Golf 3.5 km. Riding 6 km. Beach 6 km.

Open

15 May - 5 September.

At a glance

Welcome & Ambience	✓✓✓✓	Location	✓✓✓✓
Quality of Pitches	✓✓✓✓	Range of Facilities	✓✓✓✓✓

Directions

From D168 Ploubalay-Plancoet road turn onto D786 towards Matignon and St Cast. Site is very well signed 1 km. after leaving Notre Dame de Guildo.

Charges 2004

Per adult	€ 3,85 - € 5,50
child (under 7 yrs)	€ 2,30 - € 3,80
pitch incl. water and drainage	€ 8,40 - € 14,00
electricity (10A)	€ 4,70
animal	€ 3,20

Camping Cheques accepted.

Reservations

Made with deposit (€ 31) and fee (€ 15.24); min. 1 week July/Aug. Tel: 02 96 41 10 56.
E-mail: chateaugalinee@wanadoo.fr

TRAVEL SERVICE SITE
TO BOOK CALL 0870 405 4055 OR www.alanrogersdirect.com

FR22030 Camping Nautic International

Route de Beau-Rivage, 22530 Caurel (Côtes d'Armor)

This friendly family site is on the northern shore of the Lac de Guerledan. The lake is popular for all manner of watersports and there are some pleasant walks around the shores and through the surrounding Breton countryside and forests. The site is terraced down to the lake shore and offers 100 large pitches, all with electrical connections. A number of 'super pitches' (160 - 200 sq.m.) are also available. There is an imaginatively designed swimming pool and smaller children's pool, both heated by a wood burning stove (15/5-25/9). Small boats can be launched from the site, and other boating activities are available on the lake. A member of 'Sites et Paysages'.

Facilities

Washing and drying machines. Small shop (1/7-31/8). Swimming pools. Gym. Giant chess. Play area. Fishing. Tennis. Table tennis. Games room. Mobile homes for rent. Off site: Watersports. Riding. Canal from Nantes to Brest. Seaside 50 minutes by car.

Open

15 May - 25 September.

At a glance

Welcome & Ambience	✓✓✓✓	Location	✓✓✓✓
Quality of Pitches	✓✓✓✓	Range of Facilities	✓✓✓✓

Directions

From N164 Rennes – Brest road, turn off between Mur-de-Bretagne and Gouarec to the village of Caurel. Site is well signed from there.

Charges 2004

Per person	€ 3,30 - € 5,00
child (0-7 yrs)	€ 1,90 - € 3,10
pitch	€ 5,40 - € 7,00
vehicle	€ 1,60
electricity (10A)	€ 4,20
dog	€ 1,50

Reservations

Contact site. Tel: 02 96 28 57 94.
E-mail: contact@campingnautic.fr.st

FR22040 Camping Le Châtelet

Rue des Nouettes, 22380 St Cast-le-Guildo (Côtes d'Armor)

Carefully developed over the years from a former quarry, Le Châtelet is pleasantly and quietly situated with lovely views over the estuary from many pitches. It is well laid out, mainly in terraces with fairly narrow access roads. There are 216 good-sized pitches separated by hedges, all with electricity and 70 with water and drainage. Some pitches are around a little lake (unfenced) which can be used for fishing. A 'green' walking area is a nice feature around the lower edge of the site and a path leads from the site directly down to a beach (about 200 m. but including steps). Saint Cast, 1 km. away to the centre, has a very long beach with many opportunities for sail-boarding and other watersports. Used by three different tour operators (73 pitches).

Facilities

Four toilet blocks with access at different levels include plentiful washbasins in cabins and small toilets and showers for children. Three small, attractive toilet blocks have been added for the lower terraces. Some facilities may be closed outside July/Aug. Motorcaravan services. Heated swimming pool and paddling pool. Shop for basics, takeaway service, bar lounge and general room with satellite TV and pool table. Games room with table tennis, amusement machines. Small play area. Organised games and activities for all the family in season. Dancing weekly in June, July and Aug. Off site: Bicycle hire, riding and golf within 1.5 km. Beach 200 m.

At a glance

Welcome & Ambience	✓✓✓✓✓	Location	✓✓✓✓✓
Quality of Pitches	✓✓✓✓	Range of Facilities	✓✓✓✓

Directions

Best approach is to turn off D786 road at Matignon towards St Cast; just inside St Cast limits turn left at sign for 'campings' and follow camp signs on C90.

Charges 2004

Per person	€ 4,00 - € 5,80
child (under 7 yrs)	€ 2,40 - € 4,00
pitch	€ 11,55 - € 18,90
electricity (6/10A)	€ 4,00 - € 4,50
animal	€ 2,60 - € 3,60

Reservations

Necessary for July/Aug. and made (min. 1 week) with deposit (€ 60) and booking fee (€ 20).
Tel: 02 96 41 96 33. E-mail: chateletcp@aol.com

Open

1 May - 11 September.

FR22160 Camping Le Neptune

Kerguistin, 22580 Lanloup (Côtes d'Armor)

Situated on the Côte de Go'lo at Lanloup, Le Neptune offers a peaceful, rural retreat for families. The friendly owners, M. & Mme. Schira, keep the site neat and tidy. There are 84 level, grass pitches (65 for touring units) separated by trimmed hedges providing privacy and all with electricity. There are also 13 mobile homes to rent. A heated swimming pool has a retractable roof so can be open for a long season. Within walking distance is the local village, with a restaurant and shop, and sandy beaches. The site is also a good base for cycling and walking.

Facilities

The modern toilet block is of a good standard, clean and well maintained. Laundry room with washing machine and dryer. No restaurant but good takeaway (open all season). Small shop well stocked for basic needs. Bar with indoor and outdoor seating. Heated swimming pool (Easter – end Oct). Petanque. Volleyball. Table tennis, table football. Minigolf. Animation in season. Off site: Tennis 300 m. Fishing and beach 2 km. Golf and riding 8 km. Restaurant and shop within walking distance.

Open

Easter - 1 November.

At a glance

Welcome & Ambience	✓✓✓✓✓	Location	✓✓✓✓✓
Quality of Pitches	✓✓✓✓	Range of Facilities	✓✓✓✓

Directions

From Saint Brieuc (N12) take D786 Paimpol ('par la Côte'). After 28 km. on approaching Lanloup, site is well signed.

Charges 2004

Per person	€ 4,50
child (under 7 yrs)	€ 3,00
pitch	€ 7,50
electricity (6A)	€ 3,00
dog	€ 1,70

Camping Cheques accepted.

Reservations

Less 10% in low season. Tel: 02 96 22 33 35.
E-mail: contact@leneptune.com

FR22100 Camping L'Abri Côtier

Ville Es Rouxel, 22680 Etables-sur-Mer (Côtes d'Armor)

L'Abri Cotier is a well-cared-for, family run site 500 metres from a sandy beach. Small and tranquil, it is arranged in two sections separated by a lane. The pitches are marked out on part level, part sloping grass, divided by mature trees and shrubs with some in a charming walled area with a quaint, old-world atmosphere. The second section has an orchard type setting. Tim Lee and his French wife are busy with ideas to improve this very popular, friendly site. In total there are 140 pitches, all with electrical connections (long leads useful) and 60 fully serviced. The beach is within walking distance and there are restaurants in the village.

Facilities

Good clean sanitary facilities, heated in low season, include some washbasins in cabins, two units for disabled visitors (shower, washbasin and toilet) and a baby bath/shower. Dishwashing under cover. Laundry room. Well stocked shop, set menu and simple takeaway service. Bar (with TV) and outdoor terrace area. Sheltered, heated swimming pool with paddling pool and outdoor jacuzzi. Playground. Games room with billiards, darts, pinball and table tennis. Some entertainment in peak season. Gates locked at 11 pm. Off site: Restaurants and indoor pool in village. Bicycle hire and riding 1 km. Fishing 2 km. Golf 12 km. Beach 500 m.

At a glance

Welcome & Ambience	✓✓✓✓	Location	✓✓✓✓
Quality of Pitches	✓✓✓✓	Range of Facilities	✓✓✓✓

Directions

From N12 after Saint Brieuc take D786; site is well signed before Saint Quay Portrieux.

Charges 2004

Per person	€ 4,00 - € 4,50
child (under 7 yrs)	€ 2,50 - € 3,00
pitch	€ 6,00 - € 7,00
serviced pitch	€ 6,50 - € 8,00

Reservations

Advised in season; made with deposit (€ 40, sterling cheque acceptable £25). Tel: 02 96 70 61 57.
E-mail: camping.abricotier@wanadoo.fr

Open

12 April - 15 September.

FR22080 Yelloh! Village Le Ranolien

Ploumanach, 22700 Perros Guirec (Côtes d'Armor)

Le Ranolien has been attractively developed around a former Breton farm – everything here is either made from, or placed on or around the often massive pink rocks. The original buildings have been sympathetically converted into site facilities and there is an imaginative pool complex with terraces and water toboggans, with water cascading over boulders into smaller pools and a covered, heated pool which can be opened. It is all quite impressive and is overlooked by the bar terrace. The site is on the coast, with beaches and coves within walking distance and there are spectacular views from many pitches. The 540 pitches are of a variety of sizes and types, mostly large and flat but some are quite small. Some are formally arranged in rows with hedge separators, but most are either on open ground or under trees, amongst large boulders. With many holiday caravans and tour operator tents around the site (318 pitches), there are 70 pitches for tourists, most with electricity and some with water and drainage. Reservation is recommended for high season. This site can be noisy in high season and is not for those seeking a calm and peaceful holiday.

Facilities

The main toilet block, heated in cool weather, is supplemented by several other more open type blocks around the site. Washbasins in cabins, mostly British style WCs and good showers. Dishwashing facilities are mainly in the open. Laundry. Motorcaravan service facilities. Supermarket and gift shop (1/5-18/9). Restaurant, crêperie and bar (all open over a long season). Disco some nights in high season. Minigolf. Tennis. Table tennis. Games room. Play area. Cinema. Gym and steam room. Mobile homes for hire.

Open

2 April - 17 September.

At a glance

Welcome & Ambience	✓✓✓✓	Location	✓✓✓✓✓
Quality of Pitches	✓✓✓	Range of Facilities	✓✓✓✓✓

Directions

From Lannion take D788 to Perros Guirec. Follow signs to 'Centre Ville' past main harbour area and then signs to Ploumanach, La Clarté. Pass through village of La Clarté and around sharp left hand bend. Site is immediately on the right.

Charges 2005

Per unit incl. 2 persons	
and electricity	€ 13,00 - € 29,00
with water and drainage	€ 15,00 - € 37,00
extra person	€ 5,00 - € 7,00
child (2-7 yrs)	free - € 5,00
animal	€ 2,00

Reservations

Contact site. Tel: 02 96 91 65 65.
E-mail: leranolien@yellohvillage.fr

FR22130 Camping de Port l'Epine

Venelle de Pors Garo, 22660 Trélévern (Côtes d'Armor)

Port L'Epine is a pretty little site in a unique situation on a promontory. There is access to the sea, therefore, on the south side of the site, with views across to Perros Guirec, and just outside the entrance on the north side is a further sandy bay with little boats moored and facing an archipelago of seven small islands. It is charming – you can sail or swim from both sides. However, in spite of this, the site has its own small heated pool. The area covered by the site is not large but there are 160 grass pitches, all with electricity, which are divided by pretty hedging and trees. Some are used for mobile homes. Access is a little tight in parts. This site is ideal for families with young children (probably not for teenagers). The site is used by tour operators (17 pitches).

Facilities

The original toilet block is well equipped and a second block has been refurbished in modern style, including facilities for disabled visitors. Unusual dishwashing sinks in open air stone units. Shop and bar/restaurant with takeaway facility (both 1/7-31/8). Small heated swimming pool and paddling pool. Fenced play area near the bar/restaurant. Table tennis and video games. Bicycle hire. Site's own beach has rock pools, jetty and slipway for small boats or fishing. Barrier closed 23.00-07.00 hrs. Off site: Riding or golf 15 km. Useful small supermarket up-hill from site. Many coastal paths to enjoy.

Open

1 April - 30 September.

At a glance

Welcome & Ambience	✓✓✓✓✓	Location	✓✓✓✓✓
Quality of Pitches	✓✓✓✓	Range of Facilities	✓✓✓✓

Directions

From roundabout south of Perros Guirec take D6 towards Tréguier. After passing through Louannec, take left turn at crossroads for Trélévern. Go through village following camp signs – Port L'Epine is clearly marked as distinct from the municipal site. On first arrival, you must park outside in the car park and walk to reception, as there is now a barrier which requires an access code.

Charges 2005

Per pitch incl. 2 persons	
and electricity	€ 14,50 - € 27,50
serviced pitch	€ 2,30
extra person	€ 5,00
child (2-7 yrs)	€ 2,50
animal	€ 2,50

Camping Cheques accepted.

Reservations

Made with deposit (€ 90 or € 45 for stay of less than 3 nights). Tel: 02 96 23 71 94.
E-mail: camping-de-port-lepine@wanadoo.fr

FR22140 Camping de Port La Chaine

22610 Pleubian (Côtes d'Armor)

The Palvadeau family have worked hard to establish Camping de Port La Chaîne as a comfortable, quiet, family site. In a beautiful location on the 'Untamed Peninsula' between Paimpol and Perros Guirec, attractive trees and shrubs provide a balance of sun and shade, edging the central road and the grassy bays or fields which branch off on the gradual decline towards the bay and the sea (a sandy bay with rocks). To the right are mostly French-owned mobile homes, quite discreet, with the left side for independent units. Most of the bays have a slight slope, so those with motorcaravans will need to choose their pitch carefully. More open, level pitches nearer the sea are useful for tents. In all there are 200 pitches with electricity said to be available everywhere (a long lead may be useful). There are good opportunities for walking and cycling, with a way-marked footpath running along the coast to the Sillon du Talbert that juts out into the sea opposite the Island of Bréhat.

Facilities

Two traditional style toilet blocks are comfortable and fully equipped, both now completely renovated. Washbasins in cabins, British and Turkish style toilets. Cabins for families or disabled visitors. Plentiful dishwashing sinks. Laundry sinks with cold water only. Washing machines and dryer. Bar and terrace (1/7-1/9) overlooking a heated pool (2/6-15/9), play area and petanque pitch. Children's entertainer in July/Aug. Beach. Off site: Village 2 km. for tennis, market, shops and restaurants. Good fishing and diving.

Open

1 May - 15 September.

At a glance

Welcome & Ambience	✓✓✓✓✓	Location	✓✓✓✓✓
Quality of Pitches	✓✓✓✓	Range of Facilities	✓✓✓✓

Directions

Leave D786 between Lézardrieux and Tréguier to go north to village of Pleubian (about 8 km). Continue on D20 towards Larmor Pleubian and site signed on left, 2 km. from Pleubian.

Charges 2004

Per person	€ 5,20
child (under 7 yrs)	€ 3,20
pitch	€ 9,00
electricity	€ 3,60
dog	€ 2,10

Less 10-20% in low seasons.

Reservations

Contact site. Tel: 02 96 22 92 38.
E-mail: info@portlachaine.com

FR22010 Camping Les Capucines

Kervourdon, 22300 Tredrez-Locquémeau (Côtes d'Armor)

A warm welcome awaits at Les Capucines which is quietly situated about a kilometre from the village of Saint Michel with its good, sandy beach and also very near Locquémeau, a pretty fishing village. This attractive, family run site has 100 pitches on flat or slightly sloping ground. All are well marked out by hedges, with mature trees and with more recently planted. There are 70 pitches with electricity, water and drainage, including 10 for larger units. All the amenities are open all season. A good value restaurant/crêperie can be found at Trédrez, others at Saint Michel. A Sites et Paysages member.

Facilities

Two modern toilet blocks, clean and very well kept, include washbasins mainly in cabins, facilities for babies and disabled people. Laundry with washing machines and dryer. Small shop for essentials (bread to order). Takeaway, bar with TV and a general room with table tennis and table football. Swimming and paddling pools. Playground. Tennis. Minigolf. Chalets and mobile homes to rent. Dogs are not accepted. Off site: Fishing 1 km. Riding 2 km. Golf 15 km. Beach 1 km.

At a glance

Welcome & Ambience	✓✓✓✓✓	Location	✓✓✓✓
Quality of Pitches	✓✓✓✓✓	Range of Facilities	✓✓✓✓

Directions

Turn off main D786 road northeast of St Michel where site is signed, and 1 km. to site.

Charges 2004

Per unit incl. 2 persons	€ 13,00 - € 18,40
incl. electiricty (7A) and water	€ 17,40 - € 24,50
extra person	€ 3,60 - € 5,00
child	free - € 3,26

Reservations

Advised for high season and made for any length with deposit (€ 70). Tel: 02 96 35 72 28.
E-mail: les.capucines@wanadoo.fr

Open

1 May - 11 September.

FR22210 Camping Bellevue

Route de Pléneuf Val-André, 22430 Erquy (Côtes d'Armor)

Situated a mile from the beaches between Erquy and Pléneuf Val-Andre, Camping Bellevue offers a quiet country retreat with easy access to the cliffs of Cap Fréhel, Sables d'Or and St Cast le Suildo. There are 140 pitches of which 120 are available for touring units, most with electricity (6/10A) and 15 with water and drainage. Children are well catered for at this campsite – there are heated swimming and paddling pools, three play areas and minigolf, petanque and volleyball. Indoor entertainment for all includes theme evenings, Breton dancing and visits to a local cider house. There are numerous walks in the area and a vast range of aquatic sports at nearby Erquy. The site also has 20 mobile homes, chalets and bungalows to rent.

Facilities

Two modern, unisex toilet blocks are of a high standard. Some washbasins in cubicles. Facilities for disabled visitors. Dishwashing and laundry facilities. Shop and bar (1/6-10/9). Restaurant and takeaway (12/6-31/8). Swimming and paddling pools (15/5-10/9). Play areas. Pool table. TV room. Table football, video games and library. Minigolf. Petanque. Volleyball. Entertainment and organised activities in high season. Off site: Beach and fishing 2 km. Golf 3 km. Nicycle hire and boat launching 5 km. Riding 6 km.

At a glance

Welcome & Ambience	✓✓✓✓✓	Location	✓✓✓✓
Quality of Pitches	✓✓✓✓	Range of Facilities	✓✓✓✓

Directions

From St Brieuc road take D786 towards Erquy. Site is adjacent to the D786 at St Pabu and is well signed.

Charges 2005

Per person	€ 3,70 - € 4,70
child (7-13 yrs	€ 3,20 - € 4,20
pitch	€ 6,40 - € 8,00
electricity	€ 3,20 - € 4,20
dog	€ 1,20

Reservations

Contact site. Tel: 02 96 72 33 04.
E-mail: campngbellevue@yahoo.fr

Open

31 March - 30 September.

FR29280 La Pointe Superbe Camping

Route de St Coulitz, 29150 Châteaulin (Finistère)

La Pointe, just outside Châteaulin, has been lovingly and impressively brought back to life by its delightful English owners Colin Grewer and Sue Dodds. Châteaulin is a bustling market town, 15 km. from the beach at Pentrez and within easy reach of Quimper, mediaeval Locronan and the Crozon peninsula. Although not endowed with a great deal in terms of amenities, this very tranquil site does boast particularly large, grassy pitches in a quiet valley leading down to the River Aulne, which makes up part of the Nantes - Brest canal. The 60 pitches all have electricity with water close by. As a bonus, Colin offers painting demonstrations and tuition on Sundays. This small site is well suited to those who like peace and quiet.

Facilities

The first-class toilet block, kept very clean at all times, has many washbasins in cubicles. Shower cubicles are somewhat small but have full adjustable hot and cold taps. Large room with facilities for disabled visitors. Baby bathroom. Motorcaravan service point. Play area. Table tennis, volleyball and large activity room with basketball, badminton and children's corner. Off site: Châteaulin has a wide range of shops (700 m), as well as plenty of restaurants and bars. Riding and tennis nearby. Woodland walks and fishing possible in the Aulne (permit needed). Beach 9 km.

Open

6 March - 31 October.

At a glance

Welcome & Ambience	✓✓✓✓	Location	✓✓✓✓
Quality of Pitches	✓✓✓✓✓	Range of Facilities	✓✓✓✓

Directions

Site is just southeast of Châteaulin. From the bridge over the river in town centre follow signs for St Coulitz and Quimper. Shortly turn left signed St Coulitz. Site is clearly signed at this point and is a further 100 m. on the right.

Charges 2004

Per unit incl. 2 persons	€ 13,00
extra person	€ 3,00
child (under 7 yrs)	€ 2,00
animal	€ 1,00
electricity (10A)	€ 2,00

No credit cards.

Reservations

Advised for high season and made with deposit (€ 15). Tel: 02 98 86 51 53.

FR29130 Camping des Abers

Mobile homes page 364

Dunes de Ste. Marguerite, 29870 Landéda (Finistère)

This delightful twelve acre site is beautifully situated almost at the tip of the Sainte Marguerite peninsula on the north-western shores of Brittany in a wide bay formed between the mouths (abers) of two rivers, L'Aber Wrac'h and L'Aber Benoit. With soft, white sandy beaches and rocky outcrops and islands at high tide, the setting is ideal for those with younger children and this quiet, rural area provides a wonderful, tranquil escape from the busier areas of France, even in high season. Camping des Abers is set just back from the beach, the lower pitches sheltered from the wind by high hedges or with panoramic views of the bay from the higher places. There are 180 pitches arranged in distinct areas, partly shaded and sheltered by mature hedges, trees and flowering shrubs, all planted and carefully tended over 30 years by the Le Cuff family. Landscaping and terracing where appropriate on the different levels avoids any regimentation or crowding. Easily accessed by good internal roads, electricity is available to all (long leads may be needed). Speaking several languages, the family who own and run this site with 'TLC' will make you very welcome.

Facilities

Three toilet blocks (one part of the reception building and all recently refurbished) are very clean, providing washbasins in cubicles and roomy showers (token from reception 0.80). Good facilities for disabled visitors and babies have been added at the reception block. Dishwashing sinks. Fully equipped laundry. Motorcaravan service point. Mini-market stocks essentials (1/6-15/9). Simple takeaway dishes (1/7-31/8). Pizzeria and restaurant next door. Table tennis. Good play area (on sand). Games room. Live music, Breton dancing and Breton cooking classes, and guided walks arranged. Splendid beach reached direct from the site with good bathing (best at high tide), fishing, windsurfing and other watersports. Torch useful. Gates locked 22.30-07.00 hrs. Off site: Miles of superb coastal walks. Tennis and riding close. The nearby town of L'Aber Wrac'h, a well known yachting centre, has many memorable restaurants.

At a glance

Welcome & Ambience	✓✓✓✓✓	Location	✓✓✓✓✓
Quality of Pitches	✓✓✓✓	Range of Facilities	✓✓✓✓

Directions

From Roscoff (D10, then D13), cross river bridge (L'Aber Wrac'h) to Lannilis. Go through town taking road to Landéda and from there signs for Dunes de Ste Marguerite, 'camping' and des Abers.

Charges 2005

Per person	€ 3,30
child (1-7 yrs)	€ 1,80
pitch	€ 5,50
car	€ 1,50
electricity	€ 2,40
dog	€ 1,60

10% reduction outside 15 June - 31 August.
Camping Cheques accepted.

Reservations

Write to site. Tel: 02 98 04 93 35.
E-mail: camping-des-abers@wanadoo.fr

Open

1 May - 30 September.

FR29210 Camping Municipal Bois de la Palud

29250 Plougoulm (Finistère)

This delightful, small municipal site is on the edge of the little village of Plougoulm, about ten kilometres southwest of Roscoff. It sits on the brow of a hill with lovely views across the Guillec valley and the sandy bay and estuary to which there is access by footpath. There are 34 reasonably level, numbered pitches grouped in small hedged bays and most have access to 6A electricity (although long leads may be necessary). A small building near the entrance houses reception and sanitary facilities. The season is short – only 15 June - 15 September.

Facilities

All necessary toilet facilities are provided. Play area.
Off site: Fishing, bicycle hire, riding and golf, all within 4 km.

Open

15 June - 15 September.

At a glance

Welcome & Ambience	✓✓✓	Location	✓✓✓✓
Quality of Pitches	✓✓✓	Range of Facilities	✓✓

Directions

On leaving Roscoff, follow signs for Morlaix. After 6 km. take D10 (westward) signed Plouescat and after 3 km. watch for clear camp signs in the village of Plougoulm.

Charges guide

per adult	€ 3,00
child (under 7 yrs)	€ 2,00
pitch	€ 3,50
electricity	€ 2,50

No credit cards.

Reservations

Advised in high season. Tel: 02 98 29 81 82.
When closed contact the Mairie. Tel: 02 98 29 90 76.

FR29000 Yelloh! Village Les Mouettes

Mobile homes page 362

La Grande Grève, 29660 Carantec (Finistère)

Les Mouettes is less than 15 kilometres from the Roscoff ferry port, so is well situated when heading to or from home, although it also provides many facilities for a longer family holiday. For those who do not want to drive too far, the area has plenty to offer with beautiful bays and many places of interest within easy reach. Les Mouettes is a sheltered site on the edge of an attractive bay with access to the sea at the front of the site. In a wooded setting with many attractive trees and shrubs, the 273 pitches include just 70 for touring units, the remainder being taken by tour operators and around 60 site-owned mobile homes and tents (located together at the top of the site). The touring pitches, mostly arranged in hedged areas in the lower areas of the site, are of a good size and all have electricity. The focal point of the site is an impressive heated pool complex comprising a water slide pool and three water slides, 'tropical river', swimming pool, paddling pool, a jacuzzi and a sauna.

Facilities

Three clean unisex sanitary blocks include washbasins in cabins, mainly British toilets and baby bathrooms. Facilities for disabled people. Laundry facilities. Motorcaravan services. Shop (19/5-12/9, limited hours outside the main season). Takeaway. Centrally located bar (15/5-12/9) overlooking pool complex. Games and TV rooms. Play area. Volleyball, two half-courts for tennis and minigolf (in peak season). Table tennis. Discos and other entertainment organised in main season. American style motorhomes and double axle caravans should phone first. Off site: Golf 2 km. Riding 6 km. Bicycle hire 10 km. Beach 2 km.

At a glance

Welcome & Ambience	✓✓✓✓✓	Location	✓✓✓✓
Quality of Pitches	✓✓✓✓	Range of Facilities	✓✓✓✓✓

Directions

From D58 Roscoff - Morlaix road, turn to Carantec on D173. Site is approx. 4 km. from here on the outskirts of the village, signed to the left at roundabout immediately after passing supermarket on right.

Charges 2005

Per unit incl. 2 persons, electricity and water	€ 15,00 - € 39,50
child (under 7 yrs)	free - € 4,00

Reservations

Write to site with deposit (€ 46) and fee (€ 18.29).
Tel: 02 98 67 02 46.
E-mail: camping@les-mouettes.com

Open

1 May - 11 September.

FR29080 Camping Le Panoramic

Route de la Plage-Penker, 29560 Telgruc-sur-Mer (Finistère)

This medium sized, traditional style site is situated on quite a steep, ten acre hillside, with fine views along the coast. It is well tended and personally run by M. Jacq and his family who all speak good English. The site is in two parts, divided by a fairly quiet road leading to a good beach. The main upper site is where most of the facilities are situated, with the swimming pool, terrace and a playground located with the lower pitches across the road. Some up-and-down walking is therefore necessary, but this is a small price to pay for such pleasant and comfortable surroundings. The 200 pitches are arranged on flat, shady terraces, mostly in small groups with hedges and flowering shrubs and 20 pitches have services for motorcaravans. A good area for lovely coastal footpaths. A 'Sites et Paysages' member.

Facilities

The main site has two well kept toilet blocks with another very good block opened for main season across the road. All three blocks include British and Turkish style WCs, washbasins in cubicles, facilities for disabled people, baby baths, dishwashing, plus washing machines and dryers. Motorcaravan services. Small shop (1/7-31/8). Bar/restaurant with good value takeaway (1/7-31/8). Barbecue area. Heated swimming pool, paddling pool and jacuzzi (all 15/5-7/9). Playground. Games and TV rooms. Children's club in season. Sports ground with tennis courts, volleyball. Bicycle hire. Off site: Fishing 700 m. Good sandy beach 700 m. downhill by road, bit less on foot. Riding 6 km. Golf 14 km. Sailing school nearby.

At a glance

Welcome & Ambience	✓✓✓✓✓	Location	✓✓✓✓
Quality of Pitches	✓✓✓	Range of Facilities	✓✓✓✓

Directions

Site is just south of Telgruc-sur-Mer. On D887 pass through Ste Marie du Ménez Horn. In 11 km. turn left on D208 signed Telgruc-sur-Mer. Continue straight on through the town and site is on right within 1 km.

Charges 2005

Per person	€ 5,00
child (under 7 yrs)	€ 3,00
pitch	€ 12,00
electricity (6-10A)	€ 3,10 - € 4,50
water and drainage connection	€ 2,50
dog	€ 1,60

Less 20% outside July/Aug.

Reservations

Made for any period; contact site.
Tel: 02 98 27 78 41.
E-mail: info@camping-panoramic.com

Open

1 June - 15 September.

CAMPSITE INSPECTIONS

Every campsite in this guide has been inspected and selected by one our seasonal campsite inspection teams.

Our teams are required to visit typically between 30 and 50 sites and submit detailed reports on each site visited.

We now have a number of vacancies for campsite Inspectors and would be interested to hear from candidates with a good knowledge of camping and caravanning. A fee is paid for each inspection, as well as travel expenses.

For applications for these posts and further information, please contact:

Rod Wheat
Alan Rogers Guides Ltd, Spelmonden Old Oast, Goudhurst TN17 1HE
Fax: 01580 214001 Email: contact@alanrogers.com

INSPECTED & SELECTED CAMPSITES

FR29060 Camping Caravaning Le Pil-Koad

Mobile homes page 363

Route de Douarnenez, Poullan-sur-Mer, 29100 Douarnenez (Finistère)

Pil Koad is an attractive, family run site just back from the sea near Douarnenez in Finistère. It has 190 pitches on fairly flat ground, marked out by separating hedges and of quite good quality, though varying in size and shape. With 100 pitches used for touring units, the site also has a number of mobile homes and chalets. Nearly all pitches have electrical connections and the original trees provide shade in some areas. A large, modern room, named the 'Woodpecker Bar', is used for entertainment with discos and cabaret organised in July and August. A small shop selling basics is part of the same complex. The gates are closed 10.30 - 07.00 hrs. The village is 500 m. with a choice of restaurants and the town of Douarnez is 6 km. A variety of beaches is within easy reach (the nearest sandy beach is 5 km), and this coast offers some wonderful scenery and is ideal for walking.

Facilities

Two main toilet blocks in modern style include mainly British style WCs and washbasins mostly in cabins. Laundry facilities. Motorcaravan service point. Gas supplies. Small shop for basics (15/6-11/9). Takeaway (25/6-4/9). Heated swimming pool and paddling pool (no bermuda-style shorts). Tennis court. Table tennis. Minigolf. Volleyball. Fishing. Bicycle hire. Playground. Weekly outings and clubs for children (30/6-30/8) with charge included in tariff.
Off site: Restaurants in village 500 m. Riding 4 km. Nearest sandy beach 5 km. Douarnenez 6 km.

Open

15 May - 28 September.

At a glance

Welcome & Ambience	✓✓✓✓	Location	✓✓✓✓
Quality of Pitches	✓✓✓✓✓	Range of Facilities	✓✓✓✓

Directions

Site is 500 m. east from the centre of Poullan on D7 road towards Douarnenez. From Douarnenez take circular bypass route towards Audierne; if you see road for Poullan sign at roundabout, take it, otherwise there is camping sign at turning to Poullan from the D765 road.

Charges 2004

Per person	€ 3,00 - € 4,50
child (under 7 yrs)	€ 1,50 - € 3,00
pitch	€ 6,20 - € 13,00
electricity (10A)	€ 3,50
dog	€ 2,00 - € 3,00

Camping Cheques accepted.

Reservations

Made for min. 1 week with 25% deposit and fee (€ 19). Tel: 02 98 74 26 39.
E-mail: info@pil-koad.com

FR29050 Castel Camping L'Orangerie de Lanniron

Mobile homes ▶ page 363

Château de Lanniron, 29336 Quimper (Finistère)

L'Orangerie is a beautiful and peaceful, family site in 10 acres of a XVIIth century, 42 acre country estate on the banks of the Odet river. It is just to the south of Quimper and about 15 km. from the sea and beaches at Bénodet. The family's five year programme to restore the park, the original canal, fountains, ornamental 'Bassin de Neptune' (where visitors may now fish), the boathouse and the gardens and avenues is now complete. The original outbuildings have been attractively converted around a walled courtyard. The site has 200 grassy pitches, 146 for touring units. Of three types (varying in size and services), they are on fairly flat ground laid out in rows alongside access roads with shrubs and bushes providing pleasant pitches. All have electricity and 88 have all three services. The restaurant in the beautiful XVIIth century Orangerie, and the Gardens are both open to the public and in Spring the rhododendrons and azaleas are magnificent, with lovely walks within the grounds. Used by tour operators (34 pitches). All facilities are available when the site is open.

Facilities

The main heated block in the courtyard has been totally refurbished and is excellent. A second modern block serves the newer pitches at the top of the site and includes facilities for disabled people and babies. Washing machines and dryers. Motorcaravan service point. Shop (15/5-9/9). Gas supplies. Bar, snacks and takeaway, plus restaurant (open daily from 25/5-5/9, reasonably priced with children's menu). Heated swimming pool (144 sq.m.) with paddling pool. New pool planned. Small play area. Tennis. Minigolf, attractively set among mature trees. Table tennis. Fishing. Archery. Bicycle hire. General reading, games and billiards rooms. TV/video room (cable and satellite). Karaoke. Animation provided including outdoor activities with large room for indoor activities. Off site: Two hypermarkets 1 km. Historic town of Quimper under 3 km. Beach 15 km.

At a glance

Welcome & Ambience	✓✓✓✓✓	Location	✓✓✓✓
Quality of Pitches	✓✓✓✓	Range of Facilities	✓✓✓✓

Directions

From Quimper follow 'Quimper Sud' signs, then 'Toutes Directions' and general camping signs, finally signs for Lanniron.

Charges 2004

Per adult	€ 6,00
child (2-7 yrs)	€ 4,00
pitch (100 sq.m.)	€ 14,00
with electricity (10A)	€ 18,00
special pitch (120/150 sq.m.)	
with water and electricity	€ 21,00
animal	€ 3,50

Less 15% outside July/Aug.
Camping Cheques accepted.

Reservations

Made with deposit (€ 70) and fee (€ 20).
Tel: 02 98 90 62 02. E-mail: camping@lanniron.com

Open

15 May - 15 September.

TRAVEL SERVICE SITE

TO BOOK CALL 0870 405 4055 OR www.alanrogersdirect.com

FR29120 Yelloh! Village Le Manoir de Kerlut

29740 Plobannalec-Lesconil (Finistère)

Le Manoir de Kerlut is a comfortable site in the grounds of a manor house on a river estuary near Pont l'Abbe. The old 'Manoir' is not open to the public, but is used occasionally for weddings and private functions. The campsite has neat, modern buildings and is laid out on flat grass providing 240 pitches (90 for touring units). All have electricity connections, some also have water and drainage and around ten pitches have hardstanding. One area is rather open with separating hedges planted, the other part being amongst more mature bushes and some trees which provide shade. Site amenities are of good quality. Used by tour operators (18 pitches). A 'Yelloh Village' member.

Facilities

Toilet facilities in two good blocks (each with several rooms, not all open outside July/Aug), include washbasins all in cabins, and facilities for babies and disabled people. Laundry. Small shop. Takeaway. Large modern bar with TV (satellite) and entertainment all season. Bar in the Manoir. Two heated swimming pools, paddling pool and water slide. Sauna, solarium and small gym. Play area. Tennis, volleyball, badminton and petanque. Games room. Bicycle hire. Gates closed 22.30 - 7.30 hrs. Off site: Beach 2 km. Fishing 2 km. Riding 5 km. Golf 15 km.

Open

15 May - 11 September, with all services.

At a glance

Welcome & Ambience	✓✓✓✓	Location	✓✓✓✓
Quality of Pitches	✓✓✓✓✓	Range of Facilities	✓✓✓✓✓

Directions

From Pont l'Abbé, on D785, take D102 road towards Lesconil. Site is signed on the left, shortly after the village of Plobannalec.

Charges 2004

Per unit incl. 2 persons and 5A electricity	€ 15,00 - € 36,00
extra person	€ 4,00 - € 6,00
child (under 7 yrs)	free - € 4,00
electricity (10A)	free - € 1,00
dog	€ 2,50 - € 3,50

Reservations

Write to site with 10% deposit. Tel: 02 98 82 23 89. E-mail: info@campingsbretagnesud.com

FR29110 Yelloh! Village La Plage

Rue de Men-Meur B.P. 9, 29730 Le Guilvinec (Finistère)

La Plage is a friendly site located beside a long sandy beach between the fishing town of Le Guilvinec and the watersports beaches of Penmarc'h on the southwest tip of Brittany. It is spacious and surrounded by tall trees, which provide shelter, and is made up of several flat, sandy meadows. The 410 pitches (100 for touring units) are arranged on either side of sandy access roads, mostly not separated but all numbered. There is less shade in the newer areas. Electricity is available on most pitches. Like all beach-side sites, the facilities receive heavy use. There is plenty to occupy one at this friendly site but the bustling fishing harbour at Le Guilvinec and the watersports of Penmarc'h and Pointe de la Torche are within easy travelling distance. Used by tour operators (176 pitches). A 'Yelloh Village' member.

TRAVEL SERVICE SITE

TO BOOK CALL 0870 405 4055 OR www.alanrogersdirect.com

Facilities

Five sanitary blocks are of differing designs but all provide modern, bright facilities including washbasins in cabins, good facilities for children and toilets for disabled people. Laundry facilities. Motorcaravan service point. Shop with gas supplies. Bright, airy well furnished bar, crêperie and takeaway. Heated swimming pool with paddling pool and water slide. Sauna. Play area. TV room. Tennis courts. Volleyball, basketball, minigolf, badminton, petanque, table tennis, giant chess/draughts. Bicycle hire. Beach. Off site: Fishing and watersports near. Riding 5 km. Golf 20 km.

Open

15 May - 11 September, with all facilities.

At a glance

Welcome & Ambience	✓✓✓✓✓	Location	✓✓✓✓✓
Quality of Pitches	✓✓✓	Range of Facilities	✓✓✓✓

Directions

Site is west of Guilvinec. From Pont l'Abbé, take the D785 road towards Penmarc'h. In Plomeur, turn left on D57 signed Guilvinec. On entering Guilvinec fork right signed Port and camping. Follow road along coast to site on left.

Charges 2004

Per unit incl. 2 persons and 5A electricity	€ 15,00 - € 36,00
extra person	€ 4,00 - € 6,00
child (under 10 yrs)	free - € 4,00
electricity (10A)	free - € 1,00
dog	€ 2,50 - € 3,50

Reservations

Advised and accepted until 15/6 with deposit (25%) and fee (€ 19). Tel: 02 98 58 61 90. E-mail: info@campingsbretagnesud.com

FR29020 Camping Club du Saint Laurent

Kerleven, 29940 La Forêt-Fouesnant (Finistère)

Saint-Laurent is a well established site, situated on a sheltered wooded slope bordering one of the many attractive little inlets that typify the Brittany coastline. There is direct access from the site to two small sandy bays, which empty at low tide to reveal numerous rockpools (ideal for children to explore), and the site is on the coastal footpath. The 260 pitches are on level terraces, under tall trees. All are of average size (100 sq.m) and divided by hedges and partly shaded, all with electricity connections. Pitches with the best sea views tend to be adjacent to the cliff edge and may not be suitable for families with young children. Access to some places can be a little difficult, but the friendly site owners ensure that this is not a problem by offering to site any caravan using their own 4 x 4 vehicle. The swimming pool (with paddling pool and two water slides) is overlooked by the bar terrace. With organised activities and entertainment in high season, this site is an ideal choice for a lively family holiday, particularly for older children. Around 50% of the pitches are occupied by tour operators or site owned mobile homes.

Facilities

Two sanitary blocks provide combined shower and washbasin cubicles, separate washbasin cubicles, baby changing and facilities for disabled people. Laundry and dishwashing sinks. Washing machines, dryers and ironing. Small shop at reception provides essentials. Bar, snack bar and takeaway (all 12/5-10/9). Swimming pools. Gym and sauna. Canoe hire. Basketball, two tennis courts (no charge), and table tennis. Play area. During July and August daily entertainment for adults and children is organised (in English as well as in French), with discos in the bar each evening.

Open

2 May - 10 September.

At a glance

Welcome & Ambience	✓✓✓✓	Location	✓✓✓✓✓
Quality of Pitches	✓✓✓✓	Range of Facilities	✓✓✓✓

Directions

From N165 take D70 Concarneau exit. At first roundabout take D44 (Fouesnant). After 2.5 km. turn right at T-junction, follow for 2.5 km, then turn left (Port La Forêt - 200 m. before the junction is a sign that implies Port La Forêt is straight on, and it isn't). Continue to roundabout, straight ahead (Port La Forêt) and in 1 km. turn left. In 400 m left turn to site.

Charges 2004

Per unit incl. 1 or 2 persons, electricity and water	€ 15,00 - € 33,00
extra person	€ 2,50 - € 5,50
child (2-7 yrs)	free - € 3,50

Reservations

Advised for July/Aug. and made with deposit (€ 77) and fee (€ 22.87). Tel: 02 98 56 97 65. E-mail: info@camping-du-saint-laurent.fr

FR29030 Camping du Letty

29950 Bénodet (Finistère)

Built around their former farm, the Guyader family have ensured that this excellent and attractive site, with direct beach access, has plenty to offer for all the family. The site on the outskirts of the popular resort of Bénodet spreads over 22 acres with 493 pitches, all for touring units. Groups of eight to ten pitches are set in cul-de-sacs with mature hedging and trees to divide each cul-de-sac. Markers indicate the limits of each pitch which are slightly smaller than average (none more than about 80 sq.m), although they do not feel too small since they are not hedged or fenced. Most pitches have electricity, water and drainage. At the attractive floral entrance, former farm buildings provide a host of facilities including an extensively equipped fitness room. There is also a modern, purpose built nightclub and bar providing high quality live entertainment most evenings (situated well away from most pitches to avoid disturbance). Although there is no swimming pool here, the site has direct access to a small sandy beach, and has provided a floating pontoon with a diving platform and water slides into the sea (safe bathing depends on the tides).

Facilities

Six well placed toilet blocks are of good quality and include mixed style WCs, washbasins in large cabins and controllable hot showers (charged). One block includes a separate laundry and dog washing enclosures. Four well equipped baby rooms. Separate facility for disabled visitors. Launderette. Hairdressing room. Motorcaravan service points. Well stocked mini-market. Extensive snack bar and takeaway (22/6-30/8). Bar with games room and night club. Library/reading room. Games lounge with billiard and card tables and entertainment room with satellite TV. Fitness centre (no charge). Saunas, jacuzzis and solarium (all on payment). Table tennis. Two tennis and two squash courts (charged). Boules, volleyball, basketball and archery. Well equipped play area. In July/Aug. entertainment and activities organised for the whole family.

At a glance

Welcome & Ambience	✓✓✓✓	Location	✓✓✓✓✓
Quality of Pitches	✓✓✓	Range of Facilities	✓✓✓✓

Directions

From N165 take D70 Concarneau exit. At first roundabout take D44 to Fouesnant. Turn right at T-junction. After about 2 km. turn left to Fouesnant (still D44). Continue through La Forêt Fouesnant and Fouesnant, picking up signs for Bénodet. Shortly before Benodet at roundabout turn left (signed Le Letty). Turn right at next mini roundabout and site is 500 m. on left.

Charges 2004

Per adult	€ 5,00
child (under 7 yrs)	€ 2,50
pitch	€ 7,00
car or motorcaravan	€ 1,70
m/cycle	€ 1,20
electricity (1, 2, 5 or 10A)	€ 1,50 - € 4,00

Reservations

Not made. Tel: 02 98 57 04 69.
E-mail: reception@campingduletty.com

Open

15 June - 6 September.

FR29240 Camping de Kéranterec

Route de Port la Forêt, 29940 La Forêt Fouesnant (Finistère)

The area around La Forêt Fouesnant is very much 'picture postcard' Brittany - plenty of enticing crêperies and seafood restaurants, enchanting mediaeval villages and towns and delightful hidden coves. For these and many other reasons, there are plenty of campsites to choose from and Camping de Keranterec is well worth considering. A well established family run site with a very French ambience (unlike some of the neighbouring sites which have a much higher UK presence), Keranterec has 265 grassy pitches in two distinct areas. The upper part of the site is more open and has little shade, and is also largely taken up by private mobile homes. The lower and more mature area is predominantly for tourers, with terraced pitches set in a former orchard (the trees still provide fruit for the cider produced on site, which we can highly recommend!). Some of these pitches have shade from the many trees on this part of the site, and some also overlook the little cove at the rear of the site. Spacious and divided by mature hedging, all have electrical connections (25 m. cable advised) and most also offer water and drainage. At the rear of the site a gate leads to a small beach and the coastal footpath to Concarneau (8 km).

TRAVEL SERVICE SITE

TO BOOK CALL 0870 405 4055 OR
www.alanrogersdirect.com

Facilities

Two modern, fully equipped toilet blocks kept very clean include washbasins in cubicles, baby baths and facilities for disabled visitors. Washing machines, dryers and ironing boards. Small shop and bar (15/6-7/9) and takeaway (1/7-31/8). TV room with satellite. Heated swimming pool (15/5-7/9) with paddling pool, jacuzzi and three new water slides. Tennis court, boules, volleyball and basketball, table tennis (some indoors). Play area. In July/Aug. organised daily events and activities for all the family, and a free children's club. Off site: Attractive sandy beach of Kerleven ten minutes walk. Golf 1 km. Riding 3 km.

Open

10 April - 19 September.

At a glance

Welcome & Ambience	✓✓✓✓✓	Location	✓✓✓✓✓
Quality of Pitches	✓✓✓✓	Range of Facilities	✓✓✓✓✓

Directions

From N165 take D70 Concarneau exit. At first roundabout take D44 signed Fouesnant. After 2.5 km. turn right at T-junction, and follow for 2.5 km. and turn left (Port La Forêt - take care, 200 m. before junction a sign implies Port La Forêt is straight on - it isn't). Continue to roundabout and take second exit (straight on, Port La Forêt). After 1 km. turn left (site signed), then in 400 m. turn left to site on left.

Charges 2004

Per person	€ 5,25 - € 7,00
child (under 7 yrs)	€ 2,65 - € 3,50
pitch	€ 6,75 - € 9,00
electricity	€ 3,50
dog	€ 1,75 - € 2,30

Reservations

Advised in high season and made with deposit (€ 77) and fee (€ 22). Tel: 02 98 56 98 11.
E-mail: info@camping-keranterec.com

FR29190 Camping Les Prés Verts

Kernous-Plage, 29900 Concarneau (Finistère)

What sets this family site apart from the many others in this region are its more unusual features - its stylish pool complex with Romanesque style columns and statue, and its plants and flower tubs. The 150 pitches are mostly arranged on long, open, grassy areas either side of main access roads. Specimen trees, shrubs or hedges divide the site into smaller areas. There are a few individual pitches and an area towards the rear of the site where the pitches have sea views. Concarneau is just 2.5 km. and there are many marked coastal walks to enjoy in the area, plus watersports or boat and fishing trips available nearby. A 'Sites et Paysages' member.

Facilities

Two toilet blocks provide unisex WCs, but separate washing facilities for ladies and men. Pre-set hot showers and washbasins in cabins for ladies, both closed 9 pm - 8 am. Some child-size toilets. Dishwashing and laundry sinks, washing machine and dryer. Pizza service twice weekly. Swimming pool (1/6-31/8; around 18 x 11 m.) and paddling pool. Playground (0-5 yrs only). Minigolf. Off site: Path to sandy/rocky beach (300 m.) and coastal path. Riding 1 km. Supermarket 2 km. Bicycle hire 3 km. Golf 5 km.

At a glance

Welcome & Ambience	✓✓✓	Location	✓✓✓✓✓
Quality of Pitches	✓✓✓✓	Range of Facilities	✓✓✓

Directions

Turn off C7 road, 2.5 km. north of Concarneau, where site is signed. Take third left after Hotel de l'Océan.

Charges 2004

Per unit incl. 2 adults	€ 16,48 - € 20,60
extra adult	€ 4,76 - € 5,95
child (2-7 yrs)	€ 3,12 - € 3,90
dog	€ 1,16 - € 1,45
electricity (2-6A)	€ 2,90 - € 4,43

Reservations

Contact site. Tel: 02 98 97 09 74.
E-mail: info@pres-verts.com

Open

1 May - 22 September.

FR29350 Sunêlia L'Atlantique

Mousterlin, 29170 Fouesnant (Finistère)

L'Atlantique is quietly situated just outside Beg-Meil and is a superb site for families and those looking for a beach holiday. The sandy beach faces the Glénan Islands and is a pleasant 400 m. walk away through a nature reserve. The 432 pitches are predominantly used by tour operators with about 70 for independent visitors. Level and grassy, all with electricity, they are separated by an attractive variety of low shrubs, with apple orchards used for cider production also on the site. All the facilities are grouped together at the centre of the site including an innovative play area and excellent pool complex with water slides and a paddling pool. Coastal paths await exploration and Concarneau, Pont-Aven and La Pointe du Raz are all nearby.

Facilities

Clean, modern, fully equipped toilet blocks incude facilities for disabled visitors. Shop. Bar. Snack bar with takeaway meals and pizza. Heated outdoor pool, water complex with slides (all 15/5-12/9). Tennis. TV room. Billiards, table tennis. Minigolf. Sports ground. Play area. Children's club (4-12 yrs) and evening entertainment in July/Aug. Off site: Fishing 300 m. Windsurf hire 1 km. Boat hire 3 or 5 km. Riding 3 km. Golf 8 km.

At a glance

Welcome & Ambience	✓✓✓✓	Location	✓✓✓
Quality of Pitches	✓✓✓	Range of Facilities	✓✓✓✓✓

Directions

From Fouesnant follow directions for Mousterlin for 4.5 km. Site is signed.

Charges 2004

Per unit incl. 2 persons	€ 21,00 - € 36,00
extra person	€ 2,70 - € 6,00
child (0-10 yrs)	€ 1,30 - € 3,00

Camping Cheques accepted.
Low season reductions.

Reservations

Contact site. Tel: 02 98 56 14 44.
E-mail: information@camping-atlantique.fr

Open

1 May - 15 September.

FR29310 Camping La Roche Percée

Hent Kerveltrec, Beg-Meil, 29170 Fouesnant (Finistère)

Close to the beautiful Brittany coastline, La Roche Percée combines a tranquil setting with a friendly and active family environment, only 400 metres from the beach. Under new ownership, there are 123 pitches, of which 80 are for touring units, the rest being for privately owned or site owned mobile homes. Pitches are arranged in cul-de-sacs off a central area and are of a good size, grassy and flat, all with electrical connections (some may require a long lead). All pitches are separated by mature hedging, and some benefit from the shade of the variety of trees planted around the site. The bar terrace overlooks the swimming and paddling pools, and there is a waterslide into the main pool. During high season the owners organise a variety of entertainment activities, including boules, table tennis, pool and arts tournaments, barbecues, and live music in the bar.

Facilities

The clean, tidy central toilet block includes mostly British style toilets, washbasins in cubicles, dishwashing and laundry sinks. Baby bath and changing area. Wheelchair access provided on request. Motorcaravan service point. Small shop, snack bar and bar (open 15/5-15/9, with bread to order outside these dates.) Swimming pools (all season). Two play areas. Football and volleyball. Large trampoline (parental supervision essential!) Bicycle hire. Off site: Beach 400 m. Sailing school, golf and riding nearby.

Open

2 April - 26 September.

At a glance

Welcome & Ambience	✓✓✓✓	Location	✓✓✓✓✓
Quality of Pitches	✓✓✓✓	Range of Facilities	✓✓✓✓

Directions

From N165 take D70 Concarneau exit. At roundabout take first exit on D44 (signed Fouesnant, Benodet). On D44 turn right at T-junction, after 2 km. turn left and through Forêt Fouesnant. About 2 km. after village go straight over first roundabout and turn left at second on D45 to Beg Meil. After 3 km. site is signed on left.

Charges 2004

Per adult	€ 3,00 - € 4,50
child (under 7 yrs)	€ 1,50 - € 2,50
pitch	€ 8,50 - € 11,50
electricity (6/10A)	€ 3,00

Reservations

Accepted with deposit (€ 77) and fee (€ 15.50).
Tel: 02 98 94 94 15.
E-mail: contact@camping-larochepercee.com

FR29170 Camping de la Piscine

Kerleya B.P.12, Beg-Meil, 29170 Fouesnant (Finistère)

There are many campsites in this area but La Piscine is notable for the care and attention to detail that contributes to the well-being of its visitors. Created by the Caradec family from an apple orchard, the 185 level, grass pitches are of generous size and are separated by an interesting variety of hedges and trees. Water, waste and electricity points are provided, normally one stand between two pitches. A quiet site, set back from the sea, La Piscine will appeal to families looking for good quality without too many on site activities.

TRAVEL SERVICE SITE

TO BOOK CALL 0870 405 4055 OR www.alanrogersdirect.com

Facilities

Two refurbished toilet units of differing design and size include British and Turkish style toilets and washbasins in cabins. Facilities for disabled people. Washing machines and dryers. Motorcaravan service point. Shop. Takeaway (high season). Attractive pool, three slides, waterfall and jacuzzi. Sauna and solarium. Play area. BMX track. Football, volleyball and half-court tennis. TV room. Entertainment in high season. Caravan storage. Off site: Bicycle hire, fishing and riding within 4 km. Golf 7 km. Beach 1 km.

Open

15 May - 15 September.

At a glance

Welcome & Ambience	✓✓✓✓	Location	✓✓✓✓
Quality of Pitches	✓✓✓✓✓	Range of Facilities	✓✓✓✓

Directions

Site is 5 km. south of Fouesnant. Turn off N165 expressway at Coat Conq signed Concarnau and Fouesnant. At Fouesnant join D45 signed Beg Meil and shortly turn left on D145 signed Mousterlin. In 1 km. turn left and follow signs to site.

Charges 2004

Per person	€ 3,50 - € 5,00
child (under 7 yrs)	€ 1,75 - € 2,50
pitch	€ 7,00 - € 10,00
electricity (3-10A)	€ 2,85 - € 4,20

Reservations

Made with deposit (€ 40) and fee (€ 19).
Tel: 02 98 56 56 06.
E-mail: contact@campingdelapiscine.com

FR29160 Camping Les Genets d'Or

Kermerour, Pont Kereon, 29380 Bannalec (Finistère)

A jewel of a small site, Les Genets d'Or is situated in a tiny country hamlet at the end of a road from Bannalec, 12 km. from Pont-Aven in Finistère. The spacious surroundings offer a safe haven for young children and a rural, tranquil environment for adults. The gently sloping, grassy site is edged with mature trees and divided into hedged glades with the odd apple tree providing shade. There are only 52 pitches (46 for touring units), all of a good size - some of over 100 sq.m. - and most pitches have electricity, each glade having a water point. Alan and Judy, the English owners, provide a warm friendly welcome and are justifiably proud of their site which they have improved over the last few years and keep in pristine condition. There are plans for a play area and pond.

Facilities

The good quality toilet block provides all the necessary amenities and washing facilities, including a shower for disabled campers. Washing machine and dryer. New bar area. Bread delivered in season. Ice pack service. Reception has a small library and an indoor room provides snooker and table tennis. Bicycle hire. Caravan storage. Off site: Riding 3 km. Beach 12 km. The village 15 minutes walk.

Open

Easter/1 April - 30 September.

At a glance

Welcome & Ambience	✓✓✓✓✓	Location	✓✓✓✓✓
Quality of Pitches	✓✓✓✓✓	Range of Facilities	✓✓✓✓✓

Directions

Take exit D4 from N165 towards Bannalec. In Bannalec turn right into Rue Lorec (signed Quimperlé) and follow camp signs for 1 km.

Charges 2004

Per person	€ 3,00
child (under 6 yrs)	€ 2,00
pitch	€ 5,50
electricity (6A)	€ 3,00

Less 10% for over 7 nights.

Reservations

Contact site. Tel: 02 98 39 54 35.
E-mail: enquiries@holidaybrittany.com

FR29140 Haven Camping Domaine de Kerlann

Land Rosted, 29930 Pont-Aven (Finistère)

Haven Europe have, with careful and imaginative planning, ensured that their mobile homes here blend naturally into the environment. The remaining 20% of around 110 touring pitches (some 80 sq.m, some 120 sq.m, all with electricity) have been left in a more natural situation on rough grass with a small stream flowing through and with some mature trees providing shade. Land drainage is poor due to the park being on low lying ground. The 'piece de resistance' is the amazing pool complex comprising three outdoor pools with separate toboggan, attractively landscaped with sunbathing terraces, and an indoor tropical style complex complete with jacuzzi and its own toboggan. Much holiday camp style entertainment (with a French flavour) takes place on the bar terrace with its stage overlooking the complex.

Facilities

The main large toilet block on the centre of the mobile home area includes washbasins in cubicles, outside dishwashing and laundry sinks. Good laundry. A second block in the touring section opens in high season. Mini supermarket. French style restaurant, snack restaurant, takeaway and bar. Impressive pool complex including indoor and outdoor pools with lifeguards. Well equipped play areas. All weather multi-sports court, tennis courts, minigolf. Video games room, pool tables and satellite TV in the bar. Three children's clubs for different age groups. Gas barbecues are not permitted. Off site: Pont-Aven with its Gauguin connection, art galleries and museums is well worth visiting. Small ports and villages nearby. Beach 5 km.

At a glance

Welcome & Ambience	✓✓✓	Location	✓✓✓
Quality of Pitches	✓✓	Range of Facilities	✓✓✓✓

Directions

From Tregunc - Pont-Aven road, turn south towards Névez and site is on right.

Charges 2004

Per pitch incl. up to 2 persons	
with electricity	€ 13,00 - € 34,00
extra person	€ 3,00 - € 6,00
extra vehicle	€ 1,00 - € 4,00

Reservations

Accepted at any time for min. 4 days; no booking fee. Contact site or Haven Europe in the UK on 0870 242 7777 for information or reservation.
Tel: 02 98 06 01 77. E-mail: kerlann@haven.fr

Open

18 March - 30 October.

FR29250 Camping Bois des Ecureuils

29300 Guilligomarc'h (Finistère)

Situated in beautiful countryside between the rivers Scorff and Elle, this two star site provides camping 'au naturelle' for those seeking an ideal base from which to explore southern and central Brittany. The site is set in nine acres of natural woodland and open field with oak, chestnut, birch and beech trees providing a leafy backdrop to many of the 40 pitches. With a choice of sunny or shady pitches bordered by shrubs and trees, many pitches have electrical connections. The new British owners are able to provide a wealth of information on places to visit and activities in the area, including walking, cycling, canoeing and fishing. The tranquillity and peacefulness of this rural setting, combined with the friendly reception make it ideal for anyone seeking a relaxing holiday in the countryside whilst still only a short drive from southern Brittany's finest beaches.

Facilities

Small toilet block with showers, washbasins in cubicles, British and Turkish style WCs, dishwashing and laundry facilities. Reception/shop provides basic groceries and bread to order. Play area. Large grass leisure area with boules pitch, table tennis and badminton net. Bicycle and kayak hire. Off site: Beach 17 km.

Open

15 May - 15 September.

At a glance

Welcome & Ambience	✓✓✓✓✓	Location	✓✓✓✓
Quality of Pitches	✓✓✓	Range of Facilities	✓✓✓

Directions

From south on N165 take D769 (Lorient) to Carhaix Plouguer - Morlaix road. After 24 km. turn right onto D6(E) to Meslan/Arzano. In 700 m. take next left onto D6 towards Arzano. After 1 km. turn left onto C2 to Guilligomarch and site is on left in 1.1 km.

Charges 2004

Per person	€ 2,50
child (under 7 yrs)	€ 1,35
pitch	€ 4,10
electricity (5A)	€ 2,30
animal	€ 1,00

No credit cards.

Reservations

Made with deposit (€ 15); contact site.
Tel: 02 98 71 70 98.
E-mail: bois-des-ecureuils@tiscali.fr

FR29290 Yelloh! Village Le Grand Large

48 route du Grand Large, Mousterlin, 29170 Fouesnant (Finistère)

Le Grand Large is a beach-side site situated on the Pointe de Mousterlin in natural surroundings. The site is separated from the beach by the road that follows the coast around the point. It is also protected from the wind by an earth bank with trees and a fence. The beach itself looks over the bay towards the Isles de Glénan. There are 300 pitches with just 54 rather small uneven places used for touring units. Tour operators take 70 pitches and the site itself has tents and mobile homes to rent. The ground is rather sandy in places with some shrubs and mature trees. Electricity is available everywhere (long leads useful) and some pitches have drainage. A small river runs through the site but it is fenced. Benodet (7 km.) and Fouesnant (5 km.) are near in different directions and the sandy beach is just up the steps and across the road. A family site, Le Grand Large would also suit nature lovers in the low seasons as it is next to a large tract of protected land, Marais de Mousterlin, ideal for walking, cycling and birdwatching.

TRAVEL SERVICE SITE

TO BOOK CALL 0870 405 4055 OR www.alanrogersdirect.com

Facilities

Two neat toilet blocks, the largest only opened in high season, include plenty of washbasins in cabins. Two baby baths in the larger block with children's shower and toilet and facilities for disabled people in both blocks. Washing machines, dryers and plenty of laundry and washing up sinks. Bar overlooking the sea with attractive terrace. Crêperie/grill restaurant including takeaway. Swimming pool with paddling pool, water slides in separate pool. Tennis court and multi-sport court for 5-a-side football, badminton, volleyball, handball or basketball. Small play area. TV room and games room with table tennis and billiards. Bicycle hire. Off site: Fishing 100 m. Golf and riding 5 km. Beach 100 m.

At a glance

Welcome & Ambience	✓✓✓✓	Location	✓✓✓✓✓
Quality of Pitches	✓✓	Range of Facilities	✓✓✓✓✓

Directions

Site is 7 km. south of Fouesnant. Turn off N165 expressway at Coat Conq, signed Concarneau and Fouesnant. At Fouesnant take A45 signed Beg Meil, then follow signs to Mousterlin. In Mousterlin turn left and follow camping signs.

Charges 2004

Per unit incl. 2 persons and 5A electricity	€ 15,00 - € 36,00
extra person	€ 4,00 - € 6,00
child (under 10 yrs)	free - € 4,00
electricity (10A)	free - € 1,00
dog	€ 2,50 - € 3,50

Reservations

Made with deposit (€ 45) and non-refundable fee (€ 19). Tel: 02 98 56 04 06.

Open

15 May - 8 September (with all services).

FR29010 Castel Camping Le Ty-Nadan

Mobile homes page 362

Route d'Arzano, 29310 Locunolé (Finistère)

Ty Nadan is a well organised site set amongst wooded countryside along the bank of the River Elle. The 183 pitches for touring units are grassy, many with shade and 152 with 10A electricity. An exciting and varied programme of activities is offered throughout the season – canoeing, rock climbing, mountain biking, aqua-gym, riding or walking – all supervised by qualified staff. A full programme of entertainment for all ages is provided in high season including concerts, Breton evenings with pig roasts, dancing, etc. (be warned, you will be actively encouraged to join in!) The pool complex with its slides and paddling pool is very popular and now has an attractive viewing platform. Super recent additions include a large indoor pool complex and an indoor games area with a climing wall. Several tour operators use the site (90 pitches). This is a wonderful site for families with children of all ages.

Facilities

Two older, split-level toilet blocks are of fair quality and unusual design, including washbasins in cabins and baby rooms. An impressively equipped block opened in 2002 provides easier access for disabled people. Dishwashing facilities in two attractive gazebo style units. Washing machines and dryers. Good sized restaurant, takeaway, bar and well stocked shop (all open all season). Crêperie (July/Aug). Heated outdoor pool (17 x 8 m) with water slides and paddling pool. New indoor pool. Small beach on the river (unfenced). Tennis courts, table tennis, pool tables, archery and trampolines. Indoor badminton and rock climbing facility. Exciting adventure play park and new 'Minikids' park for 5-8 yrs. Riding. Bicycle hire. Boat hire. Fishing. Canoe and sea kayaking expeditions. High season entertainment. Paintball. Off site: Beaches 20 minutes by car. Golf 12 km.

At a glance

Welcome & Ambience	✓✓✓✓✓	Location	✓✓✓
Quality of Pitches	✓✓✓✓✓	Range of Facilities	✓✓✓✓✓

Directions

Make for Arzano which is northeast of Quimperlé on the Pontivy road and turn off D22 just west of village at camp sign. Site is approx. 3 km.

Charges 2004

Per person	€ 7,10
child (under 7 yrs)	€ 4,50
pitch	€ 16,00
electricity (10A)	€ 5,70
dog	€ 4,80

Camping Cheques accepted.
Less 15-20% outside July/Aug.

Reservations

Made for exact dates with deposit (€ 50) and fee (€ 25). Tel: 02 98 71 75 47.
E-mail: TY-NADAN@wanadoo.fr

Open

15 May - 15 September.

TRAVEL SERVICE SITE
TO BOOK CALL 0870 405 4055 OR www.alanrogersdirect.com

FR29090 Camping Le Raguénès-Plage

Mobile homes ▶ page 364

19 rue des Iles, Raguénéz, 29920 Névez (Finistère)

Madame Guyader and her family will ensure you receive a warm welcome on arrival at this well kept and pleasant site. Although the entrance could best be described as more functional than beautiful, once you have passed the reception block you find yourself in an attractive and well laid out campsite with many shrubs and trees. The 287 pitches are a good size, flat and grassy, separated by trees and hedges. All have electricity, water and drainage. The site is used by one tour operator (63 pitches), and has 40 mobile homes of its own. A pool complex complete with water toboggan has recently been added. From the far end of the campsite a five minute walk along a path takes you down to a pleasant, sandy beach.

Facilities

Three clean, well maintained sanitary blocks include mixed style toilets, washbasins in cabins, baby baths and facilities for disabled visitors. Laundry and dishwashing sinks. Laundry room. Motorcaravan service point. Small shop (from 15/5). Bar and restaurant (from 1/6) with outside terrace and takeaway. Reading and TV room, internet access point. Heated pool with sun terrace and paddling pool. Sauna (charged). Play areas, table tennis, games room and volleyball. Various activities are organised in July/Aug. Currency and traveller's cheques can be exchanged at reception. Off site: Beach, fishing and watersports 300 m. Supermarket 3 km. Riding 4 km.

Open

1 April - 30 September.

At a glance

Welcome & Ambience	✓✓✓✓✓	Location	✓✓✓✓✓
Quality of Pitches	✓✓✓✓	Range of Facilities	✓✓✓✓✓

Directions

From N165 take D24 Kerampaou exit. After 3 km turn right towards Nizon and bear right at church in village following signs to Névez (D77). Continue straight over roundabout through Névez, following signs to Raguénès. Continue for about 3 km. to site entrance on left (take care - entrance is quite small and easy to miss).

Charges 2004

Per unit incl. 2 persons + car	€ 15,00 - € 25,00
extra person	€ 3,90 - € 5,50
child (under 7 yrs)	€ 2,20 - € 3,00
electricity 2/6A	€ 2,80 - € 3,30

Reservations

Advised for high season, min. 7 days preferred for July/Aug. Write with deposit (€ 100).
Tel: 02 98 06 80 69.
E-mail: info@camping-le-raguenes-plage.com

FR29180 Camping Les Embruns

Rue du Philosophe Alain, Le Pouldu, 29360 Clohars-Carnoët (Finistère)

This site is unusual in that it is located in the heart of a village, yet is only 250 metres from a sandy cove. It is also close to beautiful countryside and the Carnoët Forest. The entrance with its card operated barrier and wonderful floral displays, is the first indication that this is a well tended and well organised site, and the owners have won numerous regional and national awards for its superb presentation. The 180 pitches (100 occupied by mobile homes) are separated by trees, shrubs and bushes, and most have electricity, water and drainage. There is a covered, heated swimming pool, a circular paddling pool and a water play pool. It is only a short walk to the village centre with all its attractions and services.

Facilities

Two modern sanitary blocks, recently completely renewed, include mainly British style toilets, some washbasins in cubicles, baby baths and good facilities for disabled visitors. New family bathrooms. Dishwashing and laundry sinks under cover. Washing, drying and ironing facilities. Motorcaravan service point. Small shop (3/4-15/9). Bar and terrace (1/7-31/8) overlooking a covered, heated swimming pool (3/4-15/9) and paddling pool. Takeaway (20/6-5/9). Large games hall with pinball machines and table tennis. Play area. Football field, volleyball and minigolf. Communal barbecue area. Daily activities for children and adults organised in July/Aug. Off site: Nearby sea and river fishing and watersports. Bicycle hire 50 m. Riding 2 km. Good cycling in the surrounding countryside. Beach 250 m.

At a glance

Welcome & Ambience	✓✓✓✓	Location	✓✓✓✓
Quality of Pitches	✓✓✓✓	Range of Facilities	✓✓✓✓✓

Directions

From N165 take either 'Kervidanou, Quimperlé Ouest' exit or 'Kergostiou, Quimperlé Centre, Clohars Carnoët' exit and follow D16 to Clohars Carnoët. Then D24 for Le Pouldu and site signs in village.

Charges 2004

Per unit incl. 2 persons	€ 9,90 - € 21,50
fully serviced pitch	€ 13,90 - € 25,50
extra person	€ 3,70 - € 4,90
child (under 7 yrs)	€ 2,40 - € 3,00
electricity on ordinary pitch	€ 3,00
animal	free - € 1,00

Less in low seasons.
Use of motorcaravan services € 1.83.

Reservations

Advised for high season. Tel: 02 98 39 91 07.
E-mail: camping-les-embruns@wanadoo.fr

Open

9 April - 17 September.

FR35040 Camping Le P'tit Bois

Mobile homes page 365

35430 St Jouan des Guerets (Ille-et-Vilaine)

On the outskirts of Saint Malo, this neat, family oriented site is very popular with British visitors, being ideal for one night stops or for longer stays in this interesting area. Le P'tit Bois is a busy site providing 274 large level pitches (around 140 for touring units) which are divided into groups by mature hedges and trees, separated by shrubs and flowers and with access from tarmac roads. Nearly all have electrical hook-ups and over half have water taps. Behind reception, an attractive, sheltered terraced area around the pools provides a focus during the day along with the bar and snack bar. There are site-owned mobile homes and chalets but this does mean that the facilities are open over a long season (if only for limited hours).

Facilities

Two fully equipped toilet blocks, one in the newer area across the lane, include washbasins in cabins, baby baths and laundry facilities. Simple facilities for disabled people. Motorcaravan service point. Small shop (from 15/5). Bar where entertainment and discos are organised (July-Aug). Snack bar with takeaway, small bar, TV room (large screen for sports events) and games rooms. Swimming pool with paddling pool and two water slides (from 15/5). Indoor pool with jacuzzi and turkish bath. Playground and multi-sports court. Tennis court, minigolf, table tennis, and outdoor chess. Charcoal barbecues are not permitted. Card operated security gates (deposit). Off site: Beach 1.5 km. Fishing 1.5 km, bicycle hire or riding 5 km, golf 7 km.

At a glance

Welcome & Ambience	✓✓✓✓	Location	✓✓✓✓
Quality of Pitches	✓✓✓✓✓	Range of Facilities	✓✓✓✓✓

Directions

St Jouan is west off the St Malo - Rennes road (N137) just outside St Malo. Site is signed from the N137 (exit St Jouan or Quelmer).

Charges 2005

Per person	€ 6,00 - € 8,00
child (under 7 yrs)	€ 3,00 - € 5,00
pitch and car	€ 10,00 - € 20,00
electricity (6A)	€ 4,00
water and drainage (min 7 nights)	€ 4,00
dog	€ 4,00

Reservations

Made on receipt of 25% of total cost, plus fee (€ 30) in July and August. Tel: 02 99 21 14 30.
E-mail: camping.ptitbois@wanadoo.fr

Open

16 April - 10 September.

FR35000 Camping Le Vieux Chêne

Baguer-Pican, 35120 Dol-de-Bretagne (Ille-et-Vilaine)

This attractive, family owned site is situated between Saint Malo and Mont Saint Michel. Developed in the grounds of a country farmhouse dating from 1638, its young and enthusiastic new owner has created a really pleasant, traditional atmosphere. It offers 200 good sized pitches, most with electricity, water tap and light, in spacious rural surroundings on gently sloping grass. They are separated by bushes and flowers, with mature trees for shade. A very attractive tenting area (without electricity) is in the orchard. There are three lakes in the grounds and centrally located leisure facilities include an attractive pool complex. Some entertainment is provided in high season, which is free for children. Used by a Dutch tour operator (10 pitches).

TRAVEL SERVICE SITE

TO BOOK CALL 0870 405 4055 OR www.alanrogersdirect.com

Facilities

Three very good, unisex toilet blocks include washbasins in cabins, a baby room and facilities for disabled people. All recently been refurbished and can be heated. Small laundry with washing machine, dryer and iron. Motorcaravan services. Shop. Takeaway. Café with terrace overlooking the pools (all season). Medium sized, heated swimming pool, paddling pool, slides, etc. (17/5-14/9; lifeguard July/Aug). TV room (satellite) and games room. Tennis court, minigolf, giant chess. Play area. Riding in July/Aug. Fishing is possible in two of the three lakes. Off site: Supermarket in Dol 3 km. Golf 12 km. Beach 20 km.

At a glance

Welcome & Ambience	✓✓✓✓✓	Location	✓✓✓✓
Quality of Pitches	✓✓✓✓	Range of Facilities	✓✓✓✓✓

Directions

Site is by the D576 Dol-de-Bretagne - Pontorson road, just east of Baguer-Pican. It can be reached from the new N176 taking exit for Dol-Est and Baguer-Pican.

Charges 2004

Per person	€ 5,00
child (under 10 yrs)	€ 3,00
pitch	€ 5,50 - € 14,00
electricity (5A)	€ 4,00
dog	free

Reservations

Made with deposit (€ 30) and fee (€ 15).
Tel: 02 99 48 09 55. E-mail: vieux.chene@wanadoo.fr

Open

1 April - 1 October.

FR35060 Camping La Touesse

35800 St Lunaire (Ille-et-Vilaine)

This family campsite was purpose built and has been developed since 1987 by Alain Clement who is keen to welcome more British visitors. Set just back from the coast road, 300 m. from a sandy beach it is in a semi-residential area. It is, nevertheless, an attractive, sheltered site with a range of trees and shrubs. The 142 level, grass pitches in bays (95 for touring units) have electricity and are accessed by circular tarmac roads. The plus factor of this site, besides its proximity to Dinard, is the fine sandy beach which is sheltered - so useful in early season - and safe for children. The owners speak English.

TRAVEL SERVICE SITE

TO BOOK CALL 0870 405 4055 OR www.alanrogersdirect.com

Facilities

The central toilet block is well maintained, heated in low season and provides all modern facilities. Part of it may not be open outside July/Aug. Baby bath and toilet for disabled people. Dishwashing and laundry sinks, two washing machines and a dryer. Motorcaravan service point. Shop for basics (1/4-15/9). Pleasant bar/restaurant (or clubhouse as it is called) with TV. Volleyball, table tennis and video games for children. Sauna. Off site: Fishing 300 m. Riding 500 m. Bicycle hire 1 km. Golf 2 km. Sandy beach 300 m. Many amenities near.

Open

1 April - 30 September.

At a glance

Welcome & Ambience	✓✓✓✓	Location	✓✓✓✓✓
Quality of Pitches	✓✓✓✓	Range of Facilities	✓✓✓✓

Directions

From Dinard take D786 coast road towards St Lunaire; watch for site signs to the left.

Charges 2004

Per person	€ 3,50 - € 4,50
child (under 7 yrs)	€ 2,00 - € 2,50
pitch	€ 4,60 - € 5,90
car	€ 2,50 - € 3,00
electricity (5/10A)	€ 3,00 - € 3,20
dog	€ 1,20 - € 1,40

No credit cards.

Reservations

Tel: 02 99 46 61 13.
E-mail: camping.la.touesse@wanadoo.fr

FR35020 Castel Camping Le Domaine des Ormes

Epiniac, 35120 Dol-de-Bretagne (Ille-et-Vilaine)

This impressive site is in the northern part of Brittany, about 30 km. from the old town of Saint Malo, in the grounds of the Château des Ormes. In an estate of wooded parkland and lakes it has a pleasant atmosphere, busy in high season, almost a holiday village, but peaceful at other times, with a wide range of facilities. The 800 pitches, of which only 150 are for touring units, are divided into a series of different sections, each with its own distinctive character. They offer a choice of terrain - flat or gently sloping, wooded or open – and there are electricity connections on 200 pitches. A marvellous 'Aqua Park' with pink stone and palms and a variety of pools, toboggans, waterfalls and jacuzzi (free), is set just above the small lake with pedaloes and canoes for hire. A pleasant bar and terrace overlooks the pools and a grass sunbathing area surrounds them - almost a touch of the Caribbean! The original pools are sheltered by the restaurant building, parts of which are developed from the 600 year old water-mill. A particular feature is an 18 hole golf course, also a golf practice range and a beginners' 5 hole course. A restaurant and hotel with pool is part of the complex. A popular site with British visitors, with some 80% of the pitches occupied by tour operators and seasonal units and consequently very busy with much organised entertainment.

Facilities

Sanitary installations are of fair standard, including washbasins in cabins and ample facilities for disabled people. Motorcaravan services. Shop, bar, restaurant, pizzeria and takeaway. Games room, bar and disco. Two traditional heated swimming pools and Aqua park. New adventure play area. Golf. Bicycle hire. Fishing. Riding. Minigolf, two tennis courts, sports ground with volleyball, etc, paintball, archery and a cricket club.

Open

21 May - 10 September, with all services.

At a glance

Welcome & Ambience	✓✓✓✓	Location	✓✓✓✓✓
Quality of Pitches	✓✓✓✓	Range of Facilities	✓✓✓✓✓

Directions

Access road leads off main D795 about 7 km. south of Dol-de-Bretagne, north of Combourg.

Charges 2004

Per person	€ 6,50 - € 7,20
child (under 7 yrs)	€ 3,75 - € 4,10
pitch incl. vehicle	€ 19,00 - € 21,00
electricity 3/6A	€ 3,70 - € 4,10
water and drainage	€ 1,85 - € 2,05
animal	€ 1,40 - € 1,60

Camping Cheques accepted.
Less 10% outside July/Aug.

Reservations

Made for min. 3 nights; details from site.
Tel: 02 99 73 53 00. E-mail: info@lesormes.com

TRAVEL SERVICE SITE

TO BOOK CALL 0870 405 4055 OR www.alanrogersdirect.com

FR44030 Camping Le Pré du Château de Careil

33 rue du Château, Careil, 44350 Guérande (Loire-Atlantique)

This small site has a quiet atmosphere and is popular with couples, retired people and those with young children (it is not really recommended for families with older children or teenagers). In the grounds of the Château de Careil, a building dating from the 14th century which may be visited, the site, shaded by mature trees, contains just 50 good sized pitches. All are equipped with electricity and water, some also have drainage. There is a small swimming pool.

Facilities

The main refurbished toilet facilities in the main building are fully equipped, including four unisex shower and washbasin rooms. En-suite facilities for disabled people, baby room and washing machine. In season (15/6-5/9) some emergency provisions are kept and bread can be ordered. Small swimming pool (11 x 5 m. open 15/6-5/9). Playground. TV room. Volleyball and table tennis. Archery occasionally. Off site: Supermarket near. Bicycle hire 2 km. Beach 2.5 km. Riding 5 km. Fishing and golf 10 km. In July and August, tours of the Château are possible (€ 4.57), also by candlelight (€ 5.34).

Open

22 May - 12 September.

At a glance

Welcome & Ambience	✓✓✓✓✓	Location	✓✓✓✓
Quality of Pitches	✓✓✓✓	Range of Facilities	✓✓✓

Directions

Take D92 from Guérande to La Baule and turn east to Careil before the town. From D99 Guérande - St Nazaire road, turn onto D92, following signs to 'Intermarche' and for Château de Careil. Take care as site entrance gate is fairly narrow and located between two bends making access a little awkward.

Charges 2004

Per unit incl. 2 persons and 6A electricity	€ 18,00 - € 22,00
extra person	€ 5,00
child (under 10 yrs)	€ 3,00
electricity (10A)	€ 1,60
dog	€ 1,00

Reservations

Possible with deposit (€ 21.34) and booking fee (€ 15.24). Tel: 02 40 60 22 99.
E-mail: chateau.careil@free.fr

FR44140 Camping Municipal Henri Dubourg

Route de Rennes, 44170 Nozay (Loire-Atlantique)

This good, small site is ideal for short stays or as an overnight stop, being situated in the northern outskirts of Nozay with easy access from the N137 Rennes - Nantes road. There are 25 well hedged, level, grassy pitches with electricity (6A) and a more open area at the rear of the site. Tourist information and an ice pack service are available at reception, there is a barbecue area and a baker calls each morning. Reception opens 07.30-09.00 and 18.00-20.30 hrs.

Facilities

A neat, modern and very clean toilet block has plenty of hot water, roomy showers and includes an odd Turkish style toilet. Facilities for disabled visitors. Dishwashing area under cover, laundry sinks inside. Off site: Small lake with playground and minigolf within 5 minutes walk. Fishing or golf 400 m. Two supermarkets in Nozay.

Open

15 May - 15 September.

At a glance

Welcome & Ambience	✓✓✓✓✓	Location	✓✓✓✓
Quality of Pitches	✓✓✓✓	Range of Facilities	✓✓✓✓

Directions

From N137 take N171 Chateaubriant exit, then take first right D121 for Nozay. Site is on right after the lake (approx. 1 km).

Charges 2004

Per person	€ 2,00
child (2-9 yrs)	€ 1,00
pitch and car	€ 3,50
electricity	€ 1,50
animal	€ 1,00

Reservations

Contact site. Tel: 02 40 87 94 33.
E-mail: mairie@nozay.fr

FR44100 Sunêlia Le Patisseau

Mobile homes page 366

29 rue du Patisseau, 44210 Pornic (Loire-Atlantique)

Le Patisseau is situated in the countryside just a short drive from the fishing village of Pornic. It is a relaxed site with a large number of mobile homes and chalets, which is popular with young families and teenagers. Touring pitches, which all have electrical connections (6A), are divided between the attractive 'forest' area with plenty of shade from mature trees and the more open 'prairie' area. A number of communal barbecues are provided throughout the site, helping to create a sociable atmosphere. A railway line runs along the bottom half of the site with trains two or three times a day, but they do finish at 22.30 hrs and the noise is minimal. The site's spacious restaurant and bar overlook the indoor pool. Outside the two waterslides are cleverly concealed amongst the trees. This is a lively site and the Morice family work very hard to maintain a friendly atmosphere. A new toilet block is being built for 2005.

TRAVEL SERVICE SITE

TO BOOK CALL 0870 405 4055 OR www.alanrogersdirect.com

Facilities

There are three sanitary blocks, one of which is being rebuilt for 2005. They include washbasins in private cabins, child-size toilets, baby baths, fully equipped laundry rooms and dishwashing facilities. Maintenance can be variable so do not expect too much. Shop (main season). Bar and restaurant (3/4-12/9). Takeaway (1/7-31/8). Indoor heated pool with sauna, jacuzzi and spa (all season). Outdoor pools with water slides (1/5-12/9). Play area. Volleyball and table tennis. Bicycle hire. Off site: Fishing 1.5 km. Beach 2.5 km. Riding 4 km. Golf 5 km.

Open

3 April - 12 September.

At a glance

Welcome & Ambience	✓✓✓✓✓	Location	✓✓✓✓
Quality of Pitches	✓✓✓	Range of Facilities	✓✓✓✓

Directions

Site signed at roundabout junction of D751 (Pornic - Nantes) road. From the town centre take the Rue du General de Gaulle and then the rue de Nantes, which crosses the D751. At the next roundabout turn left and follow the signs.

Charges 2004

Per unit incl. 2 persons	€ 19,00 - € 29,00
incl. electricity (6A)	€ 23,00 - € 33,00
extra person	€ 5,00 - € 7,00
child (1-7 yrs)	€ 3,00 - € 5,00
animal	€ 4,00

Camping Cheques accepted.

Reservations

Made with deposit (€ 50) and fee (€ 30); contact site by letter, phone or fax. Tel: 02 40 82 10 39.
E-mail: contact@lepatisseau.com

FR44040 Castel Camping Le Parc Sainte-Brigitte

Domaine de Bréhet, 44420 La Turballe (Loire-Atlantique)

Sainte-Brigitte is a well established site in the grounds of a manor house, three kilometres from the beaches. It is a spacious site with 150 pitches, 106 with electricity and 25 also with water and drainage. Some are in a circular, park-like setting near the entrance, others are in wooded areas under tall trees and the rest are on more open grass in an unmarked area near the pool. One can walk around many of the areas of the estate not used for camping, there are farm animals to see and a fishing lake is very popular. A quiet place to stay outside the main season, with few facilities open; in high season, however, it is mainly used by families with its full share of British visitors and it can become very busy. Used by a tour operator (20 pitches).

Facilities

The main toilet block is of fair quality, supplemented by second block next to it. They include washbasins in cabins, with bidets for women, and two bathrooms. Washing machines and dryer (no washing to be hung out on pitches, lines provided). Motorcaravan services. Small shop for basics, bread available (baker calls). Nice little restaurant/bar with takeaway (both 15/5-15/9). Heated swimming pool and paddling pool (all season). Playground. Bicycle hire. Boules, volleyball, pool and 'baby-foot'. Table tennis. TV room and traditional 'salle de reunion' in renovated outbuildings of the manor house. Off site: Riding 2 km. Nearest beach 3 km. Golf 15 km.

Open

1 April - 1 October.

At a glance

Welcome & Ambience	✓✓✓✓✓	Location	✓✓✓✓
Quality of Pitches	✓✓✓✓	Range of Facilities	✓✓✓✓

Directions

Entrance is off the busy La Turballe-Guérande D99 road, 3 km. east of La Turballe. A one-way system operates - in one lane, out via another.

Charges 2005

Per person	€ 5,25
child (under 7 yrs)	€ 4,00
pitch	€ 5,50
with water and electricity	€ 11,00
dog	€ 1,50

No credit cards.

Reservations

Made for any length with exact dates and recommended for July/Aug, with deposit (€ 64.75) plus fee (€ 15.25). Tel: 02 40 24 88 91.
E-mail: saintebrigitte@wanadoo.fr

FR44020 Camping Municipal du Moulin

Route de Nantes, 44190 Clisson (Loire-Atlantique)

This good value, small site is conveniently located on one of the main north - south routes on the edge of the interesting old town of Clisson. A typical municipal site, it is useful for short stays. There are 47 good sized, marked and level pitches with electricity and divided by hedges and trees giving a good degree of privacy; also an unmarked area for small tents. A barbecue and camp fire area (with free wood) is to the rear of the site above the river where one can fish or canoe (via a steep path). The warden lives on site in high season. The attractive old town is within walking distance.

Facilities

The fully equipped unisex toilet block includes some washbasins in cabins and others in a separate large room, with hot and cold water. Unit for disabled people. Dishwashing and laundry sinks. Cleaning can be a bit haphazard at times. Bread delivered daily. Table tennis, volleyball, and small playground. No double axle or commercial vehicles accepted. Off site: Supermarket with cheap fuel just across the road.

At a glance

Welcome & Ambience	✓✓✓✓	Location	✓✓✓✓
Quality of Pitches	✓✓✓✓	Range of Facilities	✓✓✓

Directions

Entering Clisson from the north on N149 (Nantes - Poitiers) road, turn right at roundabout after passing Leclerc supermarket on your left. Site access is directly off roundabout.

Charges 2004

Per unit incl. 1 adult and electricity	€ 7,20
extra person	€ 2,40
child (0-7 yrs)	€ 1,60

Reservations

Contact site. Tel: 02 40 54 44 48.

Open

Easter - mid October.

FR44150 Camping La Tabardière

44770 La Plaine-sur-Mer (Loire-Atlantique)

Owned and managed by the Barre family, this campsite lies next to the family farm. Pleasant, peaceful and immaculate, this site will suit those who want to enjoy the local coast and towns but return to an 'oasis' for relaxation. It still, however, provides activities and fun for those with energy remaining. The pitches are mostly terraced either side of a narrow valley and care needs to be taken in manoeuvring caravans into position - although the effort is well worth it. Most pitches have access to electricity and water taps are conveniently situated. The site is probably not suitable for wheelchair users. Whilst this is a rural site, its amenities are excellent with swimming and paddling pools and a water slide, table tennis, volleyball, tennis, boules and a very challenging 18 hole minigolf to keep you occupied, plus a friendly bar. The beautiful beaches are 3 km. with the fishing harbour town, Pomic, some 5 km, ideal for cafes, restaurants and the evening strolls.

Facilities

Two good, clean toilet blocks are well equipped and include laundry facilities. Motorcaravan service point. Bar. Shop. Snacks and takeaway. Good sized swimming pool, paddling pool and slides (supervised). Playground. Minigolf. Table tennis. Volleyball and basketball. Half size tennis courts. Boules. Overnight area for motorcaravans (€ 9 per night). Off site: Beach 3 km. Sea fishing, golf, riding all 5 km.

Open

1 April - 30 September.

At a glance

Welcome & Ambience	✓✓✓✓✓	Location	✓✓✓✓
Quality of Pitches	✓✓✓✓	Range of Facilities	✓✓✓✓✓

Directions

Site is well signed, situated inland off the D13 Pornic - La Plaine sur Mer road.

Charges 2004

extra person	€ 3,30 - € 5,10
child (2-10 yrs)	€ 2,50 - € 3,50
dog	€ 2,60
electricity (3/6A)	€ 2,70 - € 3,60

Reservations

Made with deposit (€ 60) and fee (€ 16).
Tel: 02 40 21 58 83.
E-mail: info@camping-la-tabardiere.com

FR44170 Camping Les Ajoncs d'Or

Chemin du Rocher, 44500 La Baule (Loire-Atlantique)

This site is situated in pine woods, 1.5 km. on the inland side of La Baule and its beautiful bay. It can be difficult to find an informal campsite close to an exciting seaside resort that retains its touring and camping identity, but Les Ajoncs d'Or does this. A well maintained, natural woodland setting provides a wide variety of pitch types, some level and bordered with hedges and tall trees to provide shade and many others that maintain the natural characteristics of the woodland. Most pitches have electricity and water nearby and are usually of a larger size. A central building provides a shop and open friendly bar that serve snacks and takeaways. The English speaking Bazillails family (the owners) who live on site will welcome you to their campsite. There are only just over 200 pitches, so large areas of woodland have been retained for quiet and recreational purposes and are safe for children to roam. Enjoy the gentle breezes off the sea that constantly rustle the trees. The family are justifiably proud of their site.

Facilities

Two good quality sanitary blocks are clean and well maintained providing plenty of facilities including a baby room. Washing machines and dryers. Shop and bar (July/Aug). Snack bar (July/Aug). Good size swimming pool and paddling pool (1/6-5/9). Sports and playground areas. Bicycle hire. Reception with security barrier (closed 22.30 - 7.30 hrs). Off site: Everything for an enjoyable holiday can be found in nearby La Baule. Fishing and riding 1.5 km. Golf 3 km. Beach 1.5 km.

Open

1 April - 30 September.

At a glance

Welcome & Ambience	✓✓✓✓✓	Location	✓✓✓✓
Quality of Pitches	✓✓✓✓	Range of Facilities	✓✓✓

Directions

From N171 take exit for La Baule les Pins. Follow signs for 'La Baule Centre', then left at roundabout in front of Champion supermarket and follow site signs.

Charges 2004

with electricity	€ 21,00
with water and drainage	€ 23,00
extra person	€ 6,00
child (2-7 yrs)	€ 3,00
dog	€ 0,95

Less 15-25% outside July/Aug.

Reservations

Tel: 02 40 60 33 29. E-mail: contact@ajoncs.com

FR44090 Camping Château du Deffay

Mobile homes page 365

B.P. 18 Le Deffay, Ste Reine de Bretagne, 44160 Pontchâteau

A family managed site, Château de Deffay is a refreshing departure from the usual formula in that it is not over organised or supervised and has no tour operator units. The landscape is natural right down to the molehills, and the site blends well with the rural environment of the estate, lake and farmland which surround it. For these reasons it is enjoyed by many. However, with the temptation of free pedaloes and the fairly deep, unfenced lake, parents should ensure that children are supervised. The 142 good sized, fairly level pitches have pleasant views and are either on open grass, on shallow terraces divided by hedges, or informally arranged in a central, slightly sloping wooded area. Most have electricity. The facilities are located within the old courtyard area of the smaller château (that dates from before 1400). The larger château (built 1880) and another lake stand away from this area providing pleasant walking. The reception has been built separately to contain the camping area. Alpine type chalets overlook the lake and fit well with the environment.

Facilities

The main toilet block, housed in a converted barn, is well equipped including washbasins in cabins, provision for disabled people and a baby bathroom. Washing machines, and dryer. Maintenance can be variable and, with the boiler located at one end of the block, hot water can take time to reach the other in low season. Extra facilities are in the courtyard area where the well stocked shop, bar, small restaurant with takeaway and solar heated swimming pool and paddling pool are located (all 15/5-15/9). Play area. TV in the bar, separate room for table tennis. English language animation in season including children's mini club. Torches useful. Off site: Golf and riding 5 km. Close to the Brière Regional Park, the Guérande Peninsula, and La Baule with its magnificent beach (20 km).

At a glance

Welcome & Ambience	✓✓✓✓✓	Location	✓✓✓✓
Quality of Pitches	✓✓✓✓	Range of Facilities	✓✓✓✓

Directions

Site is signed from D33 Pontchâteau - Herbignac road near Ste Reine. Also signed from the D773 and N165.

Charges 2004

Per person	€ 2,80 - € 4,55
child (2-12 yrs)	€ 1,95 - € 3,00
pitch	€ 6,75 - € 10,25
with electricity (6A)	€ 10,40 - € 13,90
with 3 services	€ 11,90 - € 15,65

Camping Cheques accepted.

Reservations

Accepted with deposit (€ 10 per day) and fee (€ 16). Tel: 02 40 88 00 57. E-mail: info@camping-le-deffay.com

Open

7 May - 17 September.

FR44160 Camping Armor-Héol

Route de Guérande, 44420 Piriac-sur-Mer (Loire-Atlantique)

Situated only 700 metres from Piriac town and the beach, and 14 km. from Guérande, this campsite makes an ideal base for a beach holiday or for touring the beautiful Breton countryside and coastline. With considerable recent investment, the site now offers excellent facilities for visitors of all ages. There are 250 good sized (120 sq.m) level pitches all with 5A electricity. Although site owned mobiles and chalets take 160 pitches, they do not feel intrusive to the camper and caravanner. In 2002 a new facility was completed providing an outdoor swimming pool, a paddling pool and 70 m. of exciting water slides, together with a bar and restaurant with a large terrace. In 2003 a new indoor pool with water movement where you swim and stay stationary was added. This is a friendly site with English speaking reception and good amenities.

Facilities

Two clean and well maintained toilet blocks include washbasins in cabins, baby rooms, family rooms, dishwashing and laundries. Dishwashing, washing machines and dryers. Super bar and restaurant (1/6-15/9). Most activities are in one part of the site with heated pools and water slides ((1/6-15/9). Multi-sports area, tennis courts, volleyball. Playground. Off site: Beach and town, fishing, boat launching, surfing and bicycle hire 700 m. Golf 2 km. Riding 2 km.

Open

3 April - 26 September.

At a glance

Welcome & Ambience	✓✓✓✓✓	Location	✓✓✓✓
Quality of Pitches	✓✓✓✓	Range of Facilities	✓✓✓✓✓

Directions

From N165 Vannes - Nantes road, take D774 south-west at Guérande. Follow D333 signed Piriac sur Mer. Site is on left 0.5 km. before Piriac sur Mer, 4 km. from Guérande.

Charges 2004

extra person	€ 3,50 - € 7,15
child (under 4 yrs)	€ 2,10 - € 4,40
animal	€ 2,00 - € 3,85
electricity	€ 3,05 - € 3,35

Reservations

Made with deposit (€ 30 per week booked) and fee (€ 20). Tel: 02 40 23 57 80.
E-mail: armor.heol@wanadoo.fr

FR44130 Camping L'Hermitage

36 ave du Paradis, 44290 Guemene-Penfao (Loire-Atlantique)

L'Hermitage is a pretty wooded site set in the Vallée du Don and would be useful for en-route stops or for longer stays. Both Nantes and Rennes are 30 minutes away, La Baule with its beaches is 40 minutes. The enthusiastic staff, even though their English is a little limited, provide a warm welcome and maintain this reasonably priced site to a good standard. There are 110 pitches of which 80 are a good size for touring and camping. Some are formally arranged on open, level grass pitches, whereas others are informal amongst light woodland. Electricity (6A) is available to all (a long lead may be useful).

Facilities

A clean and well serviced toilet block includes some wash-basins in cabins with warm water. Laundry and dishwashing sinks under cover (cold water but a hot tap is provided. Smallish pool, paddling pool and slide, nicely maintained and carefully fenced. Small play area. Table tennis. Petanque. Games room with video games. Off site: Leisure complex with indoor pool opposite. Fishing 500 m. Village 1 km. for all facilities. Riding 2 km. Many walking trails.

Open

1 April - 31 October.

At a glance

Welcome & Ambience	✓✓✓✓✓	Location	✓✓✓
Quality of Pitches	✓✓✓✓	Range of Facilities	✓✓✓

Directions

Exit N137 at Derval (signed Châteaubriant) but take D775 for Redon. Guémené-Penfao is approx. 13 km. Watch for site signs before village centre. Site is in the outskirts in a semi-residential area to the northeast.

Charges 2004

Per unit incl. 2 adults	€ 8,15 - € 9,60
extra person	€ 2,90
child (under 10 yrs)	€ 1,90
electricity	€ 2,40
dog	€ 1,20

Reservations

Contact site. Tel: 02 40 79 23 48.
E-mail: contact@campinglhermitage.com

FR44190 Camping Le Fief

Mobile homes page 366

57, chemin du Fief, 44250 St Brévin-les-Pins (Loire-Atlantique)

This site has been recommended by our agent and we plan to inspect it during 2005 with a view to future inclusion in this guide. Le Fief is a lively family site with an excellent swimming pool area (a new pool complex is planned for 2005). A lively entertainment programme is organised here throughout the high season. Mobile homes for rent.

Facilities

Modern toilet blocks. Shop. New restaurant planned for 2005. Takeaway. Swimming pool complex with cascades, fountains and a 'lazy river'. Covered pool. Play area. Table tennis. Games room. Off site: Beach 400 m. Water sports. Fishing. Planète Sauvage safari park.

Open

26 March - 15 October.

Directions

From the St Nazaire bridge, take the St Brevin - L'Ocean exit from the D213. Continue over the first roundabout and bear right at the second, to join the Chemin du Fief. The site can be found on the right and is well signed.

Charges 2004

Per pitch incl. 2 persons	€ 12,00 - € 28,00
extra person	€ 3,50 - € 6,50
child (0-7 yrs)	€ 1,75 - € 3,25
electricity	€ 4,00

Reservations

Contact site. Tel: 02 40 27 23 86.
E-mail : camping@lefief.com

FR44180 Camping de la Boutinardière

Rue de la Plage de la Boutinardière, 44210 Pornic (Loire-Atlantique)

This campsite has it all - two kilometres from the beautiful harbour town of Pornic and 200 metres from the sea, together with the very best of amenities and facilities (unusually all open and functioning 1 May - 22 Sept). This is truly a holiday site to suit all the family whatever their age. The site has 250 individual good sized pitches, 100-120 sq.m. in size, many bordered by three metre high, well maintained hedges for shade and privacy. All pitches have electricity available. This is a family owned site and English is spoken by the helpful, obliging reception staff. Beside reception is the site shop which is excellent in size, range and quantity of goods for the holidaymaker. Across the road is a new complex of indoor and outdoor swimming pools, paddling pool and a twin toboggan water slide. Facing the water complex, the bar, restaurant and terraces are also new and serve excellent food, be it a snack or in the restaurant or perhaps a takeaway. On site there are also sports and entertainment areas. This site is difficult to better in the South Brittany, Loire Atlantic area.

Facilities

Toilet facilities are in three good blocks, one large and centrally situated and two supporting blocks. Whilst the blocks are of traditional build the quality, maintenance and cleanliness are amongst the best. Washbasins are in cabins, dishwashing is under cover. Laundry room with sinks, washing machines and dryers. Excellent shop (15/6-15/9). New complex of bar, restaurant, terraces (1/4-22/9). Three heated swimming pools, one indoor, a paddling pool and water slides (15/5-22/9). Games room. Sports and activity area. Playground. Minigolf. Table tennis. Off site: Sandy cove 200 m. Golf, riding, sea fishing, restaurants, cafes, fishing harbour, boat trips, sailing and windsurfing, all within 5 km. of site.

At a glance

Welcome & Ambience	✓✓✓✓	Location	✓✓✓✓
Quality of Pitches	✓✓✓✓✓	Range of Facilities	✓✓✓✓✓

Directions

From north or south on D213, take Nantes D751 exit. At roundabout (with McDonalds) take D13 signed Bernarie-eb-Retz. After 4 km. site is signed to right. Note: do NOT exit from D213 at Pomic Ouest or Centre.

Charges 2004

extra person	€ 3,00 - € 6,00
child (2-10 yrs)	€ 2,00 - € 4,50
electricity (3-10A)	€ 3,50 - € 5,00
animal	€ 2,00 - € 3,50

Reservations

Made with deposit (€ 62) and fee (€ 23). Tel: 02 40 82 05 68. E-mail: info@laboutinardiere.com

Open

1 April - 30 September.

FR56110 Camping du Moustoir

Route du Moustoir, 56340 Carnac (Morbihan)

Camping du Moustoir is a friendly, family run site situated about three kilometres inland from the many beaches of the area and close to the famous 'alignments' of standing stones. Pitches are grassy and separated by shrubs and hedges, with several shaded by tall pine trees. There is a popular pool area with slides, a separate swimming pool and a paddling pool with 'mushroom' fountain. The bar and terrace adjoining the pool become the social centre of the site in the evenings. A high season programme includes family entertainment and a daily 'Kid's club' which attracts children of several nationalities. Several small tour operators use the site.

Facilities

The substantial, traditional style toilet block is well maintained and clean (outside peak season some sections may be closed). Motorcaravan service facilities. Shop, bar and takeaway (all from 20/5, hours vary). Heated swimming pool (21 x 8 m), water slides with landing pool, and paddling pool (from 15/5). Adventure style playground. Tennis. Boules. Volleyball, football and basketball. Table tennis and pool table. 'Kids Club' daily in high season. Off site: Easy access to watersports at Carnac Plage. Beach 3 km. Fishing, bicycle hire or riding 2 km. Golf 5 km.

At a glance

Welcome & Ambience	✓✓✓✓✓	Location	✓✓✓✓
Quality of Pitches	✓✓✓✓	Range of Facilities	✓✓✓✓✓

Directions

From N165, take exit to D768 (Carnac and Quiberon). At second crossroads after 5 km. turn left D119) towards Carnac. After 3 km. turn left (oblique turning) after a hotel, and site is 500 m. on your left.

Charges 2004

Per person (over 2 yrs)	€ 4,10
pitch	€ 5,00 - € 14,00
electricity	€ 3,10
animal	€ 1,50

Camping Cheques accepted.

Reservations

Made with deposit (€ 75). Tel: 02 97 52 16 18. E-mail: info@lemoustoir.com

Open

2 May - 17 September.

FR44200 Camping Municipal Saint Clair

44530 Guenrouet (Loire-Atlantique)

This is a very well maintained campsite in a lovely position, next to Brest - Nantes canal making it suitable for anyone interested in boating or fishing. There are about 100 pitches of varying sizes, many within a wooded area, and all with electricity (6A). The site would be ideal for an overnight stop or for a longer stay.

Facilities

Three well maintained, modern toilet blocks provide toilets (mixed British and Turkish style), washbasins in cabins and showers. Facilities for disabled visitors. Small play area. Tennis. Petanque. Games room. Off site: Leisure complex with outdoor pool, restaurant and crêperie opposite site. Village with small supermarket and other facilities 500 m.

Open

23 June - 31 August.

At a glance

Welcome & Ambience	✓✓✓✓	Location	✓✓✓✓✓
Quality of Pitches	✓✓✓✓	Range of Facilities	✓✓✓

Directions

On the N165 from Nantes, take D773 signed St Gildas de Bois. At St Gildas, turn right on D2 for Guenrouet. Site is on right after village, just before river.

Charges 2004

Per person	€ 2,50 - € 3,50
child (0-10 yrs)	€ 1,50 - € 2,50
pitch	€ 4,00 - € 5,00
electricity	€ 2,60
dog	€ 1,00 - € 1,50

Reservations

Contact site. Tel: 02 40 87 61 52.

FR56020 Camping de la Plage

Plage de Kervilaine, 56470 La Trinité-sur-Mer (Morbihan)

The area of Carnac/La Trinité is popular with holiday makers and the two La Trinité sites of La Plage and La Baie have the great advantage of direct access to a good sandy beach. Both sites are owned by the same family, and each is very well maintained, both having a small (12 m.) heated pool with a slide. The grassy pitches, which have electricity and water (70% with drainage also), are separated by hedges and shrubs and at La Plage there are attractive flower beds. Situated on a low cliff, the terrace with its views across the bay is a very popular place for a meal or a drink. Reception areas are welcoming and friendly with tourist information on display. Both sites have a number of tour operator pitches.

Facilities

Toilet blocks have washbasins in cubicles and facilities for disabled people and small children. Washing machines and dryers. Well stocked shop with bakery. Bar, restaurant, crêperie, takeaway. Swimming pools with new water slides, etc. Good play areas including ball pool. Tennis, basketball, minigolf, table tennis. Large TV screen. Lively entertainment programme in high season for all ages and some evening entertainment in nearby disco. Bicycle hire. Beach. Guided tours on foot or bicycle. Internet access. Small communal barbecue areas (only gas ones permitted on pitches). Not suitable for American motorhomes or twin axle caravans. Off site: The village of La Trinité is 20 minutes walk along the cliff path and 10 minutes (approx) by car. Carnac is a 10-15 minutes drive in the opposite direction.

At a glance

Welcome & Ambience	✓✓✓✓	Location	✓✓✓✓✓
Quality of Pitches	✓✓✓✓	Range of Facilities	✓✓✓✓

Directions

Site is signed in different places from the D186 coast road running from La Trinité to Carnac-Plage.

Charges 2004

Per unit incl. 2 persons	€ 16,40 - € 31,10
extra adult	€ 4,00
child (2-18 yrs)	€ 2,80 - € 3,00
electricity (6/10A)	€ 2,00 - € 3,70
dog	free - € 1,20

Reservations

Contact site; when booking it is important to state size of unit in order that appropriate size pitch can be allocated. Tel: 02 97 55 73 28.
E-mail: camping@camping-plage.com

Open

7 May - 17 September.

FR56080 Camping Municipal Le Pâtis

3 chemin du Pâtis, 56130 La Roche Bernard (Morbihan)

This is another of those excellent municipal sites one comes across in France. Situated beside the River Vilaine, just below the very attractive old town of La Roche Bernard and beside the port and marina, it provides 60 level grass, part-hedged pitches in bays of four, with 10A electricity and water. Next door is a sailing school, boats to hire, fishing, tennis, archery, etc. A restaurant and bar are on the quay-side, with others uphill in the town.

Facilities

There are two fully equipped sanitary blocks, one new and very modern, the other fully refurbished. Laundry room behind reception with washing machine and dryer. Small play area. Bicycle hire. Off site: Bicycle hire 500 m. Riding 5 km. Golf 15 km.

Open

Easter/April - 30 September.

At a glance

Welcome & Ambience	✓✓✓✓	Location	✓✓✓✓
Quality of Pitches	✓✓✓✓✓	Range of Facilities	✓✓✓

Directions

Go into town centre and follow signs for the Port around a one-way system and then a sharp turn down hill.

Charges 2004

Per person	€ 3,00
child (under 9 yrs)	€ 1,50
pitch	€ 4,00
vehicle	€ 2,00
animal	€ 1,00
electricity	€ 3,00

No credit cards.

Reservations

Contact site. Tel: 02 99 90 60 13.

FR56040 Camping de Penboch

9, chemin de Penboch, 56610 Arradon (Morbihan)

Penboch is 200 metres by footpath from the shores of the Golfe du Morbihan with its many islands, where there is plenty to do including watersports, fishing and boat trips. There are also old towns with weekly markets nearby and it is 30 minutes walk to Arradon which has a good range of shops and restaurants. The site in a peaceful, rural area is divided into two parts - one in woodland with lots of shade and used mainly for mobile homes and the other main part, across a minor road on more open ground with hedges and young trees. Penboch offers 175 pitches on flat grass, mostly divided into groups; electricity is available on most pitches (6/10A) and there are plenty of water points. British tour operator (12 pitches). A 'Sites et Paysages' member.

TRAVEL SERVICE SITE

TO BOOK CALL 0870 405 4055 OR www.alanrogersdirect.com

Facilities

Three fully equipped toilet blocks, two on the main part of the site (one of which is heated) and one on the annex, include washbasins in cabins. Facilities can be under considerable pressure in peak season. Washing machines and dryers. Motorcaravan service point. Friendly bar with satellite TV, snacks and takeaway, shop with basic food supplies (all 20/5-11/9) and further TV room. Heated swimming pool with water slide, toboggan and children's pool with mushroom fountain (15/5-19/9). Good playground, visible from reception, with interesting play equipment. Games room. Caravan storage. American motorhomes accepted in low season. Off site: Beach and fishing 200 m. Sailing and windsurfing 2 km. Bicycle hire, golf and riding 6 km.

At a glance

Welcome & Ambience	✓✓✓✓	Location	✓✓✓✓✓
Quality of Pitches	✓✓✓✓	Range of Facilities	✓✓✓✓✓

Directions

From N165 at Auray or Vannes, take D101 along northern shores of the Golfe du Morbihan; or leave N165 at D127 signed Ploeren and Arradon. Take turn to Arradon and site is signed.

Charges 2004

Per unit incl. 2 persons	€ 9,95 - € 28,10
extra person	€ 3,00 - € 4,70
child (2-7 yrs)	€ 2,50 - € 3,60
electricity 6/10A	€ 3,00 - € 4,00
dog	free - € 2,00

Reservations

Advised for high season (min. 7 days 10/7-18/8). Tel: 02 97 44 71 29. E-mail: camping.penboch@wanadoo.fr

Open

9 April - 24 September.

FR56010 Castel Camping La Grande Métairie

Route des Alignements de Kermario, BP 85, 56342 Carnac (Morbihan)

La Grande Métairie is a good quality site quietly situated a little back from the sea, close to the impressive rows of the famous 'menhirs' (giant prehistoric standing stones). It has a great deal to offer on site and is lively and busy over a long season. There is a feeling of spaciousness with a wide entrance and access road, with 575 individual pitches (128 for touring units), surrounded by hedges and trees. All have electricity (30 m. cables are needed in parts). Paddocks with ponds are home for ducks, goats and ponies to watch and feed. A super swimming pool complex comprises heated pools, water slides and toboggans, a flowing river, jacuzzi and a covered pool. Services are limited before late May. The site is well known and popular and has many British visitors with 358 pitches taken by several tour operators, plus site-owned mobile homes and many British touring caravanners and campers.

Facilities

Three large toilet blocks are good and well maintained, with washbasins in cabins, and facilities for babies and disabled people. Laundry room in each block. Motorcaravan service points. Shop and boutique. Restaurant, good takeaway. Bar lounge and terrace, and adjoining TV and games rooms. Pool complex with poolside bar and terrace. Two playgrounds and large playing field with football posts. Two tennis courts. Volleyball and basketball. Minigolf. BMX track. Bicycle hire. Table tennis. Fishing (on permit). Pony rides around the site. Outside amphitheatre for musical evenings and barbecues. Organised events daytime and evening. Occasional dances (pitches near these facilities may be noisy late at night - the bar closes at midnight). American motorhomes accepted up to 27 ft. Dogs and other pets only accepted by arrangement. Off site: Riding 1 km. Nearest beach 3 km. by road. Golf 12 km. Local market at Carnac on Wednesdays and Sundays.

At a glance

Welcome & Ambience	✓✓✓✓	Location	✓✓✓✓
Quality of Pitches	✓✓	Range of Facilities	✓✓✓✓✓

Directions

From N165 take Quiberon/Carnac exit onto the D768. After 5 km. turn left on D119 towards Carnac and after 4 km. turn left onto D196 to the site.

Charges 2004

Per person	€ 3,90 - € 6,50
child (under 7 yrs)	€ 2,80 - € 4,70
pitch incl. car	€ 14,10 - € 23,50
with 6A electricity	€ 16,20 - € 27,00
water and drainage	€ 3,50

Less 20% 22/5-29/6 and after 1/9.

Reservations

Made (min. 1 week) with deposit € 120. English is spoken - office open from 2 Jan. Tel: 02 97 52 24 01. E-mail: info@lagrandemetairie.com

Open

3 April - 11 September (all services from 24/5).

FR56050 Camping de Kervilor

56470 La Trinité-sur-Mer (Morbihan)

Kervilor may be a good alternative for those who find the beach-side sites in La Trinité too busy and lively. In a village on the outskirts of the town, it has 230 pitches on flat grass and is attractively landscaped with trees (silver birches) and flowers. The 230 pitches are in groups divided by hedges, separated by shrubs and trees and 200 have electricity (6/10A). Around 174 are used for touring units. There is a medium sized swimming pool, paddling pool and new water slides. This site has a feeling of spaciousness. Used by tour operators (24 pitches).

Facilities

Two modern toilet blocks are of a good standard with further facilities in an older block by the entrance. They include many washbasins in cabins, facilities for disabled people and babies. Dishwashing under cover. Small laundry. Small shop for basics and takeaway in season. Bar with terrace (28/5-9/9). Swimming pool. Play area. Minigolf, pétanque, tennis and volleyball. Table tennis. Only charcoal barbecues are permitted. Off site: Town facilities 1.5 km. Fishing or riding 2 km. Bicycle hire 3 km. Golf 12 km. Sandy beach 2 km.

Open

8 May - 11 September.

At a glance

Welcome & Ambience	✓✓✓	Location	✓✓✓✓
Quality of Pitches	✓✓✓✓	Range of Facilities	✓✓✓✓✓

Directions

Site is north of La Trinité-sur-Mer and is signed in the town centre. From Auray take D186 Quiberon road; turn left at camp sign at Kergroix on D186 to La Trinité-sur-Mer, and left again at outskirts of town.

Charges 2004

Per person	€ 4,70
child (under 7 yrs)	€ 3,10
pitch	€ 14,50
electricity	€ 3,10 - € 3,60
dog	€ 2,50

Less 25% outside high season. 7 days for the price of 6 outside July/Aug.

Reservations

Made with deposit (€ 46) and fee (€ 18.30).
Tel: 02 97 55 76 75.
E-mail: ebideau@camping-kervilor.com

FR56090 Camping Moulin de Kermaux

56340 Carnac (Morbihan)

Only 100 metres from the famous Carnac megaliths, Le Moulin de Kermaux is an excellent base from which to see these ancient stones as they portray their ever changing mood, colour and profile. The family run site has 150 pitches (120 with 6-10A electricity) and its compact nature offers a safe environment for parents and children alike. The 70 pitches for touring units are mostly separated by hedges and numerous mature trees offer welcome shade. Keen distance walkers and families with young children alike, will enjoy the numerous footpaths in the area.

Facilities

The fully equipped toilet block has high standards of cleanliness and washbasins in cabins. Toilets are a mix of (mainly) British and (a few) Turkish types. Facilities for disabled visitors. Baby bath. Laundry and dishwashing sinks. Washing machine and dryer - washing line provided. Motorcaravan service point. Well stocked shop (26/6-31/8). Bar (12/6-31/8). Swimming and paddling pools. Sauna and jacuzzi. Challenging adventure playground. Volleyball and basketball, minigolf and table tennis. Organised activities in July/Aug. Internet access (July/Aug only). Not suitable for American motorhomes or twin axle caravans.
Off site: Fishing, bicycle hire and riding within 2 km. Sandy beaches and rocky coves within 3 km. Supermarkets 3 km.

At a glance

Welcome & Ambience	✓✓✓✓✓	Location	✓✓✓✓✓
Quality of Pitches	✓✓✓✓	Range of Facilities	✓✓✓✓

Directions

From N165 take Quiberon/Carnac exit on D768. After 5 km. turn left on D781 to Carnac (site signs), turn left just before mini roundabout to site.

Charges 2004

Per person	€ 4,00
child (under 7 yrs)	€ 3,00
pitch and car	€ 13,50
electricity 6A	€ 3,00
dog	€ 2,00

Less 10-40% outside high season.

Reservations

Contact site. Tel: 02 97 52 15 90.
E-mail: moulin-de-kermaux@wanadoo.fr

Open

30 March - 15 September.

FR56100 Camping de Moulin Neuf

56220 Rochefort-en-Terre (Morbihan)

This quiet family site is in wooded countryside, 600 m. from the small medieval town. Ian and Norma Hetherington have worked hard over the last few years to develop Moulin Neuf into a neat, tidy and organised site. There is provision for 72 pitches (60 for tourers, 44 with 10A electricity) of good size (120 sq.m.) on neat grass, laid out on two levels. The top level, with a limited number of electrical hook-ups, is flat and pitches are divided by young shrubs. The entrance to the site is here and reception is located just beyond the security gate. The lower level is partly sloping but offers mature trees, shade and electricity on all the pitches. Rochefort en Terre itself is a marvellous medieval town, beautifully preserved and only ten minutes walk from the site, with a wealth of art and craft workshops, antique shops and art galleries.

Facilities

The modern heated sanitary block is on the lower level but convenient for both. Facilities are kept very clean and include large, comfortable showers, cabins with washbasins and British and Turkish style WCs. Provision for disabled people. Baby room. Dishwashing area and laundry room with sinks. Washing machine, dryer and washing lines. Bread delivered each morning. Heated swimming pool (1/6-31/8). Tennis court, table tennis, basketball, football area. Two play areas. Off site: Lake within 500 m. with watersports. Shop 600 m. Riding and golf locally. Vannes is a 30 minute drive and the beaches of Golfe du Morbihan.

At a glance

Welcome & Ambience	✓✓✓✓	Location	✓✓✓✓
Quality of Pitches	✓✓✓✓	Range of Facilities	✓✓✓

Directions

From Redon take D775 Vannes road west for 25 km. Branch north on D774 signed Rochefort en Terre. Follow road past the lake on left, in 800 m. Turn left and follow sign to site.

Charges 2004

Per person	€ 4,30 - € 5,00
child (under 8 yrs)	€ 2,60 - € 3,50
pitch	€ 7,00 - € 8,00
electricity	€ 4,40

Reservations

Made with deposit (€ 100) and fee (€ 10); contact site for booking form. Tel: 02 97 43 37 52.

Open

15 May - 16 September.

FR56200 Camping La Ferme de Lann Hoedic

Route du Roaliguen, 56370 Sarzeau (Morbihan)

Whilst still maintaining the character of 'Camping a la Ferme', the welcoming owners, Mireille and Timothy Prouten have upgraded this site to a good standard, and have attractively landscaped the site with many flowering shrubs and trees. The 108 pitches, all with electricity (10A) are large and mostly level, with maturing trees which are beginning to offer some shade. There are new toilet facilities and an excellent play area. Families are welcome to visit the working farm which produces cereal crops and raises sheep. Located in the countryside on the Rhuys Peninsula, Golfe du Morbihan, it is an ideal base for cycling, walking and water based activities.

Facilities

Two new, high quality toilet blocks with facilities for the disabled people and bathing babies. Washing machines and dryers. Playground with modern well designed equipment. Volleyball and petanque. Bread delivery (high season). Ice creams and soft drinks available at reception. Takeaway meals and traditional Breton 'soirées' (high season). Bicycle hire. Off site: Beach or boating 800 m. Fishing 600 m. Riding 2 km. Golf 6 km.

Open

1 April - 31 October.

At a glance

Welcome & Ambience	✓✓✓✓✓	Location	✓✓✓✓
Quality of Pitches	✓✓✓	Range of Facilities	✓✓✓✓

Directions

East of Vannes on the N165, join the D780 in direction of Sarzeau. Exit D780 at the 'Super U' roundabout south of Sarzeau, following signs for Le Roaliguen. Campsite is signed.

Charges 2004

per person	€ 4,10
child (under 7 yrs)	€ 2,00
pitch	€ 7,00
electricity	€ 2,60

Camping Cheques accepted.

Reservations

Made with deposit (€ 45). Tel: 02 97 48 01 73.
E-mail: contact@camping-lannhoedic.fr

FR56130 Camping Mané Guernehué

56870 Baden (Morbihan)

Located close to the Morbihan Gulf, Mané Guernehué is a smart, modern site offering a variety of pitches. Some are terraced beneath pine trees, others in a former orchard with delightful views of the surrounding countryside. The 377 pitches are generally large, 200 being occupied by mobile homes and chalets. Most pitches have 10A electricity and a few are also equipped with water and drainage. Many are level but others, particularly those in the centre of the site, slope to varying degrees. There are plenty of excellent amenities. There is a well stocked fishing lake on the edge. Used by tour operators (around 146 pitches).

Facilities

Two modern toilet blocks include washbasins in cabins. The maintenance of the blocks does seem to be under some pressure. Facilities for disabled visitors. Washing machines and dryers. Small shop, bar and takeaway. Heated swimming pool, waterslide, jacuzzi and gym. Fishing. Teenagers' room with table tennis, pool, billiards and TV. Play area. Varied entertainment programme in high season, based around a large purpose built hall.
Off site: Beach or golf 3 km.

Open

Easter - 30 September.

At a glance

Welcome & Ambience	✓✓✓	Location	✓✓✓✓
Quality of Pitches	✓✓✓✓	Range of Facilities	✓✓✓✓✓

Directions

From Auray or Vannes use the D101 to Baden and watch for signs to site.

Charges 2004

Per person	€ 3,10 - € 5,80
child (2-6 yrs)	€ 2,00 - € 4,20
pitch	€ 10,50 - € 16,00
electricity (10A)	€ 4,20
dog	€ 1,60 - € 3,40

Camping Cheques accepted.

Reservations

Advised for high season and made with deposit (€ 70) and fee (€ 20). Tel: 02 97 57 02 06.
E-mail: mane-guernehue@wanadoo.fr

FR56120 Camping Les Iles

La Pointe du Bile, 56760 Pénestin-sur-Mer (Morbihan)

You will receive a warm and friendly welcome at this family run campsite where the owner, Madame Communal, encourages everyone to make the most of this beautiful region. The 107 pitches are mostly of a reasonable size (although larger caravans and American motorhomes are advised to book) and all have electricity. All services are fully open 14/5-16/9, with a limited service at other times. There is direct access from the site to cliff-top walks and local beaches (you can even walk to small off-shore islands at low tide). Used by one tour operator (26 pitches).

TRAVEL SERVICE SITE

TO BOOK CALL 0870 405 4055 OR www.alanrogersdirect.com

Facilities

The large central toilet block has mostly British style WCs and washbasins in cabins (with hairdryers for ladies). Dishwashing and laundry sinks. Facilities for disabled people and two baby baths. Motorcaravan service point across the road at 'Parc des Iles', the mobile home section of the site. Shop. New bar and restaurant with takeaway overlooking new pool complex (14/5-16/9). Modern multi-sports pitch for football, basketball and volleyball. Tennis court across the road. Bicycle hire. Riding. Full range of activities and entertainment for adults and children in July/Aug.
Off site: Windsurfing 500 m. Sailing school 3 km.

Open

1 April - 4 October.

At a glance

Welcome & Ambience	✓✓✓✓	Location	✓✓✓✓✓
Quality of Pitches	✓✓✓✓✓	Range of Facilities	✓✓✓✓✓

Directions

From Pénestin take D201 south, taking a right fork to Pointe du Bile after 2 km. Turn right at crossroads just before beach and site is on left. Take care on arrival - the barrier is fairly close to the entrance, but there is some parking along the road outside.

Charges 2004

Per unit incl. 2 adults	€ 19,50 - € 31,50
extra person (over 10 yrs)	€ 3,20 - € 5,00
child (2-10 yrs)	€ 1,60 - € 2,50
pet	€ 1,80 - € 2,30
electricity (6A)	€ 2,80

Reservations

Made with deposit (€ 100) and fee (€ 20).
Tel: 02 99 90 30 24.
E-mail: contact@camping-des-iles.fr

FR56180 Camping Le Cénic

56760 Pénestin-sur-Mer (Morbihan)

Le Cénic is attractively set amidst trees and flowers, providing activities for all tastes. An attractive covered aquatic complex has water slides, bridges, rivers and a jacuzzi, whilst the outdoor pool comes complete with water slide, 'magic mushroom' fountain and sunbathing areas. You may fish in the pretty lake or use inflatables, watched by the peacock and the geese and turkeys. Unusually there is also a covered sports hall for ball games. A range of accommodation is on offer from tent and caravan pitches to static caravans and chalets and bungalows to rent. There are 90 pitches with electricity (6A) available. The area has much to offer from the beaches of La Mine d'Or, the harbour at Trébiguier-Pénestin, the Golf du Morbihan with its numerous islands, La Baule with its magnificent beach and the medieval city of Guérande to the unique Brière nature reserve.

Facilities

Fully equipped toilet facilities include laundry and dishwashing sinks. Washing machines and dryers. Bar, restaurant, shop, TV and games room. Indoor and outdoor swimming pools. Play area. Indoor ball area. Fishing.

Open

1 May - 30 September.

At a glance

Welcome & Ambience	✓✓	Location	✓✓✓
Quality of Pitches	✓✓✓✓	Range of Facilities	✓✓✓✓

Directions

Site is 300 m. from the D34, and 1 km. from the town, to the southwest.

Charges 2004

Per person	€ 4,00 - € 6,00
child (under 7 yrs.)	€ 2,00 - € 3,00
pitch	€ 5,00 - € 9,00
electricity	€ 3,00

Camping Cheques accepted.

Reservations

Necessary for high season. Tel: 02 99 90 33 14.
E-mail: info@lecenic.com

FR56160 Camping La Vallée du Ninian

Le Rocher, 56800 Taupont (Morbihan)

M. and Mme. Joubaud developed this peaceful family run site in central Brittany from a farm area in the eighties and take care to ensure that everyone has an enjoyable holiday. The level site falls into the three areas - the orchard with 32 large, hedged pitches with electricity, the wood with about 13 pitches more suited to tents, and the meadow by the river providing a further 35 pitches delineated by small trees and shrubs, some with electricity. The shop has, as a centre-piece, a working cider press with which M. Joubaud makes his own 'potion magique'. The adjoining covered bar area is the venue for song and dance evenings with a Breton flavour and occasional camp fire sing-songs are organised.

Facilities

The central building houses unisex toilet facilities including washbasins in cubicles, large cubicle with facilities for disabled visitors and laundry area with washing machines, dryer and ironing board. Covered dishwashing area with hot water. Shop selling basic provisions. Small (7 x 12 m) heated swimming pool. Paddling pool. Swings and slides, large trampoline, popular with children.

Open

1 May - 30 September.

At a glance

Welcome & Ambience	✓✓✓✓	Location	✓✓✓✓✓
Quality of Pitches	✓✓✓✓	Range of Facilities	✓✓✓✓

Directions

From Plo'rmel centre follow signs to Taupont north on the N8. Continue through village of Taupont and turn left (east) signed Vallée du Ninian. Follow road until 1 km. before Hellean. From Josselin follow signs for Hellean. Go through village and turn sharp right after the bridge over the river Ninian. Site is 400 m. on the right.

Charges 2004

Per person	€ 3,10
child (under 7 yrs)	€ 2,30
pitch	€ 5,00
electricity (3/6A)	€ 1,60 - € 3,10

Credit cards accepted in July/Aug. only.

Reservations

Contact site. Tel: 02 97 93 53 01.
E-mail: info@camping-ninian.com

Map 2

A striking area whose beauty lies not only in the landscape. Famed for its seafood and Celtic tradition, certain areas of Normandy remain untouched and wonderfully old fashioned.

Départements: 14 Calvados, 27 Eure, 50 Manche, 61 Orne, 76 Seine Maritime

Major cities: Caen and Rouen

Normandy is a rich landscape full of variety. From the wild craggy granite coastline of the northern Cotentin to the long sandy beaches and chalk cliffs of the south. It also boasts a superb coast line including the Cotentin Peninsula, cliffs of the Côte d'Albâtre and the fine beaches and fashionable resorts of the Côte Fleurie. Plus a wealth of quiet villages and unspoilt countryside for leisurely exploration.

The history of Normandy is closely linked with our own. The famous Bayeux Tapestry chronicles the exploits of the battle of Hastings and there are lots of museums, exhibitions, sites and monuments, including the Caen Memorial Museum, which commemorate operations that took place during the D-Day Landings of 1944.

Known as the dairy of France you'll also find plenty of fresh fish, rich cream, butter, and fine cheeses such as Camembert and Pont l'Evêque. The many apple orchards are used in producing cider and the well known Calvados, Normandy's apple brandy.

Cuisine of the region

Andouillette de Vire: small chitterling (tripe) sausage

Barbue au cidre: brill cooked in cider and Calvados

Douillons de pommes à la Normande: baked apples in pastry

Escalope (Vallée d'Auge): veal sautéed and flamed in Calvados and served with cream and apples

Ficelle Normande: pancake with ham, mushrooms and cheese

Marnite Dieppoisse: fish soup

Poulet (Vallée d'Auge): chicken cooked in the same way as Escalope Vallée d'Auge

Tripes à la Mode de Caen: stewed beef tripe with onions, carrots, leeks, garlic, cider and Calvados

Places of interest

Bayeux: home to the famous tapestry; 15th-18th century houses, cathedral, museums

Caen: feudal castle, Museum of Normandy, Museum for Peace

Omaha Beach: D-Day beaches, Landing site monuments, American Cemetery

Deauville: seaside resort, horse racing centre

Giverny: home of impressionist painter Claude Monet, Monet Museum

Honfleur: picturesque port city with old town

Lisieux: pilgrimage site, shrine of Ste Thérèse

Mont St Michel: world famous abbey on island

Rouen: Joan of Arc Museum; Gothic churches, cathedrals, abbey, clock tower

Alan Rogers tip

FOR A REAL TASTE OF WHAT NORMANDY HAS TO OFFER. FOLLOW THE WELL-TRODDEN CIDER AND CHEESE ROUTES AND STOCK UP ON ALL THOSE GOODIES!

FR14020 Camping Municipal du Bayeux

Boulevard Eindhoven, 14400 Bayeux (Calvados)

Whether or not you want to see the tapestry, this site makes a very useful night stop on the way to or from Cherbourg, and in addition it is only a few kilometres from the coast and the landing beaches. Pleasantly laid out with grassy lawns and bushes, its neat, cared for appearance make a good impression. The 140 pitches are in two areas (many are on hardstanding), and are well marked, generally of good size and with electricity. The site is busy over a long season - early arrival is advised as reservations are not taken. There is a full time site warden from 15/6-15/9, otherwise reception is open from 08.00-10.00 and 17.00-19.00 hrs. There may be some road noise on one side of the site.

Facilities

The two good quality toilet blocks have British and Turkish style WCs, washbasins in cabins in the main block, and units for disabled people. Motorcaravan service point. Laundry room. Takeaway food and snacks. Two children's playgrounds. Volleyball. Reading room with TV. Games room. Off site: Large public indoor swimming pool adjoins site with children's pool and jacuzzi. Large supermarket very close (closes 8 pm). Bicycle hire 1 km. Riding 5 km. Golf or fishing 8 km. Beach 8 km.

At a glance

Welcome & Ambience	✓✓✓✓	Location	✓✓✓✓
Quality of Pitches	✓✓✓✓	Range of Facilities	✓✓✓

Directions

Site is on the south side of northern ring road (D613) to town, and just west of the junction with the D516 to autoroute.

Charges 2005

Per person	€ 3,04
child (under 7 yrs)	€ 1,62
pitch and car	€ 3,75
electricity	€ 3,08 - € 3,08

Less 10% for stay over 5 days.

Reservations

Not made. Tel: 02 31 92 08 43.

Open

1 May - 30 September.

FR14030 Castel Camping Le Château de Martragny

14740 Martragny (Calvados)

Martragny is an attractive site in a parkland setting adjoining the château and close to D-Day beaches. It is a particularly convenient location for both the ports of Caen and Cherbourg, and has the facilities and charm to encourage both long stays and stopovers. The pleasant lawns surrounding and approaching the chateau take 160 units, with electricity connections for 140. The majority of the pitches are divided by either a small hedge or a couple of trees, only a few not marked out. Bed and breakfast (en-suite) are available in the château all year (reservation essential). Madame de Chassey takes great pride in the site and takes care that the peace and quiet is preserved. This is a perfect place for a quiet relaxing holiday yet only twelve kilometres from the sea, the wartime landing beaches, the excellent museum at Arromanche, the Bayeux tapestry or the Calvados 'Cider Route'.

Facilities

Two recently modernised sanitary blocks include washbasins in cabins, sinks for dishes and clothes and two baby baths. Disabled people are well catered for. Good laundry. Well stocked shop and takeaway food bar open 15/5-15/9. Bar. Swimming pool (20 x 6 m.) and paddling pool heated in poor weather. Play areas, one new. Tennis courts. Minigolf, games and TV room, table tennis and billiards. Fishing. Bicycle and buggy hire. Off site: Riding 1 km. Beach 15 km. Golf 20 km.

Open

1 May - 15 September.

At a glance

Welcome & Ambience	✓✓✓✓	Location	✓✓✓✓
Quality of Pitches	✓✓✓✓	Range of Facilities	✓✓✓✓

Directions

Site is off N13, 8 km. southeast of Bayeux. Take Martragny exit from dual carriageway.

Charges 2005

Per person	€ 4,70
child (under 7 yrs)	€ 2,70
pitch for caravan or motorcaravan	€ 10,60
tent pitch	€ 10,00
electricity (6A)	€ 3,00

Camping Cheques accepted.
Less 15% outside 1/7-31/8.

Reservations

Made for min. 3 nights; deposit and small fee required. Tel: 02 31 80 21 40.
E-mail: chateau.martragny@wanadoo.fr

FR14070 Camping de la Vallée

88 rue de la Vallée, 14510 Houlgate (Calvados)

Camping de la Vallée is an attractive site with good, well maintained facilities. Situated on a grassy hillside overlooking Houlgate, the 355 pitches (98 for touring units) are large and open. Hedges have been planted and all have electricity. Part of the site is sloping, the rest level, with gravel or tarmac roads. An old farmhouse has been converted to house a new bar and comfortable TV lounge and billiards room. English is spoken in season. Used by tour operators (87 pitches). Very busy in high season, maintenance and cleaning could be variable at that time. There are 130 mobile homes on site and around 40 seasonal units are also taken.

Facilities

Three good toilet blocks include washbasins in cabins, mainly British style toilets, facilities for disabled people and baby bathroom. Dishwashing, laundry with machines, dryers and ironing boards (no washing lines allowed). Motorcaravan services. Shop (from 1/5). Bar. Small snack bar with takeaway in season (from 15/5). Heated swimming pool (from 15/5; no shorts). Games room. Playground. Bicycle hire. Volleyball, football field, tennis, petanque and table tennis. Organised entertainment in Jul/Aug.
Off site: Riding 500 m. Beach, town or fishing 1 km. Championship golf course 2 km.

Open

1 April - 30 September.

At a glance

Welcome & Ambience	✓✓✓✓	Location	✓✓✓✓
Quality of Pitches	✓✓✓✓	Range of Facilities	✓✓✓✓

Directions

From A13 take exit for Cabourg and follow signs for Dives/Houlgate going straight on at roundabout. Follow road straight on at next roundabout, and then four sets of traffic lights. Turn left along seafront. After 1 km. at lights turn right, carry on for about 1 km. and over mini-roundabout - look for site sign and flag poles on right.

Charges 2004

Per unit incl. 2 persons and electricity	€ 20,00 - € 26,00
extra adult	€ 4,00 - € 6,00
child (under 7 yrs)	€ 3,00 - € 4,00

Camping Cheques accepted.
Credit card minimum € 35. Barrier card deposit € 20.

Reservations

Made with deposit and fee. Tel: 02 31 24 40 69.
E-mail: camping.lavallee@wanadoo.fr

FR14060 Camping Les Hautes Coutures

Route de Ouistreham, 14970 Bénouville (Calvados)

Les Hautes Coutures is a useful site near the Caen-Portsmouth ferry terminal suitable for overnight stays. It is 2 km. from the sea (and ferry port) and 10 km. from Caen - the site gates are opened at 6 am. for early ferries and there can be movement on site late into the evening. There are 110 grass touring pitches of 100 sq.m, clearly marked by mature hedges with tarmac roads. There are also over 150 mobile homes on the site. Ouistreham is within walking distance along the canal and the Pegasus Bridge Airborne Division Museum. A pedestrian gate leads on to the towpath (a code is needed for re-entry).

Facilities

Two toilet blocks include showers, washbasins in cabins (warm water only). Facilities can be under pressure at peak times and the hot water supply can be variable. Dishwashing and laundry facilities with washing machine and dryer. Motorcaravan service point. Small shop keeps basic items. Bar and takeaway. Small heated swimming pool (from May) which is kept locked - ask for access. Small lounge/TV area and games room. Play area on sand. Two tennis courts. Volleyball. Minigolf. Boules. Table tennis. Off site: Riding or beach 2 km. Golf 4 km.

At a glance

Welcome & Ambience	✓✓✓	Location	✓✓✓✓
Quality of Pitches	✓✓✓	Range of Facilities	✓✓✓

Directions

Site is just off the D514 dual-carriageway, north of Benouville. From Caen, follow Ouistreham car ferry signs and take first exit from D514 after Benouville.

Charges 2005

Per person	€ 7,50
pitch	€ 7,60
electricity (2/10A)	€ 5,80 - € 8,00

Reservations

Contact site. Tel: 02 31 44 73 08.
E-mail: camping-hautes-coutures@wanadoo.fr

Open

1 April - 30 September.

FR14080 Camping Le Puits

La Groudière, 14350 St Martin des Besaces (Calvados)

This traditional little site in the heart of historic Normandy is becoming very popular. Situated on the edge of the village, it only has 40 pitches in two areas, either individual ones divided by flowers and shrubs, or marked out by hedges and trees on an open grassy field. All have electricity and are slightly sloping. The Ashworth family are gradually upgrading the facilities on what was originally an 'á la ferme' site. The site has its own newsletter to keep guests informed and a comprehensive stock of tourist information in reception. A museum with a difference is close to the site featuring a unique account of the Battle of Normandy with displays, sound and light presentations, artefacts and personal memorabilia (some belonging to regular visitors to the campsite).

Facilities

Simple, basic toilet facilities at the rear of the farmhouse are being upgraded with additional toilets and showers. Sinks for dishwashing and laundry, plus washing machine and dryer. Motorcaravan services. In renovated barns are a small shop, bar with a snack bar serving pizzas, chips and quiches to order with a café style eating area outside. Bread, croissants or breakfast can be ordered. One barn provides a function room and games room. Minigolf, table tennis, billiards, volleyball and fishing in pond. Small playground. Activities organised or available in the area in season - barbecues, murder mysteries, quizzes and visits to local cider makers - even bungee jumping! Off site: Bicycle hire 5 km. Riding 10 km. Market in St Martin des Besaces on Saturday morning. Beach 50 km.

Open

1 March - 31 October.

At a glance

Welcome & Ambience	✓✓✓✓	Location	✓✓✓✓
Quality of Pitches	✓✓✓✓	Range of Facilities	✓✓✓✓

Directions

From Caen take A84 at Porte de Bretagne towards Rennes to St Martin des Besaces (exit 41). Follow signs to village on D53. At lights turn right on D675 and site is signed to left at far end of village. From Cherbourg follow N13 towards St Lô and Vire. At motorway junction with A84 take Caen direction to junction 41 St Martin des Besaces and site is signed to right at entrance to village.

Charges 2004

Per adult	€ 3,00
child (3-9 yrs)	€ 1,50
pitch	€ 8,00
electricity (6A)	€ 4,00

Credit cards are accepted with a 2% surcharge.

Reservations

Advised for high season and made with deposit of 1 nights fees. Tel: 02 31 67 80 02.
E-mail: camping.le.puits@wanadoo.fr

FR14090 Castel Camping du Brévedent

Le Brévedent, 14130 Pont-l'Evêque (Calvados)

Le Brévedent is a well established, traditional site with 140 pitches (100 for tourists) set in the grounds of an elegant 18th century hunting pavilion. Level pitches are set around the fishing lake or in the lower gardens, others are in the old orchard. All have electricity. Reception provides a vast amount of tourist information, with organised tours in the main season to Paris, Disney, a cider farm and a local distillery. The site is used by a tour operator (40 pitches). It is an excellent holiday destination within easy reach of the Channel ports. The church bells ring out every morning at 07.00 hrs, but the otherwise peaceful, friendly environment makes it ideal for mature campers or families with younger children (note the lake is unfenced). Particularly popular are the Saturday evening talks, the Sunday countryside rambles and the evening family meal.

Facilities

Three toilet blocks of varying ages (one new) include washbasins in cubicles, dishwashing and laundry sinks, and new facilities for babies and disabled people. Good motorcaravan service point. Laundries with washing machines and dryers. Well stocked shop. Baker calls each morning. Small bar in the hunting lodge itself, open each evening (1/5-26/9). Restaurant including snacks and traditional Normandy cuisine (24/5-19/9). Takeaway (1/5-26/9). Clubroom with TV and library. Swimming and paddling pools (unsupervised) are heated and in separate enclosures. Playground in the old walled garden, with table tennis tables in open fronted barns alongside. Minigolf, boules, volleyball, games room with games machines, and a pool table. Fishing is free (but put the fish back). Rowing boats (with lifejackets). Bicycle and buggy hire. Organised activities for children including pony lessons. Dogs are not accepted. Off site: Discounts arranged for riding (1 km), the nearby St Julien golf club and tennis on the local court. Pont L'Evêque 14 km. Château de Betteville with motor museum. Beach 25 km.

At a glance

Welcome & Ambience	✓✓✓✓	Location	✓✓✓✓
Quality of Pitches	✓✓✓✓	Range of Facilities	✓✓✓✓

Directions

From Pont L'Evêque take D579 toward Lisieux for 4 km. then D51 towards Moyaux. At Blangy le Château turn right (still on D51) to Le Brévedent.

Charges 2004

Per adult	€ 5,50
child 1-6 yrs	€ 3,00
child 7-12 yrs	€ 4,00
pitch	€ 8,00
electricity	€ 3,00

Camping Cheques accepted.

Reservations

Advised for the main season; contact site.
Tel: 02 31 64 72 88.
E-mail: contact@campinglebrevedent.com

Open

1 May - 25 September.

FR14120 Camping Les Ammonites

Auberville, Route de la Corniche, 14640 Villers-sur-Mer (Calvados)

Les Ammonites is a friendly, family owned site with a total of 140 pitches in a location that slopes gently downwards towards the cliffs. On entering the site you pass through an area with about 100 mobile homes, 60 privately owned, and 40 to rent. The 40 tourist pitches are at the far end of the site with the most wonderful panoramic views over the Channel. All on grass with electric hook-ups (10A), most are slightly sloping, although the views do compensate for the inconvenience. The heated swimming pool with sunbathing terrace and a shallow area for children, is next to the reception building. On the other side of the road, opposite reception, is a parking area, the bar/brasserie and takeaway. Also on this side are a basic children's playground, giant chess and draughts, table tennis, basketball net, two tennis courts (on payment), and some more pitches. The main site is unsuitable for large units and American RVs, although the pitches by the tennis courts may be accessible.

Facilities

The single sanitary unit is positioned quite near the top of the site (so quite a walk from the touring pitches) with separate facilities for men and women at the front, some unisex facilities including well refitted showers, and a dishwashing room at the rear. Laundry with washing machines and dryer, plus facilities for disabled people are at one end. Motorcaravan service point. Reception has a small shop with basic essentials. Bar/brasserie and takeaway. Swimming pool (15m x 8 m). Playground. Small games room. Animation in July/August. Off site: Houlgate (4 km.) and Villers-sur-Mer (3 km.) both have good sandy beaches. The fashionable resort of Deauville is 11 km. and within easy day trip distance are Caen and picturesque Honfleur.

Open

1 April - 31 October.

At a glance

Welcome & Ambience	✓✓✓✓	Location	✓✓✓✓
Quality of Pitches	✓✓✓	Range of Facilities	✓✓✓✓

Directions

Auberville is on the D513 mid-way between Houlgate and Villers-sur-Mer. It is best approached from the D27, which is now the primary route from Deauville to Caen (some uneven sections, but avoids coastal towns). Turn north on D163 to Auberville. At lights, turn left and almost immediately right towards coast, still on D163 signed Auberville. Site entrance is 500 m. on right.

Charges 2004

Per unit incl. 2 persons	€ 20,00
extra person	€ 3,00
electricity	€ 3,00

Reservations

Advisable for peak season. Made with deposit of 50% of total fees. Tel: 02 31 87 06 06.
E-mail: camping.lesammonites@wanadoo.fr

FR14130 Camping Le Fanal

Rue de Fanal, 14230 Isigny-sur-Mer (Calvados)

A useful informal spacious site, Le Fanal is on the outskirts of a fairly typical small town. There are 112 pitches, of which 97 are touring pitches, all on grass with around 42 electric hook-ups (16A), arranged in several large bays, surrounded by mature trees. Some areas could be a little soft in inclement weather, so the site is not really suitable for American RVs. The small, fenced swimming pool (8 x 4 m) may look like a child's pool, but is in fact between one and two metres deep - only supervised children are permitted (open July and Aug, ask for key). The town is noted for its dairy products, with visits possible to factories producing cheese, butter, cream, and caramels.

Facilities

The main sanitary unit provides washbasins in cubicles, pre-set hot showers, plus facilities for disabled people. Motorcaravan service point. The reception building has a dining room with a microwave and soft drink dispensing machines, a lounge with TV, a laundry with washing machine, dryer and ironing facility, plus more toilets and washbasins. Small swimming pool. Playground. Tennis, table tennis, volleyball, boules. Off site: Fishing and boating are possible in the adjacent lake, with a fitness course in the surrounding parkland. Site is close to the D-day landing beaches. Isigny market on Wednesday, small market Saturday a.m.

At a glance

Welcome & Ambience	✓✓✓✓	Location	✓✓✓✓
Quality of Pitches	✓✓✓	Range of Facilities	✓✓✓

Directions

Isigny-sur-Mer is just off N13, mid-way between Cherbourg and Caen, (10 km. east of Carentan). Site is west of town centre off D197A, and is well signed.

Charges 2004

Per pitch	€ 3,05 - € 4,60
adult	€ 3,05 - € 3,35
child under 16 yrs (third free)	€ 1,55
electricity	€ 3,05
dog	€ 0,75

No credit cards.

Reservations

Contact site. Tel: 02 31 21 33 20.
E-mail: camping@isigny-sur-mer.fr

Open

1 April - 15 October.

FR14100 Camping Municipal du Château

3 rue du Val d'Ante, 14700 Falaise (Calvados)

The location of this site is really quite spectacular, lying in the shadow of the Château de Falaise, in the old part of the town. The site itself is small, with only 66 pitches (all with 5A electricity). It has a rather intimate 'up-market' feel about it, rather different from the average municipal site. With good shade, tarmac roads and easy access, whatever this site lacks in size and facilities it makes up for in its situation, close to the town centre and near the river for fishing. The charges are reasonable and the reception friendly.

Facilities

The sanitary facilities could be insufficient in terms of quantity when the site is full - perhaps it never is and campers we met felt they were adequate. The quality is good and they are clean. Unit for disabled visitors. Access to showers, laundry and dishwashing closed 22.00-07.30. Play area. Table tennis. TV room. Fishing. Off site: Tennis courts adjacent. Bicycle hire 300 m. Riding 500 m.

Open

1 May - 30 September.

At a glance

Welcome & Ambience	✓✓✓✓	Location	✓✓✓✓
Quality of Pitches	✓✓✓✓	Range of Facilities	✓✓✓

Directions

Site is on western side of town, well signed from the ring road. From N158 heading south take first roundabout into Falaise (site signed), then pass through residential suburb to site.

Charges 2005

Per person	€ 3,00
pitch	€ 3,00
electricity	€ 2,50

No credit cards.

Reservations

Advised for July/Aug. Tel: 02 31 90 16 55.
E-mail: camping@falaise.fr

FR14150 Sunelia Le Port'land

Chemin du Castel, 14520 Port en Bessin (Calvados)

Le Port'land is a new site lying to the east of the little resort of Port en Bessin, one of Normandy's busiest fishing ports. A coastal path leads to the little town and the nearest beaches (the sandy Omaha Beach – 4 km. away). The 254 pitches are large and grassy. Most offer 10A electricity although there is a separate area for tents (without electricity). The camping area has been imaginatively designed with the creation of a number of distinct zones, some overlooking a series of small fishing ponds, and another radiating out from a central barbecue area. The central building houses reception, the shop, bar and restaurant, as well as a large TV and games room from where there are fine views of the Normandy coast. The heated swimming pool is adjacent and is covered in low season. In peak season a range of entertainment is organised including disco and karaoke evenings, and a range of children's activities. Mobile homes for hire. A member of the Sunelia group.

Facilities

The two sanitary blocks are modern and well maintained. Special disabled facilities. Covered swimming pool and paddling pool. Bar, restaurant. Takeaway food. Multisports pitch. Fishing. Play area. Off site: Nearest beach 4 km. 27 hole Omaha Beach International golf course adjacent. D-Day beaches. Colleville American war Cemetary. Bayeux.

Open

1 April - 4 November.

At a glance

Welcome & Ambience	✓✓✓✓	Location	✓✓✓✓
Quality of Pitches	✓✓✓✓	Range of Facilities	✓✓✓✓

Directions

Site is clearly signed off the D514 4 km. west of Port en Bessin.

Charges 2004

Per unit incl. 2 persons, electricity	€ 24,40 - € 32,30
extra person	€ 4,80 - € 7,30
child (2-10 yrs)	€ 2,80 - € 4,20

Reductions for stays over 7 nights.

Reservations

Contact site. Tel: 02 31 51 07 06.
E-mail: campingportland@wanadoo.fr

FR27050 Camping Municipal Saint Paul

2 route de St Paul, 27480 Lyons la Foret (Eure)

The village of Lyons-La-Foret, with its medieval covered market and magnificently preserved half-timbered buildings is regarded as one of the most beautiful in France. Within walking distance (900 metres), next to the stadium and public swimming pool, this quiet municipal site provides a pleasant respite. There are 100 level grass pitches with 45 for tourists. Each has access to electricity, water and drainage. They are separated by mature trees providing shade. The site is edged by fast-flowing, shallow (unfenced) streams.

Facilities

Two well maintained toilet blocks include facilities for people with disabilities. Laundry and dishwashing sinks. Washing machine. Drying lines. Play area. Separate tent area.
Off site: All facilities in village. Walking and cycling routes.

Open

1 April - 1 November.

At a glance

Welcome & Ambience	✓✓✓	Location	✓✓✓✓
Quality of Pitches	✓✓✓✓	Range of Facilities	✓✓✓

Directions

Site is to the north of Lyons-La-Foret on the D921 road.

Charges 2004

Per adult	€ 3,70
child (4-13 yrs)	€ 2,20
pitch	€ 2,20 - € 5,55
electricity	€ 2,55

Reservations

Contact site. Tel: 02 32 49 42 02.

FR27020 Camping du Domaine Catinière

Route de Honfleur, 27210 Fiquefleur-Equainville (Eure)

A peaceful, friendly site, convenient for Le Havre ferries, this is a developing site with owners who are intent on improving this countryside site which lies in the middle of a very long village. The site is steadily achieving a modern look, whilst retaining its original French flavour. There are 12 rental and 30 privately owned mobile homes, but there should be around 75 pitches for tourists including a large open field for tents and units not needing electricity. Caravan pitches are separated, some with shade, others are more open and all have electricity hook-ups. The site is divided by well fenced streams, popular with young anglers. It is a good base for visiting this part of Normandy, with the pretty harbour town of Honfleur less than five kilometres and the nearby Vallée de la Risle. It is only a short distance from the ferry terminal, and makes every effort to meet the demands of ferry users.

Facilities

Already modernised, the toilet facilities include some washbasins in cubicles, and facilities for disabled people and babies. Dishwashing sinks. Washing machine and dryer. Reception with shop. Small bar/restaurant with regional dishes and snacks. Heated swimming pool (mid-June - end Aug). Two playgrounds, trampoline. Table tennis. Boules. New barrier (card deposit). Off site: Large supermarket is also close to the southern end of the bridge. Smaller supermarket in Beuzeville (7 km). Beach 7 km.

Open

8 April - 25 September.

At a glance

Welcome & Ambience	✓✓✓✓	Location	✓✓✓✓
Quality of Pitches	✓✓✓✓	Range of Facilities	✓✓✓✓

Directions

From Le Havre ferry terminal and the north, follow signs to the Pont de Normandie crossing (with toll). Take first exit on leaving the bridge (junction 3, A29) signed Honfleur. At roundabout turn left under the motorway in the direction of Le Mans and Alencon. Take the second exit on the right after about 2 km, signed Beuzeville. The site is on the right after 1 km.

Charges 2005

Per adult	€ 4,00 - € 5,00
child (under 7 yrs)	€ 2,80 - € 3,30
pitch	€ 14,00 - € 20,00
electricity (8/13A)	€ 1,00 - € 1,50
dog	€ 2,00

Reservations

Advised for high season, made with deposit of 50% of total amount due. Tel: 02 32 57 63 51.
E-mail: info@camping-catiniere.com

FR50100 Camping Municipal Le Pont-Roulland

50370 Brécey (Manche)

Comfortable and good value, this little site is set in an old orchard of apple and cherry trees and is ideal for a relaxing short break, perhaps before heading further south or west. Various possible outings include Villedieu-les-Poêles 14 km.), Avranches (16 km.) and Mont St Michel (30 km). The 50 numbered tourist pitches are on lush grass, with electric hook-ups (6A) for all, although some may need long leads. The entire site has a slight slope, so motorcaravans will probably need levelling blocks. There is good site lighting and tarmac roads. Although off-ground barbecues are allowed on the pitch, a large communal barbecue is provided in a traditional style 'storehouse'. The guardienne lives on site and reception is open 9.00-22.00 (July/Aug), 17.00-22.00 (low season) - just choose your pitch and pay later if she is not around. The usual small country town hustle and bustle and swimming pool noise during the day gives way to quiet nights after 8 pm.

Facilities

A traditional Normandy stone building houses toilet facilities with modern fittings including British-style toilets, spacious hot showers, some basins in cubicles, dishwashing and laundry sinks, and a washing machine, but no dedicated facilities for disabled visitors. Table tennis. Playground for young children. Off site: Town centre and shops 1 km. Reception issues vouchers for free admission to adjacent municipal swimming pool (June 16.30-19.00, July/Aug 14.00-19.00) and tennis (balls and rackets for hire). Small park with free paddling pool also adjacent. River fishing nearby. Golf 18 km. Beaches 25 km.

Open

1 April - 30 September.

At a glance

Welcome & Ambience	✓✓✓✓	Location	✓✓✓✓
Quality of Pitches	✓✓✓✓	Range of Facilities	✓✓✓

Directions

Brécey is 16 km. east of Avranches. Site is 1 km. east of town centre just off D911. Turn south on D79 towards Les Cresnays (site signed). Site entrance is adjacent to the swimming pool, off a public car park.

Charges 2004

Per person	€ 2,35
child (under 7 yrs)	€ 1,20
pitch	€ 2,20
electricity	€ 2,00
dog	€ 0,45

No credit cards.

Reservations

Contact site. Tel: 02 33 48 60 60.
E-mail: tourisme-brecey@wanadoo.fr

FR50000 Camping L'Etang des Haizes

43 rue Cauticotte, 50250 St Symphorien-le-Valois (Manche)

This is an attractive and very friendly site which has recently added a swimming pool complex with four-lane slides, jacuzzi and a paddling pool. L'Etang des Haizes has 98 good size pitches, of which 60 are for touring units, on fairly level ground and all with electricity (10A). They are set in a mixture of conifers, orchard and shrubbery, with some very attractive slightly smaller pitches overlooking the lake and 38 mobile homes inconspicuously sited. The fenced lake has a small beach (swimming is permitted!), ducks and pedaloes, and offers good coarse fishing for huge carp (we are told!): believe it or not, a turtle can sometimes be seen on a fine day!

Facilities

Two well kept toilet blocks are of modern construction, open plan and unisex. They have British-style toilets, washbasins in cabins and units for disabled people. Dishwashing under cover, small laundry. Motorcaravan services. Milk, bread and takeaway snacks are available on site (no gas). Snack-bar/Bar with TV and terrace overlooking the lake and pool complex (all 20/5-10/9). Two play areas. Bicycle hire. Table tennis, pool table, petanque and volleyball. Entertainment and activities organised for all ages, including treasure hunts, archery and food tasting (10/7-25/8). Off site: La Haye-du-Puits (1 km) has two supermarkets, good restaurants and a market on Wednesdays. Good sandy beach 10 km. Normandy landing beaches 25 km.

At a glance

Welcome & Ambience	✓✓✓✓✓	Location	✓✓✓✓
Quality of Pitches	✓✓✓✓	Range of Facilities	✓✓✓✓

Directions

The site is located just north of La Haye du Puits which is on the primary route from Cherbourg to Mont St Michel, St Malo and Rennes, 24 km south of N13 at Valognes and 29 km north of Coutances: leave D900 at roundabout at northern end of by-pass (towards town) and site is signed almost immediately on the right.

Charges 2004

Per person over 4yrs	€ 3,50 - € 5,50
pitch	€ 6,00 - € 16,00
electricity (10A)	€ 3,50 - € 5,50
dog	€ 1,00 - € 2,00

Camping Cheques accepted.

Reservations

Made with 25% deposit. Tel: 02 33 46 01 16.
E-mail: etang.des.haizes@wanadoo.fr

Open

1 April - 15 October.

FR50030 Castel Camping Le Château de Lez Eaux

Saint Aubin des Préaux, 50380 St Pair-sur-Mer (Manche)

Set in the spacious grounds of a château, Lez Eaux lies in a rural situation just off the main route south, under two hours from Cherbourg. It is a very pleasant location from which to explore this corner of the Cotentin peninsula, with swimming pools on site and beaches nearby. There are 229 pitches of which 113 are tourist pitches all with electricity (5 or 10A) and 70 fully serviced. Most pitches are of a very good size, partly separated by trees and shrubs on either flat or very slightly sloping, grassy ground overlooking Normandy farmland or beside a small lake (with carp and other fish). Although there is a considerable tour-operator presence, these units by no means dominate the site, being generally tucked away in their own areas.

Facilities

Three modern toilet blocks (cleaned continually from early till late by a team of contractors) include British-style toilets, hot showers and washbasins in cabins, good facilities for children and babies, and full provision for disabled people. Shop, small bar, snacks and takeaway (all from 15/5). Small heated swimming pool (12 x 6 m.) and attractive, indoor tropical-style fun pool with slides and a glass roof (from 15/5, no T-shirts or Bermuda style shorts). Adventure play area. Good tennis court. Football, volleyball. Games room with table tennis, and TV room. Bicycle hire. Lake fishing. Torches might help at night. Only one dog per pitch accepted. Off site: Nearest beach is 4 km. St Pair is 4 km. and Granville 7 km. Riding 5 km. Golf 7 km.

At a glance

Welcome & Ambience	✓✓✓✓✓	Location	✓✓✓✓
Quality of Pitches	✓✓✓✓	Range of Facilities	✓✓✓✓✓

Directions

Lez-Eaux is just to the west of the D973 about 17 km. northwest of Avranches and 7 km. southeast of Granville. Site is between the two turnings east to St. Aubin des Préaux and is well signed.

Charges 2004

Per pitch incl. 2 persons	€ 12,00 - € 28,00
extra person	€ 7,00
child (under 7 yrs)	€ 5,00
electricity (5A)	€ 6,00
all services	€ 9,00

Reservations

Advisable for high season and made with 25% deposit. Tel: 02 33 51 66 09. E-mail: lez.eaux@wanadoo.fr

Open

1 May - 15 September.

FR50050 Camping Le Cormoran

Ravenoville-Plage, 50480 Sainte-Mère-Eglise (Manche)

Set in a flat and open landscape and only separated from the beach by the coast road, Le Cormoran is ideal for a holiday or short break quite near to Cherbourg (33 km), with the Landing Beaches close by. Holiday mobile homes, many privately owned, take 136 places and include 40 for rent. The remaining 80 pitches for touring units are sheltered from the wind by neat hedges and have 6A electricity available. With a narrow frontage, decorated with flags and a fountain, it is a fairly long site with most of the amenities at the entrance. This is a well run, family managed site with many regular visitors, which gets full in peak season. Those only staying for one night may be asked to pitch on the overflow area adjacent to the main site. A 'Sites et Paysages' member.

Facilities

Four toilet blocks are of varying styles and ages. Washbasins are in cabins. Dishwashing sinks. Washing machine and dryer in three blocks. The smallest block is of the mobile type and serves 15 extra large pitches (150 sq.m.) at the back of the site. Small shop, bar with snacks (all season) and takeaway. Swimming pool (heated 1/5-15/9, unsupervised). Three small play areas. Tennis court. Boules pitch. Entertainment and games room. Bicycle and shrimp net hire. Communal barbecue. Off site: Archery, riding and day trips to the Channel Islands can be organised. Golf 5 km. Utah Beach 5 km. Sports field and storage for up to 60 boats adjacent to the site. Beach 50 m.

At a glance

Welcome & Ambience	✓✓✓✓	Location	✓✓✓✓
Quality of Pitches	✓✓✓✓	Range of Facilities	✓✓✓✓

Directions

From N13 take Ste Mère Eglise exit and in centre of town take road to Ravenoville (6 km), then Ravenoville-Plage (3 km). Just before beach turn right and site is 500 m.

Charges 2005

Per unit incl. 1 or 2 persons	€ 16,20 - € 23,00
extra person	€ 4,60 - € 6,50
child (3- 7 yrs)	€ 1,80 - € 2,20
electricity (6A)	€ 3,80
dog	€ 2,80 - € 3,00
motorhome overnight (18.00-10.00 hrs)	€ 13,00

Camping Cheques accepted.

Reservations

Essential for July/Aug. and made with 25% deposit. Tel: 02 33 41 33 94. E-mail: lecormoran@wanadoo.fr

Open

1 April - 25 September.

FR50070 Castel Camping & Caravaning L'Anse du Brick

Route du Val de Saire, 50330 Maupertus-sur-Mer (Manche)

A friendly, family site, L'Anse du Brick overlooks a picturesque bay on the northern tip of the Cotentin peninsula, eight kilometres east of Cherbourg Port. This quality site makes a pleasant night halt, or an ideal longer stay destination for those not wishing to travel too far. Its pleasing location offers direct access to a small sandy beach, also to a woodland walk where only the noise of a cascading stream disturbs the peace. Beyond the site lie miles of walking tracks through the gorse-covered hills which, together with a stark rock face, cluster around the site and make it a sheltered sun-trap. This is a mature, terraced site with magnificent sea and hill views from certain pitches. Tarmac roads lead to the 117 touring pitches (all with 10A electricity) which are level, separated and mostly well shaded by the many trees, bushes and shrubs.

Facilities

Two sanitary blocks, although not ultra-modern, are kept spotlessly clean and are well maintained. British-style toilets, washbasins mainly in cubicles and push-button showers, provision for disabled visitors, laundry and dishwashing areas, motorcaravan service point. Swimming pool complex (15/5-15/9). Shop (1/4-15/9). Restaurant and popular bar/pizzeria (1/5-10/9). Tennis court. Play area. Organised entertainment in season. Mini-club for children (6-12 yrs). Bicycle and kayak hire. Off site: Fishing 100 m. Riding 4 km. Golf 10 km. Gourmet restaurant outside campsite gates.

Open

1 April - 30 September.

At a glance

Welcome & Ambience	✓✓✓✓✓	Location	✓✓✓✓
Quality of Pitches	✓✓✓	Range of Facilities	✓✓✓✓

Directions

From Cherbourg port follow directions for Caen and Rennes. After the third roundabout, take slip road to right and under road towards Bretteville-en-Saire (D116). From southeast on N13 at first (Auchan) roundabout, take slip road to right towards Tourlaville (N13 car ferry - route for Poids Lourds), ahead at next roundabout then turn right at third lights onto D116 to Bretteville. Continue for 7 km. to site.

Charges 2004

Per person	€ 4,00 - € 6,00
child (3-12 yrs)	€ 2,80 - € 3,80
pitch	€ 8,70 - € 12,50
dog	€ 1,90 - € 2,10
electricity (10A)	€ 4,00

Camping Cheques accepted.

Reservations

Advised for July/Aug. Tel: 02 33 54 33 57.
E-mail: welcome@anse-du-brick.com

TRAVEL SERVICE SITE

TO BOOK CALL 0870 405 4055 OR www.alanrogersdirect.com

FR61040 Camping Municipal du Champ Passais

61700 Domfront (Orne)

Situated on the edge of the old fortified town of Domfront, this small site has 34 pitches on a series of level terraces and a separate open grassy area for tents. The nine pitches nearest the entrance are all hardstandings with10A electricity. Grass pitches on the lower levels, divided by well tended shrubs and hedges, have 5A electricity. The site is lovingly cared for by an energetic lady warden who keeps everything immaculate and is justifiably proud of the amazing entries in her visitors book.

Facilities

Excellent sanitary facilities, housed in a modern building, include British-style toilets, some washbasins in cubicles. Facilities for disabled people. Washing machine. No separate chemical disposal point, but a notice tells visitors where to empty toilet cassettes. Boules. Play area. Double axle caravans are not accepted; American RVs are accepted. Off site: Supermarket 800 m. Fishing 1 km.

Open

1 April - 30 September.

At a glance

Welcome & Ambience	✓✓✓✓✓	Location	✓✓✓✓✓
Quality of Pitches	✓✓✓✓✓	Range of Facilities	✓✓✓

Directions

Domfront is on the N176 Alen≤on-Mont St. Michel road. The site is just off this road to the south of the town; it is signed to the right as you climb the hill towards the town centre - or the left as you leave town heading west.

Charges 2004

Per unit incl. 1 adult	€ 3,70
extra adult	€ 2,00
electricity (5/10A)	€ 1,80 - € 3,00

No credit cards.

Reservations

Not normally necessary. Tel: 02 33 37 37 66.

FR50060 Camping Le Grand Large

50340 Les Pieux (Manche)

Le Grand Large is a well established, quality family site with direct access to a long sandy beach and within a 20 km. drive of Cherbourg. A neat, tidy site with both touring and mobile home pitches which are divided and separated by hedging, giving an orderly well laid out appearance. At the entrance, alongside the security barrier, stands the modern reception area. Decorating the forecourt are low brick walls with sunken flower beds, the toilet blocks also having their share of flower troughs. To the rear of the site and laid out in the sand-hills is an excellent play area for children, with swings, slides and climbing frame. However, the sandy beach is the big attraction. Roads around the site are tarmac and there are pleasant views across the bay to the tip of the Cherbourg peninsula.

TRAVEL SERVICE SITE

TO BOOK CALL 0870 405 4055 OR www.alanrogersdirect.com

Facilities

The two toilet blocks are well maintained, the main one modern and colourful including washbasins in cubicles and some family rooms. WCs are mostly to the outside of the building. Provision for people with disabilities is good. Baby bathroom, dishwashing sinks, laundry area, and motorcaravan services. Shop for basic groceries. Bar/café and take-away (snacks 15/6-31/8). Swimming pool and children's pool. Play area. Tennis, table tennis, volleyball and boules. TV room. Animation in July/Aug.
Off site: Bicycle hire or riding 5 km. Golf 15 km.

Open

2 April - 18 September.

At a glance

Welcome & Ambience	✓✓✓✓	Location	✓✓✓✓
Quality of Pitches	✓✓✓✓	Range of Facilities	✓✓✓✓✓

Directions

From Cherbourg port take N13 south for approx. 2 km. Branch right on D650 road (previously D904) signed Cartaret. Continue for 18 km to Les Pieux. Take D4 in town and turn left just after Super 'U' supermarket and follow camp signs via D117/517.

Charges 2005

Per unit incl. 2 persons	€ 17,00 - € 25,00
extra person	€ 4,00 - € 6,00
child (under 7 yrs)	€ 2,50 - € 3,50
electricity (6A)	€ 4,00

Camping Cheques accepted.
Less 20% in low seasons (excl. electricity).

Reservations

Made with deposit (€ 80). Tel: 02 33 52 40 75.
E-mail: le-grand-large@wanadoo.fr

FR50090 Camping La Gerfleur

Rue Guillaume Le Conquérant, 50270 Barneville Carteret (Manche)

La Gerfleur is a very pleasant little site with a warm welcome from the owners, a new heated pool, a fishing lake and reasonable sanitary facilities. There are 44 mobile homes, but these are separated from 49 individual tourist pitches. On grass with small dividing hedges, these all have electric hook-ups (6 or 10A) and some shade from mature trees. A few are in a newly-created, more open area next to the lake, and will need more time to fully mature. The new outdoor, heated pool has a separated circular paddling pool. La Gerfleur makes a good holiday base, being an easy cycle ride from the large sandy beach at Barneville Plage, or from the harbour and the smaller cove at Carteret (both only 1.5 km). Day trips to the Channel Islands are also possible. French and a little English spoken.

Facilities

Clean facilities include British style WCs, chain operated showers and some washbasins, all in modern cubicles, units for disabled visitors, laundry and dishwashing sinks. Washing machine and dryer. Basic motorcaravan service point. Swimming pool (6.5 x 14 m). Fishing lake. Table tennis, boules, games room with snooker and table football. Enclosed small playground. In July and August extra services include a bar, 'frites' and bread supplies. Off site: Barneville town centre 300 m. Sandy beach and sailing at Barneville Plage 1.5 km. Golf 4 km. Riding 7 km.

Open

1 April - 31 October.

At a glance

Welcome & Ambience	✓✓✓✓	Location	✓✓✓✓
Quality of Pitches	✓✓✓✓	Range of Facilities	✓✓✓

Directions

Barneville-Carteret is 37 km. SSW of Cherbourg. From the north turn off the D904 Barneville-Carteret by-pass, and use the old road to the town. After 1 km. at 'figure of eight' roundabout, continue on D903E towards Barneville town centre, and site entrance is immediately on your right. From south, continue round by-pass and approach as from north.

Charges 2004

Per adult	€ 4,30
child (under 13 yrs)	€ 3,00
pitch	€ 5,20
electricity (6A)	€ 3,50

Reservations

Advisable for July/August and made with deposit (€ 76). Tel: 02 33 04 38 41.
E-mail: alabouriau@aol.com

FR50080 Camping Haliotis

Chemin des Soupirs, 50170 Pontorson (Manche)

In the past year the Duchesne family have achieved a remarkable transformation of this former municpal site. Situated on the edge of the little town of Pontorson and next to the river Couesnon, Haliotis is within walking, cycling and canoeing distance of Le Mont Saint-Michel. The site has 110 pitches, including 95 for tourers, and there are plans to extend the site for 2004. Most pitches have electricity. A new swimming pool with a jacuzzi has been built, and the large, comfortable reception area developed to incorporate a bar and restaurant.

Facilities

Very clean, renovated and well-equipped wash block. Bar and restaurant. No shop or takeaway on site, facilities available in nearby town. Swimming pool with jacuzzi, separate paddling pool. Good fenced play area. Large games room. Free tennis court. Free fishing in the River Couesnon. Off site: Local services in Pontorson within walking distance. Bicycle hire 1 km. Riding 5 km. Golf 18 km. Beach 30 km.

Open

25 March - 15 November.

At a glance

Welcome & Ambience	✓✓✓✓✓	Location	✓✓✓✓
Quality of Pitches	✓✓✓✓	Range of Facilities	✓✓✓✓

Directions

Site is 300 m. from the town centre, west of D976, alongside the river, and is well signed from the town.

Charges 2005

Per adult	€ 4,20 - € 5,00
child (under 7 yrs)	€ 1,95 - € 2,50
caravan or tent, and car	€ 4,00 - € 4,50
motorcaravan	€ 4,00 - € 4,50
electricity	€ 2,50 - € 3,00

Camping Cheques accepted.
No credit cards.

Reservations

Contact site. Tel: 02 33 68 11 59.
E-mail: info@camping-haliotis-mont-saint-michel.com

FR61010 Camping La Campière

bvd. du Docteur Dentu, 61120 Vimoutiers (Orne)

This small, well kept site is situated in a valley to the north of the town, which is on both the Normandy Cheese and Cider routes. Indeed the town is famous for its cheese and has a Camembert Museum, five minutes walk away in the town centre. The 40 pitches here are flat and grassy, separated by laurel hedging and laid out amongst attractive and well maintained flower and shrub beds. There is some shade around the perimeter and all pitches have electricity.

Facilities

The single central sanitary block is clean and heated, providing open washbasins, good sized, well designed showers, children's toilets and a bathroom for disabled visitors. Dishwashing and laundry facilities under cover. Off site: No shop but a large supermarket is 300 m. Tennis courts and a park are adjacent. Water sports facilities or riding 2 km.

Open

March - October.

At a glance

Welcome & Ambience	✓✓✓✓	Location	✓✓✓✓
Quality of Pitches	✓✓✓✓	Range of Facilities	✓✓✓

Directions

Site is on northern edge of town, signed from main Lisieux-Argentan road next to large sports complex

Charges guide

Per person	€ 2,65
child (under 10 yrs)	€ 1,55
pitch	€ 1,85
car	€ 1,85
animal	€ 1,05
electricity	€ 1,85 - € 2,25

Reductions for 7th and subsequent days.

Reservations

Not normally necessary. Tel: 02 33 39 18 86. E-mail: mairie.vimoutiers@wanadoo.fr

FR76040 Camping La Source

Petit Appeville, 76550 Hautot-sur-Mer (Seine-Maritime)

This friendly, attractive, site is just four kilometres from Dieppe and is useful for those using the Newhaven - Dieppe ferry crossing either as a one-night stop-over or for a few days' break before heading on further. The 120 pitches are flat and there is some shade; the site is quietly located in a valley with the only disturbance the occasional passing train. A fast-flowing small river runs along one border (not protected for young children), with opportunities for fishing (including eels), rowing or canoeing. There are hardstandings for motorcaravans and electricity is available. The site is well lit and stays open for late night ferries, although such arrivals are fairly rare and disturbance is minimal.

Facilities

A good, clean single toilet block (men to the left, ladies to the right) includes washbasins in cubicles and mainly British style WCs. Well equipped en-suite unit for disabled people but the unmade gravel roads may cause problems. Dishwashing under cover and laundry. Small bar and terrace (15/3-15/10). Small play field. TV room and room for young people with table tennis and amusement machines. Volleyball, basketball and badminton. Fishing. Bicycle hire. Off site: Riding 2 km. Beach 3 km. Golf 4 km.

Open

15 March - 15 October.

At a glance

Welcome & Ambience	✓✓✓✓	Location	✓✓✓
Quality of Pitches	✓✓✓	Range of Facilities	✓✓✓

Directions

From ferry terminal, follow main exit road (town centre should be avoided) to roundabout and turn west on D925 signposted first Dieppe and then Fécamp. At foot of long descent at traffic lights in Petit Appeville turn left (site is signed). From west, turn right (signed D153 St Aubin and site). Just after passing station, turn left under bridge and ahead on narrow road. Site is on left in short distance.

Charges 2005

Per person	€ 4,00
child (under 7 yrs)	€ 3,00
caravan	€ 7,00
tent	€ 5,00
car	€ 1,00
motorcaravan	€ 8,00

Reservations

Write to site Tel: 02 35 84 27 04.

FR76090 Camping Municipal d'Etennemare

Hameau d'Etennemare, 76460 St Valery-en-Caux (Seine-Maritime)

This comfortable, neat municipal site is two kilometres from the harbour and town, 30 km. west of Dieppe. Quietly located, it has 116 pitches of which 49 are available for touring units. The grassy pitches are all on a slight slope, all with electricity (6A), water and drain, but there is very little shade. Reception is open all day in July and August, but in low season is closed 12.00-15.00 hrs daily and all day Wednesdays: there is a card operated security barrier. The site is close to the municipal sports complex with tennis and football field, and there are shops and restaurants in the bustling town and a Casino, pools and plenty of entertainment along the sea-front.

Facilities

Two modern, clean and well maintained sanitary buildings are side by side, one containing showers and the other, more recently refitted, has toilets, both open and cubicled washbasins and facilities for disabled people. Both blocks can be heated in winter. Washing machines. Small shop (July/Aug). Playground. Table tennis. Off site: Hypermarket 1.5 km. Harbour and beach 2 km.

Open

All year.

At a glance

Welcome & Ambience	✓✓✓✓	Location	✓✓✓✓
Quality of Pitches	✓✓✓✓	Range of Facilities	✓✓✓

Directions

From Dieppe keep to D925 Fécamp road by-passing town (not D925 through town), at third roundabout turn right on D925E towards town and Lecierc hypermarket. From Fécamp turn left on D925E as before. Take first right almost immediately, signed to campsite which is on left in about 1 km.

Charges 2004

Per unit incl. 2 adults and electricity	€ 13,15
extra person	€ 2,70
child (under 10 yrs)	€ 1,70

Reservations

Essential for July/Aug; contact site. Tel: 02 35 97 15 79.

FR76100 Camping Municipal Cany-Barville

76450 Cany-Barville (Seine-Maritime)

This good quality site, first opened in 1997 next to the municipal sports stadium, has a floral entrance and tarmac roads. Of the 100 individual hedged pitches 75 are available for tourists. There are around 40 concrete hardstandings (awnings can be a problem) and the remainder are on grass: all are fully serviced with water, drain and electric hook-ups (10A). Shade from recently-planted specimen trees is still very limited. Cany-Barville is a bustling small town.

Facilities

The modern, centrally located, sanitary unit can be heated and has British-style toilets, controllable showers and washbasins in cubicles. Separate suites for disabled people. Drive-over motorcaravan service point with chemical disposal facility. Table tennis, volleyball, boules. Games room with pin-ball machine and ski-simulator.
Off site: Bakery, restaurants 600 m. Supermarket 1 km. Sailing and windsurfing centre 2 km. Beach 10 km.

Open

1 April - 1 October.

At a glance

Welcome & Ambience	✓✓✓✓	Location	✓✓✓✓
Quality of Pitches	✓✓✓✓	Range of Facilities	✓✓✓

Directions

Cany-Barville is 20 km. east of Fécamp on D925 to Dieppe. From traffic lights on eastern side of town turn south on D268 towards Yvetot. Go under railway arch and site is 600 m. from town centre on right, just after sports stadium.

Charges 2004

Per person	€ 2,65
child (under 14 yrs)	€ 1,10
pitch	€ 2,65
electricity (10A)	€ 2,65

Reservations

Advisable in July and August. Tel: 02 35 97 70 37.

FR76110 Camping Municipal Les Boucaniers

76470 Le Tréport (Seine-Maritime)

This large, good quality, municipal site has an attractive entrance and some floral displays, tarmac roads and site lighting. The 300 pitches are on level grass, some with dividing hedges, and a variety of trees to provide a little shade. There are 22 good quality wooden chalets for rent, and some privately owned mobile homes, which leaves around 262 pitches for tourists, all with electric hook-ups (6A). A small unit acts as shop, bar and takeaway and operates all season, the baker calls daily in high season, and every day except Monday in low season. The town centre is within walking distance.

Facilities

Three well equipped sanitary blocks (one can be heated) provide mainly British style WCs, washbasins in cubicles, pre-set hot showers, with facilities for small children and disabled persons in one block. Multi-sport court. Minigolf. Boules. Off site: Fishing, golf and beach 2 km. Riding 3 km.

Open

1 April 30 September.

At a glance

Welcome & Ambience	✓✓✓✓	Location	✓✓✓✓
Quality of Pitches	✓✓✓✓	Range of Facilities	✓✓✓

Directions

Site is north of the D925 Abbeville - Dieppe road; take D1915 towards Le Tréport town centre, (from Dieppe, at second roundabout) and at first set of lights turn right into Rue Pierre Mendès-France. Site is on that corner and entrance is immediately on right.

Charges 2004

Per person	€ 2,65
pitch with electricity	€ 6,15

Reservations

Contact site. Tel: 02 35 86 35 47.
E-mail: ville.le.treport@wanadoo.fr

FR76120 Camping Municipal Veulettes-sur-Mer

8 Rue de Greenock, 76450 Veulettes-sur-Mer (Seine-Maritime)

A good value, well kept municipal site in an attractive little coastal town, just 500 m. from the beach and all town services. There are 116 marked pitches on open level grass, 40 of which are seasonal pitches, which leaves 76 pitches for tourists, all with electric hook-ups, water and waste water drain. Reception keeps soft drinks and ices during July/August. Also on site is an attractive 'salle' (open all day in July/August) with a library and TV, a games area with electronic game, table tennis, babyfoot and further toilet facilities.

Facilities

Three good modern sanitary units in traditional style buildings are of varying ages (one can be heated). These provide pre-set hot showers, washbasins in cubicles, and facilities for disabled people in the smallest unit on the far side of the site. Laundry room with washing machine. Playground. Boules court. TV, library and table tennis. Off site: Public park with tennis courts and large playground, beach (pebble), watersports centre and all shops and services are within 500 m. level walk. Traffic free cycle path to the next village (4 km).

At a glance

Welcome & Ambience	✓✓✓✓	Location	✓✓✓✓
Quality of Pitches	✓✓✓✓	Range of Facilities	✓✓✓

Directions

Veulettes-sur-Mer is on the coast approx. 45 km. west of Dieppe. Site is central in town, lying about 500 m. back from the main promenade (signed).

Charges 2004

per person	€ 2,55
child (4-10 yrs)	€ 1,30
pitch	€ 2,20
car	€ 1,00
electricity (10A)	€ 2,50
animal	€ 0,50

Reservations

Contact site. Tel: 02 35 97 53 44.

Open

1 April - 31 October.

FR76130 Camping de la Forêt

Mobile homes page 367

Rue Mainberthe, 76480 Jumieges (Seine-Maritime)

This is a pretty family site with a friendly laid back atmosphere. It is located just ten kilometres from the A13 Paris – Caen autoroute, and is best accessed by ferry across the River Seine. The great abbey at Jumieges was founded in 654 by St Philibert, rebuilt by the Normans and consecrated in the presence of William the Conqueror – well worth a visit! The site was formerly a municipal and has recently been taken on by the Joret family. The 90 grassy pitches (76 for tourers) are attractively located in woodland. Virtually all pitches are reasonably shaded and most have electrical connections. A good range of shops, cafes, restaurants etc. can be foung in Jumieges, just 600 m. away.

Facilities

Two toilet blocks, both of modern construction and maintained to a good standard with British toilets and pre-set showers. Washing and drying machines. Shop. Small swimming pool (heated 1/6-30/8). Playground. Chalets and mobile homes to let.

Open

2 April - 30 October

At a glance

Welcome & Ambience	✓✓✓✓	Location	✓✓✓
Quality of Pitches	✓✓✓✓	Range of Facilities	✓✓

Directions

Jumieges is around 10 km. north of the A13 Paris – Caen autoroute (Bourg-Achard exit). Take D313 towards Caudebec-en-Caux. Then, either take the ferry across the Seine (with toll) from Heurtauville to Jumieges, or continue over the Pont de Brotonne and double back on D982 to Jumieges. Site is clearly signed in the village.

Charges 2005

Pitch incl. 2 persons	€ 14,20 - € 15,00
extra person (over 4 yrs)	€ 3,40 - € 3,80
electricity	€ 2,50

Camping Cheques accepted.
Reduced charges in low season.

Reservations

Conatct site. Tel: 02 35 37 93 43.
E-mail: info@campinglaforet.com

Map 3

Northern France, with its lush countryside and market towns, is much more than just a stop off en-route to or from the ports. The peaceful rural unspoilt charms of the region provide a real breath of fresh air.

Nord/Pas de Calais: 59 Nord, 62 Pas-de-Calais
Major City: Lille

Picardy: 02 Aisne, 60 Oise, 80 Somme
Major City: Amiens

This is a region where centuries of invaders have left their mark. At Vimy Ridge near Arras, World War One trenches have been preserved intact, a most poignant sight. Elsewhere almost every village between Arras and Amiens has its memorial. It is also the birthplace of Gothic architecture with six cathedrals, including Laon, Beauvais and Amiens, arguably the grandest in France.

The area however is predominately rural. Inland and south are long vistas of rolling farmland broken by little rivers and well scattered with pockets of forest woodland. The coastline is characterised by sandy beaches, shifting dunes and ports. It is a quiet and sparsely populated area with peaceful villages and churches that provide evidence of the glorious achievements of French Gothic architecture. Le Touquet combines the modernity of its sports facilities with an old world charm. Boulogne is home to Nausicaa, the world's largest sea-life centre and from Cap Griz-Nez you may be able to see the White Cliffs of Dover. There are also many huge hypermarkets where you may stock up on wine, beer and cheese.

Cuisine of the region

Carbonnade de Boeuf à la Flamande: braised beef with beer, onions and bacon

Caudière (Chaudière, Caudrée): versions of fish and potato soup

Ficelles Picardes: ham pancakes with mushroom sauce

Flamiche aux poireaux: puff pastry tart with cream and leeks

Hochepot: a thick Flemish soup with virtually everything in it but the kitchen sink

Soupe courquignoise: soup with white wine, fish, moules, leeks and Gruyère cheese

Tarte aux Maroilles: a hot creamy tart based on Maroilles cheese

Waterzooï: a cross between soup and stew, usually of fish or chicken

Places of interest

Amiens: Notre Dame cathedral, monument to 1918 Battle of the Somme

Chantilly: Château of Chantilly with a 17th century stable with a 'live' Horse museum.

Compiègne: Seven miles east of the town is Clairière de l'Armistice. The railway coach here is a replica of the one in which the 1918 Armistice was signed and in which Hitler received the French surrender in 1942

Laon: 12th century cathedral, WW1 trenches, Vauclair Abbey

Marquenterre: one of Europe's most important bird sanctuaries

Alan Rogers tip

A COLONY OF CALF SEALS LIVE IN THE SOMME BAY. THE TOWNS OF CROTOY AND ST VALÉRY ARE PARTICULARLY GOOD FOR OBSERVING THE SEALS.

FR02060 Camping Municipal Guignicourt

14 Bis Rue Godins, 02190 Guignicourt (Aisne)

This very pleasant little municipal site has 100 pitches, 50 for long stay units and 50 for tourists. These two sections are separated by the main facilities on a higher terrace. Pitches are generally large and level, although you might need an extra long electricity lead for some, but there are few dividing hedges. Pitches along the river bank have most shade, with a few specimen trees providing a little shade to some of the more open pitches. The town is quite attractive and is worthy of an evening stroll. At the junction of the N44 and D925, 7 km. west of the town, is the Chemin des Dames, Monument des Chars d'Assaut - a memorial to the WW1 tank campaign at Berry-au-Bac, with two remarkably well preserved tanks. Further to the west is the Caverne du Dragon, a former stone quarry which sheltered troops during the 1914-18 conflict, which is now a museum depicting everyday life on the front line. You may notice a low level hum from the nearby Generale Sucrière factory, a major industry of the town, but you may also hear the site's nightingales.

Facilities

The modern sanitary unit has British and Turkish style toilets, washbasins (cold only except for the one in a cubicle), push-button hot showers, dishwashing and laundry sinks. Bar (1/4-30/9). Playground. Tennis and boules courts. Fishing. Off site: The town has all services including a supermarket and bank. Golf 3km. Beach 15 km.

Open

1 April - 30 September.

At a glance

Welcome & Ambience	✓✓✓✓	Location	✓✓✓✓
Quality of Pitches	✓✓✓✓	Range of Facilities	✓✓✓

Directions

Guignicourt is about 20 km. north of Reims, just east of the A26, junction 14. The site is well signed from D925 in the village.

Charges 2004

Per adult	€ 2,00
child (2-10 yrs)	€ 1,20
pitch incl. electricity (6/10A)	€ 7,80 - € 15,60
animal	€ 1,00

Reservations

Contact site. Tel: 03 23 79 74 58.
E-mail: camping.guignicourt@free.fr

FR02000 Camping Caravaning du Vivier aux Carpes

10 rue Charles Voyeux, 02790 Seraucourt-le-Grand (Aisne)

Vivier aux Carpes is a small quiet site, close to the A26, two hours from Calais, so it is ideal for an overnight stop but is also worthy of a longer stay. A neat, purpose designed site is imaginatively set out taking full benefit of large ponds which are well stocked for fishing. There is also abundant wild life. The 60 well spaced pitches, are at least 100 sq.m. on flat grass with dividing hedges. The 45 for touring units all have electricity (6A), some also with water points, and there are special pitches for motorcaravans. This peaceful site has a comfortable feel and is close to the village centre. The enthusiastic owners and the manager speak excellent English and are keen to welcome British visitors. Although there is no restaurant on site, good and reasonable hotels are close. The cathedral cities of St Quentin, Reims, Amiens and Laon are close, Disneyland just over an hour away, Compiegne and the WW1 battlefields are near and Paris easily reached by train (1 hr 15 mins from St Quentin). This site is good for couples or fishing enthusiasts.

Facilities

The spacious, clean toilet block has separate, heated facilities for disabled visitors, which are made available to other campers in the winter months. Laundry facilities. Motorcaravan service point (fresh water for large vans is charged). Above the toilet block is a large TV/games room with table tennis and snooker. Small play area. Bicycle hire. Petanque. Fishing (about 5.50 p/day). Gates close 22.00 hrs, office open 09.00-21.30. Rallies welcome. Off site: Village has post office, doctor, chemist and small supermarket. Riding 500 m. Golf 12 km.

Open

1 March - 30 October.

At a glance

Welcome & Ambience	✓✓✓✓	Location	✓✓✓✓
Quality of Pitches	✓✓✓✓	Range of Facilities	✓✓✓

Directions

Leave A26 (Calais - Reims) road at exit 11 and take D1 left towards Soissons for 4 km. Take D8 and on entering Essigny-la-Grand (4 km.) turn sharp right on D72 signed Seraucourt-le-Grand (5 km). Site is clearly signed - it is in the centre of the village.

Charges 2004

Per unit incl. 2 persons and electricity	€ 16,00
extra person	€ 3,30
child (under 10 yrs)	€ 2,50
pet	€ 0,60

Monthly, weekly or weekend rates available.
Discounts for students with tents. No credit cards.

Reservations

Advised for peak season. Tel: 03 23 60 50 10.
E-mail: camping.du.vivier@wanadoo.fr

FR02030 Caravaning La Croix du Vieux Pont

Mobile homes page 367

02290 Berny-Riviere (Aisne)

Attractively located on the banks of the River Aisne, La Croix du Vieux Pont is a very smart, modern site offering a high standard of facilities. Many pitches are occupied by mobile homes and tour operator tents, but there are 52 pleasant touring pitches, some on the banks of the Aisne. The 34 hectare site is maintained to a high standard with some excellent amenities, notably four heated swimming pools, one indoors with a waterslide and jacuzzi. There are two tennis courts, an amusement arcade and volleyball court. At the heart of the site is a well-stocked fishing lake which is also used for pedaloes and canoes.

Facilities

The six toilet blocks are modern and kept very clean, with washbasins in cabins and free hot showers. Washing and drying machines. Facilities for disabled visitors. Large supermarket. Bar, takeaway and good value restaurant (most amenities 1/4-30/9). Swimming pool complex (covered pool 1/4-30/10, outdoor 1/5-30/9). Play area. Fishing. Bicycle hire. Coach trips organised to Paris, Parc Asterix and Disneyland. Apartments to let. Dogs are not accepted. Off site: Riding 100 m. Golf 30 km.

Open

1 January - 31 December.

At a glance

Welcome & Ambience	✓✓✓✓	Location	✓✓✓✓
Quality of Pitches	✓✓✓✓✓	Range of Facilities	✓✓✓✓✓

Directions

From Compiegne take N31 towards Soissons. At Vic-sur-Aisne turn right, towards Berny-Riviere and site is on right after 400 m.

Charges 2005

Oer unit incl. 2 persons and electricity	€ 19,00 - € 21,50
incl. 4 persons	€ 27,00 - € 29,50

Camping Cheques accepted.

Reservations

Essential for high season and made with deposit (€ 40). Tel: 03 23 55 50 02.
E-mail: info@la-croix-du-vieux-pont.com

TRAVEL SERVICE SITE

TC BOOK CALL 0870 405 4055 OR www.alanrogersdirect.com

FR59010 Camping-Caravaning La Chaumière

529 langhemast Straete, 59285 Buysscheure (Nord)

This is a very friendly, pleasant site, tucked away in the département du Nord with a strong Flanders influence, well worth considering for those using the local Channel crossings. There is a real welcome here and the owners, Guy and Bernadette, are much liked by the regular British visitors. Set just behind the village of Buysscheure (with a shop and two cafés), the site has just 22 individual pitches separated by young trees and bushes. With 16 for touring units, mostly quite large and with some slope, they are on grass with a gravel hardstanding area for the car. Each pair of pitches shares a brick-built unit, decorated with flowers, incorporating a light, electricity connections, water points and rubbish container. A small, fenced fishing lake contains some large carp (seen!) and the ducks will help you eat your baguettes. A bonus is that Bernadette works for the local vet and can arrange all the documentation for British visitors' pets. English is spoken.

Facilities

Although modern, the unisex toilet facilities are simple with two WCs, one shower and one washbasin cabin. Facilities provided for disabled visitors may also be used (a toilet and separate washbasin/shower room). Dishwashing room. Laundry room. Motorcaravan services. Bar (daily) and restaurant (weekends only, all day, all season). Dog exercise area - with jumps etc. Heated swimming pool planned for 2004. Off site: Interesting local market (Monday) at Bergues. St Omer is an old town. This is a popular area for cycling. Shop and café/restaurants in village. Beach 30 km.

Open

1 April - 31 October.

At a glance

Welcome & Ambience	✓✓✓✓✓	Location	✓✓✓✓
Quality of Pitches	✓✓✓	Range of Facilities	✓✓✓✓

Directions

From Calais take N43 towards St Omer for 25km. Just beyond Nordausques take D221 left to Watten. In Watten turn left for the centre, then right onto D26 towards Cassel. Soon after Lederzeele the site is signed to the right (just before railway bridge). When you reach Buysscheure turn left and then right from where the site is signed again.

Charges 2004

Per unit incl. 2 persons and electricity	€ 14,00
extra person	€ 7,00
child (under 7 yrs)	€ 3,50
dog	€ 1,00

No credit cards.

Reservations

Contact site. Tel: 03 28 43 03 57.
E-mail: camping.LaChaumiere@wanadoo.fr

FR59050 Camping Municipal Mauberge

Route de Mons, 59600 Maubeuge (Nord)

This is an attractive site convenient for a night-stop or for longer stays close to the RN2 road. It is a neat and tidy municipal site with 92 marked pitches of fair size. Mainly on level ground and separated by trim hedges, most have electricity (6/10A) and some have hardstanding. A variety of trees provide shade when needed. There are few amenities but the interesting town centre of Maubeuge is only 1 km.

Facilities

Two circular sanitary blocks provide good modern facilities. Washing machines. The block used in winter can be heated. Motorcaravan service point. Small playground. Fishing. Off site: Riding and bicycle hire 2 km. Golf 2.5 km.

Open

All year.

At a glance

Welcome & Ambience	✓✓✓✓	Location	✓✓✓✓
Quality of Pitches	✓✓✓✓	Range of Facilities	✓✓✓

Directions

Site is on the RN2 road (known as the N6 in Belgium) north of the town, on the right going towards Mons.

Charges guide

Per person	€ 3,05
pitch	€ 3,05
electricity	€ 4,15 - € 5,03

Reservations

Not normally made or necessary, but if in doubt telephone site. Tel: 03 27 62 25 48.

FR62050 Camping Caravaning St Louis

Rue Leulène, 62610 Autingues par Ardres (Pas-de-Calais)

Convenient for the ferry port at Calais, this is a peaceful little site with 84 pitches. Many are taken by privately owned holiday homes, but there are around 25 pitches for tourists. In a garden-like setting, they are individual and grassy with some shade. Electricity hook-ups are available for all. In high season the site is usually full by 17.00 hrs, so arrive early.

Facilities

Rather old but clean and tidy unisex toilet facilities which provide showers on payment (€ 1 token) and washbasins mostly in cubicles. Facilities for disabled people. Baby room. Dishwashing and laundry sinks, washing machine. Motorcaravan service point free to campers (€ 4 for non-residents). Snack bar and takeaway every evening in July/Aug. Playground. Games room with table football, table tennis. Off site: Beach 20 km.

At a glance

Welcome & Ambience	✓✓✓	Location	✓✓✓✓
Quality of Pitches	✓✓✓✓	Range of Facilities	✓✓✓

Directions

From Calais take N43 towards St Omer for 15 km, and just east of Ardres, turn south on D224, where site is signed.

Charges 2004

Per adult	€ 2,50
pitch incl. electricity	€ 8,50

Reservations

Advised for high season. Tel: 03 21 35 46 83.

Open

1 April - 31 October.

FR62060 Caravaning L'Orée du Bois

Mobile homes page 368

Chemin Blanc, 62180 Rang-du-Fliers (Pas-de-Calais)

This fairly peaceful but extensive campsite is in a natural woodland setting, and only 3 km. from a large sandy beach. From reception you pass through a corner of the mobile home (privately owned) section, then through an area of natural, preserved woodland which separates the touring area. This has 80 individual, touring pitches, all with shade and electric hook-ups. On sandy grass which can be slightly undulating, most are separated by hedges and bushes, but the emphasis is on 'nature'. Also on the touring site are 67 wooden camping lodges. A separate clearing in the woodland is reserved for tents, and useful for cyclists or backpackers is 'Camp Sherpa' comprising eight 2-berth wooden tents. A modern sanitary unit is central in the touring area, with a second smaller unit in the mobile homes area, useful when walking between your pitch and the bar/brasserie with takeaway, tennis courts, pétanque etc. Berck Plage is only 3 km. and has a magnificent sandy beach and promenade, with extensive free parking areas, with many bays for disabled motorists. Indeed the site and the area are well suited to disabled visitors of all ages.

Facilities

Modern facilities with open and cubicle washbasins, controllable hot showers, a laundry with washing machines and dryer, and good facilities for disabled persons (with low level dishwashing and laundry sinks), small children and babies. Note: water for the toilets is obtained from a borehole, and has a slight brownish colour. Basic motorcaravan service point by reception, with a full service area located close to the nearby Intermarché. Bar/brasserie (30/3-20/10). Animation and dancing in July/Aug. Multi-court tennis. Several playgrounds. The woodland area conceals a football field, volleyball, a fitness trail, a course for quads and all terrain bikes, and a fishing lake.
Off site: Small supermarket adjacent, large Intermarché complex 700 m. Sports centre at Berck-Plage. Also close by is Le Parc de Bagatelle, the largest amusement park in northern France. Beach 3 km. Cycle hire 2km, horse riding 1.5km, boat launching 3km, golf 8km. Market in Berck-Plage Tues/Wed/Thurs/Sat/Sun, and in Rang du Fliers Thursday.

At a glance

Welcome & Ambience	✓✓✓✓	Location	✓✓✓✓
Quality of Pitches	✓✓✓	Range of Facilities	✓✓✓✓

Directions

Rang du Fliers is just east of Berck Plage and about 15 km. south of Le Touquet. From Berck Plage take D917 east to roundabout by Intermarché supermarket, turn left (north) at next roundabout (site signed), site entrance is 500 m. on left. From A16 exit 25, follow D917 towards Berck Plage. After four roundabouts, a railway crossing, and two more roundabouts, turn right at the seventh roundabout (site signed), site entrance is 500 m. on left.

Charges 2004

extra person	€ 3,00 - € 5,50
child (3-7 yrs)	€ 2,00 - € 3,50
animal	€ 2,00

Discounts for stays of 14 days.
Barrier card deposit €50.

Reservations

Essential for July/Aug, and advisable at other times. Made with deposit of 25% of total fees.
Tel: 03 21 84 28 51. E-mail: oree.du.bois@wanadoo.fr

Open

30 March - 20 October.

FR62030 Camping Château du Gandspette

62910 Eperlecques (Pas-de-Calais)

This friendly, comfortable, family run site is in the grounds of the Château du Gandspette. It is conveniently situated for the channel ports and tunnel, providing useful overnight accommodation and a range of facilities for a longer stay. The 17th century building adjacent to the château now houses an attractive bar/restaurant. A gravel road gives access to three different camping areas and a central open space. There are 170 pitches (100 or 150 sq.m), of which 55 are taken by semi-permanent French holiday caravans which intermix with some of the touring pitches giving a real French ambience. All pitches have electricity and are delineated by trees and some hedging. Mature trees form the perimeter of the site, through which there is access to woodland walks. Used by tour operators (10 pitches), and there are also 8 site owned rental mobile homes. A 'Sites et Paysages' member.

Facilities

A partially renovated sanitary block provides satisfactory facilities with a mixture of open and cubicled washbasins in the older part of the site. The newer area is now served by a stylish modern unit which also contains facilities for disabled people and a baby changing area. Covered dishwashing sinks. Washing machines and dryers. Good motorcaravan service point. Bar, grill restaurant and takeaway (all 15/5-15/9). Two swimming pools, one large and one smaller (15/5-30/9). Adventure style playground, and play field. Tennis, petanque and a children's room with table tennis and electronic games. Entertainment is organised in season. Off site: Fishing 3 km. Riding and golf 5 km. Beach 30 km. Bicycle hire 9 km. Small supermarket in village 1 km. Market Watten (Friday) and St Omer (Saturday). The WW2 'Blockhaus◊ nearby is worthy of a visit, as is La Coupole at St Omer which also dates from WW2 and is equally fascinating.

At a glance

Welcome & Ambience	✓✓✓✓	Location	✓✓✓✓
Quality of Pitches	✓✓✓✓	Range of Facilities	✓✓✓✓

Directions

From Calais follow N43 towards St Omer for 25 km. Southeast of Nordausques take D221 (east) and follow camp signs for 5-6 km. From St Omer follow N43 to roundabout at junction with D600. Turn right onto D600 towards Dunkirk and after 5 km. turn left on D221. Site is 1.5 km. on right.

Charges 2005

Per unit incl. 2 persons	€ 16,00 - € 21,00
extra person (over 6 yrs)	€ 5,00 - € 6,00
electricity (6A)	€ 4,00
child (3-6yrs)	€ 3,00 - € 4,00
animal	€ 1,00

Camping Cheques accepted.

Reservations

Necessary for July/Aug - write to site.
Tel: 03 21 93 43 93.
E-mail: contact@chateau-gandspette.com

Open

1 April - 30 September.

FR62010 Castel Camping Caravaning La Bien-Assise

D231, 62340 Guines (Pas-de-Calais)

A mature and well developed site, the history of La Bien-Assise goes back to the 1500s. The château, farm and mill now form the focal point for this popular campsite which is under new ownership. The farm buildings house the facilities and pool complex, with the entrance to a more formal and excellent restaurant, 'La Ferme Gourmande' in the mellow farmyard opposite the dovecote. There are 220 grass pitches mainly set among mature trees with others on a newer field. Connected by gravel roads and of a good size (up to 300 sq.m), shrubs and bushes divide most of the pitches. The site's position, 15 minutes from Calais, the Channel Tunnel exit 6 km. and 20 minutes from Boulogne, make it a good stopping point en-route north or south, but it is well worth a longer stay. Reception opens for long hours to meet the needs of those crossing the Channel and the site can have heavy usage at times (when maintenance can be variable). Used by tour operators (50 pitches).

TRAVEL SERVICE SITE

TO BOOK CALL 0870 405 4055 OR www.alanrogersdirect.com

Facilities

Three well equipped toilet blocks provide many washbasins in cabins, mostly British style WCs and provision for babies, laundry and dishwashing. The main block is in four sections, two unisex. Motorcaravan service point. Shop. Restaurant. Bar/grill and takeaway (evenings from 1/5). TV room. Pool complex (10/5-10/9) with a fun pool/toboggan, covered paddling pool and outdoor pool with sliding roof to suit all weather conditions. Play areas. Minigolf. Tennis court. Bicycle hire. Off site: Local market and walks from the site. Fishing 8 km. Riding 10 km. Beach 9 km.

Open

25 April - 20 September.

At a glance

Welcome & Ambience	✓✓✓✓	Location	✓✓✓✓
Quality of Pitches	✓✓✓✓	Range of Facilities	✓✓✓✓

Directions

From ferry terminal follow A16 south (Boulogne) for junction 15, turning towards St Pierre de Calais to immediately pick up Guînes signs before going under autoroute following the D127. Continue beside canal to Guînes. Site is just southwest of village on D231 Marquise road. From Tunnel also follow A16 south (Boulogne) to immediately pick up Guînes signs at junction 11 and following D215 past St Tricat to Guînes. From south on A26, use exit 2 (Ardres, Guînes) onto N43 and D231 (15 km).

Charges 2004

Per adult	€ 3,00 - € 4,60
child (under 9 yrs)	€ 2,00 - € 3,60
pitch	€ 8,00 - € 11,50
electricity (6A)	€ 3,00 - € 3,80
dog	€ 1,00 - € 2,00

Less 10% in low seasons

Reservations

Advised for July/Aug. or if arriving late in the evening. Made for any length with deposit (€ 39) and fee (€ 7.62) for stays 5 days or more. Tel: 03 21 35 20 77. E-mail: castel@bien-assise.com

FR80010 Castel Camping Le Château de Drancourt

B.P. 22, 80230 St Valéry-sur-Somme (Somme)

A popular, busy and lively holiday site within easy distance of Channel ports, between Boulogne and Dieppe, Domaine de Drancourt is in four sections. The original section has 100 marked and numbered, grassy pitches of good size, with good shade. An extension taking some 90 units is in light woodland and two newer touring sections are on flat or gently sloping meadow, with little shade as yet. There are 356 pitches in total, of which 220 are occupied by several tour operators. The site also has 30 units for rent which leaves 80 pitches for touring units. Electricity is available in all areas. It can be dusty around the reception buildings and château in dry weather. The pools and toilet blocks can become stretched at times in peak season and maintenance and cleaning can be variable, as can the pressure and temperature of the water. English is spoken and the site is run personally by the energetic owner and his staff.

TRAVEL SERVICE SITE

TO BOOK CALL 0870 405 4055 OR www.alanrogersdirect.com

Facilities

Three modern, well equipped toilet blocks include washbasins in cubicles, family bathrooms and facilities for disabled visitors. Laundry and dishwashing sinks, washing machines and dryers. Drainage difficulties can still cause occasional problems. Shop, restaurant and takeaway (from 25/3) closed Tuesday in low season). Bar in château, new large first floor bar and pool-side bar with karaoke in season. Three TV rooms, one for children. Disco (free entry). Games room with table tennis. Two heated swimming pools, one indoor (from 25/3) and one open air with water slide and heated paddling pool. Tennis court, golf practise range and minigolf. Bicycle hire. Pony riding in season (stables 15 km). Fishing (free). Off site: Beach 14 km.

At a glance

Welcome & Ambience	✓✓✓✓	Location	✓✓✓✓
Quality of Pitches	✓✓✓✓	Range of Facilities	✓✓✓✓

Directions

Site is 2.5 km. south of St Valéry and is signed from the D940 Berck - le Tréport road. Turn south on the D48 Estreboeuf road and turn immediately left to Drancourt and the site.

Charges 2004

Per unit incl. 2 persons	€ 19,90 - € 28,90
extra person	€ 6,40
child (under 5 yrs)	€ 4,60
electricity (6A)	€ 3,10
dog	free

Reservations

Advised for the main season and made for any length, with deposit for longer stays. Tel: 03 22 26 93 45. E-mail: chateau.drancourt@wanadoo.fr

Open

Easter - 31 October.

FR80070 Camping La Ferme des Aulnes

Mobile homes page 369

1 rue du Marais, Fresne-sur-Authie, 80120 Nampont-St Martin

This peaceful site has been developed on the grassy meadows of a small, 17th century farm on the edge of the village of Fresne and is lovingly cared for by its enthusiastic owner and his hard-working team. Restored outbuildings house reception and the site's facilities, arranged around a central, landscaped courtyard that now boasts a fine heated swimming pool. Of the 120 pitches, 55 are available for touring units, with most of the remainder occupied by or for sale to private owners for holiday mobile homes. All tourist pitches have electricity (6A) and are fairly level. Many are individual and divided by shrubs and young trees, others are on an open, slightly sloping, grassy area.

Facilities

Sanitary fittings are smart, modern and well maintained, including washbasins in cubicles with a large cubicle for disabled people. Facilities are uni-sex but there are four new individual cabins for ladies. Dishwashing and laundry sinks. Small shop with local produce and necessities (all season, as are all other facilities). Piano bar and restaurant. TV room. Swimming pool from 26 March (16 x 9 m; heated and with cover for cooler weather). Fitness room. Aquagym and Balneo therapy. Playground for small children. Beach volleyball, table tennis, boules and archery. Off site: Fishing is possible in river 50 m. from site. Golf 3 km. Riding 8 km.

Open

26 March - 1 November.

At a glance

Welcome & Ambience	✓✓✓✓✓	Location	✓✓✓✓✓
Quality of Pitches	✓✓✓✓	Range of Facilities	✓✓✓✓

Directions

At Nampont St Martin (on the N1 between Montreuil and Abbeville)turn west off the N1 on to the D485 (site is signed), towards Villers-sur-Authie. Site is on right after about 3 km in village of Fresne.

Charges 2004

Per adult	€ 7,00
child (under 7 yrs)	€ 4,00
pitch	€ 6,00
dog	€ 4,00
electricity (6A)	€ 5,00

Camping Cheques accepted.

Reservations

Contact site for details. Tel: 03 22 29 22 69.
E-mail: contact@fermedesaulnes.com

TRAVEL SERVICE SITE

TO BOOK CALL 0870 405 4055 OR www.alanrogersdirect.com

FR80030 Camping du Port de Plaisance

Route de Paris, 80200 Péronne (Somme)

Run by a non-profit making association under the auspices of the Chamber of Commerce, this is a good quality site. Formerly a municipal site, it is informally laid out beside the Canal du Nord on the outskirts of the small town of Peronne, on the river Somme. The associations with the Great War (including a museum) are strong and the WW1 battlefields and cemeteries are numerous in this area. Only some two or three hours drive from the Channel ports, Péronne is convenient for overnight stops en-route to or from destinations further south or east. The site is attractive and surrounded by trees, with 90 marked pitches (87 have 6/10A electricity) of varying shapes and sizes on mainly level grass, some being seasonal.

Facilities

The modernised toilet block is kept spotlessly clean, well maintained and heated in winter. Excellent provision for people with disabilities. Laundry area with washing machine and dryer. Motorcaravan service point. Reception building includes a small shop (1/5-31/8), bar and TV room (bread orders are taken). Attractive swimming pool (June-Sept). Play area. Fishing. Off site: Bicycle hire 2 km. Riding 10 km.

Open

1 March - 31 October.

At a glance

Welcome & Ambience	✓✓✓✓	Location	✓✓✓✓
Quality of Pitches	✓✓✓✓	Range of Facilities	✓✓✓✓

Directions

From north and the ferries, on the A1 autoroute, take exit 14 and follow N17 south to Peronne. Take signs for town centre and continue through watching out for camp signs. Pass over river Somme and Canal du Nord and site is on right just past garage at Porte du Plaisance (2 km. from town centre). Alternatively continue to exit 13. From south use exit 13 and follow RN29 to Villers Carbonnel to pick up the N17 going north. Look for signs on left after traffic lights.

Charges 2004

Per unit incl. 1-3 persons	€ 12,80 - € 19,00
extra person	€ 3,20 - € 4,10
child (under 7 yrs)	free
electricity (6/10A)	€ 3,30 - € 6,85

Reservations

May be needed in main season. Tel: 03 22 84 19 31. E-mail: contact@camping-plaisance.com

FR80080 Camping Municipal Le Bois des Pêcheurs

Route de Forges Les Eaux, 80290 Poix-de-Picardie (Somme)

In an area where good municipal sites are hard to find, the municipal site at Poix-de-Picardie is excellent for a one night stop, or even a few days to explore the region. Tourist Information for the town is housed in the Campsite Reception where visitors are able to find out more about the area. The 135 pitches are on level, neatly mown grass, either individual or in hedged bays of four. The pitches at one end are often occupied by long stay or holiday groups, but there are up to 125 pitches available for tourists, all with electricity (10A).

Facilities

The well maintained, central toilet block includes pushbutton showers, and some washbasins in cubicles. Two separate rooms provide ample dishwashing and laundry sinks. Washing machine and dryer. Small playground. Bicycle hire. Volleyball, boules and table tennis. TV room. Caravan storage. Off site: Supermarket 200 m. Fishing 1 km. Shops, services and swimming pool in Poix de Picardie 1.5 km.

Open

1 April - 30 September.

At a glance

Welcome & Ambience	✓✓✓✓	Location	✓✓✓✓
Quality of Pitches	✓✓✓✓	Range of Facilities	✓✓✓

Directions

The town is 27 km south west of Amiens just off the N29. Site is southwest of the town on the D919 road, and is signed from the D901 Grandvilliers road. Approaching from Grandvilliers, there are no signs; turn left at bottom of hill as you approach town.

Charges 2005

Per unit incl. 1 or 2 adults	€ 11,00
extra person	€ 2,00
electricity	€ 3,80
No credit cards.	

Reservations

Write for details. Tel: 03 22 90 11 71. E-mail: mairie.poix.de.picardie@wanadoo.fr

FR80040 Camping Le Royon

1271 route de Quend, 80120 Fort-Mahon-Plage (Somme)

This busy family run site, some two kilometres from the sea, has 300 pitches of which 100 are used for touring units. Of either 95 or 120 sq.m, the marked and numbered pitches are divided by hedges and arranged either side of access roads. Electricity (6A) and water points are available to all. The site is well lit, fenced and guarded at night (€ 30 deposit for barrier card). Entertainment is organised for adults and children in July/Aug. The site is close to the Baie de l'Authie which is an area noted for migrating birds.

Facilities

Four toilet blocks provide mostly unisex facilities with British or Turkish style WCs and some washbasins in cubicles. Units for disabled people. Baby baths. Dishwashing and laundry sinks under cover. Small shop (July/Aug). Mobile takeaway calls each evening in July/Aug. Friendly clubroom and bar serves drinks and ices, sells bread and newspapers and has the usual games machines. Attractive, heated, covered swimming pool (16 x 8 m; 1/5-15/9) with open air children's pool and sun terrace. Playground. Table tennis, multi-court, tennis court and boules. Bicycle hire. Off site: Fishing, riding or golf within 1 km. Windsurfing, sailing, sand yachting, canoeing, swimming, climbing and shooting nearby. Cinema, disco and casino near.

At a glance

Welcome & Ambience	✓✓✓	Location	✓✓✓✓
Quality of Pitches	✓✓✓	Range of Facilities	✓✓✓✓

Directions

Site is on outskirts of Fort Mahon Plage, on D32 from Quend (which is on D940 Berck - Le Tréport road).

Charges 2004

Per pitch 95 sq.m.	
incl. electricity and 3 persons	€ 16,00 - € 25,00
pitch 120 sq.m, as above	€ 19,00 - € 28,00
extra person (over 1 yr)	€ 6,80
dog	€ 2,50

Reservations

Essential for July/Aug; made with deposit (€ 40 per week) and fee (€ 10). Tel: 03 22 23 40 30. E-mail: info@campingleroyon.com

Open

5 March - 1 November.

FR80090 Camping Caravaning Le Val d'Authie

20 route de Vercourt, 80120 Villers-sur-Authie (Somme)

In a village location, this well organised site is fairly close to several beaches, but also has its own excellent pool complex, small restaurant and bar. The owner has carefully controlled the size of the site, leaving space for a leisure area. There are 170 pitches in total, but with many holiday homes and chalets, there are only 60 for touring units. These are on grass, some divided by small hedges, with electricity and 15 with full services. Ideas for excursions include the 15/16th century chapel and the Aviation Museum at Rue and the steam railway which runs from Le Crotoy to Cayeux-sur-Mer around the Baie de Somme.

Facilities

Good modern toilet facilities include some shower and washbasin units, washbasins in cubicles, and limited facilities for disabled people and babies. Facilities may be under pressure in high season and a reader reports poor cleaning at that time. Ice pack service. Shop for basics (not in October). Bar/restaurant serving good value meals (1/5-15/9; hours vary according to season). Swimming pool with small jacuzzi and paddling pool (1/5-15/9, with lifeguards in July/Aug). Good playground for small children, club room with TV, and weekend entertainment in season (discos may be noisy until late). Multi-court, beach volleyball, football, boules and tennis court (all free). Fitness trail and running track, mountain bike circuit. Barbecues are not permitted.

At a glance

Welcome & Ambience	✓✓✓✓	Location	✓✓✓✓
Quality of Pitches	✓✓✓✓	Range of Facilities	✓✓✓✓

Directions

Villers-sur-Authie is about 25 km. NNW of Abbeville. From A16 junction 24 take N1 to Vron, then left on D175 to Villers-sur-Authie. Or use D85 from Rue, or D485 from Nampont St Martin. Site is at southern end of village at junction of minor road (easy to miss).

Charges 2004

Per person	€ 6,00
child (under 7 yrs)	€ 3,00
pitch	€ 5,00
electricity (4-10A)	€ 4,00 - € 8,00

Camping Cheques accepted.

Reservations

Advisable for high season, peak weekends and B.Hs. Tel: 03 22 29 92 47. E-mail: camping@valdauthie.fr

Open

1 April - 31 October.

FR80060 Camping Le Val de Trie

Mobile homes ▶ page 368

Bouillancourt-sous-Miannay, 80870 Moyenneville (Somme)

Le Val de Trie is a natural countryside site in a woodland location, near a small village. It is maturing into a well managed site with modern facilities. The 100 numbered, grassy pitches are of a good size, divided by hedges and shrubs with mature trees providing good shade in most areas, and all have electricity and water. Access roads are gravel (the site is possibly not suitable for the largest motorcaravans). There are good walks around the area and a notice board keeps campers up to date with local market, shopping and activity news. The site has a friendly, relaxed atmosphere and English is spoken. Very much off the beaten track, it can be very quiet in April, June, September and October. If you visit at these times and there is no-one on site, just choose a pitch or call at the farm to book in. There are a few Dutch tour operator tents (5).

Facilities

The two sanitary buildings are well maintained and cleaned, and include washbasins in cubicles, units for disabled people, babies and children, plus laundry and dishwashing facilities (and a microwave to warm babies food). Washing machine and dryer. Basic motorcaravan services. Extended shop (from 1/5) provides basic necessities, farm produce and wine, bread can be ordered each evening and butcher visits twice weekly in season. Plans include an extended bar, and snack-bar (with takeaway), with the addition of a TV room (15/5-15/9). There is a terrace and (in high season) a children's club. Pleasant, heated small swimming pool (6 x 12 m. open 1/5-31/8), fenced with large paddling pool and jacuzzi. Table tennis, boules and volleyball. Fishing lake (free). Bicycle hire. Children's play areas and small animal enclosure. Off site: Riding 2 km. Golf 10 km. Beach 12 km.

At a glance

Welcome & Ambience	✓✓✓✓✓	Location	✓✓✓✓✓
Quality of Pitches	✓✓✓✓	Range of Facilities	✓✓✓✓

Directions

From exit 2 on A28 near Abbeville take D925 to Miannay and turn left on D86 to Bouillancourt sous Miannay: site is signed in village

Charges 2005

Per unit incl. 2 persons	€ 12,00 - € 17,60
with electricity	€ 15,00 - € 21,00
extra person	€ 2,90 - € 4,40
child (under 7 yrs)	€ 1,90 - € 2,80
dog	€ 0,80 - € 1,30

Camping Cheques accepted.

Reservations

Made with dates, plus deposit (€ 31; no fee for AR readers). Tel: 03 22 31 48 88.
E-mail: raphael@camping-levaldetrie.fr

Open

1 April - 1 November.

FR80100 Camping Parc des Cygnes

111 rue de Montières, 80080 Amiens (Somme)

Formerly Camping de L'Ecluse, this is now a new 3.2 hectare site which has been completely levelled and attractively landscaped. Bushes and shrubs divide the site into areas and it is planned to plant some 20 mature trees to provide some shade. The 145 pitches are all dedicated to the touring trade, with plans for just a handful of mobile homes for rent. All the pitches are grassed with plenty of space on the tarmac roads in front of them for motorcaravans to park in wet conditions. There are 42 pitches with electricity (6/16A), water and drainage and further water points throughout the rest of the site. The enthusiastic manager is working very hard to make sure everything is fully up and running for 2005 – and is planning a swimming pool for 2006! The site is just a few minutes from the N1, the A16 Paris - Calais motorway and the A29/A26 route to Rouen and the south, so would useful as a stop-over being about 50 km. from the ports. Amiens itself is an attractive cathedral city where you can eat out on the waterfront of the 'Venice of the North' or take a boat trip around the 'floating gardens' of 'Les Hortillonnages'.

Facilities

Two identical toilet blocks (one open only when site is busy) with separate toilet facilities but unisex shower and washbasin area. Dishwashing and laundry sinks under cover. Everything is smart and clean with hot and cold water throughout. Facilities for disabled people. The reception building also houses toilets, showers and washbasins (heated when necessary). Laundry room with washing machine, dryer and ironing. Small shop (1/4-15/9). Bar and takeaway (1/5-15/9; weekends only in low season). Games and TV room, also used for occasional music events in high season. Bicycle hire. Fishing. Off site: Golf and riding 5 km. Beaches 70 km.

Open

1 April - 31 October.

At a glance

Welcome & Ambience	✓✓✓✓✓	Location	✓✓✓✓
Quality of Pitches	✓✓✓✓	Range of Facilities	✓✓✓

Directions

Site is signed on all approaches to Amiens. From A16, leave at exit 20. Take the Rocade Nord (northern bypass) to exit 40, follow signs for Amiens Longpré and at roundabout take second exit to Parc de Loisirs and then right to campsite (signs all the way).

Charges 2004

Per person	€ 5,40
child (0-7 yrs)	€ 4,40
pitch	€ 6,10 - € 8,90
car	€ 2,90
electricity	€ 3,10
dog	€ 1,60

Low season price for 2 persons and pitch € 13.

Reservations

Made for min. 2 nights with deposit (€ 25) and fee (€ 15.10). Tel: 03 22 43 29 28.
E-mail: camping.amiens@wanadoo.fr

FR80120 Camping les Aubépines

Saint-Firmin, 80550 Le Crotoy (Somme)

This peaceful, family-run site is on the edge of the Parc Ornithologique du Marquenterre and is just 1 km. from a beach on the Baie de Somme, a river estuary famous for its resident population of seals. It is an attractively laid out site which has a relaxed and very French feel and should appeal to those seeking a quiet holiday close to nature. There are 196 pitches, although around 100 are occupied by privately-owned mobile homes with a few available for rent. Consequently there are just 76 touring pitches scattered throughout the site. All on level ground, they are of a reasonable to good size, separated by hedges and trees and with water taps and electricity (3-10A) close by. For 2005 there is to be an elegant swimming pool with a paddling pool and sunbathing area – a bar is part of future plans.

Facilities

Two unisex toilet blocks are fairly basic but are kept clean and in good order. British stylets (seatless), washbasins in cubicles, push-button showers and some larger cubicles with shower and basin. Baby bath and tiny toilet. Facilities for disabled visitors are minimal (no grab-rails) Redevelopment of the older block is planned. Dishwashing sinks. Laundry room. Small shop. Table tennis and other indoor games. Morning club for younger children, afternoon activities for older ones and some evening family events (all in high season). Small play area. Bicycle hire. Off site: Riding adjacent. Beaches: tidal estuary 1 km; open sea 10 km. Nautical base 500 m. Golf 10 km. Tennis 3 km. Fishing 2 km. Bird sanctuary 3 km.

Open

1 April - 1 November.

At a glance

Welcome & Ambience	✓✓✓✓	Location	✓✓✓✓
Quality of Pitches	✓✓✓✓	Range of Facilities	✓✓✓

Directions

Le Crotoy is on the D940 Berck – Le Tréport road. At roundabout for town, take D4 to St Firmin, turning right at next roundabout. Immediately after sign for village, turn left (site signed) to site which is on right in about 500 m.

Charges 2004

Per unit incl. 2 persons	€ 15,00
incl. 3A electricity	€ 17,30
extra person	€ 3,70
child (2-7 yrs)	€ 2,70
electricity 6/10A	€ 1,80 - € 4,20
pet	€ 1,10

Less 10% in low season.

Reservations

Made for min. 6 days with deposit (€ 50).
Tel: 03 22 27 01 34.
E-mail: contact@camping-lesaubepines.com

Paris & Ile de France

Map 3

With its tree lined boulevards, museums, art galleries, the Arc de Triomphe and of course the famous Eiffel Tower, this cosmopolitan city has plenty to offer. Less than 30 miles from the heart of the capital, a fun-packed trip to Disneyland Paris is also within reach.

Départements: 75 Paris, 77 Seine-et-Marne, 78 Yvelines, 91 Essone, 92 Hauts-de-Seine, 93 Seine-St-Denis, 94 Val de Marne, 95 Val d'Oise

Major cities: Paris, Versailles, Ivry, Melun, Nanterre, Bobigny, Creteil and Pontoise.

One of the most chic and culturally rewarding cities in the world, Paris has something for everyone. The list of things to do is virtually endless and could easily fill many holidays - window shopping, the Eiffel Tower, Notre Dame, Montmartre, trips on the Seine, pavement cafés and the Moulin Rouge, the list goes on.

As a peaceful retreat, you can relax and enjoy the lush scenery of surrounding hills and secret woodlands of the Ile de France. Square bell towers in gentle valleys, white silos on endless plains of wheat; soft and harmonious landscapes painted and praised by La Fontaine, Corot and all the landscape painters. Paris is surrounded by forests, Fontainebleau, Compiègne, Saint-Germain-en-Laye and majestic châteaux such as Fontainbleau and Vaux-le-Vicomte.

Disneyland Resort Paris provides a great day out for all the family. It has two fantastic theme parks with over 70 attractions and shows to choose from. On the outskirts of Paris is Parc Asterix. The park has one of the most impressive roller-coasters in Europe offering breathtaking views.

Cuisine of the region

Although without a specific cuisine of its own, Paris and Ile de France offer a wide selection of dishes from all the regions of France. Paris also has a wide choice of foreign restaurants, such as Vietnamese and North African.

Places of interest

Fontainebleau: château and national museum, history of Napoléon from 1804-1815

Malmaison: château and national museum

Meaux: agricultural centre, Gothic cathedral, chapter house and palace

Paris: obviously! The list of places is too extensive to include here

St Germain-en-Laye: château, Gallo-roman and Merovingian archeological museum

Sèvres: ceramics museum

Thoiry: château and Parc Zoologique, 450-hectare park with gardens and African reserve containing 800 animals

Versailles: Royal Castle, Royal Apartments, Hall of Mirrors, Royal Opera and French History Museum

Alan Rogers tip

USE THE RIVER BUS TO EXPLORE. WITH REGULAR DEPARTURES THROUGHOUT THE SUMMER A CRUISE ALONG THE SEINE IS A RELAXING WAY TO ENJOY THE SIGHTS.

FR75020 Camping du Bois de Boulogne

2 allée du Bord de l'eau, 75016 Paris (Paris)

A busy site and the nearest to the city, this site is set in a wooded area between the Seine and the Bois de Boulogne. One can reach the Champs Elysees in 10-15 minutes by car or, from April to Oct, a shuttle bus runs every half hour from the site to the Metro station. The site is quite extensive but nevertheless becomes very full with many international visitors of all ages. There are 510 pitches (including mobile homes and a few chalets) of which 280 are marked, with electricity (10A), water, drainage and TV aerial connections. At the entrance is a functional, modern reception building (open 24 hrs) with a card operated barrier system. The site has undergone a huge improvement and re-development programme including the refurbishment of all toilet blocks. Reservations are made for the pitches - if not booked, arrive early in season (in the morning). Note: you are in a major city environment - take care of valuables.

Facilities

All toilet blocks have British and Turkish style WCs, washbasins in cubicles and showers with divider and seat with hot water throughout. All these facilities suffer from heavy use in season. Washing machines and dryers. Motorcaravan service point. Mini-market. Bar and restaurant (1/4-15/10). Bar open 7 am. - midnight at most times and until 2 am. in peak season. Pizza bar and takeaway service. Playground. Information service. Off site: Organised excursions (July/Aug). Fishing 1 km. Bicycle hire 2 km. Ticket sales for Disneyland, Asterix Parc, etc.

Open

All year.

At a glance

Welcome & Ambience	✓✓✓	Location	✓✓✓✓
Quality of Pitches	✓✓✓✓	Range of Facilities	✓✓✓

Directions

Site is on east side of Seine between the river and the Bois de Boulogne, just north of the Pont de Suresnes. Easiest approach is from Port Maillot, watch for traffic lights at site entrance. Follow signs closely and use a good map.

Charges 2004

Per unit incl. 2 persons	€ 18,50 - € 24,50
with electricity, water and drainage	€ 22,50 - € 31,70
tent incl. 2 persons	€ 11,00 - € 15,40
extra adult	€ 4,40 - € 6,20
child (under 7 yrs)	€ 2,20 - € 3,00
dog	€ 2,00 - € 2,50

Reservations

Contact site. Tel: 01 45 24 30 00.
E-mail: camping-boulogne@stereau.fr

FR77040 Caravaning des 4 Vents

77610 Crévecoeur-en-Brie (Seine-et-Marne)

This peaceful, pleasant site has been owned and run by the same family for over 35 years and is within easy reach of Disneyland (just 16 km. by road). There are around 200 pitches, with many permanent or seasonal units, however, there are 130 spacious grassy pitches for tourists, well separated by good hedges, all with 6A electricity and most with a water tap. The whole site is well landscaped with flowers and trees everywhere. This is a great family site with pool and games facilities located at the top end of the site so that campers are not disturbed. Crevecoeur-en-Brie celebrates the 'feast of small villages' on 21/22 June each year. Central Paris is just a 40 minute train ride from the nearest railway station (8 km) and there are also trains to Disneyland.

Facilities

Three modern sanitary units provide an adequate number of British style WCs, washbasins (mainly in cubicles) and pushbutton showers. Facilities for disabled people. Washing machine and dryer. Good motorcaravan service point. In high season (July/Aug) an excellent mobile snack bar and pizzeria is on site and is open from 16.00-23.00, and a baker is there from 07.30-11.00. Well fenced, circular swimming pool (16 m. diameter) (June to Sept). Excellent playground, a large games room with table tennis and table football, volleyball court, a billiard hall and a boules court. Off site: La Houssaye (1 km) has a grocer, bakery and post office. Fontenay (5 km) has a supermarket and all other services.

At a glance

Welcome & Ambience	✓✓✓✓	Location	✓✓✓✓
Quality of Pitches	✓✓✓✓✓	Range of Facilities	✓✓✓✓

Directions

Crèvecoeur is just off the D231 between the A4 exit 13 and Provins. From north, after passing a large obelisk turn right in 3 km, and from south 19 km. after junction with N4, turn left at signs to village and follow signs to site. Site is on western side of village.

Charges 2004

Per unit incl. 2 persons and electricity	€ 22,00
extra person	€ 5,00
child (under 5 yrs)	€ -2,00

Reservations

Essential for July/Aug. Tel: 01 64 07 41 11.
E-mail: f.george@free.fr

Open

1 March - 1 December.

FR77030 Camping International de Jablines

Base de Loisirs, 77450 Jablines (Seine-et-Marne)

Redesigned in 1997, Jablines replaces an older site in an upmarket, modern style which, with the accompanying leisure facilities of the adjacent 'Espace Loisirs', provides an interesting, if a little impersonal alternative to other sites in the region. The whole complex close to the Marne has been developed around old gravel workings. Man-made lakes provide marvellous water activities – dinghy sailing, windsurfing, canoeing, fishing and supervised bathing, plus a large equestrian centre. In season the activities at the leisure complex are supplemented by a bar/restaurant and a range of very French style group activities. The 'Great Lake' as it is called, is said to have the largest beach on the Ile-de-France! The site itself provides 132 pitches, most of a good size with gravel hardstanding and grass, accessed by tarmac roads and clearly marked by fencing panels and newly planted shrubs. All have 10A electrical connections, 60 with water and waste connections also.

Facilities

Two identical toilet blocks, heated in cool weather, are solidly built and well equipped. They include some washbasins in cubicles, indoor dishwashing and laundry facilities with washing machine and dryer. Motorcaravan service (charged). Shop (all season). Play area. Bar/restaurant adjacent at leisure centre/lake complex along with a range of watersports including 'water cable ski', riding activities, tennis and minigolf. Whilst staying on the campsite, admission to the leisure complex is free. Internet point. Ticket sales for Disneyland, Asterix and Sea Life.

Open

25 March - 30 October.

At a glance

Welcome & Ambience	✓✓✓✓	Location	✓✓✓✓
Quality of Pitches	✓✓✓✓	Range of Facilities	✓✓✓✓

Directions

From A4 Paris - Rouen take A104 before Disneyland. Take exit 8 on D404 Meaux/Base de Loisirs Jablines. From the A1 going south, follow signs for Disneyland after Charles de Gaulle airport using the A104. Take exit 6A Clay-Souilly on N3 (Meaux). After 6 km. turn right on D404 and follow signs.

Charges 2005

Per unit incl. 2 persons, electricity	€ 19,00 - € 22,00
luxury pitch incl. water and waste	€ 22,00 - € 24,00
extra person	€ 3,00 - € 5,50

Camping Cheques accepted.

Reservations

Essential for July/Aug. and made with booking form from site and 30% deposit. Tel: 01 60 26 09 37. E-mail: welcome@camping-jablines.com

FR77080 Camping Municipal les Prés

77880 Grez sur Loing (Seine-et-Marne)

A typical municipal site, although now leased to a French/English couple, Les Prés has 136 grassy pitches and a fair number of long stay units. However, there are usually around 35 pitches available for tourists, all with 5A electricity hook-ups. The town of Grez sur Loing dates back to medieval times and is well worth investigating. The site makes an ideal base for fishing, cycling (the warden can provide a booklet with five suggested routes - in French, of course), walking and rock climbing in Fontainebleau.

Facilities

A two storey building has separate male and female facilities on the upper level and unisex facilities at ground level. British and Turkish style toilets, dishwashing and laundry facilities, Excellent suite for disabled people in separate building. Small shop and limited takeaway (pizza and chips, 15/3-11/11). Off site: Bicycle hire 200 m. Riding 5 km. Golf 10 km.

Open

15 March - 11 November.

At a glance

Welcome & Ambience	✓✓✓✓	Location	✓✓✓✓
Quality of Pitches	✓✓✓✓	Range of Facilities	✓✓✓

Directions

Grez sur Loing is just off the N7 north of Nemours, south of Fontainebleau. From both directions turn east at roundabout north of town (Montcourt), cross river bridge and almost immediately turn right (signed). This access road is one-way. From south, do not follow campsite signs south of the village as the roads are too narrow for most units.

Charges 2004

Per person	€ 2,50
pitch	€ 4,30 - € 5,50
electricity (5A)	€ 2,50

Reservations

Advised for July/Aug. Tel: 01 64 45 72 75. E-mail: camping-grez@wanadoo.fr

FR77070 Camping La Belle Etoile

Quai Joffre, La Rochette, 77000 Melun (Seine-et-Marne)

Ideally situated for visiting Fontainebleau and Paris, and alongside the River Seine, this site has an overall mature and neat appearance, although the approach road along the banks of the river is somewhat off putting with several industrial plants. Continue past this point and you discover that La Belle Etoile enjoys a pleasant position with pitches to the fore of the site within view of the barges which continually pass up and down the Seine. This is a friendly, family run site with English speaking owners who are pleasant and helpful. The 170 touring pitches, with electricity connections (6/10A), are on grass and laid out between the many shrubs and trees. There are ten units for hire.

Facilities

The toilet blocks are not new but they are kept very clean and the water is very hot. Laundry room. Baby bath. Facilities for disabled visitors (shower, washbasin and WC). Motorcaravan service point. Small bar, snacks and shop with limited stock (28/6-30/8). Takeaway (1/5-15/9). Swimming pool (1/5-15/9). Play area. Fishing. Bicycle hire. Tickets for Disney and Vaux le Vicomte are sold by the site.
Off site: Fontainebleau is a short drive away and Paris easily accessible by train. Golf 15 km.

Open

1 April - 31 October.

At a glance

Welcome & Ambience	✓✓✓✓	Location	✓✓✓
Quality of Pitches	✓✓✓	Range of Facilities	✓✓✓

Directions

Travelling north on N6 Fontainebleau - Melun road, on entering La Rochette, pass Total petrol station on left and turn immediately right into Ave de la Seine. Continue to end of road and turn left at river, site on left in approx. 500 m.

Charges 2005

Per person	€ 4,65 - € 5,10
baby (0-2 yrs)	€ 2,10 - € 2,30
child (3-11 yrs)	€ 2,90 - € 3,20
pitch	€ 4,70 - € 5,10
electricity (6A)	€ 3,00 - € 3,20

Camping Cheques accepted.

Reservations

Made for a minimum of 3 nights. Tel: 01 64 39 48 12. E-mail: info@campinglabelleetoile.com

FR77090 Camping Les Etangs Fleuris

Route Couture, 77131 Touquin (Seine et Marne)

This is a pleasant, peaceful site which is near enough to both Paris (50 km.) and Disneyland (23 km.) to provide a practical alternative to the busier sites nearer the centre. It has a very French feel despite the presence of a fair number of tour operator mobile homes, since these occupy their own areas round the periphery. The touring pitches are grouped on the level ground around the attractive lakes which are home to some sizeable carp as well as being restocked daily with trout (fishing 5 for half a day). The life of the site centres round a smart bar/function room which doubles as reception and a shop, as well as the lakes and an attractive, irregularly shaped pool. There are 60 touring pitches, all with electricity (10A) and water, separated by hedges and with plenty of shade from the mature trees.

Facilities

The fairly basic toilet has British-style toilets, push-button showers, and open washbasins (with dividers and hooks) for men but mainly in cubicles for ladies. Cleaning could be a bit hit-and-miss at busy times for the hardworking owner. No facilities for disabled visitors. A second heated block among the mobile homes is only opened in cold weather or when the site is very busy. Washing machine and dryer. Very limited shop (bread and basics) in bar (both 28/3-30/9). Heated pool with paddling section (15/5-15/9). A trailer on site provides takeaway meals and snacks (15/6-15/9).
Off site: Riding 5 km. Golf 15 km.

At a glance

Welcome & Ambience	✓✓✓✓	Location	✓✓✓✓
Quality of Pitches	✓✓✓✓	Range of Facilities	✓✓✓

Directions

Touquin is off the D231, 21 km from exit 13 of the A4 motorway and 30 km northeast of Provins. From D231 follow signs for Touquin, then Etangs Fleuris and site which is 2.5 km west of the village along a single-track road with passing places.

Charges 2004

Per person	€ 7,00 - € 8,00
child (0-9 yrs)	€ 3,50 - € 4,00

Camping Cheques accepted.

Reservations

Contact site. Tel: 01 64 04 16 36. E-mail: etangs.fleuris@libertysurf.fr

Open

15 March - 15 October.

FR77020 Camping Le Chêne Gris

24, Place de la Gare de Faremoutiers-Pommeuse, 77515 Pommeuse (Seine-et-Marne)

Le Chêne Gris is a peaceful, attractive, Dutch owned site just 20 minutes drive from Disneyland Paris. The site entrance is close to the station of Faremoutiers-Pommeuse, from where commuters (and holidaymakers!) are whisked into Paris. Pommeuse can be found in the valley of the Grand Morin, amidst the characteristic hilly landscape of the Brie region. There are are 160 large, shady, mostly terraced pitches here, all with electricity, and many with water and drainage. This is a relatively simple site and most amenities, notably shops and restaurants, can be found in the surrounding villages. A swimming pool complex is planned for 2005.

Facilities

One central sanitary block. Washing machines. Play area. Table tennis. Games room. Barbecue rental. Mobile homes and tents for rent. Off site: Bar 100 m. Supermarket and restaurants nearby. River 500 m. Disneyland Paris 8 km. Trains to Paris (approx. 45 minutes).

Open

1 March - 31 October.

At a glance

Welcome & Ambience	✓✓✓	Location	✓✓✓✓
Quality of Pitches	✓✓✓	Range of Facilities	✓✓✓

Directions

From A4 autoroute take exit 16 and join the N34 towards Coulommiers. Site is well signed.

Charges 2004

Per person	€ 4,00
child (3-10 yrs	€ 3,00
pitch	€ 10,00
electricity (10A)	€ 3,00

Reservations

Contact site. Tel: 01 64 04 21 80.

FR78050 Camping Le Val de Seine

Base de Loisirs, Chemin du Rouillard, 78480 Verneuil-sur-Seine (Yvelines)

This is an excellent little site located in a large leisure and country park on the western outskirts of Paris. It has been completely refurbished to high standards (although with a few teething problems to be sorted out when we visited) and offers a pleasant alternative to the busier sites closer to Paris for those wishing to visit the city. Trains and RER services from nearby stations take you there in less than half an hour and even on to Disneyland and Versailles is easily reached by motorway. The site has 87 pitches in two sections, one end for campers (mainly groups) with its own toilet block, the other for caravans and tents. Here there are 37 level pitches each with electricity (6A), water and drainage. Campers here have free access to the huge country park (800 m. from site) which has three large lakes, one with a beach for swimming, others for sailing and pedalo hire. There are miles of paths and cycle tracks and many other activities.

Facilities

Two modern toilet blocks (not uni-sex) have British-style toilets, controllable showers and some washbasins in cubicles. Facilities for disabled visitors. Excellent dishwashing provision. Small block (low-level toilets, basins and showers) for children plus baby room. Washing machines and dryers planned, also motorcaravan service point. Reception sells bread (to order) and basic supplies. Country park with lakes, 9-hole practice golf (free), other sports facilities, a self-service restaurant and brasserie serving beer and cold drinks. Also (not free) bicycle hire, tennis courts, 18 hole minigolf. Off site: Riding adjacent. Golf 7 km.

At a glance

Welcome & Ambience	✓✓✓	Location	✓✓✓✓
Quality of Pitches	✓✓✓	Range of Facilities	✓✓✓✓

Directions

From A13 take exit 8 (Meulan-les Mureaux) and follow signs for 'Base de Loisirs du Val de Seine'. Go through Les Mureaux and bear right on D154 towards Verneuil. At roundabout turn left (signed 'Base de Loisirs') to site.

Charges 2004

Per person (4 yrs and over)	€ 3,00 - € 3,50
pitch	€ 3,50 - € 5,00
electricity	€ 4,00
pet	€ 1,50 - € 2,00

Reservations

Contact site. Tel: 01 39 28 16 20.
E-mail: sce-client@valdeseine78.com

Open

1 April - 30 September.

FR94000 Camping du Tremblay

Boulevard des Alliés, 94507 Champigny-sur-Marne (Val-de-Marne)

This is a very useful site for those wishing to visit Paris and is also convenient for Disneyland Paris as there is a bus service from the campsite gates to the Metro RER station serving both destinations. It is also close to the A4 motorway which is free as far as Disneyland. The site is on flat land beside the River Marne with 450 pitches, 76 of which are occupied by mobile homes and chalets to rent. The 220 touring pitches are on gravel and are separated by hedges. All have electricity (10A) but water has to be fetched from the toilet blocks except for the 32 serviced pitches which have taps and waste water points. There is also a large area of grass pitches for camping where there are water points but no electricity. It is very much a short-stay site but seems well run.

Facilities

The three toilet blocks are old-fashioned and lacking in any refinements, but they are apparently cleaned three times a day and this process seemed fairly thorough. Toilets are mainly segregated with many Turkish-style but some British and with the occasional seat! One block had unisex toilets which are seat-less British style. Showers are pre-set and washbasins in cubicles with warm and cold water. Facilities for disabled visitors (some en-suite) are fairly basic and there are no grab rails. Dishwashing sinks mainly under cover. Laundry sinks not recommended! Washing machines and dryers. Small, well stocked shop, bar and snack bar (15/3-15/10). Fishing.

Open

All year.

At a glance

Welcome & Ambience	✓✓✓	Location	✓✓✓✓
Quality of Pitches	✓✓✓	Range of Facilities	✓✓✓

Directions

From A4 take exit 5 onto D45 south (towards Champigny). At lights, turn right on N303 towards St Maur. At next lights continue ahead (now N4 to Vincennes) and immediately turn right at next lights onto Boulevard de Polangis. As you approach (but before you reach) the motorway flyover, turn right along Boulevard des Allies. Site entrance is on the left (passing under motorway). There are signs for Camping IDF at most points if you can spot them! It is suggested that you check your route back to the motorway before you leave if heading east.

Charges 2004

Per unit incl. 2 persons	€ 15,60 - € 21,10
incl. electricity	€ 17,90 - € 23,90
incl. water and drainage	€ 18,90 - € 25,80
extra person	€ 4,10 - € 5,50
child (0-7 yrs)	€ 2,40 - € 2,90
pet	€ 2,00 - € 2,50

Reservations

Made with deposit and € 12 fee. Tel: 01 43 97 43 97. E-mail: receptcc@stereau.fr

FR78010 Camping Caravaning International

1 rue Johnson, 78600 Maisons-Laffitte (Yvelines)

This busy site on the banks of the Seine is convenient for Paris – you can walk to the RER station and be in the centre in 20 minutes; the same line goes on through to Disneyland (55 minutes). Versailles is a short drive away. Maisons-Laffitte is a pleasant suburb with a château, a racecourse and some large training stables. The site has multilingual and friendly reception staff and occupies a grassy, tree covered area bordering the river. There are 351 pitches, 66 occupied by mobile homes and 90 used by tour operators, plus two areas dedicated to tents. Most pitches are separated by hedges, are of a good size with some overlooking the Seine (unfenced access), and all 195 touring pitches have 6A electricity hook-ups. The roads leading to the site are a little narrow so large vehicles need to take care. Being so close to Paris this site is consistently busy. Train noise can be expected.

Facilities

There are three sanitary blocks, two insulated for winter use. The third, more open in style is only used in July/and August. The facilities are clean and well maintained but with the volume of visitors, constant supervision is needed. Provision for people with disabilities. Laundry and dishwashing. Motorcaravan service point - jeton available at reception. Self-service shop. Restaurant/bar with takeaway food and pizzeria. TV room, table tennis, billiards and football area. Internet point. SNCF representative on site each morning 15/6-15/8 for travel advice. Off site: Sports complex adjoins the site. Riding 500 m. Bicycle hire 5 km.

Open

At a glance

Welcome & Ambience	✓✓✓✓	Location	✓✓✓✓
Quality of Pitches	✓✓✓	Range of Facilities	✓✓✓✓

Directions

Site is best approached from A13 or A15 autoroute. From A13 take exit 7 (Poissy)and follow D153 to Poissy, the D308 to Maisons-Laffitte, then site signs on right before town centre. From A15 exit 7 take D184 towards St Germain, after 11 km. turn left on D308 to Maisons-Laffitte and follow site signs as above. From A1 take the A86, then at exit 2 (for Bezons) take D308 to Maisons-Laffitte and follow signs to site on left.

Charges 2004

Per unit incl. 2 persons	€ 19,00 - € 22,00
with electricity	€ 21,00 - € 24,00
tent incl. 2 persons	€ 11,00 - € 12,00
extra adult	€ 5,00 - € 5,60
child (5-10 yrs)	€ 2,30 - € 2,70
animal	€ 2,50

Reservations

Advisable for July/Aug. and made with deposit (€ 10). Tel: 01 39 12 21 91. E-mail: ci.mlaffitte@wanadoo.fr

FR95000 Parc de Séjours de L'Etang

10 chemin des Bellevues, 95690 Nesles-la-Vallée (Val-d'Oise)

Parc de Sejour de L'Etang is small, informal site 33 km. northwest of Paris. It is situated on the southern outskirts of the village of Nesles-la-Vallée in a pretty, tree-lined river valley not far from L'Isle-Adam, which is a popular destination for Parisiens at weekends. Many of the 165 pitches are occupied by seasonal caravans but there are 65 large, flat pitches available for touring units of which 25 have electricity (3/9A). The site is informally arranged around a duck pond with many trees to provide shelter and shade and semi-tame rabbits competing with the ducks for food and attention. Chantilly, Parc Asterix and Disneyland are easily reached by car. By far the best way to visit Paris is by train from Valmondois, 5 minutes away via the D15 road (trains every half hour, journey time about 50 minutes).

Facilities

The main, central toilet block (heated in cooler weather) is a plain substantial building including washbasins in rather small cubicles and, in separate rooms, rather older style British and Turkish WCs. Covered dishwashing and laundry sinks. Washing machine. Smaller, much older unit includes fairly basic facilities for disabled people. Good playground, volleyball and basketball areas, and under cover play barn with table tennis. Off site: Village and restaurant within walking distance. Fishing permits for the river available in village. Riding 500 m, golf 7 km.

Open

1 March - 15 November.

At a glance

Welcome & Ambience	✓✓✓✓	Location	✓✓✓✓
Quality of Pitches	✓✓✓✓	Range of Facilities	✓✓✓

Directions

From A15 exit 10 take D915 to Pontoise, avoiding town centre, then D27 to Beauvais which joins the D927 and then D79 to Nesles-la-Vallée. Site is on left as you leave village on D64. From N1 or A16 (exit 11) take the D922 southwest towards L'Isle Adam, and then D64 northwest to Nesles la Vallée. Site is on the right as you enter the village.

Charges 2005

Per person	€ 4,00
child (1-6 yrs)	€ 3,00
pitch	€ 4,00
with electricity (3/9A)	€ 7,15 - € 8,10
animal	€ 1,00

No credit cards.

Reservations

Contact site. Tel: 01 34 70 62 89.
E-mail: brehinier1@hotmail.com

FR60010 Camping Campix

B.P. 37, 60340 St Leu-d'Esserent (Oise)

Opened in 1991, this informal site has been unusually developed in a former sandstone quarry on the outskirts of the small town. The quarry walls provide very different boundaries to most of the site, giving it a sheltered, peaceful environment. Trees have grown to soften the slopes. Not a neat, manicured site, the 160 pitches are arranged in small groups on the different levels with stone and gravel access roads (some fairly steep and possibly muddy in poor weather). Electricity (6A) is available to approximately 140 pitches. Torches are advised. There are very many secluded corners mostly for smaller units and tents and plenty of space for children to explore (parents must supervise - some areas, although fenced, could be dangerous). A footpath leads from the site to the town where there are shops, restaurants and an outdoor pool (in season). This site is best suited to those not needing sophisticated on-site facilities, or for visiting local places of interest and the friendly, English speaking owner will advise. These include Chantilly, the Asterix Park and the Mer de Sable, a Western theme amusements park, both 20 km. Disneyland is 70 km. It is also possible to visit Paris by train (information at reception).

Facilities

At the entrance to the site a large building houses reception and two clean, heated sanitary units - one for tourers, the other usually reserved for groups. Two suites for disabled people double as baby rooms. Laundry facilities with washing machine and dryer. At quieter times only one unit is opened but facilities may be congested at peak times. Motorcaravan service facilities. Bread and milk delivered daily. Basic snack bar operates from mobile unit (July/Aug). Off site: Fishing 1 or 5 km, riding or golf 5 km.

Open

7 March - 30 November.

At a glance

Welcome & Ambience	✓✓✓	Location	✓✓✓
Quality of Pitches	✓✓✓	Range of Facilities	✓✓✓

Directions

St Leu-d'Esserent is 11 km. west of Senlis, 5 km. northwest of Chantilly. From the north on the A1 autoroute take the Senlis exit, from Paris the Chantilly exit. Site is north of the town off the D12 towards Cramoisy, and is signed in the village.

Charges 2005

Per unit	€ 3,50 - € 5,00
person	€ 3,00 - € 5,00
child (under 9 yrs)	€ 2,00 - € 3,00
small tent	€ 2,50 - € 4,00
electricity	€ 2,50 - € 3,50
dog	€ 1,00 - € 2,00

Reservations

Advisable for July/Aug. Tel: 03 44 56 08 48.
E-mail: campixfr@aol.com

Map 4

Home to the Champagne region, the varied landscapes of Eastern France include dense forests, vineyards and winding rivers. The whole area is dotted with fascinating ancient churches and castles, towns and villages.

Eastern France is defined as:
Champagne-Ardenne: 08 Ardennes, 51 Marne, 10 Aube, 52 Haute-Marne.
Lorraine Vosges: 54 Meurthe-et-Moselle, 55 Meuse, 57 Moselle, 88 Vosges.
Alsace: 67 Bas-Rhin, 68 Haut-Rhin

Situated on the flatlands of Champagne are the most northerly vineyards in France where special processing turns the light, dry wine into 'le Champagne' and names such as Moet et Chandon and Veuve Clicquot spring to mind. Nowhere else in the world are you allowed to make sparkling wine and call it champagne. Travelling further east you come across the spa towns such as Vittel, Bains-les-Bains and Plombières and the birth place of St Joan of Arc at Domrémy.

Today you can descend from the mountains into the Alsace vineyards and fairy tale wine villages. The 'Route des Vins' follows the vineyards along the Rhine valley from Mulhouse to Colmar and north almost to Strasbourg. Alsace and Lorraine have been frequently fought over and today there are many poignant reminders of the turbulent past. You'll find noticeable German influence in architecture, cuisine and language. There are also numerous little wine towns, medieval villages and a host of ruined castles stretching along the north eastern margins of the Vosges.

Cuisine of the region

Quiche Lorraine: made only in the classical manner with cream, eggs and bacon.

Potage Lorraine: potato. leek and onion soup

Tarte (aux mirabelles): golden plum tart. Also made with other fruits

Tarte à l'oignon Alsacienne: onion and cream tart

Places of interest

Épernay: home of champagne production

Le Linge: trenches including rusty barbed wire have been left as they were

Reims: 13th century Gothic cathedral

Riquewihr: traditional town, fortifications and medieval houses

Verdun: hill forts such as Fort de Vaux and Fort de Douaumont, large military cemetery at Douaumont

Alan Rogers tip

TAKE ADVANTAGE OF THE FREE LOCAL ENTERTAINMENT IN REIMS THROUGHOUT JULY AND AUGUST. THE FLÂNERIES MUSICALES D'ÉTE HAS OVER 120 CONCERTS TO ENJOY.

FR08010 Camping Municipal du Mont Olympe

Rue des Paquis, 08000 Charleville-Mezieres (Ardennes)

Attractively situated alongside the Meuse River, within easy walking distance across a footbridge to the centre of the pleasant large town, this site was completely rebuilt in 2001/2, just a short distance from the old one. It now offers excellent facilities, with 128 grass pitches, all with electricity (10A), water and waste water connections, 66 will be from 108 to 219 sq. metres, 48 up to 106 sq. metres and 12 smaller pitches especially for camping-cars.

Facilities

Three heated buildings provide first class showers, private cabins, baby rooms and facilities for the disabled, plus inside dishwashing (including one for the disabled) and a well-equipped laundry room. Motorcaravan service point. Children's play area and paddling pool. TV and games room. Off site: Municipal pool next door. Boat trips on the river. Attractive town centre close by.

Open

1 April - 15 October.

At a glance

Welcome & Ambience	✓✓✓	Location	✓✓✓✓✓
Quality of Pitches	✓✓✓✓	Range of Facilities	✓✓✓

Directions

Site is north of Charleville on the island of Montcy St Pierre and is signed from the city centre 'Mont Olympe'. From the north D988/D1 follow the river, over the bridge, then immediately left. From the southeast (A203/N51/N43) take 'centre' exit, head for 'Gare' then follow Avenue Forest north and sharp left after the bridge. The site entrance is 150 metres further on from where the old site was situated.

Charges guide

Per person	€ 4,10
child (5-17yrs)	€ 2,80
pitch and vehicle	€ 4,50 - € 5,50
dog	€ 1,35
electricity (6/10A)	€ 2,50 - € 3,50
motorcaravan overnight	€ 10,00

Reservations

Contact site. Tel: 03 24 33 23 60.

FR08040 Camping La Samaritaine

Mobile homes page 369

08240 Buzancy (Ardennes)

What a surprise and a pleasure it was to arrive at such a delightful new site in the heart of the Ardennes. It is peacefully situated just outside the village beside a stream, although there may be some high season noise from the nearby lake where you can swim or fish. Flowers decorate the entrance and bushes and saplings have been planted to separate the pitches, although there is not much shade at present. The 101 numbered touring pitches all have electricity (10A) and are on level grass off hard access roads. They vary in size up to 130 sq.m. 55 have water and waste water, and there are attractive small wooden containers for waste. There are also 10 mobile homes and 9 chalets for rent on the site.

Facilities

A modern building houses the usual sanitary facilities, with private cabins, baby bath, washing machine and dryer, inside dishwashing and facilities for the disabled. A large recreation room houses some games and there are tables to sit at. Table tennis is under cover. Bread is delivered daily. A few essentials are kept in reception. Snack bar/takeaway (mid-May - end-Sept). High season accompanied walks and entertainment programme. Motorcaravan Service Point and an "Aire Exterieur" are beside the entrance road to the site. Off site: Just along from the site towards the lake is the volleyball court and boules, whilst at the lake is some play equipment 'under adult supervision only'. Lake swimming is supervised only at certain times (2 metres deep), with a paddling area up to 1.2 metres depth. Restaurant in village.

At a glance

Welcome & Ambience	✓✓✓✓	Location	✓✓✓✓
Quality of Pitches	✓✓✓✓	Range of Facilities	✓✓✓✓

Directions

The village of Buzancy is about 22 km. east of Vouziers on the RD947 towards Stenay and Montmédy. The site is 1.5 km from the centre of the village down a small road, and is well signed.

Charges 2005

Per person	€ 3,00 - € 4,00
child (under 10 yrs)	€ 2,00 - € 3,00
pitch	€ 4,50 - € 5,00
water and waste water	€ 2,00
electricity (10A)	€ 3,50
animal	€ 1,50 - € 2,50

Camping Cheques accepted.

Reservations

Contact site. Tel: 03 24 30 08 88.
E-mail: info@campinglasamaritaine.com

Open

28 April - 25 September.

FR51020 Camping Municipal en Champagne

Rue de Plaisance, 51000 Châlons-en Champagne (Marne)

The location of Châlons, south of Reims and near both the A4 and A26 autoroutes, about 200 miles from Calais and Boulogne, make this an ideal stopover. It is also ideally situated for exploring this famous region in the plain of the River Marne and its historical connections. This site on the southern edge of town is an example of a good municipal site. The wide entrance with its well tended appearance of neatly mown grass and flower beds sets the tone for the rest of the site. Ninety-five of the 148 pitches, accessed from tarmac roads, are on a gravel base with the rest on grass. The majority have electricity (10A). The generously sized gravel pitches are separated by hedges and 48 of these are multi-serviced. Trees abound although there is no shade in some parts. The newest area of pitches overlook the small lake.

Facilities

Two toilet blocks, one behind reception which can be heated, the other at the far end of the site. These facilities are of varying standards due to an ongoing programme of refurbishment. Some washbasins in cabins, baby roóm and hairdressing station, facilities for disabled visitors including some special pitches adjacent, plus a washing machine and dryer and dishwashing room. Numerous refuse bins enclosed by wooden palings which enhance the general appearance of the site. Bread to order. Bar, snack bar and takeaway (1/6-31/9 evenings plus lunchtime July/Aug). Gas supplies. Games and TV rooms. Playground. Mini golf, tennis, table tennis, volleyball, boules and place for mini-football. Motorcaravan Service Point. Off site: Fishing (free for campers) nearby. Bus stop at site entrance. Town has number of notable buildings, churches and half timbered houses.

At a glance

Welcome & Ambience	✓✓✓✓	Location	✓✓✓✓
Quality of Pitches	✓✓✓✓	Range of Facilities	✓✓✓✓

Directions

From the north on the A4, take La Veuve exit (27) onto the N44 which by-passes the town. Leave at last exit signed St Memmie and follow camping signs. From the south on A26, take exit 18 onto N77 and, head towards town. Site is well signed 'Camping', and is south of town centre on te D60.

Charges 2004

Per person	€ 4,50
child (under 7 yrs)	€ 1,70
pitch	€ 4,50
vehicle	€ 3,00
electricity	€ 3,00

Reservations

Write to site. Tel: 03 26 68 38 00.

Open

1 April - 31 October.

FR52020 Castel Camping La Forge de Sainte Marie

52230 Thonnance-les-Moulins (Haute-Marne)

The département of Haute-Marne is situated between the better known areas of Champagne and the Vosges. It is a sleepy land of rolling hills, forests and farmland. In the heart of this lies Thonnance-les-Moulins, twelve kilometres east of Joinville and the north-south N67 main road between St Dizier and Chaumont. This most attractive campsite has been created from the remains of old forge buildings and their surroundings in this secluded valley. As soon as one enters through the arched gateway, one is impressed by the setting. A picturesque bridge links the upper part of the site with a lower road going to the section near the river. Opposite reception, another old building has been skilfully converted into Gites for lettting. Grass pitches, 165 for touring units, are of a very generous size on terraces amongst the trees or in more open areas. Electricity (6A) and water are available and 120 pitches are fully serviced. There is much of interest in the area - Joan d'Arc and General de Gaulle lived near and it is not too far to the Champagne vineyards and cellars at Reims. Nigloland for the children is within range and Joinville is worth exploring. It is also possible to visit the largest man-made lake in Europe at Giffaumont-Champaubert. There are also 30 mobile homes and chalets, and 59 tour operator units on site. The enthusiastic British and Dutch managers are determined to make a success of the site.

Facilities

There are two modern sanitary blocks which do come under pressure at peak times and in high season. However, additional facilities are available at reception or in the pool complex. Shop and excellent restaurant and bar with terrace. Splendid heated indoor pool with a smaller one for children (all open 30/4-15/9). Four children's play areas imaginatively placed around the site. Level open grass area for football and volleyball. Bicycle hire. Free fishing. Games room. Internet terminal. Organized games for children in high season. Varied programme for adults including a farm visit by tractor with a barbecue, music, dancing and excursions. Organised golfing holidays arranged.
Off site: Horse riding 15km, golf 45km. A visit to Grand (20km) with its Gallo-Roman amphitheatre and mosaic is a must.

At a glance

Welcome & Ambience	✓✓✓✓	Location	✓✓✓✓
Quality of Pitches	✓✓✓✓	Range of Facilities	✓✓✓✓✓

Directions

Site is about 12 km. southeast of Joinville between Poissons and Germay on road D427. The site entrance may be a little tight for large units.

Charges 2004

Per pitch incl. 2 persons and electricity	€ 15,00 - € 25,00
extra person	€ 3,00 - € 6,00
child (2-7 yrs)	€ 1,50 - € 3,00
animal	free

Camping Cheques accepted.
Less 20% outside July/Aug.

Reservations

Contact site for details. Tel: 03 25 94 42 00.
E-mail: la.forge.de.sainte.marie@wanadoo.fr

Open

30 April - 15 September.

FR52030 Camping Lac de la Liez

Mobile homes page 371

Peigney, 52200 Langres (Haute-Marne)

Managed by the enthusiastic Baude family, this newly renovated lakeside site is near the city of Langres. With its old ramparts and ancient city centre, Langres was elected one of the 50 most historic cities in France. Situated only 10 minutes from the A5, Camping Lac de la Liez provides an ideal spot for an overnight stop en-route to the south of France. There is also a lot on offer for a longer stay, including the lake and an impressive indoor pool complex, with a sauna. The site provides 144 fully serviced, terraced pitches with panoramic views of the lake. The 200 hectare lake has a sandy beach for play and swimming, a play area and a small harbour where boats and pedaloes may be hired. Access to the lake from the campsite is down steps and across what is quite a fast road (in total 150 m).

TRAVEL SERVICE SITE

TO BOOK CALL 0870 405 4055 OR www.alanrogersdirect.com

Facilities

Two new toilet blocks have all facilities in cabins. Facilities for disabled people. Laundry facilities. Motorcaravan services. Shop, bar and restaurant (with takeaway food). Indoor pool complex with spa and sauna. Extensive games area and tennis court (free in low season). Off site: Lake with beach and boat hire. Bicycle hire and cycle tracks around the lake. Riding 5 km. Fishing 100 m. Golf 40 km.

Open

1 April - 1 November

At a glance

Welcome & Ambience	✓✓✓✓	Location	✓✓✓✓
Quality of Pitches	✓✓✓✓	Range of Facilities	✓✓✓✓

Directions

From Langres take the N19 towards Vesoul. After approximately 3 km. turn right, straight after the large river bridge, then follow site signs.

Charges 2005

Per person	€ 6,00
child (under 7 yrs)	€ 3,00 - € 3,00
pitch	€ 8,00
electricity	€ 4,00 - € 4,00
dog	€ 1,50

Camping Cheques accepted.
Reductions in low season.

Reservations

Contact site. Tel: 03 25 90 27 79.
E-mail: campingliez@free.fr

FR54000 Camping Le Brabois

Avenue Paul Muller, 54600 Villers les Nancy (Meurthe-et-Moselle)

This former municipal site, within the Nancy city boundary and 5 km. from the centre, was taken over by the Campeole group in 1998. Situated within a forest area, there is shade in most parts and, although the site is on a slight slope, the 185 good-sized, numbered and separated pitches are level. Of these, 160 pitches have electrical connections (5/15A) and 30 also have water and drainage. Being on one of the main routes from Luxembourg to the south of France, Le Brabois makes a good night stop. However, Nancy is a delightful city in the heart of Lorraine and well worth a longer stay, not only for the interesting 18th century Place Stanislas and 11th century city centre, but for the many other attractions of the area. The British manager has a wide range of tourist literature, publishes a monthly English newsletter and is pleased to help plan visits and day trips. Horse racing takes place every two weeks at the Nancy race track next to the campsite, and good wine is produced nearby.

Facilities

Six sanitary blocks spread around the site are old and due for refurbishment over the next few years. They have a mix of British and Turkish style WCs and some washbasins in cubicles. One block can be heated in cool weather. Two units for disabled visitors. Washing machine and dryer. Motorcaravan service point. Small shop (all season). Bread to order. Restaurant incorporating bar and small shop (15/6-31/8). Small library for book exchange. Playground for young children. Area for ball games and table tennis under cover. Off site: Restaurants and shops about 1 km. Excellent walks and cycle rides. Buses to Nancy every 15 minutes.

Open

1 April - 15 October.

At a glance

Welcome & Ambience	✓✓✓✓	Location	✓✓✓✓
Quality of Pitches	✓✓✓✓	Range of Facilities	✓✓✓✓

Directions

Take exit 2b 'Brabois' from autoroute A33, continue for about 500 m. to 'Quick' restaurant on left. Turn left here, pass the racetrack to T-junction, turn right and after about 400 m. turn right on to site entrance road.

Charges 2004

Per unit incl. 2 persons	€ 9,60 - € 11,20
extra person	€ 3,60
child (2-7 yrs)	free - € 2,10
electricity	€ 3,30
hiker	€ 6,60 - € 6,75
dog	€ 1,85 - € 1,90

Credit cards minimum € 15.
Barrier card deposit € 20.

Reservations

Advised for July but site say no-one is turned away.
Tel: 03 83 27 18 28.
E-mail: campeoles.brabois@wanadoo.fr

FR55010 Camping Les Breuils

Allée des Breuils, 55100 Verdun (Meuse)

Thousands of soldiers of many nations are buried in the cemeteries around this famous town and the city is justly proud of its determined First World War resistance. Les Breuils is a neat site beside a small fishing lake and close to the famous town and Citadel. It provides 166 flat, pitches of varying sizes on two levels (144 for touring units), many with shade. Separated by trees or hedges, they are beside the lake and 120 offer the possibility of electricity connection (6A) although some long leads will be necessary for some. The overall appearance of this busy site is attractive.

Facilities

Sanitary facilities, in two blocks, are a mixture of old and new, the newer parts being of a better standard, including washbasins in cabins for ladies, washing machines and dryers, facilities for the disabled and babies. Conveniently sited among the pitches are sets of four dishwashing sinks under pitched roofs (cold water only; hot water at the blocks). Cleaning and maintainance variable. Motorcaravan services. Small shop, (1/5-30/9) selling wines and essentials, reception has various local guide books for sale (1/5-31/8). Restaurant serves breakfast, evening and lunchtime snacks and takeaway (Mid June-31/8), bar (Eves 1/5-30/9). Swimming pool (200 sq.m.) and children's pool (1/6-31/8). Large fenced play area on gravel. New multi-sports complex (football, volleyball, basektball). Off site: Bicycle hire and town centre 1 km. Riding 5 km. The Citadelle Souterraine is well worth a visit and is within walking distance of the site.

At a glance

Welcome & Ambience	✓✓✓	Location	✓✓✓
Quality of Pitches	✓✓✓✓	Range of Facilities	✓✓✓✓

Directions

The RN3 forms a sort of ring road round the north of the town. Site is signed from this on the west side of the town (500 m. to site).

Charges 2004

Per person	€ 4,20
child (under 10 yrs)	€ 2,80
caravan or motorcaravan	€ 4,20
double axle caravan	€ 15,00
tent	€ 2,80
electricity (5A)	€ 3,80

Discounts for low season and longer stays.
Double axle caravans €15 per night.
Credit cards accepted for minimum of €15.

Reservations

Advised for high season. Tel: 03 29 86 15 31.
E-mail: contact@camping-lesbreuils.com

Open

1 April - 30 September

FR57050 Camping Municipal de Metz-Plage

Allée de Metz-Plage, 57000 Metz (Moselle)

As this site is just a short way from the autoroute exit and within easy walking distance for the city centre, it could make a useful night stop if travelling from Luxembourg to Nancy or for a longer stay if exploring the area. By the Moselle river, the 151 pitches are on level grass, most are under shade from tall trees and 73 have electricity (10A) and water. Tent pitches have a separate place on the river banks.

Facilities

The two sanitary blocks, one newer than the other, are acceptable if not luxurious. Baby room. Shop. Bar, restaurant and takeway. 3 pitches for overnight stops for motorhomes. Off site: Fishing near. Riding 5 km. Golf 8 km.

Open

5 May - 26 September.

At a glance

Welcome & Ambience	✓✓✓✓	Location	✓✓✓✓✓
Quality of Pitches	✓✓✓✓	Range of Facilities	✓✓✓

Directions

From autoroute take Metz-Nord - Pontiffray exit (no. 33) and follow camp signs

Charges guide

Per person	€ 2,45
child (4-10 yrs)	€ 1,20
pitch incl. electricity	€ 4,25 - € 6,40

Reservations

Not possible. Tel: 03 87 68 26 48.
E-mail: jmwingerter@mairie-metz.fr

FR67010 Camping L'Oasis

3, Rue du Frohret, 67110 Oberbronn (Bas Rhin)

This is an attractively situated, inexpensive site, set amidst the mountains and forests of northern Alsace, not far from the German border. There are good views over the valley to one side and the pretty village with trees sheltering the other. The circular internal road has pitches around the outside (120 for touring units, 30 for seasonals), as well as space in the centre where there is also a children's playground. The solar-heated swimming pool and children's pool are of excellent quality. A 'Centre de Vacances' provides a covered swimming pool, sauna and fitness room, with a minimum entry age of 17 years.

Facilities

The first well appointed toilet block, heated in cool weather, has some washbasins in cabins for ladies, washing machines and dryers, a baby room and facilities for disabled people. The second block is unisex and small. Small shop. General room with table football and air hockey. Swimming and paddling pools (July/Aug). Indoor pool next to site. Playground. Tennis court. Off site: Supermarket in the village 1 km. Riding 700 m. Fishing 3 km.

Open

14 March - 13 November.

At a glance

Welcome & Ambience	✓✓✓✓	Location	✓✓✓✓
Quality of Pitches	✓✓✓✓	Range of Facilities	✓✓✓✓

Directions

Travel northwest from Haguenau on N62 for approx. 20 km. South of Niederbronn turn left on D28 for Oberbronn-Zinswiller - site is signed from here. From A4 take exit 42 to Sarreguemines, then N62 and D620 towards Haguenau and as above.

Charges 2005

Per person	€ 3,50
child (under 7)	€ 2,10
pitch and vehicle	€ 4,00
electricity	€ 3,70

Less 5% outside 1/7-31/8. No credit cards.

Reservations

Advised for high season. Write with precise dates; no deposit required. Tel: 03 88 09 71 96.

FR67050 Camping Municipal Wasselonne

Route de Romanswiller, 67310 Wasselonne (Bas Rhin)

A good quality municipal site with a resident warden, the facilities here include a well stocked small shop, a créperie in season and the bonus of free admission to the superb indoor heated swimming pool which is adjacent to the site. There are 70 tourist pitches and around 30 seasonal units, on grass with a slight slope and all with electricity hook-ups (5/10A). Four new rental chalets are in a separate fenced area. A full programme of events is offered in the town by the Tourist Office, including welcome evenings, guided tours, concerts, musical festivals, food tasting evenings. This could be anexcellent base from which to visit Strasbourg.

Facilities

The single, large, and well maintained sanitary unit behind reception has unisex facilities with ample sized showers and washbasins in cubicles. Laundry room with washing machine and dryer and covered dishwashing sinks. No specific facilities for disabled visitors but the rooms are spacious and should be accessible to many. Excellent drive-over motorcaravan service point. Off site: Heated swimming pool, hotel with restaurant, one indoor and four outdoor tennis courts, plus an athletics stadium and running track are all adjacent to the site. A fitness trail and horse riding within 1 km. Supermarket 500 m.

At a glance

Welcome & Ambience	✓✓✓✓	Location	✓✓✓✓
Quality of Pitches	✓✓✓✓	Range of Facilities	✓✓✓✓

Directions

Wasselonne is 25 km. west of Strasbourg. Site lies southwest of town centre on D224 towards Romanswiller, and is well signed.

Charges 2004

Per unit incl. 1 person	€ 7,30
extra person	€ 3,30
child (0-10 yrs)	€ 1,70
electricity	€ 2,10 - € 3,50
animal	€ 0,60

Reservations

Possible, contact site for details. Tel: 03 88 87 00 08.

Open

15 April - 15 October.

FR67030 Camping Caravaning du Ried

Route de Rhinau, 67860 Boofzheim (Bas Rhin)

The area between the main road from Strasbourg to Colmar and the river Rhine is usually bypassed by those who are exploring Alsace or passing through to Switzerland and Italy. However, if looking for a night stop or a different base in the region, Camping du Ried could well fit the bill. Situated on the edge of a small, picturesque village, it has 100 tourist pitches (with 5A electricity) amongst the 120 rental and 55 private static caravans. Most of these are under tall trees, on grass and separated by hedges. One might think that this is just another reasonable campsite until one sees the excellent pool complex just inside the site entrance which has an attractive outdoor pool for use in July and August and a heated indoor one open from May to September. There is also a lake and small beach on site. We found this a pleasant site with very friendly management who would like to welcome more British visitors even although no English is spoken.

Facilities

The main, heated toilet block is quite a large building and was refurbished in 2002. It is well tiled and has all the usual facilities including those for disabled people. Washing machines and dryer. Additional small units by lake or reception. Bar/restaurant (weekends 1/4-30/6 & 1/9-30/9, daily 1/7-31/8). Splendid indoor and outdoor pools (bracelets must be worn). These also have toilets and showers. Motorcaravan Service Point. Playground. Boules. Minigolf. Canoeing. High season animation for children and daily programme including a variety of excursions, guided canoe trips and competitions. Library. Archery. Fitness trail around lake. Volleyball. Fishing. Off site: Large Super 'U' supermarket outside gates, also has an ATM, fuel station and car wash (open 08.00-20.00). Markets at Benfeld Mondays and Selestat Tuesdays. Cycle hire 1 km. Riding 4 km. Golf 18 km.

At a glance

Welcome & Ambience	✓✓✓✓	Location	✓✓✓
Quality of Pitches	✓✓✓✓	Range of Facilities	✓✓✓✓

Directions

Leave N83 Strasbourg - Colmar road at Benfeld and go east on D5 to Boofzheim. Site is 500 m. beyond village towards Rhinau.

Charges 2005

Per unit incl. 2 persons	€ 13,00 - € 17,50
extra person	€ 3,00 - € 5,50
hiker	€ 7,00 - € 9,00
dog	€ 2,50 - € 3,00
electricity	€ 5,00

Security barrier card deposit €30.
Discount for longer stays.

Reservations

Made with deposit and fee; contact site.
Tel: 03 88 74 68 27. E-mail: info@camping-ried.com

Open

1 April - 2 October.

FR68030 Camping Municipal Masevaux

3 rue du Stade, 68290 Masevaux (Haut-Rhin)

Masevaux is a pleasant little town in the Haut-Rhin département of Alsace, just to the north of the A36 Belfort - Mulhouse motorway in the Des Ballons region. The municipal camping site is situated in a quiet edge of town next to the sporting complex which has a good indoor pool and other sporting opportunities. The pretty flower decked entrance promises a neat, excellent site and one is not disappointed. The neatly mown 120 pitches for tourists are on level grass, of reasonable size, marked by trees and hedges, and all have electricity (3/6A). Most are well shaded by a variety of trees and have good views of the surrounding hills. The pleasant and helpful Scottish Gardiens, who take pride in the site, would like to welcome more British visitors. The attractive town is a short walk. This is a good choice for one night or a longer stay to explore this interesting region, and is an ideal destination for serious walkers.

Facilities

A modern, well designed and well equipped sanitary block has most washbasins in private cabins. Baby room. Laundry and covered dishwashing area. Baker calls in high season. Ice-creams and soft drinks available at reception. TV room, small library, Boules. Children's play area. Tennis courts (extra charge), volleyball, table tennis. Off site: Supermarket, restaurants and indoor pool near. Fishing. A network of walking routes complete with overnight shelter cabins has been set up in the mountains around the area. These overnight cabins are free of charge. Market in Masavaux Wednesdays.

At a glance

Welcome & Ambience	✓✓✓✓	Location	✓✓✓✓
Quality of Pitches	✓✓✓✓	Range of Facilities	✓✓✓

Directions

From D466 in Masevaux follow sign for Belfort and then 'Camping Complexe Sportif'.

Charges 2004

Per person	€ 2,60
child (under 7 yrs)	€ 1,35
pitch	€ 2,60
electricity (3/6A)	€ 2,60 - € 4,90
dog	€ 0,70

Credit cards accepted.

Reservations

Made with € 31 deposit; contact site.
Tel: 03 89 82 42 29.
E-mail: camping-masevaux@tv-com.net

Open

1 March - 31 October.

FR68060 Camping Intercommunal Riquewihr

Route des Vins, 68340 Riquewihr (Haut-Rhin)

Surrounded by vineyards and minutes from the delightful village of Riquewihr, this is a well run site which has earned its good reputation. Situated in the heart of the Alsace wine region the site covers three hectares with views across the open countryside. Immediately to the right of the security barrier stands a modern, part-timbered building housing reception and information area. Close by is a small summer house and both are heavily garlanded with flowers. The 161 spacious individual grass pitches, many with shade and divided by hedging, have electrical connections (6A).

Facilities

Three sanitary blocks, one more modern, include private cabins with basins, good nursery room and excellent facilities for disabled people. Dishwashing and laundry areas. Motorcaravan services. Campers' room with tables and chairs. Shop for basic necessities (from 1/5). Off site: Play area adjacent. Fishing 3 km. Bicycle hire 5 km.

Open

1 April - 31 December.

At a glance

Welcome & Ambience	✓✓✓✓	Location	✓✓✓✓
Quality of Pitches	✓✓✓✓	Range of Facilities	✓✓✓

Directions

From N83 north of Colmar take D4 westwards to Bennwihr. Turn north on D18 for 2 km. towards Ribeauvillé. Site is signed off roundabout at southern end of Riquewihr bypass. Do not enter village.

Charges 2004

Per person	€ 3,35 - € 3,70
child (under 7 yrs)	€ 1,50 - € 1,70
pitch	€ 3,60 - € 4,00
electricity	€ 4,10

Reservations

Not accepted. Tel: 03 89 47 90 08.
E-mail: camping.riquewihr@tiscali.fr

FR68080 Camping Clair Vacances

Route de Herrlisheim, 68127 St Croix-en-Plaine (Haut-Rhin)

Alsace is a popular and picturesque area of lovely villages, large vineyards, mountains and forests, and is also on the route taken by many heading for Switzerland or Italy. Clair Vacances, opened in '97, and extended in '03 is a very neat, tidy and pretty site with 130 level pitches of generous size which are numbered and most are separated by trees and shrubs. All have electricity connections (8-13A) and 10 are fully serviced with water and drainage. The quiet, family site has been imaginatively laid out with the pitches reached from hard access roads. The friendly couple who own and run it will be pleased to advise on the attractions of the area. The site is 1 km. from the A35 exit, not far from Colmar.

Facilities

Two excellent, modern toilet blocks include washbasins in cabins, well equipped baby rooms and good facilities for disabled visitors. Laundry and dishwashing facilites. Shop with limited supplies. Swimming pool and children's pool with large sunbathing area. Playground. Table tennis. Volleyball. Community room. Archery in high season. Dogs are not accepted in July/Aug. Camping Gaz stocked. Off site: Colmar with restaurants and shops is not far away.

At a glance

Welcome & Ambience	✓✓✓✓	Location	✓✓✓✓
Quality of Pitches	✓✓✓✓	Range of Facilities	✓✓✓✓

Directions

Site is signed from exit 27 of the A35 south of Colmar on the Herrlisheim road (D1).

Charges 2005

Per unit incl. 2 adults, electricity	€ 15,00 - € 19,00
extra adult	€ 3,00 - € 5,00
child (under 7 yrs)	€ 1,50 - € 3,00

Reservations

Made with deposit of € 50 and € 14 fee per week. Tel: 03 89 49 27 28. E-mail: clairvacances@wanadoo.fr

Open

Week before Easter - 25 October.

FR88090 Base de Loisirs du Lac de la Moselotte

Les Amias - B.P. . 34, 88290 Saulxures-sur-Moselotte (Vosges)

This spacious lakeside site, part of a leisure village complex, has 75 generously sized individual hedged pitches. All have electrical hook-ups (10A) and 25 of these are multi-serviced with electricity, water and waste water drain. The site is fully fenced with a security barrier and a key for the pedestrian gates (to site and lakeside) issued by reception. The adjacent 'base de loisirs' has a wide variety of activities on offer, plus supervised swimming in the lake (July/Aug), and pedalo, canoe, kayak and bicycle rental. Also on site are a snack bar and bar (all year), a children's club in high season and fishing in the lake.

Facilities

The heated modern toilet block is light and airy with controllable hot showers, some washbasins in cubicles and good facilities for babies and disabled campers. Shop for basic supplies (July/Aug). Bar/snackbar. Bicycle hire. Fishing. Playground. 30 chalets for rent. Off site: The town is an easy level walk and has all services. Attractions in the region include the Route des Vins in summer, and skiing in winter.

Open

All year.

At a glance

Welcome & Ambience	✓✓✓✓	Location	✓✓✓✓
Quality of Pitches	✓✓✓✓	Range of Facilities	✓✓✓✓

Directions

Saulxures-sur-Moselotte is about 20 km. east of Remiremont. From Remiremont take D417 east to St. Ame, then turn right (east) on D43 towards La Bresse for 10.5 km. Turn left into Saulxures (site is signed), and site entrance is on right after 0.5 km. by lake.

Charges guide

Per person	€ 5,00
pitch	€ 5,00
electricity	€ 5,00 - € 6,00

Reservations

Contact site. Tel: 03 29 24 56 56.
E-mail: info@ville-saulxures-mtte.fr

FR68070 Camping Les Sources

Route des Crêtes, 68700 Wattwiller (Haut-Rhin)

Wattwiller is just off the N83 Alsace 'Route du Vins - Route des Crêtes', tucked away in the forest hills beyond the vineyards, but not far from them, in the popular region of the Vosges. Camping Les Sources occupies a very steep slope above the village under a covering of tall trees. Of the 350 pitches, 100 are occupied by mobile home pitches for rent and 20 by seasonal units, leaving 230 for touring units. All these pitches have electricity (5A) and most are on terraces of gravel hardstanding. The trees mean that the site is very shady, so it can be rather gloomy in overcast or wet weather. A narrow hard road meanders between pitches and is very steep in places making it difficult for large units, although staff will assist with a tractor if required. Les Sources would suit those who are fit (there is much up and down walking) and wish to enjoy the quiet, secluded location although there would appear to be plenty on offer during high season. The site issues a map for walking in the area and a sheet in English with places to visit, and staff will be pleased to give further information.

Facilities

Three old toilet blocks are spread around the site and are fully equipped, but cleaning and maintenance is variable. No provision for disabled visitors who would find the steep roads too difficult. Washing machines and dryers. Shop. Good restaurant. Two swimming pools, one outdoor (July/Aug. only) and another heated and covered (all season). Arena for horse riding activities. Tennis court, table tennis, minigolf and volleyball. Bicycle hire. Entertainment area. Play area. Games room. Internet point. Organised programme with walking, games and creative activities.

Open

9 April - 30 September.

At a glance

Welcome & Ambience	✓✓✓	Location	✓✓✓
Quality of Pitches	✓✓✓	Range of Facilities	✓✓✓✓

Directions

From N66 Thann - Mulhouse road, go north to Cernay and continue through Uffholtz to Wattwiller. Turn left at roundabout on southern edge of village, left again and follow D5 for 2 km. uphill to site.

Charges 2005

Per unit incl. 2 persons	€ 15,00 - € 22,00
extra person	€ 5,00 - € 7,00
child (1-7 yrs)	€ 3,50 - € 4,50
electricity (5A)	€ 3,90

Camping Cheques accepted.
Less 15-20% in low seasons.

Reservations

Made with deposit (€ 80) and fee (€ 8).
Tel: 03 89 75 44 94.
E-mail: camping.les.sources@wanadoo.fr

FR68050 Camping Municipal Pierre de Coubertin

23, rue de Landau, 68150 Ribeauvillé (Haut-Rhin)

The fascinating medieval town of Ribeavillé on the Alsace Wine Route is within walking distance of this attractive, quietly located site. Popular and well run, the site has 226 tourist pitches, all with electricity hook-ups (2/ 6A) and some separated by shrubs or railings. There are tarmac or gravel access roads. This is a site solely for tourists – there are no mobile homes or seasonal units here. The well small shop is open daily for most of the season (hours vary) and this provides bread, basic supplies and some wines. Only breathable groundsheets are permitted.

Facilities

Large, centrally located heated block provides modern facilities with washbasins in cubicles. Baby changing facilities. Large laundry and dishwashing rooms with a generous supply of sinks. A smaller, unit at the far end of the site is opened for July/Aug. Very good facilities for disabled campers at both units. Recycling. Excellent adventure style playground with a rubber base. Tennis court. Two boules pitches. Table tennis. TV room. Off site: Outdoor pool (June-Aug) with reduced price tickets for campers available from reception. Nearby sports complex with indoor pool (all year). Worth a visit is Ferme l'Hirondelle at Ribeauvillé Gare which makes its own cheese, farm shop for milk, cheese, butter, yoghurt, and regional products, and the children can visit the animals whilst you relax on the shady terrace of the bar/restaurant.

At a glance

Welcome & Ambience	✓✓✓✓	Location	✓✓✓✓✓
Quality of Pitches	✓✓✓✓	Range of Facilities	✓✓✓

Directions

Ribeauvillé is about 13 km. southwest of Sèlestat. Site is well signed, turn north off D106 at traffic lights by large car park, east of town centre.

Charges 2004

Per person	€ 3,80
child (0-7 yrs)	€ 1,90
pitch	€ 4,00
electricity	€ 2,50 - € 4,00

Reservations

Not made - arrive early in season. Tel: 03 89 73 66 71.
E-mail: camping.ribeauville@wanadoo.fr

Open

15 March - 15 November.

FR88080 Camping Domaine des Bans

Rue James Wiese, 88430 Corcieux (Vosges)

Corcieux is in the heart of the Vosges mountains, near the lakeside resort of Gerardmer, the Alsace 'Route de Vin' and on the edge of the Ballons des Vosges National Park. Domaine des Bans is a large, busy campsite with around 600 pitches in a country setting, where there are plenty of opportunities to be active. There is a very high percentage of static and tour operator units, but room for about 50 tourist units. Pitches (with electricity, water and drainage), numbered and separated by hedges, vary in size with some on low terraces. There is good shade. Some pitches are tucked away in quiet areas with others nearer to where activities take place. A new pool complex was under construction at the time of our visit. The older swimming pool is partly covered and is surrounded by a terrace with snack bar. Domaine des Bans is not really a site for short stays, but is a base for exploring the varied and interesting countryside, Haut Koenigsbourg Castle with Colmar, Épinal and Strasbourg within range for day trips.

Facilities

Three functional toilet blocks are spread around the site. Some washbasins are in cabins. Cleaning and mainrenance is variable. Shop (15/6-31/8). Bar, restaurant and takeaway (all 1/6-10/9). Swimming pool (1/6-10/9). Playground and open area for ball games. Tennis, table tennis, badminton, minigolf, volleyball and archery. Bicycle hire. Riding. Lakes for fishing and boating. High season entertainment programme including discos (sound-proof underground room), theatre performances and other live music. 'Goats Castle' with about two dozen goats provides interest for children. Off site: Smaller restaurant just outside the site boundary with others a short distance away in the village.

At a glance

Welcome & Ambience	✓✓	Location	✓✓✓✓
Quality of Pitches	✓✓✓	Range of Facilities	✓✓✓

Directions

From D8 St Dié - Gerardmer road, turn west on D60 just north of Gerbepal to Corcieux.

Charges guide

Per person	€ 4,00 - € 7,00
child (under 6 yrs)	€ 2,00 - € 4,00
pitch incl. electricity	€ 12,00 - € 15,00

Reservations

Advised in high season and made with 25% deposit and € 12 fee. Tel: 03 29 51 64 67.
E-mail: les-bans@domaine-des-bans.com

Open

26 April - 25 October.

FR88040 Camping Club du Lac de Bouzey

Mobile homes ▶ page 371

19 rue du Lac, 88390 Sanchey (Vosges)

Camping-Club Lac de Bouzey is eight kilometres west of Epinal, overlooking the lake, at the beginning of the Vosges Massif. It is well placed for exploring the hills, valleys, lakes and waterfalls of the south of Alsace Lorraine. The word 'Club' has been added to the name to indicate the number of activities organised in high season. The 160 individual 100 sqm. back-to-back grass pitches are arranged on either side of tarmac roads with electricity (6 -10A). They are on a gentle slope, divided by trees or beech hedging, under a cover of tall, silver birch trees and some overlook the 130 ha. lake. Units can be close together when the site is busy. The lake has a number of sandy beaches. Many water sports may be enjoyed, from pedaloes to canoes, windsurfing and sailing. The large, imposing building at the entrance to the site houses a restaurant and bar with terraces overlooking the lake. Two bars by the lake would indicate that the lake-side is popular with the public in summer but the camping area is quiet, separated by a road and well back and above the main entrance. An 'all year' site, there is lots going on for teenagers. English is spoken. A 'Sites et Paysages' member.

Facilities

The central sanitary block, partly below ground level, includes a baby room and one for disabled people (although there is up and down hill walking on the site). In winter a small, heated section in the main building with toilet, washbasin and shower is used. Good laundry and dishwashing facilites. Motorcaravan service point. Well stocked shop. Bar, restaurant. Heated swimming pool (1/5-30/9) of an original shape and backed by two sunbathing terraces. Fishing, riding, volleyball, games room, archery and bicycle hire on site. Below ground, under the restaurant, is a sound-proof room for cinema shows and discos for those staying on site only. Staff escort young people back to their pitch at the end of the evening. High season programme of activities for all ages, including excursions, entertainment, sports and a mini-club.
Off site: Golf 8 km.

At a glance

Welcome & Ambience	✓✓✓✓	Location	✓✓✓✓
Quality of Pitches	✓✓✓	Range of Facilities	✓✓✓✓✓

Directions

Site is 8 km. west of Épinal on D460 and is signed from some parts of Épinal. Follow signs for Lac de Bouzey and Sanchey.

Charges 2005

Per unit incl. 2 adults	€ 15,00 - € 23,00
extra person	€ 5,00 - € 7,00
child (4-10 yrs)	free - € 5,00
electricity (6/10A)	€ 4,00 - € 5,00
dog	free - € 3,00

Camping Cheques accepted.

Reservations

Made with deposit (€ 12 per day booked) and fee (€ 25). Tel: 03 29 82 49 41.
E-mail: camping.lac.de.bouzey@wanadoo.fr

Open

All year.

FR88120 Camping Le Clos de la Chaume

21, rue d'Alsace, 88430 Corcieux (Vosges)

Corcieux is in the heart of the 'Ballons des Vosges' and this site would make a good base to explore the area. Within walking distance of the town and on level ground with a small stream adjacent, it is very pleasant. The friendly family owners live on site and do their best to ensure campers have an enjoyable relaxing stay. There are 100 level grassy pitches of varying sizes, with some holiday homes (private and rental) leaving 70 pitches for tourists. All have electricity hook-ups (6/10A) and some are divided by shrubs and trees. Access roads are sandy and large units or American RVs should telephone first to check pitch availability. The site boasts an attractive, well fenced, small swimming pool and an excellent small adventure style playground. The site has some excellent and informative leaflets (available in several languages) which give details of walks and mountain biking routes in the surrounding countryside.

Facilities

Two units provide well maintained facilities including a laundry with washing machines and dryers, a dual purpose family/disabled room and dishwashing sinks. Good motorcaravan service point. Recycling. Reception keeps basic supplies during July/August. Campingaz stocked. Swimming pool (13 x 7m, June-Sept). Games room with table football and a pool table. Table tennis, boules and volleyball. Off site: Bicycle hire 800 m. in the town. Riding 2 km. Fishing 3 or 10 km. Golf 30 km. Corcieux market on Mondays.

Open

1 May - 20 September.

At a glance

Welcome & Ambience	✓✓✓✓	Location	✓✓✓✓
Quality of Pitches	✓✓✓✓	Range of Facilities	✓✓✓✓

Directions

Corcieux is about 17 km. south-south-west of St. Dié des Vosges. Site is on D6, east of town centre, by the town boundary sign.

Charges 2005

Per unit incl. 2 persons	€ 10,80
extra person	€ 3,10
child (0-7 yrs)	€ 1,60
electricity	€ 2,70
animal	€ 1,20

Reservations

Made with deposit (€ 5 per day. Tel: 03 29 50 76 76.
E-mail: info@camping-closdelachaume.com

FR88130 Camping La Vanne de Pierre

5, rue du camping, 88100 St Dié-des-Vosges (Vosges)

La Vanne de Pierre is a neat and attractive site with 118 pitches, many of which are individual with good well trimmed hedges giving plenty of privacy. There are 9 chalets and mobile homes (for rent) and a few seasonal units, leaving around 105 tourist pitches, all multi-serviced with water, drain and electricity hook-up (6/10A). The reception building has been recently refitted and provides a well stocked small shop plus a restaurant/bar with a takeaway facility (all operating all year but opening hours may vary). A small L-shaped outdoor swimming pool (max depth 1.5 m) is well fenced and a programme of children's entertainment is arranged in July and August. The city centre is an easy 2 km. cycle ride or a level walk alongside the river.

Facilities

The main unit is a modern, heated and well tiled building with good facilities including washbasins in cubicles. Three family rooms each with WC, basin, and shower and two similar units fully equipped for disabled campers. Dishwashing room. Laundry room with washing machine and dryer. A second unit, slightly older in style, towards the far end of the site, is opened for July/Aug. Small shop. Bar/restaurant and takeaway. Swimming pool (1/4-30/9, weather permitting). Internet terminal in reception. Campingaz stocked. Bicycle hire. Off site: Golf course, tennis courts (indoor and outdoor), archery, horse riding all within 1 km. Fishing on nearby river. Places to visit include the St Dié Cathedral, Museum Pierre-No'l, Liberty Tower. Two large supermarkets (Cora & LeClerc) on town outskirts have 2.5 m. height barriers. The Intermarché on N420 (Rue d'Alsace) within the town does not.

At a glance

Welcome & Ambience	✓✓✓✓	Location	✓✓✓✓
Quality of Pitches	✓✓✓✓	Range of Facilities	✓✓✓✓

Directions

St Dié is south east of Nancy. Site is east of town centre on the north bank of the river Meurthe and just south of the D82 to Nayemont les Fosses. Site is well signed from most routes around the town.

Charges 2005

Per unit incl. 2 persons	€ 15,00 - € 20,00
extra person	€ 4,00 - € 6,00
child (4-10 yrs)	free - € 4,00
electricity	€ 4,00 - € 5,00

Camping Cheques accepted.

Reservations

Contact site. Tel: 03 29 56 23 56.
E-mail: vannedepierre@wanadoo.fr

Open

All year.

Vendée & Charente

Map 5

It's not only the fine beaches that make this holiday region so appealing. Sleepy fishing harbours, historic ports and charming towns all create a great holiday atmosphere.

We have exercised a little license with this area taking one département from the official Western Loire region, 85 Vendée, and one from the Poitou-Charentes region, 17 Charente-Maritime

With a sunshine record to rival the south of France, the Vendée and Charente regions are among the most popular areas in France. Running alongside the coastal area stretching down from La Rochelle past Rochefort to Royan, it boasts gently shelving sandy beaches, warm shallow waters and fragrant pine forests. Explore the coasts for traditional fishing villages or head inland for fields of sunflowers and unspoilt rural villages.

The Vendée was the centre of the counter-revolutionary movement between 1793 and 1799 and a *'son et lumière'* extravaganza held at the Chateau Puy-du-Fou tells the whole story. Les Sables d'Olonne is its main resort renowned for its excellent sandy beach. The area between the Vendée and Charente, the Marais Poitevin, is one of the most unusual in France – a vast tract of marshland with a thousand or more tree-lined canals and slow moving streams. The port of La Rochelle, with massive medieval towers, buzzes with life and the island of Ré is popular with those seeking beaches and small, quiet ports.

Cuisine of the region

Fish predominates, both fresh water (eel, trout, pike), sea water (shrimps, mussels, oysters). Drink includes light fruity wines from Haut-Poitou, Deux-Sèvres and Charente, and Cognac and Pineau des Charentes – an aperitif of grape juice and Cognac

Cagouilles: snails from Charentes

Chaudrée: ragout of fish cooked in white wine, shallots and butter

Mouclade: mussels cooked in wine, egg yolks and cream, served with Pineau des Charentes

Soupe de moules à la Rochelaise: soup of various fish, mussels, saffron, garlic, tomatoes, onions and red wine

Sourdons: cockles from the Charentes

Places of interest

Marais Poitevin: marshes known as the 'Green Venice'

Angoulême: Hill-top town surrouded by ramparts, cathedral, Renaissance château

La Rochelle: port, Porte de la Grosse Horloge (clock gate), Museum of the New World

Le Puy-du-Fou: 15th-16th century castle, sound and light show involving over 700 participants

Les Sables d'Olonne: fishing port and seaside resort

Noirmoutier: linked to the mainland by a 3 mile bridge

Saint Savin: 17th century abbey, mural painting

Alan Rogers tip

FOR LESS CROWDED BEACHES AND GENERAL PEACE AND QUIET VISIT THE ISLANDS OF RÉ, A HAVEN FOR CYCLISTS, AND OLÉRON.

FR17020 Airotel Le Puits de L'Auture

151 avenue de La Grande-Côte, 17420 St Palais-sur-Mer (Charente-Maritime)

This popular region has a very sunny climate and Le Puits de l'Auture is well situated with the sea outside the gates, just across the road, and a long sandy beach starting 400 m. away. It is situated at the start of a pleasant coastal development down to Royan and beyond. The flower beds at the entrance to the site, with the shop and overnight parking opposite reception, welcome you in. Of the 400 numbered pitches, 240 are for touring units, all these being level and having electricity (6A). A fair number are separated by bushes with some trees giving shade and all have access to water and drainage. Mobile homes occupy the rest of the site, a few used by a tour operator. Considering its close proximity to the beach and its popularity, there is a remarkably calm and relaxed atmosphere and the site is well worth considering.

Facilities

Well maintained toilet blocks are more than adequate for the number of visitors. Most WCs are British type and all washbasins are in cabins, showers are adjustable and hot water is plentiful. Baby baths and showers, and full facilities for disabled people. Washing machines and ample sinks for dishwashing and laundry. Well stocked shop (1/5-30/9). Takeaway and bar (1/6-15/9). Swimming pool complex with sunbathing areas (most attractive with banana plants making a backdrop with a difference). Volleyball. Table tennis. Games room. Play area. Bicycle hire. Barbecues are only allowed in a special area. Dogs are not accepted.
Off site: Riding and golf 800 m. Several restaurants nearby specialise in sea food.

At a glance

Welcome & Ambience	✓✓✓✓	Location	✓✓✓✓✓
Quality of Pitches	✓✓✓✓	Range of Facilities	✓✓✓✓

Directions

Site is on the coast, 2 km. from St Palais and 8 km. from Royan. From Royan take D25 past St Palais following signs for La Palmyre. At two lane junction system turn back left signed Grande Côte and St Palais and site is 800 m.

Charges 2004

Per unit incl. 2 persons	€ 15,50 - € 31,00
with 6A electricity	€ 20,00 - € 35,00
with 10A electricity	€ 23,00 - € 39,00
with water and drainage	€ 30,00 - € 43,00
extra person (over 3 yrs)	€ 5,00 - € 7,00

Reservations

Made for min. 5 days with deposit and fee.
Tel: 05 46 23 20 31.
E-mail: camping-lauture@wanadoo.fr

Open

1 May - 30 September.

FR17040 Camping International Bonne Anse Plage

La Palmyre, 17570 Les Mathes (Charente-Maritime)

On the edge of the Forêt de la Coubre, just beyond the popular resort of La Palmyre, Bonne Anse has a lovely setting amongst pine trees, just a short stroll from an extensive tidal inlet. It is a spacious, gently undulating site, carefully designed to provide 865 level, marked pitches, of which 460 are for touring units, all with electricity. Most are shaded by the pines, the ones nearer the sea less so (these are rather more sandy). The site's amenities are centred around the entrance and reception building and include a restaurant and bar with a spacious outdoor terrace and an impressive pool complex. This forms the social focus of the site and overlooks the boules area with the pool complex opposite. English and Dutch is spoken and rallies welcomed with visit programmes organised. Used by tour operators (35 pitches). With plenty to do for the active, the site is perhaps a little impersonal.

Facilities

Seven sanitary blocks include some washbasins in cabins, British style toilets with a few Turkish, hot and cold showers. Facilities for disabled visitors and babies. Launderette. Washing up and laundry sinks under cover. Motorcaravan service point. Shopping centre (all season) includes a supermarket, excellent delicatessen and takeaway, crêperie, shops for bread and pastries, holiday goods and papers, plus visiting traders' stalls (wines, seafood, etc) in high season. Restaurant and bar (20/6-30/8). Takeaway (19/5-5/9). Splendid, lively swimming pool complex with heated pool (35 x 25 m), three water toboggans and a water slide. Playground, large video games room, TV (satellite), minigolf and table tennis. Enclosed area with an all-weather surface for football, volleyball or basketball. Direct access to cycle tracks (bicycle hire available) that avoid the main road. Entertainment in season. Internet access. Only gas barbecues are permitted. Dogs are not accepted.
Off site: Fishing and riding 1 km. Golf 5 km. Facilities for watersports and tennis nearby. Supervised, safe beaches 500 m. Fitness track.

At a glance

Welcome & Ambience	✓✓✓✓	Location	✓✓✓✓
Quality of Pitches	✓✓✓	Range of Facilities	✓✓✓✓✓

Directions

Leave A10 autoroute at Saintes and head for Royan (N150). In Royan take signs for La Palmyre (D25). At La Palmyre roundabout follow signs for Ronce-les-Bains and site is 1 km. on the left.

Charges 2005

Per unit incl. 1 or 2 persons	€ 30,00
extra person (over 1 yr)	€ 8,20
electricity (6A)	€ 5,80

Reservations

Min. 5 days - phone, fax or write for details.
Tel: 05 46 22 40 90. E-mail: Bonne.Anse@wanadoo.fr

Open

21 May - 5 September.

FR17010 Camping Bois Soleil

Mobile homes page 372

2 avenue de Suzac, 17110 St Georges-de-Didonne (Charente-Maritime)

Close to the sea and the resort of St Georges, Bois Soleil is a fairly large site in three separate parts, with 165 serviced pitches for touring units and a few for tents. All touring pitches are hedged, and have electricity, with water and a drain between every two. There are a few pitches with lockable gates for late night entry and exit. The main part, 'Les Pins', is mature and attractive with ornamental trees and shrubs providing shade. Opposite is 'La Mer' which has direct access to the beach. It has some areas with rather less shade and a raised central area for tents. The sandy beach here is a wide public one, sheltered from the Atlantic breakers although the sea goes out some way at low tide. The third part of the site, 'La Forêt', is for static holiday homes. The areas are well tended with the named pitches (not numbered) cleared and raked between clients and with an all-in charge including electricity and water. This lively site offers something for everyone, whether they like a beach-side spot or a traditional pitch, plenty of activities or the quiet life – it is best to book for the area you prefer. It can be full mid-June - late August.

Facilities

Each area is served by one large sanitary block, supplemented by smaller blocks providing toilets only Another heated block is near reception. Well designed and appointed buildings, cleaned twice daily, they include washbasins in cubicles, facilities for disabled people (WC, basin and shower) and for babies. Launderette. Nursery for babies. Supermarket, bakery (July/Aug) and beach shop. Restaurant and bar by pool. Excellent takeaway (from April). Heated swimming pool. 'Parc des Jeux' with tennis, table tennis, bicycle hire, boules and children's playground. TV room and library. Comprehensive tourist information and entertainment office. Internet terminal. Charcoal barbecues are not permitted but gas ones can be hired by the evening. Pets are not accepted. Off site: Fishing and riding within 500 m. Golf 20 km.

At a glance

Welcome & Ambience	✓✓✓✓✓	Location	✓✓✓✓✓
Quality of Pitches	✓✓✓✓✓	Range of Facilities	✓✓✓✓✓

Directions

From Royan centre take coast road (D25) along the sea-front of St Georges-de-Didonne towards Meschers. Site is signed at roundabout at end of the main beach.

Charges 2004

Per unit incl. 2 persons, 6A electricity	€ 16,00 - € 27,50
3 persons	€ 19,00 - € 27,50
tent incl. 2 persons	€ 13,00 - € 24,50
extra person	€ 3,50 - € 5,00
child (3-7 yrs)	€ 1,50 - € 3,50
electricity (10A)	€ 3,40 - € 5,00

Camping Cheques accepted.
Less 20% outside July/Aug.

Reservations

Made with 25% deposit and € 26 fee.
Tel: 05 46 05 05 94.
E-mail: camping.bois.soleil@wanadoo.fr

Open

3 April - 30 November.

FR17110 Camping Caravaning Monplaisir

Route de la Palmyre, 17570 Les Mathes - La Palmyre (Charente-Maritime)

Monplaisir provides a small, quiet haven in an area with some very hectic campsites. It is ideal for couples or families with young children. The site is quite close to the town set back from the road, and the entrance leads through an avenue of trees, past the owners home to a well kept, garden-like site with many varieties of trees and shrubs. There are only 114 level, marked pitches and all but 9 have electrical connections (6A). On 14 there are caravans for rent and a modern building attached to the site provides flats and studios for rent. There is no shop, bar or restaurant but it is a happy, friendly site with visitors who return year after year.

TRAVEL SERVICE SITE

TO BOOK CALL 0870 405 4055 OR www.alanrogersdirect.com

Facilities

The toilet block has good facilities including some washbasins in cabins and excellent facilities for disabled people. Laundry and dishwashing sinks outside, but under cover. Washing machine and dryer. Ice pack service in reception. Bread delivered daily. TV, games room and library. Heated swimming pool and paddling pool (early May - 30/9). Small play area. Minigolf adjacent (owned by the site). Winter caravan storage. Off site: Fishing 500 m. Riding 1 km. Golf 5 km. Supermarket short walk.

Open

1 April - 1 October.

At a glance

Welcome & Ambience	✓✓✓✓	Location	✓✓✓✓
Quality of Pitches	✓✓✓✓	Range of Facilities	✓✓✓

Directions

Follow the D25 to La Palmyre and, in the town, turn north to Les Mathes. At roundabout turn right to town centre and site is on left. From north on D14 La Tremblade road turn onto D268 signed Les Mathes and Palmyre at roundabout just before Arvert. Keep straight on to Les Mathes when road becomes D141 and turn left (north) at roundabout. Site is 600 m. on left.

Charges 2004

Per unit incl. 2 persons	€ 16,00
incl. 3 persons	€ 18,00
extra person	€ 4,50
baby under 2 yrs	€ 2,00
electricity	€ 3,00
dog	€ 1,50

Less 20% outside July/Aug.

Reservations

Made with deposit and fee, min. stay 4 nights.
Tel: 05 46 22 50 31.

Bois Soleil

Camping ★★★★
Charente-Maritime

Surrounded by pine trees and a sandy beach on the Atlantic Coast, with one direct access to the beach, Bois Soleil proposes to you many attractions like tennis, tabletennis, children playgrounds and entertainment.
Shops, take-away and snack-bar with big TV screen.

Campings-Caravanings Les pieds dans l'eau®
www.lespiedsdansleau.com

Camping Cheque

Camping Qualité

Spring and Summer 2005

2, avenue de Suzac - 17110 ST GEORGES DE DIDONNE
Tel: 0033 546 05 05 94 - Fax: 0033 546 06 27 43
www.bois-soleil.com / e-mail: camping.bois.soleil@wanadoo.fr

FR17140 Castel Camping Sequoia Parc

Mobile homes ▶ page 372

La Josephtrie, 17320 St Just-Luzac (Charente-Maritime)

Approached by an impressive avenue of flowers, shrubs and trees, Séquoia Parc is a Castel site set in the grounds of La Josephtrie, a striking château with beautifully restored outbuildings and a spacious courtyard. The site itself is designed to a high specification with reception in a large, light and airy room retaining its original beams and leading to the courtyard area where you find the shop, bar and restaurant. The pitches are 140 sq.m. in size with 6A electricity connections and separated by young shrubs. The pool complex with water slides, A large paddling pool and sunbathing area is impressive. The site has some 400 mobile homes and chalets, of which 125 are used by tour operators. This is a popular site with a children's club and entertainment all season and reservation is necessary in high season.

TRAVEL SERVICE SITE

TO BOOK CALL 0870 405 4055 OR www.alanrogersdirect.com

Facilities

Three luxurious toilet blocks, maintained to a high standard, include units with washbasin and shower, a laundry, dishwashing sinks, facilities for disabled visitors and baby baths. Motorcaravan service point. Gas supplies. Shop. Restaurant/bar and takeaway. Impressive swimming pool complex with paddling pool. Tennis, volleyball, football field. Games and TV rooms. Bicycle hire. Pony trekking. Organised entertainment all season.

Open

15 May - 11 September, with all services.

At a glance

Welcome & Ambience	✓✓✓✓	Location	✓✓✓✓
Quality of Pitches	✓✓✓✓✓	Range of Facilities	✓✓✓✓✓

Directions

Site is 2.5 km. southeast of Marennes. From Rochefort take D733 south for 12 km. Turn west on D123 to Ile d'Oléron. Continue for 12 km. and turn southeast on D728 towards Saintes. Site signed (1 km. on the left).

Charges 2004

Per unit incl. 2 persons and electricity	€ 15,00 - € 35,00
extra person	€ 6,00 - € 8,00
child (3-7 yrs)	€ 3,00 - € 5,00

Camping Cheques accepted.

Reservations

Made with 25% deposit and € 30 booking fee.
Tel: 05 46 85 55 55. E-mail: sequoia.parc@wanadoo.fr

FR17050 Camping L'Orée du Bois

225 route de la Bouverie, La Fouasse, 17570 Les Mathes (Charente-Maritime)

L'Orée du Bois has 388 pitches of about 100 sq.m. in a very spacious, pinewood setting. There are 150 for touring units, mainly scattered amongst the permanent chalets and tents. They include 40 large pitches with hardstanding and individual sanitary facilities (built in small, neat blocks of four and containing your own shower, toilet, washbasin and dishwashing sink). The pitches are on flat, fairly sandy ground, separated by trees, shrubs and growing hedges and all have electrical connections (6A). The forest pines offer some shade. A very lively site in high season, suitable for all age groups, it can be noisy but is tranquil in low season with large, spacious pitches.

Facilities

Four main toilet blocks have good fittings, including some washbasins in cabins. Three blocks have laundry rooms. Fully equipped units for disabled people. Well stocked shop. Excellent bar, restaurant, crêperie and takeaway. Large swimming pools, including water slide and paddling pool (proper trunks, not shorts). Play areas. Tennis court, boules, volleyball, table tennis, football and basketball areas. Games room and TV lounge (with satellite). Bicycle hire. Twice weekly discos and free, all day children's entertainment in July/Aug. Internet access. Barbecues allowed in special areas. Off site: Riding 300 m. Fishing 4 km. Golf 20 km.

Open

12 April - 28 September.

At a glance

Welcome & Ambience	✓✓✓✓	Location	✓✓✓
Quality of Pitches	✓✓✓	Range of Facilities	✓✓✓✓

Directions

From north follow D14 La Tremblade road. At roundabout just before Arvert turn onto D268 signed Les Mathes and La Palmyre. Site is on right in Fouasse. From the south, at Royan take D25 towards La Palmyre and in the town turn north to Les Mathes. At first roundabout in Les Mathes follow sign for Fouasse and La Tremblade. Site is on left after 2 km.

Charges 2004

Per unit incl. 2 persons	€ 15,00 - € 38,00
extra person (over 3 yrs)	€ 6,00

Camping Cheques accepted.
Min. stay 7 days in high season.

Reservations

Made with 30% deposit plus fee (€ 21).
Tel: 05 46 22 42 43.
E-mail: info@camping-oree-du-bois.fr

FR17150 Camping Municipal du Château Benon

17170 Benon (Charente-Maritime)

Benon was once the capital of this area and had strong English connections, its castle being built in 1096, although now all that remains is a single round tower. However, the mayor and villagers are still anxious to welcome English visitors and local information is provided in reception (part of the toilet block). The municipal site is beautifully kept, with open and shady areas and is ideal for those wanting a peaceful stay. There are 70 pitches on neat grass, 40 with 10A electricity, although many are sloping or uneven. This is a pretty, quiet site where visitors are made welcome.

Facilities

The reasonably modern toilet block is fully equipped, with hot water always available and facilities for disabled visitors. Tennis court. Reception may only be open in the mornings. Off site: Village 250 m. La Rochelle is within easy reach (25 minutes) for shopping, beaches, etc. Riding 5 km. Fishing or bicycle hire 7 km. Golf 13 km.

Open

1 May - 30 September.

At a glance

Welcome & Ambience	✓✓✓✓	Location	✓✓✓✓
Quality of Pitches	✓✓✓✓	Range of Facilities	✓✓✓

Directions

Benon is 28 km. east of La Rochelle on the N11. Turn south at 'Relais de Benon', Benon 2 km. and site is in centre of village.

Charges 2004

Per adult	€ 2,50
pitch	€ 1,50
electricity	€ 2,10

No credit cards.

Reservations

Advised for 14 July - 15 Aug; contact the Mairie. Tel: 05 46 01 61 48. E-mail: mairie-benon@smic17.fr

FR17160 Camping Le Clos Fleuri

8 impasse du Clos Fleuri, 17600 Médis (Charente-Maritime)

Camping Le Clos Fleuri really does live up to its name. The profusion of different trees and, in the more open area, the lawns and flower beds give this small site a very rural atmosphere. There is always a warm welcome from the Devais family who created the site in 1974. The 123 touring pitches are mostly of generous size (a little uneven in places), varying in the amount of shade they receive (from full sun to well shaded) and 100 have electrical connections. The bar/restaurant is a converted barn with chalk and stone walls and a high timbered ceiling - a cool haven on hot days and a very convivial venue for evening gatherings and entertainment. The surrounding countryside is very pleasant with crops of sunflowers, wheat and maize, while beaches of all sorts are within easy reach. All in all the Clos Fleuri combines a great deal of charm, beauty and friendliness with a location from which the attractions of the Charente Maritime may be discovered.

Facilities

Toilet facilities are in two blocks which are kept scrupulously clean. One block is segregated male and female, the other is unisex with each unit in its own cubicle. Baby baths, washing machines and dryers. Attractive small pool with separate paddling pool and sunbathing terrace. Sauna. Good shop with fresh meat and vegetables, restaurant (both 1/7-31/8) and bar (1/7-15/9) are housed in the old farm buildings, which form the nucleus of the site. In high season there are twice weekly 'soirees' and boules and archery competitions. Minigolf. Small football pitch. Security barrier closed at night. Off site. Shops in Médis 2 km.

Open

1 June - 15 September.

At a glance

Welcome & Ambience	✓✓✓✓✓	Location	✓✓✓✓
Quality of Pitches	✓✓✓✓	Range of Facilities	✓✓✓✓

Directions

Médis is on the N150 from Saintes, halfway between Saujon and Royan. Site is signed to south at various points in Médis and is about 2 km. outside the village.

Charges 2005

Per pitch incl. 2 adults	€ 23,50
extra person	€ 7,20
child (2-7 yrs)	€ 5,00
electricity (5/10A)	€ 4,10 - € 5,30
dog	€ 3,20

Less 20% in June and Sept.

Reservations

Essential for high season and made with deposit (€ 100) and fee (€ 20). Tel: 05 46 05 62 17. E-mail: clos-fleuri@wanadoo.fr

FR17180 Haven Camping La Pignade

45 avenue de Monard, 17390 Ronce les Bains (Charente-Maritime)

If you are looking for a busy, active well appointed site offering a wide range of facilities and daily entertainment all season, then La Pignade, a Haven Europe park, may be just what you want. The 500 or so pitches, of which 150 are reserved for tourers, are located around well spaced pine trees which, while giving some shade, also give an open aspect. The ground is sandy but site roads are tarmac so dust is not a problem. The pitches are generous in size, most separated by low, evergreen hedges with planting continuing. The number of mobile homes is increasing each year. Entertainment and catering facilities are central, well constructed and maintained to a high standard with an impressive range of pools and water slides. The English speaking French staff are welcoming and helpful. Good sandy beaches are nearby, while the fascinating oyster producing area of Marennes is only a few kilometres away. Also close by is the island of Oléron, reached by a magnificent road bridge, where there are more beaches and a number of historic buildings, pretty villages and excellent facilities for cycling and horse riding. All in all La Pignade offers a great holiday base in an area full of attractive and interesting places.

Facilities

Four refurbished, fully equipped toilet blocks are centrally placed in four separate areas. Open style dishwashing and laundry sinks. Baby packs for hire. Washing machines and dryers. Separate provision for disabled people. Large mini-market and gift shop. Choice of food outlets, waiter service restaurant or takeaway. Spacious well stocked and attractively staffed bar. Barbecue areas. Swimming pools (heated and supervised). Practice golf, crazy golf, archery and bicycle hire (charged). Clubs for children (free all season) and a daily programme of games, competitions, activities and entertainment. Dogs and other animals are not accepted. Off site: Nearby riding, tennis and watersports.

At a glance

Welcome & Ambience	✓✓✓✓✓	Location	✓✓✓✓
Quality of Pitches	✓✓✓✓	Range of Facilities	✓✓✓✓✓

Directions

Ronce-les-Bains is on the D25 north of La Tremblade and the D728 from Marennes. The site is clearly signed from all directions.

Charges 2004

Per pitch incl. 2 persons with electricity	€ 13,00 - € 27,00
extra person	€ 3,00 - € 6,00

Reservations

Accepted at any time for min. 4 days; no booking fee. Contact site or Haven Europe in the UK on 0870 242 7777 for information or reservation.
Tel: 05 46 36 15 35.
E-mail: europe.website@bourne-leisure.co.uk

Open

30 April - 19 September.

FR17170 Domaine des Charmilles

St Laurent de la Prée, 17450 Fouras (Charente-Maritime)

Fouras is a relatively little known resort situated between La Rochelle and Rochefort which retains much of the charm missing from larger, more heavily commercialised resorts in the area. Les Charmilles is located about a mile from the town centre. It is very easily accessed from the main La Rochelle to Rochefort road (N137). There are 270 large pitches, of which only 60 are touring pitches. The remainder are occupied by mobile homes, chalets and tour operators. All touring pitches have electricity (10A) and many have water and drainage. Ten are specically for disabled visitors. Roughly a third are well shaded, with the remainder in a sunnier, more open setting. The latter area is also away from the busy road which runs past the front of the site. A variety of entertainment is provided in high season which can mean that the site is noisy until at least midnight. Recent improvements include the attractive refurbishment of the bar and restaurant, the upgrading of the main pool with extra slides and a new pool with sliding doors. These changes have created a high quality focal point for the site.

TRAVEL SERVICE SITE

TO BOOK CALL 0870 405 4055 OR www.alanrogersdirect.com

Facilities

Three modern toilet blocks provide most washbasins in cubicles and facilities for babies and disabled people. Washing machines and dryers. Small shop (1/6-15/9). Bar and takeaway (15/5-15/9). Restaurant (1/6-15/9). Heated swimming pools, water slides and large sunbathing terrace (15/5-30/9). Sauna. Jacuzzi. Good playground. Minigolf, table tennis and multisports court. Bicycle hire. Entertainment. Minibus service to the beach in July/Aug. Charcoal barbecues are not permitted. Off site: Fishing 3 km. Golf 5 km. Riding 15 km.

Open

1 April - 25 September.

At a glance

Welcome & Ambience	✓✓✓✓	Location	✓✓✓
Quality of Pitches	✓✓✓✓	Range of Facilities	✓✓✓✓

Directions

Leave N137 at exit for Fouras and St Laurent de la Prée, joining D937 towards Fouras. Site is on left in about 800 m.

Charges 2004

Per pitch incl. 2 adults	€ 12,00 - € 25,00
extra adult	€ 5,50
child (under 5 yrs)	€ 3,50
with electricity	€ 15,50 - € 28,50
animal	€ 2,90

Reservations

Necessary for high season with deposit and fee.
Tel: 05 46 84 00 05.
E-mail: charmilles17@wanadoo.fr

FR17200 Camping-Caravaning Au Fil de l'Eau

6 Rue de Courbiac, 17100 Saintes (Charente-Maritime)

Saintes is a 2,000 year old Gallo-Roman city, well worth a couple of days to visit the Cathedral, the Abbey, the Arch of Germanicus, the Amphitheatre and several museums, all of which are within walking distance of the campsite (reception can provide a city map). Do take a stroll through the well tended, very pretty public gardens by the riverside. There is a fresh produce market in the town centre every morning except Monday. This pleasant, well run site has 214 mostly shady and generally grassy level pitches, with 132 electric hook-ups, and a few mobile homes and caravans for rent.

Facilities

The main toilet block is a large and modern building, with two smaller older units opened at peak times. Washbasins in cubicles. Facilities for disabled people are in a unit by the laundry building. Motorcaravan service point. Bar, restaurant and takeaway (July/Aug). TV room. Boules pitch, table tennis, badminton, volleyball and minigolf. Small playground. Off site: Adjacent open air Olympic-sized swimming pool complex is free for campers (23/6-10/9).

Open

1 May - 30 September.

At a glance

Welcome & Ambience	✓✓✓✓	Location	✓✓✓
Quality of Pitches	✓✓✓✓	Range of Facilities	✓✓✓✓

Directions

From east and northeast follow signs for town centre and site, turning right after crossing river. From all other directions, use bypass following signs for N137 La Rochelle to large roundabout at northern end and turn right signed town centre and Camping Municipal (at this roundabout coming from La Rochelle on N137, go straight on). Turn left at next roundabout, ahead at two more and right at next.

Charges 2004

Per adult	€ 4,20
pitch	€ 4,30
electricity	€ 3,20

Reservations

Advisable for high season. Tel: 05 46 93 08 00.

FR17190 Le Logis du Breuil

17570 St Augustin-sur-Mer (Charente-Maritime)

Space - no, not the final frontier, but the first impression on arrival at this impressive campsite. Between the site buildings and pool, and the camping area is a 200 metre expanse of farm pasture where (on different areas) cattle graze and children play. The camping areas themselves are set among rows of mature and shady trees which give a very restful, dappled effect to the tents, caravans and grassy pitches. The 320 pitches (with 3/6A electricity) are very large and have direct access to wide, unpaved alleys, which lead on to the few tarmac roads around the site. The campsite amenities are centred around the reception area and pool complex. The area around the site is very pleasant agricultural land and the beaches of the Atlantic coast are nearby, as are the oyster and the mussel beds of Marennes and La Tremblade. The Gagnard family started the campsite about 25 years ago and obviously take great pride in what it has now become a peaceful, friendly and very pleasant site from which to explore a delightful holiday area. A 'Sites et Paysages' member.

Facilities

Four very well maintained toilet blocks are well spaced around the camping area. Laundry facilities. Shop, bar and snacks and takeaway (franchised) are well run. Swimming pools. No evening entertainment. Play area. Indoor area providing archery, pool and table tennis. Bicycle hire. Tennis and basketball. Free archery. Excursions organised.

Open

1 May - 30 September.

At a glance

Welcome & Ambience	✓✓✓✓✓	Location	✓✓✓✓
Quality of Pitches	✓✓✓✓✓	Range of Facilities	✓✓✓✓

Directions

On approaching Royan follow signs to St Palais sur Mer, bypassing Royan centre. Continue straight on past first set of traffic lights and roundabout. At second set of lights turn right towards St Augustin. Site is 2 km on left, before village centre.

Charges 2005

Per unit incl. 2 adults	€ 13,60 - € 16,30
with 3A electricity	€ 16,95 - € 19,90
extra person	€ 3,20 - € 5,00

Reservations

Advised for high season and made with deposit (€ 46) and booking fee (€ 8). Tel: 05 46 23 23 45.
E-mail: camping.Logis-du-Breuil@wanadoo.fr

FR17260 Camping Le Cormoran

Route de Radia, Ars en Ré, 17590 Ile de Ré (Charente-Maritime)

This site has been recommended by one of our readers, and we plan to include a full report on this popular family site in a future inspection programme. Le Cormoran is located 500 m. from the sea and offers 140 shady pitches, most with electrical connections, and a good range of leisure facilities, of which the swimming pool is the focal point. Mobile homes for rent.

Facilities

Bar, restaurant and takeaway meals, Small shop. Swimming pool (covered in low season), Gym and sauna. Bicycle hire. Tennis. Volleyball, Games room. Play area. Entertainment programme in high season. Off site: Nearest beach 500 m. Riding 4 km. Ars-en-Ré 800 m. (shops, restaurants etc).

Open

3 April - 3 October.

Directions

Cross the toll bridge from La Rochelle onto the Ile de Re and continue on the D735 to Ars en Ré, from where the site is well signposted.

Charges 2004

Per unit incl. 2 persons	€ 15,50 - € 22,50
fextra person	€ 5,15 - € 10,00
child (0-10 yrs)	€ 3,10 - € 10,00
electricity (10A)	€ 3,75

Reservations

Contact site. Tel: 05 46 29 46 04.
E-mail: info@cormoran.com

FR17220 Camping La Brande

Route des Huitres, 17480 Le Château-d'Oléron (Charente-Maritime)

A quality site, run and maintained to the highest standard, La Brande offers an ideal holiday environment on the delightful Ile d'Oleron, famed for its oysters. La Brande is situated on the oyster route and close to a sandy beach. The Barcat family ensure that their visitors not only enjoy quality facilities, but Gerard Barcat offers guided bicycle tours and canoe trips. This way you discover the nature, oyster farming, vineyards and history of Oléron, which is joined to the mainland by a three kilometres bridge. Pitches here are generous and mostly separated by hedges and trees, the greater number for touring outfits. All are on level grassy terrain and have electricity hook-ups, some are fully serviced. A feature of this site is the heated swimming pool which can be covered under a sliding roof in cool weather and is open all season. The many activities during the high season, plus the natural surroundings, make this an ideal choice for families.

Facilities

Three heated, bright and clean sanitary blocks have spacious, well equipped showers and washbasins (mainly in cabins). Baby bath/changing area. Excellent facilities for people with disabilities (separate large shower, washbasin and WC). Laundry room with hot water and sinks, plus washing machine and dryers. Drive over motorcaravan service point. Restaurant/takeaway and bar in July/Aug. Shop with basics in low season, but well stocked in main season. Play area on grass. Football field, tennis, minigolf, fishing and archery. Bicycle hire. Canoe hire. Internet access. Off site: Beach 300 m.

Open

15 March - 15 November.

At a glance

Welcome & Ambience	✓✓✓✓	Location	✓✓✓✓
Quality of Pitches	✓✓✓✓	Range of Facilities	✓✓✓✓✓

Directions

After crossing bridge to L'Ile d'Oléron turn right towards Le Château d'Oléron. Continue through village and follow sign for Route des Huitres. Site is on left after 3 km.

Charges 2004

Per unit incl. 2 persons	€ 16,00 - € 24,00
large 125 sq.m. pitch	€ 16,00 - € 32,00
extra person	€ 5,00 - € 7,00
electricity (6-10A)	€ 3,20 - € 3,80
dog	€ 2,50

Camping Cheques accepted.

Reservations

Advised in high season and made with 25% deposit and € 16 fee. Tel: 05 46 47 62 37.
E-mail: info@camping-labrande.com

FR17210 Camping Interlude

Plage de Gros Jonc, 17580 Le Bois-Plage-en-Ré (Charente-Maritime)

The island of Ré, which is no more than 30 km. long and 5 km. wide, lies off the coast at La Rochelle and is reached by a toll bridge. It is a paradise for cyclists, walkers and those who wish to commune with nature. Camping Interlude enjoys a pleasant location with access to an excellent beach. A popular site even in low season, (may become very crowded with overstretched facilities in high season), it is has 387 pitches, 136 of which are for touring units. Pitches are sand based, vary in size from 80-120 sq.m. and are mostly divided by hedged on part undulating, sandy terrain. Many are placed to the left of the site in a pine forest setting, others mingle with the tour operators and mobile homes. Choosing a shady pitch is not a problem for there are many trees. Interlude makes an ideal base for exploring the island of Re and for those planning an early holiday, the facilities on site are all operational from the beginning of April. It is a suitable site for all ages, with plenty of recreational pursuits to keep families happy, both on and off site.

Facilities

Two modern, clean and well equipped sanitary blocks provide washbasins in cabins and some shower units suitable for families with twin washbasins. Baby room, child size toilets, en suite facilities for disabled visitors, laundry sinks, washing machines and dryers, plus dishwashing areas. Motorcaravan service point. Restaurant/bar and shop (all season). Two swimming pools, one outdoor and one inside. Play area. Volleyball, boules. Organised events and entertainment for young and old. Games/TV room. Tennis courts. Bicycle hire. Communal barbecues. New multi-sport area.

Open

9 April - 2 November.

At a glance

Welcome & Ambience	✓✓✓✓	Location	✓✓✓✓✓
Quality of Pitches	✓✓✓	Range of Facilities	✓✓✓✓✓

Directions

After crossing toll bridge to Ile de Ré follow sign for Le Bois Plage. Turn left at first roundabout and continue straight on at next two, then left at fourth roundabout where site is signed.

Charges 2005

Per unit incl. 2 persons, 100 sq.m. pitch	€ 17,00 - € 27,50
120 sq.m. pitch incl. water and electricity	€ 21,00 - € 31,50
140 sq.m. pitch incl. drainage also	€ 21,00 - € 34,50
extra person	€ 3,90 - € 9,15
pet	€ 2,00 - € 7,00

Camping Cheques accepted.

Reservations

Advisable all season. Tel: 05 46 09 18 22.
E-mail: infos@interlude.fr

FR17230 Camping de L'Océan

Mobile homes page 374

La Passe, La Couarde sur Mer, 17670 Ile de Ré (Charente-Maritime)

L'Océan lies close to the centre of the Ile de Ré, just 50 metres from a sandy beach. There are 338 pitches here with around 200 for touring units, the remainder occupied by mobile homes and chalets. The camping area is well shaded and pitches are of a reasonable size, most with electricity (10A) and 60 with water and drainage. Pride of place goes to the large heated swimming pool which is surrounded by an attractive sunbathing terrace. Bicycle hire is popular here as the island offers over 100 km. of interesting cycle routes. There is a pleasant bar/restaurant with a terrace overlooking the pool. In peak season a range of entertainment is organised including disco evenings. Future plans include a new toilet block, internet access in the bar and an indoor pool.

Facilities

The sanitary blocks are modern and well maintained with facilities for disabled visitors and a dog shower. Shop. Bar/restaurant and takeaway (all season). Swimming pool. Riding. Bicycle hire. Tennis court. Fishing pond adjacent. Basketball. Play area. Charcoal barbecues are not permitted. Off site: South facing beach 50 m. La Couarde (nearest restaurants, shops etc.) 2.5 km. Golf 5 km.

Open

25 March - 25 September.

At a glance

Welcome & Ambience	✓✓✓✓	Location	✓✓✓✓
Quality of Pitches	✓✓✓✓	Range of Facilities	✓✓✓✓

Directions

After crossing the toll bridge onto the island, join D735 which runs along the north side of the island until you pass La Couarde. The site is 2.5 km beyond the village (in the direction of Ars en Re).

Charges 2004

Per unit incl. 2 persons	€ 14,00 - € 35,00
extra person	€ 4,00 - € 8,80
electricity	€ 5,00
dog	€ 1,70 - € 4,20

Camping Cheques accepted.

Reservations

Contact site. Tel: 05 46 29 87 70.
E-mail: campingdelocean@wanadoo.fr

FR17060 Airotel Oléron

Domaine de Montravail, 17480 Le Château-d (Charente-Maritime)

The site is on the outskirts of Le Château d'Oléron, shortly after leaving the bridge joining Ile d'Oléron to the mainland. The entrance appears to be in a residential area but the site itself is surrounded by paddocks and backs onto the Marais. With the horses, stables and indoor riding school on one side of the approach and the geese and ducks on the other it has a rural feeling. The many peacocks add novelty, and noise! This is a mature site with about 270 pitches of medium to large size, with varying degrees of shade provided by an attractive selection of trees and ornamental shrubs. It is well laid out with the touring pitches (130) and mobile homes each in several separate groups. Most touring pitches have electricity (10A) and four have their own water and waste as well. There is an attractive swimming pool complex and a range of other sporting facilities, with a full entertainment programme in high season. This family run site offers a friendly, attentive, laid-back atmosphere in which to enjoy campsite life – especially equestrian activities – and the exploration of the island with its fine sandy beaches on the Atlantic coast and the miles of flat tracks for walking, cycling or horse riding.

Facilities

Two toilet blocks are well maintained and clean with toilets of both styles, and washbasins in cabins. Washing machines plus laundry and dishwashing sinks at each block. Motorcaravan service point. Fridge hire. Well stocked shop with pleasant staff. Bar, restaurant and takeaway (15/6-15/9). TV and games room. Internet access in reception. Heated swimming and paddling pools. Two tennis courts. Table tennis and play area. Bicycle hire. Riding (hard hats can be supplied, but probably best to take your own).

Open

15 April - 30 September.

At a glance

Welcome & Ambience	✓✓✓✓	Location	✓✓✓✓
Quality of Pitches	✓✓✓✓	Range of Facilities	✓✓✓✓

Directions

Immediately after the viaduct turn right onto the D734 to Le Château and follow camp signs at junctions.

Charges 2004

Per unit incl. 2 persons	€ 13,00 - € 21,00
extra person	€ 4,00 - € 6,00
electricity (8A)	€ 3,80
dog	€ 2,40

Reservations

Made for exact dates (min. about one week in Aug.) with deposit (€71,65) and booking fee (€19,82). Tel: 05 46 47 61 82.
E-mail: info@camping-airotel-oleron.com

FR17270 Camping L'Anse des Pins

397 Chemin Rateau Domino, 17190 Saint Georges d'Oleron (County)

Recommended by our agent, we hope to include a full report on this popular seaside campsite in a future inspection programme. L'Anse des Pins is a bustling site on the Ile d'Oléron, just 50 m. from the beach. Pitches are mostly sunny, and most offer electricity - some are also equipped with water and drainage. Mobile homes for rent.

Facilities

Restaurant and takeaway meals. Small shop. Swimming pool and childrens' pool. Archery and tennis. Playground. Table tennis. Games room. Entertainment programme in high season. Off site: Beach 50 m,. Riding. Fishing, oyster beds, Fort Boyard, La Palmyre zoo.

Open

1 April - 15 October.

Directions

Having crossed the bridge onto the Ile d'Oléron, continue on the D734 to St Georges d'Oléron, from where the site is well signed.

Charges 2004

Per unit incl. 2 persons and electricity	€ 23,00
extra person	€ 6,00
child (0-4 yrs)	€ 3,00
water and drainage	€ 3,00

Reservations

Contact site. Tel: 05 46 76 55 97.
E-mail : camping-apv@wanadoo.fr

FR85510 Camping Le Bois Joli

2 rue de Châteauneuf, 85710 Bois de Céné (Vendée)

This site is a hidden gem in a small village away from the hustle and bustle of the seaside resorts. Suitable for people looking for a quiet holiday, it is still within driving distance of the Vendée coast (20 km). A warm welcome is given by the English speaking Urvoy family, who make every effort to make your stay enjoyable. On site is a small lake with free fishing (carp and eels), and a very large sports field (with a new portacabin style toilet block). The site also has a small swimming pool and paddling pool. A local farmer visits the site three times a week offering local produce. There are 130 pitches of which 90 are for touring units. All pitches have 6A electricity, although not every pitch is serviced with water.

Facilities

Three toilet blocks - old, but with modem, bright tiles and very clean. All are unisex with some washbasins in cubicles, some controllable showers, two baby baths, two washing machines, dishwashing and laundry sinks. Bar with evening entertainment. Children's activities. Good play area with swings. Table tennis. Tennis court. Volleyball. Petanque. Bicycle hire. Off site: Supermarket in the village (two minutes walk). Walking, cycling and canoeing near. Riding 5 km.

Open

Easter - 15 September.

At a glance

Welcome & Ambience	✓✓✓✓	Location	✓✓✓✓
Quality of Pitches	✓✓✓✓	Range of Facilities	✓✓✓✓

Directions

From Challans take D58 direct to Bois de Céné (10 km). Turn left at road junction in centre of village and site is immediately on right.

Charges 2004

Per pitch incl. 2 persons	€ 9,00 - € 13,20
with electricity (6A)	€ 10,70 - € 15,90
extra person	€ 2,60 - € 3,60
child (under 7 yrs)	€ 1,35 - € 1,90
animal	€ 1,45 - € 2,00

Reservations

Advised and made with deposit (€ 80 per week) and fee (€ 15). Tel: 02 51 68 20 05.
E-mail: campingboisjoli@free.fr

FR85200 Camping La Petite Boulogne

12 rue du Stade, 85670 St Etienne-du-Bois (Vendée)

Set in countryside 24 km. northwest of La Roche sur Yon, St Etienne-du-Bois is a quiet village, well away from the hustle and bustle of the big Vendée resorts. This campsite, owned by the local council, has 40 grassy pitches (most slightly sloping), all with electricity, water and drainage. Pitches are marked by low hedges giving the site an open and sunny aspect. Although the site is inland, it is only 20 km. to the coast with its large sandy beaches, but there are also many attractions and places to visit inland in the Vendée, and this good value municipal site provides a great base from which to explore the whole region.

Facilities

The modern, heated toilet block includes some washbasins in cabins. Laundry and dishwashing sinks. Room for disabled people with toilet and shower. Washing machine and dryer. Reception sells bread and a few other essentials. Small unheated pool (June - Aug). TV room. Table tennis. Small play area. Two free tennis courts. Bicycle hire. Daily events in area listed in reception and occasional animation organised in high season, introducing the region and its produce. Off site: Open-air, heated pool nearby. Bar and restaurant both few minutes walk away in village. Fishing possible in the nearby Petite Boulogne river. Volleyball and petanque at local sports centre (300 m). Supermarket 8 km at Legé.

At a glance

Welcome & Ambience	✓✓✓✓	Location	✓✓✓✓
Quality of Pitches	✓✓✓✓	Range of Facilities	✓✓✓

Directions

From Legé take D978 south towards Palluau for 7 km. then turn left on D94 towards St Etienne-du-Bois. Go straight through village and, as you come out the other side, cross a small bridge over the river. Site is 50 m. further on, on the right.

Charges guide

Per unit incl. 2 persons	€ 10,00
extra person	€ 3,00
child (under 7 yrs)	€ 2,00
dog	€ 2,00
electricity (6A)	€ 2,50

No credit cards.

Reservations

Made with deposit (€ 31). Tel: 02 51 34 54 51.
E-mail: la.petite.boulogne@wanadoo.fr

Open

1 May - 31 October.

FR85540 Domaine de L'Eden

La Railliere, 85600 Boissière de Montaigu (Vendée)

Hidden in the Haut Bocage area of the Vendée region, Le Domaine de l'Eden is a haven of tranquility in the traditional manner. This 35 acre site has 56 large, level touring pitches made up of grass and sand (long electricity cables may be needed) with mature trees providing varying amounts of shade. There are 44 mobile home pitches scattered throughout the site. The majority of visitors are French, many returning year after year, and there are no tour operators on the site. A limited programme of entertainment is provided in July and August and a good network of well marked footpaths and cycleways is easily accessible. Le Domaine de l'Eden offers the chance to taste the real France for oneself.

Facilities

Two well-maintained, heated toilet blocks include some washbasins in cabins; lighting is by time switch. Facilities for disabled visitors are opened on request. Washing machine and dryer. Dishwashing under cover. Small shop (11/4-31/10). Restaurant (1/6-30/9). Bar with TV open all year. Games room. Heated swimming pool with paddling area (15/6-15/9). Play areas. Tennis courts, multisports area, football pitch, minigolf and fitness course. Fishing in lake. Off site: Walking and cycling trails. Puy du Fou theme park.

Open

All year.

At a glance

Welcome & Ambience	✓✓✓	Location	✓✓✓✓
Quality of Pitches	✓✓✓✓	Range of Facilities	✓✓✓✓

Directions

Site is signed from N137 Nantes - La Rochelle road, 7 km. south of Montaigu and 30 km. north of Chantonnay. At tourist office and Arrivé factory, take D62 northeast for 5 km. and follow signs.

Charges 2005

Per unit incl. 1 or 2 persons,	€ 11,50 - € 14,50
with services	€ 14,50 - € 17,50
extra person	€ 4,00 - € 4,10
child (2-7 yrs)	€ 2,00 - € 2,10
animal	€ 2,00

Reservations

Contact site. Tel: 02 51 41 62 32.
E-mail: domaine.eden@free.fr

FR85630 Camping Maison Blanche au Perrier

85300 Le Perrier (Vendée)

A new venture in 2003 for an experienced campsite owner, Maison Blanche is undergoing a replanting program to eventually provide more shade and privacy to the 176 grassy touring pitches here. All are flat and of good size, most have electricity (6A) and water, but there are no dividing hedges. The pool is attractive and there are two tennis courts, an off site football field and small playground. When we visited, the site was peaceful for high season, with no evening entertainment. A young English family described the site as a 'Little Paradise'! Situated only 500 m. from the small town of Le Perrier, bars and restaurants are an easy stroll away, whilst Challans and St Jean de Monts (both about six kilometres) offer a wider range of facilities.

Facilities

Two toilet blocks provide washbasins (some open, some in cubicles), British and Turkish style toilets, showers, a baby room and toilet for disabled campers. Washing machine. No bar or restaurant, but a limited takeaway is provided. Heated swimming pool. TV/games room. Bicycle hire.Tennis. Football in a separate field. Some children's entertainment in high season. Off site: Small town 500 m. Beach within 6 km.

Open

1 May - 15 September.

At a glance

Welcome & Ambience	✓✓✓✓	Location	✓✓✓✓
Quality of Pitches	✓✓✓✓	Range of Facilities	✓✓✓✓

Directions

From the D753 St Jean de Monts - Challans road, at traffic lights in the small town centre, turn north on D59. Turn left almost immediately and site is straight ahead.

Charges 2004

Per unit incl. 2 persons	€ 9,50 - € 10,60
with electricity	€ 12,50 - € 13,60
extra person	€ 3,30
child (under 7 yrs)	€ 1,90
animal	€ 1,00

Reservations

Made with 25% deposit and € 20 fee.
Tel: 02 51 49 39 23.
E-mail: camping.maisonblanche@wanadoo.fr

FR85370 Camping Les Mancellières

Route de Longeville-sur-Mer, 85440 Avrillé (Vendée)

This is a family run site on the edge of the small town of Avrillé, on the road between La Rochelle and Noirmoutiers, yet only a short drive from some of the delightful beaches of the southern Vendée. It is a simple and well-established site with 130 pitches (73 touring pitches), most with a mixture of sun and shade, but some very shaded. The fact that the snack bar is not licensed might appeal to those who prefer a simple life! Organised events include a weekly outdoor disco, accompanied by moules-frites and other activities including pétanque, volleyball, water polo and table-tennis competitions (all July/Aug).

Facilities

The two sanitary blocks are kept clean, with mainly British style WCs, washbasins (some in cubicles), baby bath in the ladies' wash rooms, an en-suite unit for disabled visitors. Sinks for dishwashing and laundry. Washing machine. Small shop and adjacent snack bar open in July/Aug. Swimming pool and water slide (until 15 Sept). A jacuzzi is planned. Play area and good sized sports area. Two games rooms. Not suitable for American motorhomes or twin axle caravans. Off site: Tennis 800 m. Sea 5 km. Riding 7 km. Golf 10 km. Children's theme park 10 km.

At a glance

Welcome & Ambience	✓✓✓✓	Location	✓✓✓✓
Quality of Pitches	✓✓✓✓	Range of Facilities	✓✓✓✓

Directions

Avrillé is on the D949 Les Sables d'Olonne - Luçon road, 23 km. from Les Sables. Site is about 1 km. south of the town, on D105 to Longeville-sur-Mer.

Charges 2004

Per unit incl. 2 persons	€ 10,15 - € 14,50
extra person	€ 2,80 - € 3,20
electricity (6A)	€ 3,20

Reservations

Advised for high season. Tel: 02 51 90 35 97. E-mail: camping.mancellieres@tiscali.fr

Open

1 May - 30 September.

FR85550 Camping Le Port de Moricq

Le Port de Moricq, 85750 Angles (Vendée)

Nestling amongst the marshes, this site was bought in 2002 by Mme Louche who is slowly but surely exerting her influence in carrying out improvements to the facilities. The 60 touring pitches are level and grassy and spread amongst the mobile homes. There is little shade but hedges divide the pitches all of which have easy access to water and electricity (10/16A). Outside high season the site is very quiet but in July and August there is a children's club twice a day and a varied evening entertainment programme. Fishing is possible in the canal near the site. It is 2 km. from Angles and 7 km. from the beach.

TRAVEL SERVICE SITE

TO BOOK CALL 0870 405 4055 OR www.alanrogersdirect.com

Facilities

One traditional style, well maintained toilet block (a second is planned), has Turkish and British style toilets, washbasins in cubicles and open plan. Unit for disabled visitors. Washing machine and dryer. Bar (15/3-15/10), Restaurant and take-away (1/6-15/10). Heated outdoor pool (15/6-30/9). TV and games room. Playground. Multi-sports pitch. Bicycle hire. Off site: Fishing. Beaches, golf and riding within 15 km.

Open

15 March - 15 October.

At a glance

Welcome & Ambience	✓✓✓	Location	✓✓✓✓
Quality of Pitches	✓✓✓	Range of Facilities	✓✓✓

Directions

Site is signed from roundabout on D747 (La Roche-sur-Yon - La Tranche), 7 km. south of the junction with D949 (Les Sables - Lucon) road.

Charges 2004

Per unit incl. 2 persons	€ 14,00 - € 19,00
with electricity	€ 16,00 - € 23,00
extra person	€ 4,00 - € 5,00

Reservations

Made with deposit (€ 80) and fee (€ 15). Tel: 02 51 28 95 21. E-mail: infos@camping-port-moricq.com

FR85580 Camping Les Blancs Chenes

Route de la Roche sur Yon, 85360 La Tranche-sur-Mer (Vendée)

Part of the Vagues Océanes group, this is a very well managed site with good facilities, excellent children's activities and a varied programme of high season entertainment for all the family. The manager and his staff take a real pride in their work. The 40 level touring pitches are on sandy grass, are separated by hedges and have access to electricity (5A). They are scattered around the site and some have shade. The site is 1.8 km. from the town of La Tranche with its many shops, restaurants and sandy beach. In high season a free bus service to the beach is provided.

Facilities

Three modern toilet blocks have washbasins in cabins, good baby units and facilities for disabled visitors. Shop (15/4-30/9). Bar with TV (15/4-30/9). Restaurant and take-away (15/4-30/9). Indoor pool (15/4-30/9), outdoor pool (15/6- 15/9) with jacuzzi, paddling pool and slides. Tennis (charged), minigolf, table tennis. Bicycle hire.

Open

15 April - 30 September.

At a glance

Welcome & Ambience	✓✓✓✓	Location	✓✓✓
Quality of Pitches	✓✓✓	Range of Facilities	✓✓✓✓

Directions

Site is well signed on the western side of the D747 (La Tranche - La Roche) road, 2 km. north of La Tranche.

Charges guide

Per unit incl. 2 persons	€ 17,00 - € 21,00
extra person	€ 3,00 - € 6,00
electricity (5A)	€ 5,00

Reservations

Contact Vagues Océanes reservations office at Rte. de la Roche-sur-Yon, 85360 La Tranche-sur-Mer. Tel: 02 51 30 41 70. E-mail: vagues.oceanes@wanadoo.fr

FR85320 Camping Caravaning Val de Vie

Rue du Stade, 85190 Maché (Vendée)

Opened in 1999, Val de Vie is a small, good quality site run with enthusiasm and dedication by its English owners on the outskirts of a rural village back from the coast. There are currently 52 pitches for touring units (42 with electricity; 4, 6 or 10A) that vary in size from 80-137 sq.m. on mostly level grass with newly planted hedging. The ground can become very hard so steel pegs are advised. The pitches are arranged in circular fashion around the toilet block which, with reception, is built in local style with attractive, red tiled roofs. The owners, Peter and Shelagh McClearns, want you to experience real French village life and culture and encourage you to enjoy the local amenities. If you are looking for a beach, the Vendée coast is 20 km.

Facilities

The toilet block provides excellent, modern facilities including some washbasins in cabins, baby bath, facilities for disabled people, dishwashing and laundry sinks, and washing machine. Reception also offers wine, beer, soft drinks and ice cream. Small play area for young children. Swimming pool (from mid May). Bicycle hire. Not suitable for American motorhomes. Off site: Opposite site are a heated outdoor municipal pool and tennis courts. Shops, bar, tabac, etc. all within walking distance, with a good restaurant 2 km. away. Lake d'Apremont (300 m.) and Apremont itself with Renaissance château are 4 km. Vendée coast 20 km.

At a glance

Welcome & Ambience	✓✓✓✓✓	Location	✓✓✓✓✓
Quality of Pitches	✓✓✓✓	Range of Facilities	✓✓✓

Directions

From D948 at Aizenay take D107 northwest to Maché (6 km). Site signed in the village.

Charges 2004

Per unit incl. 2 persons	€ 17,00
extra person	€ 4,00
child (under 10 yrs)	€ 3,00
electricity (4-10A)	€ 2,90 - € 3,50
dog	€ 2,00

Less 20% in low season (excl. electricity).
No credit cards.

Reservations

Contact site. Tel: 02 51 60 21 02.
E-mail: campingvaldevie@aol.com

Open

1 May - 30 September.

FR85020 Camping du Jard

123 Mal de Lattre de Tassigny, 85360 La Tranche-sur-Mer (Vendée)

Camping du Jard is a well maintained site between La Rochelle and Les Sables d'Olonne. First impressions on booking in are good, with a friendly welcome from M. Marton or his staff and each new arrival being personally shown to their pitch. The 350 pitches are level and grassy, hedged on two sides by bushes. The smallest are 100 sq.m. (the majority larger) and most are equipped with electricity, half with water and drainage. It is a comparatively new site, but the large variety of trees is beginning to provide a little shade. An impressive pool complex has a toboggan, paddling pool and an indoor pool with jacuzzi. The site is 700 m. from a sandy beach with many shops and restaurants near. Used by British tour operators (150 pitches).

Facilities

Three toilet blocks, well designed and maintained, are light and airy with excellent facilities for babies and disabled people and most washbasins are in cabins. Washing machines and dryer. Dishwashing and laundry sinks. Small shop for basics (1/6-10/9), restaurant and bar (both 25/5-10/9). Heated swimming pool with toboggan and paddling pool, plus good heated indoor pool with jacuzzi (no bermuda-style shorts in the pools). Sauna, solarium and fitness room with instructors. Tennis court, minigolf, table tennis. Bicycle hire. Play area, games room and TV room. Card operated barrier with outside parking. American motorhomes are not accepted. Dogs allowed with papers.

At a glance

Welcome & Ambience	✓✓✓✓	Location	✓✓✓✓
Quality of Pitches	✓✓✓✓	Range of Facilities	✓✓✓✓✓

Directions

Site is east of La Tranche-sur-Mer on the D46. From D747 (La Roche-sur-Yon to La Tranche) follow signs for La Faute-sur-mer along the new bypass. Take exit for La Grière and then turn east to site.

Charges 2005

Per standard pitch incl. 2 persons, electricity (10A)	€ 20,70 - € 27,60
child (under 5 yrs)	€ 2,70 - € 3,60
extra person	€ 3,90 - € 5,10

Reservations

Advisable for July/Aug. (min. 1 week, Sat.- Sat.) with deposit (€ 100). Tel: 02 51 27 43 79.
E-mail: info@camping-du-jard.fr

Open

25 May - 15 September.

FR85420 Camping 'Bel

Rue du Bottereau, 85360 La Tranche-sur-Mer (Vendée)

Camping 'Bel's owner, M. Guicau, who has a very dry sense of humour, takes an individual approach. The first priority is the contentment of the children, who receive various small gifts during their stay. The site is popular with a large proportion of returning French clients, despite the large presence of British tour operators (130 pitches). The 70 touring pitches are on level, sandy grass. They are separated by hedges with some mature trees giving shade. All of the pitches have electrical connections (10A). It is only 150 m. from a good sandy beach and in the seaside town of La Tranche sur Mer with all amenities within walking distance. This is a good site for a family beach holiday.

Facilities

Two modern toilet blocks have washbasins in cabins, very good baby units and facilities for disabled visitors. Shop with basic provisions. Bar. Heated outdoor pool with jacuzzi. Plenty of entertainment for children aged 6-14 yrs (July/Aug). Table tennis. Fitness area. Tennis and badminton. Pets are not accepted. Not suitable for American motorhomes or twin axle caravans. Off site: Bicycle hire 100 m. Supermarket with fuel 200 m. Fishing 150 m. Watersports 150 m. Riding 5 km.

At a glance

Welcome & Ambience	✓✓✓✓✓	Location	✓✓✓✓
Quality of Pitches	✓✓✓✓	Range of Facilities	✓✓✓✓✓

Directions

Follow signs from the roundabout on the La Tranche bypass, near 'Super U' supermarket onto avenue General de Gaulle. Turn left after 50 m. onto rue du bottereau. Site is on right after 100 m.

Charges 2004

Per unit with 2 persons and water	€ 20,00
with electricity (6A)	€ 24,00
extra person	€ 4,30
child (under 5 yrs)	€ 3,40

Reservations

Contact site. Tel: 02 51 30 47 39.

Open

29 May - 7 September with all services.

FR85440 Camping Les Brunelles

Le Bouil, 85560 Longeville-sur-Mer (Vendée)

This is a well managed site with good facilities and a varied programme of high season entertainment for all the family. The owner, M. Guinard is justifiably proud of his campsite. The leaflet given to all visitors on arrival (together with a bottle of wine) explains in detail the workings of the campsite and the standards of behaviour expected. In mid July the site was very busy but there was an atmosphere of well ordered calm. M. Guinard believes that if the children are happy and occupied then the parents are also happy. This approach certainly seems to work. This has to be one of the cleanest and neatest sites on the Vendée. The 60 touring pitches are all level on sandy grass and separated by hedges, away from most of the mobile homes on site. There is a mixture of sunny and shaded pitches and all have easy access to electricity (6A). Water points are not so frequent. A good supervised sandy beach is just 900 m. away. The village of St Vincent sur Jard (two kilometres) has shops, bars and restaurants and the pleasant seaside town of Jard sur Mer with its market is just four kilometres.

TRAVEL SERVICE SITE

TO BOOK CALL 0870 405 4055 OR www.alanrogersdirect.com

Facilities

Four old but well maintained and modernised toilet blocks have British and Turkish style toilets, washbasins both open style and in cabins, plenty of sinks for dishwashing and laundry, five washing machines, two dryers and ironing. Shop (from 1/6). Takeaway (l5/6-7/9). Large modern, airy bar (15/6-15/9) with games area overlooks the impressive pool complex. New covered pool with jacuzzi (all season). Outdoor pool with slides and paddling pools (from 15/5), both pools are heated but unsupervised. Fenced area for football, volleyball and basketball. Table tennis. Tennis. Bicycle hire. Off site: Golf, riding, karting and numerous other activities within 15 km.

Open

3 April - 8 September.

At a glance

Welcome & Ambience	✓✓✓✓	Location	✓✓✓
Quality of Pitches	✓✓✓	Range of Facilities	✓✓✓✓✓

Directions

From the D21 Talmont - Longeville road, between St Vincent and Longueville, site is well signed south from the main road towards the coast. Turn left in village of Le Bouil (site signed) and site is 800 m. on left.

Charges 2004

Per unit incl. 2 persons	€ 14,00 - € 20,00
with electricity	€ 17,00 - € 25,00
extra person	€ 5,00
child (under 5 yrs)	free - € 3,00
animal	€ 2,00

Camping Cheques accepted.

Reservations

Made with 25% deposit and € 20 fee.
Tel: 02 51 33 50 75.
E-mail: camping@les-brunelles.com

FR85210 Camping Les Ecureuils

Route des Goffineaux, 85520 Jard-sur-Mer (Vendée)

Les Ecureuils is a wooded site in a quieter part of the southern Vendée. It is undoubtedly one of the prettiest sites on this stretch of coast, with an elegant reception area, attractive vegetation and large pitches separated by low hedges with plenty of shade. Of the 261 pitches, some 120 are for touring units, each with water and drainage, as well as easy access to 10A electricity. Jard is rated among the most pleasant and least hectic of Vendée towns. The harbour is home to some fishing boats and rather more pleasure craft, and has a public slipway for those bringing their own boats. This site is very popular with tour operators (126 pitches). And in case you are curious, yes there are squirrels on site, including red ones! A new indoor pool and spa were added in 2002.

Facilities

Two toilet blocks, well equipped and kept very clean, include baby baths, and laundry rooms. Small shop. Takeaway service (pre-order). Snacks and ice-creams available from the friendly bar. Good sized L-shaped swimming pool and separate paddling pool. New indoor pool. Modern play area. Minigolf, table tennis and a pool table. Club for children (5-10 yrs) daily in July/Aug. Bicycle hire. Only gas barbecues are allowed. Dogs are not accepted. Off site: Nearest beach 400 m. Fishing 400 m. Many places to eat at nearby marina or in town which has good supermarket and weekly market.

Open

15 May - 15 September.

At a glance

Welcome & Ambience	✓✓✓✓	Location	✓✓✓✓✓
Quality of Pitches	✓✓✓✓	Range of Facilities	✓✓✓✓

Directions

Jard-sur-Mer is on the D21 road between Talmont St Hilaire and Longeville sur Mer. Site is well signed from the main road - caravanners will need to follow these signs to avoid tight bends and narrow roads.

Charges 2005

Per person	€ 6,50
child (0-4 yrs)	€ 2,00
child (5-9 yrs)	€ 4,50
per pitch with water and drainage	€ 11,50
with electricity (10A)	€ 15,50

Less 10% outside 30/6-1/9.

Reservations

Advised for July/Aug. Tel: 02 51 33 42 74.
E-mail: camping-ecureuils@wanadoo.fr

FR85430 Camping Club La Bolée D'Air

Route de Longeville, 85520 St Vincent sur Jard (Vendée)

This is a well managed site with good facilities and a varied programme of high season entertainment. The 120 touring pitches are all level and well grassed on sandy soil. Many are situated around the perimeter of the site and are separated by trimmed hedges giving good privacy but little shade. Long electricity cables may be required on some pitches. The main road runs along one side of the site and may cause traffic noise at some times although when we visited in July there did not appear to be a problem. A refurbished complex at the entrance houses all the amenities. A good, sandy, supervised beach is just 900 m. away. The village of St Vincent sur Jard (1.5 km.) has shops, bars and restaurants and the pleasant seaside town of Jard sur Mer with its market is just 3.5 km.

TRAVEL SERVICE SITE

TO BOOK CALL 0870 405 4055 OR www.alanrogersdirect.com

Facilities

Three modernised, unisex sanitary blocks provide washbasins in cabins, plenty of sinks for dishwashing and laundry, washing machines and dryers. Shop and takeaway (1/6-31/8). Bar (1/5-30/9). Heated indoor pool, outdoor pool (1/6-30/9) with slide, jacuzzi and paddling pool. Tennis. Minigolf. Bicycle hire. Table tennis. Good multi-sport all-weather terrain. Off site: Golf, riding, karting and many other activities within 1.5 km.

Open

2 April - 25 September.

At a glance

Welcome & Ambience	✓✓✓✓	Location	✓✓✓
Quality of Pitches	✓✓✓	Range of Facilities	✓✓✓✓

Directions

Site is just off the D21 Les Sables La Franche road, just east of St Vincent-sur-Jard and is well signed from the main road.

Charges 2005

Per unit with 2 persons and car	€ 12,00 - € 22,50
with electricity	€ 16,50 - € 27,00
extra person	€ 5,70
child (under 5 yrs)	€ 3,70
animal	€ 2,80

Reservations

Made with deposit (€ 40 p/week), fee (€ 25) and cancellation insurance. Tel: 02 51 90 36 05. E-mail: info@chardotel.com

FR85240 Camping Caravaning Jarny-Ocean

Le Bouil, 85560 Longeville-sur-Mer (Vendée)

Jarny Ocean is the sort of the site the French love - wooded (though less so than before the storms of Dec. 99) and with many pitches separated by thick hedges giving plenty of privacy. There are other areas, however, which are more open and with plenty of sun. There are 303 large, grassy pitches on level ground, of which 200 are for touring units, around 25% well shaded. All have electrical connections (6/10A) and about 30 also with water and drainaway. A beach is within easy walking distance (800 m) or a beach with lifeguards (and parking) is four kilometres. English is spoken.

TRAVEL SERVICE SITE

TO BOOK CALL 0870 405 4055 OR www.alanrogersdirect.com

Facilities

Five toilet blocks of differing ages have a mix of British and Turkish style WCs. Small shop for basics in July/Aug, but bread, croissants, etc. can be ordered from reception all season. Takeaway in the Centre de Vacances that shares the site (from 1/5). Bar (weekends in low season, 11.00 - 01.00 hrs in July/Aug). Heated swimming pool (1/5 -15/9). Large central play area. Table tennis. Tennis (free in low season) including short court tennis. Bicycle hire. Volleyball and basketball. Off site: Bars, restaurants and minigolf short walk. Riding or fishing 4 km. Golf 20 km.

At a glance

Welcome & Ambience	✓✓✓	Location	✓✓✓✓
Quality of Pitches	✓✓✓	Range of Facilities	✓✓✓

Directions

From D21 Talmont - Longeville road, soon after Jard, pass through St Vincent and very shortly the site is signed towards the coast (before Longeville). Turn left in village of Le Bouil (site signed) and site is on left in 800 m.

Charges 2004

Per unit incl. 2 adults	€ 9,25 - € 20,00
with 6A electricity	€ 11,00 - € 22,80
with water and drainage	€ 12,70 - € 24,40
extra adult	€ 2,05 - € 3,20

Reservations

Made with deposit (€ 45.73) and fee (€ 15.24). Tel: 02 51 33 42 21. E-mail: jarny-ocean@wanadoo.fr

Open

1 May - 30 September.

FR85450 Camping Les Roses

Rue des Roses, 85100 Les Sables d'Olonne (Vendée)

Les Roses has an urban location, with the town centre and the beach just a short walk away. There is an informal air with the 210 pitches arranged interestingly on a knoll. Mature trees give good shade to parts of the site. There are 107 touring pitches of varying size, many more suitable for tents than caravans. All pitches have access to electricity and water but long cables may be needed. In high season caravanners might find access to the site tricky at times due to overloaded town centre traffic systems. The site has 103 mobile homes and chalets, but no tour operators. An entertainment programme is arranged in high season. Les Sables with its lively night life is readily accessible.

Facilities

There are three well maintained toilet blocks with washbasins in cubicles, unit for disabled visitors, baby room, washing machines and dryers. Bar (15/5-15/9). Simple shop. Small attractively laid out, heated, outdoor swimming pool with water slide and paddling pool (1/5-30/9). Play area. Volleyball, basketball, petanque and table tennis. Bicycle hire. Electric barbecues are not permitted. Off site: Golf, riding, karting, water sports, zoo, sea and river fishing all within easy reach.

At a glance

Welcome & Ambience	✓✓✓	Location	✓✓✓✓✓
Quality of Pitches	✓✓✓	Range of Facilities	✓✓✓✓

Directions

Site is signed from the D949 Les Sables to La Rochelle road, north of the 'Géant Casino' roundabout. Turn south at minor junction.

Charges 2004

Per pitch incl. 2 persons	€ 14,00 - € 22,50
with electricity	€ 28,00 - € 26,50
extra person	€ 3,50 - € 5,50

Reservations

Contact site. Tel: 02 51 33 05 05.
E-mail: info@chadotel.com

Open

1 April - 31 October.

FR85570 Camping Caravaning Le Pomme de Pin

Rue Vincent Auriol, 85520 Jard-sur-Mer (Vendée)

This family run site, set amongst the pines, is just 150 metres from a sandy beach in a residential area and within easy reach of the town of Jard with its lively weekly market and fishing harbour. It specialises in mobile homes (over 140) but there are 10 small touring pitches. These are well shaded as the site has a cover of the pine trees from which it gets its name. The compact, attractively laid out swimming pool is overlooked by the bar terrace. There is a good entertainment programme in high season.

Facilities

Three unisex toilet blocks provide washbasins in cabins (warm water) and preset showers. Simple facilities only for babies and disabled vsitors. Washing machines and dryer. Bar, restaurant, takeaway (1/6-30/9). Small well-stocked shop (15/6-30/9). Play area. No charcoal barbecues.

Open

1 April - 30 September.

At a glance

Welcome & Ambience	✓✓✓✓	Location	✓✓✓
Quality of Pitches	✓✓✓	Range of Facilities	✓✓✓

Directions

From the D21 (Talmont - Longeville) road, site is signed to the south.

Charges 2004

Per unit incl. 2 persons	€ 14,50 - € 22,00
with electricity	€ 18,00 - € 26,00
extra person	€ 3,50 - € 5,40

Reservations

Contact site. Tel: 02 51 33 43 85.
E-mail: info@pommedepin.net

FR85270 Chadotel Camping L'Oceano d'Or

58 rue Georges Clémenceau, BP 12, 85520 Jard-sur-Mer (Vendée)

This site should appeal to families with children of all ages. It is very lively in high season but appears to be well managed, with a full programme of activities (it can therefore be noisy, sometimes late at night). The site is only 999 metres from the excellent beach. There are 430 flat, grass and sand pitches of which 40% are occupied by tour operators and mobile homes. The 260 for touring units, all with 6A electricity, are quite large (about 100 sq.m.). Some are separated by high hedges, others are more open with low bushes between them. A modern complex at the entrance houses all the facilities. There are shops, bars and restaurants, and a weekly market in the pleasant little town of Jard-sur-Mer.

Facilities

Four modern, unisex toilet blocks include washbasins all in cabins, plenty of dishwashing and laundry sinks and washing machines and dryers. Small shop (1/6-10/9). Bar and snack bar (both 1/6-10/9, but limited hours outside high season). Swimming pool (15/5-15/9) with 3 water slides, 2 waterfalls and children's pool. Walled (three sides) play area with lots of recently refurbished equipment. Tennis, table tennis, volleyball, pétanque and minigolf. Electric barbecues are not allowed. Internet access. Off site: Golf, riding, karting and numerous other activities within 15 km. Excellent beach within walking distance.

At a glance

Welcome & Ambience	✓✓✓	Location	✓✓✓✓✓
Quality of Pitches	✓✓✓✓	Range of Facilities	✓✓✓✓✓

Directions

Site is on the D21 Talmont St Hilaire - Longeville sur Mer, just east of the turning to the town centre.

Charges 2004

Per pitch incl. 2 adults	€ 14,00 - € 22,50
with electricity	€ 18,00 - € 26,50
extra person	€ 3,50 - € 5,50

Reservations

Necessary for high season with deposit (€ 39) and fee (€ 22.87). Central reservations: Siege Social - Centrale de Reservation, BP 12, 85520 Jard-sur-Mer.
Tel: 02 51 33 05 05. E-mail: chadotel@wanadoo.fr

Open

1 April - 25 September.

TRAVEL SERVICE SITE
TO BOOK CALL 0870 405 4055 OR www.alanrogersdirect.com

FR85470 Camping Les Pirons

Rue des Marchais, La Pironnière, 85180 Château-d'Olonne (Vendée)

This is a modern, well run site of which the new owner M. Chailloleau is very proud. The site is a short walk from the sandy beach and within easy reach of the many facilities of the attractive seaside town of Les Sables d'Olonne. The 105 touring pitches are grassed and either level or on a slight slope. They are concentrated in one central area of the campsite away from the large number of mobile homes (over 300). The large new sanitary block has all facilities, as has the swimming pool complex overlooked by the bar's sun terrace. There are several small French tour operators on the site (56 pitches). At the start of the season the site is quiet and facilities are limited. In high season there is an excellent animation programme for all ages with evening entertainment nightly.

Facilities

Four toilet blocks, of which three are new, have washbasins in cubicles and units for disabled people, babies and dogs. Washing machines and dryers. Bar (29/6-31/8) with sun terrace overlooking the pool. Shop (29/6-31/8). Takeaway (29/6-31/8). Covered, heated pool, outdoor pools with slide and children's pool, large sun terrace. Good children's play area. Table tennis, volleyball, football. Tennis. Pétanque. Indoor games area. Bicycle, scooter and motorbike hire. Activities day and evening for all ages (29/6-31/8).
Off site: Beach, sea fishing, horse riding and sailing all within 5 km.

Open

27 March - 8 November.

At a glance

Welcome & Ambience	✓✓✓	Location	✓✓✓✓
Quality of Pitches	✓✓✓	Range of Facilities	✓✓✓✓

Directions

From D949 Les Sables - La Rochelle road, site is well signed at traffic lights near Toyota garage on the western outskirts of Les Sables d'Olonne.

Charges 2004

Per unit incl. 3 persons	€ 15,00 - € 21,00
with electricity (6A)	€ 18,00 - € 25,00
with water and drainage	€ 20,00 - € 27,00
extra person	€ 3,00 - € 4,00
child (under 7 yrs)	€ 1,00 - € 2,00
animal	€ 2,50

Reservations

Made with 30% deposit and € 18.29 fee.
Tel: 02 51 95 26 75.
E-mail: camping.les.pirons@wanadoo.fr

FR85400 Camping Bois Soleil

Chemin des Barres, 85340 Olonne-sur-Mer (Vendée)

This site has a very French feel, the majority of the population when we visited seeming to be French. It is a traditionally laid out site with 199 marked pitches, separated by hedges, on flat or gently sloping ground. There are just two tour operators and a scattering of mobile homes and chalets, leaving some 87 pitches available for tourers and tents. All have electricity (6A, French style sockets) and water points adjacent and many also have waste water pipes. The main buildings house a small reception and tourist information room as well as the bar and attached shop. There is an excellent new swimming pool complex with sunbathing areas, paddling pool and a separate pool for the two water slides and impressive flume. In July and August a range of daily activities is organised for adults and children.

Facilities

The two well equipped and maintained toilet blocks have copious hot water, mainly British style toilets, with washbasins in cubicles in the new block. This block is locked overnight, but basic toilet facilities are provided. Covered dishwashing and laundry sinks. Two washing machines. Shop (July/Aug. only) with 'eat in' or takeaway service; bread (and cooked chicken) must to be ordered the previous day. Swimming and paddling pools. Sandy play area (caged), trampoline and table tennis. Off site: Beaches are just 2 km. The thriving resort of Les Sables d'Olonne is 5 km. along the coast

At a glance

Welcome & Ambience	✓✓✓✓	Location	✓✓✓
Quality of Pitches	✓✓✓	Range of Facilities	✓✓✓✓

Directions

Site is off the D80 coast road between Olonne-sur-Mer and is clearly signed on the inland side.

Charges guide

Per unit incl. 2 persons	€ 14,00 - € 17,00
with electricity	€ 17,00 - € 20,00
extra person	€ 2,00 - € 2,50
child (under 7 yrs)	€ 2,00 - € 2,50
animal	€ 2,50

Reservations

Advised for July/Aug. and made with 25% deposit and booking fee in July/Aug of € 18.
Tel: 02 51 33 11 97.
E-mail: camping.boissoleil@wanadoo.fr

Open

5 April - 28 September.

FR85260 Village de la Guyonnière

La Guyonnière, 85150 St Julien-des-Landes (Vendée)

La Guyonnière is a spacious, rural site, away from the hertic coast. It is popular for many reasons, the main ones being the free and easy atmosphere and its reasonable pricing. It is Dutch owned but English is spoken and all visitors are made very welcome. It is a farm type site with five different fields, each being reasonably level and each having a toilet block albeit the fifth block is a 'Portakabin' style construction (a new toilet block is planned). The 183 pitches have a mix of sun and shade, they are very large (the few smaller ones are cheaper) and are separated by a tree and a few bushes. All have access to electricity connections. Bar/restaurant facilities are housed in the original farm buildings attractively converted. Entertainment is provided in the bar on high season evenings. A perfect place for families, with large play areas on sand and grass,and paddling pond with shower. Being in the country it is a haven for cyclists and walkers, with many signed routes from the site. A pleasant 500 m. walk takes you to the Jaunay lake where fishing is possible (permits from the village), canoeing (lifejackets from reception) and pedaloes to hire. There are no tour operators and, needless to say, no road noise.

Facilities

Toilet blocks are modern, functional and central for each area. Most cubicles are quite small but they serve their purpose and were very clean when we visited; however, perhaps not adequate in high season. Washbasins are in cubicles. Limited provision for babies and disabled visitors. Dishwashing and laundry sinks at each block. Shop (1/5-15/9; order bread from reception outside these dates). Bar with TV and pool table and pleasant restaurant (1/5-15/9). Pizzeria with takeaway. Small swimming pool, new heated pool with jacuzzi and slide, very attractive and can be covered in cool weather. Paddling pool. Play areas, sand pit. Table tennis, volleyball and football fields. Bicycle hire. Car wash. Off site: Riding 3 km. Golf 8 km. Beaches 10 km.

At a glance

Welcome & Ambience	✓✓✓✓✓	Location	✓✓✓✓✓
Quality of Pitches	✓✓✓✓✓	Range of Facilities	✓✓✓✓

Directions

Site is off the D12 road (La Mothe Achard - St Gilles Croix de Vie), approx. 4 km. west of St Julien-des-Landes. It is signed about 1 km. from the main road.

Charges 2004

Per unit incl. 2 persons and electricity	€ 15,00 - € 27,45
extra person	€ 4,20 - € 5,00
child (3-9 yrs)	€ 2,70 - € 3,00
animal	€ 2,50

Less 10-20% outside high season.

Reservations

Made with 25% deposit. Tel: 02 51 46 62 59. E-mail: info@laguyonniere.com

Open

1 May - 30 September.

FR85050 Le Village de Florine

La Grouinière, 85220 Coëx (Vendée)

Le Village de Florine has been recommended by a reader and we hope to include a full report for this site in a future edition. This country site offers some large, grassy pitches all of which are equipped with electrical connections (10A). The principal site buildings are converted farm buildings and lend to the rural ambience. Mobile homes for rent.

Facilities

Toilet block with special facilities for disabled visitors and babies. Bar. Takeaway. Swimming and paddling pools. TV room. Play area. Entertainment in high season.
Off site: Coëx 2 km (shops, restaurants etc). Golf, tennis, fishing.

Open

April - October.

Directions

From St Gilles Croix-de-Vie take the D6 to Coëx. Then take the D40 towards La Chaize-Giraud - the site is on the right after 2km.

Charges year

Per unit incl. 2 persons and electricity	€ 17,80
extra person	€ 3,50
child (0-7 yrs)	€ 3,00

Reservations

Contact site. Tel: 02 51 60 19 51.
E-mail: le-village-de-florine@wanadoo.fr

FR85040 Castel Camping La Garangeoire

Mobile homes page 374

St Julien-des-Landes, 85150 La Mothe-Achard (Vendée)

La Garangeoire is one of a relatively small number of seriously good sites in the Vendée, situated some 15 km. inland near the village of St Julien des Landes. One of its more memorable qualities is the view of the château through the gates as you drive in. Imaginative use has been made of the old Noirmoutiers 'main road' which passes through the centre of the site and now forms a delightful, quaint thoroughfare, nicknamed the Champs Elysée. Providing a village like atmosphere, it is busy at most times with the facilities opening directly off it. The site is set in the 200 ha. of parkland surrounding the small château of La Garangeoire. The peaceful fields and woods, where campers may walk, include three lakes, one of which is used for fishing and boating (life jackets supplied from reception). With a spacious, relaxed atmosphere, the main camping areas are arranged on either side of the old road, edged with mature trees. The 300 pitches, each with a name not a number and individually hedged, are especially large (most 150-200 sq.m.) and are well spaced. Most have electricity (12A), some water and drainage also. The site is popular with tour operators (144 pitches).

Facilities

Ample sanitary facilities are of good standard, well situated for all areas. One excellent block has facilities for babies and disabled people. All have washbasins in cabins. Good laundry facilities. Motorcaravan service point. Good shop. Full restaurant, takeaway and a separate crêperie with bars and attractive courtyard terrace overlooking the swimming pool complex (from 1/5) with water slides, fountains and a children's pool. Large play field with play equipment for children's activities, whether organised or not. Games room. Two tennis courts. Bicycle hire. Table tennis, crazy golf, archery and volleyball. Riding in July/Aug. Fishing and boating. Off site: Beaches 15 km.

At a glance

Welcome & Ambience	✓✓✓✓✓	Location	✓✓✓✓
Quality of Pitches	✓✓✓✓	Range of Facilities	✓✓✓✓✓

Directions

Site is signed from St Julien; the entrance is to the east off the D21 road, 2.5 km north of St Julian-des-Landes.

Charges 2004

Per unit incl. 2 persons	€ 14,00 - € 27,00
with electricity	€ 17,00 - € 30,00
with services	€ 18,50 - € 33,50
extra person	€ 4,50 - € 6,00
child (under 10 yrs)	€ 2,50 - € 3,00
dog	€ 3,00

Camping Cheques accepted.

Reservations

Made for min. 7 days with deposit (€ 61) and fee (€ 22.87). Tel: 02 51 46 65 39.
E-mail: garangeoire@wanadoo.fr

Open

5 April - 24 September.

FR85530 Camping La Parée Préneau

23 Avenue de la Parée Préneau, 85270 St Hilaire-de-Riez (Vendée)

This site was founded in 1968 by the grandfather of the present owner. It has been gradually and thoughtfully expanded to its present size (206 pitches). Of these, 150 are touring pitches of varying shapes and sizes, interestingly arranged. Mature trees proliferate to give varying amounts of shade to the undulating site, although the pitches are level. All have electricity (6A) and many also have water and drainage. The calm atmosphere is enhanced by the absence of tour operators. All amenities are very clean and well maintained. The cosy welcoming bar overlooks the pool area. The friendly welcome in campsite reception is indicative of the caring attitude of those running the site.

Facilities

The two sanitary blocks are modern and include washbasins (some in cubicles), facilities for babies and disabled visitors. WCs are a mixture of British, seatless and Turkish, all thoroughly cleaned twice a day. Laundry and dishwashing sinks, washing machine and dryer. No restaurant or shop but bread, milk and other essentials are available. Mobile takeaway vendors call in high season. Heated indoor and outdoor swimming pools with jacuzzi and paddling pool surrounded by wide sun terrace. Large play area with football, volleyball/basketball pitch. Table tennis (indoor). Bicycle hire. Not suitable for American motorhomes or twin axle caravans. Off site: Beach 1 km. Riding 3 km. Shops, bars, restaurants 5 km. Fishing, golf and sailing 7 km.

At a glance

Welcome & Ambience	✓✓✓✓	Location	✓✓✓✓
Quality of Pitches	✓✓✓✓	Range of Facilities	✓✓✓

Directions

From large roundabout on D38 just north of St Hilaire-de-Riez, turn south signed St Hilaire for 400 m. Take first exit at next roundabout signed Les Plages and after another 400 m. continue straight on at junction. Site is on left after 3 km.

Charges 2004

Per unit incl. 2 persons	€ 13,40 - € 17,80
with electricity	€ 15,50 - € 20,00
extra person	€ 3,30 - € 4,20
child (under 5 yrs)	€ 2,10 - € 2,50
dog	€ 1,40 - € 2,00

Reservations

Made with deposit (€ 35) and fee (€ 15).
Tel: 02 51 54 33 84.
E-mail: camplapareepreneau@free.fr

Open

1 May - 12 September.

FR85310 Chadotel Camping La Trévillière

Rue de Bellevue, 85470 Bretignolles-sur-Mer (Vendée)

A member of the Chadotel group, La Trévillière has a pleasant semi-rural setting on the edge of the little resort town of Bretignolles. Although just 2 km. from the nearest beach and less than 5 km. from the Plage des Dunes (one of southern Vendée's best beaches), La Trévillière has a more 'laid-back' feel than many other sites in the area, particularly in low season. After a new extension, there are now 203 pitches, all with easy access to electricity and water. The original area provides either level or slightly sloping pitches separated by hedges or low bushes and there is a mix of shady or more open positions. The new area has no shade as yet from newly planted trees and bushes. The site has around 50 mobile homes and chalets and is used by three small tour operators, but it remains very much a camping and caravanning site. There is a heated swimming pool with water slide, a small paddling pool and a large sunbathing terrace with plenty of loungers. Overlooking the pool is the building housing the bar and reception. In early season the site is very quiet, becoming much livelier in July and August when there is a good range of morning activities for children, afternoon events for families and evening entertainment for all.

Facilities

Three modern, clean toilet blocks include washbasins in cubicles, a unit for disabled people and baby room with bath, shower and toilet. Washing machines and dryers. Bar (limited opening in low season). Small independently operated shop and snack bar with takeaway (20/6-8/9). New restaurant. Heated outdoor pool (15/5-15/9) with slide and paddling pool. Play area. Mingolf, table tennis. Charcoal barbecues are not allowed. Off site: Golf, riding, karting, water sports and water parks are all within easy reach.

Open

1 April - 25 September.

At a glance

Welcome & Ambience	✓✓✓✓	Location	✓✓✓✓
Quality of Pitches	✓✓✓✓	Range of Facilities	✓✓✓✓

Directions

Bretignolles is on the D38 coast road (Noirmoutier - Les Sables d'Olonne). From north, after St Gilles go through Bretignolles-La Sauzaie (take left fork) and before reaching Bretignolles itself turn left (sign for site) on sharp right hand bend, heading for water tower. Site is on right in 800 m. From south, after centre of Bretignolles, turn right (sign 'Ecoles') and then left (signs for sports centre and site). Site is signed to left after stadium.

Charges 2005

Per pitch incl. 2 adults	€ 12,00 - € 22,50
with electricity	€ 16,50 - € 27,00
extra adult	€ 5,70
child (under 5 yrs)	€ 3,70
animal	€ 2,80

Reservations

Necessary for high season with deposit and fee. Central reservations: Siege Social - Centrale de Reservation, BP 12, 85520 Jard sur Mer.
Tel: 02 51 33 05 05. Fax: 02 51 33 94 04.
E-mail: chadotel@wanadoo.fr. Tel: 02 51 33 05 05.

TRAVEL SERVICE SITE

TO BOOK CALL 0870 405 4055 OR www.alanrogersdirect.com

FR85520 Camping Domaine des Renardières

13 Chemin du Chêne Vert, 85270 Notre-Dame-de-Riez (Vendée)

Just seven kilometres from the busy coastal strip with its many large, multi-activity campsites, Domaine des Renardières is an oasis of calm in the traditional French manner. Converted from the family farm in 1970 by the present owner's father, the site consists of three fields with varying amounts of shade and two further open fields in full sun. The visitors are 65% French, many of whom, together with British visitors, return year after year. The 100 touring pitches are well grassed and level; torches and long cables are advisable. Mme. Raffin's benevolent authority is to be seen everywhere. There is an abundance of flowers and plants, the facilities are scrupulously maintained and all arriving clients are provided with a set of campsite rules which are also explained at the regular Monday Aperitif welcome meeting. A doctor calls twice a day in high season and Mme. Raffin is highly qualified in first aid. The welfare of her clients is of paramount importance to her. The site is very well organised with a soft touch.

Facilities

The new unisex sanitary block has private wash cubicles, baby changing room and a bathroom for disabled visitors. Showers are closed at night except for one cold shower. Dishwashing under cover. Washing machine and dryer. Small shop and takeaway (1/7-30/8). Air-conditioned bar with TV, video games and pool (1/7-30/8). Small outdoor pool attractively laid out (1/5-4/9). Play area. Only gas barbecues are permitted. Motorhome service point. Not suitable for American motorhomes. Off site: Fishing 700 m. Bicycle hire 6 km. St Hilaire de Riez (7 km) has shops, bars, restaurants and all entertainments as well as a good sandy beach. Riding 9 km. Golf 11 km.

At a glance

Welcome & Ambience	✓✓✓✓✓	Location	✓✓✓✓
Quality of Pitches	✓✓✓	Range of Facilities	✓✓✓✓

Directions

Site is well signed from the centre of the village of Notre Dame de Riez.

Charges 2004

Per unit incl. 2 persons	€ 14,00
with electricity (6A)	€ 17,00
extra person	€ 3,50
child (under 5 yrs)	€ 2,50
dog	€ 1,50 - € 3,00

Less 10-20% outside 15/7-21/8.
No credit cards.

Reservations

Made with deposit and € 10 fee. Tel: 02 51 55 14 17. E-mail: caroline.raffin@free.fr

Open

1 May - 4 September.

FR85130 Camping Pong

Rue du Stade, 85220 Landevieille (Vendée)

A comfortable family run site, Camping Pong is in a rural situation on the edge of a neat village, twelve kilometres southeast of St Gilles-Croix-de-Vie, and five kilometres from the coast at Brétignolles. It has 230 pitches, all with electricity (4/6A) and of a good size with some larger ones costing a little more. The redeveloped entrance and reception area provides an efficient welcome and the bar, restaurant, function room, games room, gym and shop have all recently been rebuilt. The original part of the site around the small, lightly fenced fishing lake (there are warning signs) has a mixture of mature trees, whereas, in the newer areas the vegetation is less developed. An attractive pool area includes a delightful paddling pool with many fascinating features for children and a pretty patio area overlooked by the bar. There are no tour operator pitches.

TRAVEL SERVICE SITE

TO BOOK CALL 0870 405 4055 OR www.alanrogersdirect.com

Facilities

Four modern, unisex sanitary blocks provide toilets of mixed styles and some washbasins in cabins. Facilities for disabled people, separate baby room, dishwashing under cover and laundry room. Maintenance can be variable. New shop, takeaway, bar and restaurant (15/6-15/9). Swimming pools including heated pool with jacuzzi, toboggan and paddling pool (from 15/5). Small gym, TV lounge and games room. Bicycle hire. Exciting new fenced play area and regular children's club. Off site: Tennis 200 m. Large Lac du Jaunay 2.5 km.(canoeing and pedaloes). Golf or riding 5 km. Nearest beach 6 km. Lac d'Apremont and its XV1 century château 14 km.

At a glance

Welcome & Ambience	✓✓✓✓	Location	✓✓✓✓
Quality of Pitches	✓✓✓✓	Range of Facilities	✓✓✓✓

Directions

Site is on the edge of Landevieille and is signed from both the D32 (Challons-Les Sables d'Olonne) and D12 (La Mothe Achard-St Gilles Croix de Vie) roads.

Charges 2004

Per unit incl. 2 persons	€ 12,00 - € 18,00
extra person	€ 3,00 - € 4,50
child (under 5 yrs)	€ 2,25 - € 3,30
electricity 4-6A	€ 3,00 - € 4,00
water and drainage	€ 1,10
dog	€ 1,75 - € 2,00

Reservations

Made with dates of arrival and departure, plus deposit and fee. Tel: 02 51 22 92 63. E-mail: lepong@free.fr

Open

1 April - 30 September.

FR85070 Camping Les Biches

Mobile homes ▶ page 375

Route de Notre-Dame-de-Riez, 85270 St Hilaire-de-Riez (Vendée)

Les Biches is a popular, quality site four kilometres from the sea. It is set in a pinewood so nearly everywhere has shade. There are 434 pitches with around 60 available for touring units. The large, spacious pitches are mostly hedged and on fairly sandy ground, all with electricity, water and drainage. The majority for tents and caravans are in the far part of the campsite behind the tennis courts, although a few others are scattered through the rest of the site. A very attractive pool complex is near the site entrance, overlooked by the bar and terraces. Various activities such as boules tournaments and sporting events are organised during high season. It is a useful site for families with children and, as it is popular with British tour operators (65%), it tends to be busy and active all season.

Facilities

The four sanitary blocks are clean and well maintained, with extremely spacious cubicles for pre-set showers. Some washbasins are in cabins with a bidet alongside. All blocks have laundry and dishwashing facilities. Washing machines and dryers. Facilities for disabled visitors. Shop (all season) with ice service. Large bar (all season). Restaurant and crèperie (1/6-10/9).Takeaway (20/5-10/9). Two heated swimming pools (unsupervised), children's pool, water slide with splash pool, jacuzzi and indoor pool. Tennis courts. Volleyball, table tennis and minigolf. Games room with amusement machines. Large adventure type playground. Bicycle hire. Disco. TV room with satellite TV. Internet terminal at Reception. Not suitable for American motorhomes. Off site: Private fishing lake 1.5 km. Beach 4 km. Riding 4.5 km. Golf 6 km.

At a glance

Welcome & Ambience	✓✓✓✓	Location	✓✓✓✓
Quality of Pitches	✓✓✓✓	Range of Facilities	✓✓✓✓✓

Directions

Site is about 2 km. north of St Hilaire, close to and well signed from the main D38 road.

Charges 2004

Per unit incl. 3 persons	€ 37,00
with electricity	€ 41,00
extra person	€ 10,00
child (under 7 yrs)	€ 5,00
dog	€ 2,00

Less 30% May, June and Sept.

Reservations

Required for high season and made with deposit (€ 61) and fee (€ 15.24). Tel: 02 51 54 38 82. E-mail: campingdesbiches@wanadoo.fr

Open

15 May - 15 September.

FR85300 Camping La Grand' Métairie

Mobile homes ▶ page 376

8 rue de la Vineuse en Plaine, 85440 St Hilaire la Forêt (Vendée)

Just five kilometres from the super sandy beach at Jard sur Mer, La Grand' Métairie offers many of the amenities of its seaside counterparts, but with the advantage of being on the edge of a delightful, sleepy village, otherwise untouched by tourism. It is a busy well run site with a lively entertainment programme in high season. The site has 180 pitches (69 for touring), all with electricity, water and drain. As yet there is little shade but pitches are separated by small trees and bushes and are reasonable in size.

Facilities

Two modern toilet blocks are kept very clean and include washbasins mainly in cabins. Units for disabled people. Washing machines and dryers. Fridge hire. Basic provisions kept with village store just 100 m. Smart bar/restaurant (1/5-10/9). Attractive, kidney-shaped heated pool, indoor pool, jacuzzi and paddling pool. Tennis, minigolf (both free in low season). Internet access. Not suitable for American motorhomes. Off site: Riding and fishing within 5 km.

Open

1 April - 30 September.

At a glance

Welcome & Ambience	✓✓✓✓✓	Location	✓✓✓✓
Quality of Pitches	✓✓✓✓	Range of Facilities	✓✓✓✓

Directions

Site is in centre of St Hilaire la Forêt. From Les Sables d'Olonne take D949 (La Rochelle) towards Talmont St Hilaire and Luçon 7 km. after Talmont turn right on D70 to St Hilaire la Forêt. Site is on the left before village centre.

Charges 2004

Per unit incl. 2 persons and electricity (6A)	€ 16,00 - € 24,00
extra person	€ 4,00 - € 7,00

Reservations

Advised for high season with 25% deposit and fee (€ 25). Tel: 02 51 33 32 38. E-mail: grand-metairie@wanadoo.fr

FR85330 Camping Naturiste Cap Natur'

Mobile homes ▶ page 376

151 ave de la Faye, 85270 St Hilaire-de-Riez (Vendée)

Situated on the northern outskirts of the busy resort of St Hilaire-de-Riez, and only about one kilometre from the nearest beach (six kilometres from the nearest official naturist beach beside Plage des 60 Bornes) this family campsite for naturists is in an area of undulating sand dunes and pine trees. The 140 touring pitches nestle among the dunes and trees and offer a wide choice to suit most tastes, including the possibility of electrical connections (10A), although in some cases long leads are needed. Despite the undulating terrain, some pitches are quite level and thus suitable for motorcaravans. The modern facilities are excellent and include both open air and indoor pools, and a jacuzzi. Around the pool is an ample paved sunbathing area, including a stepped 'solarium'. The whole of the indoor complex is a designated non-smoking area. In season a regular Saturday evening 'soirée' is held with a set Vendéen meal, wine and entertainment. There is an air of peace and quiet about this site which contrasts with the somewhat frenzied activity which pervades many of the resorts in this popular tourist area, with a friendly, warm welcome from the family that own it. A number of apartments, tents and mobile homes are on site.

Facilities

Sanitary facilities are basic, but clean, consisting of one indoor (heated) and one outdoor (but roofed) block. Both blocks have open plan hot showers, British style WCs, washbasins, baby baths and children's toilets. Small shop (with takeaway pizza's) and restaurant (menu includes some local specialities), good sized bar, with TV, pool tables and various indoor table games. Indoor and outdoor swimming pools. Fitness classes in high season. Massage room. Play area on soft sand. Volleyball and archery. Torches useful. Bicycle hire. Not suitable for American motorhomes.
Off site: Beach 2 km. Fishing 5 km. Naturist beach 6 km. Golf, riding and boat launching 10 km.

Open

9 April - 1 November.

At a glance

Welcome & Ambience	✓✓✓✓	Location	✓✓✓✓
Quality of Pitches	✓✓✓✓	Range of Facilities	✓✓✓✓

Directions

Site is on the north side of St Hilaire-de-Riez. From Le Pissot roundabout go south on the D38, follow signs for St Hilaire at first roundabout you come to (first exit off roundabout), then at second roundabout turn right signed 'Terre Fort'. At third Y-shaped junction right again signed 'Parée Prèneau' (also site sign here). Site is 2 km along this road on left.

Charges 2004

Per unit incl. 2 adults	€ 14,50 - € 26,50
extra person	€ 2,50 - € 5,70
child (under 13 yrs)	€ 1,60 - € 4,10
animal	€ 2,20
electricity (10A)	€ 4,20

Camping Cheques accepted.

Reservations

Advised in high season and for French holidays. Made with 25% deposit and booking fee (€ 27.44). Single male visitors are not accepted. Tel: 02 51 60 11 66. E-mail: info@cap-natur.com

FR85080 Hotellerie de Plein Air La Puerta del Sol

Les Borderies, Chemin de Hommeaux, 85270 St Hilaire-de-Riez (Vendée)

La Puerta del Sol is a good quality campsite a short distance away from the busy coast. It is suitable not only for families with teenage children to entertain, but also for those seeking a more peaceful and relaxing holiday. There are 216 pitches, of which 158 are used for touring units. Pitches are level with dividing hedges and many receive shade from the mature trees on the site. Each pitch is fully serviced with water, waste water point and electricity. A self-service restaurant and takeaway with reasonably priced food overlooks the pool and terrace. In July/Aug. a range of activities is provided for adults and children, including a children's club, aqua aerobics, swimming lessons, tournaments and games, with evening entertainment in the bar. There is one small French tour operator on site (20 pitches).

TRAVEL SERVICE SITE

TO BOOK CALL 0870 405 4055 OR www.alanrogersdirect.com

Facilities

Three well maintained toilet blocks of identical design have a mix of Turkish and British style WCs, washbasins in cabins and baby baths. Dishwashing and laundry sinks. Laundry with washing machines and irons. Fully equipped rooms for disabled visitors. Small shop (1/7-31/8). Bar (15/5-15/9). Self-service restaurant and takeaway (1/7-31/8). Swimming pool, new slide and paddling pool (15/5-15/9; no bermuda style shorts). Play area. Tennis court. Bicycle hire. Volleyball, table tennis and video games. American motorhomes are accepted in limited numbers with reservation.
Off site: Riding, fishing and golf within 5 km. Nearest sandy beach 5 km. St Jean de Monts 7 km.

Open

1 May - 15 September.

At a glance

Welcome & Ambience	✓✓✓✓	Location	✓✓✓✓
Quality of Pitches	✓✓✓✓	Range of Facilities	✓✓✓✓

Directions

From Le Pissot (7 km. north of St Gilles Croix-de-Vie on D38) take the D59 towards Le Perrier. Site is 2 km. along this road on the right down a short side road. A large sign for the site is 200 m. before the turn with another on the left directly opposite the turning.

Charges 2004

Per unit incl. up to 3 persons and services	€ 17,50 - € 33,00
extra person	€ 4,70 - € 6,30
child (under 7 yrs)	€ 2,30 - € 3,20
animal	€ 2,00

Reservations

Advised for high season and made for any period with deposit (€ 138) and fee (€ 30.49).
Tel: 02 51 49 10 10.
E-mail: puerta-del-sol@wanadoo.fr

FR85390 Camping des Batardières

85440 St Hilaire-la-Foret (Vendée)

Camping des Batardières is a haven of tranquillity on the edge of an unspoilt village, yet just five kilometres from the sea. It is an attractive, unsophisticated little site, lovingly maintained by its owners for the past 23 years. Many visitors return year after year. There are 75 good-sized pitches (a few up to 130 sq.m.) and all are available for touring units (there are no mobile homes and no tour operators!) All have easy access to water and electricity (6A, or 2A for tents). Otherwise there are few facilities on site.

Facilities

The centrally positioned sanitary block is kept very clean and visitors are encouraged to keep it that way (no shoes in the shower cubicles, for instance) - it seems to work. Some washbasins in cubicles for ladies. Dishwashing and laundry facilities, including a washing machine and a dryer. TV room, table tennis and a tennis court. Play area and a huge field for games, kite-flying etc. Not suitable for American motorhomes. Off site: Village shop and bar only a short walk (200 m.) from the entrance. Nearby Jard-sur-Mer (5 km.) has good supermarkets, shops, bars, restaurants, a weekly market and the sea.

At a glance

Welcome & Ambience	✓✓✓✓	Location	✓✓✓✓✓
Quality of Pitches	✓✓✓✓✓	Range of Facilities	✓✓✓

Directions

Site is on edge of St Hilaire-la-Forêt. From Les Sables d'Olonne take D949 (la Rochelle) road towards Talmont St Hilaire and Luçon 7 km. after Talmont turn right on D70 to St Hilaire-la-Forêt and site is signed to the right as you approach the village.

Charges 2004

Per unit incl. 2 persons	€ 19,00
with electricity	€ 22,00
extra person	€ 3,00
child (under 5 yrs)	€ 2,00
dog	€ 1,50

Reservations

Contact site. Tel: 02 51 33 33 85.

Open

27 June - 2 September.

FR85350 Camping Caravaning La Ningle

Chemin des Roselières 66, 85270 St Hilaire-de-Riez (Vendée)

Camping La Ningle is well situated to explore the beautiful port of St Gilles Croix de Vie, with its abundance of restaurants (where seafood is served direct from the morning's catch) and pedestrianised shopping area with a variety of individual boutiques. You are guaranteed to receive a warm welcome at this site from M. & Mme. Guibert, who have established a very pleasant campsite with a friendly, family atmosphere. There are 155 pitches, 80 available for touring units. All have electricity (6A) and a limited number are fully serviced (electricity, water and drainage). Pitches are spacious with dividing hedges and all have some shade. The nearest beach is a 500 m. walk through a pine forest, but there are also three small swimming pools on site.

Facilities

Two regularly cleaned toilet blocks include some washbasins in cubicles. Well equipped toilet/shower room for disabled people and large family shower room in the main block. Laundry and dishwashing facilities. Washing machines and dryer. Bread available July/Aug. Takeaway three evenings per week. Bar (July/Aug) with entertainment twice a week in high season. Main swimming pool, larger children's pool, paddling pool and water slide. Small fitness suite with range of equipment (no instructor, but free). Tennis court. Games field with volleyball and table tennis. Games room with pinball and arcade machines. Small lake for fishing (free). Children's activities (July/Aug), and regular petanque and tennis competitions. Off site: Small supermarket and takeaway 200 m.

Open

15 May - 15 September.

At a glance

Welcome & Ambience	✓✓✓✓✓	Location	✓✓✓✓
Quality of Pitches	✓✓✓✓	Range of Facilities	✓✓✓✓

Directions

Driving south on D38 St Jean de Monts - St Gilles road, turn right at L'Oasis hotel/restaurant in Orouet (6 km. outside St Jean de Monts), signed Les Mouettes. After 1.5 km. you come to a roundabout. Turn left here signed St Hilaire de Riez. After passing two campsites (Les Ecureuils and Bois Tordu) take next left turn, signed La Ningle. Site is approx. 150 m. on the left.

Charges 2004

Per pitch incl. 2 persons	€ 13,80 - € 19,50
with 6A electricity	€ 15,90 - € 22,30
with 10A electricity	€ 17,90 - € 24,50
extra person	€ 3,00 - € 4,10
child (under 7 yrs)	€ 1,60 - € 2,50
dog	€ 1,85

No credit cards.

Reservations

Made with deposit (€ 77.50) and fee (€ 15.25).
Tel: 02 51 54 07 11.
E-mail: campingdelaningle@wanadoo.fr

TRAVEL SERVICE SITE

TO BOOK CALL 0870 405 4055 OR www.alanrogersdirect.com

FR85610 Camping Les Aventuriers de la Calypso

Route de Notre-Dame-de-Monts, Les Tonnelles, 85160 St Jean-de-Monts (Vendée)

This site is ideally situated within 700 metres of the beautiful, sandy Vendée beaches and close to St Jean de Monts (four kilometres) with its wide variety of shops and restaurants. Although there are 253 pitches, only a limited number are for touring units, and these are situated amongst the site's own mobile homes (there are no tour operators here). The pitches are level, grassy and of good size, and are either in the open or shade, with hedges providing privacy. All have electricity (3-10A) and some have water and drainage. The site is neatly maintained with an attractive pool complex and amenities. There is a good variety of entertainment for all ages during the high season. A useful complex with facilities is 150 m. from the site which includes a pizzeria, supermarket and a popular seafood shop.

TRAVEL SERVICE SITE

TO BOOK CALL 0870 405 4055 OR www.alanrogersdirect.com

Facilities

The modern sanitary block is fully equipped including facilities for babies and disabled campers. A 'portacabin' style block has WCs, showers and washbasins. Both are very clean and well maintained. Laundry. Bar with restaurant area (high season). Very small shop with basic supplies. Games area. Tennis court. Bicycle hire. Entertainment in July and August. Off site: Commercial centre 150 m. Nearest beach 700 m. Notre Dame de Monts 3 km. St Jean de Monts 4 km. Numerous cycle routes.

Open

1 April - 30 September.

At a glance

Welcome & Ambience	✓✓✓✓	Location	✓✓✓✓
Quality of Pitches	✓✓✓✓	Range of Facilities	✓✓✓✓

Directions

Site is on the D38 St Jean de Monts - Notre Dame de Monts road, at the Les Tonnelles roundabout.

Charges 2004

Per unit incl. 2 persons	€ 21,00
serviced pitch	€ 24,00
extra person	€ 5,00
child (under 5 yrs)	€ 2,50
electricity	€ 2,50 - € 4,00

Reservations

Made with deposit (€ 100) and fee (€ 15).
Tel: 02 51 97 55 50.
E-mail: camping-apv@wanadoo.fr

FR85590 Camping Plein Sud

246 route de Notre-Dame-de-Monts, 85160 St Jean-de-Monts (Vendée)

Plein Sud is a small welcoming site with 110 grassy pitches, many with adequate shade and separated by hedges. All are of about 100 sq.m. and have electricity (4/6A), water and drainage. There is one main drive through the site and site owned and private mobile homes are mostly positioned nearer the entrance. Touring pitches are situated further from the main road and bar area and are more pleasantly peaceful. The pool is inviting with a small children's pool and fountain alongside. Only 800 metres away is the beautiful long stretch of safe sandy beach, which is accessed via a pleasant walk through pines and sand dunes. In high season there is a security guard and gate. There are no tour operators.

TRAVEL SERVICE SITE

TO BOOK CALL 0870 405 4055 OR www.alanrogersdirect.com

Facilities

Two modern, clean sanitary blocks provide washbasins in cabins. One block has a baby room. Dishwashing facilities. Washing machines and dryers. Small bar with TV and terrace. Heated pool (no Bermuda style shorts). Play area with volleyball and table tennis. Bread and milk can be ordered daily at reception. Outside caterers provide regular takeaways. Bicycle hire. Daily pony and trap rides for young children (free). Children's entertainment organised in high season. Off site: Small supermarket, bar and restaurants within 500 m. Golf, fishing and riding all within 5 km.

At a glance

Welcome & Ambience	✓✓✓✓	Location	✓✓✓✓
Quality of Pitches	✓✓✓✓	Range of Facilities	✓✓✓✓

Directions

Site is 1 km. north of St Jean de Monts on the D38, Route de Notre Dame de Monts, on the right almost opposite Camping L'Abri des Pins.

Charges 2004

Per unit incl. 3 persons	€ 12,00 - € 22,00
incl. 4A electricity	€ 14,00 - € 24,00
incl. water and drainage	€ 16,00 - € 26,00
extra person	€ 2,50 - € 4,50
child (2-5 yrs)	free - € 2,50

Reservations

Made with deposit (€ 53) and fee (€ 23). Tel: 02 51 59 10 40. E-mail: camping-pleinsud@club-internet.fr

Open

1 May - 15 September.

FR85150 Camping La Yole

Mobile homes ▶ page 375

Chemin des Bosses, Orouet, 85160 St Jean-de-Monts (Vendée)

La Yole is an attractive, popular and well run site, two kilometres from a sandy beach. It offers 278 pitches (100 touring pitches), the majority under trees with ample shade and separated by bushes and the trees. All have electricity (10A), water and drainage and are of 100 sq.m. or more. The pool complex is surrounded by a paved sunbathing area and overlooked by a new bar and restaurant which have a large terrace. A pleasant walk through pine woods then by road leads to two sandy beaches. The security barrier is closed at night. Used by tour operators (50%). A 'Sites et Paysages member'. This a friendly, popular site with welcoming owners.

Facilities

Two toilet blocks of older design, one refurbished, include washbasins in cabins, units for disabled people and baby baths, all kept very clean. The third block in the newer part of site is very modern with baby room. Laundry with washing machine, dryer and iron. Well stocked shop. Takeaway. Bar (1/5-1/9) and restaurant (18/5-31/8). Swimming pool with water slide, paddling pool and an indoor heated pool with jacuzzi. Play area on sand, large field for ball games and a club room. Tennis. Table tennis, pool and video games. Organised entertainment in high season. Only gas barbecues are permitted. Off site: Fishing, golf and watersports 6 km. at St Jean.

At a glance

Welcome & Ambience	✓✓✓✓✓	Location	✓✓✓✓
Quality of Pitches	✓✓✓✓	Range of Facilities	✓✓✓✓✓

Directions

Signed off the D38, 6 km. south of St Jean de Monts in the village of Orouet.

Charges 2005

Per unit incl. 2 persons, electricity, water and drainage	€ 17,00 - € 28,70
tent incl. 2 persons, electricity and water	€ 15,00 - € 23,00
extra person	€ 3,65 - € 5,90
child (2-9 yrs)	€ 2,05 - € 4,30
baby (0-2 yrs)	free - € 3,25

Camping Cheques accepted.

Reservations

Advised, particularly for June, July and Aug. Tel: 02 51 58 67 17. E-mail: contact@la-yole.com

Open

2 April - 30 September.

FR85120 Haven Camping Le Bois Masson

149 rue des Sables, 85160 St Jean-de-Monts (Vendée)

Le Bois Masson is a large, lively site with modern buildings and facilities in the seaside resort of St Jean-de-Monts. As with other sites here, the long, sandy beach is a few minutes away by car, reached through a pine wood. This site, popular with tour operators, offers 500 good sized pitches, all with electricity. Most are occupied by mobile homes. Pitches are of sandy grass, mostly separated by hedges, with medium sized trees providing some shade. There are some pitches with water and drainage and an area kept for those who prefer a quieter pitch. There is plenty of on-site entertainment over a long season. The pool complex is impressive and includes a large outdoor pool, a paddling pool, a separate slide and landing pool and, for cooler weather, an indoor pool, with sliding doors to the outside. A jacuzzi, sauna and fitness room are also provided together with many other sports. Very busy in high season, this is not a site for those seeking somewhere quiet, but there is plenty to do for those perhaps with older children.

Facilities

Four sanitary blocks of excellent design provide modern showers with mixer taps, washbasins in cabins and British style WCs. Facilities for disabled visitors and babies. Dishwashing room (with dishwashers). Laundry. Comprehensive amenities housed in modern buildings fronting on to the road include a good supermarket, a large, lively bar with entertainment room, overlooking the pools, a restaurant and a creperie. Many activities including tennis, volleyball, table tennis and bicycle hire. Gas barbecues only are permitted. Mobile homes and rooms to rent. Off site: Riding, golf, squash, watersports near.

At a glance

Welcome & Ambience	✓✓✓✓✓	Location	✓✓✓✓
Quality of Pitches	✓✓✓✓	Range of Facilities	✓✓✓✓✓

Directions

From the roundabout at the southeast end of the St Jean de Monts bypass road, turn into town following signs to 'Centre Ville' and site, which is on the right after 400 m.

Charges 2004

Per pitch (incl. 2 persons and electricity € 13,00 - € 34,00

Reservations

Contact site. Tel: 02 51 58 62 62. E-mail: boismasson@haven.fr

Open

19 March - 10 October.

FR85090 Camping L'Abri des Pins

Route de Notre-Dame-de-Monts, 85160 St Jean-de-Monts (Vendée)

L'Abri des Pins is situated on the outskirts of the pleasant, modern resort of St Jean-de-Monts and is separated from the sea and long sandy beach by a strip of pinewood. From the back entrance of the site it is a pleasant 15 minute walk to the beach. Bathing is said to be safer here than on most of the beaches on this coast, but is nevertheless supervised in July/August. The site has 218 pitches, 78 of which are for touring units with 30 larger than average, with electricity, water and drainage. Electricity is also available to the other pitches which are around 100 sq.m, fully marked out with dividing hedges and quite shady. Many pitches are occupied by privately owned mobile homes, but there are no tour operators on the site. Throughout the season visitors may use the facilities at Les Places Dorées (under the same family ownership) across the road.

Facilities

The two sanitary blocks have been modernised and include washbasins in cabins, laundry and dishwashing sinks. Good small shop and bar/restaurant on the far side of the site provides good quality, value for money meals, both to eat in and take away (all 1/7-31/8). Outdoor, heated swimming pool and water slide, plus small pool for children, with decked sunbathing area (1/6-15/9; no bermuda style shorts). Daily children's club, football, petanque, aqua aerobics. Off site: Supermarket 10 minutes walk. Walking, cycling, fishing and riding within 1 km.

Open

1 June - 15 September.

At a glance

Welcome & Ambience	✓✓✓✓	Location	✓✓✓✓
Quality of Pitches	✓✓✓	Range of Facilities	✓✓✓✓

Directions

Site is 4 km. from the town centre on St Jean-de-Monts - Notre Dame-de Monts/Noirmoutiers road (D38), on left heading north, just after Camping les Amiaux.

Charges guide

Per unit incl. 3 persons	
and electricity	€ 18,20 - € 28,00
with water	€ 19,00 - € 29,00
extra person	€ 2,80 - € 4,70
child (under 5 yrs)	€ 1,70 - € 3,00
pet	free - € 2,80

Deposit required for armband for access to pool and site (high season only).

Reservations

Advised for high season; min. stay 12 nights between 14/7-15/8. Made with deposit (€ 92) and fee (€ 23). Tel: 02 51 58 83 86. E-mail: abridespins@aol.com

FR85280 Camping Les Places Dorées

Route de Notre-Dame-de-Monts, 85160 St Jean-de-Monts (Vendée)

Les Places Dorées is owned by the same family as L'Abri des Pins (8509) which is just across the road. It is a much newer site, but maturing trees are gradually beginning to offer some shade. The site has a range of facilities, including a pool complex, but one of the main reasons for visiting the Vendée is for its beaches and the closest beach to Les Places Dorées is a pleasant 15 minute walk away (through L'Abri des Pins and then alongside the pine forest and sand dunes). The site has 245 grassy pitches, the quietest being towards the back of the site. Each one is separated, all have electrical connections (6A) and some are also equipped with water and drainage. One small British tour operator is on site (18 pitches). In low season the site is quiet but it can be noisy in high season with the bar and disco closing late.

Facilities

Three modern toilet blocks include washbasins in cubicles. Facilities for disabled visitors. Laundry and dishwashing sinks. Washing machines and dryers. Swimming pool complex with water slides, jacuzzi area and waterfall (no bermuda style shorts). In high season the site becomes quite lively with plenty of organised entertainment, most based around the bar/restaurant area. High season children's club at L'Abri des Pins, also organised activities for adults (petanque tournaments, aqua aerobics, etc). The facilities at L'Abri des Pins may be used - well stocked shop (July/Aug), tennis , fitness room, swimming pools and a games room.

At a glance

Welcome & Ambience	✓✓✓	Location	✓✓✓✓
Quality of Pitches	✓✓✓✓	Range of Facilities	✓✓✓✓

Directions

Site is 4 km. north of St Jean de Monts on the D38 St Jean de Monts - Notre Dames de Monts road on the right hand side, almost opposite L'Abri des Pins.

Charges 2004

Per pitch incl. 3 persons	
and electricity	€ 21,00 - € 30,00
extra person	€ 3,50 - € 5,00
child	€ 2,30 - € 3,30
dog	free - € 2,80

Reservations

Advised for high season; min. stay 12 nights between 14/7-15/8. Tel: 02 51 59 02 93. E-mail: abridespins@aol.com

Open

16 June - 1 September.

FR85360 Camping La Forêt

190 chemin de la Rive, 85160 St Jean-de-Monts (Vendée)

Camping La Forêt has been owned by M. and Mme. Jolivet for the past few years and they work hard to provide a small, quality site. Well run and attractive, with a friendly, family atmosphere, it provides just 61 pitches with 50 for touring units. Of 100 sq.m. in size, the pitches are surrounded by mature hedges and have water and electricity. Over 50 species of trees are planted on the site, providing shade to every pitch, and the Jolivets provide an information panel by reception to help you identify the various types. There is one tour operator on the site (13 pitches), but their presence is in no way intrusive and the site has a quiet and relaxed atmosphere, ideal for couples or families with young children.

Facilities

The central toilet block is kept very clean and includes washbasins in cubicles. Laundry and dishwashing sinks. Baby bath. Facilities for disabled people. Washing machine and although clothes lines are prohibited, free-standing clothes airers are loaned for drying. Motorcaravan waste tanks can be emptied on request. Basic provisions sold in reception, including fresh bread. Takeaway at excellent prices all season. Small, but inviting swimming pool (15/5-15/9). Play area. Table tennis. Bicycle hire. Only gas and electric barbecues allowed, communal barbecue in centre of site. Not suitable for American motorhomes. Off site: Local beach 400 m. along forest path. Network of cycle paths runs through the forest and local marshland.

Open

15 May - 28 September.

At a glance

Welcome & Ambience	✓✓✓✓✓	Location	✓✓✓✓
Quality of Pitches	✓✓✓✓	Range of Facilities	✓✓✓✓

Directions

Site is 5.5 km. from town centre, just off the D38. Follow D38 out of St Jean de Monts, towards Notre Dame de Monts. After 4.5 km. you come to a roundabout with a pizzeria called Les Tonnelles. Go straight over the roundabout, and in 1 km. turn left at sign for site and 'Plage de Pont d'Yeu'. Follow road as it almost doubles back on itself and site is on left in about 100 m.

Charges 2004

Per pitch incl. 2 persons	€ 16,00 - € 23,50
extra person	€ 3,00 - € 4,50
child (under 7 yrs)	€ 3,00
dog	€ 2,00
electricity (6A)	€ 3,80

No credit cards.

Reservations

Advised, particularly for high season and made with € 34 deposit; min. 15 nights 2/7-19/8.
Tel: 02 51 58 84 63.
E-mail: camping-la-foret@wanadoo.fr

FR85620 Camping Le Caravan'ile

B.P. No.4, La Guérinière, 85680 Ile de Noirmoutier (Vendée)

This well appointed, 8.5 hectare, family run site is reached by crossing the bridge on the D38 to the pretty island of Noirmoutier. It is also accessible via the causeway (Le Gois) at low tide. Not far from the town centre, with an adjoining sandy beach, the site offers indoor and outdoor swimming pools, a popular sauna, jacuzzi and mini-gym and a variety of entertainment in high season to suit all ages. The level touring pitches are mainly situated near the beach (shielded by the sand dune) and all have electricity (6A). Some also have a water point, but no dividing hedges or shade. A few are situated on a ridge with sea views to the front and rear. Camping Le Caravan'ile has a very French ambience, with no tour operators.

Facilities

Three immaculately clean sanitary blocks, each with showers, British toilets, some enclosed wash cabins and facilities for disabled people. Hot showers only available 0800-1200 and 1700-2100 hrs. Laundry. Dishwashing. Heated indoor and outdoor swimming pools, paddling pools and flume. Fitness room, sauna and jacuzzi. Bar/takeaway (July/August). Games and sports area. Organised entertainment in July/August. Off site: Bar, restaurant, ATM, small supermarket and minigolf, all 500 m. Riding, cycling, windsurfing, aquarium, water theme park and salt marshes within close proximity.

At a glance

Welcome & Ambience	✓✓✓✓	Location	✓✓✓✓✓
Quality of Pitches	✓✓✓	Range of Facilities	✓✓✓✓

Directions

Take D38 road from the mainland, crossing bridge to Ile de Noirmoutier. Site is at the roundabout at La Guérinière, on the left.

Charges 2004

Per unit incl. 2 persons	€ 9,10 - € 17,20
incl. 5A electricity	€ 11,10 - € 20,30
extra person	€ 2,70 - € 4,20
child (2-7 yrs)	€ 1,70 - € 2,70
animal	€ 1,60 - € 2,60

Reservations

Contact site. Tel: 02 51 39 50 29.
E-mail: contact@caravanile.com

Open

1 March - 15 November.

FR85660 Camping Le Pont Rouge

Rue Clemenceau, 85220 St Reverend (Vendée)

This small, tranquil site is situated down a short tree-lined country lane just 600 metres from a small village. Suitable for people who prefer to be away from the frenzy of activity at the nearby coastal resorts. Owned and run by a young, enthusiastic, English-speaking and a very friendly couple, M. and Mme. Pousse, who make great efforts for an enjoyable stay. The pitches are grassy, varied in shape and size with most located near mature trees giving ample shade and separated by tall hedges, some flowering, ensuring peace and privacy. The 13 mobile homes, most with timber terraces, are situtated, with some touring pitches, in an open sunny aspect. All pitches have electricity but long leads may be required on some. Ample water points are situated close to all pitches.

Facilities

Two toilet blocks, one wihtin the main reception building with bright modern tiles has segregated showers, toilets, and wash cubicles. The second new block has segregated showers and wash cubicles with a uni-sex toilet section and includes a washing machine, and washing and ironing facilities. All very clean. Two play area - one with swings, slides and adventure frames set on a sandy base and one near new toilet block set on grass. Small sports field at rear of site. Small, neat, fenced-off pool complex at rear of reception with separate children's pool and slide. Bicycle hire. Basic provisions available in reception. Off site: Shops, restaurant and bakery in village - 600 m. Country walks, cycling. Golf and riding nearby.

At a glance

Welcome & Ambience	✓✓✓✓	Location	✓✓✓✓✓
Quality of Pitches	✓✓✓✓✓	Range of Facilities	✓✓✓

Directions

From the D6 Aizenay to St Gilles-Croie-de-Vie turn north onto D94 signed St Révérend about 4 km west of Coëx. Site is on left 400 m. just before village.

Charges 2004

Per unit incl. 2 persons and car	€ 11,82 - € 13,90
with electricity	€ 13,86 - € 16,30
person	€ 2,98 - € 3,50
child (under 8 yrs)	€ 2,13 - € 2,50
animal	€ 1,70 - € 2,00

Reservations

Contact site. Tel: 02 51 54 68 50.
E-mail: camping.pontrouge@wanadoo.fr

Open

1 April - 31 October.

FR85690 Camping Moncalm

85700 Angles (Vendée)

This site is a member of the Atlantique Pellerin Vacances group and has been recommended by our agent with a view to inclusion in our 2005 campsite inspection programme. Moncalm is a popular family site, sharing some amenities with its sister site L'Atlantique, across the road. There is a lively entertainment programme here and the site boasts an impressive pool complex. Mobile homes for rent.

Facilities

Shop. Bar, Takeaway food. Covered pool, paddling pool, water slides, sauna and jacuzzi. Gym. Tennis. Basketball. Play area. Games room. Football pitch. Minigolf. Children's club. Entertainment. Shuttle bus to beach. Off site: Nearest beach 7 km. Angles centre 300 m. (shops, restaurants etc). Golf. Fishing.

Open

May - September.

Directions

Angles can be found close to the D747 La Tranche-sur-Mer - La Roche sur Yon road. The site is close to the village centre, and clearly indicated.

Charges year

Per unit incl. 2 persons and electricity	€ 21,00
extra person	€ 5,00
child (0-4 yrs)	€ 2.50

Reservations

Advised for high season; contact site.
Tel: 02 51 97 55 50. E-mail: camping-apv@wanadoo.fr

Loire Valley

Maps 6 & 7

With over one hundred of France's finest châteaux, this is a region to inspire the imagination. The Loire valley is a charming region of lush countryside, fields of sunflowers, rolling vineyards and of course the great river itself.

Our tourist regions includes all the Loire Valley: 18 Cher, 28 Eure-et-Loir, 36 Indre, 37 Indre-et-Loire, 41 Loir-et-Cher, 45 Loiret. From Western Loire: 49 Maine-et-Loire, 53 Mayenne, 72 Sarthe. And from Poitou-Charentes: 79 Deux Sèvres, 86 Vienne

For centuries the Loire valley was frequented by French royalty and the great river winds its way past some of France's most magnificent châteaux: Amboise, Azay-le-Rideau, Chenonceau, with its famous arches that span the river and appear to 'float' on the water, and the fairytale Ussé with myriad magical turrets are just some of the highlights. *'Son et Lumière'* shows are also a wonderful experience.

Known as the Garden of France, the Loire's mild climate and fertile landscape of soft green valleys, lush vineyards and fields of flowers makes it a favourite with the visitors. Renowned for its wines, with hundreds to choose from, all are produced from vineyards stretching along the main course of the River Loire. Imposing abbeys, troglodyte caves, tiny Romanesque churches, woodland areas such as the Sologne and sleepy, picturesque villages reward exploration. Cities like Blois and Tours are elegant with fine architecture and museums and Paris is only one hour by TGV. One of the oldest towns of Loire valley is Saumur. Its old quarter, grouped around the riverbank beneath the imposing château, is particularly pleasant to wander around.

Cuisine of the region

Wild duck, pheasant, hare, deer, and quail are classics and fresh water fish such as salmon, perch and trout are favourite. Specialities include rillettes, andouillettes, tripes, mushrooms and the regional cheeses of Trappiste d'Entrammes and Cremet d' Angers, Petit Sable and Ardoises d'Angers cookies

Bourdaines: apples stuffed with jam and baked

Tarte a la citrouille: pumpkin tart

Tarte Tatin: upside down tart of caramelised apples and pastry

Places of interest

Amboise: château, Leonardo da Vinci museum

Beauregard: château with Delft tiled floors

Blois: château with architecture from Middle Ages to Neo-Classical periods

Chambord: Renaissance château

Chartres: cathedral with stained glass windows

Chinon: old town, Joan of Arc museum

Loches: old town, château and its fortifications

Orléans: Holy Cross cathedral, house of Joan of Arc

Tours: Renaissance and Neo-Classical mansions, cathedral of St Gatien,

Vendôme: Tour St Martin, La Trinité

Villandry: famous renaissance gardens

Alan Rogers tip

PUBLIC TRANSPORT IS LIMITED IN THIS REGION SO RENT A CAR OR BIKE - THIS IS EASY CYCLING COUNTRY, AND A BIKE RIDE ALONG THE RIVER BANKS WILL PROVE ENJOYABLE.

FR28110 Camping Municipal de Bonneval

Bois de Chievre, 28800 Bonneval (Eure et Loir)

On the outskirts of Bonneval and within walking distance of the centre, this municipal site offers good facilities in peaceful surroundings. The site has thick cover from trees in most parts with some pitches entirely hidden for those who like lots of privacy. Nearly all the pitches are marked out on grass in clearings, some on a slope, but the majority fairly flat. Of the 130 pitches, 120 have 6A electricity, some hardstanding. The site has no bar, restaurant or shop, but all are available in Bonneval itself or, when open, in the municipal swimming pool and tennis complex adjacent (reduced rates for campers). Caravans with double axles or more than 5.6 m. are not accepted.

Facilities

Sanitary facilities consist of one large block, plus three smaller units without showers. The large block has mostly chain operated hot showers, some washbasins in cubicles and facilities for disabled people. Laundry room with washing machine and ironing facilities. Motorcaravan services. Large TV/games room. Playground. Bicycle hire. Fishing. Boules court. Off site: Swimming pool and tennis adjacent.

Open

1 April - 31 December.

At a glance

Welcome & Ambience	✓✓✓✓	Location	✓✓✓✓
Quality of Pitches	✓✓✓✓	Range of Facilities	✓✓✓✓

Directions

Site signed from Bonneval town centre on N10 from Châteaudun to Chartres (on Rte de Vouvray).

Charges 2004

Per person	€ 2,80
child (2-7 yrs)	€ 1,50
pitch	€ 3,00
electricity	€ 3,00 - € 4,00

No credit cards. Barrier card deposit € 15.

Reservations

Contact site. Tel: 02 37 47 54 01.
E-mail: camping.bonneval@wanadoo.fr

FR28120 Camping Municipal du Pré de l'Eglise

Avenue du Pré de l'Eglise, 28380 St Remy-sur-Avre (Eure et Loir)

This neatly kept, useful little site has only 45 pitches, but is quite popular as a short stay or transit site with many nationalities as it lies just off the main N12 cross country route. The pitches are on level grass and divided by hedges, with electricity, and are arranged around a circular access road, with some shade from specimen trees. The guardian lives adjacent to the site. Double axle caravans are not accepted.

Facilities

The sanitary unit, in the older style, is adequate and includes facilities for disabled people. Dishwashing and laundry sinks are under cover. Washing lines. Salle with TV. Off site: Supermarket 2 km. in the direction of Nonancourt.

Open

1 April - 30 September.

At a glance

Welcome & Ambience	✓✓✓✓	Location	✓✓✓✓
Quality of Pitches	✓✓✓✓	Range of Facilities	✓✓✓

Directions

St Remy-sur-Avre is 9 km. west of Dreux on N12 and site is signed from N12 at traffic lights. Turn towards town centre and almost immediately turn right, then following signs turn left., and then left again. Site is on right with parking space outside the barrier.

Charges guide

Per person	€ 2,46
pitch	€ 3,27
electricity	€ 2,46 - € 6,00

Reservations

Contact site. Tel: 02 37 48 93 87.

FR36050 Camping Municipal Les Vieux Chênes

36310 Chaillac (Indre)

A delightful site on the outskirts of an attractive village, this is another little gem - a small site within walking distance of the centre, where there are shops, bars, cafés, restaurants, etc. The 34 grass pitches, all with electricity (15A), are very generous in size, slightly sloping, with hedging and some mature trees. The well manicured appearance and relaxed atmosphere add to the attraction of this peaceful environment. The adjacent lake is for fishing only, although there is access to a larger lake just one kilometre away where varied watersports - swimming, windsurfing, canoeing and pedaloes - can be enjoyed. The small water toboggan is free of charge. In high season it is possible some noise may carry from this area to the site.

Facilities

Heated sanitary facilities are insulated for winter use and include washbasins in private cabins. Bicycle hire. Winter caravan storage. Off site: Shops 200 m. Watersports 1 km. Fishing 25m.

Open

All year.

At a glance

Welcome & Ambience	✓✓✓✓	Location	✓✓✓✓
Quality of Pitches	✓✓✓✓	Range of Facilities	✓✓✓

Directions

From the north leave A20, south of Argenton sur Creuse, take D1 to St Benoit (16 km.) and then west to Chaillac on D36 (8.5 km). From the south leave A20 at exit 21, take D10 to St Benoit, then D36 as before. Go through the village and turn left by the Mairie.

Charges 2004

Per person	€ 1,55
pitch	€ 2,05 - € 2,55
electricity	€ 1,55

Reservations

Not made. Tel: 02 54 25 61 39.

FR37010 Camping de la Mignardière

22 avenue des Aubépines, 37510 Ballan-Miré (Indre-et-Loire)

Southwest of the city of Tours, this site is within easy reach of several of the Loire châteaux, notably Azay-le-Rideau. In addition, there are many varied sports amenities on the site or very close by. The site has 177 numbered pitches of which 139 are for touring units, all with electricity (6/10A) and 37 with drainage and water. The pitches are of a good size on rather uneven grass with limestone gravel paths (which are rather 'sticky' when wet). The site's facilities are supplemented by a small 'parc de loisirs' just across the road which provides a bar and refreshments, pony rides, minigolf, small cars, playground and other amusements. The barrier gates (coded access) are closed 22.30 - 07.30 hrs. Reservation is essential here for most of July/August.

Facilities

Two toilet blocks, one new near the site entrance, the other totally refurbished, include washbasins in private cabins, a unit for disabled people, baby bath and laundry facilities. Motorcaravan service point. Shop (15/5-15/9). Takeaway (1/7-31/8). Two large, heated swimming pools (15/5-15/9). Good tennis court. Table tennis. Bicycle hire. Off site: Attractive lake catering particularly for windsurfing 300 m. (boards can be hired or use your own) and family fitness run. Fishing 500 m. Riding 1 km. Golf 3 km. Tours centre 8 km.

Open

10 April - 25 September.

At a glance

Welcome & Ambience	✓✓✓✓✓	Location	✓✓✓✓
Quality of Pitches	✓✓✓✓	Range of Facilities	✓✓✓✓

Directions

From A10 autoroute take exit 24 and D751 towards Chinon. Turn right after 5 km. at Campanile Hotel following signs to site. From Tours take D751 towards Chinon.

Charges 2004

Per unit incl. 2 persons	€ 13,50 - € 19,00
with electricity, water and drainage	€ 19,00 - € 26,50
extra person	€ 4,00 - € 5,00
child (2-10 yrs)	€ 2,60 - € 3,00

Camping Cheques accepted.

Reservations

Made for any length with 30% deposit (min. € 40). Tel: 02 47 73 31 00. E-mail: info@mignardiere.com

FR37070 Camping de L'Ile Auger

Quai Danton, 37500 Chinon (Indre-et-Loire)

This is a well-placed site for exploring the old medieval town of Chinon and its impressive castle that was a home of England's Henry II and includes a museum to Joan of Arc. Alongside the River Vienne, it is a five minute walk over the main bridge to the town centre. The 277 pitches are numbered but not separated, with electricity (4/8/12A). A few are shaded by tall shrubs.

Facilities

Six toilet blocks around the site have British style WCs. A very good new block is next to the office building. Washing up sinks. Barrier locked 22.00 - 07.00 hrs. Off site: Tennis. Indoor and outdoor swimming pools nearby. Bicycle hire 1 km. Shop 1 km. Fishing 3 km. Riding 10 km.

Open

15 March - 15 October.

At a glance

Welcome & Ambience	✓✓✓✓	Location	✓✓✓✓✓
Quality of Pitches	✓✓✓✓	Range of Facilities	✓✓✓

Directions

From Chinon town cross the river and turn right at the end of the bridge. The campsite entrance is about 100 m. on the right.

Charges 2004

Per unit incl. 2 persons and electricity	€ 10,50 - € 13,50

Reservations

Contact site or the Mairie. Tel: 02 47 93 53 00. Tel: 02 47 93 08 35.

FR37060 Camping L'Arada Parc

Mobile homes page 377

Rue de la Baratière, 37360 Sonzay (Indre-et-Loire)

A good, well maintained site in a quiet location, Camping L'Arada Parc is a popular base from which to visit the numerous châteaux in this beautiful part of France. The 81 grass pitches all have electricity and 22 have water and drainage. The clearly marked pitches, some slightly sloping, are separated by maturing trees and shrubs that will, in time, provide some shade. An attractive, heated pool is on a pleasant terrace beside the restaurant and campers can enjoy their meal or a drink overlooking the pool. Entertainment, themed evenings and activities for children are organised in July/August. This is a new site with modern facilities which is developing well.

Facilities

Two modern toilet blocks provide unisex toilets, showers and washbasins in cubicles. Excellent baby room, Facilities for disabled visitors (wheelchair users may the gravel in front of the lower block difficult). Dishwashing and laundry sinks under cover at each block. Laundry with washing machine, dryer and ironing board. Shop, bar, restaurant and takeaway (27/3-31/10). Swimming pool (no Bermuda style shorts; 1/5-13/9). Play area, covered games area. Boules, volleyball, badminton and table tennis. TV room. Bicycle hire.
Off site: Tennis 200 m. Riding 7 km. Fishing 9 km. Golf 12 km.

At a glance

Welcome & Ambience	✓✓✓✓✓	Location	✓✓✓✓
Quality of Pitches	✓✓✓✓	Range of Facilities	✓✓✓✓✓

Directions

Sonzay is northwest of Tours. Take D959 Tours - Château-la-Vallière road, then D6 to Sonzay and follow camping signs. Site is signed from the D959.

Charges 2004

Per unit incl. 2 persons	€ 14,50
extra person	€ 4,50
child (2-7 yrs)	€ 3,00
electricity (10A)	€ 3,00

Camping Cheques accepted.

Reservations

Made with deposit (30%); contact site.
Tel: 02 47 24 72 69. E-mail: laradaparc@free.fr

Open

1 April - 1 November.

FR37110 Camping Municipal Au Bord du Cher

RN 76, 37270 Veretz (Indre-et-Loire)

This is an inexpensive, well laid out site on the banks of the River Cher with views through tall elm trees to the Château of Veretz. Monsieur Menard and his wife live in a caravan on site during the season and are always pleased to welcome British tourists. With 64 pitches, most divided by small hedges and all with at least 6A electricity, the site is just outside the town of Veretz where shops, restaurants, bars, etc. can be found. A wooden chalet houses reception and plenty of tourist information, with notice boards giving weather forecasts, etc. In addition, the manager is always willing to offer information and advice about where to go and what to see in the area. Of particular interest for railway enthusiasts are restored steam trains and track in the area. River trips are possible in the replica of a boat used to carry goods (mainly wine) on the river until the '20s. English is spoken.

Facilities

Large, modern sanitary block includes British and Turkish style WCs, dishwashing under cover, laundry and washing machine. Motorcaravan service point. Takeaway with covered area to sit and eat (from mid-June). Communal barbecue. Playground. Table tennis. Not suitable for American motorhomes. Off site: Baker 700 m. Tennis 1 km. Riding 3 km. Outdoor swimming pool (July/Aug) 4 km. Bicycle hire 12 km. Bus service from Tours station to Bleré passes site entrance. Fishing nearby.

At a glance

Welcome & Ambience	✓✓✓✓	Location	✓✓✓✓
Quality of Pitches	✓✓✓	Range of Facilities	✓✓✓

Directions

Site is at Veretz, via the N76, 10 km. southeast of Tours (much better than the municipal at St Avertin).

Charges 2004

Per adult	€ 2,00
pitch	€ 3,50 - € 6,00
electricity	€ 2,60 - € 4,60

No credit cards.

Reservations

Contact site. Tel: 02 47 50 50 48.

Open

22 May - 26 September.

FR37090 Camping du Château de La Rolandière

37220 Trogues (Indre-et-Loire)

This is charming little site set in the grounds of a small château which has the appearance of a Queen Anne style dolls house. There are 30 medium sized, flat pitches, some gently sloping front to rear, and all separated by neat hedges. All but four have 10A electricity and water taps nearby and the parkland trees give shade. The château and adjoining buildings contain rooms to let and a small swimming pool serves them and the campsite. An eighteen hole minigolf meanders through the parkland and there is an area set aside for ball games, swings and slides for younger children. Sabine Toulemonde and her husband, who bought the château in 2002, offer a very warm welcome. Situated on the D760 between Ille Bouchard and St Maure-de-Touraine, the site is five kilometres west of the A10, convenient for an overnight break or for longer stays to explore the châteaux at Chinon, Loches or Azay-le-Rideau and the villages of Richelieu and Crissay-s-Manse.

Facilities

The refurbished French style toilet block provides showers, washbasins, dishwashing and laundry areas around central British style WCs with a separate provision for disabled visitors. There is a single washbasin cabin in both the male and female units. Washing machine and dryer available via reception. Bar with terrace and snacks. Small shop in reception for basic provisions. Swimming pool. Minigolf. Play area. Bicycle hire. Off site: Fishing 1 km. to River Vienne. Restaurant 5 km. adjacent to A10 junction. Full range of shops and commercial facilities in St Maure 8 km.

Open

15 April - 30 September.

At a glance

Welcome & Ambience	✓✓✓✓✓	Location	✓✓✓✓
Quality of Pitches	✓✓✓✓	Range of Facilities	✓✓✓✓

Directions

The site is 5 km. west from junction 25 on A10 at St Maure-de-Touraine on the D760 towards Chinon. The entrance is clearly signed and marked by a model of the château.

Charges 2005

Per adult	€ 5,00 - € 6,00
child	€ 2,50 - € 3,00
pitch	€ 7,00 - € 8,50
animal	€ 1,50 - € 2,00
electricity	€ 3,50

No credit cards.

Reservations

Contact site. Tel: 02 47 58 53 71.
E-mail: contact@larolandiere.com

FR37050 Camping Caravanning La Citadelle

Avenue Aristide Briand, 37600 Loches en Touraine (Indre-et-Loire)

A pleasant, well maintained site, La Citadelle is within walking distance of Loches, noted for its perfect architecture and its glorious history, at the same time offering a rural atmosphere in the site itself. Most of the 97 level, good-sized pitches (all with electricity) offer some shade from trees, although sun lovers can opt for a more open spot. Campers are given free entry to the adjacent municipal pool and tennis courts and there are many organised activities during July and August. Loches, its château and dungeons, is 500 m. A free bus/little train runs from the site to the centre in summer. A 'Sites et Paysage' member.

Facilities

Three toilet blocks provide British and Turkish style WCs, washbasins (most in cabins) and showers. Laundry facilities. Motorcaravan service area at the block nearest reception. Two excellent baby units and provision for disabled people. Play equipment for children. Boules, volleyball and games room. Small snack bar (July/Aug). Off site: Riding 3 km. Supermarket 3 km. Golf 7 km.

Open

19 March - 19 October.

At a glance

Welcome & Ambience	✓✓✓✓	Location	✓✓✓✓✓
Quality of Pitches	✓✓✓✓✓	Range of Facilities	✓✓✓✓

Directions

Site is south of Loches. From RN143 Châteauroux - Tours, follow signs to Loches centre at roundabout (look for Leclerc supermarket). Campsite is about 3 km. on right (well signed from ring road).

Charges 2004

Per pitch incl. 2 adults	€ 12,40 - € 17,30
with water and drainage	€ 16,50 - € 21,50
extra person	€ 2,00 - € 4,20
electricity (10A)	€ 3,10

Camping Cheques accepted.

Reservations

Advised in July/Aug. Tel: 02 47 59 05 91.
E-mail: camping@lacitadelle.com

FR37120 Castel Camping Parc de Fierbois

Ste Catherine de Fierbois, 37800 St Maure-de-Touraine (Indre-et-Loire)

Parc de Fierbois has an impressive entrance and a tree lined driveway – all rather beautiful and grand. Set among 250 acres of lakes and forest in the heart of the Loire Valley, the site itself is a lively family holiday site with a super pool complex and a sandy beach on the shores of the lake. In all, there are 320 pitches including 100 for touring units, the remainder being used by tour operators and for chalets and mobile homes. There are 80 touring pitches, mostly level and separated by low hedging or small trees, with water, drainage and electricity hook-ups (2-8A). The other pitches are small or medium in size, many unmarked and some sloping and in the shade. There is plenty here to occupy and entertain children and this site would be good for family holidays. English is spoken in reception.

Facilities

Three toilet blocks provide British style WCs, hot showers and washbasins in cubicles. Baby room. Dishwashing under cover. Washing machines and dryers. Motorcaravan service point. Shop. Bar. Restaurant. Takeaway. Pizzas. Indoor heated swimming pool. Water park complex with pools, long slides, paddling pool, etc. and grass sunbathing areas. New indoor entertainment and games bar with paved terrace overlooking the pools. Tennis. Volleyball. Badminton. Football pitch. Petanque area. Minigolf. Bicycle hire. Go-karts, electric cars and red London buses on a small circuit. TV and video room (French and English). Fishing. Pedaloes and canoeing in July/Aug. Entertainment programme in July/Aug. Off site: Riding 10 km. Golf 30 km.

At a glance

Welcome & Ambience	✓✓✓	Location	✓✓✓✓
Quality of Pitches	✓✓✓	Range of Facilities	✓✓✓✓

Directions

Travelling south on N10 from Tours, go through Montbazon and continue towards Ste Maure and Chatellerault. Site is signed about 16 km. outside Montbazon near the village of Ste Catherine. Turn off main road and follow signs to site. From A10 auto-route use Ste Maure exit and turn north up N10.

Charges 2004

Per unit incl. 2 persons	€ 15,00 - € 33,00
extra person	€ 5,00
electricity	€ 3,80

Reservations

Made with 25% deposit and fee (€ 15).
Tel: 02 47 65 43 35. E-mail: parc.fierbois@wanadoo.fr

Open

15 May - 15 September.

FR41030 Yelloh! Village Le Parc des Alicourts

Domaine des Alicourts, 41300 Pierrefitte-sur-Sauldre (Loir-et-Cher)

A secluded holiday village set in the heart of the forest and with many sporting facilities, Parc des Alicourts is midway between Orléans and Bourges, to the east of the A71. There are 490 pitches (just under half used by tour operators and with a number of mobile homes and chalets). All pitches have electricity connections (6A) and good provision for water, and most are 150 sq.m. (min. 100 sq.m). Locations vary from wooded to more open areas, thus giving a choice of amount of shade. All facilities are open all season and the leisure amenities are exceptional. Competitions are organised for adults as well as children and, in high season organised activities include a club for children with an entertainer twice a day, a disco once a week and a dance for adults. An inviting water complex (all season) includes two swimming pools, a pool with wave machine and beach area, and a spa, not forgetting three water slides.

Facilities

Three modern sanitary blocks include some washbasins in cabins and baby bathrooms. Washing machines and dryers. Excellent facilities for disabled visitors in one block (but with shallow step to reach them). Motorcaravan services. Shop with good range of produce (the nearest good-sized town is some distance). Restaurant with reasonable prices, plus takeaway in a pleasant bar with terrace. Water complex. 7 hectare lake with fishing, bathing, canoes, pedaloes and play area. Nine hole golf course (very popular). Well equipped play area. Football pitch, volleyball, tennis, mini-golf, table tennis, boules. Roller skating/skateboard area (bring your own equipment). Bicycle hire with cyclo-cross and mountain bikes and a way-marked path for walking and cycling.

At a glance

Welcome & Ambience	✓✓✓✓	Location	✓✓✓✓✓
Quality of Pitches	✓✓✓✓	Range of Facilities	✓✓✓✓✓

Directions

From A71, take Lamotte Beuvron exit (no 3) or from N20 Orléons to Vierzon (which runs parallel with the A71) turn left on to D923 towards Aubigny. After 14 km, turn right at camping sign on to D24E. Site is clearly marked from there in about 4 km.

Charges 2005

Per unit incl. 2 persons and electricity	€ 15,00 - € 38,00
extra person	€ 6,00 - € 8,50
child 7-17 yrs	€ 4,00 - € 6,50
child 1-6 yrs	free - € 5,50
dog	€ 7,00

Reductions for low season longer stays.

Reservations

Made for min. 7 days for July/Aug. only, with 25% deposit. Tel: 02 54 88 63 34.
E-mail: parcdesalicourts@wanadoo.fr

Open

17 May - 7 September.

FR37030 Camping Le Moulin Fort

37150 Francueil-Chenonceaux (Indre-et-Loire)

Camping Le Moulin Fort is a tranquil, riverside site that has been redeveloped by British owners, John and Sarah Scarratt. The 137 pitches are enhanced by a variety of trees and shrubs offering some shade and 80 pitches have electricity (6A). The attractive (unheated) swimming pool is accessed by a timber walkway over the mill race from the snack bar terrace adjacent to the restored mill building. The picturesque Chateau of Chenonceaux is little more than one kilometre along the Rive Cher and many of the Loire châteaux are within easy reach, particularly Amboise and its famous Leonardo de Vinci museum. Although not intrusive there is some noise from the railway line across the river and a few trains run at night. The site is more suitable for couples and families with young children.

Facilities

Two toilet blocks with all the usual amenities of a good standard, including washbasins in cubicles and baby baths. Shop, bar, restaurant and takeaway (all 15/5-30/9). Swimming pool (15/5-30/9). Minigolf. Games room and TV. Regular family entertainment including wine tasting, quiz evenings, activities for children and light-hearted games tournaments. Fishing. Bicycle hire. Off site: Riding 12 km. Golf 20 km.

Open

1 April - 31 October.

At a glance

Welcome & Ambience	✓✓✓✓✓	Location	✓✓✓✓✓
Quality of Pitches	✓✓✓✓✓	Range of Facilities	✓✓✓✓

Directions

Site is well signed from the N76 Tours - Vierzon road. From the D40 Tours - Chenonceaux road, go through the village and after 2 km. turn right on D80 to cross the river at Chisseaux. Site is on left just after the bridge.

Charges 2005

extra adult	€ 4,00 - € 5,00
child (4-112 yrs)	€ 2,00 - € 4,00
electricity (6A)	€ 4,00
dog	€ 2,00 - € 3,00

Reservations

Advised for high season and for large units at any time; contact site. Tel: 02 47 23 86 22.
E-mail: lemoulinfort@wanadoo.fr

FR41020 Castel Camping Château de la Grenouillière

41500 Suèvres (Loir-et-Cher)

Château de la Grenouillère is a comfortable site with good amenities on the N152 midway between Orléans and Tours. It is well situated for visiting many of the Loire châteaux and there are enough attractions on site and locally to make it suitable for a longer stay holiday. It is set in a 28-acre park and the 260 pitches (including 130 for tour operators and mobile homes) are in three distinct areas. The majority are in a well wooded area, with about 60 in the old orchard and the remainder in open meadow, although all pitches are separated by hedges. There is one water point for every four pitches and only 10 lack an electric hook-up (5A). Additionally, there are 14 'grand confort' pitches with a separate luxury sanitary block in the outbuildings of the château itself. A weekly trip to Paris, a canoe-kayak trip, wine cellar and cheese tasting visits, musical evenings and children's entertainment are organised in high season.

Facilities

Three sanitary blocks, one for each area, are modern and well appointed, including some washbasins in cabins. Washing machines and dryers in a small laundry. Shop. Bar. Pizzaria and pizza takeaway. Restaurant and Chicken Grill takeaway (1/6-5/9). Swimming complex of four pools (one covered) and a water slide. Tennis, squash, table tennis, pool, baby foot and video games. Internet point. Bicycle and canoe hire (July/Aug). Guided tours organised once a week. Off site: Fishing, riding, and aqua sports 5 km. Golf 10 km. Suèvres 3 km.

Open

1 May - 5 September.

At a glance

Welcome & Ambience	✓✓✓✓	Location	✓✓✓✓
Quality of Pitches	✓✓✓✓	Range of Facilities	✓✓✓✓✓

Directions

Site is between Suevres and Mer on north side of N152 and is well signed.

Charges 2004

Per unit incl. 2 persons	€ 18,50 - € 28,00
with 5A electricity	€ 22,50 - € 32,00
with full services	€ 26,00 - € 40,00
extra person	€ 5,00 - € 6,50
child (under 7 yrs)	€ 3,00 - € 4,50
dog	€ 3,00 - € 4,00

Less 10% during middle season, and 35% during low season.

Reservations

Booking fee €20. Deposit €90. Tel: 02 54 87 80 37.
E-mail: la.grenouillere@wanadoo.fr

Mobile homes ▶ page 378

Le Moulin Fort
CAMPING ★★★
37150 FRANCUEIL-CHENONCEAUX
éléphone : +33 (0) 2 47 23 86 22 - Fax : +33 (0) 2 47 23 80 93 - E-mail : lemoulinfort@wanadoo.fr
Camping
LE MOULIN FORT
offers you :
An unbeatable location within walking distance of Chenonceau castle
An ideal base for exploring the Loire region of France
A warm welcome from the English owners
A perfect place for relaxing by the river or enjoying the wide range of facilities and animation available on site
A good stopover point within easy reach of the UK ports, well-signposted and easy to find
On-site facilities :
*Shop *Bar *Take-away *Swimming pool
*TV room *Animation *Play-area
*Themed evenings *Bicycle hire
*Canoe hire *Barbecues permitted
*Motorcaravan service area
**Covered caravan storage available
***Reservation recommended for high season

FR41010 Le Parc du Val de Loire

Mobile homes page 378

Route de Fleuray, 41150 Mesland (Loir-et-Cher)

Between Blois and Tours, quietly situated among vineyards away from the main roads and towns, this family owned site is nevertheless centrally placed for visits to the châteaux; Chaumont, Amboise and Blois (21 km.) are the nearest in that order. There are 232 touring pitches of reasonable size, either in light woodland marked by trees or on open meadow with separators. All of the pitches have electricity (6A), and 100 of them also have water and drainage. Sports and competitions are organised in July/Aug. with weekly disco and dance for adults. Wine tasting opportunities each Friday. There are local walks and bike rides on marked paths (free maps available).

Facilities

Two original toilet blocks of varying standards include washbasins in cabins. Units for disabled visitors, baby bathrooms and laundry facilities. Motorcaravan service point. Large shop with bakery. Bar next to the pools, with restaurant, snack service, pizzeria and takeaway, TV room and large recreation room. Three swimming pools, the two smaller ones heated all season, one with popular water slide, (the newest 200 sq.m.). Tennis court with floodlighting, good playgrounds with skate board facilities, bicycle hire, table tennis, minigolf, BMX track, tennis training wall, football pitch, volleyball, badminton and basketball. Pony rides. Barbecue area. Off site: Fishing 2 km. Golf 4 km. Riding 10 km.

Open

26 March - 13 November.

At a glance

Welcome & Ambience	✓✓✓✓	Location	✓✓✓✓
Quality of Pitches	✓✓✓	Range of Facilities	✓✓✓

Directions

The village of Mesland is 5 km. northwest of Onzain, accessible from the Château-Renault/Amboise exit of A10 autoroute via D31 to Autrèche, continue 5 km. then left at La Hargardière at camp sign and 8 km. to site.

Charges 2005

Standard pitch (100 sq.m.) incl. 2 persons	€ 10,00 - € 21,70
large pitch (150 sq.m.) with water and drainage	€ 13,80 - € 27,30
extra person	€ 2,00 - € 5,60
child (2-7 yrs)	€ 1,50 - € 3,20
electricity 6-10A	€ 3,80
animal	€ 2,20

Reservations

Made for min. 4 days with deposit (25%) and fee (€ 20). only in high season Tel: 02 54 70 27 18. E-mail: parc.du.val.de.loire@wanadoo.fr

FR41090 Camping Municipal de la Varenne

41210 Neung-sur-Beuvron (Loir-et-Cher)

This is a particularly well organised site in a peaceful location, yet within easy walking distance of the town centre. It is a good economic base for visiting Orleans, Blois or the Chateaux of the Loire. The site has a slight slope but most of the 69 grass touring pitches are fairly level, all with electricity (10A). Some pitches are individual, others in bays of four, and some for tents amongst the trees. There is good shade in most areas. At the rear of the site is a large open field which slopes down to the small river. Each evening the warden visits every pitch to take the bread orders. Four mobile homes are for rent.

Facilities

An excellent, clean and well equipped modern building includes spacious showers, baby facilities, a suite for disabled people, and a washing machine. A second older unit at the rear of the reception building has additional good facilities. Freezer for Ice blocks. Motorcaravan service point. Playground. Volleyball. Two tennis courts. Table tennis. Bicycle hire. River fishing adjacent to site. Off site: The town has all services.

Open

Easter - 30 September.

At a glance

Welcome & Ambience	✓✓✓✓	Location	✓✓✓✓
Quality of Pitches	✓✓✓✓	Range of Facilities	✓✓✓✓

Directions

Neung-sur-Beuvron is about 40 km. east of Blois, and is 2 km. west of the 0922 about 22 km. north of Romarantin-Lanthenay. Site is 1 km. northeast of town centre (well signed}.

Charges 2004

Per adult	€ 1,80
child (5-16 yrs)	€ 0,95
pitch	€ 2,45
electricity	€ 2,30

Reservations

Contact site. Tel: 02 54 83 68 52. E-mail: mairie-neungsurbeuvron@wanadoo.fr

FR41070 Camping Caravanning La Grande Tortue

Mobile homes page 379

3 route de Pontlevoy, 41120 Candé-sur-Beuvron (Loir-et-Cher)

This is a pleasant, rustic site that has been tastefully developed in the surroundings of an old forest. It provides 169 touring pitches set amongst trees which provide shade as well as some sunshine. The majority of the pitches are more than 100 sq.m. and all have 6/10A electricity. The family owners continue to develop the site with a new multi-sports court already created and a covered swimming pool planned. During July and August, they organise a programme of trips including wine/cheese tastings, canoeing and horse riding excursions. Used by tour operators.

Facilities

Three sanitary blocks offer British style WCs, washbasins in cabins and push-button showers. Very basic chemical emptying point. Laundry with deep sinks, washing machine, dryer and ironing board. Shop selling provisions. Terraced bar and restaurant with reasonably priced food and drink (15/5-15/9). Swimming pool and two shallower pools for children (15/5-30/9). Trampolines, a ball crawl with slide and climbing wall, bouncy castle, table tennis. New multi-sport court. Off site: Walking and cycling. Bicycle hire 1 km. Fishing 500 m. Golf 7 km. Riding 8 km.

Open

9 April - 30 September.

At a glance

Welcome & Ambience	✓✓✓✓✓	Location	✓✓✓✓
Quality of Pitches	✓✓✓	Range of Facilities	✓✓✓✓

Directions

Site is just outside Candé-sur-Beuvron on the D651, midway between Amboise and Blois. From Amboise, turn right just before entering Candé, then immediately left into the campsite (well signed from the road).

Charges 2004

Per unit incl. 2 persons	€ 13,00 - € 21,00
incl. electricity	€ 17,00 - € 24,00
extra adult	€ 4,50 - € 5,90
child (under 9 yrs)	€ 3,20 - € 4,20
animal	€ 2,90

Camping Cheques accepted.

Reservations

Necessary in July and August. Tel: 02 54 44 15 20.
E-mail: grandetortue@libertysurf.fr

FR41040 Camping Château des Marais

27 rue de Chambord, 41500 Muides-sur-Loire (Loir-et-Cher)

The Château des Marais campsite is well situated to visit the chateau at Chambord (its park is impressive) and the other châteaux in the 'Vallée des Rois'. The site, providing 133 large touring pitches, all with electricity (6/10A), water and drainage and with ample shade, is situated in the oak and hornbeam woods of its own small château (in which there are rooms to let). An excellent swimming complex offers pools and two flumes. English is spoken and the reception from the enthusiastic owners and the staff is very welcoming. In high season, canoe trips on the Loire are popular: campers are taken by coach to Muides-sur-Loire and are collected three hours later at Boire. Used by tour operators (90 pitches). A 'Sites et Paysages' member.

Facilities

Four modern, purpose built sanitary blocks have good facilities including some large showers and washbasins en-suite. Washing machine. Motorcaravan service point. Shop and takeaway. Bar/restaurant with large terrace. Swimming complex with heated and unheated pools, water slide and cover for cooler weather. TV room. Bicycle hire. Fishing lake. Excursions by coach to Paris, an entertainment programme and canoe trips organised in high season. Off site: Riding 5 km. Golf 12 km. Village of Muides sur Loire, with a variety of small shops, etc. five minutes walk.

Open

15 May - 15 September.

At a glance

Welcome & Ambience	✓✓✓✓	Location	✓✓✓✓
Quality of Pitches	✓✓✓✓	Range of Facilities	✓✓✓✓✓

Directions

From A10 autoroute take exit 16 to Mer, then cross the Loire to join the D951 and follow signs. Site is signed off D103 to southwest of village. 600 m. from junction with the D112.

Charges 2004

Per pitch incl. 2 persons	€ 22,00 - € 28,00
extra person	€ 6,00
child (under 5 yrs)	€ 4,00
electricity (6/10A)	€ 4,00 - € 6,00
dog	€ 4,00

Credit cards accepted for amounts over € 80.

Reservations

Advised July/Aug. Tel: 02 54 87 05 42.
E-mail: chateau.des.marais@wanadoo.fr

FR41060 Camping de Dugny

CD 45 (la Cabinette), 41150 Onzain (Loir-et-Cher)

This well organised campsite started life as an 'a la ferme' back in 1976. Since then it has grown into an eight hectare camping site surrounded by many acres of wonderfully quiet farmland. Still under the same ownership, it now opens all year round. There are 300 pitches, with mobile homes (privately owned and to rent) leaving 190 tourist pitches. Generously sized, they are partially separated, some with shade and others open. All but 30 have electricity (10A), water and drainage. This is a campsite for active people, both young and older. Play areas and sports fields includes equipment for youngsters, a trampoline, mini golf, football and basket ball. A marquee provides entertainment for up to 12 year-olds and a large barn offers undercover table tennis. Adult and children's quad bikes can be hired or you can take a flight in a microlight from the site landing strip. Most activities take place away from the camping area to guard a quiet atmosphere. Coach trips to chateaux, wine cellars and other places of interest are arranged in July and August or when numbers are adequate.

TRAVEL SERVICE SITE

TO BOOK CALL 0870 405 4055 OR www.alanrogersdirect.com

Facilities

Three sanitary units include some washbasins in cubicles and provision for disabled people. Dishwashing and laundry sinks. Bread, ices, soft drinks and gas are stocked. Small restaurant and takeaway, with barbecue evenings organised on the terrace. Heated outdoor swimming pool complex with two pools (one with slides) and paddling pool. Large play areas for 4-12 year olds. Minigolf, table tennis, volleyball, basketball and a pétanque court. Internet point. Pony and horse riding around the farmland. Microlight flights. Pedaloes and row boats for hire. Varied activity programme including children's disco, boules and table tennis tournaments and camp-fire evenings. Off site: Local markets at Onzain, Montrichard, Blois and Amboise. A little train takes guests to a nearby wine cave, and a local farm that produces goats cheese.

At a glance

Welcome & Ambience	✓✓✓✓	Location	✓✓✓✓
Quality of Pitches	✓✓✓	Range of Facilities	✓✓✓✓✓

Directions

Onzain is southwest of Blois (15km) and on the opposite side of the river from Chaumont-sur-Loire. Take N152 Blois to Tours road, turn right onto D1 signed Onzain. Site is signed after the railway bridge. Turn right onto D58, then left onto D45. Keep following signs.

Charges 2004

Per adult	€ 5,80 - € 8,90
child (5-14 yrs)	€ 4,00 - € 5,00
child (under 5)	free
pitch	€ 3,10 - € 3,60
electricity	€ 3,60 - € 5,10

Camping Cheques accepted.

Reservations

Not normally required, but made with 25% deposit. Tel: 02 54 20 70 66.
E-mail: info@camping-de-dugny.fr

Open

All year.

FR45010 Sunêlia Les Bois du Bardelet

Mobile homes page 377

Route de Bourges, Poilly, 45500 Gien (Loiret)

This attractive, lively family site, in a rural setting, is well situated for exploring the less well known eastern part of the Loire Valley. A lake and the pool complex have been attractively landscaped in 12 hectares of former farmland, blending old and new with natural wooded areas and more open field areas with rural views. Bois du Bardelet provides 260 pitches with around 140 for touring units. All are larger than 100 sq.m. and have electrical connections, with some fully serviced. The communal areas are based on attractively converted former farm buildings with a wide range of leisure facilities. A family club card can be purchased to make use of the many activities on a daily basis (some high season only). Various activities and excursions are organised, the most popular being to Paris on Wednesdays.

Facilities

Three sanitary blocks (only one open outside 15/6-31/8) include washbasins in cabins and facilities for people with disabilities and babies. Washing machines. Shop (1/4-15/9). Pleasant terraced bar. Snack bar, takeaway and restaurant (1/4-15/9) and pizzeria. Three swimming pools, one outside for serious swimmers (1/5-31/8), one indoor child's pool, both free, and another indoor pool, heated and needing the club card. Aqua gym, fitness and jacuzzi room. New pool and games area for children. Archery. Lake for canoeing and fishing. Tennis, minigolf, boules and table tennis. Bicycle hire. Playground (under-8 yrs. Internet access. Off site: Supermarket 5 km. Riding 7 km. Golf 25 km. Walking and cycling routes from reception. Gien 5 km.

Open

Easter - 12 September.

At a glance

Welcome & Ambience	✓✓✓✓✓	Location	✓✓✓✓
Quality of Pitches	✓✓✓✓	Range of Facilities	✓✓✓✓✓

Directions

From Gien take D940 towards Bourges. After 5 km. turn right (signed) and right again to cross the road and follow signs to site. From Argens sur Sauldre take D940 towards Gien and site is signed to right after approx. 15 km. (narrow road). The entrance is about 200 yd. past what looks like the first site opening.

Charges 2004

Per unit incl. 2 persons	€ 23,00
electricity	€ 5,00
extra person (over 2 yrs)	€ 5,60
animal	€ 4,00
family leisure card (per week)	€ 38,00 - € 48,00

Camping Cheques accepted.
Less 15-25% in low seasons (20-40% for over 60s).

Reservations

Made with deposit (€ 54) and fee (€ 30).
Tel: 02 38 67 47 39. E-mail: contact@bardelet.com

FR41100 Camping Les Saules

D102 route de Contres, 41700 Cheverny (Loir-et-Cher)

Set in the heart of the châteaux region, this former municipal site had been allowed to run down and was eventually closed, but has recently been revitalised and re-opened by a local family. The tastefully renovated traditional reception buildings in their lakeside setting give a very pleasant welcome. There are 166 good size, level pitches with 159 available for touring units. All have shade from the many trees on the site, 150 have electricity (a few require leads longer than 25 m.) and there are ample water taps.

Facilities

Two sanitary blocks with toilets (mostly modern style, but two Turkish in the older block), showers, washbasins in cubicles and facilities for disabled visitors. Dishwashing and laundry sinks. Washing machine. The older block is due to be refurbished. Motorcaravan service point. Gas supplies. Shop selling local produce. Restaurant (set meal only). Bar. Snack bar and takeaway. Swimming and paddling pools. TV/social room. Two play areas. Large grass area for ball games. Minigolf. Table tennis. Fishing. Bicycle hire. Off site: Golf 3 km. Riding 3 km.

At a glance

Welcome & Ambience	✓✓✓✓✓	Location	✓✓✓✓
Quality of Pitches	✓✓✓✓	Range of Facilities	✓✓✓✓

Directions

From Cheverny take D102 south towards Contres. Site is on the right after about 2 km.

Charges 2004

Per unit incl. 2 persons	€ 17,00 - € 21,50
extra person	€ 4,50
electricity	€ 3,50 - € 7,00

Reservations

Can be made at any time with 25% deposit.
Tel: 02 54 79 90 01.
E-mail: contact@camping-cheverny.com

Open

1 April - 31 October.

FR49000 Camping du Lac de Maine

Avenue du Lac de Maine, 49000 Angers (Maine-et-Loire)

Set in the heart of the Anjou region, the Lac de Maine site has the advantage of being at the southern end of the Parc de Loisirs du Lac de Maine which is a leisure area with all sorts of activities. Most of the level 141 touring pitches are part grass and part gravel hardstanding, with the remainder being all gravel. All have water, drain and electricity. The main park entrance has a height restriction of 3.2 m, although there is an alternative gate. The adjacent 100-acre lake has a sandy beach for swimmers, windsurfing, sailing and pedaloes, while the park provides tennis courts and a nature reserve. This is a useful site, only five minutes from the centre of Angers. It is also suitable for American RVs.

Facilities

Two sanitary blocks, one which can be heated and includes some washbasins in cubicles. British style WCs (no seats). Facilities for babies and visitors with disabilities. Washing machines. Excellent motorcaravan service point. Reception stocks gas. Restaurant/bar (both early June - mid Sept). Heated L-shaped swimming pool. Volleyball. Pétanque. Bicycle hire. Playground. Internet point. Barrier card deposit € 20. Off site: Lake beach 0.5 km. Fishing 1 km. Riding 3 km. Golf 5 km.

Open

25 March - 10 October.

At a glance

Welcome & Ambience	✓✓✓✓	Location	✓✓✓✓✓
Quality of Pitches	✓✓✓✓	Range of Facilities	✓✓✓✓

Directions

Leave N23 (Angers ringroad) at signs for Quartier de Maine and Lac de Maine. Follow signs for Pruniers and Bouchemaine. Site is on the D111 and is well signed. Site also signed from centre of Angers (5 km).

Charges 2005

Per unit incl. 2 persons	€ 10,70 - € 14,90
extra person	€ 2,10
child (under 7 yrs)	€ 1,35
electricity (10A)	€ 3,10

Camping Cheques accepted.

Reservations

Advised for July/Aug. and made with deposit (€ 8 per night of stay) and fee (€ 6).
Tel: 02 41 73 05 03. E-mail: camping@lacdemaine.fr

FR49040 Camping de l'Etang

Mobile homes ▶ page 379

Route de St Mathurin, 49320 Brissac (Maine-et-Loire)

Originally the farm of the Château de Brissac (yet only 24 km. from the lovely town of Angers), this rural campsite retains the tranquillity and ambience of by-gone days and added the necessary comforts expected by today's campers. The 150 level touring pitches have pleasant views across the countryside. Separated and numbered, some have shade and all have electricity with water and drainage nearby. A small bridge crosses the river Aubance which runs through the site and there are two lakes where fisherman can enjoy free fishing. The site has its own vineyard and the wine produced can be purchased on the campsite and is highly recommended. Tour operators use 18 pitches.

TRAVEL SERVICE SITE

TO BOOK CALL 0870 405 4055 OR www.alanrogersdirect.com

Facilities

Three well maintained toilet blocks provide all the usual facilities. Laundry room with washing machines and dryers. Excellent baby room. Disabled visitors are well catered for. Motorcaravan service point. The adapted farmhouse houses reception, small shop and takeaway (from 19/5). Across the courtyard is a bar/restaurant serving crêpes, salads, etc (evenings form 15/6, all day 1/7-31/8). Swimming pool (heated and covered) and paddling pool. Fishing. Play area. Bicycle hire. Variety of evening entertainment in high season. Off site: Adjacent Parc de Loisirs (free for campers) is a paradise for young children with many activities including boating, pedaloes, pony rides, miniature train, water slide, bouncy castle and swings. Golf and riding 10 km.

At a glance

Welcome & Ambience	✓✓✓✓✓	Location	✓✓✓✓
Quality of Pitches	✓✓✓✓	Range of Facilities	✓✓✓✓

Directions

Take D748 south from Angers. Follow signs to Brissac-Quincé but do not enter the town, proceed to site along D55 (well signed) in direction of St Mathurin.

Charges 2005

extra person	€ 4,50 - € 6,00
child (0-10 yrs)	€ 3,00 - € 3,50
electricity	€ 3,00
dog	€ 2,00

Reservations

Contact site. Tel: 02 41 91 70 61.
E-mail: info@campingetang.com

Open

14 May - 10 September.

FR49010 Castel Camping L'Etang de la Brèche

Route Nationale 152, 5 Impasse de la Breche, 49730 Varennes-sur-Loire (Maine-et-Loire)

The Saint Cast family has developed L'Etang de la Brèche with loving care and attention on a 25-hectare estate four kilometres northeast of Saumur on the edge of the Loire behind the dykes. It is a peaceful base from which to explore the famous châteaux, abbeys, wine cellars, mushroom caves and Troglodyte villages in this region. The site provides 201 large, level pitches with shade from mixed tall trees and bushes, facing central, less shaded grass areas used for recreation. There are electrical connections to all pitches (in some cases a long cable may be required due to the size of the pitches), with water and drainaway on 63 of them. The restaurant, also open to the public, blends well with the existing architecture and, together with the bar area and terrace, provides a social base and is probably one of the reasons why the site is popular with British visitors. The swimming complex includes three pools: one with a removable cover, one outdoor, and a lovely pool for toddlers. The site includes a small lake (used for fishing) and wooded area ensuring a quiet, relaxed and rural atmosphere and making L'Étang de la Brèche a comfortable holiday base for couples and families. Used by tour operators (85 pitches).

Facilities

Three toilet blocks, modernised to good standards, include facilities for babies with two units for people with disabilities. Washing up sinks and laundry. Shop and epicerie. Restaurant, pizzeria and takeaway. Three heated pools. Tennis, basketball, minigolf and a field for football. Bicycle hire. General room, games and TV rooms. Well organised, varied sporting and entertainment programme (10/7-25/8). Child minding is arranged in afternoons. Internet point. Torch useful. Off site: Riding 2 km. Golf 8 km.

Open

15 May - 15 September.

At a glance

Welcome & Ambience	✓✓✓✓✓	Location	✓✓✓✓
Quality of Pitches	✓✓✓✓	Range of Facilities	✓✓✓✓✓

Directions

Site is 100 m. north off the main N152, about 4 km. northeast of Saumur on the north bank of the Loire.

Charges 2004

Per unit incl. 2 persons	€ 16,50 - € 27,00
incl. 3 persons	€ 20,50 - € 33,00
extra person	€ 4,00 - € 6,00
child (under 10 yrs)	€ 2,50 - € 3,00
electricity (10A)	free - € 3,00
water and drainage	€ 2,50

7th night free in low season.

Reservations

Made for min. 7 nights in high season (3 days in low season) with deposit and fee. Tel: 02 41 51 22 92. E-mail: mail@etang-breche.com

FR49020 Camping de Chantepie

St Hilaire-St Florent, 49400 Saumur (Maine-et-Loire)

The drive along the winding road bordered by apple orchards and vineyards is well rewarded on arriving at the colourful, floral entrance to Camping de Chantepie. A friendly greeting awaits at the attractive reception office set beside the tastefully restored farmhouse. Linked by gravel roads (which can be dusty), the 150 grass pitches are level and spacious, with some new larger ones for long units (state preference when booking). Most pitches have electricity (5/10A) and are separated by low hedges of flowers and trees which offer some shade. The panoramic views over the Loire from the pitches on the terraced perimeter of the meadow are stunning and from here a footpath leads to the river valley. Leisure activities for all ages are catered for in July/Aug. by the Chantepie Club, including wine tastings, excursions and canoeing. This is a good site for families.

Facilities

The toilet block is very clean and the provision of facilities is adequate with washbasins in cubicles, new showers (men and women separately) and facilities for disabled visitors. Well stocked shop. Bar, terraced café and takeaway (from 19/5). Covered and heated pool, outdoor pool and paddling pool protected from the wind by a stone wall. Play area. Terraced minigolf. Volleyball, TV, video games and table tennis. Pony rides. Bicycle and mountain bike hire. Off site: Fishing 200 m. Golf 2 km. Riding 6 km.

Open

14 May - 10 September.

At a glance

Welcome & Ambience	✓✓✓✓✓	Location	✓✓✓✓
Quality of Pitches	✓✓✓	Range of Facilities	✓✓✓✓✓

Directions

From Saumur take D751 signed Gennes. Turn right at roundabout in St Hilaire-St Florent and continue until you reach Le Poitrinea and campsite sign, then turn left. Continue for about 3 km. and then turn right into road leading to site.

Charges 2005

Per unit incl. 2 persons	€ 15,00 - € 24,00
extra person	€ 4,50 - € 6,00
child (010 yrs)	€ 3,00 - € 3,50
electricity	€ 3,00
dog	€ 2,00

Reservations

Made with € 11 fee; contact site. Tel: 02 41 67 95 34.

FR49070 Camping Caravaning La Vallée des Vignes

La Croix Patron, 49700 Concourson-sur-Layon (Maine-et-Loire)

The enthusiasm of the English owners here comes across instantly in the warm welcome received by their guests. The attention to detail in all they do and the improvements they have made shows how keen they are to make this site prosper. The site entrance with flowers, vines and wine press welcomes visitors – even the dog has a wine barrel for a kennel! Bordering the Layon river, the 54 good sized touring pitches are reasonably level and fully serviced (electricity, water tap and drain). Five pitches have a hardstanding for cars. Attractions include a newly enclosed bar and restaurant with folding doors to open in good weather, a generously sized sun terrace surrounding the pool and high season activities for children and adults. These include wine tasting, a hog roast (or similar) followed by competitions and treasure hunts. This is also an ideal base for visiting the châteaux of the Loire and the many caves and vineyards in the area.

Facilities

The toilet block includes washbasins in cabins, with dish-washing facilities at either end, under cover. Baby room. facilities for disabled visitors. Washing machine and dryer. Bar (from 15/5 or on request) serving meals, snacks and takeaway (from 1/6). Swimming and paddling pools (from 15/5). Playground, games area and small football pitch. Minigolf, volleyball, basketball, table tennis. Internet access. Fishing possible from 2005. Caravan storage. Off site: Zoo and rose gardens at Doué-la-Fontaine. Parc Puy du Fou.

Open

Easter - 31 October.

At a glance

Welcome & Ambience	✓✓✓✓✓	Location	✓✓✓✓✓
Quality of Pitches	✓✓✓✓	Range of Facilities	✓✓✓✓

Directions

Site signed off D960 Doué - Vihiers road, just west of Concourson-sur-Layon.

Charges 2004

Per unit incl. 2 persons	€ 15,00 - € 20,00
extra person	€ 3,50 - € 4,50
child (2-12 yrs)	€ 2,00 - € 2,50
electricity (10A)	€ 3,00
dog	€ 2,50

Special offers available.

Reservations

Contact site. Tel: 02 41 59 86 35.
E-mail: Campingvdv@wanadoo.fr

FR49080 Camping Ile d'Offard

Rue de Verden, Ile d'Offard, 49400 Saumur (Maine-et-Loire)

Situated on an island between the banks of the Loire and within walking distance of the centre of Saumur, this site is useful as an overnight stop en-route south or as a short-term base from which to visit the numerous châteaux in the region. The 200 touring pitches are on grass at the far end or hardstanding nearer the entrance. Some 23 pitches are occupied by tour operators and caravan holiday homes and these can be intrusive in some areas. As the site only closes from mid December until mid January, it is ideal for winter travellers. Some pitches have access to a 5A electricity hook-up. The adjacent municipal swimming pools and minigolf (open in July/Aug) are free for campers.

TRAVEL SERVICE SITE

TO BOOK CALL 0870 405 4055 OR www.alanrogersdirect.com

Facilities

Three sanitary blocks, one heated in winter, include provision for disabled visitors. Toilet facilities in all blocks are unisex. Block one has a well equipped laundry. The other blocks are only open in high season. Basic restaurant and bar (early May - late Sept) with takeaway. Table tennis, volleyball. Play area. Some activities with a children's club, wine tastings, etc. in high season. Off site: Thursday market 500 m. Saturday morning market 2 km. Riding 5 km. Fishing in the Loire (permits from Saumur).

Open

1 March - 31 October.

At a glance

Welcome & Ambience	✓✓✓✓	Location	✓✓✓✓✓
Quality of Pitches	✓✓✓✓	Range of Facilities	✓✓✓✓

Directions

From N147 take exit for 'Saumur Centre'. At round-about follow signs for Châtellerault and Chinon (keeping McDonalds on left) and continue alongside river towards town centre. At next roundabout (Office du Tourisme in front) turn left over bridge (Pont Cessart) onto island. Drive through shops and just before next bridge turn right past Hotel Adagio. Site is ahead beside municipal pool and sports stadium.

Charges 2005

Per unit incl. 2 adults	€ 14,50 - € 19,50
extra person	€ 4,00
child (2-10 yrs)	€ 2,00
electricity	€ 3,00

Camping Cheques accepted.

Reservations

Advised for July/Aug. with 25% deposit plus charge for registration. Tel: 02 41 40 30 00.
E-mail: iledoffard@wanadoo.fr

FR49060 Camping Parc de Montsabert

Montsabert, 49320 Coutures (Maine-et-Loire)

Owned and run by a friendly Dutch family who continually looking to improve it, this extensive campsite has a rural atmosphere in the shadow of Montsabert château, from where visiting peacocks happily roam in the spacious surroundings. The main features are the heated swimming pool (with cover) and the adjoining refurbished, rustic style restaurant. There are 82 large, well marked touring pitches, divided by hedges and all with water tap, drain and electricity (5/10A). Picnic tables are provided in the shade near the entrance with a communal barbecue area. Partially wooded by impressive redwood trees, this site offers the peace of the countryside and yet easy access to both Saumur and Angers. It is an ideal base for exploring, whether by foot, bicycle or car. Used by two tour operators (30 pitches).

Facilities

The main central toilet block can be heated and has washbasins and bidets in cabins and a baby room. Outside dishwashing and laundry facilities. Washing machines and dryer. A second block serves the pool. Shop (15/6-30/8). Restaurant and takeaway (15/6-15/9). Bar (1/6-15/9). Large 25 m. heated swimming pool which can be covered (20/5-12/9; no bermuda shorts) and paddling pool. Sports hall, minigolf, volley and basketball, table tennis and tennis. Play area. Bicycle hire. Entertainment (high season). Barrier key deposit (€ 10). Off site: Fishing and golf 5 km. Riding 8 km.

Open

30 April - 16 September.

At a glance

Welcome & Ambience	✓✓✓✓✓	Location	✓✓✓✓
Quality of Pitches	✓✓✓✓✓	Range of Facilities	✓✓✓✓✓

Directions

From Le Mans going towards Angers, take exit 12 (Seiches-sur-Loire). Turn left on D74 signed Bauné, Château Montgeoffroy and Mazé. In Mazé take D55 towards St Maturin-sur-Loire. Pass bridge and follow signs for 'Montsabert' and Européen.

Charges 2004

Per pitch incl. 2 persons	€ 14,50 - € 19,50
extra person	€ 4,50
child (1-10 yrs)	€ 2,90
electricity (5/10A)	€ 2,75 - € 3,85
dog	€ 3,00

Reservations

Made with 30% deposit and fee (€ 10).
Tel: 02 41 57 91 63.
E-mail: camping@parcdemontsabert.com

FR49090 Camping l'Isle Verte

Avenue de la Loire, 49730 Montsoreau (Maine-et-Loire)

This friendly, natural site, with pitches overlooking the Loire, is just 100 m. from the centre of Montsoreau, an ideal starting point to visit the western Loire area. Most of the 86 shaded, level and good-sized pitches are separated by low hedges. Fishermen are particularly well catered for here, there being an area to store their equipment and live bait (permits are available in Saumur). Attractions within walking distance include the château (500 m), Troglodyte mushroom caves and restaurant 500 m, wine tasting in the cellars opposite the site, and a Sunday market. Excellent English is spoken in the reception and bar.

Facilities

A single building provides separate male and female toilets. Washbasins, some in cabins, and showers are unisex. Separate facilities for disabled campers. Baby room. Laundry room with deep sinks, washing machine and dryer. Dishwashing area under cover at the front of the building. Bar and snack bar (1/5-30/9). Heated swimming and paddling pools (15/5-30/9). Small play area. Table tennis, volleyball. Bicycle hire (June - August or by special request). Fishing. Off site: Golf 6 km. Riding 15 km.

Open

1 April - 30 September.

At a glance

Welcome & Ambience	✓✓✓✓	Location	✓✓✓✓
Quality of Pitches	✓✓✓	Range of Facilities	✓✓✓✓

Directions

Take D947 from Saumur to Montsoreau and site is clearly signed on left along the road into town.

Charges 2004

Per unit incl. 1 or 2 persons	€ 12,50 - € 16,00
extra adult	€ 3,00
child (2-10 yrs)	€ 1,50
electricity	€ 3,00
motorcaravan services (free if camping).	€ 4.50 - € 7.50

Camping Cheques accepted.

Reservations

Advised for July/Aug. with 25% fee and booking fee.
Tel: 02 41 51 76 60. E-mail: isleverte@wanadoo.fr

FR72020 Camping Municipal du Lac

Rue du Lac, 72120 St Calais (Sarthe)

St Calais is a small town 37 km. east of Le Mans. Camping du Lac has 59 marked pitches, most separated by hedges and all with electricity (3/6A), water and drain. A separate area is for tents. Pizzas are sold on Saturday evenings and in high season there are theme evenings (crêpes or pizzas), walks, competitions, children's activities, and communal meals with music. Reception is welcoming, the value is excellent and this would make a good night stop or base for visiting the Le Mans 24 hour race. There is some road noise.

Facilities

Two sanitary blocks provide some washbasins in private cabins. Washing machine in larger block. Bread and croissants (to order), post cards and T-shirts available at reception. Two small play areas. Off site: Swimming pool adjacent. Local supermarket just a short walk.

Open

1 April - 15 October.

At a glance

Welcome & Ambience	✓✓✓✓	Location	✓✓✓✓
Quality of Pitches	✓✓✓✓	Range of Facilities	✓✓✓

Directions

Well signed from N157, site is beside lake north of the town, near the station. Follow signs for 'Camping Plan d'eau'.

Charges guide

Per person	€ 2,30
child (under 10 yrs)	€ 1,10
pitch	€ 2,05
electricity (3/6A)	€ 1,50 - € 2,45

Reservations

Made with deposit (€ 15.24). Tel: 02 43 35 04 81.

FR72030 Castel Camping Le Château de Chanteloup

72460 Sillé-le-Philippe (Sarthe)

A peaceful, pleasant site with a certain rural charm, 15 km. from Le Mans, Chanteloup is situated in the park of a 19th century château in the heart of the Sarthe countryside. There are 148 pitches, some along the edge of the woods, many on the lawn and completely open, and a few overlooking the lake, so the degree of shade varies. The pitches are open and all have electricity although long leads will be required in some instances. This lack of regimentation enhances the atmosphere of spaciousness in the grounds surrounding the old château. Tours of the grounds and the village by pony and cart can be arranged.

TRAVEL SERVICE SITE

TO BOOK CALL 0870 405 4055 OR www.alanrogersdirect.com

Facilities

Sanitary facilities in the château outbuildings are a long way from some pitches and cleaning and maintenance can be variable. Washbasins in cabins. Washing machine. Small shop. Pleasant bar (31/5-6/9) with terrace in the château with breakfast, lunch and dinner served (all 10/6-22/8). Swimming pool. Play area (parental supervision essential). Games room, tennis, volleyball, table tennis. Mountain bike hire. Organised activities in high season Off site: Riding 7 km. Golf 14 km.

Open

1 June - 8 September.

At a glance

Welcome & Ambience	✓✓✓✓	Location	✓✓✓✓
Quality of Pitches	✓✓✓	Range of Facilities	✓✓✓✓

Directions

Site is 15 km. northeast of Le Mans. From autoroute take exit 23 and follow signs for Le Mans and Tours, then Le Mans and Savigne l'Evèque. Site is halfway between Bonnétable and Savigne l'Evèque (road is narrow) on western edge of Sille-le-Phillippe village.

Charges 2005

Per person	€ 5,00 - € 6,50
child (under 7 yrs)	€ 3,00
pitch	€ 7,50 - € 11,00
electricity	€ 3,00

Less 10% outside 24/6-20/8.

Reservations

No minimum length. Tel: 02 43 27 51 07.
E-mail: chanteloup.souffront@wanadoo.fr

FR72060 Camping Municipal du Val de Sarthe

Rue de l'Abreuvoir, 72170 Beaumont sur Sarthe (Sarthe)

This delightful, inexpensive riverside site is conveniently located just a short walk from the pretty little town and its shops and services. The 73 level, grassy individual pitches are large, divided by growing hedges and all have electricity (5A). Some of the pitches including those along the river's edge may require a longer cable. An excellent activity area provides swings and other play equipment, boules pitches, tennis, netball, and a fitness trail. Those intending to stay longer than one night require a barrier card (refundable deposit). Reception opens 08.00-22.00 daily in high season, 10.00-20.00 in low season.

Facilities

The central sanitary unit is accessed by a flight of steps although there is a long and fairly steep ramp for disabled people. Modern facilities include some washbasins in cubicles and spacious showers. Washing machine. Motorcaravan service point. Bread and croissants to order. River fishing. Room for campers' use (July/Aug). Double axle caravans not accepted. Off site: Sports centre with outdoor pool. Riding 10 km. Bicycle hire 15 km.Golf 25 km.

Open

1 May - 30 September.

At a glance

Welcome & Ambience	✓✓✓✓	Location	✓✓✓✓
Quality of Pitches	✓✓✓✓	Range of Facilities	✓✓✓

Directions

Site is well signed from approach roads and from the town centre.

Charges 2004

Per person	€ 1,57
child (under 7 yrs)	€ 0,78
pitch	€ 1,23
electricity	€ 2,06
dog	€ 0,32

Barrier card deposit € 30.
Credit cards accepted, minimum amount € 20.

Reservations

Not normally necessary. Tel: 02 43 97 01 93.
E-mail: beaumont.sur.sarthe@wanadoo.fr

FR79040 Camping de la Venise Verte

178, route des Bords de Sèvre, 79510 Coulon (Deux-Sèvres)

This family run site on the edge of the Sevre Nortaise and the Marais Poitevin is ideal for short or long stays. With canoe and cycle hire on site you have no excuse for not exploring the local area. In the Deux Sevres, the 'department of discovery', so named because it has two rivers named Sevre, the Noirtaise and Nantaise, the Venise Verte provides an excellent site. The flat pitches are of a good size with electricity, water and drainage and with some shade. To try a real local flavour walk into Coulon and taste, and then perhaps buy, some 'Pissenlit', dandelion liqueur.

Facilities

Modern, heated toilet facilities are of a high standard with free showers. Washing machine and dryer. Motorcaravan services. Restaurant/bar. Heated swimming pool (high season) Bicycle and canoe hire. Boules area. Off site: Boat trips in the Marais. Ideal for walking, cycling or canoeing.

Open

1 April - 31 October.

At a glance

Welcome & Ambience	✓✓✓✓	Location	✓✓✓✓
Quality of Pitches	✓✓✓✓	Range of Facilities	✓✓✓✓

Directions

From Niort take N11 towards La Rochelle. Turn on the D3 towards Sansais and then north on the D1 towards Coulon. At traffic lights head towards 'centre ville' (Coulon) at mini-roundabout turn slightly right. Follow the Sevre Noirtaise for about 1.5 km. to site.

Charges 2004

Per unit incl. 2 persons and electricity	€ 14,50 - € 19,00
extra person	€ 3,20 - € 4,50
child (3-5 yrs)	€ 1,50 - € 1,90

Reservations

Advised for high season. Tel: 05 49 35 90 36.
E-mail: accueil@camping-laveniseverte.com

FR86030 Camping Le Relais du Miel

Mobile homes page 380

Route d'Antran, 86100 Châtellerault (Vienne)

With very easy access from the A10 and N10 roads, in the northern outskirts of Châtellerault, this site is being developed in the 10 acre grounds of a grand house dating from Napoleonic times. It is surrounded by majestic old trees beside the River Vienne. Twin barns form two sides of a courtyard behind the house, one of which has already been converted very stylishly into reception, a high ceilinged function and games room, and a bar. Beams taken from the original ceiling now form part of the bar top and act as arm rests. There is also an orchard and stone gateposts leading onto ground, previously the home farm, that now forms 80 large, flat pitches. Divided by trees and bushes, now maturing well and some providing shade, all the pitches have electricity and water, 15 with drainage. You may fish on the river bank with access through a gate in the walled grounds. Mobile homes and apartments to rent.

Facilities

Excellent toilet facilities include washbasins in cabins, facilities for disabled people, dishwashing sinks, and a washing machine and dryer. Basic essentials and gas are kept. Bar and restaurant serving good value meals. Pizzas to order (from local pizzeria). Takeaway. Small snack bar with outdoor tables, sheltered by canopy, open in the evenings 1/7-31/8. Swimming and paddling pools (15 x 7 m). Playground. First class tennis courts. Volleyball, basketball. Bicycle hire. Boules and games room with electronic games, pool and table tennis. Observatory with telescope. Internet access. Torch useful. Off site: Supermarket 400 m. Riding 5 km. Golf 11 km. Futuroscope 16 km.

At a glance

Welcome & Ambience	✓✓✓✓✓	Location	✓✓✓✓
Quality of Pitches	✓✓✓✓	Range of Facilities	✓✓✓✓✓

Directions

Take exit no. 26 from the A10 autoroute (Châtellerault-Nord) and site is signed just off the roundabout. From the N10 follow signs for Antran north of the town.

Charges 2004

Per unit incl. 2 persons, electricity	€ 19,00 - € 21,00
extra person over 5 yrs	€ 3,00 - € 5,00
extra tent	€ 3,00 - € 5,00

Less 15% for 1 week, 20% for 2 weeks

Reservations

Made with 10% deposit. Tel: 05 49 02 06 27.
E-mail: camping@lerelaisdumiel.com

Open

15 May - 2 September.

FR86010 Castel Camping Le Petit Trianon

Saint Ustre, 86220 Ingrandes-sur-Vienne (Vienne)

A family owned site for many years, quaint and rustic are words that spring to mind on arrival here. Situated between Tours, Poitiers and Futuroscope, the approach to Le Petit Trianon is through a grand, narrow, gateway leading onto a slightly sloping meadow surrounded by trees in front of the château, plus a newer, large, more open field with a woodland area between. The 99 spacious, open but marked pitches are arranged to leave plenty of free space and there is shade in parts. All have electricity. Reception is housed in the 18th century château which was once a hunting lodge. The pool area is located on the sunny side of a rather picturesque castled facade in which is a large, very cool reading room. This is an attractive campsite with many well tended plants around the site. Futuroscope at Poitiers is well worth at least a day's visit (if you stay for the after dusk laser, firework and fountain show, remember your late night entry code for the site gate).

Facilities

The original toilet unit is dated but immaculate. It includes washbasins in cabins, some washbasin and shower units, baby baths, laundry with washing machines and dryer, and sinks for dishwashing. Smaller blocks serve the newer parts of the site and one contains facilities for disabled people. Motorcaravan service point. Shop with essentials, bread to order. Takeaway. Heated swimming pool and paddling pools. Playground. Table tennis. Minigolf. Badminton, croquet, volleyball and boules. TV room with satellite, books and games. Bicycle hire. Local wine and cognac tastings on site and organised excursions. Internet access. Caravan storage. Off site: Restaurant (menu displayed on site) 50 m. Fishing 3 km. Riding 15 km.

Open

20 May - 20 September.

At a glance

Welcome & Ambience	✓✓✓✓✓	Location	✓✓✓✓
Quality of Pitches	✓✓✓	Range of Facilities	✓✓✓✓

Directions

Ingrandes is signed from the N10 north of the town, which is between Dangé and Châtellerault. From autoroute A10 take exit 26 for Châtellerault-Nord and at roundabout follow signs for Tours to Ingrandes where site is signed.

Charges 2004

Per person	€ 6,60
child (0-6 yrs)	€ 1,10 - € 3,30
pitch incl. car	€ 7,70 - € 10,35
electricity (5/10A)	€ 3,95 - € 4,95
dog	€ 2,10

Less 10-20% for longer stays.

Reservations

Made with 25% deposit and fee (€ 12.50); minimum 5 days in July/Aug. Tel: 05 49 02 61 47. E-mail: chateau@petit-trianon.fr

FR86080 Camping Caravaning Les Peupliers

86700 Couhé (Vienne)

Family owned and run since 1968, Les Peupliers is located in a valley south of Poitiers. The site is arranged on the banks of a river (unfenced), the 130 pitches on both sides or around a fishing lake. On level grass, most are separated and all have electricity, while 55 are fully serviced. There is a good pool complex (open until mdinight) that includes impressive water slides and new toboggans, a heated main pool, a paddling pool and a lagoon with two slides for younger children (under 10 yrs), plus water games. There is a local market for each day of the week (Chaunay, Lezay, Civray, Rouillé or Vivonnet). Nearby Vaux has an ostrich farm and at Romagne there is La Vallée des Singes with 25 species of monkey, ape and gorilla.

Facilities

The three toilet blocks are in Mediterranean style, with washbasins in cubicles and facilities for babies and disabled people. Dishwashing and laundry sinks. Washing machines and dryers. The newest block is in regular use, with the other two opened as the season progresses. Fridge rental. Small, well stocked shop. Snack bar, restaurant and bar with covered terrace and entertainment in peak season. Swimming pool complex (2/5-30/9). Playground. Fishing lake. Minigolf, table tennis and some pedaloes. Off site: Tennis court 800 m. Bicycle hire 1 km. Riding 5 km.

Open

1 May - 30 September. Chalets for hire all year.

At a glance

Welcome & Ambience	✓✓✓	Location	✓✓✓
Quality of Pitches	✓✓✓	Range of Facilities	✓✓✓✓

Directions

Couhé is about 30 km. south of Poitiers on the N10. From the north, follow the signs for Couhé and the campsite, which is a short distance on the right.

Charges 2005

Per person	€ 6,00
child (2-10 yrs)	€ 3,50
pitch	€ 8,50
electricity	€ 3,50
electricity, water and drainage	€ 5,00

Camping Cheques accepted.
Less 30% in low season.

Reservations

Contact site. Tel: 05 49 59 21 16. E-mail: info@lespeupliers.fr

FR86090 Camping du Parc de Saint Cyr

Mobile homes page 382

86130 Saint Cyr (Vienne)

This well organised, five hectare campsite is part of a 300 hectare leisure park, based around a large lake with sailing and associated sports, and an area for swimming (supervised July/Aug). Land-based activities include tennis, two half-courts, table tennis, fly fishing, badminton, pétanque, beach volleyball, TV room, and a well equipped fitness suite, all of which are free of charge. In high season there are extra free activities including a kids club, beach club, archery and an entertainment programme. Also in high season, but charged for, are sailing school, aquatic toboggan, windsurfing, canoe, kayak, water bikes and stunt bikes. Campers can also use the 9 and 18 hole golf courses (with 20% discount for the 18 hole). If all this sounds a bit too exhausting, you could escape to the small, peaceful formal garden in the centre of the site. The campsite has around 179 tourist pitches and 11 mobile homes for rent. The marked and generally separated pitches are all fully serviced with electricity (10A), water and drain.

Facilities

The main toilet block is modern and is supplemented for peak season by a second, recently refitted unit, which should prove adequate for demand, although they do attract some use by day-trippers to the leisure facilities. They include washbasins in cubicles, dishwashing and laundry sinks, washing machines and dryers, and facilities for babies and disabled persons. Shop, restaurant and takeaway (April - Sept). Playground on the beach. Bicycle hire. Barrier locked 22.00-07.00 hrs (10 deposit for card).

Open

1 April - 30 September.

At a glance

Welcome & Ambience	✓✓✓✓	Location	✓✓✓✓
Quality of Pitches	✓✓✓	Range of Facilities	✓✓✓✓

Directions

Saint Cyr is approx. midway between Châtellerault and Poitiers. Site is signed to the east of the N10 at Beaumont along the D82 towards Bonneuil-Matours, and is part of the Parc de Loisirs de Saint Cyr.

Charges 2004

Per pitch incl. electricity, water and drainage	€ 6,00 - € 12,00
adult	€ 2,50 - € 5,00
child (1-7 yrs)	€ 1,50 - € 2,00
animal	free - € 1,50

Reservations

Advisable for high season, made with fee (€ 7.62). Tel: 05 49 62 57 22.

E-mail: contact@parcdesaintcyr.com

FR86040 Camping Le Futuriste

Mobile homes page 382

86130 St Georges-les-Baillargeaux (Vienne)

On raised ground with panoramic views over the strikingly modern buildings and night-time bright lights that comprise the popular attraction of Futuroscope, Le Futuriste is a neat, modern site, open all year. It is ideal for a short stay to visit the park which is only 1.5 km. away (tickets can be bought at the site) but it is equally good for longer stays to see the region. With a busy atmosphere, there are early departures and late arrivals. Reception is open 08.00-22.00 hrs. There are 112 individual, flat, grassy pitches divided by young trees and shrubs which are beginning to provide some shelter for this elevated and otherwise rather open site (possibly windy). There are 28 pitches without electricity for tents, 22 with 6A electricity and a further 62 with electricity, water, waste water and sewage connections. All are accessed via neat, level and firmly rolled gravel roads. Of course, the area has other attractions and details are available from the enthusiastic young couple who run the site. Note: it is best to see the first evening show at Futuroscope otherwise you will find youself locked out of the site - the gates are closed at 23.30 hrs.

Facilities

Excellent, very clean sanitary facilities are housed in two modern blocks which are insulated and can be heated in cool weather. The facilities in the newest block are unisex. and include some washbasins in cabins and facilities for disabled people. Dishwashing and laundry sinks. Washing machine and dryer. Small shop (1/5-30/9) provides essentials (order bread the night before). New bar/restaurant. Snack bar and takeaway. Two outdoor pools, one with a slide and paddling pool (1/5-30/9). Free fishing in lake on site. Youth groups are not accepted. Off site: Bicycle hire 500 m. Golf 5 km. Riding 10 km. Supermarkets near.

Open

All year.

At a glance

Welcome & Ambience	✓✓✓✓	Location	✓✓✓✓
Quality of Pitches	✓✓✓✓	Range of Facilities	✓✓✓✓

Directions

From either A10 autoroute or the N10, take Futuroscope exit. Site is located east of both roads, off the D20 to St Georges-Les-Baillargeaux. From all directions follow signs to St Georges. The site is on the hill; turn by the water tower and site is on the left.

Charges 2004

Per pitch incl. 1-3 persons	€ 12,75 - € 17,50
extra person	€ 1,65 - € 2,35
electricity	€ 2,35 - € 3,20
dog	€ 1,60

Camping Cheques accepted.

Reservations

Phone bookings accepted for min. 2 nights.
Tel: 05 49 52 47 52.
E-mail: camping-le-futuriste@wanadoo.fr

Map 8

Burgundy is a wonderfully evocative region offering breathtaking chateaux and cathedrals, rolling hills and heady mountain views, vineyards and superlative cuisine, not to mention of course, a wide variety of world renowned wines.

Départements: 21 Côte d'Or, 58 Nièvre, 71 Saône-et-Loire, 89 Yonne

Major city: Dijon

In the rich heartland of France, Burgundy was once a powerful independent state and important religious centre. Its golden age is reflected in the area's magnificent art and architecture: the grand palaces and art collections of Dijon, the great pilgrimage church of Vézelay, the Cistercian Abbaye de Fontenay and the evocative abbey remains at Cluny, once the most powerful monastery in Europe.

However Burgundy is best known for its wine, including some of the world's finest, notably from the great vineyards of the Côte d'Or and Chablis, and also for its sublime cuisine.You'll also notice how driving through the country villages is like reading a wine merchant's list with plenty of opportunities for tasting and choosing your wine.

The area is criss-crossed by navigable waterways and includes the Parc Régional du Morvan; good walking country amidst lush, rolling wooded landscape.

Cuisine of the region

Many dishes are wine based, including *Poulet au Meursault* and *Coq au Chambertin*. Dijon is known for its *pain d'épice* (spiced honey-cake) and spicy mustard

Boeuf Bourguignon: braised beef simmered in a red wine-based sauce

Charolais (Pièce de): steak from Charolais cattle

Garbure: heavy soup, a mixture of pork, cabbage, beans and sausages

Gougère: cheese pastry based on Gruyère

Jambon persillé: parsley-flavoured ham, served cold in jelly

Matelote: fresh-water fish soup, usually based on a red wine sauce

Meurette: red wine-based sauce with small onions, used with fish or poached egg dishes

Places of interest

Autun: 12th century St Lazare cathedral

Beaune: medieval town; Museum of Burgundy Wine

Cluny: Europe's largest Benedictine abbey

Dijon: Palace of the Dukes, Fine Arts Museum, Burgundian Folklore Museum.

Fontenay: Fontenay Abbey and Cloister

Joigny: medieval town

Mâcon: Maison des Vins (wine centre)

Paray-le-Monial: Romanesque basilica, pilgrimage centre

Sens: historic buildings, museum with fine Gallo-Roman collections

Vézelay: fortified medieval hillside

Alan Rogers tip

GET ON YOUR BIKE! BURGUNDY HAS PLENTY OF LONG-DISTANCE CANAL PATHS, GREAT FOR CYCLING.

FR21010 Camping Municipal Louis Rigoly

Esplanade St Vorles, 21400 Châtillon-sur-Seine (Côte d'Or)

This well kept, small, hillside municipal site has 54 pitches. Mainly individual and separated, they are on fairly flat grass, 48 with electricity (4A) with mature trees providing shelter. Adjoining the site is the municipal swimming pool complex with both indoor and outdoor pools (on payment). There is no shop, but the town is close. The site, which has much transit trade, can become full by evening in season.

Facilities

The main toilet block at the lower end of the site is satisfactory. A smaller heated unit behind reception contains facilities for babies, a washing machine and dryer. Facilities for disabled visitors provided in a separate block. Snack bar July/Aug. Play area. Off site: Fishing or bicycle hire 1 km. Riding 4 km.

Open

1 April - 30 September.

At a glance

Welcome & Ambience	✓✓✓✓	Location	✓✓✓✓
Quality of Pitches	✓✓✓	Range of Facilities	✓✓✓

Directions

On northeast outskirts of town; site is signed from centre (steep hills approaching site, narrow roads).

Charges 2005

Per person	€ 3,00
child (under 7 yrs)	€ 1,30
pitch and vehicle	€ 4,00 - € 4,20
electricity (4A)	€ 2,15 - € 4,30

No credit cards.

Reservations

Not officially made, but write just before your visit, they will reserve until 7 p.m. Tel: 03 80 91 03 05. E-mail: tourism-chatillon-sur-seine@wanadoo.fr

FR21020 Camping Municipal Les Cent Vignes

10 rue Auguste Dubois, 21200 Beaune (Côte d'Or)

The Côte de Beaune, situated southeast of the Côte d'Or, produces some of the very best French wines. Beaune is also a city of art and has a charm all of its own and there are several 'caves' in the town just waiting to be visited. Les Cents Vignes is a very well kept site offering 116 pitches of good size, separated from each other by neat beech hedges high enough to keep a fair amount of privacy. Over half of the pitches are on grass, ostensibly for tents, the remainder on hardstandings with electricity for caravans. A popular site, within walking distance of the town centre, Les Cent Vignes becomes full mid-June to early Sept. but with many short-stay campers there are departures each day and reservations can be made.

Facilities

Two modern, fully equipped and well constructed, sanitary blocks, one of which can be heated, should be large enough. Nearly all washbasins are in cabins. Dishwashing and laundry sinks. Washing machines. Shop, restaurant with takeaway (all 1/4-15/10). Playground. Sports area with tennis, basketball, volleyball, boules and table tennis. TV room. Barbecue area. Off site: Bicycle hire 1 km. Fishing, golf or wind surfing 4 km. Centre of Beaune 1 km.

Open

15 March - 31 October.

At a glance

Welcome & Ambience	✓✓✓✓	Location	✓✓✓✓✓
Quality of Pitches	✓✓✓✓	Range of Facilities	✓✓✓✓

Directions

From autoroute exit 24 follow signs for Beaune centre on D2 road, camping signs to site in approx. 1 km. Well signed from other routes.

Charges 2005

Per person	€ 3,05
child (2-7 yrs)	€ 1,50
pitch	€ 4,20
electricity (6A)	€ 3,00

Reservations

Made before 30 May without deposit. Tel: 03 80 22 03 91.

FR21030 Camping Municipal Les Premier Pres

Route De Bouilland, 21420 Savigny-les-Beaune (Côte d'Or)

This popular site is ideally located for visiting the Burgundy vineyards, for use as a transit site or for spending time in the town of Beaune. During the high season it is full every evening, so it is best to arrive by 4 pm. The 90 level pitches are marked and numbered, with electric hook-ups and room for an awning. If reception is closed when you arrive, you find a pitch and report later, otherwise 'Madame' will allocate a place. Whilst the famed wine region alone attracts many visitors, Beaune, its capital, is unrivalled in its richness of art from times gone by. Narrow streets and squares are garlanded with flowers, pavement cafés are buzzing and overlooking the scene is the glistening Hotel Dieu.

Facilities

Well kept sanitary facilities are housed in a modern building behind reception. Additional WCs and water points are conveniently placed towards the middle of the site. Table tennis. Motorcaravan service point. Torch useful. Off site: Sunday market in the village 1 km. Beaune 7 km.

Open

1 May - 30 September.

At a glance

Welcome & Ambience	✓✓✓✓	Location	✓✓✓✓
Quality of Pitches	✓✓✓✓	Range of Facilities	✓✓✓

Directions

From A6 autoroute take exit 24 signed Beaune and Savigny-lès-Beaune onto D2. Turn right towards Savigny-lès-Beaune (3 km) and follow signs to site.

Charges 2004

Per person	€ 2,00
child (under 7 yrs)	€ 1,10
pitch	€ 2,95
electricity	€ 3,25

No credit cards.

Reservations

Not accepted. Tel: 03 80 26 15 06.

FR21040 Camping de l'Etang de Fouche

Mobile homes ▶ page 383

Rue du 8 Mai 1945, 21230 Arnay le Duc (Côte d'Or)

Useful as an overnight stop en-route to or from the Mediterranean or indeed for longer stays, this quite large but peaceful, lakeside site has good facilities and the added advantage of being open all year. It can be very busy during the school holidays, and is probably better visited outside the main season. There are 190 good sized pitches, on fairly level grass and all with 10A electricity (some with water). This part of Burgundy is popular and Arnay le Duc itself is an attractive little town with an interesting history and renowned for its gastronomy, with many hotels and restaurants. The pitches, many hedged, offer a choice of shade or more open aspect. In July/August there are regular activities for children and adults.

Facilities

At the time of the inspection, only two of the four sanitary blocks were open. They are reasonably modern and well maintained, including some British style WCs, washbasins in cabins, facilities for disabled visitors. Washing machines and dishwashing under cover. Shop (with bread), bar, restaurant, takeaway (all 15 May to 15 Sep). TV/games room. Boules. Table tennis. Playground. Off site: Site is within 800m of the town centre, which has tennis courts, shops etc. At the supervised lakeside beach next to the site - small playground, water slides, pedaloes, canoes, soft drinks.

Open

15 April - 15 October.

At a glance

Welcome & Ambience	✓✓✓✓	Location	✓✓✓✓
Quality of Pitches	✓✓✓✓✓	Range of Facilities	✓✓✓✓

Directions

Site is on east side of town (well signed), 15 km. from A6 autoroute (exit at péage de Pouilly en Auxois).

Charges 2004

Per unit incl. 2 persons	€ 8,50 - € 11,70
extra person	€ 2,50 - € 3,20
child (under 7 yrs)	€ 1,24 - € 1,60
electricity	€ 3,30
animal	€ 1,00

Reservations

Advised for Jul/Aug; contact site. Reservation fee €10, deposit €30. Tel: 03 80 90 02 23.
E-mail: info@campingfouche.com

FR21050 Camping La Grappe d'Or

2 route de Volnay, 21190 Meursault (Côte d'Or)

Mersault, the capital of the great white wines of Burgundy, is southwest of Beaune and Camping de la Grappe d'Or offers terraced pitches overlooking acres of vineyards. Most of the 125 touring pitches are flat, of varying sizes, and some have shade from mature trees. They all have electricity (15A). There is an outdoor pool and flume and, during July and August, aqua gym and other water activities are organised. There is a play area for youngsters and, just across the road from the entrance, there are two tennis courts. A second part of the site is located 100 m. towards the village in the grounds of the owners' house. Here there are caravan holiday homes for rent as well as those used by tour operators.

Facilities

Sanitary facilities are in three blocks with some washbasins in cabins. Child/baby room, facilities for visitors with disabilities, laundry and undercover dishwashing sinks. Shop, bar, restaurant, takeaway and swimming pool, all open 1/5-30/9 (pool heated 15/6 - 15/9) although hours may vary. Play area, volleyball, tennis courts. Bicycle hire. Off site: Golf or riding 7 km. Fishing 8 km. Beaune 9 km.

Open

25 March - 15 October.

At a glance

Welcome & Ambience	✓✓✓✓	Location	✓✓✓✓
Quality of Pitches	✓✓✓	Range of Facilities	✓✓✓✓

Directions

Site is north of Mersault. Take N74 from Beaune and follow the sign for Mersault; campsite is well signed from the town.

Charges 2005

Per unit incl. 2 persons	€ 15,50
extra person	€ 3,70
child (under 7 yrs)	€ 1,90
electricity	€ 3,50

Camping Cheques accepted.

Reservations

Made with € 25 deposit plus € 5 fee.
Tel: 03 80 21 22 48.
E-mail: camping.lagrappedor@wanadoo.fr

FR21060 Camping Les Bouleaux

21200 Vignoles (Côte d'Or)

Les Bouleaux is an excellent little campsite at Vignolles, northeast of Beaune. There are just 46 pitches, all with an electrical connection (long leads may be required on some pitches). The large flat pitches are attractively laid out and most are separated by hedges and trees giving some shade. M. Rossignal takes great pride in his campsite, keeping the facilities very clean and tidy, and by planting bright flowers near reception. The nearest shops and restaurants are 3 km. - there are none on-site.

Facilities

An older unisex building provides Turkish style WCs, while the adjacent modern block houses British style WCs (no paper in either). Washbasins in cabins or communal; push-button controllable showers, excellent facilities for visitors with disabilities. Laundry and dishwashing sinks but no washing machines. The only water point is at the central toilet blocks. No shop, but wine and basic groceries can be bought at reception. Gas exchange. Off site: Bicycle hire, fishing or golf 3 km. Riding 6 km. Beaune 3 km.

Open

All year.

At a glance

Welcome & Ambience	✓✓✓✓✓	Location	✓✓✓✓
Quality of Pitches	✓✓✓✓✓	Range of Facilities	✓✓✓

Directions

Leave A6 autoroute at exit 24.1 south of Beaune. Turn right at roundabout, straight on at traffic lights (centre lane), then turn right at next roundabout. Cross the autoroute, turn left at sign for Vignolle and follow the campsite signs.

Charges 2004

Per adult	€ 3,30
child (under 7 yrs)	€ 2,40
electricity (3/6A)	€ 2,00 - € 4,10
pitch and vehicle	€ 4,00

No credit cards.

Reservations

Not usually required, but phone during July/August to confirm availability. Tel: 03 80 22 26 88.

FR21070 Camping Municipal Les Grèbes

21330 Marcenay (Côte d'Or)

This attractive, peacefully located and very spacious lakeside site has 85 level, grassy pitches all with 6A electricity hook-ups. They are arranged in small clearings with dividing shrubs and hedges. The stylish reception building has a small shop, a snack bar with drinks, a small library, some games machines and a pool table. The site has access via pedestrian gates onto the lakeside path, there is a small beach and swimming area and one can use non-powered boats or fish. The nearby Haut Fourneau is worth a visit.

Facilities

Two good modern sanitary units. The main one can be heated, the second at the rear of the site is open for peak season. Both provide washbasins in cubicles and spacious hot showers. Good units for disabled people. Washing machine and dryer. Motorcaravan service point. Shop. Snackbar. Games room. Canoe hire. Playground. Volleyball, basketball and boules. Off site: Riding 500 m.

Open

1 April - 15 September.

At a glance

Welcome & Ambience	✓✓✓✓	Location	✓✓✓✓
Quality of Pitches	✓✓✓✓	Range of Facilities	✓✓✓

Directions

Marcenay is 35 km. east of Tonnerre. From Tonnerre take D965 east to Laignes, then D102 northeast to Marcenay, and follow signs to campsite and lake.

Charges guide

Per person	€ 2,30
child (under 7 yrs)	€ 1,30
pitch and car	€ 4,30
electricity	€ 2,75

Reservations

Advised for July/Aug. No deposit required.
Tel: 03 80 81 61 72.

FR21000 Camping Lac de Panthier

Mobile homes ▶ page 383

21320 Vandenesse-en-Auxois (Côte d'Or)

An attractively situated lakeside site in Bungundy countryside, Camping Lac de Panthier is divided into two distinct campsites. The first, smaller section houses the reception, shop, restaurant and other similar facilities. The second, larger area is 200 m. along the lakeside road and is where the site activities take place and the pool can be found. The 200 pitches (136 for touring units) all have electricity connections and are mostly on level grass, although in parts there are shallow terraces. The most obvious attraction here is the proximity to the lake with its many watersports facilities. The site's restaurant has panoramic views over the lake. Used by tour operators. A 'Sites et Paysages' member.

Facilities

Four unisex toilet blocks (two for each site) also provide for babies and disabled people. Shop, bar and restaurant (all from 15/5). Swimming pool, children's pool and water-slide (15/5-15/9). Indoor pool, sauna and fitness equipment. Fishing. Riding. Watersports. Off site: Boat excursions from Pouilly en Auxois (8 km). Dijon, Autun and Beaune are also within easy reach.

Open

24 April - 29 September.

At a glance

Welcome & Ambience	✓✓✓✓	Location	✓✓✓✓
Quality of Pitches	✓✓✓✓	Range of Facilities	✓✓✓✓

Directions

From the A6 join the A38 and immediately exit at junction 24. Take N81 towards Arnay Le Duc (back over the A6), then almost immediately turn left on D977 for 5 km. Fork left again for Vandenesse en Auxois. Continue through village on D977 for 2.5 km, turn left again and site is on left.

Charges 2004

Per adult	€ 3,70 - € 6,10
child (under 7 yrs)	€ 1,80 - € 3,00
pitch	€ 4,10 - € 6,80
electricity	€ 4,00
dog	€ 1,50

Camping Cheques accepted.

Reservations

Contact site. Tel: 03 80 49 21 94.
E-mail: info@lac-de-panthier.com

TRAVEL SERVICE SITE

TO BOOK CALL 0870 405 4055 OR www.alanrogersdirect.com

FR58010 Camping des Bains

Mobile homes ▶ page 380

15 avenue Jean Mermoz, 58360 St Honoré-les-Bains (Nièvre)

You are assured of a warm welcome at this attractive family run site, which is well situated for exploring the Morvan area in the heart of Burgundy – an area of rolling countryside, woods, rivers and villages, ideal for walking or cycling. The spacious 120 level grassed pitches (all with 6A electricity) are mostly separated by hedges with a variety of mature trees offering shade. Next to the site is the 'thermal spa' where there are opportunities to 'take the waters' for a three day session or a full blown cure of three weeks! Details are at reception. An excellent restaurant is almost opposite the entrance. A 'Sites et Paysages' member.

Facilities

The two main sanitary units have mostly British style WCs, washbasins in separate cabins and ample hot showers. Laundry. Facilities for disabled people. Family bar (1/6-30/9) also provides food and a takeaway service (15/6-15/9). Small swimming pool (12 x 12 m) with a separate slide and new paddling pool (15/6-15/9). Excellent play area and two small streams for children to fish. Table tennis. Minigolf. Entertainment weekly for children in July/Aug. Off site: Bicycle hire or riding 500 m. Fishing 5 km. Canal-side cycle route runs for 50 km. from Vandenesse (6 km).

Open

1 May - 10 October.

At a glance

Welcome & Ambience	✓✓✓✓	Location	✓✓✓✓
Quality of Pitches	✓✓✓✓	Range of Facilities	✓✓✓✓

Directions

From Nevers, travel east on D978; turn right onto D985 towards St Honoré-les-Bains, from where site is signed 'Camping des Bains', on entering town. Care is needed at narrow site entrance.

Charges 2005

Per unit incl. 2 persons	€ 15,50
extra person	€ 4,50
child (2- 7 yrs)	€ 2,85
electricity (6A)	€ 3,20
dog	€ 1,50

Reservations

Write to site with deposit (€ 65) and fee (€ 12.20). Tel: 03 86 30 73 44. E-mail: camping-les-bains@wanadoo.fr

FR58030 Castel Camping Manoir de Bezolle

58110 St Pereuse-en-Morvan (Nièvre)

Manoir de Bezolle is well situated to explore the Morvan Natural Park and the Nivernais area. It has been attractively landscaped to provide a number of different areas, some giving pleasant views over the surrounding countryside. Pitches of varying sizes are on level grass with shade, some with terracing and most have access to electricity (6A or more). There are two small lakes, stocked with many fish for anglers. This site is good for families with a range of activities provided for them.

Facilities

Two main toilet blocks provide washbasins in cabins, mostly British style WCs, bath, provision for disabled visitors and a baby bath. Two tiny family suites for rent. Laundry. Motorcaravan services. Shop (15/5-15/9; bread to order at other times). Bar and restaurant (15/5-15/9). Pizza and takeaway (main season). Internet. Two swimming pools with sunbathing terrace (1/6-15/9). Pony rides (June-Sept). Table tennis, minigolf. Fishing. Animation is organised in season.

Open

15 April - 30 September.

At a glance

Welcome & Ambience	✓✓✓✓	Location	✓✓✓✓
Quality of Pitches	✓✓✓✓	Range of Facilities	✓✓✓✓

Directions

Site is between Nevers and Autun (mid-way between Châtillon-en-Bazois and Château-Chinon), just north of the D978 by the small village of St Péreuse-en-Morvan.

Charges 2004

Per pitch incl. 2 persons	€ 15,00 - € 21,00
extra person	€ 5,00 - € 6,00
child (3-7 yrs)	€ 3,00 - € 4,00
electricity (10A)	€ 4,00

Camping Cheques accepted.

Reservations

Made with deposit (€ 45.70) and fee (€ 15.20). Tel: 03 86 84 42 55. E-mail: info@bezolle.com

FR71110 Camping du Lac

Le Fourneau, 71430 Palinges (Saône-et-Loire)

Monsieur Labille, this site's owner, thinks of the site as his home and every visitor as his guest. Adjacent to a lake with a beach and safe bathing, he provides tables and chairs for tent campers and freezes bottles of water for cyclists (free of charge). Guests can also use the washing machine and fridge free of charge. The site contains 47 good sized grass touring pitches, each with a small hardstanding. All but 8 of the pitches have two 10A electricity connections, and 24 have water and waste points.

Facilities

The central sanitary block provides showers, washbasins in cubicles, facilities for campers with disabilities and two family rooms. Washing machine and fridge. Bread to order. Boules. Play area. TV room. Sports field, lake beach adjacent. Bicycle and pedalo hire in July/Aug. Off site: Just outside the gates is a bar/snack bar. Riding 200 m.

Open

1 April - 30 September.

At a glance

Welcome & Ambience	✓✓✓✓✓	Location	✓✓✓✓✓
Quality of Pitches	✓✓✓✓✓	Range of Facilities	✓✓✓✓

Directions

Palinges is midway between Montceau les Mines and Paray le Monial. From Montceau take N70, then turn left on D92 to Palinges. Follow site signs. Site also well signed from the D985 (Toulon-sur-Arroux - Charolles).

Charges 2004

Per unit incl. 2 persons	€ 12,00 - € 15,00
extra person	€ 1,50
child (under 10 yrs)	€ 0,80

No credit cards.

Reservations

Advised in July/August. Tel: 03 85 88 14 49.

FR71020 Le Village des Meuniers

Mobile homes page 381

71520 Dompierre-les-Ormes (Saône-et-Loire)

In a tranquil setting with panoramic views, the neat appearance of the reception building sets the tone for the rest of this attractive site. The main part has 113 terraced, grassy pitches, some with hardstanding, are all fairly level, each with electricity and ample water points. Of these, 75 also have waste water outlets. A second section, used only in high season contains 16 standard pitches. All pitches enjoy stunning views of the surrounding countryside - the Beaujolais, Maconnais, Charollais and the Clunysois. An extensive sunbathing area surrounds the attractively designed swimming pool complex. This is a superb site, tastefully landscaped, with a high standard of cleanliness in all areas. As the hedges and trees mature they will offer more shade. This is an area well worth visiting, with attractive scenery, interesting history, excellent wines and good food. Used by tour operators (12 pitches) and 15 chalets to rent.

Facilities

Sanitary facilities mainly in an unusual, purpose designed hexagonal block, with modern fittings, of high standard. Smaller unit in the lower area of the site, plus further toilets in the main reception building. Motorcaravan service point in car park. Café (high season). Bar, shop and takeaway from 1/6. Swimming pool complex with three heated pools and toboggan run (from 1/6). Children's activities organised in high season. Football. Minigolf. Internet access.
Off site: Village 500 m. for all services (banks and some shops, closed Sun/Mon). Fishing 1.5 km. Riding 10 km.

Open

15 May - 15 September.

At a glance

Welcome & Ambience	✓✓✓✓	Location	✓✓✓✓
Quality of Pitches	✓✓✓✓✓	Range of Facilities	✓✓✓✓

Directions

Town is 35 km. west of Macon. Follow N79/E62 (Charolles, Paray, Digoin) road and turn south onto D41 to Dompierre-les-Ormes (3 km). Site is clearly signed through village.

Charges 2005

Per person	€ 5,00 - € 7,00
child (2-12)	€ 3,00 - € 4,00
pitch	€ 6,00 - € 8,50
electricity	€ 3,00 - € 4,00
dog	€ 1,50
car	€ 1,00

Reservations

Advised for July/Aug. Tel: 03 85 50 36 60.
E-mail: levillagedesmeuniers@wanadoo.fr

FR71050 Camping Moulin de Collonge

71940 St Boil (Saône-et-Loire)

This well run, family site offers an 'away from it all' situation surrounded by sloping vineyards and golden wheat fields. It has an instant appeal for those seeking a quiet, relaxing environment. There are 57 level pitches, most with electrical hook-ups although long cables may be required. Hanging flower arrangements are in abundance and, like the shrubs and grounds, are constantly being attended by the proprietor and his family (M. Gillot's other interest is the restoration of classic cars). Beyond the stream that borders the site are a swimming pool, patio and a pizzeria (also open to the public all year). A new lake, 1.8 m. deep, has been created for leisure activities.

Facilities

Toilet facilities housed in a converted barn are tastefully decorated and well kept. Some washbasins are in cubicles. Washing machine and dryer under cover. Freezer. Shop for basics, ices and cool drinks (1/6 - 3/9). Pizzeria/ snack bar (1/7 - 31/8). Swimming pool covered by plastic dome. Playgrounds. Bicycle hire. Table tennis. Fishing. Pony trekking. Off site: Riding 4 km. Chateaux, wine route.

Open

1 March - 30 September.

At a glance

Welcome & Ambience	✓✓✓✓	Location	✓✓✓✓
Quality of Pitches	✓✓✓	Range of Facilities	✓✓✓✓

Directions

From Chalon-sur-Saône travel 9 km. west on the N80. Turn south on D981 through Buxy (6 km). Continue south for 7 km. to Saint-Boil and site is signed at south end of the village.

Charges 2004

Per person	€ 4,50 - € 5,50
pitch	€ 5,50 - € 8,00
electricity	€ 3,00 - € 3,50

Camping Cheques accepted.
Less 20% outside July/Aug.

Reservations

Accepted - contact site. Tel: 03 85 44 00 40.
E-mail: millofcollonge@wanadoo.fr

FR71060 Camping Caravaning Château de Montrouant

71800 Gibles (Saône-et-Loire)

This is a small, pretty site beside a lake in the grounds of an imposing chateau, located in a steep valley in the rolling Charolais hills. There is ample shade from the many mature trees and the 45 pitches (12 used by tour operators) are on reasonably flat grassy terraces, mainly separated by small hedges. All have electrical connections. The overall appearance is attractive with some pitches overlooking the lake and some next to a field where ponies graze. This site is probably best for smaller units as the access roads are very steep and not in very good condition; caravans (and motorcaravans) are towed off site if required. The enthusiastic owner organises several unusual and interesting activities during the main season, including stone masonry, model boat building, walks, wine tours, etc. Good fishing is possible in the site's lakes and is a feature of the site. Regrettably the season here is short and the site becomes quickly full mid-July - mid-Aug. and is very popular with the Dutch. The best times could be from late June - mid July or the second half of August. Motorcaravan owners should always check in advance as there may not be a suitable pitch. Used by a Dutch tour operator.

Facilities

The sanitary facilities, not too well designed and with maintenance that can be variable, are housed in a part of the château. They include washbasins in cabins. Washing machine and dryer. Basic supplies available at reception. Very small open-air bar/restaurant/takeaway for evening barbecues (only open certain evenings). Swimming pool (1/6-10/9)with secluded sunbathing area, has been sympathetically landscaped. Half-court tennis. Fishing. Pony riding. Free bicycle loan. Torches useful. Off site: Village of Gibles, with shops, restaurant, etc. is 2 km. Riding 10 km.

Open

1 June - 4 September.

At a glance

Welcome & Ambience	✓✓✓✓	Location	✓✓✓✓
Quality of Pitches	✓✓✓	Range of Facilities	✓✓✓✓

Directions

Site is to the west of Mâcon and can be reached from the A6 (Macon Sud) via the N79 to Charolles (approx. 55 km). Take exit for Trivy - Dompierre-les-Ormes and D41 towards Montneland and Gibles.

Charges 2004

Per person	€ 5,00
child (under 7 yrs)	€ 3,50
pitch	€ 4,50
vehicle	€ 4,50
electricity (6A)	€ 4,50

Camping Cheques accepted.
Special weekly charges. 10% reduction outside 1/7 - 31/8.

Reservations

Essential for high season (8/7-25/8) and made with 25% deposit. Tel: 03 85 84 54 30.

FR71080 Camping de L'Etang Neuf

L'Etang Neuf, 71760 Issy-l'Évêque (Saône-et-Loire)

This quiet and tranquil campsite overlooking a lake, with a forest on one side and a view of the 19th century Château de Montrifaut on another, is a real countryside haven for relaxation. Separated by low hedges, there are 64 clearly marked grass pitches with 5A electricity and a small hardstanding area on which to park a car. Some young trees offer a little shade. A separate area is set aside for tents. Visitors come here to relax and enjoy the surroundings. There is no organised entertainment but a play area, fenced swimming and paddling pools and plenty of space will keep children happily amused. Many walks and mountain bike trails start from the site and free maps are provided by the friendly manager, Marc Pille.

Facilities

Two very clean sanitary blocks include British and Turkish style WCs and washbasins in cabins. Washing machine. Baby room. Separate shower and toilet rooms for disabled people are in the lower block. Motorcaravan service point. Bar/restaurant. Bread and croissants to order. Boules pitch. TV and games room. Table tennis. Volleyball. Off site: Minigolf. Riding 500 m. Nearest shop 1 km.

Open

1 May - 30 September.

At a glance

Welcome & Ambience	✓✓✓✓	Location	✓✓✓✓
Quality of Pitches	✓✓✓✓	Range of Facilities	✓✓✓✓

Directions

From D973 (Luzy - Bourbon-Lancy) turn left onto D25 (just west of Luzy) and continue for about 12 km. Turn right on D42 in centre of Issy l'Évêque, signed to campsite. Take care as the road narrows considerably as you approach the site entrance on the right.

Charges 2005

Per unit incl. 2 adults	€ 17,00
with 5A electricity	€ 20,00
extra adult	€ 4,50
child (3-8 yrs)	€ 3,00

Camping Cheques accepted.

Reservations

Advised for July and August. Tel: 03 85 24 96 05.
E-mail: info@camping-etang-neuf.com

FR71070 Castel Camping Château de l'Epervière

71240 Gigny-sur-Saône (Saône-et-Loire)

Peacefully situated on the edge of the little village of Gigny-sur-Saône, yet within easy distance of the A6 autoroute, this site nestles in a natural woodland area near the Saône river (subject to flooding in winter months). With 135 pitches, nearly all with 10A electricity, the site is in two fairly distinct areas. The original part has semi-hedged pitches on part-level ground with plenty of shade from mature trees, close to the château and fishing lake - you may need earplugs in the mornings because of the ducks! The centre of the second area has a more open aspect, with large hedged pitches and mature trees offering shade around the periphery and central open grass area. A partly fenced road across the lake connects the two areas of the site (care is needed with children). The managers, Gert-Jan and Francois, and their team enthusiastically organise a range of activities for visitors that includes wine tastings in the cellars of the château and a Kids' Club in July/Aug. Used by tour operators (60 pitches). A member of 'Les Castels' group.

Facilities

Two well equipped toilet blocks, one beside the château and a newer one on the lower section include washbasins in cabins, dishwashing and laundry areas under cover. Washing machine and dryer. Shop providing bread and basic provisions (1/5-30/9). Tastefully refurbished restaurant in the château with a distinctly French menu (1/4-30/9). Second restaurant with more basic menu and takeaway. A converted barn houses an attractive bar, large screen TV and games room. Unheated swimming pool (1/5-30/9), with many sunloungers, partly enclosed by old stone walls protecting it from the wind, plus a smaller indoor heated pool with jacuzzi, sauna and paddling pool. Well equipped play area. Outdoor paddling pool. Bicycle hire.
Off site: Riding 15 km. Golf 20 km.

At a glance

Welcome & Ambience	✓✓✓✓✓	Location	✓✓✓✓
Quality of Pitches	✓✓✓✓	Range of Facilities	✓✓✓✓✓

Directions

From N6 between Châlon-sur-Saône and Tournus, turn east on D18 (just north of Sennecey-le-Grand) and follow site signs for 6.5 km. From A6, exit Châlon-Sud from the north, or Tournus from the south.

Charges 2004

Per person	€ 5,40 - € 6,40
child (under 7 yrs)	€ 3,30 - € 4,30
pitch	€ 6,90 - € 9,60
dog	€ 2,20 - € 2,70
electricity	€ 3,30 - € 4,30

Camping Cheques accepted.

Reservations

Contact site. Tel: 03 85 94 16 90.
E-mail: domaine-de-leperviere@wanadoo.fr

Open

1 April - 30 September.

TRAVEL SERVICE SITE

TO BOOK CALL 0870 405 4055 OR www.alanrogersdirect.com

FR71090 Camping Intercommunal du Lac de Saint Point

71520 St Point (Saône-et-Loire)

On the banks of the lake, this site is managed by a young husband and wife team. It would make a convenient overnight stop, but its location on the lake may influence you to stay longer. The area is renowned for its wine and cheese as well as Roman churches, abbeys and châteaux. There are 35 reasonably level, serviced touring pitches, mostly separated by low hedges, and 46 tent pitches on a sloping and partly terraced field behind. On-site activities include swimming in the lake (lifeguard on duty during July and August), with pedaloes for hire and fishing.

Facilities

Two sanitary blocks, one adjoining the reception and the other towards the back of the site up a slope, provide all the usual facilities and a washing machine. Shower and toilet/washbasin in separate cabins for disabled campers. Bar and snacks (1/6-30/9). Play area. Volleyball, basketball and badminton. Table tennis. Games room. Boules. Mountain bike hire. Off site: Nearest shop 300 m. Tennis 4 km. Organised walks on Wednesdays 4 km. Riding 5 km.

Open

1 April - 31 October.

At a glance

Welcome & Ambience	✓✓✓	Location	✓✓
Quality of Pitches	✓✓	Range of Facilities	✓✓✓✓

Directions

Leave A6 at junction 29 and take the N79 as far as the Cluny exit. Bear left and follow the signs to Saint-Point; campsite is on the village outskirts on the right.

Charges 2004

Per unit incl. 2 adults, 2 children	€ 11,50
with electricity	€ 14,50 - € 17,00
extra person	€ 2,00
extra child (up to 7 yrs)	€ 1,50
dog	€ 1,50

No credit cards.

Reservations

Advised in July/August. Tel: 03 85 50 52 31.
E-mail: camping.stpoint@wanadoo.fr

FR71120 Camping La Heronnière

Lac de Laives, 71240 Laives (Saône-et-Loire)

La Herronière is a quiet, relaxing site on the edge of a leisure lake in pleasant rolling woodland countryside. The 90 touring pitches are good sized, grassy and level. About half have shade, with electrical connections for 81. A pleasant walk, reached directly from the campsite, runs along the edge of the lake. The site is within easy reach of Châlon-sur-Saône, Tournus and the Chalonnais vineyards and wine route. The Voie Verte, a 117 km. long linear cycling route, is 15 km. to the west.

Facilities

The modern sanitary block provides toilets, showers, washbasins and facilities for campers with disabilities. Baby rooms. Washing machine. Snack bar near pool with hot food (June - Aug). Basic provisions kept. Heated outdoor pool. Volleyball. Table tennis. Boules. Bicycle hire. Fishing. Playground. Off site: Popular, guarded part of the lake for swimming with grass area and beach, bar and restaurant 300 m. Golf 15 km. Riding 10 km.

Open

1 May - 15 September.

At a glance

Welcome & Ambience	✓✓✓✓	Location	✓✓✓✓
Quality of Pitches	✓✓✓✓	Range of Facilities	✓✓✓✓

Directions

Leave N6 (Châlon-sur-Saône - Mâcon) at Sennecy-le-Grand (about 18 km. south of the centre of Châlon), taking D18 west to Laives (4 km.). Site is signed from Laives, 4 km. to the northwest, initially along the D18.

Charges 2004

Per person	€ 4,00
child (0-7 yrs)	€ 2,80
pitch incl. car	€ 4,50 - € 7,00
electricity (6A)	€ 3,70

Camping Cheques accepted.
No credit cards.

Reservations

Advisable in July and August. Tel: 03 85 44 98 85.
E-mail: camping.laives@wanadoo.fr

FR89060 Camping Les Ceriselles

Route de Vincelottes, 89290 Vincelles (Yonne)

A distinctive, modern site, Les Ceriselles was created in 1998 on land adjacent to the Canal du Nivernais and is owned by a group of communities. A very level site, it has 84 pitches on grass, all with electricity and 37 with full services. A covered terrace houses a small snack bar with a good range of snacks, takeaway and drinks. Staff live on site and the gates are locked 22.00 - 07.00 hrs. Cars are parked on the secure on-site car park and not on the pitches. Double axle caravans are not accepted. This good value site is just off the popular N6 route and ideal for exploring the Yonne valley and Auxerre region.

Facilities

Four small heated toilet blocks each provide 1 WC, 2 washbasins in cubicles and 2 showers per sex, with a unit for disabled visitors in block one (nearest reception). Chemical toilet disposal is on the fully serviced pitches at present. Snack bar (all season). Playground. Bicycle hire. Fishing. Boules. Off site: Supermarket and restaurant within walking distance. Cycle path along canal for 8 km.

Open

1 April - 30 September.

At a glance

Welcome & Ambience	✓✓✓✓	Location	✓✓✓✓
Quality of Pitches	✓✓✓✓	Range of Facilities	✓✓✓

Directions

Vincelles is 10 km. south of Auxerre. From A6 take 'Auxerre Sud' exit and follow N65 towards Auxerre. After 4 km. turn south on N6 towards Avallon and after 10 km. left on D38. Entrance is on left.

Charges 2004

Per person	€ 2,20
pitch	€ 4,00 - € 6,00
electricty	€ 1,80

Reductions for longer stays.

Reservations

Contact site. Tel: 03 86 42 39 39.
E-mail: lesceriselles@wanadoo.fr

Franche Comté

Located to the south of Alsace, the historic province of Franche Comté boasts a varied landscape ranging from flat plains to dense woodlands, rugged dramatic mountains and limestone valleys.

Départements: 25 Doubs, 39 Jura, 70 Haute-Saône, 90 Tre. de Belfort

Major city: Besançon

Franche Comté is really made up of two regions. The high valley of the Saône is wide, gently rolling farmland with a certain rustic simplicity, while the Jura mountains are more rugged with dense forests, sheer cliffs, craggy limestone escarpments and torrents of clear, sparkling water gushing through deep gorges. It is for this thrilling scenery that Franche Comté is best known. Nature lovers can climb, bike and hike in the mountains or explore the hills honeycombed with over 4,000 caves. The streams and lakes provide world-class fishing. The spa towns of Salins les Bains and Besançon offer relaxation and a chance to 'take the waters'.

The region has a rich architectural heritage dating from many different periods, including medieval abbeys and châteaux and a poignant chapel in memory of the war. Roman remains, fortresses perched on cliff tops and elegant spa towns can all be explored at leisure. The region's position, bordering Switzerland and close to Germany, is reflected in its culture and also the great diversity of architectural style in the many fine buildings.

Cuisine of the region

Freshwater fish such as trout, grayling, pike and perch are local specialities. The region has a rare wine known as *vin de paille* as well as *vin jaune* (deep yellow and very dry) and *vin du jura*, Jura wine.

Brési: water-thin slices of dried beef; many local hams

Gougére: hot cheese pastry based on the local *Comté* cheese

Jésus de Morteau: fat pork sausage smoked over pine and juniper

Kirsch: cherry flavoured liqueur

Pontarlier: aniseed liqueur

Poulet au vin jaune: chicken, cream and *morilles* (chestnuts) cooked in *vin jaune*

Places of interest

Arbois: Pasteur Family Home and Museum, Museum of Wine and Wine Growing

Belfort: sandstone lion sculpted by Bartholdi; Memorial and Museum of the French Resistance

Besançon: citadel with good views over the city

Champlitte: Museum of Folk Art

Dole: lovely old town, Louis Pasteur's birthplace

Gray: Baron Martin Museum

Luxeuil-les-Bains: Tour des Echevins Museum

Ornans: Gustave Courbet birthplace, museum

Ronchamp: Chapel of Notre-Dame du Haut de Ronchamp designed by Le Corbusier

Salins-les-Bains: Salt mines and tunnels

Sochaux: Peugeot Museum

Alan Rogers tip

THE 150 KM. TRAIL AROUND THE JURA LAKES OFFERS SPECTACULAR SCENERY AND POINTS OF INTEREST. OR SIMPLY SIT BACK AND ENJOY A CRUISE ALONG ONE OF THE MANY LAKES.

FR25000 Castel Camping Le Val de Bonnal

Bonnal, 25680 Rougemont (Doubs)

This is an impressive, well managed site in a large country estate, harmoniously designed in keeping with the surrounding countryside, well away from main roads and other intrusions. Having said that, the site itself is very busy, with a wide range of activities and amenities. The 350 pitches, all of a good size and with electricity (5A), are separated by a mixture of trees and bushes, carefully landscaped. Some of the newer pitches are less secluded, but the ambience generally is peaceful despite the size of the site (300 pitches in a large area) and its deserved popularity. The main attraction must be the variety of water-sports on the three large lakes and nearby river which include swimming, pedaloes, and fishing as well as water skiing, windsurfing and canoeing. In fact, the range of activities available in high season is almost inexhaustible, not to say exhausting! Used by tour operators (150 pitches).

Facilities

Five clean toilet blocks include washbasins in cabins. Separate washing up blocks. Washing machines, ironing boards and sinks for laundry. Riverside restaurant, snack bar/takeaway, bar and terrace, shop (all 20/5-8/9), sympathetically converted from former farm buildings. New swimming pool complex features water slides. Well equipped children's play areas. Range of sport facilities including table tennis, boules, bicycle hire, and water sports, etc. Fishing on the river and lake. Off site: Golf 6 km. Day trips to Switzerland.

Open

4 May - 4 September.

At a glance

Welcome & Ambience	✓✓✓✓	Location	✓✓✓✓
Quality of Pitches	✓✓✓✓	Range of Facilities	✓✓✓✓✓

Directions

From Vesoul take D9 towards Villersexel. After approx. 20 km. turn right in the village of Esprels at sign for Val de Bonnal. Follow for 3.5 km. and site is on the left. From autoroute A36 take exit for Baume-les-Dames; go north on D50, then D486 to Rougemont and follow signs to site.

Charges 2005

Per unit incl. 2 persons and electricity	€ 27,00 - € 32,00
extra person	€ 8,00
child (3-8yrs)	€ 2,00

Less 20% outside July/Aug.

Reservations

Only made for pitches with electricity.
Tel: 03 81 86 90 87.
E-mail: val-de-bonnal@wanadoo.fr

FR25030 Camping du Bois de Reveuge

25680 Huanne (Doubs)

As Bois de Reveuge was only opened in 1992, it still has a new look about it, in as much as there is little shade yet from the young trees. Being on a hillside, the pitches are on terraces with good views across the surrounding countryside and leading down to two lakes which may be used for fishing and canoeing. The site also has private use of a ten hectare lake set in a park ten kilometres away where there are swimming and boating opportunities. Tall trees have been left standing at the top of the hill. 190 pitches available for tourers have a water supply as well as electricity and some are extra large (150 - 180 sq.m). There is a good solar heated swimming pool which can be covered in cool weather and another pool with four water slides. Several supervisors are in attendance during the summer.

TRAVEL SERVICE SITE

TO BOOK CALL 0870 405 4055 OR www.alanrogersdirect.com

Facilities

Four modern sanitary blocks are nicely spaced around the site and have British and Turkish style WCs and washbasins mainly in cabins. Kiosk for basic food supplies (open all season) and restaurant/pizzeria with terrace (1/6-3/9). Swimming pools. Four play areas. High season 'baby club' with a large tent for wet weather, large video screen and some music and other entertainment for adults. Bowling alley. Shooting range. Pony club. Groups may request a ctivities such as orienteering. A package deal includes use of canoes as well as archery, fishing, bicycle hire and pedaloes.

Open

23 April - 17 September.

At a glance

Welcome & Ambience	✓✓✓✓	Location	✓✓✓✓
Quality of Pitches	✓✓✓	Range of Facilities	✓✓✓✓

Directions

Site is well signed from the D50. From A36 autoroute south of the site, take exit for Baume-les-Dames and head north on D50 towards Villersexel for about 7 km. to camp signs

Charges 2005

Per unit incl. 2 persons	€ 17,00 - € 35,00
extra person	€ 3,00 - € 6,00
child (2-5 yrs)	€ 2,00 - € 4,00
animal	€ 2,00

Camping Cheques accepted.

Reservations

Made with 30% deposit and fee (€ 20).
Tel: 03 81 84 38 60.
E-mail: info@campingduboisdereveuge.com

FR25050 Camping Municipal de Saint Point-Lac

8 rue du Port, 25160 St Point-Lac (Doubs)

A good example of a municipal campsite in which the village takes a pride, this site is on the banks of a small lake with views to the distant hills. The 84 level, numbered pitches are on grass and 60 have electricity (16A). It is worth making a detour from the Pontarlier - Vallorbe road or for a longer stay. The village shop and restaurant are an easy 200 m. walk from the site entrance.

Facilities

Good central sanitary block has British style WCs and free hot water. Hot snacks and takeaway in high season (July/Aug). Fishing. Off site: Bicycle hire 5 km.

Open

1 May - 30 September.

At a glance

Welcome & Ambience	✓✓✓	Location	✓✓✓✓
Quality of Pitches	✓✓✓	Range of Facilities	✓✓✓

Directions

From north, take D437 south of Pontarlier and keep on west side of the lake to the second village (Saint Point-Lac); from south exit N57 at Les Hopitaux-Neufs and turn west to lake.

Charges guide

Per pitch incl. 2 persons	€ 7,50 - € 9,00
with electricity	€ 11,50 - € 13,00

Reservations

Made with deposit (€ 45) and fee (€ 7.60). Contact site from 1 May. Tel: 03 81 69 61 64.
E-mail: camping-saintpointlac@wanadoo.fr

FR39010 Camping La Plage Blanche

3 rue de la Plage, 39380 Ounans (Jura)

Situated in open countryside, along the banks of the River Loue, this site has 220 good sized, marked pitches on level ground, all with electricity (6A). Trees provide both fully shaded and semi-shaded pitches. Approximately a kilometre of riverside and beach provide the ideal setting for children to swim and play safely in the gently flowing, shallow water - inflatables are popular and there is a canoe/kayak base. The site also has a swimming pool.

Facilities

Modern, well kept sanitary facilities in three unusual blocks include separate washing cabins. Dishwashing facilities are in blocks of 8 sinks. Launderette. Motorcaravan service area. Bar/restaurant with terrace (1/4-30/9). Pizzeria and takeaway (all season). TV room. Swimming pool and children's pool. Play area. River fishing. Table tennis. Off site: Bicycle hire 200 m. Riding 700 m. Golf 10 km.

Open

1 April - 15 October.

At a glance

Welcome & Ambience	✓✓✓✓	Location	✓✓✓✓
Quality of Pitches	✓✓✓	Range of Facilities	✓✓✓✓

Directions

Ounans is 20 km southeast of Dole. On A36 from Besancon, take Dole exit then D405 to Parcey. After Parcey take N5 to Mont Sous Vaudrey (8 km) then D472 towards Pontarlier to Ounans from where site is signed. From A9 Dole exit follow signs for N5, Poligny and Lons le Saunier. From Parcy follow as above.

Charges 2004

Per person	€ 4,70
child (1-7 yrs)	€ 2,90
pitch	€ 5,90
electricity	€ 3,00

Camping Cheques accepted.

Reservations

Made with deposit (€ 31) and fee (€ 8).
Tel: 03 84 37 69 63.
E-mail: reservation@la-plage-blanche.com

FR39050 Camping Fayolan

B.P. 52, 39130 Clairvaux-les-Lacs (Jura)

This modern site, backed by wooded hills, is situated on the shores of Le Petit Lac about a mile from the town of Clairvaux-les-Lacs amid the lakes and forests of the Jura. Here one can relax, enjoy the peaceful countryside, explore the interesting villages, historic towns and museums of the area by car or cycle or take to the water where you can swim, windsurf and canoe. The neat, tidy site is in two parts, with pitches from 80-100 sq.m. either on terraces overlooking the lake or on the flatter area near the shore. There are electrical connections (6A) for those who want them and 200 pitches have electricity, water, drainage and sewage connections. The upper part has little shade until the young trees grow but there is some on the lower section. Used by tour operators (130 pitches).

Facilities

Four modern toilet units spread around the site have warm water from push-button taps in washbasins and showers. Shop. Restaurant. Two good swimming pools (heated from mid-May), one with a slide, and smaller one for children (trunks, not shorts). Playground. Organised activities. Fishing. Entertainment. Off site: Bicycle hire 800 m. Riding 4 km.

Open

3 May - 15 September.

At a glance

Welcome & Ambience	✓✓✓✓	Location	✓✓✓✓
Quality of Pitches	✓✓✓✓	Range of Facilities	✓✓✓✓✓

Directions

Clairvaux-les-Lacs is on the N78 between Lons-le-Saunier and Morez. In Clairvaux follow signs for 'Lacs Campings' and Fayolan.

Charges 2004

Per unit incl. 2 persons	€ 15,00 - € 28,00
extra person	€ 5,00 - € 6,00
child (4-20 yrs)	free - € 3,00
serviced pitch	€ 4,60

Reservations

Made with 30% deposit and € 19 fee.
Tel: 03 84 25 26 19.
E-mail: Relais.Soleil.Jura@wanadoo.fr

FR39030 Camping Domaine de Chalain

39130 Doucier (Jura)

Doucier lies east of Lons-le-Saunier among the wooded hills of the Jura and rather away from the main routes. This large, park-like site (804 pitches) is on the edge of the Lac de Chalain surrounded on three sides by woods and some cliffs. Large areas are left for sports and recreation. The lake shelves gently at the edge but then becomes deep quite suddenly. Day visitors can be very numerous during fine week-ends. The site also has an attractive, well equipped pool complex. The site is divided into two parts, one (nearer the lake) with larger pitches (costing more). You should find room in the other part, but for July and August, it is better to reserve to make sure. There are over 200 electrical connections; little shade. Used by tour operators (100 pitches).

Facilities

Nine sanitary blocks, improved over the years, include washbasins with warm water (all in cabins). Showers are in separate blocks. One block can be heated with facilities for babies and disabled people. Washing machines. Shops (15/5-15/9). Bar, takeaway and snacks (1/5-20/9) and a community room. New pool complex with heated indoor pool, outdoor pools with slide, sauna and spa. Tennis, table tennis, minigolf and pedaloes for hire. Fishing. Bicycle hire. Animals and birds in enclosures. Cinema and organised activities, plus a disco for the young. Dogs are not permitted on the lake beach Off site: Riding 2 km. Golf 25 km.

Open

1 May - 20 September.

At a glance

Welcome & Ambience	✓✓✓✓	Location	✓✓✓✓
Quality of Pitches	✓✓✓	Range of Facilities	✓✓✓✓

Directions

Site can only be approached via Doucier: from Switzerland via N5 (from Geneva), then the N78 and D39; from other directions via Lons-le-Saunier or Champagnole.

Charges 2004

Per unit incl. 3 persons acc. to location and services	€ 19,25 - € 32,77
extra adult	€ 6,22 - € 7,80
child (4-15 yrs)	€ 3,96 - € 4,78
electricity	€ 2,60
dog	€ 2,60

Reservations

Made for min. 7 days with 30% deposit (min. € 61). Sat.-Sat. only in high season. Tel: 03 84 25 78 78. E-mail: chalain@chalain.com

FR39040 Sunêlia La Pergola

Mobile homes page 381

39130 Marigny (Jura)

Close to the Swiss border and overlooking the sparkling waters of Lac de Chalain, La Pergola is a neat, tidy and terraced site set amongst the rolling hills of the Jura. Awaiting discovery as it is not on the main tourist routes, La Pergola is very well appointed, with 350 pitches, mainly on gravel and separated by small bushes, and all with electricity, water and drainage. Arranged on numerous terraces, connected by steep steps, some have shade and the higher ones have good views over the lake. A tall fence protects the site from the public footpath that separates the site from the lakeside but there are frequent access gates. The entrance is very attractive and the work that Mme. Gicquaire puts into the preparation of the flower-beds is very evident. The bar/restaurant terrace is beautiful, featuring grape vines for welcome shade and a colourful array of spectacular flowers leading on to a landscaped waterfall area next to the three swimming pools and entertainment area. English is spoken. Used by tour operators (120 pitches).

TRAVEL SERVICE SITE

TO BOOK CALL 0870 405 4055 OR www.alanrogersdirect.com

Facilities

The latest sanitary block serving the lower pitches is well appointed with private cabins. Slightly older blocks serve the other terraces. Visitors with disabilities are advised to select a lower terrace where special facilities are provided. Washing machines and dryers. Bar. Restaurant. Pool complex, two pools heated. Good play area and children's club. Table tennis and volleyball. Windsurfing, pedaloes and small boats for hire. Organised programme in high season includes cycle tours, keep fit sessions and evening entertainment with disco twice weekly. Off site: Riding 3 km.

Open

30 April - 11 September.

At a glance

Welcome & Ambience	✓✓✓✓	Location	✓✓✓✓
Quality of Pitches	✓✓✓✓	Range of Facilities	✓✓✓✓✓

Directions

Site is 2.5 km. north of Doucier on Lake Chalain road D27.

Charges 2004

Per unit incl. 2 persons and electricity	€ 20,00 - € 35,00
extra person	€ 4,50 - € 5,50
child (2-6 yrs)	free - € 4,50
dog	€ 2,00

Camping Cheques accepted.
Various special offers available.

Reservations

Made with deposit (€ 122) and fee (€ 27). Tel: 03 84 25 70 03. E-mail: contact@lapergola.com

FR39060 Camping La Marjorie

640 Bvd. de l'Europe, 39000 Lons-le-Saunier (Jura)

La Marjorie is a spacious site set on the outskirts of the spa town of Lons-le-Saunier. A former municipal site, it has 200 level pitches. Mainly on hardstanding, they are separated by well trimmed hedges interspersed with tall trees which give privacy plus a little shade at some part of the day. Bordering one area of the site are open fields and woodlands. All pitches have electricity and a few are fully serviced. The site is 2.5 km. from the centre of the town which is the capital town of the Jura region. A bicycle path from the site leads into town and a mountain bike track behind the site. English is spoken.

Facilities

Three well maintained toilet blocks, two modern and heated, have individual cubicles with washbasins and large showers. Baby baths, good facilities for disabled people, washing and ironing. Motorcaravan service point (charge). Small shop (15/6-31/8). Small bar with takeaway meals (all 15/6-31/8). TV room, table tennis, small play area, boule pitch, volleyball and football field. Archery, canoeing and riding can be arranged (fee). Off site: Local swimming pool 200 m. Restaurants 500 m. Golf 5 km. Caves and waterfalls 17 km.

Open

1 April - 15 October.

At a glance

Welcome & Ambience	✓✓✓✓	Location	✓✓✓✓
Quality of Pitches	✓✓✓✓	Range of Facilities	✓✓✓✓

Directions

Site is off the N83 Lons-le-Saunier - Besancon road. Approaching Lons on the D52 or the N78 or D471, site is signed from the first roundabout on the outskirts of the town. When approaching from Bescancon on N83, follow signs for Club Nautique on outskirts of Lons - this takes you under the N83 to the site.

Charges 2004

Per unit incl. 2 persons	€ 9,78 - € 14,00
with electricity (6A)	€ 11,22 - € 16,50
extra person	€ 2,38 - € 3,50
child (under 10 yrs)	€ 1,28 - € 2,00
dog	€ 1,00

Less 10% for stays over 7 days.

Reservations

Made with deposit (€ 130) and fee (€ 9.15).
Tel: 03 84 24 26 94.
E-mail: info@camping-marjorie.com

FR39080 Camping du Domaine de l'Epinette

15, rue de l'Epinette 39130 Chatillon (Jura)

This quiet site has the same owners as FR39040, but is more recently established and less than half the size. It is set in charming wooded countryside on land sloping down to the river Ain, which here is shallow and slow moving. There are 150 grassy pitches, of which 8 are occupied by a Dutch tour operator and 126 (including 4 with hardstanding) are available for touring units. These are arranged on terraces and separated by hedges and young bushes and trees, about half being shaded and half in the open. The number of slightly sloping and level pitches is about equal. Nearly all have electricity hookups nearby, although some long leads might be needed. There is an attractive swimming pool, paddling pool and surrounds. An activity club for children takes place in July/August. Guided canoe trips on the river start and finish at the campsite.

Facilities

Two modern toilet blocks provide some Turkish toilets, showers and washbasins (some in cubicles). Unit for disabled visitors. Baby bath. Dishwashing and laundry sinks, all with warm or hot and cold water. Washing machine and dryer. Small shop for basics in reception. Snack bar and takeaway (evenings). A bar, restaurant, TV room and larger shop are planned. Playground. Table tennis under marquee. Boules. Direct access to river for swimming and canoeing (at your own risk). Off site: Riding 6 km. Golf 25 km. Shops, etc. in Dorcier 6 km.

Open

Mid-June - mid-September.

At a glance

Welcome & Ambience	✓✓✓✓	Location	✓✓✓✓✓
Quality of Pitches	✓✓✓✓	Range of Facilities	✓✓✓✓

Directions

From Lons-le-Saunier take D471 eastwards towards Champagnole. After about 8 km. fork right onto D39 towards Doucier. After about 11 km at Chatillon turn right onto D151 south towards Blye. Site is less than 2 km. on the left.

Charges 2004

Per unit incl. 2 persons and electricity	€ 12,00 - € 24,50
extra person	€ 2,00 - € 4,00
child (2-7 yrs)	free - € 2,50

Camping Cheques accepted.
Less 10% for 10 days or longer.

Reservations

Made with 25% deposit and € 30 fee for high season bookings. Tel: 03 84 25 71 44.
E-mail: contact@domaine-epinette.com

FR70020 Camping International du Lac Vesoul

70000 Vesoul (Haute-Saône)

This is one of the better examples of a municipal site and is part of a leisure park around a large lake. A five kilometre path has been created around the lake for jogging, walking and cycling and there is a large open space for ball games or sunbathing, along with a good playground for children and a bar and restaurant. A map at the entrance shows the water areas for swimming, boating and windsurfing. Watersports are organised by the Club Nautique Haut-Saonois Vesoul and there is also tennis, table tennis, archery, basketball and night-time carp fishing. The campsite does not have direct access to the lake as it is separated by a security fence, but access is possible at the site entrance. There are 160 good sized, level, grass pitches, all with electricity (10A). Access is from hard roads and pitches are separated by shrubs and bushes. There is a large hard area in the centre of the site brightened by flowers and young trees.

Facilities

Three good quality toilet blocks, one heated, are well spaced around the site. They have a mix of British and Turkish style WCs and free, pre-mixed warm water from push-button taps in the washbasins and showers. Baby room. Facilities for disabled visitors. Washing machines and dryers.

Open

1 March - 31 October.

At a glance

Welcome & Ambience	✓✓✓✓	Location	✓✓✓✓
Quality of Pitches	✓✓✓✓	Range of Facilities	✓✓✓

Directions

On road D457 to west of Vesoul on route to Besançon, well signed around the town.

Charges guide

Per person	€ 3,00
child (under 7 yrs)	€ 1,30
pitch	€ 3,10
pitch with electricity	€ 5,10
vehicle	€ 2,10
dog	€ 1,60

No credit cards.

Reservations

Contact site. Tel: 03 84 76 22 86.

FR90000 Camping L'Etang des Forges

11 rue Béthouart, 90000 Belfort (Tre. de Belfort)

Belfort (known as the City of the Lion) is an historic fortified town with much history. The region is well endowed with footpaths and cycle trails and this site would make a good base for a longer stay. There are also opportunities for ballooning and hang-gliding. Although 178 pitches are marked out, this very spacious site only uses 90 of them, and you should always be able to find room here. The pitches are all on level, mostly open ground divided by low bushes. A few trees around one end give a little shade to some pitches and there are electricity hook-ups (6A) to all pitches and a good supply of water taps. The reception building also contains a small shop and cafe.

Facilities

A single modern sanitary building (heated in cool weather) provides washbasins in cubicles, a suite for disabled people, dishwashing and laundry sinks, a washing machine and dryer. Motorcaravan service point. Outdoor swimming pool. Volleyball. Table tennis. Small playground. TV Room. Shop and cafe (117-31/8). Internet terminal. Off site: Large supermarket is on edge of town on the Mulhouse road.

Open

14 April - 30 September.

At a glance

Welcome & Ambience	✓✓✓✓	Location	✓✓✓✓✓
Quality of Pitches	✓✓✓✓	Range of Facilities	✓✓✓✓

Directions

Site is northeast of town centre, adjacent to the lake and sports facilities (well signed).

Charges 2004

Per person	€ 3,10 - € 3,80
child (4-9 yrs)	€ 2,50 - € 3,10
pitch	€ 7,00 - € 8,00
electricity	€ 3,00
animal	€ 1,00 - € 1,50

Reservations

Not usually necessary. Tel: 03 84 22 54 92.
E-mail: contact@campings-belfort.com

Map 9

Deep valleys dividing mountain slopes, covered in lush alpine pastures and evergreen woods - this is the Savoy Alps bordering Switzerland. Further south you'll come across the Dauphiné Alps which, although they can appear harsh and forbidding, offer spectacular scenery.

Départements: 38 Isère, 73 Savoie, 74 Haute-Savoie

Major city: Grenoble

Lying between the Rhône Valley and the Alpine borders with Switzerland and Italy are the old provinces of Savoie and Dauphiné. This is an area of enormous granite outcrops, deeply riven by spectacular glacier hewn and river etched valleys. One of the world's leading wintersport playgrounds there is also a range of outdoor activities in the summer. Despite development, great care has been taken to blend the old with the new and many traditional villages still retain their charm and historical interest. For many, it is an opportunity to escape the crowds and enjoy some clean air, unusual wildlife, stunning views, hidden lakes and sometimes isolated villages in spectacular mountain settings.

From Chambéry, north to the shores of Lac Léman (Lake Geneva) are many towns and villages that, since Roman times, have attracted visitors to take the waters. Aix-les-Bains, Evian and Annecy were three major lakeside spa resorts of the Victorians; while Chamonix and Grenoble attracted the 19th century travellers who pioneered modern skiing and 'alpinism'. To the north is the region of Chartreuse famous for its monastery and liqueur!

Cuisine of the region

Plat gratiné applies to a wide varity of dishes, in the Alps this means cooked in breadcrumbs.

Farcement (Farçon Savoyard): potatoes baked with cream, eggs, bacon, dried pears and prunes

Féra: a freshwater lake fish

Fondue: hot melted cheese and white wine

Gratin Dauphinois: potato dish with cream, cheese and garlic

Gratin Savoyard: another potato dish with cheese and butter

Lavaret: a freshwater lake fish, like salmon

Longeole: a country sausage

Lotte: a burbot, not unlike an eel

Tartiflette: potato, bacon, onions and Reblochon cheese

Places of interest

Aix-les-Bains: spa resort on the Lac du Bourget, boat excursions to the Royal Abbey of Hautecombe

Albertville: 1992 Winter Olympics, museum, now has an active night-life!

Annecy: canal-filled lakeside town, 12th century château, old quarter

Bourg-St-Maurice: centre of Savoie café society

Chambéry: old quarter, Dukes of Savoie château, Savoie museum.

Chamonix: site of first Winter Olympics in 1924, world capital of mountain climbing

Evian-les-Bains: spa and casino on Lake Geneva

Grenoble: University city, Fort de la Bastille

Alan Rogers **tip**

WATCH THE FAMOUS CYCLE RACE, THE TOURS DE FRANCE, WHICH PASSES THROUGH THIS AREA IN JULY; AND HUSKY DOG TREKKING WHICH ALSO TAKES PLACE IN SUMMER.

FR38090 Camping Caravaning Belle Roche

38930 Lalley (Isère)

Belle Roche, a good, small municipal site, has extremely pleasant views all round and is a convenient overnight stop, or even for a longer stay. The level site is only a few years old, so is rather open at present with very little shade, but it is nonetheless neat and well maintained throughout. There are 65 spacious pitches, many part grass with a gravel hardstanding. All have 16A electricity and there are ample water points. This is a convenient base for enjoying this scenic but relatively unknown Trièves part of the Isère.

Facilities

Two sanitary blocks provide some washbasins in private cabins. Facilities for disabled visitors. Laundry and dishwashing. Good motorcaravan service point. Bar and terrace serving simple, good value meals. Bread from reception. Swimming pool (19 x 12 m; June-Sept.) with large sunbathing area and sunbeds. Play area. Off site: Village shop. Cycling, walking, climbing.

Open

1 May - 30 September.

At a glance

Welcome & Ambience	✓✓✓✓✓	Location	✓✓✓✓
Quality of Pitches	✓✓✓✓	Range of Facilities	✓✓✓✓

Directions

Follow N75 south from Grenoble (approx. 65 km.) turn left onto D66, signed Lalley and follow camping signs through the village. The campsite is on the right just beyond the village.

Charges guide

Per unit incl. 2 persons	€ 10,90 - € 13,20
child (8 - 16 yrs)	€ 3,00
child (under 7 yrs)	€ 1,50

Camping Cheques accepted.

Reservations

Advised for July/Aug. Tel: 04 76 34 75 33.
E-mail: camping-belleroche@joliefrance.com

FR38010 Le Coin Tranquille

Mobile homes ▶ page 384

38490 Les Abrets (Isère)

Set in the Dauphiny countryside north of Grenoble, Le Coin Tranquille is truly a 'quiet corner', especially outside school holiday times, although it is still popular with families in high season. Les Abrets is well placed for visits to the Savoie regions and the Alps. It is an attractive and well maintained site of 192 grass pitches (160 for touring units), all with electricity. They are separated by well maintained hedges of hydrangea, flowering shrubs and a range of trees to make a lovely environment doubly enhanced by the rural aspect and marvellous views across to the mountains. This is a popular, family run site with friendly staff that makes a wonderful base for exploring the area, especially in low season. The Chartreuse caves at Voiron are well worth a visit. Used by a tour operator (17 pitches). A 'Sites et Paysages' member.

Facilities

The central large sanitary block is of good quality and well kept, heated in low season. It includes washbasins in cabins, facilities for children and disabled people and a laundry room. Two other blocks on either edge of the site have been refurbished to a high standard. Busy shop. Excellent restaurant, open all year (closed two days weekly in low season) and attracting local clientele. Swimming pool and paddling pool (15/5-30/9; no Bermuda style shorts) with sunbathing areas. Play area. TV/video room with balcony, games room and quiet reading room. Supervised games for children, slide shows of the region's attractions and weekly entertainment for adults including live music (not discos) arranged mid-May - end-August. Bicycle hire. Off site: Riding 6 km. Fishing 8 km. Golf 25 km. Les Abrets with shops and supermarket 2 km. Wonderful old towns and villages, fantastic gastronomy. Morestel withits colourful flowers and market 21 km.

At a glance

Welcome & Ambience	✓✓✓✓✓	Location	✓✓✓✓
Quality of Pitches	✓✓✓✓✓	Range of Facilities	✓✓✓✓

Directions

Site is east of Les Abrets. From the roundabout in the centre of town take N6 towards Chambery, turning left in just under 2 km. (signed Restaurant and Camping). Follow signs along country lane for just over 1 km. and entrance is on right.

Charges 2004

Per pitch incl. 2 persons	€ 14,00 - € 26,00
extra person	€ 4,00 - € 6,50
child (2-7 yrs)	€ 2,30 - € 4,50
electricity (2/6A)	€ 1,30 - € 3,00
pet	€ 1,00

Camping Cheques accepted.

Reservations

Write with deposit (€ 134) and fee (€ 16).
Tel: 04 76 32 13 48.
E-mail: contact@coin-tranquille.com

Open

26 March - 31 October.

FR38030 Camping La Cascade

Route de l'Alpe d'Huez, 38520 Bourg-d'Oisans (Isère)

Camping La Cascade is close to and within sight and sound of the waterfall from which it takes its name. The friendly owners keep this very pleasant site neat and tidy. Bourg d'Oisans lies in the Romanche valley 725 m. above sea level surrounded by high mountains. It is a real sun trap and gets very hot in summer. The ski resorts of Alpe d'Huez and Les Deux Alpes are close by. The Alpe d'Huez road past the campsite with its 21 hairpin bends is revered by serious cyclists as it is often used as the 'king of the mountain' stage for the Tour de France. La Cascade has 133 individual pitches, 106 for touring units on mainly flat ground. Of varying but quite adequate size with 16A electricity, many have little shade.

Facilities

Two heated sanitary blocks are of good quality with mainly British style toilets and washbasins in cabins. Washing machine. Bar and snack bar (1/7-31/8). Good sized, heated and sheltered swimming pool and paddling pool (15/5-30/9) surrounded by large, enclosed sunbathing area. Small playground. General room with TV. Games room. Table tennis, volleyball and boules. Evening entertainment and lots of activities organised in season. Off site: Supermarket or fishing 500 m. Bicycle hire or riding 1 km. Bourg d'Oisans 1 km, with bars, restaurants, shops and banks etc. Ski resorts of Alpe d'Huez 13 km. and Les deux Alpes 25 km.

Open

20 December - 30 September.

At a glance

Welcome & Ambience	✓✓✓✓	Location	✓✓✓✓
Quality of Pitches	✓✓✓✓	Range of Facilities	✓✓✓✓

Directions

Leave Bourg d'Oisans on the N91 towards Brianson. Shortly after crossing the river, on a sharp right hand bend, turn left onto the D211, signed Alpe d'Huez. Site is on right in 400 m.

Charges 2004

Per unit incl. 2 persons	€ 14,80 - € 22,00
extra person (over 5 yrs)	€ 4,00 - € 5,50
electricity	€ 3,50
electricity for heating in winter	€ 3,50
animal	free

Reservations

Essential for July/Aug; made for minimum 8 days with deposit (€ 64) and fee (€ 16). No reservations by phone. Tel: 04 76 80 02 42.
E-mail: lacascade@wanadoo.fr

FR38040 Camping La Rencontre du Soleil

Route de l'Alpe d'Huez, 38520 Bourg-d'Oisans (Isère)

This part of the Isère is an attractive and popular region with some exceptional scenery for which this site proves a good base from which to explore. Pleasant, friendly and family run, it nestles between two impressive mountain ranges, at the base of France's largest National Park, Le Parc des Ecrins. Only 2 km. from Bourg d'Oisans, a regular staging point for the Tour de France, it offers some serious and exciting cycling. The site has 73 level, hedged pitches, most of average size, with mature trees offering good shade. Electricity is available (2, 6 or 10A). Canoeing, rafting, riding and many other activities are possible nearby. The site is used by a tour operator (20 pitches). A 'Sites et Paysages' member.

Facilities

A large heated toilet block provides all the usual amenities, all of high quality and extremely clean and well maintained. Washing machine and dryer. Motorcaravan service point. Bread to order. Restaurant and takeaway (all season). Sitting room with TV and children's play room adjoining. Small, sheltered swimming pool (all season). Play area. Programme of activities in high season includes walking, mountain biking and a mini-club for children. Off site: Supermarket 1 km. towards Bourg d'Oisans. Fishing 1 km. Bicycle hire 1.2 km. Canoeing, rafting, riding, hiking and climbing nearby. Cable car at Alpe d'Huez. Some skiing normally possible until mid-July at Les Deux Alpes (16 km).

Open

11 May - 15 September.

At a glance

Welcome & Ambience	✓✓✓✓✓	Location	✓✓✓✓
Quality of Pitches	✓✓✓✓	Range of Facilities	✓✓✓✓

Directions

Leave Bourg d'Oisans on the N91 towards Briancon. Shortly after crossing the river, on a sharp right hand bend, turn left on D211 signed Alpe d'Huez. Site is on left just beyond Camping la Piscine. Entrance is on a sharp bend - take care.

Charges 2004

Per unit incl. 2 persons	€ 14,30 - € 22,85
incl. 3 persons	€ 15,85 - € 25,15
extra person	€ 5,30 - € 5,55
child (2-5 yrs)	€ 3,70 - € 3,95
electricity (2/10A)	€ 2,90 - € 4,00
dog	free - € 0,80

Camping Cheques accepted.

Reservations

Advised in high season with 20% deposit and fee (€ 15.25) Tel: 04 76 79 12 22.
E-mail: rencontre.soleil@wanadoo.fr

FR38050 Camping Caravaning Le Temps Libre

38150 Bouge-Chambalud (Isère)

You will receive a warm welcome at this spacious, family run site which is close to the A7 motorway, between Lyon and Valence, making it ideal for an overnight stay. It would also make a base to discover this interesting region – discover the rolling countryside, vineyards, orchards and picturesque villages. There are 160 pitches, with 80 available for tourers, the mobile homes and seasonal pitches being in a separate section. The medium to large, party sloping, grassy pitches are mostly separated by high hedges and trees giving privacy and some shade. All have 9A electricity and water close by. Most are in cul-de-sacs, in groups of 8, and a few have tricky access. There is a large hardstanding area with electricity for motorcaravans and overnight stays. The site has a large pool complex and sunbathing area comprising a swimming pool plus three other pools with toboggans to suit all ages (no Bermuda style shorts). There is a large area adjacent for youngsters to let off steam.

Facilities

Three toilet blocks, two (both refurbished) for tourers, one near the entrance and one in the centre by the pool. They provide all the necessary facilities. Motorcaravan service point. Good shop, bar/restaurant and takeaway (all 1/7-31/8). Swimming pools (15/5-31/8). Two playgrounds. Club/TV room. Football pitch. Volleyball. Boules. 3 tennis courts (free). Fishing. Minigolf. Organised activities for all ages and pony cart rides (July and Aug). Internet access. Off site: Golf and riding 10 km. Canoeing. Foothills of the Alps. Shops, supermarket and the Lafuma factory shop at Anneyron 8 km.

At a glance

Welcome & Ambience	✓✓✓✓	Location	✓✓✓✓
Quality of Pitches	✓✓✓	Range of Facilities	✓✓✓✓

Directions

From A7 motorway take exit 12 (Chanas) or from the N7 take D510 east towards Grenoble for about 7 km to Bougé Chambalud. Turn right in the village (site signed) and entrance is a few hundred metres.

Charges 2004

Per unit incl. 2 persons	€ 12,10 - € 18,30
extra person	€ 4,00 - € 6,10
electricity (9A)	€ 3,80

Camping Cheques accepted.

Reservations

Contact site. Tel: 04 74 84 04 09.
E-mail: camping.temps-libre@libertysurf.fr

Open

1 April - 30 September.

FR38100 Camping Belledonne

Rochetaillée, 38520 Bourg-d'Oisans (Isère)

This extremely neat site, run by the Arnaud family, takes its name from the nearby Belledonne mountain range, and one of the six valleys of the Oisans area. All are impressive, but there is something rather magnificent about the views surrounding this site; furthermore it enjoys sunshine for most of the day. Access roads are tarmac and each of the 150 grassy pitches, 105 for touring, are not only level and well drained, but also generously sized, with electricity (3/6A). The site is divided into six areas, each named after one of the local valleys. High hedges and abundant mature trees provide ample privacy and shade. Next to this is an attractive pool complex surrounded by well tended gardens. This is a friendly and well run site (English spoken). There is some noise from the nearby road. A 'Sites et Paysages' member.

Facilities

Two toilet blocks include washbasins in cabins, a mixture of British and Turkish style toilets, laundry, baby changing rooms and facilities for disabled visitors. Shop. Bar/restaurant (all season). Takeaway. TV room. Swimming and paddling pools. Tennis. Volleyball. Small play area and a large grass meadow with comprehensive fitness course. Bicycle hire.

Open

21 May - 4 September.

At a glance

Welcome & Ambience	✓✓✓✓	Location	✓✓✓✓✓
Quality of Pitches	✓✓✓✓	Range of Facilities	✓✓✓✓

Directions

From Grenoble take N85 to Vizille, then N91 towards Bourg d'Oisans. Branch left on D526 and site is approx. 250 m. on right.

Charges 2005

Per pitch incl. 2 persons	€ 15,10 - € 22,40
extra person	€ 4,00 - € 5,80
electricity (3-6A)	€ 2,80 - € 3,90

Camping Cheques accepted.

Reservations

Made with € 15 fee; contact site. Tel: 04 76 80 07 18.
E-mail: belledon@club-internet.fr

FR38110 Camping Le Champ du Moulin

Bourg d'Arud, 38520 Venosc (Isère)

With steep-sided mountains on all sides, Le Champ du Moulin nestles comfortably on the floor of the narrow Vénéon valley. Even though the bustling town of Le Bourg d'Oisans is only a 15 minute drive away, this peaceful campsite is enjoyed by visitors in both winter and summer. When we visited in early spring, it proved to be a good base for skiing. A cabin chairlift near the entrance transports visitors to Les 2 Alpes. This renowned resort lies out of sight over a sharp rise and offers miles of ski runs in season and extensive glacier skiing in summer. Watching over the site is the more traditional village of Venosc which clings to the hillside a short walk away. Its church, narrow streets, old buildings and notable craft shops are a delightful alternative to the more recently developed glitzy ski towns. On site, generous pitches and large trees are features to note. However, when the mountain snows starts to melt in late May/early June, the River Vénéon adjacent to the site changes from its winter trickle to an impressive torrent. Parents with small children need to be especially vigilant. With its location on the edge of the Ecrins National Park, this is a peaceful location with stunning scenery and miles of marked cycling and walking trails. It is not really suitable for teenagers seeking late-night revelry and nightly disco dancing.

Facilities

A well heated toilet block is welcome after a day of winter sport, and clothes soon dry on the racks provided. Excellent baby room. Laundry. Motorcaravan service point. Chalet restaurant/bar with very good home cooking at easy-on-the-pocket prices. Small shop sharing reception with bread each morning. Play area. TV room. Computer room with internet access. Fishing. Off site: Municipal heated outdoor pools and flume next door open in summer, together with a play-ground, tennis courts and tree-top adventure park. White water rafting, paragliding, bungee jumping and hill walking available nearby. Discounted ski passes. Riding 0.5 km, golf 3 km (both summer only).

Open

15 December - 15 September.

At a glance

Welcome & Ambience	✓✓✓✓	Location	✓✓✓✓
Quality of Pitches	✓✓✓✓	Range of Facilities	✓✓✓✓

Directions

From Grenoble, leave on the southeast side of the city following signs for Oisans. At Bourg d'Oisans (40 km), go through village following signs for Les 2 Alpes and Briancon. After 3 km. turn right at sharp bend for Venosc. In 8 km. along the twisting valley road, pass the bottom ski station on the left. Site is on right after 400 m.

Charges 2005

Per unit incl. 1 or 2 persons	€ 13,00 - € 18,00
extra person	€ 3,80 - € 4,60
child (3-7 yrs)	€ 2,30 - € 2,80
electricity (3/6/10A)	€ 2,50 - € 8,00
dog	€ 0,50 - € 1,00

Less 10% for 14 nights, 15% for 21 nights. Special ski arrangements.

Reservations

Made with deposit (and high season € 15 booking fee). Tel: 04 76 80 07 38.
E-mail: christian.avallet@wanadoo.fr

FR38120 Camping du Bontemps

38150 Vernioz (Isère)

This spacious, attractive and well cared for site is enhanced by a wide variety of coniferous and deciduous trees planted by the dedicated owner nearly 30 years ago. The 200 large, level and grassy pitches are arranged in groups, partly separated by neat hedges, all with water and electricity. Seven pitches are used for mobile homes and chalets and a group at the back is used by weekenders. The shop, bar/restaurant, landscaped swimming pool and superb children's play pool, including toboggan, mushrooms and fountain are conveniently placed near to the entrance. The large sports area and excellent activity hall are off to one side minimising noise problems. There is a field and stable for horses, a small river and fishing lake next to the site. This is an excellent site for both short and long stays.

Facilities

The excellent two main toilet blocks and the smaller block near the pool are modern, kept very clean and contain all the necessary facilities. Two motorcaravan service points. Shop. Bar/restaurant (all season). Swimming pools (June - 30 Sept). Several play areas. Minigolf. Table tennis. Tennis. Badminton, archery, volleyball and football. Riding. Electronic games. Extensive list of activities for all the family (high season). Off site: The small village of Vernioz (shops, restaurant and bar) 2 km. Bicycle hire 7 km. Historic old market town of Vienne 20 km. Golf 20 km. City of Lyons.

Open

1 April - 30 September.

At a glance

Welcome & Ambience	✓✓✓✓✓	Location	✓✓✓✓
Quality of Pitches	✓✓✓✓	Range of Facilities	✓✓✓✓

Directions

Exit A7 south of Lyons at junction 11. Continue south for about 7 km. on the N7. Just north of Auberives turn left on D37 and follow campsite signs for 7 km. Entrance is on the right just beyond Vernioz.

Charges 2005

Per adult	€ 5,00
child (under 7 yrs)	€ 2,50
pitch	€ 6,50 - € 9,00
electricity	€ 2,50
dog	€ 2,00

Reservations

Essential in high season, contact site. There are usually a few spaces available each day for overnight stops, but arrive early. Tel: 04 74 57 83 52.
E-mail: info@campinglebontemps.com

FR38080 Camping Caravaning Au Joyeux Réveil

Le Château, 38880 Autrans (Isère)

The small town of Autrans is set on a plateau, 1,050 m. high, in the Vecors region. Au Joyeux Réveil is run by a very friendly family (English is spoken). It is ideally situated for any of the activities that this wonderful area has to offer - from walking, mountain biking and pot-holing in summer to downhill and cross-country skiing in winter, it is all there for you in magnificent scenery. The site is on the outskirts of the town, set below a ski jump and short lift. The 111 pitches, 80 for touring are mainly on grass, reasonably level with small trees giving only a little shade. All have electricity and are in a sunny location with fantastic views over the surrounding wooded mountains. Plans for 2005 include a new swimming pool area with river and slide. The D531 road and then the D106 look a little daunting on the map but they are good roads with reasonable gradients.

Facilities

The new toilet block is very well appointed, with under-floor heating and all the expected facilities. Another new building houses a bar with terrace, snack bar/takeaway (July and August). New pool area planned to replace small, kidney-shaped swimming pool with sunbathing area and a large paddling pool with toboggan for children. Small play area and large chess table. TV room Off site: Short ski lift is near the site and a shuttle bus runs regularly the 5 km. to the longer runs. Fishing, bicycle hire or riding 300 m.

Open

1 December - 31 March and 1 May - 30 September.

At a glance

Welcome & Ambience	✓✓✓✓✓	Location	✓✓✓✓
Quality of Pitches	✓✓✓	Range of Facilities	✓✓✓✓

Directions

Exit autoroute A48, northwest of Grenoble at exit 13 (going south) or 3A (going north). Follow N532 to Sassenage, turn west on D531 to Lans en Vercors. At the roundabout turn right on D106 signed Autrans. On entering village turn right at roundabout and very shortly right again. Site is on your left.

Charges 2005

Per unit incl. 1 or 2 persons	€ 15,00 - € 17,00
extra person	€ 4,50
child (under 6 yrs)	€ 3,20
electricity (2-10A)	€ 2,00 - € 7,70

Camping Cheques accepted.
Winter prices - apply to site.

Reservations

Write to site with 20% deposit and € 12 fee.
Tel: 04 76 95 33 44.
E-mail: camping-au-joyeux-reveil@wanadoo.fr

FR73020 Camping Caravaneige Le Versoyen

Route des Arcs, 73700 Bourg-St Maurice (Savoie)

Bourg-St-Maurice is on a small, level plain at an altitude of 830 m. on the River Isère, surrounded by high, often snow-capped mountains. For many years a winter ski resort, it now caters for visitors all year round. The Parc National de la Vanoise is nearby, along with a wealth of interesting places. Le Versoyen itself attracts visitors all year round (except for a month when they close). The site's 205 unseparated, flat pitches (180 for touring) are marked by numbers on the tarmac roads and all have electrical connections (4/6A). Most are on grass but some are on tarmac hardstanding making them ideal for use by motorcaravans or in winter. Trees typically seen at this altitude give shade in some parts, although most pitches have almost none. Duckboards are provided for snow and wet weather. This is a good base for winter skiing, summer walking, climbing, rafting or canoeing, or for car excursions.

Facilities

Two acceptable toilet blocks can be heated, although the provision may be hard pressed in high season. British and Turkish style WCs. Laundry. Motorcaravan service facilities. Heated restroom with TV. Small bar with takeaway in summer. Free shuttle in high season to funicular railway. Off site: Fishing or bicycle hire 200 m. Riding 1 km. Golf 15 km. Commercial centre (500 m.) with a variety of shops. Tennis and swimming pool 500 m. (free for campers during July/Aug). Bourg-st-Maurice 1.5 km. Les Arcs (15 minutes by funicular railway) with ski lifts, some for bikes, to wonderful mountain tracks for bikes and ramblers (15 km). Cross country ski track (up to 30 km. in winter) just behind the site.

At a glance

Welcome & Ambience	✓✓✓✓	Location	✓✓✓✓
Quality of Pitches	✓✓✓✓	Range of Facilities	✓✓✓

Directions

Site is 1.5 km. east of Bourg-St-Maurice on CD119 Les Arcs road.

Charges 2004

Per unit incl. 2 person	€ 10,20 - € 13,68
extra person	€ 3,50 - € 4,74
child (7-13 yrs)	€ 1,50 - € 4,70
electricity (4-12A)	€ 4,20 - € 5,90
dog	€ 1,00

Reservations

Write to site with deposit (€ 30) and fee (€ 10).
Tel: 04 79 07 03 45. E-mail: leversoyen@wanadoo.fr

Open

All year except 7/11- 14/12 and 2/5-15/5.

FR73030 Camping Les Lanchettes

Mobile homes page 384

73210 Peisey-Nancroix (Savoie)

This site is in the beautiful Vanoise National Park and at 1,470 m. is one of the highest campsites in this guide. There is a steep climb to the site, not recommended for underpowered units, although the spectacular scenery is well worth the effort. A natural, terraced site, it has 90 good size, reasonably level and well drained, grassy/stony pitches, with 80 used for touring units, 70 having electricity (3-10A). Because it is very cold in winter and quite cold on some spring and autumn evenings (warm bedding necessary) there are no outside taps. In winter about 30 of the pitches at the bottom of the site are unused as they become part of a cross country ski run. For those who love mountains, wonderful scenery, flora and fauna and for those wanting a walking/biking summer holiday, from novice to expert, this is the site for you. In winter it is ideal for the serious skier being close to the famous resort of Les Arcs (via free bus service and cable car).

Facilities

Comprehensive facilities are all in the basement of the house, very cosy in winter. The large, open entrances are closed during cold weather and when the evenings are cold allowing the building to be heated. Motorcaravan service point. Restaurant with takeaway (July/Aug. and mid Dec-mid April). Playground. Club/TV room. Large tent/marquee used in bad weather for a meeting place and as a dormitory by those with small tents. In winter a small bus (free) runs to all the hotels, bars, ski tows etc. and calls at the campsite. A wide range of footpaths and mountain bike rides is available in the valley and mountains around. Some chair lifts carry bikes up to the walking/bike tracks high up in the mountains; the descent is breathtaking. The roads around are ideal for the serious road cyclist.
Off site: Accompanied walks (one free) in the National Park. Riding next to site. Village of Peisey-Nancroix with a few restaurants, bars and shops 3 km. Les Arcs winter sports centre 6 km. Outdoor swimming pool and bicycle hire 6 km. Golf and indoor pool 8 km.

At a glance

Welcome & Ambience	✓✓✓✓	Location	✓✓✓✓
Quality of Pitches	✓✓✓✓	Range of Facilities	✓✓✓

Directions

From Albertville take N90 towards Bourg-St-Maurice, through MoΩtiers and Aime and 9 km. further turn right on D87, signed Landry and Peisey-Nancroix. Follow road down and then up a reasonably wide, steep, winding hill (with hairpin bends) for 10 km. Pass through Peisey-Nancroix and Nancroix; site is on right about 1 km. beyond Nancroix.

Charges 2004

Per unit incl. 2 persons	€ 11,10 - € 12,80
extra person	€ 3,80 - € 4,30
child (2-7 yrs)	€ 2,30 - € 2,50
electricity (3-10A)	€ 2,90 - € 7,30
dog	€ 1,00 - € 1,20

Camping Cheques accepted.

Reservations

Made with 25% deposit and fee (€ 10).
Tel: 04 79 07 93 07. E-mail: lanchettes@free.fr

Open

15 December - 15 October.

FR73040 Camping Municipal Le Savoy

Avenue du Parc, 73190 Challes-les-Eaux (Savoie)

This attractive, well run and easily accessible municipal site is surrounded by mountains and only a few hundred metres from the centre of the spa town of Challes-les-Eaux. There are 100 level pitches, mostly for touring and 91 with electricity (5A). Some are separated by beech hedges and mature trees offer some shade. There are 12 pitches with hardstanding for motorcaravans, 47 part hardstanding super pitches with water, drain and 10A electricity with the remainder on grass. Rock pegs are advised for hardstanding areas. This site is a very good base for touring this scenic region and makes an ideal stop over for those on route to the Fréjus Tunnel and Italy.

Facilities

Two modern, very clean and well equipped toilet blocks with all the necessary facilities although they may be stretched in high season. Facilities for disabled visitors. Most of the facilities are near to the entrance but there is also a small toilet block in the middle of the site. Bar, snacks and a meal every Friday (15/6-30/8). Good sized playground. Boules, table tennis and table football. Off site: Adjacent is a small park with a small lake for swimming and the municipal tennis and volleyball courts. Challes-les-Eaux, with shops, banks, bars, restaurants, spar, casino and minigolf, a few hundred metres. Interesting town of Chambery 6 km. Fréjus Tunnel 96 km. and Bardonecchia (Italy) 110 km.

Open

1 May – 30 September.

At a glance

Welcome & Ambience	✓✓✓	Location	✓✓✓✓
Quality of Pitches	✓✓✓✓	Range of Facilities	✓✓✓

Directions

Leave autoroute A43 at exit 20 and head towards Challes-les-Eaux. Site is on the N6 at the northern edge of the town, just before a small park and lake. Turn right at traffic lights, site well signed.

Charges 2004

Per person	€ 3,05
child (0-12 yrs)	€ 1,25
piych	€ 3,55 - € 4,00
electricity (5A)	€ 2,45
electricity (10A), water and drain	€ 5,00

Reservations

Made with deposit (€ 30.5) and fee (€ 10,70).
Tel: 04 79 72 97 31.
E-mail: camping73challes-les-eaux@wanadoo.fr

FR74010 Camping Les Deux Glaciers

Route des Tissiéres, Les Bossons, 74400 Chamonix (Haute-Savoie)

A pleasant and well kept, naturally laid out, small mountain site for summer and winter use. Les Deux Glaciers lies at the foot of two glaciers and is close to the well known ski resort of Chamonix. This is a magnificent region, the summer flowers, walking, bike rides and winter skiing are almost beyond description. Explore the high mountain passes in the area and visit Italy (Courmeveur 21 km) and Switzerland (Martigny 48 km). The site has 135 individual pitches on terraces, 110 for touring, levelled out of quite steeply rising ground, with electricity (2-10A) available for 100 pitches. Rock pegs are advised. It is pleasantly laid out with different trees and floral displays in their season. Access may be difficult for large outfits. There are magnificent views of Mont Blanc Range and the Aiguille-de-Midi. With a good position and adequate amenities, the site becomes full for much of July/Aug. The temperature drops as soon as the sun sets and it can be quite cold at night. There is significant road noise. Reservations are not taken in summer, so arrive early.

Facilities

Two small, clean sanitary blocks, both heated in cool weather, have dated facilities. At least half the washbasins are in cabins. Facilities for disabled visitors, although the site is not ideal for those with walking difficulties. Washing machine and drying room. Restaurant/takeaway (June - mod Sept). Mobile traders call in season. General room (for winter use only). Table tennis. Small play area.
Off site: Village shop 500 m. Fishing, bicycle hire or riding within 2 km. Golf 4 km. Chamonix, swimming, hang-gliding, cable cars, ski lifts, funicular railway all within 3 km. Walks and bike rides. Bus to Chamonix and other villages all season. Fantastic skiing in winter.

Open

All year.

At a glance

Welcome & Ambience	✓✓✓	Location	✓✓✓✓✓
Quality of Pitches	✓✓✓	Range of Facilities	✓✓✓

Directions

From west turn right off main Geneva - Chamonix road (N205) at second exit for Les Bossons; site is on right in a few hundred metres. From east turn right at sign for Les Bossons, then left at T-junction and pass under the main road; site is on the right in few hundred metres.

Charges 2004

Per unit incl. 2 persons	€ 12,50
extra person	€ 4,70
child (7-13 yrs)	€ 4,00
child (0-7 yrs)	€ 2,30
electricity (2-10A; higher in winter)	€ 2,30 - € 6,50

Reservations

Not made for summer. Tel: 04 50 53 15 84.
E-mail: glaciers@clubinternet.fr

FR74060 Camping La Colombière

St Julien-en-Genevois, 74160 Neydens (Haute-Savoie)

La Colombière, a family owned site is on the edge of the small residential village of Neydens, a few minutes from the A40 autoroute and only a short drive from Geneva. It is an attractive site with only 107 pitches (72 for touring), all reasonably level and separated by fruit trees, flowering shrubs and hedges. There are views to the east and west of the mountain ridges. M. Bussat owns a small vineyard close to the site, has the wine made in Switzerland and sells it by the glass or bottle in the restaurant (a very nice rosé). One of France's long-distance footpaths (GR65) passes close to the site. The village of Neydens is the first stage for pilgrims from Northern Europe on the pilgrim route to Santiago de Compostella on their way to cross the Pyrénées at St Pied de Port. The site has a dormitory with eight beds for pilgrims or for anyone else who may need a bed, for example, motorcyclists or a family en-route south. Neydens makes a good base for visiting Geneva and the region around the lake. It is a very pleasant, friendly site where you may drop in for a night stop – and stay for several days! English is spoken. A 'Sites et Paysages' member.

TRAVEL SERVICE SITE

TO BOOK CALL 0870 405 4055 OR www.alanrogersdirect.com

Facilities

Three good sanitary blocks (one can be heated) include all the necessary facilities and units for disabled people. Motorcaravan service point. Fridge hire. Gas supplies. Very good bar/restaurant (all season) and terrace overlooking the heated pool (15/5-15/9). Low season organised visits of discovery, in high season one daily event including visits to Geneva, organised mountain walks and guided cycle tours (bicycle hire on site). Archery, volleyball and boules competitions. Playground. French country music evenings. Off site: Fishing 2 km. Riding 3 km. Golf 6 km. Tennis (reduced price). St Julien-en-Genevois (5 km) has many bars, restaurants, shops and supermarkets. Switzerland 3 km. Geneva with its magnificent old town, Lake Geneva and beautiful surrounding area with many walks and cycle rides.

At a glance

Welcome & Ambience	✓✓✓✓✓	Location	✓✓✓✓
Quality of Pitches	✓✓✓✓	Range of Facilities	✓✓✓✓

Directions

Take exit 13 from A40 autoroute south of Geneva, and then N201 towards Annecy. Turn left through village of Neydens and follow campsite signs to site in just over 1 km.

Charges 2004

Per unit incl. 2 persons	€ 14,00 - € 22,00
extra person	€ 3,50 - € 5,50
child (2-7 yrs)	€ 3,00 - € 4,00
electricity (5/6A)	€ 3,50
dog	€ 1,70

Camping Cheques accepted.

Reservations

Made with fee (€ 12). Less 3% for 11th and subsequent days. Tel: 04 50 35 13 14.
E-mail: la.colombiere@wanadoo.fr

Open

1 April - 30 September.

FR74030 Camping Belvédère

8 route du Semnoz, 74000 Annecy (Haute-Savoie)

Annecy is a very interesting town in a beautiful setting at the head of the lake of the same name. The old centre has historical interest and is intersected by flower decked canals with many restaurants and shops to visit. There is much to see and do in this region in both summer and winter, with Geneva, Chamonix and the high Alps close by. Le Belvédère, as its name implies, overlooks the lake and some of the pitches have stunning views over the lake to the mountains beyond. This municipal site is the nearest campsite to the town which can be reached in 15 minutes by a quiet, but steep footpath. There are 120 good sized pitches with electricity (10A). Of these 80 with part hardstanding are fully serviced with water and a drain and there are 50 grass pitches for tents (rock pegs essential). Space may be limited if the site is busy. One small area is reserved for groups. Tall pines and a steep hillside to the west provide a backdrop to the site and a variety of trees provide decoration and some shade. This site is ideally placed for visiting Annecy but it is not suitable for large units.

Facilities

Three modern toilet blocks, two recently refurbished to a high standard, are situated around the site and were very clean. One is heated in cold weather, with a washroom for visitors with disabilities. Laundry facilities. Small shop, bar and restaurant (June-Aug). Large games/wet weather room. Good playground. Swimming is possible in the lake and municipal pool. Bicycle hire. Communal area for barbecues. Sporting activities can be booked from the site. Bus to Annecy in July/Aug. Off site: Boat launching 600 m. Lakeside beach 800 m. Swimming pool 800 m. Many other activities on and around Lake Annecy. Boat trips. Lakeside cycle track. Hang-gliding and canyoning.

Open

4 April - 10 October.

At a glance

Welcome & Ambience	✓✓✓✓	Location	✓✓✓✓
Quality of Pitches	✓✓✓✓	Range of Facilities	✓✓✓✓

Directions

Leave A41 at Annecy Sud and take N508 towards Albertville and drive around the town. Just after some traffic lights descend a hill looking for 'H' and 'Silence' signs for the hospital. Very soon after, on left hand bend, turn right up the hill, signed Le Semnoz. Keep right at the fork. Take care at next junction – do not take right hand road signed Belvédère (this leads down a very steep and narrow hill. Turn left, signed Camping Belvédère, to site shortly on right.

Charges 2004

Per unit incl. 2 persons	€ 13,80 - € 17,80
tent/car incl. 2 persons	€ 10,00 - € 13,30
extra person	€ 3,90 - € 4,70
child (2-10 yrs)	€ 2,40 - € 2,80
electricity (10A)	€ 2,50

Reservations

Necessary for July/Aug. - write with 30% deposit to Mairie d'Annecy, B.P. 2305, 74011 Annecy Cedex. Tel. 04 50 33 87 96. Tel: 04 50 45 48 30.
E-mail: camping@ville-annecy.fr

FR74040 Camp de la Ravoire

Bout-du-Lac, Route de la Ravoire, 74210 Doussard (Haute-Savoie)

De la Ravoire is a high quality site, some 800 m. from Lake Annecy, noted for its neat and tidy appearance and the quietness of its location in this popular tourist region. The 112 numbered and level pitches are on well mown grass with some shade and separated by small shrubs and some hedging. The 90 pitches for touring units (21 with water and drain) have electricity connections (5-15A). Those looking for a quiet campsite in this most attractive region without the 'animation' programmes that so many French sites feel are necessary will find this a peaceful base although disco noise from a site by the lake may drift across under some weather conditions. Take to the back roads and explore the ancient villages and wonderful countryside. Used by a tour operator (18 pitches).

Facilities

The very good central toilet block includes washbasins in cabins, facilities for disabled people, and a laundry room with washing machines, dryers and irons. Bar and snack bar with takeaway. Shop. Outdoor pool with separate water slide and paddling pool. All open all season. Good young play area. Sports areas. Off site: Fishing, boat launching, bicycle hire 1 km. Riding 6 km. Golf 8 km. Good restaurant on the lakeside where the camp road leaves the main road, with others near, plus shops in Doussard village and Annecy. Cycle track (20 km) almost to Annecy passes close by. Canyonong and hangliding close. Boat trips on the lake.

Open

15 May - 15 September.

At a glance

Welcome & Ambience	✓✓✓✓✓	Location	✓✓✓✓
Quality of Pitches	✓✓✓✓	Range of Facilities	✓✓✓✓

Directions

Site is signed from the N508 Annecy - Albertville road, just north of Bout-du-Lac. About 2 km. south of the traffic lights in Brédannaz turn right (west, site signed) and then very shortly right again. Site is on right in about 1 km.

Charges 2004

Per unit incl. 2 adults and electricity (5A)	€ 27,20
pitch with water and drainage	€ 30,40 - € 31,20
extra adult	€ 5,75
child (0-15 yrs)	€ 2,55 - € 3,80
electricity (10/15A)	€ 2,00 - € 3,10

Camping Cheques accepted.
Less 20% outside July/Aug.

Reservations

Essential for July/Aug; made for min. 10 days with deposit (€ 130-150). Tel: 04 50 44 37 80.
E-mail: info@camping-la-ravoire.fr

FR74100 Village Camping Europa

1444 Route Albertville, 74410 St Jorioz (Haute-Savoie)

You will receive a friendly welcome at this quality, family run site. The flowers, shrubs and trees (giving some shade) are lovely and everything is kept neat and tidy. There are 210 medium to large size pitches (110 for touring) on level stony grass. Rock pegs are advised. All pitches have electricity (6A) close by and 18 have water and a drain. The static units are separated from the touring section by high hedges giving the impression that you are on a small site. There may be some noise from the adjacent main road. Europa should suit those families who like to make their own entertainment although there are some activities for children and a weekly soirée (high season) and a pool complex with slides, jacuzzi, cascade and paddling pool. This is a good base from which to tour the Lake Annecy area with its beautiful old villages and the fantastic countryside of the region.

Facilities

Two very good toilet blocks, recently modernised to a high standard, have all the necessary facilities including some large cubicles with both showers and washbasins. Motorcaravan service point. Good bar and restaurant (1/6-31/8). Swimming pool complex (entry bracelet € 2 each). Volleyball. Basketball. Football. Bicycle hire. Internet access. Mini-club. Some musical evenings. Off site: Fishing 300 m. Boat launching 500 m. Lakeside beach 2 km. Riding 3 km. Golf 8 km. Lakeside bike ride (40 km long). Lake Annecy and all its activities. St Joriz has shops, etc. Canyoning and hang-gliding nearby. Boat trips.

Open

8 May - 12 September.

At a glance

Welcome & Ambience	✓✓✓✓	Location	✓✓✓✓
Quality of Pitches	✓✓✓✓	Range of Facilities	✓✓✓✓

Directions

From Annecy take N508 signed Albertville. Site is well signed on the right on leaving Saint-Jorioz.

Charges 2004

Per unit incl. 2 persons and electricity	€ 18,00 - € 27,00
serviced pitch	€ 21,20 - € 30,20
extra person	€ 3,50 - € 5,50
child (2-6 yrs)	free - € 4,40
dog	free - € 2,00

Reservations

Made with deposit (30%) and fee (€ 16).
Tel: 04 50 68 51 01.
E-mail: info@camping-europa.com

FR74110 Camping Le Taillefer

1530 Route de Chaparon, 74210 Doussard (Haute-Savoie)

This excellent, small site is family run and friendly. It is only 1.5 km. from Lake Annecy, yet it offers a quiet, very relaxing and beautiful environment all at a very good price. The views over the lakeside mountains are stunning. This site is terraced and abounds with flowers, shrubs and small trees. It only has 32 average to good sized, grassy, level and sunny pitches, 28 with electricity (6A). In high season the site is quiet as there are no organised events, although there are plenty on and around the lake close by.

Facilities

The modern toilet block with very good separate facilities for ladies and men is near reception. Facilities for disabled visitors. Very small shop selling bread, drinks, etc. Small bar in high season. Playground. Small club/TV room. Torches needed (no site lighting). Off site: Nearby village of Doussard has shops. Lake Annecy with beaches (2 km). Minigolf, bicycle hire, boat launching. Canyoning and hang-gliding. Boat trips. Golf 8 km. Riding 7 km.

Open

1 May - 30 September.

At a glance

Welcome & Ambience	✓✓✓✓	Location	✓✓✓✓
Quality of Pitches	✓✓✓✓	Range of Facilities	✓✓✓

Directions

From Annecy take N508 signed Albertville. At traffic lights in Brédannaz turn right and then immediately left for 1.5 km. and site is on the left. Do not turn in by reception (this is a dead end) – wait in road until directions are received.

Charges 2004

Per unit incl. 2 persons	€ 11,50 - € 12,80
extra person	€ 2,80
child (under 10 yrs)	€ 2,20
electricity (6A)	€ 3,20

Reservations

Made with € 30 booking fee. Tel: 04 50 44 30 30.
E-mail: info@campingletaillefer.com

FR74130 Camping de la Plage

304 rue de la Garenne, 74500 Amphion-les-Bains (Haute-Savoie)

This very good, family run site is small, quiet and friendly. It has a very long season and is only a few hundred metres from Lake Geneva and the village of Amphion making it an excellent centre to relax and explore this wonderful region. Madame Frossard loves gardening and the site does her credit with its flowers, trees, hedges and beautifully mown grass. The 53 pitches, only a few used by mobile homes, are level, medium to large and separated by trees. They all have water points, drains and electricity. In addition to the very small pool on the site, there is a super centre in the adjacent park (with a large pool, paddling pool, diving pool, wave pool and a giant slide), plus an excellent playground and plenty of space to enjoy. The site does not accept large unit or double-axle caravans.

Facilities

The ample facilities are comprehensive and first class, with fully controllable showers, washbasins in cabins, facilities for children and disabled people, sinks for dishwashing and laundry. One block is heated off season. Washing machine, dryer and iron. Small bar and takeaway (high season). Small heated swimming pool, covered in cool weather and with invigorating pressure jets. Small playground for young children. Table tennis, boules. TV room. Well equipped exercise room with superb play area for young children. Off site: Lake Geneva with beaches, restaurants, snack bars, fishing and many water sports. Ferry service around lake incl. Geneva and Lausanne. Small shops, restaurants and supermarket within walking distance in village. Hypermarket 1 km. Golf 3 km.

At a glance

Welcome & Ambience	✓✓✓✓✓	Location	✓✓✓✓✓
Quality of Pitches	✓✓✓✓	Range of Facilities	✓✓✓✓

Directions

Site is between Thonon les Bains and Evian les Bains. Turn north off the N5 at Amphion les Bains (at roundabout with statue and fountains) and follow site signs - site is a few hundred metres on the right.

Charges 2004

Per unit incl. 2 persons	€ 16,00 - € 21,00
extra person	€ 6,00 - € 6,10
child (under 8 yrs)	€ 3,00
electricity (2-6A)	€ 1,52 - € 3,80

Reductions for long stay in low season.

Reservations

Essential in high season and made with 25% deposit and € 11 booking fee. Tel: 04 50 70 00 46. E-mail: info@camping-dela-plage.com

Open

All year excl. 2 November - 24 December.

FR74070 Camping Caravaning L'Escale

74450 Le Grand-Bornand (Haute-Savoie)

You are assured a good welcome from the Baur family at this beautifully maintained, picturesque site. Situated at the foot of the Aravis mountain range, beside the picture postcard ski resort of Le Grand-Bornand, L'Escale has wonderful views, is surrounded by fields of flowers in summer and is clearly popular all year round. The 149 fairly sunny pitches (142 for touring) are of average size, clearly marked with a part grass, part gravel surface and separated by trees and shrubs. All have electricity and 86 pitches are fully serviced. Rock pegs are essential. The village (200 m.) has all the facilities of a major resort with ongoing activity for summer or winter holidays. In summer a variety of well signed footpaths and cycle tracks provide forest or mountain excursions of all degrees of difficulty. In winter the area provides superb facilities for down-hill and cross-country skiing and apres-ski entertainment. La Maison du Patrimoine is a must to visit. A 'Sites et Paysages' member.

Facilities

The very good toilet blocks (heated when cold) have all the necessary facilities. Two chalet buildings provide further facilities. Large drying room with sinks, dryer and washing machines. Separate room for skis and boots. Superb new complex with interconnected indoor and outdoor pools and paddling pools (June-Aug). Bar/restaurant (July/Aug). Play area. Tennis and table tennis. Torches essential (no street lighting). Off site: The village (5 minutes walk) has shops, bars, restaurants, municipal pool complex, archery, para-gliding, hang-gliding, 150 km. of signed walks. Activities are organised for children and adults. Ice skating and ice hockey in winter. Bicycle hire 200 m. Riding and golf 3 km.

Open

All year excl. October and November.

At a glance

Welcome & Ambience	✓✓✓✓✓	Location	✓✓✓✓✓
Quality of Pitches	✓✓✓✓	Range of Facilities	✓✓✓✓✓

Directions

Probably the best access is via Annecy following the D16 and D909 roads towards La Clusaz. Shortly before La Clusaz, at St Jean-de-Sixt, turn left at roundabout on D4 signed Le Grand Bornand. Just before entering village turn right signed Vallée de Bouchet and camping. Site is just over 1 km. at a roundabout on right.

Charges 2005

Per unit incl. 1 or 2 persons	€ 15,50 - € 21,00
extra person	€ 4,30 - € 5,50
electricity (2-10A)	€ 3,30 - € 7,90
animal	€ 2,20 - € 2,30

Camping Cheques accepted.

Reservations

Made with deposit (€ 71) and fee (€ 10). Tel: 04 50 02 20 69. E-mail: contact@campinglescale.com

FR74090 Camping Le Plan du Fernuy

Route des Confins, 74220 La Clusaz (Haute-Savoie)

The pretty little village of La Clusaz is 32 km. east of Annecy at 1,200 m. above sea level and in the heart of the Savoie Alps. Le Plan du Fernuy, 2 km. east of the village lies just to the north of the Avaris mountain range in a peaceful, scenic location. The wild flowers in early summer are a joy to behold. The neat and open site has separate summer and winter seasons. It has 80 pitches, 58 for tourists. All of reasonable size and with electricity connections, and 22 fully serviced, the pitches are stony with some grass. Arranged in rows on either side of hard access roads, there are good mountain views but little shade. Rock pegs are essential. The site's crowning glory is an excellent indoor heated pool with large windows looking out on to the mountains and sunbeds beside them. This is a good site for ski-ing in winter (with access to a ski-tow from the campsite and a free bus to other centres). In summer it is a good base for walking and cycling with other sporting opportunities nearby. The pleasant owners speak good English.

Facilities

The large apartment building at the entrance houses very good sanitary provision on the ground floor and is heated in cool weather. Some washbasins in cabins. Baby room. Facilities for disabled visitors. Separate rooms for dishwashing and laundry with washing machine and dryer. Drying room for ski clothing and boots, etc. Motorcaravan service point. Small shop and bar with snacks, takeaway, basic food supplies. Video games and TV room. Heated indoor pool and paddling pool. Skiing from site and ski excursions organised. Off site: Shops and restaurants in village 2 km. Riding 800 m. Golf, bicycle hire and fishing 1.5 km.

Open

4 June - 4 September and 18 December - 24 April.

At a glance

Welcome & Ambience	✓✓✓✓	Location	✓✓✓✓
Quality of Pitches	✓✓✓✓	Range of Facilities	✓✓✓✓

Directions

From Annecy take D909 to La Clusaz and at roundabout turn towards Les Confins. Site is on right after 2 km. (well signed). It is best to avoid using D909 from Flumat particularly with caravans or motorhomes.

Charges 2004

Per pitch incl. 2 persons	€ 16,00 - € 18,00
with electricity (4-13A)	€ 21,00 - € 24,50
extra person	€ 5,50
child (2-7 yrs)	€ 4,00
animal	€ 1,50

Winter prices are higher and may be quoted per week only.

Reservations

Advised for mid-July - mid-Aug. and winter.
Tel: 04 50 02 44 75. E-mail: info@plandufernuy.com

FR74140 Camping Les Dômes de Miage

197 route des Contamines, 74170 St Gervais-les-Bains (Haute-Savoie)

Saint Gervais is a pleasant spa town, 22 km. west of Chamonix-Mont Blanc and this site is 2 km. to the south on just about the only level land available by the road into the mountains. On its 3 hectares (7.5 acres) are 150 reasonably sized flat grassy pitches, about half with shade. The 75 or so nearest the reception block have individual electricity points (3, 6 or 10A) . The remainder are on terraced ground, and are used for tents. There are few water taps and some pitches are up to 80 m. from one. The region is good for walking and there is a bus service into Saint Gervais, from where there is a frequent shuttle bus to its spa and a tramway to the Mont Blanc range. There is also good public transport between the town and Chamonix.

Facilities

Two centrally placed sanitary blocks, one heated, with WCs, washbasins (H&C) and showers together in cubicles, a suite for disabled visitors and baby room. Dishwashing sinks (H&C), laundry sinks (mostly H&C), washing machines and dryer. Motorcaravan service point. Small shop area in reception for basics, wine, ice cream and gaz. Social and TV room with library and ironing board. Excellent playground. Playing field with table tennis, volleyball, basketball basket, goal net. Off site: Fishing 100 m. Bicycle hire 1 km. Riding 8 km. Shops, etc. and outdoor swimming pool in St Gervais.

At a glance

Welcome & Ambience	✓✓✓✓	Location	✓✓✓✓
Quality of Pitches	✓✓✓✓	Range of Facilities	✓✓✓

Directions

From St Gervais take D902 towards Les Contamines and site is on left after 2 km.

Charges 2004

Per unit incl. 1 or 2 persons	€ 14,00 - € 19,00
extra person	€ 2,50 - € 3,50
child (2-10 yrs)	€ 2,00
electricity (3/6A0	€ 2,90 - € 3,50
dog	€ 2,00

Camping Cheques accepted.

Reservations

Made with deposit (€ 50) and booking fee (€ 10, includes cancellation insurance).
Tel: 04 50 93 45 96.
E-mail: camping.st.gervais@wanadoo.fr

Open

1 June - 15 September.

FR74150 Camping de la Mer de Glace

200 Chemin de la Bagna, Les Praz, 74400 Chamonix (Haute-Savoie)

This attractive site is convenient for Chamonix but is in a tranquil setting away from its hustle and bustle. Set in a large level clearing, with a view of the Mont Blanc range, it has been kept as natural as possible without a pool, restaurant, bar or disco, etc. and is well suited to those looking for quiet and relaxation. For those more interested in exercise, the area is rich in trails for walking and mountain biking, and many pass near the site. The buildings are of typical regional timber construction, decorated with traditional painted flower designs. Inside, they have modern facilities and are well maintained and clean. There are 150 pitches of varying sizes, of which 75 have electricity connections (3, 6 or 9A) and are suitable for caravans and camper vans. The others are usually allocated for tents. There are sufficient water points.

Facilities

Three sanitary blocks, all unisex: one with toilets (some Turkish), one with washbasins (some in cubicles) and baby room, one with showers. Facilities for disabled visitors. Dishwashing and laundry sinks (H&C). Two washing machines and a dryer. Motorcaravan service point (not WC tank). Bread can be ordered for the following morning. Pizza van twice weekly in July/Aug. Meeting room and snack room. Small playground for young children. Off site: Fishing and golf 500 m. Bicycle hire 1 km. Riding 5 km. Shops, etc. 700 m. in Les Praz or 1.5 km. in Chamonix. Indoor and outdoor swimming pools in Chamonix 1.5 km.

Open

29 April - 2 October.

At a glance

Welcome & Ambience	✓✓✓✓	Location	✓✓✓✓
Quality of Pitches	✓✓✓✓	Range of Facilities	✓✓✓

Directions

From Chamonix take N506 northeast towards Les Praz. After about 1 km. site is signed to the right. NOTE: the first two signs direct you under a 2.4 m. high bridge. It is best to wait until you reach a small roundabout at the entrance to Les Praz, turn right there and follow the signs.

Charges 2004

Per person	€ 5,30 - € 6,10
child (0-3 yrs)	€ -2,00
pitch	€ 5,00 - € 6,90
electricity (3A)	€ 2,70

Reservations

Not made. Tel: 04 50 53 44 03.
E-mail: campingmdg@tiscali.fr

FR74160 Camping l'Ile des Barrats

185, chemin de l'le des Barrat, 74400 Chamonix (Haute-Savoie)

A delightful neat and tidy, small and tranquil site, Ile de Barrats is run by the third generation of a very friendly family who speak good English. It is within easy walking distance of the beautiful town of Chamonix, although there are bus and train services close by if needed. It is surrounded by magnificent mountains with views over the Mont Blanc Range and the Aiguille de Midi. In summer the mountain flowers are second to none. There are several cable cars and chair lifts close by which operate during the summer high season giving access to Alpine walks ranging from the casual stroll to the full mountain hike. Switzerland and Italy are easily accessible via the Col de la Forclaz mountain pass and the Mont Blanc Tunnel. There are 53 slightly sloping, grassy pitches all for touring mostly separated by small hedges and a variety of trees offering some shade. All have electricity (5/10A) and 32 have water and a drain. This is an ideal site for those wishing to roam the mountain trails and for those seeking a peaceful and relaxing holiday in a most superb setting. No twin axle caravans.

Facilities

A modern and very clean toilet block offers all the necessary facilities, including those for disabled visitors. Covered picnic area with table and benches, ideal for those with small tents. Cans of soft drinks and beer sold from reception. Ice pack service. Motorcaravan service point. Store room for those leaving tents and other equipment on site whilst in the mountains. Daily visits from a mobile shop in July/Aug. No organised activities on site. Off site: Baker 500 m. Chamonix (800 m level walk) with all the amenities of a high class summer and winter resort and a colourful Saturday market. Hang gliding, funicular railway, cable cars and chair lifts nearby.

At a glance

Welcome & Ambience	✓✓✓✓✓	Location	✓✓✓✓✓
Quality of Pitches	✓✓✓✓	Range of Facilities	✓✓✓

Directions

On entering Chamonix on the main road from Geneva, turn left at the first roundabout after the turn off for the Mont Blanc Tunnel (follow signs for Hospital). Shortly turn left, at next roundabout and the campsite is on the right opposite the hospital.

Charges 2004

Per person	€ 5,40
child (0-7 yrs)	€ 4,00
pitch incl. car	€ 7,10
electricity	€ 3,00
dog	€ 1,00

Reservations

Contact site. Tel: 04 50 53 51 44.

Open

1 May - 3 October.

FR74170 Camping Moulin de Dollay

Rue du Moulin-Dollay, 74570 Groisy (County)

This small site has been recommended by a reader and we hope to undertake a full inspection in 2005. Located on the edge of a forest and alongside a river, Le Moulin de Dollay has 25 grassy pitches, most of which are shaded and offer electrical connections and water and drainage. Mobile homes for rent.

Facilities

Toilet block with special facilities for disabled people and for babies. Bar, Play area. Sports field. TV room. Fishing. Volleyball. Off site: Supermarket 800 m. Takeaway food 800 m. Tennis 2 km. Restaurant 3 km. Golf 4 km. Swimming pool 5 km.

Open

15 May - 15 September.

Directions

Groisy is best accessed from the N203 Annecy to Bonneville road. Heading north, leave this road at Le Plot, following signs to Groisy, from where the site is clearly signposted.

Charges year

Per unit incl. 2 persons and electricity	€ 14,00
extra person	€ 3,80
child (under 7 yrs)	free

Reservations

Contact site. Tel: 04 50 68 00 31.

La Clef Verte - Green Holidays in France

La Clef Verte (or 'green key') is France's principal campsite environmental scheme. Many of the campsites in this guide are accredited members and will display the green key logo.

La Clef Verte was first established in Denmark in 1994, and then adopted for French campsites by the French Foundation for Environmental Education in 1998.

The Clef Verte label encourages site owners to adopt an environmentally sound approach in the running of their site. It takes account of 7 major elements:

- ✓ **Landscape and overall quality of life:** (traffic management, availability of open spaces, control of noise pollution etc.
- ✓ **Environmental management** (sound, environmentally friendly management methods, e.g. wash block maintenance)
- ✓ **Waste management** (general waste reduction, waste collection for recycling)
- ✓ **Water management** (water treatment, irrigation methods, reduction in water usage)
- ✓ **Energy management** (general reduction in usage, energy saving devices etc.)
- ✓ **Environmental education** (information about the Green Key scheme, staff training, creation of awareness about local fauna and flora)

These criteria are strictly monitored, and only those campsites able to prove that they have sound environmental policies will succeed in obtaining accreditation. However, it's good to note that, every year, more and more campsites are seeking membership.

Map 10

Endless shimmering beaches, huge sand dunes, watersports aplenty, fragrant pine forests, the fine wines of Bordeaux, and the chic city of Biarritz: it's easy to see the allure of the Atlantic Coast.

The coastal départements of the official region of Aquitaine, stretching from Bordeaux in the north to the Pyrénées and the Spanish border are included in our 'tourist' region: 33 Gironde, 40 Landes, 64 Pyrénées Atlantiques

The Atlantic Coast stretches north from Biarritz to Arcachon. The most notable features are the uninterrupted line of vast sandy beaches, over 100 miles long, and the endless pine woods in the hinterland - this is Europe's largest man-made forest. There are also many lakes to see, ideal for watersports activities.

The département of the Gironde covers the area from the Bassin d'Arcachon, famed for its oysters and Europe's highest sand dune, to the Gironde estuary and Bordeaux. The vineyards of Bordeaux are world famous and especially well known for their Médoc, Sauternes, and St Emilion wines.

The Pays Basque area in the southwest corner is much influenced by Spain. The most famous Basque towns are Biarritz, Bayonne and the picturesque old port of St-Jean-de-Luz. Further inland and nearer the Pyrénées is the attractive town of St-Jean-Pied-de-Port on the pilgrims' route to northern Spain and Santiago de Compostela, close to the forest of Iraty with its lakes and ski runs.

Cuisine of the region

Seafood is popular, local specialities include carp stuffed with foie gras and mullet in red wine

Cèpes: fine, delicate mushrooms; sometimes dried

Chorizos: spicy sausages

Chou farci: stuffed cabbage, sometimes *aux marrons* (with chestnuts)

Foie Gras: specially prepared livers of geese and ducks, seasoned and stuffed with truffles

Gâteau Basque: shallow custard pastry with fillings

Jambon de Bayonne: raw ham, cured in salt and sliced paper thin

Lamproie: eel-like fish with leeks, onions and red Bordeaux wine

Places of interest

Bayonne: old streets and fortifications; Basque Museum

Bordeaux: 14,000 piece Bohemian glass chandelier in foyer of the Grand Theatre, 29 acre Esplanade des Quinconces

Pau: famous motor racing circuit on (closed) public highway; stadium for the Basque game of *pelota*

St Emilion: visit the castle ramparts or drink premier cru St Emilion at pavement cafés

St Jean-de-Luz: seaside resort and fishing village

St Jean-Pied-de-Port: ancient city with citadel, bright Basque houses in steep streets

Alan Rogers **tip**

TOUR THE VINEYARDS OF THE BORDEAUX REGION AND SAMPLE THE LOCAL WINES. THERE ARE PLENTY TO VISIT INCLUDING THOSE AT MÉDOC, ST-ÉMILION, AND SAUTERNES.

FR33010 Camping de la Dune

Route de Biscarrosse, 33115 La Pyla-sur-Mer (Gironde)

La Dune is a good example of a busy French family site. It is informal, friendly and lively, with a comprehensive range of amenities. From its situation at the foot of the enormous dune (the highest in Europe) you can reach the beach either by climbing over the dune - a ladder goes up nearly to the top - or driving round. The 325 marked pitches, some sloping, some terraced but level, vary somewhat in size but all are hedged with shade from pine trees. Nearly half are caravan pitches with electricity, water and drainaway. Some of the site roads are quite narrow and parts are quite sandy. English is spoken. There are no tour operators. A busy site with good security.

Facilities

Modern toilet blocks include one small one and one that can be heated in cool weatherwith make roomy showers and washbasins en-suite. WCs are of British and Turkish types, many washbasins are in private cabins. Some blocks may be closed at night. Motorcaravan service point. Small supermarket. Pleasant little bar and restaurant with takeaway - (opens June, all other facilities are all season). Medium-size swimming pool. Playground. Open-air theatre, sports and tournaments organised July -end Aug. Purpose built barbecue (only gas individual ones are allowed). Fridge hire. Off site: Riding 2 km, fishing 3 km, golf 10 km.

Open

1 May - 30 September.

At a glance

Welcome & Ambience	✓✓✓✓	Location	✓✓✓✓
Quality of Pitches	✓✓✓✓	Range of Facilities	✓✓✓✓

Directions

The D259, signed from the N250 to Biscarrosse and Dune du Pilat, just before La Teste, avoids Pyla-sur-Mer. At end of new road turn left at roundabout on D218 coast road. La Dune is second site on right.

Charges 2004

Per tent incl. 2 persons	€ 12,00 - € 23,00
caravan incl. 2 persons, electricity and water	€ 15,00 - € 26,00
extra person	€ 4,00 - € 8,00
child (under 7)	€ 1,50 - € 4,50
dog	€ 1,00 - € 3,50

Reservations

Made for min. 1 week in high season with 25% deposit and fee (€22,87) at least 1 month in advance. Tel: 05 56 22 72 17. E-mail: campingdeladune@wanadoo.fr

FR33020 Camping Caravaning Fontaine-Vieille

4 boulevard du Colonel Wurtz, 33510 Andernos-les-Bains (Gironde)

Fontaine Vieille is a large, traditional site that has been operating for over 50 years. The site stretches along the eastern edge of the Bassin d'Arcachon under light woodland in the residential area of the small town of Andernos. Popular with the French, it has nearly 700 individual pitches, of which 520 are touring pitches (about 400 with electricity). On flat, grassy or sandy ground, they are marked by stones in the ground or young trees. A beach runs alongside the tidal 'Bassin' which can be used for boating when the tide is in. When it is out, there is sand and mud but it is claimed that swimming in the channels is still possible. A full range of entertainment is organised in high season.

Facilities

Seven sanitary blocks of rather unusual design provide an adequate number of hot showers, plus facilities for people with disabilities and children. Shop (1/6-15/9). Bar with terrace and takeaway (all season). Restaurant (1/6-15/9). Swimming pool complex. Four tennis courts. TV room. Two play areas for little ones and adventure area for older children. Minigolf. Boats, sailboards for hire. Sports organised in high season. Communal barbecue areas (only gas may be used on pitches). Off site: Golf 3 km. Riding 5 km. Town shops near

At a glance

Welcome & Ambience	✓✓✓✓	Location	✓✓✓✓
Quality of Pitches	✓✓✓	Range of Facilities	✓✓✓✓

Directions

Turn off D3 at southern end of Andernos towards Bassin at camp sign.

Charges 2004

Per unit incl. 2 persons	€ 13,00 - € 20,00
with electricity (5A)	€ 16,00 - € 24,00
extra person	€ 3,00 - € 5,00
child (2-7 yrs)	€ 2,00 - € 3,00

Reservations

Made for any length with deposit (€ 80) and fee (€ 20). Tel: 05 56 82 01 67. E-mail: contact@fontaine-vieille.com

Open

1 April - 30 September.

FR33050 Camping Les Ourmes

Avenue du Lac, 33990 Hourtin (Gironde)

Located only 500 metres from the largest fresh water lake in France, only 10 minutes drive from the beach and with its own pool, this is essentially a holiday site. Of the 270 pitches, 240 are for tourers, marked but in most cases not actually separated, and arranged amongst tall pines and other trees which give good shade. All have electricity connections. The site's amenities are arranged around a pleasant entrance courtyard with an evening entertainment programme in season. This site has a busy, cosmopolitan feel, with visitors of many different nationalities.

Facilities

Three recently refurbished toilet blocks are of a good standard including some washbasins in cabins. Washing machine in each block and dryer, with hot water taps for washing up. Small shop (1/6-15/9). Bar/restaurant with outdoor tables serving takeaway snacks and a range of reasonably priced meals (1/7-31/8). Medium sized swimming pool and new paddling pool (1/5-15/9). Separate large leisure area with play area, volleyball and basketball courts and table tennis tables (under cover). TV, games rooms. Boules. Off site: Watersports and fishing possible on the lake, with bicycle hire, tennis and riding within 500 m.

At a glance

Welcome & Ambience	✓✓✓✓	Location	✓✓✓✓
Quality of Pitches	✓✓✓	Range of Facilities	✓✓✓✓

Directions

Follow Route du Port (Ave du Lac) from the town centre and site is signed on left.

Charges 2005

Per unit incl. 2 persons	€ 11,00 - € 18,50
incl. electricity	€ 14,00 - € 21,50
extra person (over 2 yrs)	€ 1,80 - € 3,00
dog	€ 1,20 - € 1,50

No credit cards.

Reservations

Necessary in high season. Tel: 05 56 09 12 76. E-mail: lesourmes@free.fr

Open

1 April - 30 September.

FR33090 Camping Le Pressoir

Petit Palais et Cornemps, 33570 Lussac (Gironde)

Buried in the famous wine producing countryside of the Lussac, Pomerol and St Emilion area north of Bordeaux, Le Pressoir is surrounded by fields of vines. With a manicured entrance featuring attractive trees, shrubs and flowers, together with preserved equipment from its former role as a wine farm, it is a neat site with good quality facilities. The 100 large pitches are arranged on either side of a gravel road leading up a slight hill and many are shaded by attractive trees. They are over 100 sq.m. and equipped with electricity (blue EC plugs) and interspersed with five Trigano type tents for hire. The old barn has been converted into a stylish bar and a really charming, separate restaurant. A quiet, family site, Le Pressoir provides a comfortable base for a holiday in this area famous for good food and wine.

Facilities

Very good fully equipped toilet facilities in purpose built block near the farmhouse include hair and make-up area for ladies, facilities for disabled visitors, and washing machine. Bar. Restaurant (all season). Swimming pool (14 x 7 m; 15/5-15/9, no bermuda shorts). Playground with timber equipment. Petanque, volleyball and table tennis. Gates locked 22.00 - 08.00 hrs. Off site: Tennis nearby. Fishing 5 km. Riding and bicycle hire 10 km.

Open

26 March - 3 October.

At a glance

Welcome & Ambience	✓✓✓✓	Location	✓✓✓✓✓
Quality of Pitches	✓✓✓✓	Range of Facilities	✓✓✓✓

Directions

From N89 Bordeaux - Périgueux turn at Saint Médard de Guizières towards Lussac on the D21. Site is signed here and also from Lussac.

Charges 2005

Per person	€ 6,00
child (2-6 yrs)	€ 3,50
pitch	€ 6,90
with 6A electricity	€ 9,90

Camping Cheques accepted.

Reservations

Contact site. Tel: 05 57 69 73 25. E-mail: camping.le.pressoir@wanadoo.fr

FR33110 Airotel Camping de la Côte d'Argent

Mobile homes page 385

33990 Hourtin-Plage (Gironde)

Spread over 20 hectares of undulating sand-based terrain and in the midst of a pine forest, this large site is well placed and well equipped for leisurely family holidays. It also makes an ideal base for walkers and cyclists, with over 100 km. of cycle lanes leading through the Medoc countryside. Hourtin-Plage is a pleasant invigorating resort on the Atlantic coast and a popular location for watersports enthusiasts, or those who prefer spending their days on the beach. More appealing though may be to stay on site, for Côte d'Argent's top attraction is its pool complex with wooden bridges connecting the pools and islands, on which there are sunbathing patios and play areas. A super new indoor heated pool is a recent addition. There are 750 touring pitches which are not clearly defined and in the trees, some on soft sand-based ground. The site is well organised and ideal for children. Entertainment takes place at the bar near the entrance (until 12.30). There are 48 hardstandings for motorcaravans outside the site, providing a cheap stop-over, but with no access to site facilities.

TRAVEL SERVICE SITE

TO BOOK CALL 0870 405 4055 OR www.alanrogersdirect.com

Facilities

Five very clean sanitary blocks of various ages include provision for disabled visitors. Plenty of laundry machines. Motorcaravan service points. Large supermarket, restaurant, takeaway and pizzeria bar. Four outdoor pools with waterslides and flumes. New indoor pool. Massage. Astronomy once a week. Two tennis courts. Pool tables. Four play areas. Mini-club and organised entertainment in season. Charcoal barbecues are not permitted. Fishing. Riding. Bicycle hire. Off site: Path to the beach 300 m. Golf 30 km.

Open

13 May - 18 September.

At a glance

Welcome & Ambience	✓✓✓✓	Location	✓✓✓✓
Quality of Pitches	✓✓✓	Range of Facilities	✓✓✓✓✓

Directions

Turn off D101 Hourtin-Soulac road 3 km. north of Hourtin. Then join D101E signed Hourtin-Plage. Site is 300 m. from the beach.

Charges 2004

Per unit incl. 2 persons	€ 19,00 - € 30,00
tent incl. 2 persons	€ 15,00 - € 25,00
extra person	€ 3,00 - € 5,00
child (2-10 yrs)	€ 2,00 - € 4,00
electricity (6A)	€ 5,00
dog	€ 2,00 - € 4,00

Camping Cheques accepted.

Reservations

Necessary for July/August. Tel: 05 56 09 10 25. E-mail: info@camping-cote-dargent.com

FR33080 Domaine de la Barbanne

Route de Montagne, 33330 St Emilion (Gironde)

La Barbanne is a pleasant, friendly, family-owned site in the heart of the Bordeaux wine region, only 2.5 km. from the famous town of St Emilion. With 160 pitches, the owners have transformed it into a carefully maintained, well equipped site. The original parts of the site bordering the lake have tarred roads, good shade and pleasant surroundings, whilst the newer area has younger trees, some shade and gravel access roads. The pitches are being re-numbered and are all large, level and grassy with dividing hedges and electricity connections. La Barbanne has an attractive entrance and reception area with ample space for parking or turning. The owners run a free minibus service three times a day to St Emilion and also organise excursions to local places of interest, including Bordeaux. A 'Sites et Paysages' member.

TRAVEL SERVICE SITE

TO BOOK CALL 0870 405 4055 OR www.alanrogersdirect.com

Facilities

Two toilet blocks, the original one fully refurbished, the other in the newer area being very modern. Most washbasins are in private cabins. Visitors with disabilities are well catered for. Motorcaravan service point. Small, well stocked shop. Bar with terrace, takeaway and restaurant (1/7-31/8). Two landscaped swimming pools, one heated with cork-screw water slide (15/4-20/9). Fully enclosed play area with seats for parents and an organised children's club (from 1/7). Tennis, boules, volleyball, table tennis and minigolf. The lake provides superb free fishing, pedaloes, canoes and lakeside walks. Bicycle hire. Off site: St Emilion and shops 2.5 km. Riding 8 km.

At a glance

Welcome & Ambience	✓✓✓✓✓	Location	✓✓✓✓✓
Quality of Pitches	✓✓✓✓	Range of Facilities	✓✓✓✓

Directions

At St Emilion take D122 for 2.5 km. Turn right just before Montagne and site is on left after 400 m. Caravans and motorhomes are forbidden through the village of St Emilion. They must approach the site by taking the D243 from Libourne or from Castillon on the D936 via D130/D243.

Charges 2004

Per person	€ 4,00 - € 6,50
child (under 7 yrs)	€ 2,50 - € 5,20
pitch incl. electricity	€ 14,00 - € 21,00
animal	free - € 2,00

Camping Cheques accepted.

Reservations

Made for min. 4 days. Tel: 05 57 24 75 80. E-mail: barbanne@wanadoo.fr

Open

1 April - 20 September.

FR33120 Camping La Cigale

Route de Lège, 33740 Arès (Gironde)

La Cigale is an attractive little site with charm and ambience where the owners extend a very warm welcome. Small and beautifully maintained, it is set amid pine trees and M. Pallet's floral displays. The 95 level, grassy pitches, most with electricity and of 100 sq.m. in size, are divided by hedges and flower borders. The majority have shade from the pine trees. There are two small swimming pools in a pleasant setting and under the ample shade of a large plane tree, where drinks, meals and snacks are served on the bar terrace. This is an exceptional area for cycling, with designated routes. Across the bay lies bustling Arcachon and the enormous Dune de Pilat, easily reached by ferry from Cap Ferret. Used by tour operators (18%).

Facilities

The central, flower-bedecked, unisex toilet block includes a family room with two showers, facilities for disabled visitors and a laundry with a washing machine and dryer. All is meticulously maintained. Motorcaravan services. Simple shop. Bar terrace with meals and snacks. Pizza takeaway at front of the site. Two small swimming pools. Small play area. Full-time entertainers for children and adults in July/Aug. Free donkey cart rides every Sunday. Off site: Site is convenient for a wide choice of beaches. Village centre 800 m. Fishing or riding 1 km.

Open

29 April - 2 October.

At a glance

Welcome & Ambience	✓✓✓✓✓	Location	✓✓✓✓
Quality of Pitches	✓✓✓✓	Range of Facilities	✓✓✓✓

Directions

Leave Bordeaux ringroad at exit 10 (D213) or exit 11 (D106) and continue on good roads direct to Arès. Turn into Arès following road to church square. Turn right following signs for Lège/Cap Ferret. Site is 800 m. on left.

Charges 2004

Per unit incl. 1 or 2 persons	€ 16,50 - € 22,80
extra person	€ 4,20 - € 4,80
child (7 yrs)	€ 2,60 - € 2,80
electricity (4/6A)	€ 4,80

Reservations

Advised for July/Aug. and made with deposit (€ 79) and fee (€ 16). Tel: 05 56 60 22 59. E-mail: campinglacigaleares@wanadoo.fr

FR33140 Camping Le Grand Pré

Route de Casteljaloux, 33430 Bazas (Gironde)

In a rural position, this is a developing site where the owners stated phiolosophy of tranquility in nature is realised. There are only 30 grass pitches at present, which are separated by low shrubs and bushes, some of which have yet to mature. All have electricity hook-ups (6-16A), water and drainage. Reception facilities and a bar are in a very tastefully converted old barn, where you may have breakfast or collect bread if ordered the day before. There is a traffic free footpath direct from the site to the town, which we can recommend. The fortified town is notable for the magnificent Cathedral (illuminated at night), the annual festival of the Bazardais cattle, the bonfires of St Jean, and the weekly Saturday market, and is on the Pilgrims Route. A new cycle path runs from Bazas to the Atlantic coast (on 80 km. of old railway track). Reservation is advisable for July and August.

Facilities

The single, high quality toilet block may not be adequate for demand, but we are told more units will be built. It includes open and cubicle washbasins, washing machine and dryer, dishwashing and laundry sinks, an excellent baby room, and full facilities for disabled persons. Motorcaravan service point. Unusual swimming pool and paddling pool. Sunbathing area. Small playground. Volleyball, boules. Library with some English books. B&B nearby at the Château.

Open

1 April - 30 September.

At a glance

Welcome & Ambience	✓✓✓✓✓	Location	✓✓✓✓
Quality of Pitches	✓✓✓✓	Range of Facilities	✓✓✓✓

Directions

Bazas is around 55 km. southeast of Bordeaux, and 15 km. south of Langon. From Bazas centre take the D655 east towards Casteljaloux, and the site entrance is about 1 km. on your right (well signed).

Charges 2004

Per unit incl. 1 or 2 persons	€ 7,88 - € 18,85
incl. 3 persons	€ 9,48 - € 22,00
electricity (6-16A)	€ 3,20 - € 4,74
extra person over 10 yrs	€ 2,37 - € 3,93
dog	free - € 3,00
Discounts for longer stays	

Reservations

Advisable for July and August. Tel: 05 56 65 13 17. E-mail: legrandpre@wanadoo.fr

FR33130 Camping Caravaning Les Grands Pins

Mobile homes page 385

33680 Lacanau-Océan (Gironde)

This Atlantic coast holiday site with direct access to a fine sandy beach, is on undulating terrain amongst tall pine trees. A large site, it provides 570 pitches, with about 44 private and rental mobile homes, leaving around 525 pitches of varying sizes for touring units. The site is well served by tarmac access roads, and although not noticeably divided, one half of the site is a traffic free zone (except for arrival or departure day, caravans are placed on the pitch, with separate areas outside the zone for car parking). There is a good number of tent pitches, those in the centre of the site having some of the best views, and especially useful for tenters are safety deposit and fridge boxes which are available for rent. The large sandy beach is a 350 m. stroll from the gate at the back of the site.

Facilities

Five toilet blocks include washbasins in cubicles, dish-washing and laundry sinks, a dog and wetsuit washing area, baby room and facilities for disabled people (not all units are open in low season). Well equipped launderette. Motorcaravan services. Good sized supermarket, surf boutique. Bar, restaurant and snack bar with takeaway. Heated swimming pool (20 x 10 m, from 1/5 with lifeguard in July/Aug) with large paved sunbathing surround. Jacuzzi. Free fitness activities (aquagym, etc). Games room. Fitness suite. Tennis (charge in July/Aug). Two playgrounds. Bicycle hire. Organised activities for children (July/Aug). Entrance barrier with keypad access. Only gas barbecues permitted. Off site: Fishing, golf, riding and bicycle hire 5 km.

Open

1 May - 15 September

At a glance

Welcome & Ambience	✓✓✓✓	Location	✓✓✓✓✓
Quality of Pitches	✓✓✓	Range of Facilities	✓✓✓✓

Directions

From Bordeaux take N125/D6 west to Lacanau, continue on D6 to Lacanau Ocean. At second roundabout, take second exit: Plage Nord and follow signs to camps sites. Les Grand Pins is signed to the right at the far end of the road. If approaching from northern France you could use the ferry from Royan to Le Verdon.

Charges 2004

Pitch incl. 2 persons and electricity	€ 20,00 - € 34,00
extra person	€ 6,00 - € 9,00
child (2-12 yrs)	free - € 4,00
dog	€ 3,00 - € 4,00

Reservations

Essential for high season, made with deposit and fee. Discounts for early booking. Tel: 05 56 03 20 77. E-mail: reception@lesgrandspins.com

FR33150 Camping Municipal Les Gabarreys

Route de la Rivière, 33250 Pauillac (Gironde)

An attractive, small site with well tended flower beds, Les Gabarreys is surrounded by the many vineyards of the Médoc region. An excellent site, it has 59 pitches, 41 with hardstanding for caravans or motorcaravans, 14 grass pitches for tents and 4 mobile homes, all with electricity (some may require long leads). The 'Maison du Tourisme et du Vin' should be your first port of call, the surrounding area is well supplied with wine caves, and being fairly level you could perhaps cycle to some of them. The site is popular with the grape pickers in September, but the warden always keeps some pitches for tourists.

Facilities

Two immaculate toilet blocks provide open and cubicle washbasins and excellent facilities for disabled people. Motorcaravan services. General room with satellite TV, fridge-freezer and small library. Minigolf (free). Volleyball.

Open

26 March - 11 October.

Reservations

Advisable for July-September. Tel: 05 56 59 10 03.
E-mail: camping.les.gabarreys@wanadoo.fr

At a glance

Welcome & Ambience	✓✓✓✓	Location	✓✓✓✓
Quality of Pitches	✓✓✓	Range of Facilities	✓✓✓✓

Directions

Pauillac is on the western side of the Gironde estuary, NNW of Bordeaux. From Bordeaux take the D1 to St Laurent, then the D206 to Pauillac. At roundabout turn right to Pauillac Guais, then straight on at next roundabout and turn right just before the Maison du Tourisme. Site is 800 m. on the left. If approaching from the north, you could use the ferry from Royan to Le Verdon, or Blaye to Lamarque (cheaper).

Charges 2004

Per unit incl. 2 persons	€ 11,00 - € 12,00
extra person	€ 3,60 - € 4,00
electricity (5/10A)	€ 3,50 - € 4,80

FR33220 Sunêlia Le Petit Nice

Route de Biscarosse, 33115 Pyla-sur-Mer (Gironde)

Le Petit Nice is a traditional seaside site, just south the great Dune de Pyla (Europe's largest sand dune, and a genuinely remarkable sight). It is a friendly, if relatively unsophisticated, site with direct (steep) access to an excellent sandy beach. The 225 pitches are for the most part terraced, descending towards the sea. Many are quite small, with larger pitches generally occupied by mobile homes. For this reason it is likely to appeal more to campers and those with small motorcaravans and very small caravans. Most pitches are shaded by pine trees but those closest to the sea are unshaded. Unusually, the site also has a private hang-gliding and paragliding take-off strip (very popular activities here).

Facilities

Two refurbished toilet blocks include washbasins in cubicles, baby rooms and facilities for disabled people. New, very smart bar/restaurant. Well stocked shop. Games room. Attractive swimming pool with small slide, children's pool and jacuzzi. Tennis, table tennis and boules court.

Open

1 April – 30 September.

At a glance

Welcome & Ambience	✓✓✓	Location	✓✓✓✓✓
Quality of Pitches	✓✓	Range of Facilities	✓✓✓✓

Directions

The site is on D218 (Arcachon – Biscarosse) south of Dune de Pyla; it is the fifth site after the Dune.

Charges 2004

Per adult	€ 3,50 - € 6,00
child	€ 2,00 - € 4,00
pitch with electricity	€ 16,00 - € 30,00

Camping Cheques accepted.

Reservations

Essential in high season. Tel: 05 56 22 74 03.
E-mail: camping.petit.nice@wanadoo.fr

FR33240 Camping Airotel de L'Océan

33680 Lacanau (Gironde)

Its location on the Atlantic coast, only 600 metres from a lovely sandy beach makes this site extremely popular. Set in 10 hectares of wooded sand dunes, the site offers the total holiday experience with over 500 pitches set amongst pine trees with areas for peace and quiet and areas for those who want to be on top of it all. The pitches are quite spacious, some level and others requiring blocks. At the time of our visit everywhere was very dry and there was very little grass. There is a large pool complex, a bar and disco (in a soundproof building). Lacanau-Océan has many weekend visitors and is popular for surfing.

Facilities

Six toilet blocks provide spacious facilities including washbasins in cabins, a room for disabled visitors in each block (although the site is quite hilly in places), baby rooms, and washing machines. Motorcaravan service point. Supermarket. Bar, restaurant and takeaway. Large pool complex. Various sports facilities. Fitness gym. TV and games rooms. Internet access. Bicycle hire. Barbecue area. Off site: Beach 600 m. Shops 1 km.

Open

9 April - 25 September.

At a glance

Welcome & Ambience	✓✓✓✓	Location	✓✓✓✓✓
Quality of Pitches	✓✓✓✓	Range of Facilities	✓✓✓✓

Directions

From Bordeaux take D106 then onto D3 to Royan and through the wooded areas of the Atlantic coast. At Lacanau join D6 to Lacanau Ocean. At roundabout before village turn right. Site is 800 m. on the right.

Charges 2005

Per unit incl. 2 persons	€ 21,00 - € 34,00
with electricity	€ 21,00 - € 37,00
extra person	€ 4,50 - € 7,50
child (under 12 yrs)	free - € 4,00

Reservations

Made with 25% deposit and € 28 fee.
Tel: 05 56 03 24 45.
E-mail: airotel.lacanau@wanadoo.fr

FR33320 Camping Talaris Vacances

Route de l'Océan, 33680 Lacanau (Gironde)

This is a typically French campsite where the owner is anxious to welcome more British visitors. It is located near a large lake and just six kilometres from the Atlantic coast at Lacanau Océan, so there are opportunities for swimming in either lake or sea, for surfing, water-skiing or sailing. There are plenty of cycle tracks and horse riding is available nearby. On site, there is plenty going on for youngsters – the many activities take place in front of the bar, restaurant and swimming pool area, so it is probably not the place for parents to relax! However, the part of the campsite allocated to the 150 tourist pitches is amongst mature trees (mainly oak, silver birch and the inevitable pines) at the far end of the site, so is surprisingly peaceful and relaxed (depending, of course, on one's neighbours!) Some 100 mobile homes and chalets are available for rent, grouped in another part of the site.

Facilities

Two similar almost identical toilet blocks, one serving mainly the area occupied by tour operators providing activity holidays for young people, but the one in the touring area is adequate, with pre-set showers, washbasins in cubicles and solar heating used for water. Dishwashing and laundry sinks under cover. Washing machines and dryers. Baby room. Facilities for disabled people. Shop (July/Aug). Bar/restaurant and takeaway with covered terrace (1/5-13/9). Swimming pools (1/5-13/9). Off site: Riding 1 km. Golf 3 km. Lake 1 km. Sea beach 6 km.

At a glance

Welcome & Ambience	✓✓✓✓	Location	✓✓✓✓
Quality of Pitches	✓✓✓	Range of Facilities	✓✓✓✓

Directions

From Bordeaux, take N125/D6 west to Lacanau and continue on D6 towards Lacanau Océan. Site is on right in about 7 km.

Charges 2005

Per unit incl. 2 persons	€ 16,25 - € 26,50
extra person	€ 3,00 - € 5,50
child (4-10 yrs)	free - € 3,30
animal	€ 2,50 - € 3,00
electricity (6A)	€ 3,00

Reservations

Contact site. Tel: 05 56 03 04 15.
E-mail: talarisvacances@free.fr

Open

1 May - 17 September.

FR33210 Sunêlia La Pointe du Medoc

Route de la Pointe de Grave, 33123 Le Verdon-sur-Mer (Gironde)

La Pointe du Medoc, part of the Sunelia group, was established four years ago close to the tip of the Medoc peninsula and it benefits from some excellent, modern amenities. This site has 260 pitches, with around half taken by mobile homes or chalets. It is situated roughly equi-distant between the sandy Atlantic beach (accessed by a pleasant walk through the forest opposite the site) and that of the Gironde estuary, both around one kilometre away. Pitches are generally large (100–150 sq.m). Some are in full sun (the site lost many trees in the great storm of 1999) but those towards the rear of the site offer much more shade. All are equipped with electricity (6A), and many have water and drainage. A little used railway line passes by the front of the site, as well as the main road to Le Verdon. The site is well located for excursions to the Medoc chateaux or marshland.

Facilities

Two modern toilet blocks are maintained to a high standard, with good hot showers and washbasins in private cabins. Pleasant bar and restaurant with takeaway. Heated swimming pool with small waterfalls, split-level paddling pool. Massage room. Beach volleyball. Minigolf. Multi-sport terrain. Bicycle hire. Communal barbecue area. Wide range of organised entertainment and imaginative children's club in high season. Off site: Sea fishing 1 km. Riding 5 km.

Open

9 April - 30 September

At a glance

Welcome & Ambience	✓✓✓✓	Location	✓✓✓✓
Quality of Pitches	✓✓✓✓	Range of Facilities	✓✓✓✓✓

Directions

Site is on the RN215 just south of Le Verdon and can be accessed either from the south (Bordeaux or the Blaye ferry), or from the north using the regular Royan – Pointe de Grave car ferry.

Charges 2004

Per unit incl. 2 persons and electricity	€ 14,00 - € 22,00
extra person (over 1 yr)	€ 2,00 - € 5,00
dog	€ 4,00

Camping Cheques accepted.

Reservations

Essential for high season – contact site.
Tel: 05 56 73 39 99.
E-mail: info@camping-lapointedumedoc.com

FR33310 Yelloh! Village Le Panorama

Grande Dune du Pyla, Route de Biscarrosse, 33260 Pyla-sur-Mer (Gironde)

Many campsites set amongst pine trees have a rather untidy look, but Panorama is different. Here the entrance is very inviting with well tended flower beds and a pleasant, airy reception. From the entrance there is a steep climb up to the pitches, passing the swimming pool and play area. The touring pitches are a mix of those suitable for caravans and motorcaravans and those suitable only for tents. They are set on terraces amongst the tall pines outnumbering the pitches used for mobile homes and most have electricity (3-10A). Access to the toilet blocks may involve a steep climb (the site is probably not suitable for people with disabilities or with very young children). There are many activities and entertainments organised in high season, even classical concerts. All potentially noisy activities – pool, play areas, shop, discos, concerts, bar and takeaway – are grouped on the entrance side of the dune, away from the pitches. A track leads down to the beach with a staircase and right next door is Europe's largest dune, the Dune de Pyla, a favourite with parascenders. The area is a maze of off road cycle tracks. A Yelloh Village member.

Facilities

Seven toilet blocks (progressively being renovated) are clean and well maintained with free hot showers, baby rooms and facilities for disabled people. Fridge hire. Laundry facilities. Motorcaravan service point. Bar/restaurant with panoramic view of the ocean. Attractive pool area with three heated swimming pools and jacuzzi (1/5-30/9). Adjacent play area. Tennis. Minigolf and table tennis. Organised entertainment in high season for all ages.
Off site: Riding and golf 10 km.

Open

1 May - 30 September.

At a glance

Welcome & Ambience	✓✓✓✓✓	Location	✓✓✓✓✓
Quality of Pitches	✓✓✓✓	Range of Facilities	✓✓✓✓

Directions

From the N250, just before La Teste, take D259 signed Biscarrosse and Dune de Pilate. At roundabout at end of road turn left (south) on D218 coast road signed Biscarrosse and Dune de Pyla. Site is 4 km. on right.

Charges 2004

Per person	€ 3,50 - € 8,00
child (under 12 yrs)	€ 1,50 - € 2,50
pitch	€ 8,00 - € 17,00
electricity (3-10A)	€ 3,00 - € 5,00
animal	€ 2,00 - € 5,00

Reservations

Made with deposit (€ 120) and fee (€ 30); min. 10 days in high season. Tel: 05 56 22 10 44. E-mail: mail@camping-panorama.com

FR40020 Camping Les Chênes

Bois de Boulogne, 40100 Dax (Landes)

Dax is not a place that springs at once to mind as a holiday town but, as well as being a 'spa', it promotes a comprehensive programme of events and shows during the summer season. Les Chênes is a well established site, popular with the French themselves and situated on the edge of town amongst parkland (also near the river) and close to the spa for the thermal treatments. The 183 touring pitches are of two types, some large and traditional with hedges, water and electricity connections, and others more informal, set amongst tall pines with electricity if required. This is a reliable, well run site, with a little of something for everyone, but probably most popular for adults taking the 'treatments'.

Facilities

Two very different toilet blocks, one new and very modern with heating, washbasins in cubicles, facilities for disabled people and babies and young children. The older block has been refurbished. Laundry room. Ample laundry and dishwashing sinks. Reasonably well stocked shop also providing takeaway food (3/4-30/10). Unusual and attractive swimming and paddling pools (1/5-18/8). Good play area. Table tennis and boule pitch. Bicycle hire. Mini-club for children (July/Aug). Occasional evenings for adults with meals and dancing. Charcoal barbecues are not permitted. Off site: Restaurant opposite site entrance. Fishing 100 m. Riding and golf 300 m. Beaches 28 km.

Open

27 March - 6 November.

At a glance

Welcome & Ambience	✓✓✓✓	Location	✓✓✓
Quality of Pitches	✓✓✓✓	Range of Facilities	✓✓✓

Directions

Site is west of town on south side of river, signed after main river bridge and at many junctions in town (Bois de Boulogne 1.5 km). In very wet weather the access road to the site may flood (but not the site).

Charges 2004

Per pitch incl. 1 or 2 persons and electricity (5A)	€ 13,00 - € 15,60
with water and drainage	€ 15,50 - € 18,20
extra person	€ 5,00
child (0-12 yrs)	€ 3,00
animal	€ 1,00

Reservations

Made with deposit (€ 46.50) and fee (€ 7.50); contact site. Tel: 05 58 90 05 53.
E-mail: camping-chenes@wanadoo.fr

FR40030 Les Pins du Soleil

Départementale 459, 40990 St Paul-lès-Dax (Landes)

This site will appeal to families, particularly those with younger children, or those who prefer to be some way back from the coast within easy reach of shops, cultural activities, etc. and well placed for touring the area. Dax is a busy spa town with many attractions – Les Pins du Soleil is actually at St Paul lès Dax, some 3 km. from Dax itself. The site has 145 good sized pitches, 99 for touring units of which 59 have electricity and drainage. Although new, the site benefits from being developed in light woodland so there is a fair amount of shade from the many small trees. A range of excursions is possible by bus to St Sebastian, Lourdes, etc. and the nearby Calicéo aquatic centre is recommended. English is spoken.

Facilities

Modern sanitary facilities include facilities for babies, disabled visitors and laundry. Small supermarket. Bar. Takeaway (2/6-15/9). Attractive, medium sized swimming pool with café (both 2/6-15/9). Playground. Children's mini-club in high season. Volleyball. Table tennis. Bicycle hire. Off site: Fishing 1 km. Riding 3 km. Bus to thermal baths.

Open

2 April - 29 October.

At a glance

Welcome & Ambience	✓✓✓✓	Location	✓✓✓
Quality of Pitches	✓✓✓	Range of Facilities	✓✓✓✓

Directions

From west on N124, avoid bypass and follow signs for Dax and St. Paul. Almost immediately turn right at roundabout on D459 and follow signs. It is also well signed from town centre, north of the river.

Charges 2004

Per pitch incl. 2 persons	€ 8,00 - € 17,00
with electricity, water, drainage	€ 15,00 - € 23,00
extra person	€ 6,00
child (4-10 yrs)	€ 3,50

Camping Cheques accepted.

Reservations

Made with deposit (€ 35) and fee (€ 6).
Tel: 05 58 91 37 91. E-mail: pinsoleil@aol.com

FR40040 Yelloh! Village La Paillotte

40140 Azur (Landes)

La Paillotte, in the Landes area of southwest France, is a site with a character of its own. The campsite buildings (reception, shop, restaurant, even sanitary blocks) are all Tahitian in style, circular and constructed from local woods with the typical straw roof (and layer of waterproof material underneath). Some are now being replaced but still in character. It lies right beside the Soustons lake, 1.5 km. from Azur village, and has its own sandy beach. This is particularly suitable for young children because the lake is shallow and slopes extremely gradually. For boating the site has a small private harbour where you can keep your own non-powered boat (of shallow draught). All 310 pitches at La Paillotte are marked, individual ones and are mostly shady with shrubs and trees planted. The 132 pitches for touring units vary in price according to size, position and whether they are equipped with electricity, water, etc. La Paillotte is an unusual site with its own atmosphere which appeals to many regular clients. Used by tour operators (45 pitches). Member 'Yelloh Village'.

TRAVEL SERVICE SITE

TO BOOK CALL 0870 405 4055 OR www.alanrogersdirect.com

Facilities

Circular rustic-style toilet blocks are rather different from the usual campsite amenities, but are modern and fully tiled. They include individual washbasins, partly enclosed, some toilets and basins en-suite and separate 'mini' facilities for children. Outside washing-up sinks. Washing machines and dryers. Motorcaravan service points. Shop (1/6-29/9). Good restaurant with pleasant terrace overlooking the lake, bar, takeaway (all 13/4-26/9). Swimming pool complex (13/4-26/9). Sports, games and activities organised for children and adults. 'Mini-club' room, with 'mini' equipment. TV room, library. Fishing. Bicycle hire. Table tennis. Sailing, rowing boats and pedaloes for hire. Torches useful. No dogs are accepted. Off site: Riding 5 km. Golf 10 km. Atlantic beaches 10 km.

At a glance

Welcome & Ambience	✓✓✓✓	Location	✓✓✓✓✓
Quality of Pitches	✓✓✓✓	Range of Facilities	✓✓✓✓✓

Directions

Coming from the north along N10, turn west on D150 at Magescq. From south go via Soustons. In Azur turn left before church (site signed).

Charges 2004

Per unit incl. 2 persons	
with 10A electricity	€ 15,00 - € 34,00
with electricity and water	€ 17,00 - € 36,00
pitch by the lake	€ 20,00 - € 42,00
extra person (over 4 yrs)	€ 3,00 - € 6,50

Reservations

Advised for high season; made for Sat. to Sat. only 2/7- 27/8, with deposit (€ 38.11 per week) and fee (€ 25). Tel: 05 58 48 12 12. E-mail: info@paillotte.com

Open

April - September.

FR40050 Sunêlia Le Col-Vert

Lac de Leon, 40560 Vielle-St Girons (Landes)

This extensive but natural site edges a nature reserve and stretches along the Lac de Léon, a conservation area, for one kilometre on a narrow frontage. This makes it particularly suitable for those who want to practise water sports such as sailing and windsurfing. Bathing is also possible as the lake bed shelves gently making it easy for children. The site has a supervised beach, sail-boarding courses are arranged and there are some boats and boards for hire. There are some 800 pitches in total, the 380 pitches for touring units being flat and covered by light pinewood, most with good shade and many along the lake side. They are of around 100 sq.m, only partly separated and some 120 have water and electricity points. Much 'animation' is organised in season: children's games, tournaments, etc. by day and dancing or shows in the evenings. Used by tour operators (80 pitches).

TRAVEL SERVICE SITE

TO BOOK CALL 0870 405 4055 OR www.alanrogersdirect.com

Facilities

Of the four toilet blocks, one is heated in low season. Mostly British WCs, washbasins in cabins. Dishwashing sinks (mainly cold water but with hot tap to draw from). Washing machines, dryer and dishwasher. Good facilities for disabled people. Motorcaravan services. Shops (15/4-15/9). Good bar/restaurant by the lake (open to all). Simple takeaway. Two pools (all season and supervised), one open air with whirlpool and one covered and heated. Sunbathing areas. Playground. TV room, table tennis, amusement machines. Sports area with boules, tennis and volleyball. Fitness centre and sauna. Two jogging tracks. Safety deposit boxes. An overall charge is made for the leisure activities but this excludes certain facilities, eg. riding, bicycle hire, sauna, tennis, minigolf. Fishing (lessons for children). Riding. Sailing school (15/6-15/9). Several areas for barbecues. Off site: Walking and cycle ways in the forest. Atlantic beaches 5 km. Golf 10 km.

At a glance

Welcome & Ambience	✓✓✓✓	Location	✓✓✓✓✓
Quality of Pitches	✓✓✓	Range of Facilities	✓✓✓✓✓

Directions

Site is off D652 Mimizan-Léon road, 4 km. south of crossroads with D42 at St. Girons. Road to lake and site is signed at Veille.

Charges 2004

Per unit incl. 2 persons	
acc. to season, type and location	€ 11,00 - € 41,90
extra person	€ 2,00 - € 5,90
child (3-13 yrs)	€ 1,50 - € 4,90
electricity (3/10A)	€ 3,60 - € 5,00
dog	€ 1,00 - € 4,00

Camping Cheques accepted.

Reservations

Any length with UK £42 deposit per week booked and £25 fee. Tel: 05 58 42 94 06. E-mail: contact@colvert.com

Open

9 April - 25 September.

FR40160 Camping Les Vignes

Mobile homes page 388

Route de la Plage du Cap de L'Homy, 40170 Lit-et-Mixe (Landes)

Les Vignes is a large holiday site close to the Atlantic coast with 450 pitches, of which 250 are occupied by a mix of mobile homes, bungalows and tents, most of which are for rent. The 157 tourist pitches are relatively level on a sandy base, all serviced with electricity (10A) and water, some with waste water drains. The site's amenities, including a supermarket, restaurant and bar, are located at the entrance to the site. The rather stylish swimming pool complex includes a six lane water slide. A wide range of activities is provided and during July and August a great variety of entertainment options for both adults and children, some of which take place in the new entertainment 'Big Top'.

Facilities

Four virtually identical sanitary units (not all open in low season) provide combined washbasin and shower cubicles, dishwashing and laundry sinks, washing machines and dryers, facilities for babies and disabled people. Large supermarket (15/6-10/9). Restaurant and bar (15/6-10/9). Takeaway (July/Aug). Swimming pool complex (1/6-15/9). Tennis. Table tennis. Golf driving range. Minigolf. Volleyball, basketball. Pétanque. Kids club and playground. Bicycle hire. Barrier closed 23.00-07.00 hrs. Off site: Golf course, canoeing, kayaking, surfing, riding. Many cycle tracks.

At a glance

Welcome & Ambience	✓✓✓✓	Location	✓✓✓✓
Quality of Pitches	✓✓✓	Range of Facilities	✓✓✓✓

Directions

Lit-et-Mixe is on the D652 20 km. south of Mimizan. Turn west on D88 1 km. south of town towards Cap de l'Homy for 1.5 km. where site entrance is on left.

Charges guide

Per pitch incl. 2 persons incl. electricity and water	€ 14,50 - € 33,00
extra person (over 5 yrs)	€ 4,00 - € 5,00
child (under 5 yrs)	€ 1,50 - € 3,00
animal	€ 3,00

Reservations

Advisable for high season, made with deposit and fee. Tel: 05 58 42 85 60. E-mail: contact@les-vignes.com

Open

1 June - 15 September.

FR40110 Camping Caravaning Sen Yan

Le Village Tropical, 40170 Mézos (Landes)

This exotic family site is about 12 km. from the Atlantic coast in the Landes forest area, set just outside the village. There are 310 pitches marked with hedges, 190 with electricity (6A), and with ample water points. Some mobile homes and tour operator pitches are in a separate 'village'. The reception, bar and pool area is almost tropical with the luxuriant greenery of its banana trees, palm trees, tropical flowers and its straw sunshades. Evening entertainment includes a disco twice a week in high season.

Facilities

Three toilet blocks with good quality fittings have showers and washbasins in cabins and some British style WCs. The newest block is especially suitable for low season visitors with a special section for babies, plus facilities for disabled people. Shop (from 15/6). Bar, restaurant and snacks (1/7-31/8). Outdoor swimming pools (1/7-30/8). Heated indoor pool(1/6-15/9). Archery. Practice golf. Bicycle hire. Only gas barbecues are permitted. Off site: Fishing 500 m. Riding 6 km. Beach 12 km.

Open

1 June - 15 September.

At a glance

Welcome & Ambience	✓✓✓✓	Location	✓✓✓✓
Quality of Pitches	✓✓✓✓	Range of Facilities	✓✓✓✓✓

Directions

From N10 take exit 14 (Onesse-Laharie), then D38 Bias/Mimizan road. After 13 km. turn south to Mézos from where site is signed.

Charges 2004

Per pitch incl. 2 persons	€ 14,50 - € 26,00
with 6A electricity	€ 16,50 - € 31,00
extra person	€ 5,00
child (under 7 yrs)	€ 3,50

Reservations

Made with deposit (€ 84) and fee (€ 26). Tel: 05 58 42 60 05. E-mail: reception@sen-yan.com

FR40100 Camping du Domaine de la Rive

Mobile homes page 387

Route de Bordeaux, 40600 Biscarosse (Landes)

Set in pine woods, La Rive has a superb beach-side loaction on Lac de Sanguient. It provides mostly level, numbered and clearly defined pitches of 100 sq.m. all with electricity connections (6A). The swimming pool complex is wonderful, with various pools linked by water channels and bridges, the four-slide pool having a wide staircase to the top to speed up enjoyment. There is also a jacuzzi, paddling pool and two large, unusually shaped swimming pools, all surrounded by paved sunbathing areas and decorated with palm trees. An indoor pool is heated and open all season. The beach is excellent, shelving gently to provide safe bathing for all ages. There are windsurfers and small craft can be launched from the site's slipway. This is a friendly site with a good mix of nationalities.

TRAVEL SERVICE SITE

TO BOOK CALL 0870 405 4055 OR
www.alanrogersdirect.com

Facilities

Five modern, very good quality toilet blocks have washbasins in cabins and mainly British style toilets. Visitors with disabilities well catered for in three blocks. Baby baths. We found the facilities very clean. Motorcaravan service point. Well stocked shop with gas (1/5-15/9). Bar serving snacks and takeaway. Games room adjoining. Restaurant with reasonably priced family meals (1/5-10/9). Swimming pool complex supervised July/Aug (outdoor pool 1/5-15/9). Play area. Two tennis courts. Bicycle hire. Hand-ball or basketball court, table tennis, boules, archery and football. Fishing. Water skiing. Watersports equipment may be hired and tournaments in various sports are arranged in June-Aug. Skateboard park, trampolines with safety harness and an enlarged and upgraded play area. Discos and karaoke evenings organised outside bar with stage and tiered seating. Mini-club for children twice daily. Charcoal barbecues not permitted on pitches (central area available). Caravan storage.
Off site: Riding 5 km. Golf 10 km.

At a glance

Welcome & Ambience	✓✓✓✓	Location	✓✓✓✓
Quality of Pitches	✓✓✓	Range of Facilities	✓✓✓✓✓

Directions

Take D652 from Sanguinet to Biscarrosse and site is signed on the right in about 6 km.

Charges 2004

Per pitch incl. 2 persons	
and electricity	€ 20,00 - € 34,00
with water and drainage	€ 23,00 - € 37,00
extra person	€ 3,40 - € 5,90
child (3-10 yrs)	€ 2,30 - € 4,50
boat	€ 5,00 - € 6,00
dog	€ 2,10 - € 3,50

Camping Cheques accepted.

Reservations

Advised for July/Aug; write or fax site. (deposit € 100)
Tel: 05 58 78 12 33.
E-mail: info@camping-de-la-rive.fr

Open

1 April - 30 September.

FR40120 Domaine Naturiste Arnaoutchot

40560 Vielle-St Girons (Landes)

'Arna' is a large naturist site with extensive facilities and direct access to the beach. Even with 500 pitches, its layout in the form of a number of sections, each with its own character, make it quite relaxing and very natural. These sections amongst the trees and bushes of the Landes provide a variety of reasonably sized pitches, most with electricity (3/6A), although the hilly terrain means that only a limited number are flat enough for motorcaravans. The centrally located amenities are extensive and of excellent quality. The site has the advantage of direct access to a large, sandy naturist beach, although access from some parts of the site may involve a walk of perhaps 600-700 metres. The 'Arna Club' provides more than 30 activities and workshops (in the main season). English is spoken. There are chalets, mobile homes, caravans and tents for rent. The site is used by a tour operator (20 pitches). Green Key award. Member 'France 4 Naturisme'.

Facilities

Sanitary facilities include the usual naturist site type of blocks with communal hot showers and also a number of tiny blocks with one hot shower, WC and washbasin each in an individual cabin. All blocks have been upgraded to provide fully tiled, modern facilities, one block is heated in low season. Laundry. Motorcaravan service point. Large supermarket and range of other shops. Bar/restaurant, pizzeria and tapita (fish) bar. Pizza delivery to pitches or to telephone point on beach. Heated indoor pool with solarium, whirlpool and slide. Outdoor pool and terraced sunbathing area. Spa centre with sauna, steam, whirlpool and massage treatments. Arna Club (main season) including archery, golf practise, tennis, petanque, swimming, rambling, cycling, handicrafts, excursions and activities for children. TV, video and games rooms. Cinema. Library. Hairdresser and chiropodist. Cash point. Internet point. Bicycle hire. Fishing on site. Torches useful. Barbecues not permitted. American motorhomes not accepted. Off site: Riding or golf 5 km.

At a glance

Welcome & Ambience	✓✓✓✓	Location	✓✓✓✓
Quality of Pitches	✓✓✓	Range of Facilities	✓✓✓✓✓

Directions

Site is signed off the D652 road at Vielle-Saint-Girons. Follow D328 for 3-4 km.

Charges 2005

Per unit incl. 2 persons	€ 10,00 - € 32,90
extra person (over 3 yrs)	€ 2,00 - € 6,80
electricity (3A)	€ 3,60
animal	€ 1,20 - € 3,00

Camping Cheques accepted.
Deposit on arrival for accommodation € 50.
Special offers available.

Reservations

Made with 25% deposit and fee (€ 30).
Tel: 05 58 49 11 11. E-mail: contact@arna.com

Open

1 April - 25 September.

La Rive ★★★★
Le Rêve
Location de mobil homes et chalets
www.larive.fr
Création Vista Communication 06 14 23 92 32
BISCARROSSE
Camping Qualité
ANWB
Camping du Domaine de la Rive
Route de Bordeaux - 40600 Biscarrosse
Tél. 05 58 78 12 33 - Fax. 05 58 78 12 92
e-mail : info@camping-de-la-rive.fr

FR40130 Camping de la Côte

40660 Messanges (Landes)

A peaceful family site, surrounded by pine forests near the beaches of the Landes, has large, level pitches edged with newly planted trees and shrubs. A number of the 142 touring pitches are set among trees that provide shade, 118 have electricity connections (6/10A) and 12 also have water and drainage. The beach and the dunes are 20 minutes walk. M. and Mme. Moresmau are very proud of their site and do their utmost to maintain a quiet family atmosphere with customers who return year after year.

Facilities

Two modern toilet blocks built in the Landes style are of excellent quality and very well maintained. Facilities include washbasins in cabins, a baby room and provision for disabled people. Washing machines and dryer with sinks for laundry and dishes. Motorcaravan service point. Reception sells bread and milk, a few basic supplies and gas (1/7-31/8). Takeaway pizza (July/Aug). Barbecues only permitted at designated areas. Games room, play area, football, volleyball, table tennis and boules. Mobile homes to rent. Off site: Fishing or riding within 1 km. Bicycle hire 1.5 km. Golf 2 km. Supermarket and resort of Vieux-Boucau near.

At a glance

Welcome & Ambience	✓✓✓✓	Location	✓✓✓✓
Quality of Pitches	✓✓✓✓	Range of Facilities	✓✓✓

Directions

Site is signed off the D652, 1.5 km. north of Vieux-Boucau.

Charges 2004

Per unit incl. 2 persons	€ 8,50 - € 12,90
extra person	€ 2,30 - € 3,20
child (under 7 yrs)	€ 1,60 - € 2,20
electricity (6/10A)	€ 2,30 - € 4,10
water and drainage	€ 2,00 - € 3,20
pet	€ 0,80 - € 1,30

Reservations

Advised and made with deposit (€ 60). Tel: 05 58 48 94 94. E-mail: lacote@wanadoo.fr

Open

1 April - 30 September.

FR40140 Camping Caravaning Lou P'tit Poun

Mobile homes ▶ page 387

110 avenue du Quartier Neuf, 40390 St Martin de Seignanx (Landes)

The manicured grounds surrounding Lou P'tit Poun give it a well kept appearance, a theme carried out throughout this very pleasing site. It is only after arriving at the car park that you feel confident it is not a private estate. Beyond this point the site unfolds to reveal an abundance of thoughtfully positioned shrubs and trees. Behind a central sloping flower bed lies the open plan reception area. The avenues around the site are wide and the 168 pitches are spacious. All have electricity (6/10A), 30 are fully serviced and some are separated by low hedges. The jovial owners not only make their guests welcome, but extend their enthusiasm to organising weekly entertainment for young and old during high season. A 'Sites et Paysages' member.

TRAVEL SERVICE SITE
TO BOOK CALL 0870 405 4055 OR www.alanrogersdirect.com

Facilities

Two unisex sanitary blocks, maintained to a high standard and kept clean, include washbasins in cabins, a baby bath and provision for disabled people. Dishwashing sinks and laundry facilities with washing machine and dryer. Motorcaravan service point. Café, bread and ices (1/7-31/8). Swimming pool (1/6-15/9) Play area. Games room, TV. Half court tennis. Table tennis. Bicycle hire. Caravan storage. Off site: Bayonne 6 km. Fishing or riding 7 km. Golf 10 km. Sandy beaches of Basque coast ten minute drive.

Open

1 June - 15 September.

At a glance

Welcome & Ambience	✓✓✓✓✓	Location	✓✓✓✓
Quality of Pitches	✓✓✓✓✓	Range of Facilities	✓✓✓✓

Directions

Leave A63 at exit 6 and join N117 in the direction of Pau. Site is signed at Leclerc supermarket. Continue on N117 for 5.5 km. and site is then clearly signed on right.

Charges 2004

Per pitch incl. 1 or 2 persons	€ 10,00 - € 22,00
with 4A electricity	€ 12,00 - € 24,00
with water and drainage	€ 18,00 - € 28,00
extra person	€ 5,00 - € 6,00
child (under 7 yrs)	€ 2,00 - € 4,00
pet	€ 3,00 - € 4,00

Reservations

Made with deposit (25%) and fee (€ 20). Tel: 05 59 56 55 79. E-mail: ptitpoun@club-internet.fr

FR40170 Haven Camping La Réserve

Gastés, 40160 Parentis-en-Born (Landes)

La Resérve, now run by Haven Europe, is a large site set in a pine wood. It has access to a large lake with a beach and small harbour and the Atlantic beaches are nearby (20 km). The lake shelves gradually so is good fun for for children and there are good facilities for windsurfing and sailing; powered boats for water ski-ing are also permitted here. The 700 numbered pitches (200 for touring) are of above average size (mostly 120 sq.m.) set on mainly flat ground and marked by stones in the ground. Most have electricity. A variety of entertainment, sports and activities are organised in the Haven Europe tradition, often in and around the super pool complex.

Facilities

Five toilet blocks, with en-suite facilities in one, include washbasins in cabins. Washing machines. When visited they were in some need of care and maintenance - this is being addressed. Well stocked supermarket. Restaurant and large bar with entertainment all season. Swimming pool complex with water slides, paddling pools, etc. (lifeguards on duty). Children's club. Two tennis courts (floodlit in the evening), minigolf, table tennis and volleyball. Boat hire, windsurfing courses and water ski-ing. TV room, general room and amusement machines. Fishing. Bicycle hire. Dogs are not accepted. Off site: Atlantic beaches 20 km.

At a glance

Welcome & Ambience	✓✓✓✓	Location	✓✓✓✓
Quality of Pitches	✓✓✓	Range of Facilities	✓✓✓✓✓

Directions

Turn west off D652 Gastes - Mimizan road on southern outskirts of Gastes by campsite sign, then 3 km. to site.

Charges 2004

Per pitch incl. 2 persons	€ 12,00 - € 34,00
with electricity	€ 14,00 - € 39,00
extra person	€ 3,00 - € 6,00

Reservations

Accepted at any time for min. 4 days; no booking fee. Contact site or Haven Europe in the UK on 0870 242 7777 for information or reservation.
Tel: 05 58 09 74 79. E-mail: lareserve@haven.fr

Open

23 April - 25 September.

FR40180 Camping Le Vieux Port

Mobile homes page 388

Plage sud, 40660 Messanges (Landes)

The area to the north of Bayonne is heavily forested and a number of very large campsites are attractively located close to the superb Atlantic beaches. Le Vieux Port is probably the largest and certainly one of the most impressive of these. A well established destination appealing particularly to families with teenage children, this lively site has no fewer than 1,406 open pitches of mixed size, most with electrical hook-ups (6/8A) and some with water and drainage. Sprawling beneath the pines, the camping area is well shaded and pitches are generally of a good size, attractively grouped around the toilet blocks. At least a third of the site is taken up with mobile homes and there are a large number of tour operators here (30%). The heated swimming pool complex is exceptional boasting no less than five outdoor pools and three large water slides. There is also a heated indoor pool. At the back of the site a path leads across the dunes to a superb beach. A little train also trundles to the beach on a fairly regular basis in high season (small charge). All in all, a lively site with a great deal to offer an active family.

TRAVEL SERVICE SITE

TO BOOK CALL 0870 405 4055 OR www.alanrogersdirect.com

Facilities

Nine well appointed toilet blocks are all of modern design and well maintained. Facilities for disabled people. Motorcaravan service point. Good shopping facilities, including a well stocked supermarket and various smaller shops. Several restaurants (including takeaway service) and bars (all open all season). Large swimming pool complex (no bermuda shorts). Three tennis courts, two football pitches, a multi-sport pitch, minigolf etc. Bicycle hire. Well run and popular riding centre. Large animation team organise a wide range of activities in high season including frequent discos and karaoke evenings. Only communal barbecues are allowed.

Open

1 April - 30 September.

At a glance

Welcome & Ambience	✓✓✓	Location	✓✓✓✓✓
Quality of Pitches	✓✓✓✓	Range of Facilities	✓✓✓✓✓

Directions

Leave RN10 at Magescq exit heading for Soustons. Pass through Soustons following signs for Vieux-Boucau. Bypass this town and site is clearly signed to the left at second roundabout.

Charges 2005

Per unit incl. 2 persons	€ 12,00 - € 33,00
extra person	€ 3,50 - € 6,00
child (under 10 yrs)	€ 2,50 - € 4,00
electricity (6/8A)	€ 4,00 - € 6,50
animal	€ 2,00 - € 3,50

Reservations

Essential in high season. Tel: 05 58 48 22 00. E-mail: contact@levieuxport.com

FR40220 Camping Les Acacias

Route d'Azur, Quartier Delest, 40660 Messanges (Landes)

A reader had recommended this family site and we hope to include a full report in a future edition of this guide. Les Acacias is a friendly site just 2 km. from the nearest beach at Messanges. Pitches are mostly well shaded, and most offer electrical connections. Mobile homes for rent.

Facilities

Toilet block with facilities for disabled visitors and babies. Small shop. Visiting takeaway. Children's play area. Table tennis. Games room. Off site: Beach 2 km. Swimming pool at Messanges. Water sports, fishing, cycle trails, riding, salt water lake at Vieux-Boucau.

Open

25 March - 25 October.

Directions

Les Acacias is situated 2 miles south of Messanges, just off the D50 road from Azur.

Charges 2005

Per unit incl. 2 persons	€ 8,30 - € 10,30
extra person	€ 2,60 - € 2,80
child (0-7 yrs)	€ 1,80 - € 2,10
electricity	€ 2,40 - € 2,60

Reservations

Advised for high season; contact site.
Tel: 05 58 48 01 78.
E-mail: lesacacias@lesacacias.com

FR40190 Camping Airotel Saint Martin

Mobile homes page 389

Avenue de l'Océan, 40660 Moliets-Plage (Landes)

A family site aimed mainly at couples and young families, Airotel St Martin is a welcome change to most of the sites in this area in that it has only a small number of mobile homes (77) compared to the number of touring pitches (583). First impressions are of a neat, tidy, well cared for site and the direct access to the beach is an added bonus. The pitches are mainly typically French in style with low hedges separating them plus some shade. There is also a 'free and easy' area under tall trees. Electric hook ups are 11-15A and a number of pitches also have water and drainage. Entertainment in high season is low key (with the emphasis on quiet nights) – daytime competitions and a 'mini-club' and the occasional evening entertainment, well away from the pitches and with no discos or karaoke.

Facilities

Six toilet blocks of a high standard and very well maintained, have washbasins in cabins, large showers, baby rooms and facilities for disabled visitors. Motorcaravan service point. Washing machines and dryers. Fridge rental. Very good supermarket and various bars, restaurants and takeaways are at the entrance, owned by the site (Easter - 30/10). Attractive indoor pool, jacuzzi and sauna (open all season, charged for in July/Aug). Large outdoor pool area with pools, jacuzzi and paddling pool (15/6-15/9). Multi sports pitch. Small play area. Internet access. Only electric barbecues are permitted. Off site: Tennis or golf 700 m. Riding 7 km. This is an excellent area for cycling.

Open

Easter - 2 November.

At a glance

Welcome & Ambience	✓✓✓✓	Location	✓✓✓✓✓
Quality of Pitches	✓✓✓✓	Range of Facilities	✓✓✓✓

Directions

From the N10 take D142 to Lèon, then D652 to Moliets-et-Mar. Follow signs to Moliets-Plage, site is well signed.

Charges 2004

Per unit incl. 1 or 2 adults, 1 child	€ 16,50 - € 26,50
with electricity	€ 19,50 - € 30,00
with services	€ 22,50 - € 36,00
extra person	€ 3,00 - € 5,00
dog	€ 2,50

Prices are for reserved pitches.

Reservations

Contact site. Tel: 05 58 48 52 30.
E-mail: contact@camping-saint-martin.fr

FR40200 Yelloh! Village Le Sylvamar

Avenue de l'Océan, 40530 Labenne Océan (Landes)

Sylvamar is less than a kilometre from the long sandy beach of Labenne Ocean. The large, light and airy reception area is very welcoming. The 500 pitches (320 for touring units) are level, numbered and mostly separated by low hedges. All have electricity (10A), many also have water and there is welcoming shade. The pool complex is absolutely superb, set in a sunny location. There are pools of various sizes with a very large one for paddling. The four toboggans are very popular, there is a fast flowing channel that youngsters find exciting, sailing down in the inflatable boats and rubber rings provided. There is ample room for sunbathing and all is overlooked by the bar/restaurant. A Yelloh! Village member.

Facilities

Four modern toilet blocks with good quality fittings have washbasins in cabins, and facilities for babies and disabled visitors. Washing machines at each block. Small shop on site but a large supermarket is only 500 m. Bar/restaurant (all season) sells bread and takeaway. Play area for young children. Mini-club in July/Aug. Fitness centre. Tennis. Bicycle hire. Table tennis. Badminton. Library. Extensive entertainment programme incl. evening shows in the outdoor amphitheatre. Fridge hire. Barbecues are not permitted (communal ones provided). Internet July-August only.

At a glance

Welcome & Ambience	✓✓✓✓	Location	✓✓✓✓
Quality of Pitches	✓✓✓✓	Range of Facilities	✓✓✓✓✓

Directions

Labenne is on the N10. In Labenne, head west on the D126 signed Labenne Océan and site is on right in 4 km.

Charges 2004

Per unit incl. 2 persons, electricity	€ 15,00 - € 34,00
extra person (over 7 yrs)	€ 3,00 - € 6,00

Reservations

Made with deposit (€ 130), fee (€ 30) and cancellation insurance (€ 16). Tel: 05 59 45 75 16. E-mail: camping@sylvamar.fr

Open

17 April - 25 September.

FR40070 Camping Lous Seurrots

Contis Plage, 40170 St Julien-en-Born (Landes)

Lous Seurrots is only a short 300 metre walk from the beach and parts of the site have views across the estuary. There are 610 pitches, mainly in pine woods on sandy undulating ground. They are numbered but only roughly marked out, most have good shade and over 80% have electrical hook-ups. The site's pool complex is in a superb setting of palm trees and flower beds and the paved sunbathing areas have wonderful views out to the estuary and the sea. For all its size, Lous Seurrots is a family site with the emphasis on peace and tranquillity (no discos). Used by tour operators.

Facilities

Six well kept, modern toilet blocks cope very well and include some washbasins in cabins, and some showers with washbasins. Baby rooms and good facilities for disabled people. Washing machines. Motorcaravan service point. Large shop (1/6-15/9). Bar, takeaway and restaurant (15/5-15/9). Swimming pool complex (15/5-30/9), four pools and jacuzzi with keep fit classes in July/Aug. Tennis, table tennis, archery, volleyball and minigolf. Canoeing. Bicycle hire. Fishing. Mini-club for younger children. Evening entertainment twice weekly in high season in open-air auditorium. Only gas barbecues permitted. Off site: Riding 3 km.

At a glance

Welcome & Ambience	✓✓✓✓	Location	✓✓✓✓
Quality of Pitches	✓✓✓	Range of Facilities	✓✓✓✓✓

Directions

Turn off D652 on D41 (15 km. south of Mimizan) to Contis-Plage and site is on left as you reach it.

Charges 2004

Per unit incl. 2 adults	€ 11,00 - € 28,00
extra person	€ 4,00 - € 6,00
child (3-7 yrs)	free - € 4,00
electricity (6A)	€ 4,00
animal	€ 3,00

Reservations

Made with deposit (€ 46) and fee (€ 18.29). Tel: 05 58 42 85 82. E-mail: info@lous-seurrots.com

Open

1 April - 30 September.

FR64080 Camping Les Tamaris Plage

Quartier Acotz, 64500 St Jean-de-Luz (Pyrénées-Atlantiques)

This is a small, pleasant and well kept site. It is situated well outside the town but just across the road from a sandy beach with 79 numbered pitches, 45 with electricity, including some mobile homes. They are of very good size and separated by hedges, on slightly sloping ground with some shade. There is no shop, but bread is available daily across the road.

Facilities

Single toilet block of superb quality and unusual design. Washbasins and showers in private cabins, mainly British style WCs, facilities for disabled people and washing machine. New covered terrace with views of the sea. TV room for adults and children's room with TV and games. Playground. Not suitable for twin axle caravans. Off site: Fishing 30 m. Bicycle hire or golf 4 km. Riding 7 km.

Open

1 April - 30 September.

At a glance

Welcome & Ambience	✓✓✓✓	Location	✓✓✓✓✓
Quality of Pitches	✓✓✓✓	Range of Facilities	✓✓✓

Directions

Proceed south on N10 and 1.5 km. after Guethary take first road on right (before motorway and Carrefour centre commercial) and follow camp signs.

Charges 2004

Per unit (100 sq.m. pitch)	
incl. 2 persons and 5A electricity	€ 23,10 - € 30,50
textra person (over 2 yrs)	€ 3,90 - € 5,60
dog	€ 3,00

Reservations

Made with 20% deposit and fee (€ 18.30). Tel: 05 59 26 55 90. E-mail: tamaris1@clubinternet.fr

FR64010 Europ Camping

Ascarat, 64220 St Jean-Pied-de-Port (Pyrénées-Atlantiques)

Europ Camping is a neat and orderly, family run site with wonderful views of the vine-covered closer hills and the distant high Pyrénées. The 111 pitches (90 for touring units) are clearly marked and separated by shrubs and all have electricity (6A), water and drainage. The area is good for walking or mountain biking and there is rafting on a local river. The site is only 20 km. from the forest of Iraty with its lakes and ski-runs, and the Spanish border on the route de St Jacques-de-Compostelle, is 8 km.

Facilities

The central, modern and well appointed toilet block includes washbasins in cubicles and facilities for disabled visitors. Two washing machines, dryer. Motorcaravan service point. Small shop. Bar/restaurant with reasonably priced meal of the day and takeaway. Swimming pool with paddling pool and sauna. Play area. Volleyball. Petanque. Barbecue area. Off site: Tennis near. Fishing 200 m. Bicycle hire 2 km. St Jean-Pied-de-Port 2 km. Riding 10 km.

Open

Easter - 30 September.

At a glance

Welcome & Ambience	✓✓✓✓	Location	✓✓✓✓
Quality of Pitches	✓✓✓✓	Range of Facilities	✓✓✓✓

Directions

Site is 2 km. northwest of St Jean-Pied-de-Port in the hamlet of Ascarat and is signed from the D918 Bayonne road.

Charges 2004

Per person	€ 5,40
child (under 7 yrs)	€ 2,70
pitch and car	€ 7,50
electricity (6A)	€ 3,80
dog	€ 2,00

Reservations

Made in writing with 30% deposit and € 21.34 fee. Tel: 05 59 37 12 78.

FR64060 Camping Le Pavillon Royal

Avenue du Prince de Galles, 64210 Bidart (Pyrénées-Atlantiques)

Le Pavillon Royal has an excellent situation on raised ground overlooking the sea, with good views along the coast to the south and to the north coast of Spain beyond. Beneath the site - and only a very short walk down - stretches a wide sandy beach. This is the Atlantic with its breakers and a central marked-out section of the beach is supervised by lifeguards (from mid-June). There is also a section with rocks and pools. If the sea is rough, the site has a large swimming pool and sunbathing area. The site is divided up into 303 marked, level pitches, many of a good size. Connected by asphalt roads, all have electricity and most are serviced with water and drainage. Much of the campsite is in full sun, although one area is shaded. Reservation in high season is advisable.

Facilities

The toilet blocks are of highest quality with mainly British style WCs, washbasins in cabins, sinks and baby baths and good units for disabled people, all thoroughly cleaned twice daily. Washing facilities are closed at night except for night units. Washing machines and dryers. Motorcaravan services. Well stocked shop (including gas). Restaurant with takeaway (all season). Swimming and paddling pools. Sauna. Playground. General room, TV room and games room with table tennis, also used for films. Fishing. Surf school. Dogs are not accepted. Barrier card with deposit (€ 20).

Open

15 May - 25 September.

At a glance

Welcome & Ambience	✓✓✓✓	Location	✓✓✓✓✓
Quality of Pitches	✓✓✓✓	Range of Facilities	✓✓✓✓✓

Directions

Don't go into Bidart as the site is on the Biarritz side. From the north, keep on main N10 bypassing Biarritz, then turn sharp back right on D911 (last possible road leading to Biarritz). After 600 m. turn left at camp sign (easy to miss). From A63 autoroute take C4 exit.

Charges 2005

Per unit incl. 2 persons, electricity and water	€ 24,00 - € 39,50
tent pitch incl. 1 or 2 persons	€ 17,50 - € 29,50
child (over 4 yrs)	€ 6,00 - € 7,50

Reservations

Made for exact dates with deposit and fee. Tel: 05 59 23 00 54. E-mail: info@pavillon-royal.com

TRAVEL SERVICE SITE

TO BOOK CALL 0870 405 4055 OR www.alanrogersdirect.com

FR64090 Camping Airotel La Chêneraie

Chemin Cazenave, 64100 Bayonne (Pyrénées-Atlantiques)

La Chêneraie is only eight kilometres from the coast at Anglet with its long sandy beach and large car park, but with the calm and tranquillity of this site you would think you were much further away from all the hustle and bustle of the coast. The distant views of the Pyrénées from various points all add to the feeling of tranquility. There are 210 pitches arranged on neat grass, with most partially divided by trees and shrubs, so quite well shaded. Many have electricity, some with water and drainage. One area is very sloping but it has been terraced to give level pitches. Wooded walks lead to a small lake which can be used for inflatable boats or fishing (no swimming). A tour operator uses 20 pitches.

Facilities

Large, central toilet block with washbasins in cabins, with three smaller blocks around the site providing additional facilities. In high season these facilities may be under pressure and maintenance and cleaning could be variable. Dishwashing and laundry sinks. Washing machine and dryers, baby baths, and facilities for disabled people. Shop, restaurant with all day snacks and takeaway (all main season). Medium sized swimming pool open June - end August (longer if the weather is good). Playground. Tennis courts (free outside July/Aug). TV room. Table tennis. Off site: Bicycle hire 5 km. Riding 6 km. Golf 7 km.

Open

Easter - 30 September (full services 1/6-15/9).

At a glance

Welcome & Ambience	✓✓✓✓	Location	✓✓✓✓
Quality of Pitches	✓✓✓	Range of Facilities	✓✓✓

Directions

Site is 4 km. northeast of Bayonne just off main N117 road to Pau, signed at traffic lights. From new autoroute A63 take exit 6 marked 'Bayonne St Esprit'.

Charges 2004

Per person	€ 3,70 - € 4,40
child (under 10 yrs)	€ 2,15 - € 2,75
pitch	€ 9,45 - € 11,43
with water and electricity	€ 13,75 - € 18,00
tent pitch	€ 7,65 - € 8,85
dog	€ 2,30

Less 10-20% outside 1/6-1/9. No credit cards.

Reservations

Made for min. 1 week with deposit (€ 62) and fee (€ 15.24). Tel: 05 59 55 01 31.

FR64040 Camping Des Gaves

64440 Laruns (Pyrénées-Atlantiques)

Des Gaves is a clean, small and well managed site, open all year, with very friendly owners and staff. It is set high in Pyrennean walking country on one of the routes to Spain. Laruns is only 25 km. from the Spanish border. There are 101 pitches including 50 level touring pitches of which 38 are fully serviced, numbered and separated (the remainder are used for seasonal units). The river runs alongside the site (well fenced) and fishing is possible and the busy little tourist town of Laruns is only a short walk. Tourist information here will suggest many and varied things to do in the area. There are also five delightful wooden chalets to rent.

Facilities

The very clean toilet block has been refurbished, can be heated in cool weather and has modern fittings. Washbasins for ladies in curtained cubicles and one shower in ladies' suitable for showering children. Dishwashing and laundry sinks. Laundry room. No shop but baker calls daily (July/Aug). Small bar with large screen TV, pool and video games (July/Aug). Larger bar with table tennis tables. Small play area. Boules. Volleyball. Fishing. Card operated barrier (€ 20 deposit). Off site: Bicycle hire 800 m.

Open

All year.

At a glance

Welcome & Ambience	✓✓✓✓	Location	✓✓✓✓
Quality of Pitches	✓✓✓	Range of Facilities	✓✓✓

Directions

Take N134 from Pau towards Olorons and branch left on D934 at Gan. Follow to Laruns and just after town, turn left following signs to site.

Charges 2004

Per person	€ 2,90 - € 3,51
child (under 10 yrs)	€ 1,83 - € 2,29
pitch	€ 4,42 - € 9,15
electricity (3-10A)	€ 2,44 - € 3,96
dog	€ 1,68

Reservations

Advised for July/Aug. and winter sports season. Tel: 05 59 05 32 37. E-mail: campingdesgaves@wanadoo.fr

FR64110 Camping du Col d'Ibardin

Mobile homes ▶ page 389

64122 Urrugne (Pyrénées-Atlantiques)

This family owned site at the foot of the Basque Pyrénées is highly recommended and deserves praise. It is well run with emphasis on personal attention, the smiling Madame, her staff and family ensuring that all are made welcome and is attractively set in the middle of an oak wood. Behind the forecourt, with its brightly coloured shrubs and modern reception area, various roadways lead to the 178 pitches. These are individual, spacious and enjoy the benefit of the shade (if preferred a more open aspect can be found). There are electricity hook-ups (4/10A) and adequate water points. From this site you can enjoy the mountain scenery, be on the beach at Socoa within minutes or cross the border into Spain approximately 14 km. down the road. Used by tour operators (20 pitches).

Facilities

Two toilet blocks, one rebuilt to a high specification, are kept very clean. WC for disabled people. Dishwashing facilities in separate open areas. Laundry unit with washing machine and dryer. Motorcaravan service point. Small shop selling basic food and gas, with orders taken for bread (1/7-31/8). Catering and takeaway in July/Aug. Bar and occasional evening entertainment which includes Flamenco dancing. Swimming pool and paddling pool. Children's playground and club with adult supervision. Tennis courts, boules, table tennis, video games. Bicycle hire. A multi-purpose sports area is planned. Not suitable for American motorhomes. Off site: Riding 2 km. Fishing 5 km. Large supermarket and shopping centre 5 km. Golf 7 km.

Open

1 April - 30 September.

At a glance

Welcome & Ambience	✓✓✓✓	Location	✓✓✓✓
Quality of Pitches	✓✓✓✓	Range of Facilities	✓✓✓✓

Directions

Leave A63 autoroute at St Jean-de-Luz sud, exit no. 2 and join the RN10 in the direction of Urrugne. Turn left at roundabout (signed Col d'Ibardin) on the D4 and site is on right after 5 km. Do not turn off to the Col itself, but carry on towards Ascain.

Charges 2004

Per unit incl. 2 persons	€ 12,00 - € 19,50
extra adult	€ 2,60 - € 4,50
child (2-7 yrs)	€ 1,55 - € 2,80
electricity (4/10A)	€ 2,75 - € 5,20
animal	€ 1,00 - € 1,60

Reservations

Are accepted - contact site. Tel: 05 59 54 31 21.
E-mail: info@col-ibardin.com

TO BOOK CALL 0870 405 4055 OR www.alanrogersdirect.com

TRAVEL SERVICE SITE

FR64210 Camping Municipal Chibaou–Berria

64500 St Jean-de-Luz (Pyrénées-Atlantiques)

The first impression of this large site beside the beach is one of neatness. From the entrance tarmac roads lead to spacious pitches which are divided by hedges with plenty of room for awnings. Pitches to the left hand side beyond reception are placed at different levels, whilst those to the right have a sea view. There are 202 pitches in all, all with electrical hook-ups. There is direct access to the beach for surfing and wind-surfing. Nearby are discos, tennis courts and often Basque folk festivities or Corridas with Landes cows.

Facilities

Toilet facilities, spotlessly clean when visited, include some showers with washbasins and individual wash cabins. Toilets are a mix of British and Turkish style. Dishwashing sinks in open position. Laundry facilities including washing machines and ironing room. There are only a few spaces suitable for motorhomes. Unsuitable for American motorhomes and twin axle caravans. The approach road is very narrow.

Open

1 June - 15 September.

At a glance

Welcome & Ambience	✓✓✓✓	Location	✓✓✓✓✓
Quality of Pitches	✓✓✓✓	Range of Facilities	✓✓✓

Directions

From A63 autoroute (St Jean de Luz Nord) take N10 towards Bayonne, then take second left signed Acotz Campings. Site signed in about 1 km. (the first left at Carrefour has a low bridge). From north, 1.5 km. after Geutherey on N10 take right at Carrefour super-marché, signed 'Plages'.

Charges 2004

Per person	€ 5,10
child (under 13 yrs)	€ 3,10
pitch	€ 5,40
electricity	€ 2,90

Reservations

Contact site. Tel: 05 59 26 11 94.

FR64140 Sunêlia Bérrua

Mobile homes page 390

Rue Berrua, 64210 Bidart (Pyrénées-Atlantiques)

Berrua Village Camping, set only 1 km. from the sea, is an ideal location for visiting the beaches here in southwest France. A neat and tidy site, it has 270 level pitches (120 for touring units) set amongst trees. Most places have electricity (6A) and some are fully serviced. The attractive swimming pool has sunbeds around for sunbathing and a paddling pool. A new complex is planned for 2005. There is some animation organised in high season for both adults and children, for example guided walks, dances, sporting competitions, bingo and karaoke. A member of the Sunêlia group.

TRAVEL SERVICE SITE

TO BOOK CALL 0870 405 4055 OR www.alanrogersdirect.com

Facilities

Toilet facilities are good (unisex) consisting of two blocks with washbasins in cabins, baby rooms, facilities for disabled visitors, washing machines and dishwashing sinks (cold water only). Motorcaravan service point. Shop (July/Aug). Bar/restaurant and takeaway (15/4-15/9). Swimming pool. Games room. Play area (3-10 yrs only). Bicycle hire. Archery and boule. Off site: Fishing 1 km. Golf or riding 3 km. Beach 1 km.

Open

6 April - 5 October.

At a glance

Welcome & Ambience	✓✓✓✓	Location	✓✓✓✓
Quality of Pitches	✓✓✓✓	Range of Facilities	✓✓✓✓✓

Directions

From A63 exit 4, take N10 south towards Bidart. At roundabout after the 'Intermarche' supermarket, turn left. Bear right then take next right (site signed).

Charges 2004

Per unit incl. 2 persons	€ 14,50 - € 23,60
extra person	€ 2,95 - € 5,30
child (2-10 yrs)	€ 2,00 - € 3,15
electricity (6A)	€ 2,65 - € 4,00
animal	free - € 4,00

Camping Cheques accepted.

Reservations

Contact site. Tel: 05 59 54 96 66.
E-mail: contact@berrua.com

FR64230 Camping Municipal de Mosqueros

64270 Salies de Bearn (Pyrénées-Atlantiques)

In scenic surroundings convenient for the A64, this 3 star municipal site is worthy of its grading and is attractively located in a parkland situation 1 km. from the pretty little town of Salies de Béarn. It has an immaculate appearance, welcoming wardens and very clean facilities. Tarmac roads lead from the entrance barrier (locked at night), past reception to spacious, numbered pitches. Most have electricity (10A), many have water taps and all are separated by tall shrubs and hedges giving privacy. Salies de Béarn, with its old houses overhanging the river and its thermal baths, is only minutes away.

Facilities

The fully equipped toilet block is in a central position and maintained to a high standard. Dishwashing and laundry area with sinks, washing machine, dryer and iron. TV and recreation room. Off site: Swimming pool (special rates for campers and tennis court adjacent. Golf and riding 2 km.

Open

15 March - 31 October.

At a glance

Welcome & Ambience	✓✓✓✓	Location	✓✓✓✓
Quality of Pitches	✓✓✓✓	Range of Facilities	✓✓✓

Directions

Site is well signed in the town and is on the D17 Bayonne road, west of the town.

Charges 2004

Per person	€ 2,55
child (1-7 yrs)	€ 1,55
pitch	€ 2,50 - € 5,00
electricity	€ 2,50

Reservations

Advisable for July/Aug. Contact site.
Tel: 05 59 38 12 94.

FR64150 Airotel Residence des Pins

Avenue de Biarritz, 64210 Bidart (Pyrénées-Atlantiques)

This is a very pleasant, reasonably priced site which will appeal greatly to couples and young families. Set on a fairly gentle hillside the top level has reception, bar restaurant and behind reception there are some of the pitches, all resonably level. Slightly lower are the paddling and swimming pools in a sunny location with sunbeds. Next comes the well stocked shop, tennis courts and the rest of the pitches. The pitches are all set under tall trees, some slightly sloping and separated by hydranga hedges. There are some electric hookups 10A, long leads required. There is some low key entertainment in July and Aug. There is a little day time road noise but not intrusive. The site is not suitable for American Motorhomes. It is used by tour operators and there are mobile homes around the outer edges of the site. Buses pass the gate.

Facilities

The two toilet blocks have washbasins in cabins, also washbasins and showers together but all are a little on the small side. Washing machines, dryers and ironing boards and full facilities for disabled people. A drive over motor-caravan service point. A games room, table tennis, and tennis to pay in July/Aug. Play area for 3-8 yrs, bike hire. Shop and bar open all season, restaurant and takeaway open 15/7-30/8. Pool open all season. Off site: A lake at 600 m. has fishing (no licence required). Golf 1 km. Riding 1 km. Beach with llifeguard 600 m.

Open

14 May - 30 September.

At a glance

Welcome & Ambience	✓✓✓✓	Location	✓✓✓✓
Quality of Pitches	✓✓✓✓	Range of Facilities	✓✓✓

Directions

Heading south on the A63 towards Spain, take exit J4 onto the N10 towards Bidart. At the roundabout straight after Intermarche turn right towards Biarritz. The site is on the right after 1 km.

Charges year

Per unit with 2 persons	€ 15,30 - € 23,40
extra person (over 2 yrs)	€ 3,10 - € 5,60
electricity	€ 3,10 - € 5,90
dog	free - € 2,30

Camping Cheques accepted.

Reservations

Contact site. Tel: 05 59 23 00 29.
E-mail: lespins@free.fr

FR64070 Castel Camping Le Ruisseau des Pyrénées

Route d'Arbonne, 64210 Bidart (Pyrénées-Atlantiques)

This pleasant, busy site, just behind the coast, is about 2 km. from Bidart and 2.5 km. from a sandy beach. It has two swimming pools - one 1,100 sq.m. pool complex with slides on the main site and an indoor heated pool on the newer area opposite. There is also a little lake, where boating is possible, in the area at the bottom of the site which has a very pleasant open aspect and now includes a large play area. Pitches on the main campsite are individual, marked and of a good size, either on flat terraces or around the lake. The terrain is wooded so the great majority of them have some shade. There are 330 here with a further 110 on a second area where shade has developed and which has its own good toilet block. Electrical connections are available throughout. Animation is provided in the main season, with organised day-time sports and evening entertainment nightly in season. The site is popular with tour operators and the site has a number of its own mobile homes.

Facilities

Toilet facilities (unisex) consist of two main blocks and some extra smaller units. With washbasins in cabins, they are regularly refurbished and maintained. Washing machines. Shop. Large self-service restaurant with takeaway and separate bar with terraces, and TV (all 15/5-12/9). Outdoor swimming pools and indoor pool (15/5-12/9). Sauna and solarium. Large play area. Two tennis courts (free outside July/Aug). Volleyball, table tennis. Fitness track. TV and games rooms. Minigolf. Fitness room. Bicycle hire. Surf board hire. Fishing. Motorhome service point. Internet access. Off site: Riding or golf 2 km.

Open

15 May - 12 September.

At a glance

Welcome & Ambience	✓✓✓✓	Location	✓✓✓✓
Quality of Pitches	✓✓✓✓	Range of Facilities	✓✓✓✓✓

Directions

Site is east of Bidart on a minor road towards Arbonne. From A63 autoroute take Biarritz exit (4), turn towards St Jean-de-Luz and Bidart on N10. After Intermarche turn left at roundabout and follow signs to site.

Charges 2004

Per unit incl. 2 persons	€ 15,00 - € 26,00
extra person	€ 4,50 - € 6,00
child (under 7 yrs)	€ 2,25 - € 3,00
electricity	€ 3,00 - € 4,00
dog	free - € 1,50

Reservations

Made for exact dates, for min. a week or so in main season, with deposit (€ 53.36), fee (€ 9.45) and cancellation insurance (€ 2.74). Tel: 05 59 41 94 50.
E-mail: francoise.dumont3@wanadoo.fr

the travel service

Save Time, **Save Money**

THE LOW COST PITCH AND FERRY RESERVATION SERVICE
FOR READERS OF THE ALAN ROGERS GUIDES

We'll book your preferred campsite(s)
Choose from 150 of the finest inspected and selected sites across Europe (look for the highlighted site descriptions in all Guides). We can even book site-owned mobile homes and chalets (visit www.alanrogersdirect.com or ask for details).

Ask about our incredible Ferry Deals:

- ✓ Caravans GO **FREE**
- ✓ Motorhomes Priced as Cars

We'll organise your low cost Channel crossing - call us for a quote or visit **www.alanrogersdirect.com**

We'll provide comprehensive information
Leave it to the experts and enjoy peace of mind.

Don't leave it to chance,
leave it to us

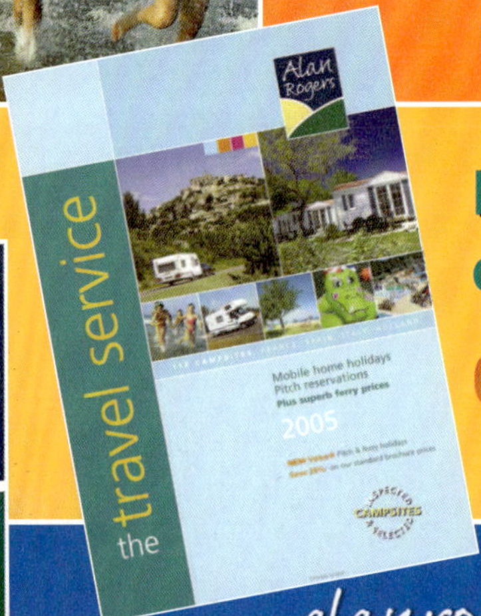

For your FREE colour brochure

0870 405 4055

Alan Rogers

alanrogersdirect.com
book on-line and save

Map 11

The Dordogne is a historical region of great beauty, full of pretty golden-stoned villages and ancient castles. Home to delicacies such as foie gras, truffles and walnuts, plus Roquefort cheese and Cognac, it is one of the gastronomic centres of France.

We have used départements from these official regions to form 'The Dordogne'.
Aquitaine: 24 Dordogne, 47 Lot-et-Garonne
Midi-Pyrénées: 12 Aveyron, 46 Lot
Poitou-Charentes: 16 Charente

The Dordogne's history goes back many thousands of years when man lived in the caves of Périgord and left cave paintings at sites such as Les Eyzies and Lascaux. Aquitaine was ruled by the English for 300 years following the marriage of Eleanor of Aquitaine to Henry Plantagenet, who became King of England in 1154.

The villages and castles of the area bear evidence of the resulting conflict between the French and English, and today add charm and character to the countryside. Monpazier is the best example of the '*bastides*' (fortified towns) and is set in a diverse region of mountains, vineyards, and fertile river valleys. The rolling grass-lands and dense forests include the beautiful valleys of the Dordogne and Vézère.

South of the cultivated fields and cliff-side villages beside the river Lot lie the higher, stony lands of the Quercy Causse and the rocky gorges of the Rivers Aveyron and Tarn. Centred around Millau, there are tortuous gorges and valleys, spectacular rivers, underground caves and grottes, and thickly forested mountains.

Cuisine of the region

Local specialities include the fish dishes: carp stuffed with foie gras, mullet in red wine and *besugo* (sea bream), plus *cagouilles* (snails from Charentes)

Cassoulet: a hearty stew of duck, sausages and beans

Cèpes: fine, delicate mushrooms; sometimes dried

Chou farci: stuffed cabbage, sometimes aux marrons (with chestnuts)

Confit de Canard (d'oie): preserved duck meat

Foie Gras: specially prepared livers of geese and ducks, seasoned and stuffed with truffles

Magret de canard: duck breast fillets

Mouclade: mussels cooked in wine, egg yolks and cream, served with Pineau des Charentes

Places of interest

Agen: rich agricultural area, famous for its prunes

Angoulême: Hill-top town surrouded by ramparts, cathedral, Renaissance château

Cognac: the most celebrated *eau de vie* in the world, cellars, Valois Castle

Cordes: medieval walled hilltop village

Monflanquin: well preserved fortified village

Rocamadour: cliffside medieval pilgrimage site

Saint Cirq-La Popie: medieval village perched on a cliff

Sarlat: Saturday market

Alan Rogers **tip**

LEARN HOW TO COOK THE REGION'S SPECIALITIES AT ONE OF THE MANY COOKERY COURSES OPEN TO VISITORS. ASK THE LOCAL TOURIST OFFICE FOR DETAILS.

FR12150 Camping Marmotel

Mobile homes page 393

12130 St Geniez-d'Olt (Aveyron)

The road into Marmotel passes various industrial buildings and is a little off-putting – persevere, as they are soon left behind. The campsite itself is a mixture of old and new. The old part provides many pitches with lots of shade and separated by hedges. The new area is sunny until the trees grow. These pitches each have a private sanitary unit, with shower, WC, washbasin and dishwashing. New and very well designed, they are reasonably priced for such luxury. All the pitches have electricity (10A). A lovely restaurant has a wide terrace with views of the hills and overlooking the heated swimming and paddling pools. These have fountains, a toboggan and sun beds either on grass or the tiled surrounds. The Lot river runs alongside the site where you can fish or canoe.

Facilities

Good sanitary facilities include baby baths and facilities for disabled visitors. Shower cubicles are a little small. Washing machines. Bar/restaurant and takeaway (all season). Swimming pools. Small play area. Multi-sports area (tennis, volleyball, basketball). Entertainment for all ages in July/Aug. including a disco below the bar, cinema screen, karaoke, dances and a mini club for 4-12 yr olds. Bicycle hire. Fishing. Canoeing. Off site: Large supermarket 500 m. Riding 10 km. Bicycle tours and canoe trips on the Lot and rafting on the Tarn are organised.

Open

1 May - 10 September.

At a glance

Welcome & Ambience	✓✓✓✓	Location	✓✓✓✓
Quality of Pitches	✓✓✓	Range of Facilities	✓✓✓✓✓

Directions

Heading south on autoroute 75 (free) take exit 41 and follow signs for St Geniez d'Olt. Site is at western end of village. Site is signed onto D19 to Prades d'Aubrac, then 500 m. on left.

Charges 2005

Per unit incl. 1 or 2 persons, and 10A electricity	€ 17,00 - € 28,80
extra person	€ 2,90 - € 5,40
child under 4 yrs	€ 1,00 - € 3,10
animal	free - € 1,60

Camping Cheques accepted.
Less 30% outside July/Aug.

Reservations

Made with deposit (€ 100) and fee (€ 16).
Tel: 05 65 70 46 51. E-mail: info@marmotel.com

FR12120 Camping du Rouergue

Avenue de Fondiès, 12200 Villefranche-de-Rouergue (Aveyron)

A spacious and well appointed site in the Vallée de L'Aveyron, Camping du Rouergue is adjacent to the municipal sports facilities. Run by the Rouergue Tourisme Service, the managers are friendly and welcoming. The site has 98 grassy individual pitches of varying sizes, served by tarmac roads, and all serviced with electricity (16A), water and drain. Some pitches are shady. There are reduced rates for campers at the municipal swimming pool and shops and restaurants are within walking distance along the riverside foot and cycle path. Villefranche-de-Rouergue is one of the larger Bastide towns of the region and is on the pilgrim route to Santiago de Compostela. The site is also ideally placed for exploring the many other historical bastides of the Rouergue and Aveyron.

Facilities

The modern spacious sanitary unit includes washbasins in cubicles. Facilities for babies and disabled persons. Dishwashing and laundry sinks. Washing machine. With two identical sections to the block, only one is open during low season. Motorcaravan service point outside campsite entrance. Small bar (June-Oct). TV room. Well equipped playground. Bicycle hire. Off site: Fishing 1 km. Riding 5 km.

Open

17 April - 15 October.

At a glance

Welcome & Ambience	✓✓✓✓✓	Location	✓✓✓✓
Quality of Pitches	✓✓✓✓	Range of Facilities	✓✓✓

Directions

Villefranche de Rouergue is about midway between Cahors and Rodez. Site is 1 km. southwest of town on D47 towards Monteils, follow signs from D911 to campsite and 'Stade'.

Charges 2004

Per pitch incl. 2 persons	€ 10,50 - € 13,50
extra person (over 10 yrs)	€ 2,30
child (4-10 yrs)	€ 1,50
electricity	€ 2,50

Reservations

Advisable for high season, made with 20% deposit.
Tel: 05 65 45 16 24. E-mail: infos@villefranche.com

FR12050 Camping Les Terrasses du Lac

Route du Vibal, 12290 Pont-de-Salars (Aveyron)

At an altitude of some 2,000 ft. on the plateau of Le Lévézou, this outlying site enjoys attractive views over Lac de Pont de Salars. The site seems largely undiscovered by the British, perhaps as it is only open for a short season. A terraced site, it provides 180 good sized, level pitches, 130 for touring, with or without shade, all with electricity. Some pitches have good views over the lake which has direct access from the site at two places - one for pedestrians and swimmers, the other for cars and trailers for launching small boats. This site is well placed for excursions into the Gorges du Tarn, Caves du Roquefort and nearby historic towns and villages. Although there are good facilities for disabled visitors, the terracing on the site may prove difficult.

Facilities

Four toilet blocks of varying ages include some washbasins in private cabins, plus dishwashing areas under cover and laundry facilities. Fridge hire. Shop. Large bar/restaurant with a lively French ambience serving full meals in high season and snacks at other times, with takeaway (all 1/7-31/8). Heated swimming pool (200 sq.m.) and children's pool (1/6-30/9). Solarium. Playground. Volleyball, pétanque, table tennis, billiards. Games and TV rooms. Entertainment and activities organised in high season. Barbecue area. Off site: Tennis 3 km. Riding 5 km. Golf 20 km.

Open

1 April - 30 September.

At a glance

Welcome & Ambience	✓✓✓✓✓	Location	✓✓✓✓
Quality of Pitches	✓✓✓✓	Range of Facilities	✓✓✓✓

Directions

Using D911 Millau - Rodez road, turn north at Pont de Salars towards the lake on the D523. Follow camp signs. Ignore first site and continue following lake until Les Terraces (approx. 5-6 km).

Charges 2005

Per pitch incl. 2 persons	€ 11,00 - € 19,90
extra person	€ 3,50 - € 4,50
child (2-7 yrs)	€ 3,20 - € 3,50
electricity (6A)	€ 3,60 - € 4,50

Reservations

American motorhomes and twin axle caravans must reserve. Made with deposit (€ 61) and fee (€ 15.24). Tel: 05 65 46 88 18. E-mail: terrasses12@aol.com

FR12070 Camping La Grange de Monteillac

Mobile homes ▶ page 391

12310 Séverac-l'Église (Aveyron)

La Grange de Monteillac is a modern, well equipped site in the beautiful, well preserved small village of Sévérac L'Église. A spacious site, it provides 105 individual pitches, 70 for touring, on gently sloping grass, separated by flowering shrubs and young trees offering little shade. All pitches have access to electricity (6A, long leads may be required), water and waste water connections. They include 35 chalets, mobile homes and tents for rent in separate areas. The friendly owner and his welcoming staff will advise about the visits to a château evening with candlelight banquet, an angora farm, and a local pottery that are run weekly in main season. An evening stroll around this delightful village is a must.

Facilities

The toilet block central to the touring area is modern, spacious and clean, with all washbasins in cubicles. Facilities for babies and disabled people. Dishwashing and laundry sinks. Washing machine and dryer. Shop at reception (1/7-31/8). Poolside restaurant/snack-bar serving pizzas, grills etc. and takeaway in high season. Music or groups feature in the bar (July-Aug). Two swimming pools with toilets and changing rooms below (1/6-15/9). Large well equipped playground. Organised activities include children's club, bicycle hire and archery lessons. Off site: Shops in village 1.5 km. Fishing 2 km. Riding 9 km.

At a glance

Welcome & Ambience	✓✓✓	Location	✓✓✓✓
Quality of Pitches	✓✓✓	Range of Facilities	✓✓✓✓

Directions

Site is on the edge of Sévérac L'É glise village, just off N88 Rodez - Sévérac Le Château road. From A75 use exit 42.

Charges 2004

Per unit incl. 2 persons and electricity	€ 21,50
extra person	€ 3,80
child (under 7 yrs)	€ 2,50
Less 30% outside July/Aug.	

Reservations

Contact site. Tel: 05 65 70 21 00.
E-mail: info@la-grange-de-monteillac.com

Open

1 May - 15 September.

FR12170 Sunêlia Le Caussanel

Lac de Parelour, 12290 Canet de Salars (Aveyron)

This large, extremely spacious site on the banks of Lac de Pareloup is greatly improved. It is ideal, in low season, for those seeking a tranquil holiday in a beautiful region of France or in high season, for those seeking an active holiday. It has 235 large, fairly level, grassy pitches, with 169 for touring. Most have 6A electricity (a few have 10A) but very long leads may be necessary, and 33 have water and a drain. The pitches are defined by a tree or boulder in each corner and offer little privacy but many have wonderful views over the lake. Most pitches have little shade with only a few having good shade. The original pool and paddling pool behind reception are quite small and are being replaced with a new pool complex with pools and slides. The adjacent lake offers a large area, 1 km. long, for swimming and all the usual watersports. One tour operator takes 20 pitches.

Facilities

Five well cleaned, modern toilet blocks have all the necessary facilities. Motorcaravan service point (€ 3) at entrance. Shop (limited hours in low season). Bar. Restaurant and takeaway (July/Aug). Swimming pool and paddling pool (from June). New pool complex. Very large play area. Boules. Tennis. Football. Volleyball. Large room for table tennis. TV room and clubhouse. Extensive programme of family events (July/Aug). Fishing. Bicycle hire (July/Aug). Motor boat launching. Various water sports (July/Aug) and swimming in adjacent lake. Internet access. Off site: Cycle and footpaths around the lake. Many other marked walks and cycle rides. Shops, banks, restaurants, etc. 8 km. Riding 10 km. Golf 30 km. Canoeing, rafting, paragliding and windsurfing.

Open

30 April - 24 September.

At a glance

Welcome & Ambience	✓✓✓✓	Location	✓✓✓✓
Quality of Pitches	✓✓✓✓	Range of Facilities	✓✓✓✓✓

Directions

From D911 Rodez - Millau road, just east of Pont de Sellars, turn south on D993 signed Salles-Curan. In about 6 km. at crossroads turn right on D538 signed Le Caussanel. Very shortly turn left and carry straight on to site.

Charges 2005

Per unit incl. 2 persons	€ 13,20 - € 21,10
extra person	€ 4,40 - € 5,40
child (2-7 yrs)	€ 3,20 - € 3,90
electricity	€ 3,10
water and drain	€ 2,40

Camping Cheques accepted.

Reservations

Essential in high season, made with deposit (€ 90) and fee (€ 10). Tel: 05 65 46 85 19.
E-mail: info@lecaussanel.com

FR12040 Castel Camping Les Tours

12460 St Amans-des-Cots (Aveyron)

This is an impressive campsite set in beautiful countryside very close to the Truyère Gorges, Upper Lot valley and the Aubrac Plateau. Efficiently run, it is situated on the shores of the Lac de la Selves. There are 275 pitches of around 100 sq.m. with 6A electrical connections, some bordering the lake, the rest terraced and hedged with views of the lake. About 100 pitches also have individual water points. The site has a spacious feel, enhanced by the thoughtfully planned terraced layout and it is well kept and very clean. The owner and his staff are friendly and helpful. Used by tour operators (70 pitches). There is some up and down walking to the facilities, especially from the upper terraces.

TRAVEL SERVICE SITE

TO BOOK CALL 0870 405 4055 OR www.alanrogersdirect.com

Facilities

Four good toilet blocks including two excellent new ones, one of an unusual round design, are fully equipped including individual washing cubicles and are more than adequate for number of campers. Attractive central complex housing the amenities. Restaurant, bar. Swimming pools (650 and 40 sq.m.). Shop (with gas), Takeaway. Play area. Volleyball, tennis courts, football area and table tennis under cover. Varied programme of daytime and evening activities, with mini-club, archery and tree climbing (all supervised). Lake activities include canoeing, pedaloes, windsurfing, water ski-ing and provision for launching small boats. Internet terminal. Off site: Riding and golf 8 km.

Open

20 May - 9 September.

At a glance

Welcome & Ambience	✓✓✓✓	Location	✓✓✓✓✓
Quality of Pitches	✓✓✓✓	Range of Facilities	✓✓✓✓✓

Directions

Take D34 from Entraygues-sur-Truyère to St Amans-des-Cots (14 km). In St Amans take the D97 to Colombez and then D599 to Lac de la Selves (site signed and is 5 km. from St Amans). Alternatively, from autoroute A75, take St Flour exit and follow D921 south for 41 km. Go 1.5 km. past Lacalm and turn right on D34 signed St Amans-des-Cots. Follow signs for 23 km.

Charges 2004

Per unit incl. 2 persons	€ 20,80 - € 26,50
extra person	€ 4,40 - € 5,50
child (under 7 yrs)	€ 3,00 - € 3,80
electricity	€ 2,40 - € 3,00

Camping Cheques accepted.

Reservations

Advised for July/Aug; contact site.
Tel: 05 65 44 88 10.
E-mail: camping-les-tours@wanadoo.fr

FR12010 Castel Camping Le Val de Cantobre

Mobile homes page 390

12230 Nant-d'Aveyron (Aveyron)

This very pleasant terraced site has been imaginatively and tastefully developed by the Dupond family over a 25 year period. In particular, the magnificent carved features in the bar create a delightful ambience, complemented by a recently built terrace. True, the ground is hard in summer but reception staff supply robust nails if your awning pegs prove a problem. Most of the 200 pitches (all with electricity and water) are peaceful, generous in size and blessed with views of the valley. The pools have a new surround, bedecked by flowers and crowned by a large urn which dispenses water into the paddling pool. But it is the activity programme that is unique at Val de Cantobre, supervised by qualified instructors in July and August, some arranged by the owners and some at a fair distance from the site. Passive recreationists appreciate the scenery, especially Cantobre, a medieval village that clings to a cliff in view of the site. Nature lovers will be delighted to see the vultures wheeling in the Tarn gorge alongside more humble rural residents. Butterflies in profusion, orchids, huge edible snails, glow worms, families of beavers and the natterjack toad all live here. It is easy to see why - the place is magnificent. Although tour operators occupy around 40% of the pitches, the terrace design provides some peace and privacy, especially on the upper levels and a warm welcome awaits from the Dupond family.

Facilities

The impressive, fully equipped toilet block is beautifully appointed with a huge indoor dishwashing area. Laundry. Fridge hire. Shop, although small, offers a wide variety of provisions; including many regional specialities (comparing well with local shops and markets). Attractive bar, restaurant, pizzeria and takeaway facility (some steepish up and down walking from furthest pitches to some facilities). Three adjoining swimming pools. Minigolf. Table tennis. Play area. Around 15 types of activity including river rafting, white water canoeing, rock climbing or jumps from Millau's hill tops on twin seater steerable parachutes. All weather sports pitch. Torch useful. Off site: Fishing 4 km. Riding 15 km. Bicycle hire 25 km.

At a glance

Welcome & Ambience	✓✓✓✓✓	Location	✓✓✓✓✓
Quality of Pitches	✓✓✓✓	Range of Facilities	✓✓✓✓

Directions

Site is 4 km. north of Nant, on D991 road to Millau. From Millau direction take D991 signed Gorge du Dourbie.

Charges 2004

Per unit incl. 2 persons and 4A electricity	€ 19,00 - € 29,00
extra person (4 yrs and over)	€ 4,00 - € 7,00
dog	free - € 2,00

Camping Cheques accepted.

Reservations

Made for any length with 25% deposit, fee (€ 25) and optional cancellation insurance. Tel: 05 65 58 43 00. E-mail: info@valdecantobre.com

Open

14 May - 11 September, with all facilities.

FR12020 Camping Caravaning Les Rivages

Mobile homes page 391

Avenue de l'Aigoual, Route de Nant, 12100 Millau (Aveyron)

Les Rivages is a large site on the outskirts of the town. It is well organised and well situated, being close to the high limestone Causses and the dramatic gorges of the Tarn and Dourbie, the latter of which runs past the back of the site. Smaller pitches, used for tents and small units, abut a pleasant riverside space suitable for sunbathing, fishing or picnics. Most of the 314 pitches are large, 100 sq.m. or more, and well shaded. A newer part of the site (on the right as you enter) has less shade but pitches are larger. All pitches have electricity (6A), and 100 have water and drainage. The site offers a very wide range of sporting activities close to 30 in all (see facilities). Millau is a bustling and pleasant town. Don't miss the night markets, but don't eat before you get there – there are thousands of things to taste, many of them grilled or spit roasted. The gates are shut 10 pm.- 8 am, with night-watchman.

TRAVEL SERVICE SITE

TO BOOK CALL 0870 405 4055 OR www.alanrogersdirect.com

Facilities

Four well kept modern toilet blocks have all necessary facilities. Special block for children with baby baths, small showers and toilets, as well as ironing facilities. Shop for most essentials (1/6-15/9). Terrace restaurant and bar overlooking a good-sized main swimming pool and children's pool (from 10/5). Play area. Much evening entertainment, largely for children, along with child-minding and a mini-club. Tennis (indoor and outdoor). Squash (can be viewed from the bar). Table tennis. Floodlit petanque. Many river activities, walking, bird watching and fishing. Off site: Rafting and canoeing arranged. Bicycle hire 1 km. Riding 10 km. Hypermarket in Millau.

At a glance

Welcome & Ambience	✓✓✓✓✓	Location	✓✓✓✓✓
Quality of Pitches	✓✓✓✓	Range of Facilities	✓✓✓✓

Directions

From Millau, take D991 road south towards Nant. Site is about 400 m. on the right.

Charges 2004

Per pitch incl. 2 persons and electricity	€ 15,50 - € 24,00
with water and drainage	€ 17,50 - € 26,00
extra person (over 3 yrs)	€ 3,00 - € 4,50
pet	free - € 3,00

Reservations

Advisable for July/Aug. with deposit (€ 61) and fee (€ 15,24). Tel: 05 65 61 01 07. E-mail: campinglesrivages@wanadoo.fr

Open

1 May - 30 September.

FR12080 Camping Club Les Genêts

Mobile homes ▶ page 393

Lac de Pareloup, 12410 Salles Curan (Aveyron)

This family run site is on the shores of Lac de Pareloup and offers both family holiday and watersports facilities. The 162 pitches include 102 grassy, mostly individual pitches for touring units. These are in two areas, one on each side of the entrance lane, and are divided by hedges, shrubs and trees. Most have electricity (6A) and many also have water and waste water drain. The site slopes gently down to the beach and lake with facilities for all watersports including waterskiing. A full animation and activities programme is organised in high season, and there is much to see and do in this very attractive corner of Aveyron. The site is not suitable for American style motorhomes. Used by tour operators (25 pitches). A 'Sites et Paysages' member.

Facilities

Two main sanitary units include washbasins in cubicles and a suite for disabled people. Refurbishment of the older unit is planned, whilst the other unit is new. Baby room. Dishwashing and laundry sinks. Laundry room. Very well stocked shop. Bar and restaurant. Snack bar serving pizzas and other snacks in main season. Swimming pool and spa pool (both from 1/6; unsupervised). Playground. Minigolf, volleyball and boules. Bicycle hire. Red Indian style tee-pees. Hire of pedaloes, windsurfers and kayaks. Fishing licences available.

Open

31 May - 11 September.

At a glance

Welcome & Ambience	✓✓✓✓	Location	✓✓✓✓✓
Quality of Pitches	✓✓✓✓	Range of Facilities	✓✓✓✓✓

Directions

From Salles-Curan take D577 for about 4 km. and turn right into a narrow lane immediately after a sharp right hand bend. Site is signed at junction.

Charges 2004

Per unit incl. 1 or 2 persons and 6A electricity	€ 11,00 - € 28,00
lakeside pitch	€ 11,00 - € 36,00
extra person	€ 4,00 - € 6,00
child (under 2 yrs)	free
pet	€ 3,00 - € 4,00

Refundable deposits for barrier card € 20 and for pool bracelet € 8 per person.

Reservations

Advised for July/Aug. and made with deposit (€ 155) and fee (€ 29). Tel: 05 65 46 35 34.
E-mail: contact@camping-les-genets.fr

FR12000 Camping Caravaning de Peyrelade

Route des Gorges du Tarn, 12640 Rivière-sur-Tarn (Aveyron)

Situated at the foot of the Tarn gorges on the banks of the river, this attractive site is dominated by the ruins of the Château de Peyrelade. Bathing from the pebble beach is safe and the water is clean. The 130 touring pitches are terraced, level and shady with 6A electricity hook-ups (long leads may be required for the riverside pitches) and nearby water points. The site is ideally placed for visiting the Tarn, Jonte and Dourbie gorges, and centres for rafting and canoeing are a short drive up the river. Other nearby attractions include the Caves of Aven Armand, the Chaos de Montpellier, Roquefort (of cheese fame) and the pleasant town of Millau. Many of the roads along and between the Gorges are breath-taking for passengers, but scaring for drivers who won't like looking down!

Facilities

The two toilet blocks have been refurbished. Young children are catered for, also people with disabilities. Washing machines and dryer. Bar, restaurant, pizzeria and takeaway (all from 1/6). Paddling pool and attractively designed swimming pool (proper swimming trunks, no shorts). Good playground. Games room and mini-club. Fishing. Off site: Bicycle hire 100 m. Riding 3 km. Facilities in the adjacent leisure centre (reduced charge). Millau nearby with hypermarket, shops and night markets but note road to/from Millau can be jammed at peak hours.

Open

15 May - 15 September.

At a glance

Welcome & Ambience	✓✓✓✓	Location	✓✓✓✓
Quality of Pitches	✓✓✓	Range of Facilities	✓✓✓✓

Directions

Take autoroute A75 to Séverac. From N9 Séverac - Millau road, turn east from Aguessac on D907 (follow Gorges du Tarn signs). Site is 2 km. past Rivière sur Tarn, on the right - the access road is quite steep.

Charges 2005

Per unit incl. 2 persons	€ 14,00 - € 21,00
extra person	€ 3,50 - € 5,00
child (under 5 yrs)	€ 2,00 - € 3,00
electricity (6A)	€ 3,00
dog	€ 1,50

Reservations

Made with deposit (€ 84) and fee (€ 16).
Tel: 05 65 62 62 54.
E-mail: campingpeyrelade@wanadoo.fr

FR12190 Camping Les Calquières

17 avenue Jean Moulin, 12150 Sévérac le Château (Aveyron)

This site is ideally situated, as it is only three kilometres from the free A75 autoroute and makes an excellent short stay for those on route to the south. It would also be a good base for those wishing to visit the nearby Cévennes National Park with its beautiful and rugged scenery. This quiet, neat, family run site nestles below the old village and medieval château and close to the lower part of the town, all within easy walking distance of the site. There are spectacular views from the Château, floodlit at night. There are 97 good sized, level, grassy pitches mostly separated by a variety of hedges with maturing trees providing some shade. All have electricity (6A).

Facilities

Two good toilet blocks, one built in 2003 to a very high standard. They contain all the necessary facilities, including those for disabled visitors, and were very clean when visited. Off site: Adjacent municipal swimming pool (July/Aug) and tennis , both free to campers. Lower part of Sévérac le Château (1 km) with a small range of shop. Old, upper part of the town, with Château, other shops etc, is a similar distance but is a good climb. Riding 1 km. Fishing 800 m.

Open

1 April - 30 September.

At a glance

Welcome & Ambience	✓✓✓✓	Location	✓✓✓✓
Quality of Pitches	✓✓✓	Range of Facilities	✓✓✓

Directions

From A75 exit 42, at roundabout, take N9 signed Sévérac le Château. Shortly turn hard right (N88) and at crossroads straight on, signed Centre Ville and Gare. At station roundabout turn left and follow road beside the railway through the town. Turn left at camp sign and immediately left again.

Charges 2004

Per unit incl. 2 persons	€ 9,20 - € 11,20
extra person	€ 3,00
child (0-7 yrs)	€ 2,00
electricity (6A)	€ 2,50

Reservations

Not needed. Tel: 05 65 47 64 82.

FR12160 Camping Caravaning Les Peupliers

Mobile homes page 394

Route des Gorges du Tarn, 12640 Rivière-sur-Tarn (Aveyron)

Les Peupliers is a friendly, family site on the banks of the Tarn river. Most of the good-sized pitches have shade, and all have electricity, water and a waste water point. The river has a landing place for canoes and a small beach. In a lovely, sunny situation is the swimming pool with a paddling pool and sun beds, all protected by a beautifully clipped hedge and with a super view to the surrounding hills and the Chateau du Preylarde perched above the village. The site has its own canoes (to hire). Some English is spoken. A treat for us at dusk was to watch beavers playing on the river bank.

Facilities

Large, light and airy toilet facilities are a good provision with adjustable showers, washbasins in cubicles and mainly British style WCs. Good baby facilities with baths, showers and WCs. Facilities for disabled visitors. Washing machines. Shop (1/6-30/9). Bar with TV and internet point. Snack bar and takeaway (1/5-30/9). Swimming pool (from 1/5). Games and competitions organised in July/Aug. Fishing. Volleyball, football, badminton. Play area. Above reception is a balcony with fitness equipment. Play area. Weekly dances organised in July/Aug. Canoe hire. Off site: Village with shops and restaurant 300 m. Riding 0.5 km. Bicycle hire 2 km. Golf 25 km.

Open

1 April - 30 September.

At a glance

Welcome & Ambience	✓✓✓✓	Location	✓✓✓✓
Quality of Pitches	✓✓✓✓	Range of Facilities	✓✓✓✓

Directions

Heading south from Claremot Ferrand to Milau on the A75 autoroute, take exit 44 signed Aguessac and Gorges du Tarn. In Aguessac follow signs to Rivière-sur-Tarn (5 km. away) and site is clearly indicated.

Charges 2004

Per person	€ 5,00 - € 7,00
child (under 5 yrs)	€ 2,00 - € 3,00
pitch	€ 4,00 - € 6,00
electricity (6A)	€ 3,00
dog	€ 1,50

Camping Cheques accepted.

Reservations

Made with deposit (€125) and fee (€25).
Tel: 05 65 59 85 17.
E-mail: lespeupliers12640@wanadoo.fr

FR16050 Camping Municipal de Cognac

Boulevard de Châtenay, Route de Ste-Sévère, 16100 Cognac (Charente)

If you are a lover of brandy this area is a must, with abundant vineyards and little roadside chalets offering tastings of Pineau (a Cognac based aperitif) and a vast range of Cognacs. This municipal site by the Charente river is convenient as a night stop or longer stay to visit the area, and for sleeping off the effects of the 'tastings' - you probably won't even notice the slight noise from the nearby road! The 175 large pitches, all with electricity, are neatly laid out and separated by shrubs and trees. The famous Cognac Houses (Pineau, Hennessy, Hine, Martell, Remy Martin, etc.) and the Cognac Museum may be visited. There is public transport to the town centre (daily July/Aug; Saturdays only at other times).

Facilities

Two fairly modern toilet blocks have mixed British and Turkish style WCs, including children's toilets, washbasins in cabins, dishwashing and laundry sinks and a washing machine. Cleaning can be variable. Motorcaravan services. Small swimming pool on site (municipal pool nearby). Snack bar and entertainment (1/7-15/9). Fishing. Volleyball. Table tennis. Play area on grass. Off site: Bicycle hire 2 km. Riverside walks. Restaurants, bars and shops in the town (2.3 km). Golf 5 km. Riding 6 km.

Open

1 May - 15 October.

At a glance

Welcome & Ambience	✓✓✓	Location	✓✓✓✓
Quality of Pitches	✓✓✓	Range of Facilities	✓✓✓✓

Directions

Site is signed from N141 Saintes - Angoulême road following signs for town centre. It is to the north of the town beside the river on the D24 to Boutiers and Ste-Sévère.

Charges guide

Per pitch incl. 2 persons	€ 10,00 - € 11,00
extra person	€ 3,00
child (0-7 yrs)	€ 2,00

Less for stays over 3 days.

Reservations

No reservations taken. Write for more information to Office de Tourisme de Cognac, 16 Rue du 14 Juillet, 16100 Cognac. Tel: 05 45 36 55 36 Fax: 0545 32 15 82 Tel: 05 45 36 55 36. E-mail: camping@cc-cognac.fr

FR16060 Camping Marco de Bignac

Lieudit 'Les Sablons', 16170 Bignac (Charente)

The small village of Bignac is set in peaceful countryside not too far from the N10 road, north of Angoulême. Since buying the campsite in 1994, the Marshall family have worked hard to improve this tranquil site which is arranged along one side of an attractive lake on a level, grassy meadow. The 89 pitches are marked at each corner by a tree so there is shade, and electricity (3/6A) is available. At the far end of the site is a hedged swimming pool and plenty of grassy space for ball games. The lake shores are home to ducks and the lake itself is used for fishing and small boats. The reception office is part of the owner's home and near to it is a bar, snack bar and restaurant with tables outside and views across the lake. This site is popular with British visitors and is a peaceful, relaxing location for couples or young families. There is no noisy entertainment and all the activities are free of charge.

Facilities

Two traditional style toilet blocks have functional facilities all in cabins opening from the outside. British style WCs. Washing machine. Bar and snack bar (1/6-31/8; closed Mon. until high season). Essentials kept in the bar and baker calls daily (high season). Swimming pool (15/6-31/8, unsupervised). Football field, badminton, tennis, table tennis, pedaloes, minigolf a boule pitch and fishing, all free. Library. Play area. Pets corner. Special evenings, outings and competitions organised in high season. A torch may be useful. Off site: Riding 5 km. Bicycle hire 10 km. Golf 25 km.

At a glance

Welcome & Ambience	✓✓✓✓	Location	✓✓✓✓✓
Quality of Pitches	✓✓✓✓	Range of Facilities	✓✓✓✓

Directions

From N10 south of Poitiers, 14 km. north of Angoulême, take D11 west to Vars and Basse. Where you turn right onto D117 to Bignac. Site is signed at several junctions and in village (Camping Bignac).

Charges 2005

Per pitch incl. 2 persons	€ 13,00 - € 19,00
extra person	€ 3,00 - € 5,00
electricity (3/6A)	€ 2,50 - € 4,00

Reservations

Made with deposit (€ 30). Tel: 05 45 21 78 41. E-mail: camping.marcodebignac@wanadoo.fr

Open

15 May - 15 September.

FR16030 Camping Municipal Le Champion

16230 Mansle (Charente)

Le Champion is a convenient stop-over from the N10 or a good base to explore the northern Charente area. Beside the Charente river, the site has a cool, relaxing atmosphere created by its attractive location and the entrance and reception are decorated with flowers. The site, with 120 average sized, separated pitches, is mostly open with little shade. All pitches have electricity (16A) and 15 have water points. A privately owned restaurant is at the site entrance, attractively canopied for 'al fresco' eating and another outlet sells snacks. Information on opportunities for cycling, walking, canoeing or fishing is available from reception with several guides and maps of suggested routes for sale. There is some road noise from the N10.

Facilities

The main modern sanitary block is well maintained and provides some washbasins in cabins and facilities for disabled people. Dishwashing and laundry areas and a small washing machine. An additional smaller, older block is in the tenting area at the rear of the site. Motorcaravan service point at entrance. Minigolf. Volleyball. Petanque. English spoken. Off site: Restaurant and snacks outside site. Town with its Roman bridge. Tourist office 500 m. Swimming pool in town (discount for campers), recreation area next to the site.

At a glance

Welcome & Ambience	✓✓✓✓	Location	✓✓✓✓
Quality of Pitches	✓✓✓	Range of Facilities	✓✓✓

Directions

Site is well signed off the N10 (in the town of Mansle), 30 km. north of Angoulême.

Charges 2004

Per adult	€ 2,10
child (under 7 yrs)	€ 1,10
pitch incl. car	€ 6,20 - € 10,50
electricity	€ 2,50

Reservations

Bookings accepted without deposit, although not usually necessary. Tel: 05 45 20 31 41.

Open

15 May - 15 September.

FR16020 Castel Camping les Gorges du Chambon

Eymouthiers, 16220 Montbron (Charente)

A welcoming and friendly, family site in pretty, rolling Périgord Vert countryside, Gorges du Chambon is arranged around a restored Charente farmhouse and its outbuildings. It provides an attractive, spacious setting with 120 large, marked pitches with electrical connections. On gently sloping grass and enjoying extensive views over the countryside, the pitches are arranged in two circular groups with a sanitary block at the centre of each. The site also offers canoe hire on the river and a footpath has been created to the river with two beaches where swimming is possible. A converted barn provides an interesting gallery arrangement in the restaurant/bar. The site owners are very helpful.

Facilities

Traditional style, unisex blocks include washbasins in private cabins, facilities for disabled people, a baby bath, laundry sinks, washing machine and tumble dryer, and good dishwashing rooms. Reception stocks some basic supplies and bread can be ordered the day before. Bar and restaurant (good food, well priced), plus takeaway including pizzas (all season). Swimming pool (18 x 7 m) and children's pool. Children's play area. Games room, TV and table tennis. Tennis, archery and minigolf, bicycle and canoe hire. Animation is organised in July/Aug. including a children's club, youth disco and teenagers' corner. Dogs are not accepted. Off site: Fishing and riding within 200 m. Golf 4 km. Visits are organised to local producers and day trips (low season).

At a glance

Welcome & Ambience	✓✓✓✓✓	Location	✓✓✓✓✓
Quality of Pitches	✓✓✓✓	Range of Facilities	✓✓✓✓

Directions

From N141 Angoulême - Limoges road at Rochefoucauld take D6 to Montbron village. Follow D6 in direction of Piegut-Pluviers and site is signed down country road past holiday complex.

Charges 2004

Per person	€ 3,50 - € 5,60
child (1-7 yrs)	free - € 2,60
pitch	€ 5,00 - € 7,00
vehicle	€ 1,50 - € 2,10
electricity (6A)	€ 3,20

Camping Cheques accepted.

Reservations

Necessary for July/Aug; contact site quoting Alan Rogers. Tel: 05 45 70 71 70.
E-mail: gorges.chambon@wanadoo.fr

Open

10 April - 25 September.

FR24000 Camping La Tuilière

St Rémy-sur-Lidoire, 24700 Montpon Ménestérol (Dordogne)

La Tuilière is a traditional and spacious site, run by a family with lots of activities for children. With a small lake, 100 pitches are arranged on a gently sloping hillside. Most pitches are reasonably level with some shade and there are 75 with electricity, although long leads may be needed. The small unfenced lake, where there is play equipment, can be used for fishing and water games. This is a typical French site with very friendly owners. St Rémy is in the western Dordogne (less crowded), not far from Ste Foy la Grande, and well positioned to visit the wine areas of St Emilion, Pomerol and Bergerac.

Facilities

Two modern toilet blocks are very clean and include some washbasins in cubicles. Baby room and unit for disabled visitors. Laundry facilities. Small shop and attractively furnished bar/restaurant for lunches and evening meals (all 1/7-31/8), overlooking the swimming pool and paddling pool. Jacuzzi. Good play area and tennis court. Archery, minigolf, table tennis and pool tables. Dances, tournaments and karaoke nights arranged in July/Aug. Off site: Riding 3 km. Supermarket 5 km. Bicycle hire.

Open

1 May - 15 September.

At a glance

Welcome & Ambience	✓✓✓✓✓	Location	✓✓✓✓✓
Quality of Pitches	✓✓✓✓	Range of Facilities	✓✓✓✓

Directions

From the north on D708 Montpon-Ménestérol to Ste Foy-la Grande road, site is 5 km. south of Montpon on the right. From the south site is 1.5 km. north of St Rémy on the D708 (on the left).

Charges 2004

Per person	€ 2,50 - € 3,10
child (under 7 yrs)	€ 1,60 - € 2,00
pitch	€ 3,60 - € 4,50
electricity (5-10A)	€ 2,30 - € 3,10
animal	€ 1,00 - € 1,20

Less 20% in low season.

Reservations

Made with € 10 deposit. Tel: 05 53 82 47 29.
E-mail: la-tuiliere@wanadoo.fr

FR24010 Castel Camping Château Le Verdoyer

Mobile homes page 394

Champs Romain, 24470 St Pardoux (Dordogne)

Le Verdoyer is a Dutch, family-owned site developed in the park of a restored château. We particularly like this site for its beautiful buildings and lovely surroundings. It is situated in this lesser known area of the Dordogne sometimes referred to as the Périgord Vert, with its green forests and small lakes. The 37 acre estate has two such lakes, one in front of the Château for fishing and one accessed by a footpath, with sandy beach and safe swimming area. There are 150 marked, level, terraced pitches (some a little rocky). Mostly of a good size (100-150 sq.m), all have electricity (5/10A), with a choice of wooded area or open field, where hedges have been planted and have grown well; 120 are 'confort' pitches with more planned. There is a swimming pool complex and in high season activities are organised for children (5-13 yrs) but there is definitely no disco! The courtyard area between reception and the bar is home to evening activities, and provides a pleasant place to enjoy drinks and relax. The Château itself has rooms to let and its excellent lakeside restaurant is also open to the public. Used by a Dutch tour operator (15 pitches).

Facilities

Recently completely renewed, three very well appointed toilet blocks include washbasins in cabins, facilities for disabled people and baby baths. Serviced launderette. Motorcaravan service point. Fridge rental. Multi-purpose shop with gas. Bar (with snacks and takeaway) and restaurant, both open all season (and also open to the public). Good value bistro serving meals (July/Aug). Two pools (25 x 10 m. and 10 x 7 m; the smaller one can be covered in low season), slide (36 m. long) and paddling pool. Play areas. All-weather tennis court. Volleyball, basketball and badminton. Table tennis. Minigolf. Bicycle hire (tennis and bicycles free in low season). Small library.
Off site: Riding 3 km.

At a glance

Welcome & Ambience	✓✓✓✓✓	Location	✓✓✓✓✓
Quality of Pitches	✓✓✓✓	Range of Facilities	✓✓✓✓

Directions

Site is 2 km. from the Limoges (N21) - Chalus (D6bis-D85) - Nontron road, 20 km. south of Chalus and is well signed from the main road. Site is on the D96 about 4 km. north of village of Champs Romain.

Charges 2004

Per unit incl. 2 persons and electricity	€ 18,00 - € 29,00
extra adult	€ 5,00 - € 6,00
child (under 4 yrs)	free
dog	free - € 3,00

Camping Cheques accepted.
Between 9/7-20/8 stay 14 nights, pay for twelve.

Reservations

Write to site. Tel: 05 53 56 94 64.
E-mail: chateau@verdoyer.fr

Open

23 April - 15 October.

FR24330 Camping de l'Etang Bleu

24340 Vieux-Mareuil (Dordogne)

Set halfway between the historic towns of Perigueux and Angoulême, this tranquil countryside site in a mature woodland setting has recently been acquired by enthusiastic British owners Mark and Jo Finch. The site has 169 pitches, with 108 available to touring units. The remainder are taken up by two small tour operators and site owned mobile homes and ready erected tents for rent. The pitches are of a good size, flat and grassy, with mature hedging and trees providing privacy and plenty of shade. All pitches have water and 90 have electricity (10/16A). At the bottom of the site is a fishing lake stocked with carp (no permit required), and various woodland walks start from the campsite grounds. The bright and cheerful 'bistro bar' provides good value food and drinks, and becomes a focal point for evening socialising on site. This site is ideal for couples or families with young children who are looking for a quiet and relaxing holiday away from the hustle and bustle of the busiest tourist areas, but still within reach of some of the area's major towns.

Facilities

Two modern, clean and well maintained toilet blocks provide mostly British style toilets, washbasins (some in cubicles), showers, facilities for babies and disabled people. Laundry. Dishwashing facilities. Small playground with paddling pool. Swimming pool (20m x 10m) with sun terrace and loungers. Pleasant bar and terrace with 'bistro' food (all season), Takeaway. Small shop (items not stocked can be ordered on request). Table tennis, boules. Canoe and bicycle hire. Various entertainments, sporting activities and excursions organised in high season. (Floodlit tennis court, minigolf and adventure type playground are planned for summer 2004). Off site: Restaurant - Auberge de L'Etang Bleu - adjacent to campsite, small supermarket, post office etc. in Mareuil (7 km).

Open

18 March - 18 October.

At a glance

Welcome & Ambience	✓✓✓✓	Location	✓✓✓✓
Quality of Pitches	✓✓✓✓	Range of Facilities	✓✓✓✓

Directions

From Angoulême take D939 south, from Perigueux take D939 north. From either direction after about 45 km. the village of Vieux Mareuil is signed on north side of the road. Turn here on D93, and follow narrow road through the village. Just after leaving village site is signed on right, just past Auberge de L'Etang Bleu. Follow signs down long gravel drive to site entrance. NOTE: American-style motorhomes and larger caravans may find it easier to access site by taking the D708 Mareuil - Nontron road, and turning south on the D93, avoiding the narrow access roads in Vieux Mareuil village.

Charges 2004

Per adult	€ 3,50 - € 5,00
child (2-7 yrs)	€ 2,00
pitch	€ 6,00 - € 7,00
with electricity	€ 7,50 - € 11,00
pet	€ 3,00

Less 30% in low seasons.

Reservations

Advisable for high season. Tel: 05 53 60 92 70.
E-mail: marc@letangbleu.com

FR24060 Camping Le Paradis

St Léon-sur-Vézère, 24290 Montignac (Dordogne)

Le Paradis is an exceptionally attractive riverside site, halfway between Les Eyzies and Montignac. Well placed for exploring the Dordogne and its prehistoric grottos and other sites, the site is very well kept and laid out with mature shrubs and bushes of different types. It has 200 individual pitches of good size on flat grass, divided by trees and shrubs (139 for touring units). All have electricity, most also have water and drainage, and there are some special pitches for motorcaravans. Canoeing on the Vézère river starts from steps which give comfortable access to the riverside, adjacent to a small beach. The site welcomes a good quota of British and Dutch clients, many through a tour operator. Organised games, competitions and evening events are aimed at maintaining a true French flavour. English is spoken. This is a site of real quality, which we thoroughly recommend.

Facilities

Two unisex toilet blocks are of outstanding quality and fully equipped. They can be heated, have baby baths and toilets, extensive laundry facilities and even outside showers for swimmers. Well stocked shop (with gas). Restaurant with extensive choice of menu with good takeaway service. Very good pool complex heated in low season, with a large deep pool (25 x 10 m), a smaller shallower one (17 x 7 m), plus a paddling pool. Two tennis courts. Football, BMX track, volleyball, table tennis and pool activities. Canoe hire. Fishing. Bicycle hire. Well designed playground. Off site: Riding 2 km. Various trips organised to surrounding area.

At a glance

Welcome & Ambience	✓✓✓✓	Location	✓✓✓✓
Quality of Pitches	✓✓✓✓	Range of Facilities	✓✓✓✓✓

Directions

Site is 12 km. north of Les Eyzies and 3 km. south of St Léon-sur-Vézère, on the east side of the D706.

Charges 2004

Per person	€ 4,90 - € 6,95
pitch	€ 7,60 - € 10,90
electricity (6A)	€ 3,00

Camping Cheques accepted.
Low season reductions. 10% discount for pensioners in low seasons.

Reservations

Made for any length with deposit (€ 80) and fee (€ 20). Tel: 05 53 50 72 64.
E-mail: le-paradis@perigord.com

Open

26 March - 25 October.

FR24250 Camping Les Tourterelles

24390 Tourtoirac (Dordogne)

This is a site with its own equestrian centre that will appeal to lovers of the countryside, in an area that is ideal for walking or horse riding. The adjacent riding stables with 30 horses is run by the owner's daughter Angélique. The horses have been selected to be ideal for the local terrain, and to be safe and dependable. There are 125 pitches in total, but the site has some chalets, bungalows and mobile homes which leaves around 87 grassy pitches for tourists. These are on several different levels most with good shade from mature trees, and all have electricity hook-ups (6A).

Facilities

Three good, fully equipped toilet blocks, one new provides a baby unit. Laundry. Bread can be ordered. Bar/restaurant serving good value meals, with takeaway. Freezer pack service. Swimming pool (20 x 10 m.) and paddling pool. Riding. Tennis, volleyball, badminton, table tennis. Animation programme in main season. Off site: Shop at Tourtoirac 1 km. Fishing 1 km. Supermarket at Excideuil.

Open

16 April - 30 September.

At a glance

Welcome & Ambience	✓✓✓✓	Location	✓✓✓✓
Quality of Pitches	✓✓✓✓	Range of Facilities	✓✓✓✓

Directions

From Limoges take D704 to St Yrieux (70 km. south), Lanouaille and Cherveix-Cubas. Just after Cherveix-Cubas turn right in village on D5 to Tourtoirac. Fork left on D73 towards Coulaures; site is on left in 1 km.

Charges 2005

Per person	€ 3,20 - € 3,80
pitch	€ 8,85 - € 10,75
electricity	€ 3,50

No credit cards.

Reservations

Advised for July/Aug; contact site.
Tel: 05 53 51 11 17. E-mail: les-tourterelles@tiscali.fr

FR24280 Camping de Barnabé

Rue des Bains, 24750 Perigeux (Dordogne)

A memorable site in a unique setting, Barnabé has a special ambience. A distinctive 1936 Art Deco style building houses the reception, bar, restaurant and games room, complete with an attractive terrace overlooking the River L'Isle, in the style of the old 'Café de Paris'. The bar has its own Wurlitzer juke box. This site has 56 pitches all for touring vans and with access to electricity (4/6A). About twelve pitches also have water and drainage. Pitches are in four areas, with 42 pitches on one side of the river. The other 14 are in an annexe on the opposite side and use a separate entrance. Pedestrian access between the two parts of the site is provided by an old fashioned, passenger operated ferry boat – a delightful way to cross the river. The entrance and access roads are a little narrow, and large units need to take great care.

Facilities

Six sanitary buildings around the site (one on the far side of the river). Not modern, but functional, simple and clean with spacious shower cubicles. Unisex facilities, with both British and Turkish style toilets (no paper). One heated block is open in winter. Off site: Périgeux town centre 2 km.

Open

All year.

At a glance

Welcome & Ambience	✓✓✓	Location	✓✓✓✓
Quality of Pitches	✓✓✓	Range of Facilities	✓✓✓✓

Directions

From the west of town, at N2089 and N221 round-about, take exit for 'centre ville'. Follow under bridge and up hill. Keep right and turn right at lights. From the east follow 'Brive' signs, cross river and in 1.5 km. turn left. Site is signed after 400 m. to the right.

Charges 2005

Per person	€ 3,50
pitch	€ 5,00 - € 5,40
electricity (4/6A)	€ 2,60 - € 2,95

Reservations

Contact site for details. Tel: 05 53 53 41 45.
E-mail: contact@barnabe-perigord.com

FR24160 Camping Le Grand Dague

Atur, 24750 Périgueux (Dordogne)

Le Grand Dague is a good quality site only a few miles from Périgueux and yet in an extremely rural and tranquil setting. The spacious, clean and attractive site has 93 pitches (68 for touring units). All have electricity (6A), and are divided by tall, mature hedging. Several large, open grassy areas provide plenty of space for youngsters. The Dutch owners have a passion for motorcycling, the 'Harley Davidson' themed campsite bar bearing witness to this! There are no tour operators. A 'Sites et Paysages' member.

Facilities

Excellent sanitary facilities provide mostly unisex facilities. Washbasins in cubicles, baby room and facilities for disabled people. Small shop for essentials (15/6-30/9). Attractive restaurant, bar and takeaway (all from June). Swimming pool, slide and paddling pool (from early May). Football, volleyball, badminton, minigolf and table tennis. Play area. Fishing. Bicycle hire. Off site: Riding 5 km. Golf 10 km.

Open

Easter - 30 September.

At a glance

Welcome & Ambience	✓✓✓✓	Location	✓✓✓
Quality of Pitches	✓✓✓✓	Range of Facilities	✓✓✓✓

Directions

From N89 Périgueux bypass or Périgueux town centre take D2 towards Atur. On reaching the village turn east on minor road (the turn is fairly sharp). Follow signs along this road for 3 km. to site.

Charges 2004

Per person	€ 4,25 - € 5,75
pitch	€ 4,95 - € 7,25
electricity (6A)	€ 3,25

Reservations

Advised for high season and made with deposit (€ 136) and fee (€ 23). Tel: 05 53 04 21 01.
E-mail: info@legranddague.fr

FR24300 Camping La Rivière Fleurie

St Aulaye de Breuilh, 24230 St Antoine de Breuilh (Dordogne)

This quiet and pleasant campsite is close to the vineyards of Pomerol and St Emilion, and not far from the extensive shopping of St Foy la Grande and Bergerac. The 60 pitches are all spacious, divided by shrubs, and maturing trees are beginning to provide shade on many. All pitches have electricity (4A and 10A) There are no tour operators, but 8 pitches are used for site owned mobile homes, and there are also studio apartments to let throughout the year. The site has a tranquil and peaceful ambience, suitable for anyone looking for a quiet and relaxing holiday.

Facilities

Sanitary facilities are plentiful and modern. Bar and terrace restaurant serving a range of basic meals. Swimming pool (100 sq.m) and toddlers' pool. Football, volleyball, table tennis, table football and TV room. Weekly 'soirées' where the owners host an evening of French food and entertainment. Bicycle hire. Canoe trips arranged. Off site: Municipal tennis court adjacent (free to campers). Fishing 100 m. Riding 4 km. Bicycle hire 8 km.

Open

1 April - 30 September.

At a glance

Welcome & Ambience	✓✓✓✓	Location	✓✓✓✓
Quality of Pitches	✓✓✓✓	Range of Facilities	✓✓✓✓

Directions

Site is in the hamlet of St Aulaye, about 3 km. south of the D936 Bordeaux – Bergerac road. Site is signed at two points off the D936 down local roads, one 6 km. east of Lamothe-Montravel, the other at the western end of St Antoine de Breuilh. Follow 'camping' signs along either road until you come to the river, and site is 500 m.

Charges 2004

Per unit incl. 2 persons	€ 12,80 - € 16,00
extra person	€ 4,00 - € 5,00
child (under 7 yrs)	€ 2,80 - € 3,50
animal	€ 1,44 - € 1,80
electricity	€ 2,90 - € 4,00

Reservations

Advised for July/August. Deposit of 30% (sterling cheques accepted as deposit). Tel: 05 53 24 82 80. E-mail: info@la-riviere-fleurie.com

FR24070 Camping Lestaubière

Pont St Mamet, 24140 Douville (Dordogne)

Set just off the main N21 road near Pont St Mamet, mid-way between Bergerac and Perigueux this quiet and charming campsite is well situataed for exploring the western side of the Dordogne and the Bergerac vineyards. There are 90 pitches, mostly on fairly flat, shaded wooded ground at the top of the site, with some on more sloping open meadow with views across the valley. Pitches are marked and all have electrical connections (4/10A) although long leads may be necessary for some pitches. The swimming pool and small lake with diving platform and beach encourage longer stays. A pleasant, shaded patio terrace under vines and maples leads to a general room with a bar and a separate room for young people with amusement machines. There are many British and Dutch visitors, but no tour operators. Good English is spoken by the friendly Dutch owners.

Facilities

Two toilet blocks include some washbasins in private cabins in the larger block. Baby baths and large family shower room. Ample dishwashing and laundry sinks. No facilities for disabled visitors. Small shop. Bar. Library. Swimming pool (unsupervised) and paddling pool. Excellent adventure style play area. Volleyball, boules and fishing. Occasional organised activities. Off site: Tennis 500 m.

Open

1 May - 1 October.

At a glance

Welcome & Ambience	✓✓✓✓	Location	✓✓✓✓
Quality of Pitches	✓✓✓	Range of Facilities	✓✓✓

Directions

Site is 19 km. north east of Bergerac. From N21 Bergerac - Perigueux road take the exit for Pont St Mamet. The site is 500 m. north of the village, on the eastern side of the road, and is well signed. After you turn off the main road at this point the site entrance is almost immediately on you left.

Charges guide

Per person	€ 4,60 - € 5,20
child (under 7)	€ 2,80 - € 3,30
pitch	€ 5,10 - € 6,90
electricity (4/10A)	€ 2,70 - € 4,00

Reservations

Advised for July and August. No deposit and booking fee. Tel: 05 53 82 98 15. E-mail: lestaubiere@cs.com

FR24290 Camping Le Moulin du Bleufond

Avenue Aristide Briand, 24290 Montignac (Dordogne)

Built on flat ground around a 17th century mill, this converted and improved former municipal site has its own pool as well as adjacent town facilities for various sports. The 84 pitches (66 for touring units) are marked and divided by mature hedges, all have electricity and most have some shade. Some pitches are quite small, so it is best to ensure when booking that you ask for one of the larger ones (in excess of 100 sq.m). Owners of the very largest caravans or motorhomes may need to think again. Montignac is at the head of what is to become a World Heritage site - the Vezère valley houses some of the planet's most important prehistoric caves and grottoes, with the Lascaux complex only minutes away. Although the original cave is now closed to the public, the replica Lascaux II is nearby. A third major cave system was discovered earlier this year. The site is separated from the river by a reasonably quiet road, but there is a sizeable bank for fishing. This is an ideal base from which to visit a fascinating and beautiful part of the Perigord.

Facilities

Modern, clean sanitary facilities are well cared for by the energetic new owners and can be heated. Bread and a few essentials available at reception. Bar, snack bar and terrace restaurant (all season). Heated swimming pool (140 sq.m) and paddling pool. Games room with table football, pool, table tennis and giant TV screen. Canoe trips and bicycle hire can be arranged. Musical evenings weekly in high season. Off site: Shops, supermarkets, bars and a range of interesting restaurants in the town.

Open

1 April - 15 October.

At a glance

Welcome & Ambience	✓✓✓✓	Location	✓✓✓✓✓
Quality of Pitches	✓✓✓	Range of Facilities	✓✓✓✓

Directions

Site is just south of Montignac town centre, on the D65 to Sergeac. Just after you cross the stone bridge on the one way system in the centre of the town turn sharp right (allow for a wide sweep!) The site is 750 m. on the left.

Charges 2005

Per person	€ 3,45 - € 4,60
child (3-8 yrs)	€ 2,06 - € 2,75
pitch	€ 4,20 - € 5,60
electricity (-10A)	€ 3,00 - € 3,00
animal	€ 1,52

10% discount for senior citizens in low season (for advance bookings).

Reservations

Advised for July/Aug with 30% deposit (no booking fee). Tel: 05 53 51 83 95.
E-mail: le.moulin.du.bleufond@wanadoo.fr

FR24180 Camping Caravaning Saint Avit Loisirs

Le Bugue, 24260 St Avit-de-Vialard (Dordogne)

Although Saint Avit Loisirs is set in the middle of rolling countryside, far from the hustle and bustle of the main tourist areas of the Dordogne, the facilities are first class, providing virtually everything you could possibly want without the need to leave the site. This makes it ideal for families with children of all ages. The site is divided into two sections. One smaller part is dedicated to chalets and mobile homes, whilst the main section of the site contains 199 flat and mainly grassy pitches, all a minimum of 100 sq.m and with electricity (6A), arranged in cul-de-sacs off a main access road. Tour operator tents and mobile homes (with lots of British visitors) occupy around half the pitches, leaving 99 for touring units. Three modern unisex toilet blocks provide high quality facilites, but could possibly become overstretched (particularly laundry and dishwashing sinks) in high season. The café, shop and bar open onto a large terrace with pergola and hanging baskets, which overlooks the excellent pool complex. In high season a variety of activities and entertainments are organised - tournaments of all sorts, aquagym, bingo and even weekly films in English.

Facilities

Clean and modern toilet blocks include washbasins in cabins. Well stocked shop, bar, restaurant, good-value cafeteria and takeaway are housed in a traditional-style stone building. Outdoor swimming pool (200 sq.m), children's pool, water slide, 'crazy river' and heated indoor pool with jacuzzi and adjacent fitness room. Disco behind bar, sound-proofed. Table tennis. Floodlit minigolf and boules area and dirt bike track. Good quality tennis court, volleyball and extensive play area. Canoe trips on the Dordogne and other sporting activities organised. Good walks direct from the site. Off site: Sarlat and Perigeux within range for markets and hypermarkets.

Open

3 April - 25 September.

At a glance

Welcome & Ambience	✓✓✓✓	Location	✓✓✓
Quality of Pitches	✓✓✓✓	Range of Facilities	✓✓✓✓✓

Directions

Site is 6 km. north of Le Bugue. From D710 Le Bugue - Perigueux road, turn west on C201 (about 2.5 km. from Le Bugue), toward St Avit de Vialard. Follow road around and through hamlet of St Avit, bearing right - site is about 1.5 km. past here, on the right. Note: the road to St Avit is narrow and bumpy in places.

Charges 2004

Per person	€ 3,50 - € 7,50
child (under 4 yrs)	free
pitch	€ 5,50 - € 11,00
with electricity	€ 9,00 - € 15,00
with water and drainage	€ 11,50 - € 18,00
dog	€ 2,00 - € 3,70

Reservations

Made with deposit (€ 46 per week) and fee (€ 15).
Tel: 05 53 02 64 00.
E-mail: contact@saint-avit-loisirs.com

FR24170 Camping Le Port de Limeuil

24480 Allés-sur-Dordogne (Dordogne)

At the confluence of Dordogne and Vézère rivers, opposite the picturesque village of Limieul, this delightful family site exudes a peaceful and relaxed ambience. There are 90 marked, grassy, flat and numbered pitches, some very spacious and all with electricity connections (5A). The buildings are in traditional Périgourdine style and surrounded with flowers and shrubs - it is a very pretty site - and the young French owners have been steadily developing the facilities. A sports area on a large open grassy space between the river bank and the main camping area adds to the feeling of space, and provides an additional recreation and picnic area (there are additional unmarked pitches for tents and camper vans along the bank here). This is an ideal location for visiting the west central part of the Dordogne département, and is recommended for long stays. It is used fairly unobtrusively by a tour operator.

Facilities

Two clean, modern toilet blocks provide excellent facilities. Bar/restaurant with snacks and takeaway (all 20/5-5/9). Small shop. Swimming pool with jacuzzi, paddling pool and children's slide (1/5-30/9). Badminton, football, boules and volleyball. Mountain bike hire. Canoe hire - launched from the site's own pebble beach. Off site: The pretty medieval village of Limeuil 200 m. Riding 1 km. Golf 10 km.

Open

1 May - 30 September.

At a glance

Welcome & Ambience	✓✓✓✓✓	Location	✓✓✓✓
Quality of Pitches	✓✓✓✓	Range of Facilities	✓✓✓✓

Directions

Site is about 7 km south of Le Bugue. From D51/D31E Le Buisson to Le Bugue road turn west onto D51 towards Limeuil. Just before you cross the bridge into the village of Limeuil, turn left (site signed here), across another bridge. Site is about 100 m. along this road on the right.

Charges 2004

Per pitch incl. 2 persons	€ 13,51 - € 19,30
extra person	€ 3,36 - € 4,80
child (under 10 yrs)	€ 2,45 - € 3,50
electricity (5A)	€ 2,13 - € 3,05
dog	€ 1,40 - € 2,00

Reservations

Advised for mid July - end August.
Tel: 05 53 63 29 76. E-mail: didierbonvallet@aol.com

FR24040 Castel Camping Le Moulin du Roch

Route des Eyzies, D47, 24200 Sarlat (Dordogne)

Le Moulin du Roch is set on natural sloping woodland in the grounds of a former water mill and the Dutreux family have worked hard to ensure that it is an attractive and well run family campsite, fully deserving of its place in the Castels and Camping chain. Only 10 km. from the charming medieval town of Sarlat and 52 km. from Pèrigueux – the capital town of the Périgord region – this campsite is well situated for exploring the natural, historical, cultural and gastronomic riches of the Dordogne. The site has 199 pitches, of which 104 are for touring units. Pitches are mostly flat (some slope slightly) and grassy, and all have electricity (6A). Pitches on the upper levels have plenty of shade, whilst those on the lower level near the amenities and the fishing lake are more open. Entertainment and activities are organised from June to September, with something for everyone from craft workshops and sports tournaments to canoeing and caving for the more adventurous. An excellent multi-lingual children's club runs in July and August. Walking and mountain biking lead from the site through surrounding woodland.

TRAVEL SERVICE SITE

TO BOOK CALL 0870 405 4055 OR www.alanrogersdirect.com

Facilities

Three modern toilet blocks provide clean and well maintained facilities. Washing machines and dryers. Shop (30/4-17/9) stocks a good range of groceries and fresh food, and is very reasonably priced. Bar with terrace (1/6-31/8). Takeaway (30/4-17/9). Superb restaurant (14/5-11/9, closed Mondays). Attractive swimming pool, paddling pool and sun terrace with loungers (30/4-17/9). Fishing lake (carp and roach - no charge), tennis, table tennis, boules area, volleyball pitch, playground, discos twice weekly in high season. Dogs and other animals are not accepted. Off site: Supermarkets, banks, etc. at Sarlat 10 km. Bicycle hire and riding 10 km. Golf 15 km.

At a glance

Welcome & Ambience	✓✓✓✓✓	Location	✓✓✓✓
Quality of Pitches	✓✓✓✓	Range of Facilities	✓✓✓✓✓

Directions

Site is 10 km. west of Sarlat la Canéda, on south side of D47 Sarlat - Les Eyzies road.

Charges 2004

Per pitch incl. 2 persons	€ 13,00 - € 24,00
with electricity	€ 17,00 - € 28,00
with full services	€ 13,00 - € 28,00
extra person	€ 3,00 - € 7,20
child (4-9 yrs)	free - € 2,60

Camping Cheques accepted.

Reservations

Essential from June - August, with deposit (20%) and fee (€ 9 in low season, € 19 in July/Aug).
Tel: 05 53 59 20 27.
E-mail: moulin.du.roch@wanadoo.fr

Open

30 April - 17 September.

FR24240 Camping Les Bo-Bains

24150 Badefoils-sur-Dordogne (Dordogne)

Offering a limited number of touring pitches, but a good range of facilities and activities, Les Bo-Bains is a well kept site in an attractive location alongside the Dordogne river. The flat, grassy and larger than average pitches are all set along the river bank (families with young children need to consider this), and are divided by hedges, shrubs and bushes of different types. All pitches have electricity, with water taps and drainaway points between each pair. River bathing is possible, although in places the current can be quite strong. Canoeing can be arranged from reception and there are places to launch one's own small craft. The site welcomes a good quota of French and Dutch clients, but not many British as yet. Mobile homes and chalets are available to rent.

Facilities

The two main toilet blocks are of good quality with baby rooms and laundry facilities. Small shop. Bar (open all season) and restaurant with a choice of menu and comprehensive takeaway service (15/5-15/9). Swimming pool complex with a main pool (18 x 9 m), another shallower one (5 x 5 m), plus two slides and landing pool (14 x 7 m). Several small play areas. TV room. Multi-gym. Small football field. Minigolf, archery, boules, trampoline, volleyball, badminton, table tennis and basketball courts. Children's club. Games, competitions and evening events. Quad bike and bicycle hire. Tennis. Riding. Canoeing excursions. Off site: The small village of Badefols is within easy walking distance, and has a restaurant, bar, tobacconist and an historic château.

At a glance

Welcome & Ambience	✓✓✓	Location	✓✓✓✓
Quality of Pitches	✓✓✓✓✓	Range of Facilities	✓✓✓✓

Directions

Site is on D29 Bergerac - Sarlat road, about 4 km. east of Lalinde, on the north side of the road.

Charges 2004

Per pitch incl. 2 persons and electricity (5A)	€ 16,00 - € 28,00
extra person over 4 yrs	€ 3,00 - € 7,50
animal	free - € 3,00

Reservations

Advised for July and August. Made for any length with deposit (30% - minimum € 45) and booking fee (€ 16). Tel: 05 53 73 52 52.
E-mail: info@bo-bains.com

Open

15 April - 30 September.

FR24100 Sunêlia Le Moulinal

24540 Biron (Dordogne)

A lakeside site with a wide range of activities, not only does Le Moulinal provide a good base for exploring the southern Dordogne, but it also has extensive wooded grounds to explore with picnic areas. Of the 280 grassy pitches, only around 40 are available for touring units, and these are spread amongst the site's own mobile homes, chalets and some tour operator tents. All pitches are flat, grassy and have electricity (3/6A), but vary considerably in size from 75 sq.m. to over 100 sq.m. The five-acre lake has a sandy beach and is suitable for boating (canoes available), swimming and fishing. Ambitious, well organised animation is run throughout the season - including a 'baby club' (ages 2-6), tennis, mountain biking, canoeing, riding, archery, rock climbing, potholing and craft activities (all charged), and children's activities, sports tournaments, discos and fishing (free of charge). The site is also popular with tour operators (80 pitches), although the owner has reduced their presence.

Facilities

Toilet facilities, built to harmonise with the surroundings, include British and Turkish style toilets (most in one block), some washbasins in cabins, and dishwashing sinks. Facilities for disabled people and babies. Laundry with washing machines and dryers. Motorcaravan service point. Excellent restaurant serving regional meals. Bar serving snacks and light meals (all season). Snack bar/takeaway on the other side of the lake. Large, heated swimming pool with jacuzzi and children's pool. Rustic play area on grass. Volleyball, table tennis, football and hockey. Bicycle hire. Excursions organised on foot, on horseback, by car or bicycle. Full programme of evening entertainment in high season.

Open

5 April - 14 September with all services.

At a glance

Welcome & Ambience	✓✓✓✓✓	Location	✓✓✓✓
Quality of Pitches	✓✓✓✓	Range of Facilities	✓✓✓✓✓

Directions

Site is 53 km southeast of Bergerac. From D104 Villeréal -; Monpazier road take the D53/D150 south to Lacapelle Biron. Just before Lacapelle Biron turn right onto the D255 towards Dévillac, (site is well signed here), and site is 1.5 km along on the left.

Charges 2004

Per pitch incl. 2 persons and electricity	€ 17,00 - € 34,00
electricity, water and drainage	€ 20,00 - € 40,00
pitch near lake with electricity	€ 18,00 - € 38,00
extra person	€ 3,00 - € 8,20
child (2-7 yrs)	free - € 7,50
animal	€ 4,00

Low season offer - 14 nights for price of 10.

Reservations

Made with deposit (€ 92) and for high season, fee (€ 28). Tel: 05 53 40 84 60.
E-mail: lemoulinal@perigord.com

FR24080 Camping Caravaning Le Moulin de David

Mobile homes page 395

Gaugeac, 24540 Monpazier (Dordogne)

Owned and run by a French family who continually seek to improve it, this pleasant and attractive site is one for those who enjoy peace, away from the hustle and bustle of the main Dordogne attractions, yet sufficiently close for them to be accessible. Set in a 14 hectare. wooded valley, it has 160 pitches split into two sections; 102 are available for touring vans - 33 below the central reception complex in a shaded situation, and 69 above on partly terraced ground with varying degrees of shade. All pitches have electricity (3-10A). Spacing is good and there is no crowding. The site has been planted with a pleasing variety of shrubs and trees, and combined with the small stream that runs through the centre of the site they create a beautiful and tranquil setting. There is a delightful wooded walk via a long distance footpath (GR 36) to Château Biron, about two to three kilometre distance. A 'Sites et Paysages' member.

TRAVEL SERVICE SITE

TO BOOK CALL 0870 405 4055 OR www.alanrogersdirect.com

Facilities

All three toilet blocks are good, including washbasins in cabins, facilities for disabled visitors and babies in each. Adequate dishwashing and laundry sinks. Laundry room. Good shop. Bar/restaurant with shaded patio and takeaway. Swimming pool and children's paddling pool, plus freshwater pool with waterslide. Play area. Boules, half-court tennis, table tennis, volleyball, basketball, trampolining and football area. Library. Bicycle hire. Events, games and canoe trips organised (1/7-31/8). Off site: Small supermarket and cash point in Monpazier 2.5 km.

Open

14 May - 10 September.

At a glance

Welcome & Ambience	✓✓✓✓	Location	✓✓✓✓
Quality of Pitches	✓✓✓✓✓	Range of Facilities	✓✓✓✓

Directions

From Monpazier take the D2 Villeréal road. Take third turning left (after about 2 km), signed to Moulin de David and 'Gaugeac mairie'. Site is about 500 m. along this road on the left.

Charges 2004

Per person (over 2 yrs)	€ 3,65 - € 6,40
normal pitch	€ 5,00 - € 9,30
large pitch incl. water and drainage	€ 8,00 - € 12,00
extra child's tent	€ 1,35 - € 3,15
electricity (3/10A)	€ 3,35 - € 5,65
animal	€ 1,35 - € 2,50

Camping Cheques accepted.

Reservations

Advisable for Jul/Aug, with deposit (€ 65 per week reserved) and fee (€ 19) for stays between 26/6 and 21/8). Tel: 05 53 22 65 25.
E-mail: courrier@moulin-de-david.com

FR24030 Camping Les Périères

Route Ste Nathalène, 24203 Sarlat (Dordogne)

Les Périères is a good quality small site in an attractive setting within walking distance of the beautiful medieval town of Sarlat. The 100 pitches arranged on wide terraces around the semi-circle of a fairly steep valley, overlooking central leisure area that includes indoor and outdoor pools and tennis courts. The pitches are of a very good size, all with electricity (6A), water and drainage and many have dappled shade from the numerous walnut trees on the site (the walnuts can be bought in the shop). Reservations are advised for high season, although a few pitches are made available on a 'first come first serve basis'. The site has a refreshingly spacious and open feel, quite free from overcrowding, even at busy times.

Facilities

The toilet blocks of varying styles and sizes should be quite sufficient, including washbasins in cabins, facilities for disabled visitors, a good baby bathroom in one block and washing machines and dryers. Motorcaravan service point. Small shop. Pleasant bar. Small snack bar/takeaway (July/August). Outdoor swimming pool (no shorts) and paddling pool and heated indoor spa pool and sauna. Two tennis courts. Table tennis (indoors or out), football pitch and fitness track with exercise halts. Stone cottages to rent. No electric barbecues allowed. Off site: Bicycle hire 1 km. Fishing 5 km. Riding or golf 7 km.

At a glance

Welcome & Ambience	✓✓✓✓	Location	✓✓✓✓✓
Quality of Pitches	✓✓✓✓	Range of Facilities	✓✓✓✓

Directions

Site is on the east side of Sarlat, on the D47 to Ste Nathalene. (Negotiating Sarlat town centre is best done outside of peak hours).

Charges 2004

Per unit incl. 2 persons	€ 18,20 - € 24,60
with electricity	€ 22,00 - € 28,50
extra person	€ 6,00
child (under 7 yrs)	€ 3,70

Reservations

Advised for high season and made for min. 1 week with deposit (€ 100 p/week) and fee (€ 15). Tel: 05 53 59 05 84. E-mail: les-perieres@wanadoo.fr

Open

Easter - 30 September.

FR24110 Camping Caravaning Aqua Viva

Route Sarlac-Souillac, Carsac-Aillac, 24200 Sarlat (Dordogne)

This shaded woodland site is ideally situated for visits to Rocamadour and Padirac, as well as the many places of interest in the Dordogne region, including the medieval town of Sarlat, only seven kilometres away. The site is divided into two sections, separated by a small access road. Pitches are flat, divided by shrubs, and vary from average to large size. Many have shade from the numerous trees (the shadier pitches tend to have less grass and more sand!). All have electricity (6–10A). A wide range of organised activities, clubs and entertainments run throughout the season, making this site popular with families, especially those with pre-teen and younger teenage children. English is spoken. There are no tour operators, but the site attracts a good mixture of nationalities, resulting in a very 'international' ambience.

Facilities

Each part of the site has a central, modern toilet block, with facilities for disabled people, laundry and baby areas. Bar and restaurant/takeaway with terrace. Shop selling good range of groceries. Heated swimming pool and children's pool. Small fishing lake. High quality minigolf. Half tennis court, ping pong tables, volleyball and badminton nets. Good under 7's play park. Floodlit boules pitch and multi-sports court. Bicycle hire. Off site: Arial woodland assault course 500 m. Riding and golf 5 km.

Open

15 April - 25 September.

At a glance

Welcome & Ambience	✓✓✓✓✓	Location	✓✓✓✓
Quality of Pitches	✓✓✓	Range of Facilities	✓✓✓✓✓

Directions

Site is 7 km. from Sarlat, south of the D704 road from Sarlat to Souillac. Coming from Souillac, the access road is just around a left hand bend, and is not easy to see, but if you miss the turn there is a roundabout a little further on.

Charges 2005

Per person	€ 3,90 - € 6,50
child (2-7 yrs)	€ 2,60 - € 4,70
pitch	€ 4,80 - € 9,50
electricity (3/10A)	€ 3,50

Reservations

Made with 50% deposit and € 20 fee. (Fee charged 15/6-31/08). Tel: 05 53 31 46 00. E-mail: aqua_viva@perigord.com

TRAVEL SERVICE SITE

TO BOOK CALL 0870 405 4055 OR www.alanrogersdirect.com

FR24150 Camping Les Deux Vallées

24220 Vézac (Dordogne)

This site is enviably situated almost under the shadow of Beynac castle in the heart of the Dordogne. There are 95 flat marked touring pitches, most of a good size, some large, and with electricity (6/10A). There is plenty of shade and the general feel is of unspoilt but well managed woodland. There is a small fishing lake on site, and it is only a short distance to the Dordogne river for bathing or canoeing. The site is being steadily upgraded by its Dutch owners who provide a warm and friendly welcome. English is spoken. This site would be ideal for those wanting a quiet and relatively inexpensive base from which to visit the Dordogne region, particularly in low season, as it has the advantage of being open all year.

Facilities

The main unisex toilet block is modern and very clean, and gives an ample provision, with good access for disabled people. A second smaller recently refurbished block can be heated for off-season use. Shop and bar/restaurant (both 1/6-30/9) serving good value snacks and more ambitious meals to take away, eat inside or on the terrace. Good sized pool (1.6 m. deep) and children's pool (from mid May). Bicycle hire. Volleyball, basketball, small minigolf, boules area, table tennis, table football. Quiz nights, painting lessons and barbecues are a regular feature in the main season. Facilities may open earlier than stated if demand is sufficient. Off site: Riding 2 km. Golf 8 km.

Open

All year.

At a glance

Welcome & Ambience	✓✓✓✓	Location	✓✓✓✓
Quality of Pitches	✓✓✓	Range of Facilities	✓✓✓✓

Directions

Site is on the northwest side of the D57 Beynac-et-Cazenac - Sarlat road, about 8 km from Sarlat and 2 km. from Beynac. From Beynac follow D57, pass under railway bridge and then take second turning left (by a bus shelter, small site sign). Follow road around and take first turn left over a small bridge. Turn immediately left and site is about 200 m. ahead. From Sarlat the turn off the D57 will be on your right, just past a detatched stone house.

Charges 2004

Per person	€ 3,00 - € 5,00
child (3-7 yrs)	€ 2,00 - € 3,00
pitch	€ 4,00 - € 6,50
electricity (6A)	€ 3,00
animal	€ 0,60 - € 1,00

Reservations

Advised for July/Aug. and made with deposit (€ 100) and fee (€ 15). Tel: 05 53 29 53 55.
E-mail: les2v@perigord.com

FR24090 Camping Soleil Plage

Mobile homes page 395

Vitrac, 24200 Sarlat (Dordogne)

This spacious site is in one of the most attractive sections of the Dordogne valley, right on the riverside. The site has a total of 199 pitches, divided into two sections, of which around 114 are available for touring units. The smaller section surrounds the main reception and other facilities, which are housed in a renovated Périgordin farmhouse, whilst the larger section of the site is about 250 m. from the reception and pool areas, and offers river bathing from a sizeable pebble bank. All pitches are bounded by hedges and are of good size – in the larger section there are a few bigger pitches for large families. Most pitches have some shade, all have electricity and a few have water and a drain. Various activities are organised during high season including walks and sports tournaments, and daily canoe hire is available from the site. Once a week there is a 'soirée' usually involving a barbecue or paella, with band and lots of free wine - worth catching! The site is popular, although in late August it begins to empty.

Facilities

Toilet facilities are in two modern unisex blocks. Washing machines. Motorcaravan service point. Pleasant bar with extensive and good value takeaway menu, refurbished restaurant serving excellent Périgourdine menus, and well stocked shop (all 12/5-15/9). Very impressive swimming pool complex includes main pool, paddling pool, spa pool and two water slides. Tennis court, devilish minigolf, table tennis, volleyball and football pitches. TV room. Playground. Fishing. Canoe and kayak hire. Currency exchange. Off site: Golf 1 km. Bicycle hire 2 km. Riding 5 km.

Open

1 May - 30 September.

At a glance

Welcome & Ambience	✓✓✓✓✓	Location	✓✓✓✓
Quality of Pitches	✓✓✓✓✓	Range of Facilities	✓✓✓✓

Directions

Site is 8 km. south of Sarlat. From D703 Vitrac - Carsac-Aillac road turn southeast at 'Rochebois' golf course (site signed). Follow road to the end, turn right at T-junction, and follow the road along and around to the left. Site is on left just after turning the corner.

Charges 2004

Per person	€ 4,00 - € 6,40
child (2-10 yrs)	€ 2,40 - € 3,70
pitch	€ 6,00 - € 10,60
with electricity (6A)	€ 8,50 - € 14,00
with full services	€ 11,50 - € 19,00

Reservations

Made for exact dates: min. 1 week with deposit (€ 65) and fee (€ 35); send for booking form. Tel: 05 53 28 33 33. E-mail: info@soleilplage.fr

FR24230 Camping Le Moulin de Paulhiac

24520 Daglan (Dordogne)

Daglan is a very pretty well restored village that is becoming something of a tourist centre for this quieter area of the Dordogne. You will be guaranteed a friendly welcome from the Armagnac family, who are justifiably proud of their well-kept and attractive site, built in the grounds surrounding an old mill. The 150 pitches (98 for touring) are separated by hedges and shrubs, all have electricity, some have water and drain, and there is plenty of shade. Many pitches are next to a stream running through the site to join the River Ceou along its far edge. This site will appeal to families with younger children.

Facilities

Two clean toilet blocks provide modern facilities, including those for disabled. Well-stocked shop. Restaurant and takeaway. Modern heated pool complex (no bermuda style shorts) with a main pool (sliding roof in low season; 15 x 7.5 m), children's pool (7.5 x 7.5 m), a further small pool and two slides. Volleyball, table tennis, badminton and boules. Bicycle hire. Canoe trips. Regular evening activities. Children's club. Off site: Municipal tennis courts adjoining.

Open

15 May - 15 September.

At a glance

Welcome & Ambience	✓✓✓✓✓	Location	✓✓✓✓
Quality of Pitches	✓✓✓✓	Range of Facilities	✓✓✓✓✓

Directions

Site is about 17 km south of Sarlat, and is on the east side of the D57, about 3.5 km north of the village of Daglan.

Charges 2005

Per person	€ 6,20
child under 10 yrs	€ 2,40 - € 4,55
pitch	€ 9,00
electricity (6-10A)	€ 3,35 - € 4,00
water and drainage	€ 2,30

Reservations

Made for any length with deposit (€ 72) and booking fee (€ 8). Tel: 05 53 28 20 88. E-mail: Francis.Armagnac@wanadoo.fr

FR24310 Camping Caravaning La Bouquerie

Mobile homes page 396

24590 St Geniès-en-Périgord (Dordogne)

La Bouquerie is a well maintained site, situated within easy reach of the main road network in the Dordogne, but without any associated traffic noise. The main complex is based around some beautifully restored traditional buildings. It includes a shop, and a bar and restaurant overlooking the pool complex, with a large outdoor terrace for fine weather. The excellent restaurant menu is varied and reasonably priced. Of the 165 pitches, 61 are used for touring units and these are of varying size (80-120 sq.m.), flat and grassy, some with shade, and all with electrical connections (5A). The rest of the pitches are taken up by site owned mobile homes and a UK tour operator. In high season the site offers a range of tournaments and sporting activities (aqua-gym, archery, canoeing, walks etc) as well as a children's club. La Bouquerie is ideally situated for exploring the Périgord region, and has something to offer families.

Facilities

Three unisex toilet blocks contain a mixture of new and older facilities, but are all extremely clean and well maintained. Two blocks provide facilities for disabled visitors (with fixed height shower), and dedicated baby rooms with changing mat, bath and child toilet. Separate covered laundry area with washing machines and covered drying lines. Shop (15/05-15/09) with takeaway food. Bar and restaurant (both 15/05-15/09). Pool complex (all season) with paddling pool, large shallow pool (heated) and large deep pool, as well as sunbathing areas with loungers. Carp fishing in lake on site. Bicycle hire. Off site: Shops and restaurants, etc. in the nearby village of St Geniès.

At a glance

Welcome & Ambience	✓✓✓✓	Location	✓✓✓✓
Quality of Pitches	✓✓✓	Range of Facilities	✓✓✓

Directions

Site is signed on east side of the D704 Sarlat - Montignac road, about 500 m. north of junction with D64 St Geniès road. Turn off D704 at campsite sign and take first left turn signed La Bouquerie.

Charges 2004

Per person	€ 4,60 - € 6,50
child (under 7 yrs)	€ 3,20 - € 4,50
pitch	€ 6,30 - € 9,00
electricity	€ 3,00

Reservations

Advised for high season. Tel: 05 53 28 98 22.
E-mail: labouquerie@wanadoo.fr

Open

Easter - 25 September.

FR24360 Camping Le Mondou

24370 St Julien de Lampon (Dordogne)

This quiet little Dutch owned site mid-way between Sarlat and Souillac is ideally situated for visiting a wide range of attractions in the Dordogne and Lot départments. It is set amongst countryside at the edge of the small village of St Julien, and only two kilometres from the Dordogne river. The 62 grassy pitches are of medium size (tending to be long and narrow rather than square), divided by shrubs, and with some shade from a variety of trees. All have electricity (6A). The friendly and helpful owners – John and Lia - organise regular evening entertainment in high season.

Facilities

Two sanitary blocks provide basic facilities, including facilities for disabled visitors, baby baths, washing machine, ironing board and iron. Terrace bar and snack bar with reasonably priced menu. Large swimming pool with sun terrace and children's paddling pool. Rustic style children's play area and large playing field. Boules pitch, volleyball/badminton net. Off site: Bar, restaurant and small shop in village of St Julien-de-Lampon (1 km).

Open

1 May - 15 October.

At a glance

Welcome & Ambience	✓✓✓✓	Location	✓✓✓✓
Quality of Pitches	✓✓✓	Range of Facilities	✓✓✓✓

Directions

Site is 12 km. southwest of Souillac. From D703 Sarlat-Souillac road turn south across river at Rouffillac, signed St Julien-de-Lampon. On entering village of St Julien turn left on D50, signed Mareuil and Le Roc. Follow road along (it is narrow in one or two places), and just at the end of the village the site is signed to right. Site is 500 m. on the right.

Charges 2004

Per person	€ 4,00
child (under 7 yrs)	€ 2,00
pitch	€ 4,00
electricity	€ 2,50

Reservations

Advised for July and August. Tel: 05 53 29 70 37.
E-mail: lemondou@camping-dordogne.info

FR24320 Camping Les Peneyrals

Mobile homes page 396

Le Poujol, 24590 St Crépin-Carlucet (Dordogne)

Within easy reach of all the attractions of the Périgord region, M. and Mme. Havel have created an attractive and friendly family campsite at Les Peneyrals. Set on a wooded hillside, with flowers in abundance (thanks to the dedication of Mme. Havel's mother), the site has 199 pitches, of which 87 are available for touring units. The pitches at the bottom of the hill tend to be quieter as they are further from the main facilities, but are all level and grassy (some on terraces), with electricity (5/10A), and most have some shade. An attractive bar and restaurant with terrace overlook the excellent pool complex and sunbathing areas. At the bottom of the campsite is a small fishing lake with carp (no charge to fish), and in July and August, activities are organised including archery, various sports tournaments, aqua gym, discos and a children's club. The site is used fairly unobtrusively by a UK tour operator (67 pitches).

Facilities

Two modern, unisex toilet blocks provide good quality facilities, including provision for babies and disabled visitors. Motorcaravan services. Good value shop, restaurant and takeaway. Pool complex with two large pools (one heated), paddling pool and four slides with splash pool. Bicycle hire. Minigolf, tennis (charged). Football. Badminton, volleyball. Table tennis. Play area. Games room, TV room and small library. Off site: Supermarkets, etc. in Sarlat (11 km).

Open

14 May - 10 September.

At a glance

Welcome & Ambience	✓✓✓✓	Location	✓✓✓✓
Quality of Pitches	✓✓✓✓	Range of Facilities	✓✓✓✓✓

Directions

Site is 11 km. north of Sarlat. From D704 Sarlat - Montignac road turn east on D60 towards Salignac-Eyvigues. After 4 km. turn south on D56 towards St Crépin-Carlucet. Site is about 500 m. along this road on the right.

Charges 2004

Per person	€ 4,20 - € 6,40
child (under 7 yrs)	free - € 4,10

Reservations

Advised for July and August, with € 72 deposit (and € 18 booking fee in high season).
Tel: 05 53 28 85 71.
E-mail: camping.peneyrals@wanadoo.fr

FR24350 Camping RCN Le Moulin de la Pique

24170 Belvès (Dordogne)

Set in the grounds of converted former mill and iron foundry, this impressive and well managed site offers something for every member of the family. The 135 touring pitches are flat, grassy and extremely spacious (most well over 100 sq.m.) and most have electricity (6A), water and drainage. Some pitches border the lake which can be used for both fishing and boating. The 11th century fortified town of Belvès is only 2 km. and the site is well located for access to the many other attractions of the Dordogne valley. There is a new pool with a 45 m. slide and daily activities are organised. There is even a 'fossil field', where children can become amateur archaeologists, digging for genuine fossils. Discounted golf, canoeing, bike hire and riding can be arranged through reception. Used by a tour operator (55 pitches).

Facilities

Three modern toilet blocks provide good quality unisex facilities. Baby baths and changing. Facilities for disabled visitors. Dishwashing and laundry sinks. Washing and drying machines. Bar and restaurant, snack bar and shop (open all season), Swimming pool (heated), paddling pool, four water slides with separate landing pool. Playing field, football field. Volleyball. Table tennis.Tennis. Boules. Minigolf. Various play areas. TV and games room. Toddler's playroom. Library. Internet access. Off site: Bars, restaurants and shops in the village of Belvès 2 km.

At a glance

Welcome & Ambience	✓✓✓✓	Location	✓✓✓✓
Quality of Pitches	✓✓✓✓✓	Range of Facilities	✓✓✓✓✓

Directions

Site is 35 km. southwest of Sarlat. From Siorac-en-Périgord, take D710 south (signed Belvès and Fumel). After 4.5 km. at roundabout, go straight on (D710 signed Fumel) and site is 2.5 km. on the left.

Charges 2004

Per pitch with max 6 persons incl electricity and water	€ 25,00 - € 45,00

Reservations

Advised for July/Aug. with 50% deposit.
Tel: 05 53 29 01 15.
E-mail: info@rcn-lemoulindelapique.fr

Open

20 April - 11 October.

FR24340 Camping Le Val de la Marquise

24260 Campagne (Dordogne)

This recently refurbished campsite, set between the tourist centres of Le Bugue and Les Eyzies, is in an ideal situation from which to explore the châteaux and prehistoric sites of the Perigord region. The 131 touring pitches are flat, grassy and all of a good size (mostly over 110 sq.m.). The pitches are divided by shrubs, and some have shade from mature trees, whilst others are more open. Most have electricity. The site has a good bar and snack bar, and reception stocks a range of basic groceries including bread made on site every day. Weekly entertainment and excursions are organised in high season, but the site retains a relaxed peaceful air and is an ideal retreat after a busy day of sightseeing in the area.

Facilities

The central, very clean toilet block provides first-rate facilities, including controllable showers, washbasins in cubicles, laundry and dishwashing sinks and a baby bath. A smaller block near reception houses facilities for disabled visitors (no ramp but only a half inch step into the building) and washing and drying machines. Bar (1/6-15/9) and snack bar/takeaway (15/7-15/8) with terrace. Swimming pool with sun terrace and paddling pool. Small fishing lake (free). Chalets to rent. Off site: Bars and restaurants in the village of Champagne (500 m).

Open

4 April - 15 October.

At a glance

Welcome & Ambience	✓✓✓	Location	✓✓✓✓
Quality of Pitches	✓✓✓✓	Range of Facilities	✓✓✓✓

Directions

Site is 28 km. west of Sarlat, and 4 km. southeast of Le Bugue. Take D703/D706 Le Bugue -; Les Eyzies road. At village of Champagne take D35 heading east towards St Cyprien (there is a peculiar 'Y' junction where the D703, D706 and D35 meet). Site is about 500 m. along the D35 on the right.

Charges 2005

Per unit incl. 6 persons	€ 4,20 - € 7,00
extra person	€ 3,10 - € 4,40
child (2-10 yrs)	€ 2,10 - € 3,00
electricity (15A)	€ 3,00

Reservations

Advised for July/Aug. with deposit (€ 31 per week) and fee (€ 16). Tel: 05 53 54 74 10. E-mail: val-marquise@wanadoo.fr

FR46040 Camping Moulin de Laborde

46700 Montcabrier (Lot)

Based around a converted 17th century watermill, Moulin de Laborde provides a tranquil and uncommercialised campsite for the whole family to enjoy. Bordered by woods, hills and a small river, there are 90 flat and grassy pitches, all of at least 100 sq.m. and with electricity (6A). Pretty shrubs and trees divide the pitches and provide a moderate amount of shade. A gate at the back of the site leads walkers onto a footpath which passes through the village of Montcabrier (1 km). A small lake with rafts and rowing boats, and an adventure-type play area with rope bridges and 'death slide' will keep children amused, whilst parents can relax in the charming courtyard housing the bar and restaurant.

Facilities

The centrally located and very clean toilet block has well designed showers and washbasins in cabins. Covered area provides sinks for dishwashing and laundry. Unit for disabled people. Washing machine and dryer. Shop (all season). Small bar, restaurant and takeaway. Swimming pool with sunbathing area and paddling pool (1/5-15/9). Play area. Small lake with rafts, rowing boats and fishing. Volleyball and badminton nets. Boules pitch. Covered recreation area and table tennis. Mountain bike hire. Rock climbing and archery lessons. Live music one evening a week. Dogs are not accepted. Off site: Riding 5 km. Golf 8 km. Tennis nearby and canoeing on the Lot.

At a glance

Welcome & Ambience	✓✓✓✓	Location	✓✓✓✓
Quality of Pitches	✓✓✓✓	Range of Facilities	✓✓✓

Directions

Site is on the north side of the D673 (Fumel - Gourdon) 1 km. northeast of the turn to Montcabrier.

Charges 2004

Per person	€ 5,50
child (under 7 yrs)	€ 3,00
pitch	€ 7,50
electricity (6A)	€ 2,50

Less 30% outside July/August. No credit cards.

Reservations

Accepted with deposit (€ 7.50 per night booked). Tel: 05 65 24 62 06. E-mail: moulindelaborde@wanadoo.fr

Open

1 May - 15 September.

FR46030 Camping Les Pins

46350 Payrac-en-Quercy (Lot)

Set amongst four hectares of beautiful pine forest, Camping Les Pins is well situated for exploring the historical and natural splendours of the Dordogne region, as well as being a convenient overnight stop when heading north or south. There are 125 clearly marked, level pitches (100 sq.m), of which 75 are for touring units. The pitches are well marked and separated by small shrubs or hedges. Many have shade from the abundant pine trees and all have 6A electricity connections. There is a bar and a good value restaurant with a terrace overlooking the pool area. The friendly and welcoming owners are keen to encourage visitors to explore the region and have negotiated reductions for their guests when visiting certain local attractions.

Facilities

Three toilet blocks, two recently modernised, are well maintained and include washbasins in cabins and good baby bath facilities. Dishwashing and laundry sinks, washing machines and dryers (with plenty of drying lines). Motorcaravan service point. Shop with limited range of basics (1/6-31/8). Bar/restaurant and takeaway (1/6-31/8). Swimming pool (15 x 17 m.), three water slides and smaller paddling pool (15/5-15/9). Tennis court. Table tennis, pétanque and volleyball. TV and library. Some entertainment in season, including weekly family discos. Walking routes starting from the site. English and Dutch are spoken.
Off site: Fishing 7 km. Riding 10 km.

At a glance

Welcome & Ambience	✓✓✓✓	Location	✓✓✓✓
Quality of Pitches	✓✓✓✓	Range of Facilities	✓✓✓✓

Directions

Site entrance is 16 km. from Souillac on western side of the N20 just south of Payrac-en-Quercy village.

Charges 2004

Per person	€ 2,75 - € 5,50
child (under 7 yrs)	€ 1,90 - € 3,90
pitch	€ 4,20 - € 8,40
with electricity	€ 7,00 - € 11,00
dog	€ 1,50 - € 2,00

Special low season family price.

Reservations

Made for min. 1 week with deposit (25%) plus fee (€ 15.24). Tel: 05 65 37 96 32.
E-mail: info@les-pins-camping.com

Open

1 April - 30 September.

FR46050 Camping Le Rêve

Mobile homes page 397

46300 Le Vigan (Lot)

Le Rêve is a very peaceful site situated in the heart of rolling countryside where the Perigord runs into Quercy. Le Rêve continues to impress us with its tranquillity and the young Dutch owners are keen to develop the site in such a way that this will not be lost. The 56 touring pitches are all of good size, with access to electricity (6A), and divided by shrubs. A few of the pitches are situated at the edge of the forest, and provide plenty of shade. Plenty of large grassy areas give lots of space for children to play and make this site particularly suitable for young families.

Facilities

The modern toilet block includes a heated enclosed area for cooler weather. Washbasins in cabins, special cubicles for disabled people and a baby room. Washing machine and dryers. Small shop for basics (bread, milk etc.), pleasant bar, restaurant and takeaway (all open all season). Small, clean, solar heated swimming pool and large paddling pool with
Off site: Riding 2 km. Fishing 5 km. Golf 20 km.

Open

9 April - 24 September.

At a glance

Welcome & Ambience	✓✓✓✓	Location	✓✓✓
Quality of Pitches	✓✓✓✓	Range of Facilities	✓✓✓✓

Directions

From N20 Souillac-Cahors road take D673 3 km. south of Payrac. After 2 km. site is signed down small lane on west side of the road. Turn here, and follow signs for another 2.5 km. to site.

Charges 2005

Per person	€ 2,50 - € 3,50
child (under 7 yrs)	€ 1,60 - € 2,50
pitch	€ 12,00 - € 17,00
electricity (6A)	€ 2,50

Less 20-30% outside July/Aug. No credit cards.

Reservations

Advised for high season and made for any length with deposit (€ 70) and fee (€ 5). Tel: 05 65 41 25 20.
E-mail: info@campinglereve.com

FR46010 Castel Camping Le Domaine de la Paille Basse

46200 Souillac-sur-Dordogne (Lot)

Set in a rural location some eight kilometres from Souillac, this family owned, high quality site is easily accessible from the N20 and well placed to take advantage of excursions into the Dordogne. It is part of a large domaine of 80 hectares, which is available to campers for walks and recreation. The site is quite high up and there are excellent views over the surrounding countryside. The 250 pitches are in two main areas - one is level in cleared woodland with good shade, and the other on grass in open ground without shade. Numbered and marked, the pitches are a minimum 100 sq.m. and often considerably more. All have electricity (3/6A) with about 80 also equipped with water and drainage. A wide range of activities and entertainment are organised in season (animation was of a very high standard when we stayed). For good reason, the site can get very busy in high season and is popular with tour operators (25%), but there is more space available from mid August.

TRAVEL SERVICE SITE

TO BOOK CALL 0870 405 4055 OR www.alanrogersdirect.com

Facilities

Three main toilet blocks all have modern equipment and are kept very clean. Laundry facilities. Shop for essentials. Good restaurant, bar with terrace and takeaway. Crêperie. Good pool complex, with main swimming pool (25 x 10 m), a smaller one (10 x 6 m), paddling pool (unheated) and water slides. Sun terrace with loungers. Sound-proofed disco room (twice weekly in season). TV rooms (with satellite). Cinema room below the pool area. Archery, tennis (charged), football, volleyball and table tennis. Play area. Off site: Golf 4 km.

Open

15 May - 15 September.

At a glance

Welcome & Ambience	✓✓✓✓	Location	✓✓✓✓
Quality of Pitches	✓✓✓✓	Range of Facilities	✓✓✓✓

Directions

From Souillac take D15 road leading northwest towards Salignac-Eyvignes and after 6 km. turn right at camp sign and follow steep and narrow approach road for 2 km.

Charges 2004

Per person	€ 4,70 - € 5,80
child (under 7 yrs)	€ 3,10 - € 3,80
pitch	€ 7,20 - € 8,90
incl. water and drainage	€ 8,80 - € 10,90
dog	€ 3,80

Camping Cheques accepted.
Less 20% outside 15/6-1/9.

Reservations

Advised mid-July - mid-Aug. and made for min. 1 week with deposit and booking fee.
Tel: 05 65 37 85 48. E-mail: paille.basse@wanadoo.fr

Mobile homes ▶ page 397

FR46110 Camping du Port

46600 Creysse (Lot)

Set off the beaten track this small, unassuming riverside campsite provides an unusual combination of peace and tranquillity alongside a range of sporting activities to occupy even the most adventurous of people. Pitches are mostly flat, and of a large size (100m² plus), with plenty of shade from the abundant trees, but no dividing hedges or fences. 70 of the 100 touring pitches have electricity (6A). The far side of the site slopes down to the picturesque Dordogne river, providing a launching area for canoes, and a small gravel 'beach'. The campsite owner runs daily activities including canoeing, caving, climbing, abseiling, cycling, walking and woodland assault course through the trees, all with qualified supervision. On-site entertainment includes regular paella, 'moules and frites' and barbecue evenings, live musical entertainment and open air cinema screenings (July/Aug). Despite all these activities the campsite retains a very rural 'a la ferme' ambience, and is ideal for anyone seeking a restful time away from the hustle and bustle of the larger sites along the Dordogne.

Facilities

Central toilet block contains a mix of older and more modern facilities, which are maybe a little basic, but are well cleaned, and would appear more than adequate for the number of pitches. Toilets are mostly British style, washbasins both open and in cubicles, showers pre-set pushbutton type. Dishwashing and laundry sinks, washing machine. Small shop with reasonable range of groceries, bread, camping gas etc. Open air bar and terrace, small snack bar / takeaway. Attractive swimming pool with sun terrace (no paddling pool). All facilities open 01/05-30/09, but may be limited in low season. Mobile homes to rent. Off site: Bar/restaurant in the pretty medieval village of Creysse, about 500 yds away, providing a varied menu including 'a la carte'.

At a glance

Welcome & Ambience	✓✓✓✓	Location	✓✓✓✓
Quality of Pitches	✓✓✓✓	Range of Facilities	✓✓✓✓

Directions

Site is approximately 15 km. east of Souillac. From the village of Martel on the D703 take the D23 south to Creysse. The site is signposted on the left just before you enter the village.

Charges 2005

child under 7 yrs	€ 2,90
pitch with electricity	€ 6,90
animal	€ 0,50

Reservations

Not required. Tel: 05 65 32 20 82.
E-mail: contact@campingduport.com

Open

1 May - 30 September.

FR46150 Camping La Truffière

46330 St Cirq-Lapopie (Lot)

Set in 4 hectares of mature oak woodland, only 2.5 km from the clifftop village of St Cirq-Lapopie, La Truffière is well suited to those seeking a peaceful countryside holiday amongst the stunning natural scenery of the 'Parc naturel régional des Causses de Quercy'. The 80 terraced touring pitches are of varying sizes, and a mixture of grass and gravel (larger units should reserve pitches in advance). All pitches have electricity (6A) and most have shade from the abundant trees. There are various walks and mountain bike trails in the area, and you can hire bikes on site. In high season the campsite owners organise a range of activities including guided walks, château visits, sports tournaments and a daily children's entertainment (not always in English). Due to the woodland nature of the campsite, barbecues are not permitted on individual pitches, but there are three communal barbecue areas around the site.

Facilities

Two clean and modern toilet blocks (one heated in low season) provide a full range of facilities including those for disabled visitors. Motorcaravan service point. Fridge hire. Bar/restaurant (1/6-31/8) with terrace overlooking swimming pool and playing field. Snack bar (15/5-15/9). Swimming pool and paddling pool with sun terrace and loungers (May – Sept). Small shop with essentials (open all season). Large playing field for volleyball, basketball and football. Adventure style play area. Table tennis. Trampolines. Boules pitches. English spoken. Off site: Small shop in village, hypermarkets 36 km. in Cahors. Riding 3 km. Fishing (in the River Lot) 3 km.

Open

1 April - 30 September.

At a glance

Welcome & Ambience	✓✓✓✓	Location	✓✓✓
Quality of Pitches	✓✓✓	Range of Facilities	✓✓✓

Directions

From D911 Cahors – Rodez road, turn north on the D42 at village of Concots (signed towards St Cirq-Lapopie). Site is about 5 km. along this road on the right. Approaching from the north on the D42 via St Cirq-Lapopie is not recommended due to an extremely tight left hand turn at the edge of the village.

Charges 2004

Per person	€ 4,60
child (0-7 yrs)	€ 3,00
pitch	€ 5,00
electricity	€ 3,00
dog	€ 1,00

Camping Cheques accepted.
Less 10% outside July/Aug.
Credit cards only acceptd 1/6-15/8.

Reservations

Advisable in high season and made with fee (€ 11.50). Tel: 05 65 30 20 22.
E-mail: Contact@camping-truffiere.com

FR47100 Camping Municipal Tonneins

47400 Tonneins (Lot et Garonne)

Close to the River Garonne, this small site has a rather formal charm with neat flower beds, well mown lawns and a generally extremely well cared for appearance. With a small reception, the Guardien based on site and a security barrier, it only has 40 pitches (a few occupied by seasonal units) plus a meadow for additional camping. All with electricity (15A), the pitches are of a reasonable size, partly separated by hedges and shrubs. The site is on the southern outskirts of the town with a fair choice of shops, restaurants, etc, and only a 15 minute drive from the charming old riverside town of Port Ste Marie. There is some road and rail noise at times. This is a good stopping off point.

Facilities

Sanitary facilities, very clean when seen in high season, provide British style WCs, washbasins in cabins and dishwashing sinks (H&C) under cover. Purpose built and roomy but of fairly old design, they are adequate rather than luxurious. Washing machine. No proper chemical disposal point. Ice and cold drinks available. Under cover area with fridge and freezer and tables and chairs. Small play area, sandpit and table tennis. Torch useful.

Open

1 June - 30 September.

At a glance

Welcome & Ambience	✓✓✓✓	Location	✓✓✓✓
Quality of Pitches	✓✓✓✓✓	Range of Facilities	✓✓✓

Directions

Take either exit 5 from autoroute to Marmande then the N113 south or exit 6 to Aiguillon (avoid town) and follow N113 north. Site off N113 just south of Tonneins.

Charges 2004

Per unit incl. 1 person	€ 5,10
incl. 2 persons	€ 7,24
extra person	€ 2,35
electricity	€ 3,00

Reservations

Contact site. Tel: 05 53 79 02 28.

FR47050 Camping Moulin de Campech

47160 Villefranche-de-Queyran (Lot et Garonne)

This site is run by Sue and George Thomas along with Sue's parents, Dot and Bob Dunn. A cheery welcome and a free drink awaits you and a determination to ensure that you enjoy your stay. A fabulous view also awaits as you descend the drive from the entrance. The trout lake with graceful weeping willows feeds under the restored mill house which is home to the owners, the main administration area alongside and the bar and restaurant. Enjoy the fare produced by Sue on the pretty terrace as the trout jump (fresh trout is a menu option). The river continues through one side of the site. Children will need supervision around the lake and at the pool which is on an elevated area above the mill house. The 60 pitches are mostly divided by hedges, with electricity available (2/6A, long leads may be necessary in places).

Facilities

The single, rather ordinary toilet unit has modern fittings, can be heated and includes both British and Turkish style WCs, some washbasins in cubicles with hot water, or open washbasins (cold only in men's section). Covered dishwashing and laundry sinks (H&C). Two washing machines and a dryer. Bar and restaurant. Terraced swimming pool and baby pool. Open grassy area for volleyball and other games. Table tennis and baby-foot in tent outside. Board games, boules and small library. Barbecue and gourmet nights organised in high season. Fishing (discounted rate for campers). Torch useful.
Off site: Watersports, bicycle hire, golf or riding 10 km. Markets every day in villages and towns around the region.

At a glance

Welcome & Ambience	✓✓✓✓✓	Location	✓✓✓✓
Quality of Pitches	✓✓✓✓	Range of Facilities	✓✓✓✓

Directions

Take A10 south to Bordeaux. Join A62 for Toulouse and take exit 6 for Damazan. Follow D8 to Mont de Marsan, at Cap du Bosc turn right onto D11 for Casteljaloux. The site is 10 km. on the right and signed.

Charges 2005

Per person	€ 3,60 - € 5,10
child (under 7 yrs)	€ 2,70 - € 3,60
pitch	€ 7,00 - € 8,75
electricity (2/6A)	€ 2,30 - € 3,80
dog	€ 2,40

Reservations

Advised for July/Aug. Tel: 05 53 88 72 43.
E-mail: campech@wanadoo.fr

Open

24 March - 23 October.

FR47010 Camping Caravaning Moulin du Périé

Mobile homes page 398

47500 Sauveterre-la-Lemance (Lot et Garonne)

Set in a quiet area and surrounded by woodlands this peaceful little site is well away from much of the tourist bustle. Its 125 grass pitches, divided by mixed trees and bushes, are reasonably sized and extremely well kept, as indeed is the entire site. All pitches have electricity (6A) and most enjoy good shade, with a wide variety of trees and shrubs. The picturesque old mill buildings, adorned with flowers and creepers, now house the bar and restaurant where the food is to be recommended, as is the owner's extensive knowledge of wine that he is pleased to share with visitors. The attractive front courtyard is complemented by an equally pleasant terrace at the rear. Two small, clean swimming pools overlook a shallow, spring water lake, ideal for inflatable boats and paddling, and bordering the lake, a large grass field is popular for games. A quiet, friendly site with regular visitors - reservation is advised for July/Aug. A 'Sites et Paysages' member.

Facilities

Two clean, modern and well maintained toilet blocks include facilities for disabled visitors. Motorcaravan service point. Fridge, cot, barbecue and chemical toilet hire (book in advance). Shop for essentials (with gas). Bar/reception and restaurant (including takeaway). Two small swimming pools (no bermuda-style shorts). Football and volleyball. Boules, table tennis, outdoor chess. Playground and trampoline. Small, indoor play area. Bicycle hire. In season various activities are arranged; including canoeing, riding, wine tasting visits, sight seeing trips plus weekly barbecues and gastronomic meals. Winter caravan storage.

Off site: Fishing 1 km. Small supermarket in village and larger stores in Fumel.

Open

23 April - 20 September.

At a glance

Welcome & Ambience	✓✓✓✓	Location	✓✓✓
Quality of Pitches	✓✓✓✓	Range of Facilities	✓✓✓

Directions

From D710 Fumel - Périgueux road, turn southeast into village of Sauveterre-le-Lemance across the railway line. Continue straight through village and turn left (northeast) at far end on C201 minor road signed to campsite, Château Sauveterre and Loubejec. Continue straight along this road and site is 3 km. on the right.

Charges 2004

Per unit incl. 2 persons	€ 12,10 - € 20,50
with electricity	€ 15,70 - € 24,10
extra person	€ 3,90 - € 6,10
child (under 7 yrs)	€ 1,65 - € 3,25
animal	€ 2,00 - € 3,30

Camping Cheques accepted.

Reservations

Advised for July/Aug. and made with deposit (€ 140) and fee (€ 20). Tel: 05 53 40 67 26. E-mail: moulinduperie@wanadoo.fr

FR47030 Camping Le Château de Fonrives

Rives, 47210 Villeréal (Lot et Garonne)

This is a very pleasant Dordogne site set in pretty part-farmed, part-wooded countryside, close to the delightful old town of Villeréal. The neat, orderly site is a mixture of hazelnut orchards, woodland with lake, château (mostly 16th century) and camping areas. An attractive avenue leads to the barns adjacent to the château which have been tastefully converted (the restaurant particularly so). There are 200 pitches, 160 for touring units, all of good size (100-150 sq.m.) and with electricity (4, 6 or 10A). Pitches near the woodland receive moderate shade, but elsewhere there is light shade from hedges and young trees. Former barns have been converted to provide a good quality restaurant with covered terrace and large, airy bar with an open terrace overlooking the outdoor pool. The lake can be used for fishing or boating.

Facilities

Two main sanitary units are clean and adequate including washbasins in well appointed cabins and some private bathrooms (for hire by the week). Facilities for children and babies. Laundry rooms. Motorcaravan services. Shop. Elegant restaurant, plus snacks and takeaway meals (all 10/6-10/9). Bar with disco area and terrace (15/5-15/9). Covered swimming pool (April-Oct) and outdoor pool with water slides and paddling pool (15/5-15/9; no bermuda style shorts). Play areas. Small field for volleyball and football. Reading room. Minigolf. Tennis. Bicycle hire. Activities organised for children and adults in season, including excursions and walks. Caravan storage.
Off site: Riding 8 km.

At a glance

Welcome & Ambience	✓✓✓✓	Location	✓✓✓✓
Quality of Pitches	✓✓✓✓	Range of Facilities	✓✓✓✓

Directions

Site is about 2 km. northwest of Villeréal, on west side of the D14/D207 Bergerac - Villaréal road.

Charges 2004

Per unit incl. 2 persons	€ 16,00 - € 23,00
extra person	€ 4,00
child (under 7 yrs)	€ 2,00
electricity 4-10A	€ 3,00 - € 5,50

Reservations

Advisable for July/Aug. with deposit (€ 77) and fee (€ 20). Tel: 05 53 36 63 38.
E-mail: chateau.de.fonrives@wanadoo.fr

Open

4 May - 14 September.

Map 12

These two quiet and deeply rural provinces are right in the centre of France and are surrounded by the tourist regions of the Loire Valley, the Dordogne and the Auvergne. Unknown to many, it is often 'forgotten territory' but by some it's considered close to paradise.

We have combined two official regions: Limousin with départements 19 Corrèze, 23 Creuse, 87 Haute-Vienne; and Auvergne, 03 Allier, 15 Cantal 43 Haute-Loire, 63 Puy-de-Dôme. Also included is 48 Lozère, part of the offical region of Languedoc-Roussillon

This is the home of Limoges porcelain and Aubosson tapestry, of exceptional Romanesque and Gothic Churches and fairytale Renaissance châteaux. Limousin is an unspoilt, thinly populated region on the western side of the Massif Central. With hills and gorges and lush green meadows, numerous ancient village churches dot the landscape as well as more imposing abbey churches and fortresses. The many lakes and rivers of the Limousin provide endless possibilities for canoeing, sailing, wind-surfing and other watersports. To the south, fortified cities cling to mountain sides, home to many religious events and legends.

The Auvergne, set in the heart of the Massif Central, was formed by a series of volcanic eruptions and is a dramatic region of awe-inspiring non-active volcanoes, lakes, sparkling rivers, green valleys and forests. There are also numerous underground streams that have carved out extensive and fantastic cave systems, for which the region is famous. It is a wonderful destination for nature lovers, those who enjoy active outdoor pursuits or for people who want to relax at spa resorts.

Cuisine of the region

Limousin is known for a thick soup called *bréjaude* and its beef, which is extremely tender and full of flavour. Local specialties in the Auvergne include ham and andouille sausages, stuffed cabbage, and bacon with lentil and *cèpes* (mushrooms). Le Puy is famed for its lentils and *Vereine du Velay* – yellow and green liqueurs made from over 30 mountain plants.

Aligot: purée of potatoes with Tomme de Cantal cheese, cream, garlic and butter

Friand Sanflorin: pork meat and herbs in pastry

Jambon d'Auvergne: a tasty mountain ham

Perdrix à l'Auvergnate: partridge stewed in white wine

Potée Auvergnate: a stew of vegetables, cabbage, pork and sausage

Places of interest

Aubusson: long tradition of tapestry making, Hotel de Ville tapestry collections

Clermont-Ferrand: old city centre, 11th and 12th century Notre Dame du Port Basilica, 13th century cathedral; known as *ville noire* for its houses built in local black volcanic rock

Limoges: porcelain, enamel and faience work, château, church of St Michel-de-Lions, cathedral of St Etienne

Vichy: spa, natural spring park

Alan Rogers tip

FOR THOSE FASCINATED BY CREEPY CRAWLIES, TAKE A TRIP TO THE PARC DES ABEILLES AND THE CITÉ DES INSECTES - A GREAT DAY OUT FOR CHILDREN!

FR03010 Camping de la Filature

Ile de Nieres, 03450 Ebreuil (Allier)

Near to the spa town of Vichy and beside a fine fly fishing river that borders the Massif Central region, this site makes a good base to explore the Auvergne including the nearby river gorges, medieval châteaux and extinct volcanoes. Developed on the site of a spinning mill, this rural setting is home to peacocks (including some white ones). There are 80 spacious, grassy pitches, most with shade from mature trees and many directly on the river bank. In summer the river is clean, shallow and pleasant to play in. There is a deeper swimming area 500 m. away. Most pitches have electricity (3/6A). The area is ideal for walking and cycling, especially mountain biking and touring by car on the quiet country roads. Bird watching and wild flowers are additional attractions. You will receive a warm welcome from the English owners (their superb takeaways are very popular).

Facilities

Very clean sanitary facilities are in individual cubicles in pleasantly decorated buildings. Fully equipped, they include mostly British type toilets, a bathroom and a room for disabled visitors. Washing machine and ironing facilities. Small shop for essentials (1/5-30/9). Baker calls. Bar (1/6-30/9). Excellent takeaway (1/6-30/9). Barbecues and pizza nights organised in high season. River bathing and fishing. Play area. Bicycle hire. Minigolf, table football, table tennis. Off site: Riding, canoeing and tennis nearby. Ébreuil with shops and restaurants 1 km. Parc des Volcans and Vulcania attraction,

Open

31 March - 1 October.

At a glance

Welcome & Ambience	✓✓✓✓✓	Location	✓✓✓
Quality of Pitches	✓✓✓✓	Range of Facilities	✓✓✓

Directions

Site is well signed from exit 12 of A71 autoroute to Clermont Ferrand in the direction of Ébreuil. It is about 6 km. from the A71 and 1 km. west of Ébreuil beside the river on the D915 towards the Chouvigny gorges.

Charges 2004

Per unit incl. 2 persons	€ 15,00
extra adult	€ 4,00
child (under 16 yrs)	€ 2,00
electricity (3/6A)	€ 2,00 - € 3,00

Discounts in low season.

Reservations

Made with deposit (€ 30 per week of stay or full amount if stay costs less). Tel: 04 70 90 72 01.
E-mail: camping.filature@libertysurf.fr

FR03170 Camping Municipal (Dompierre-sur-Besbre)

03290 Dompierre-sur-Besbre (Allier)

An immaculate site with a cosmopolitan clientele, this very attractive, floral site has level, individually hedged, grassy pitches. It is located next to the municipal sports fields, and within easy walking distance of the town centre and supermarket (700 m). There are 70 pitches, some very large, with only a few long stay units, leaving about 65 for tourists; 60 have electricity (10A) and most have full service facilities. The warden is very proud of his efficiently run, value for money site. The Canal Latéral de la Loire is good for boating - do visit the nearby vertical boat lift.

Facilities

The toilet block is kept very clean and includes some washbasins in curtained cubicles for ladies, Turkish and British style WCs, dishwashing and laundry sinks plus a washing machine. Excellent motorcaravan service point. New facilities under construction. Off site: The Vallée de la Besbre has a wealth of activities, with tennis and a swimming pool close by. Several rivers and small lakes nearby are suitable for fishing. Cycle tracks and footpaths, and equestrian centres in the area.

At a glance

Welcome & Ambience	✓✓✓✓	Location	✓✓✓
Quality of Pitches	✓✓✓✓	Range of Facilities	✓✓✓

Directions

Site is southeast of town centre just before the junction of N79 and D55, close to the river bridge.

Charges 2004

child (5-14 yrs)	€ 1,00
pitch	€ 1,50
motorcaravan	€ 1,80
electricity	€ 1,70

Reservations

Advised for high season. Tel: 04 70 34 55 57.

Open

15 May - 15 September.

FR03050 Camping Caravaning La Petite Valette

Sazeret, 03390 Montmarault (Allier)

Originally a working farm, La Petite Valette has been transformed by its hard working Dutch and German owners into a very attractive and peaceful campsite. There are 55 level grassy pitches of average size, many with rural views, each with an electricity point (6A) and separated by flowering bushes and trees, which gives some shade. A small lake in one of the lower fields is stocked with fish for anglers. Ponies and small livestock (rabbits, chickens and ducks) keep the farm feeling alive and restaurant tables in the cottage garden overflowing with flowers provide a tranquil atmosphere. The countryside is ideal for cycling and there are many interesting old villages nearby.

Facilities

Toilet facilities are housed in original outbuildings, each block having very good quality, modern fittings. A large separate room has full facilities for disabled people, families and babies. Laundry. Bread can be ordered. Meals and snacks served in the farmhouse restaurant (to order only). Takeaway service. New swimming and paddling pools, with sunbathing areas. Small fenced play area with seating. Table tennis in one of the barns, mountain bike hire and organised activities in July/Aug. Off site: Tennis, riding and sailing in the area. Montmarault 4 km. for shopping needs.

Open

1 April - 30 October.

At a glance

Welcome & Ambience	✓✓✓	Location	✓✓✓✓
Quality of Pitches	✓✓✓	Range of Facilities	✓✓✓✓

Directions

From N79 Montmarault - Moulins road, turn right at first roundabout onto D46 signed St Pourcain. Turn left at next roundabout onto unclassified road signed Deux-Chaises and La Valette. After 2.5 km. turn left at site sign (La Valette) and site is approx. 1 km.

Charges 2004

Per adult	€ 3,95 - € 4,95
child (0-8 yrs)	€ 2,90 - € 3,85
pitch	€ 6,05 - € 7,50
electricity (6A)	€ 2,85
dog	€ 1,68
Surcharge for one night stay motorcaravan	€ 4,00 - € 5,50

For one night stay 1/7-31/8, plus 10%.

Reservations

Essential for July/Aug. and made with 50% deposit. Tel: 04 70 07 64 57. E-mail: la.petite.valette@wanadoo.fr

FR03020 Camping Château de Chazeuil

03150 Varennes-sur-Allier (Allier)

This spacious site is set in the attractive parkland surrounding a château. Here you will be surrounded by beautiful plants, flowers and bird song (if you are lucky, you will hear the nightingale). The 60 large, marked pitches are laid out on a well maintained lawn and all have electricity (although long leads may be necessary). Mature trees provide some pitches with shade. Although the entrance is adjacent to the main N7, traffic noise should be no problem as the site is set up a long drive. A one-way road system operates to ensure a safe exit from the site. The site provides a pleasant night's stop or short stay. There are walks from the campsite and the surrounding area has several interesting towns such as Vichy and St Pourçain with its vineyards. Many châteaux, churches and museums are also in the area.

Facilities

The modern sanitary block provides washbasins and showers in cabins, a washing machine and dishwashing and laundry sinks. It is maintained to a satisfactory level. Very pleasant unheated swimming pool and sunbathing area. Play area. Table tennis. Reading/information room. Off site: Shops, restaurants, etc. in Varennes 2 km. Fishing and canoeing in River Allier 2 km. Marked walks and cycle rides.

Open

15 April - 15 October.

At a glance

Welcome & Ambience	✓✓✓✓	Location	✓✓✓
Quality of Pitches	✓✓✓✓	Range of Facilities	✓✓✓

Directions

Site is 25 km. south of Moulins and just north of Varennes on the eastern side of the main N7. The entrance is at the traffic lights at the D46 turning for St Pourçain.

Charges 2004

Per person	€ 4,50
child (under 7 yrs)	€ 2,50
pitch incl. car	€ 7,20
animal	€ 1,00
electricity (6A)	€ 2,75

Reservations

Made for min. 3 days with € 32 deposit. Tel: 04 70 45 00 10. E-mail: camping-de-chazeuil@ifrance.com

FR15010 Camping Le Belvédère du Pont de Lanau

15260 Neuvèglise (Cantal)

This is a very steeply terraced, family run site in the picturesque southern Auvergne. Of the 120 pitches around 100 are for touring. The highest pitches, affording wonderful views, have no electricity and are only suitable for tents. The lower pitches have 6A electricity and some pitches have a sink, draining board and barbecue. The pitches are of good size and separated by conifers and pines, offering good shade and privacy. The site roads are steep and have sharp bends and access may be difficult for large units. Some pitches are some distance from the toilet blocks and access may involve a large number of steep steps. The nearby lake is good for fishing and water sports but swimming is not allowed. The site has its own small pool and terrace but little space for children to play. There are many places of interest in the area, including the Viaduc de Garabit (built by Eiffel), the Cantal Mountains and Salers (one of the most beautiful villages in France). It is an excellent region for walking, cycling, mountain biking and bird watching. There are beautiful wild flowers in the spring and wonderful autumn colours. This is not an ideal site for those who are not physically fit.

Facilities

Two toilet blocks have fairly modern equipment, including some basins in cabins. Baby room. Good facilities for disabled people. Sauna. Washing machine and dryer. Good motorcaravan service point. Spacious bar/restaurant/TV room provides meals and takeaways all season. Small shop in high season. Organised activities for all the family in July/Aug. Off site: Fishing, boat launching 500 m. Bicycle hire 5 km. Riding 20 km.

Open

1 April - 15 October.

At a glance

Welcome & Ambience	✓✓✓✓	Location	✓✓✓✓
Quality of Pitches	✓✓✓	Range of Facilities	✓✓✓✓

Directions

Site is 5 km. north of Chaudes-Aigues on D921 St Flour - Rodez road. Turn west at site sign, entrance is just beyond the Belvédère Centre de Vacance.

Charges guide

Per unit incl. 1 or 2 adults	€ 10,70 - € 16,70
with electricity (6A)	€ 12,40 - € 19,10
with electricity, sink and barbecue	€ 13,90 - € 21,40
extra adult	€ 2,15 - € 3,20
child (4-9 yrs)	€ 1,70 - € 2,40

Reservations

Advised in high season. Tel: 04 71 23 50 50.
E-mail: Belvedere.Cantal@wanadoo.fr

FR15030 Camping-Caravaning Le Val Saint Jean

15200 Mauriac (Cantal)

La Val Saint-Jean is part of a typical, newly developed 'Centre de Loisirs' which the French do so well, set beside a lake in the heart of the département of Cantal. The campsite is situated at a height of 700 m. and provides 100 generously sized touring pitches (with 10A electricity), terraced with good views and organised for the maximum of privacy, on a hill above the lake. The site is well planned so that you are never far from a sanitary block and it has an impressive number of good quality facilities. Most of the activities are situated by the lake where you can use all the facilities of the leisure club (high season) including cycling, canoeing, kayaking and pedalos. The lake has a sandy beach and an area for swimming. There is a large swimming pool, plus one for children on the campsite with sunbathing areas (free to campers). Both the pool and the lake have lifeguards most of the time in high season and they can get very busy in the main season. This less well known region is well worth exploring and the local gastronomy can be experienced in the village of Mauriac with its attractive architecture typical of the area.

Facilities

The two toilet blocks (4 and 6 years old) are well equipped with hot water throughout, providing some washbasins in cabins, dishwashing sinks and a laundry room with washing machine and dryer. Facilities for people with disabilities. Limited shop. Bar, snack bar and restaurant (all May - Sept). Swimming and paddling pools (1/6-15/9). Play area, playing field and table tennis. Watersports. Fishing. Activities organised for children (8-16 yrs) in July/Aug. Off site: Nine-hole golf course next to site. Mauriac village 600 m. Riding 2 km.

At a glance

Welcome & Ambience	✓✓✓✓	Location	✓✓✓✓✓
Quality of Pitches	✓✓✓✓	Range of Facilities	✓✓✓✓

Directions

From Clermont-Ferrand take RN89 towards Bordeaux, then D922 towards Bort-les-Orgues and Mauriac. Site is well signed in Mauriac.

Charges 2005

Per unit incl. 2 persons	€ 10,00 - € 17,00
extra adult	€ 4,00 - € 5,00
child (under 10 yrs)	free - € 2,50
dog	€ 1,50
electricity (10A)	€ 3,50

Reservations

Contact site. Tel: 04 71 67 31 13.
E-mail: info@camping-massifcentral.com

Open

1 May - 18 September.

FR19070 Camping Chateau de Gibanel

St Martial Entrayguis, 19400 Argentat (Corrèze)

This slightly terraced campsite is located in a beautiful estate, dominated by the 16th century château, on the banks of a very clean lake in this lesser known part of the Dordogne valley. Boats of up to 10 hp can be used on the lake for watersports and fishing. The very friendly family (English spoken) have ensured that everything is of a very high standard. Nearly all of the 250 grassy pitches are used for touring units. All have electricity (6A) and they are separated by a variety of mature trees giving varying amounts of shade. Some have an ideal position alongside the lake. Many of the trees have low branches making access to most pitches rather difficult for large motorcaravans. The attractive bar, restaurant and disco in the château is set well away from the pitches and the swimming pool and good sized paddling pool, with large sunbathing terrace, are alongside the spacious and well equipped play area.

Facilities

Four modern, spacious and very clean toilet blocks include many large cubicles with a shower and washbasin making them ideal for families. Washing machine and dryer. Small shop for basics (all season). Bar, restaurant and takeaway (July/Aug). Wide range of family activities in July/Aug, including weekly dance evenings, folklore events, watersports, walking and cycling, Bicycle hire (July/Aug). TV room, Table tennis. Boules. Volleyball. Bus stop on site in July/Aug. Off site: Argentat with its interesting old town, shops, restaurants etc. 5 km.

At a glance

Welcome & Ambience	✓✓✓✓✓	Location	✓✓✓✓
Quality of Pitches	✓✓✓✓	Range of Facilities	✓✓✓✓

Directions

Site is 5 km. northeast of Argentat. Take D18, signed Eggletons, and after 4 km, alongside the lake, fork right at site sign. Follow lane down to site.

Charges 2004

Per person	€ 3,72 - € 4,65
child (under 7 yrs)	€ 1,88 - € 2,35
pitch	€ 4,12 - € 5,15
electricity	€ 2,80
dog	€ 1,12 - € 1,40

Reservations

Essential in high season. Tel: 05 55 28 10 11.
E-mail: contact@camping-gibanel.com

Open

1 June - 15 September.

FR19060 Camping Le Mialaret

Route d'Egletons, 19160 Neuvic (Corrèze)

Mialaret is four kilometres from the village of Neuvic and only six from the river Dordogne. It is set in the grounds of a 19th century château, now a hotel and restaurant with a good reputation for fresh lobster and with a special evening menu for campers. Most pitches are set in a sunny, gently sloping meadow type situation. Some are level and separated by small bushes, most have some shade and 6A electricity. In low season there are cooking courses with the chefs of the hotel, also at that time of the year the owner has time to take customers on a conducted tour of the estate in his 4x4 vehicle. Entertainment in high season is quite low key with a mini club, some games, tournaments or an evening sing-along around a campfire, also musical evenings by both professionals and of the do-it-yourself type. Ten pitches are used by a tour operator.

Facilities

Three refurbished sanitary blocks give an adequate provision, one heated. Washbasins in cabins and adjustable showers, baby baths, facilities for disabled people, washing machines and dishwashing sinks. Motorcaravan service point. Shop at reception with bread daily. Bar with snacks and takeaway. Dinner at the hotel at special rate for campers. Play areas. Tennis. Table tennis. Fishing. Volleyball, football. Bicycle hire. The swimming pool is virtually a national monument as it is an original art-deco example. Unfortunately no paddling pool but a swimming pool is planned. Off site: Village with shops and lake 4 km. Golf 4 km. Canoeing, cycling and riding trips organised.

Open

1 May - 31 October.

At a glance

Welcome & Ambience	✓✓✓	Location	✓✓✓✓
Quality of Pitches	✓✓✓	Range of Facilities	✓✓✓✓

Directions

From Clermont-Ferrand take N89 southwest and, at Ussel, take D982 to Neuvic. In Neuvic take D982 signed Egletons and shortly turn right (D991) signed Egletons and La Mialaret. Site is within 4 km. on right. Note: the D991 Egleton - Neuvic road is only suitable for cars and small motorcaravans.

Charges 2004

Per person	€ 4,50 - € 5,50
child (2-8 yrs)	free - € 3,00
pitch	€ 4,50 - € 6,50
electricity	€ 2,00 - € 3,00
dog	free

Camping Cheques accepted.

Reservations

Contact site. Tel: 05 55 46 02 50.
E-mail: info@lemialaret.com

FR19080 Camping Le Vianon

19160 Palisse (Corrèze)

You will receive a very warm welcome from the new Dutch owners of this spacious and peaceful site and they speak excellent English. The site is tucked away in the lesser known, very beautiful Corrèze region yet it is only a few kilometres from the river Dordogne. This region is reputed to have the purest air in France. The grassy, slightly sloping pitches are of a good size in a natural woodland setting with tall trees offering shade, and all have 6A electricity. The bar, restaurant and terrace overlook the swimming pool and sunbathing area and are open all season. One speciality is the fresh bread and croissants, etc. baked on site each morning. Activities are arranged for all the family when there are enough participants, but these do not continue too late in the evening. As an added attraction they are developing a small farm for the children including a pony, a donkey, a goat, some chickens and some rabbits.

Facilities

Two modern toilet blocks with all the necessary facilities. There are plans for further refurbishment. En-suite unit and special pitches for disabled visitors. Bar. Restaurant and takeaway. Shop. No dedicated motorcaravan service point but arrangements can be made. Boules. Table tennis. Volleyball. Play area plus plenty of other space for children to play. Bicycle hire. Lake fishing. Off site: Neuvic (9 km) is a small town with a range of shops, restaurants and a bank. Large lake near Neuvic with a good range of water sports and area for swimming. Many old towns and villages with markets and museums including Bort les Orgues, Mauriac, Tulle, Egletons and Château de Val, Canoeing in the Dordogne (30 mins). Riding and golf course at Neuvic. Large range of marked walks and cycle rides (some guided).

At a glance

Welcome & Ambience	✓✓✓✓✓	Location	✓✓✓✓
Quality of Pitches	✓✓✓✓	Range of Facilities	✓✓✓✓

Directions

Leave A89 southwest of Ussel and take N89 towards Egletons. In about 7 km, just before Combressol, turn left on D47 signed Palisse and Camping le Vianon. Site entrance is on the left in 7 km.

Charges 2005

Per person	€ 3,90 - € 5,70
child (3-9 yrs)	free - € 3,50
pitch	€ 4,20 - € 7,10
electricity (6A)	€ 3,50
dog	free - € 2,00

Special rates for long stays.

Reservations

Contact site. Tel: 05 55 95 87 22.
E-mail: camping.vianon@wanadoo.fr

Open

12 April - 12 October.

FR19100 Camping Au Soleil d'Oc

Monceaux-sur-Dordogne, 19400 Argentat (Corrèze)

Set amongst a variety of tall trees on the banks of the river Dordogne, this attractive site should appeal to lovers of water and other sports, particularly in July and August when the site organises many activities for all the family. The 120 large, level, grass pitches, 60 for tourists, all with 6A electricity, are mostly separated by neatly trimmed shrubs and hedges. They are set out on two levels; the lower level nearer the river, with fewer static pitches, being some distance from the toilet facilities and sports area. The shop, bar, restaurant and swimming pool are near the entrance and just across the little road is the large sports area. This will be a lively site in July and August. It is not recommended for very large outfits due to the narrow, winding site roads and hedges.

Facilities

Two unisex toilet blocks on the upper level of the site offer all the facilities one would expect. Shop, bar, restaurant and takeaway (mid June – Sept). Swimming pool and small sunbathing area (June – Sept). Bathing in the river Dordogne. Fridge hire. Full entertainment programme of family activities including children's club (July/Aug). Canoe hire and organised trips from site. Fishing, volleyball, football, table tennis, pool table and electronic games. Bicycle hire. Guided walks and bike rides. Off site: River Dordogne. Argentat (4 km) with a good range of shops, banks etc and water sports centre. Riding 15 km.

Open

Easter - 1 November.

At a glance

Welcome & Ambience	✓✓✓	Location	✓✓✓✓
Quality of Pitches	✓✓✓✓	Range of Facilities	✓✓✓✓

Directions

Leave Argentat on the D12 heading southwest, signed Beaulieu. In 3.5 km/ turn left across a single track bridge spanning the river Dordogne (camping signed). Immediately turn left and site entrance is a few hundred metres on the left.

Charges 2004

Per unit incl. 2 persons	€ 12,50 - € 17,60
extra person	€ 3,00 - € 4,60
child (2-7 yrs)	free - € 2,50
electricity (6A)	€ 2,80 - € 3,00
dog	free - € 1,80

Camping Cheques accepted.

Reservations

Contact site. Tel: 05 55 28 84 84.
E-mail: info@dordogne-soleil.com

FR19090 Camping Le Vaurette

Monceaux-sur-Dordogne, 19400 Argentat (Corrèze)

The Audureau family have spent over 30 years developing this beautiful campsite from an old farm. The ancient barn at the far end of the site houses the bar and a large TV room (large screen) and the terrace overlooks the good sized and attractive, but unheated, swimming and paddling pools (all season). The well stocked shop and takeaway are near reception. There are 120 large, gently sloping grass pitches, 118 for touring. Separated by a large variety of beautiful trees and shrubs offering varying amounts of shade, all have 6A electricity and many have good views over the river Dordogne as the pitches nearest the river are slightly terraced. The owners are trying to run an active campsite for all the family whilst maintaining an air of tranquillity. You are assured of a warm welcome here, as excellent English and Dutch is spoken.

Facilities

Two very clean and modern toilet blocks offer all the expected facilities, including facilities for disabled people. Further facilities are near the bar and pool. Motorcaravan service point. Shop and takeaway (July/Aug). Football. Volleyball. Badminton. Boules. Table tennis. Tennis (free in low season). Fishing. Accompanied canoe trips, walks and mountain bike rides from site. Wide range of organised activities for all the family (July and Aug) but no late night discos etc. Off site: River Dordogne. Argentat (9 km.) with a good range of shops, banks etc and a water sports centre. Riding 15 km. Many marked walks and mountain bike rides close by.

At a glance

Welcome & Ambience	✓✓✓✓✓	Location	✓✓✓✓
Quality of Pitches	✓✓✓✓	Range of Facilities	✓✓✓✓

Directions

Leave Argentat on the D12 heading southwest, signed Beaulieu. The campsite is in 9 km on the left.

Charges 2004

Per unit incl. 2 persons	€ 13,00 - € 19,00
extra person (over 2 yrs)	€ 3,00 - € 4,50
electricity (6A)	€ 2,95
dog	€ 1,20 - € 2,50

Reservations

Made with fee (€ 10) for middle and high season plus deposit (€ 6 per day). Tel: 05 55 28 09 67. E-mail: camping.le.vaurette@wanadoo.fr

Open

1 May - 21 September.

FR19050 Camping La Rivière

Route de Brive, 19270 Donzenac (Corrèze)

The Corrèze is not nearly as well known as the Dordogne to the immediate south, but it is, in fact, a beautiful area deserving of more attention. Donzenac itself is an attractive small town with a variety of shops, restaurants, etc. This former municipal site is situated on the outskirts, somewhat less than a mile from the centre (an uphill walk). The site is small and neat with 77 fairly large pitches on level grass, the majority with electricity (10A). A variety of trees and shrubs give some shade. The site is next door to the town tennis courts and swimming pool (July/Aug. only; free to campers).

Facilities

Modernised sanitary facilities are very good and include a laundry room including washing machine and microwave. Baker calls at site in July/Aug. Table tennis, boules and minigolf. Fishing. Double axle caravans are not accepted. Off site: Riding 4 km. Golf 10 km.

Open

1 April - 30 September.

At a glance

Welcome & Ambience	✓✓✓✓	Location	✓✓✓✓
Quality of Pitches	✓✓✓	Range of Facilities	✓✓✓

Directions

At roundabout at southern end of Donzenac (D920) turn southwest onto D170 signed Ussac and La Rivière, Entrance to site is shortly on the right.

Charges 2004

Per person	€ 4,00 - € 4,40
child (4-14 yrs)	€ 2,05 - € 2,55
pitch	€ 4,60
electricity (10A)	€ 2,55
dog	€ 1,00

Reservations

Probably unnecessary, but if in doubt phone. Tel: 05 55 85 63 95.

FR23010 Castel Camping Le Château de Poinsouze

Mobile homes ▶ page 401

Route de la Châtre, BP 12, 23600 Boussac-Bourg (Creuse)

Le Château de Poinsouze is a recently developed site with 145 pitches arranged on the open, gently sloping, grassy park to one side of the château's main drive - a beautiful plane tree avenue. It is a well designed, high quality site. The 112 touring pitches, some with lake frontage, all have electricity (6-25A), with water, waste water and sewage connections to many. The château (not open to the public) lies across the lake from the site. Exceptionally well restored outbuildings on the opposite side of the drive house a new restaurant, other facilities and the pool area. The site has a friendly family atmosphere, there are organised activities in main season including dances, children's games and crafts, family triathlons, and there are marked walks around the park and woods. All facilities are open all season, though times may vary. This is a top class site with a formula which should ensure a stress-free, enjoyable family holiday. Boussac (2.5 km) has a market every Thursday morning. The massive 12/15th century fortress, Château de Boussac, is open daily all year.

TRAVEL SERVICE SITE

TO BOOK CALL 0870 405 4055 OR www.alanrogersdirect.com

Facilities

The high quality, double glazed sanitary unit is entered via a large utility area equipped with dishwashing and laundry sinks, foot-pedal operated taps, sinks accessible for wheelchair users, drinks machine and two smaller rooms with washing machines, dryer and ironing. Four spacious rooms are very well equipped including some washbasins in cubicles, baby baths, changing mats and child's WC, and two suites for disabled people. Good motorcaravan service point. Well stocked shop. Takeaway, Comfortable bar with games, TV and library room above. New restaurant. Well fenced swimming pool with slide, children's pool (children wear colour coded bracelets, deposit required). Fenced playground designed with safety in mind. Table tennis, petanque, pool table and table football games. Bicycle hire. Free fishing in the lake (if you put the fish back); boats and lifejackets can be hired. Football, volleyball, basketball, badminton and other games. Dogs are not accepted in high season (9/7-19/8).

At a glance

Welcome & Ambience	✓✓✓✓✓	Location	✓✓✓✓✓
Quality of Pitches	✓✓✓✓	Range of Facilities	✓✓✓✓

Directions

Site entrance is 2.5 km north of Boussac on D917 (towards La Châtre).

Charges 2005

Per pitch incl. 2 persons	€ 12,00 - € 19,00
with electricity (6A), water, waste water	€ 18,00 - € 26,00
with electricity (10A), water, waste water, sewage connection	€ 23,00 - € 28,00
extra adult	€ 3,00 - € 5,50
child (2-7 yrs)	€ 2,00 - € 4,50
electricity 10-25A	€ 2,50 - € 5,00

Camping Cheques accepted.

Reservations

Advisable during July/Aug; made with 30% deposit and € 15 fee. Tel: 05 55 65 02 21. E-mail: info.camping-de.poinsouze@wanadoo.fr

Open

13 May - 18 September.

FR43020 Camping du Puy-en-Velay

Avenue d'Aiguilhe, 43000 Le Puy-en-Velay (Haute-Loire)

This very popular urban site is within ten minutes walk of the old town with its very interesting old centre and is well worth the trip. The Office de Tourisme is in Place du Clauzel, next to the Mairie. The site has a good security barrier and a warden who speaks good English and lives on site. Tarmac roads lead to 80 grassy pitches with 6A electricity, including 5 with water and a drain. A motorcaravan service point is adjacent with its own security barrier - apply to reception for a barrier key to use the services, or for an overnight stop (reception opens 08.00 - 21.00 hrs). Access is good and early arrival is advised.

Facilities

The main sanitary unit, recently refurbished and extended, includes some washbasins in cubicles. Facilities for disabled persons. Dishwashing and laundry sinks. An older unit at the rear of the site is only used in peak season. The facilities may be stretched in high season. Motorcaravan service point - see above. A room by reception has tourist information and a TV. Table tennis, boules, volleyball and badminton. Off site: Indoor pool and tennis adjacent. Baker and small supermarket 5 minutes walk. Several other shops, bar and restaurants close by. Fishing and golf 4 km. Riding 5 km.

At a glance

Welcome & Ambience	✓✓✓✓	Location	✓✓✓✓
Quality of Pitches	✓✓✓	Range of Facilities	✓✓✓

Directions

Site is northwest of the town centre, close to where N102 crosses the River Borne, and the Rocher St Michel d'Aiguilhe (a church on a rocky pinnacle). Site is well signed from around the town. Large blue 'Aire de Service' sign at entrance.

Charges 2004

Per unit incl. 2 persons	€ 8,75

No credit cards.

Reservations

Contact site for details. Tel: 04 71 09 55 09.

Open

Mid-April - 1 October.

FR43030 Camping du Vaubarlet

Vaubarlet, 43600 Sainte-Sigolène (Haute-Loire)

This peacefully located, spacious riverside family site has 131 marked, level, grassy and open pitches, with only those around the perimeter having shade and all having electricity (6A). With 102 pitches for tourists, the remainder are occupied by site owned tents or mobile homes. Those who really like to get away from it all can use a small 'wild camping' area on the opposite side of the river with its own very basic facilities. This area is reached either by footbridge or a separate road access. The main site is separated from the river (unfenced) by a large field used for sports activities. This is also an attractive site for those seeking a quieter late break in September when it can be warm and sunny and with the pool, rooftop sun-deck, delightful modern bar with covered terrace all open. Tourist attractions in and around the region include a textile museum in Sainte Sigolène, an 'escargot' farm in nearby Grazac, the stunning scenery, chateaux and churches of the Haute-Loire, and the annual medieval festival in Le Puy each September. A 'Sites et Paysages' member.

Facilities

Two toilet units have British and Turkish style WCs, some washbasins in cubicles for ladies, baby room, laundry with washing machine and dryer and dishwashing sinks. Two new family bathrooms (WC, basin, shower) behind the bar, are also suitable for disabled people. Basic sanitary unit and campers' kitchen with cooker in 'wild' area. Small shop (bread to order). Takeaway in main season. Bar. Fenced swimming pool with children's pool. Bicycle hire. Table tennis, boule, volleyball and space for ball games. Playground. Organised activities in main season include camp fire and music evenings, canoe lessons for children, pony riding and mini-motorbike motocross (possibly noisy). Trout fishing (licenses available). Birdwatching, walking. Barbecues on loan. Off site: Two supermarkets and other shops in Ste Sigolène 6 km. Riding 15 km. Three golf courses around 30 km.

At a glance

Welcome & Ambience	✓✓✓✓✓	Location	✓✓✓✓
Quality of Pitches	✓✓✓✓	Range of Facilities	✓✓✓✓

Directions

Site is 6 km. southwest of Ste Sigolène on the D43 signed Grazac. Turn off this road by river bridge and follow signs.

Charges 2004

Per unit incl. 2 persons	€ 12,75 - € 15,00
extra person	€ 2,55 - € 3,00
child (2-7 yrs)	€ 1,70 - € 2,00
electricity	€ 2,55 - € 3,00
pet	€ 0,85 - € 1,00

Camping Cheques accepted.
Less 15% outside July/Aug.

Reservations

Advised for high season and made with 25% deposit and fee (€ 19.82). Tel: 04 71 66 64 95.
E-mail: camping@vaubarlet.com

Open

1 May - 30 September.

FR48000 Camping Caravaning Le Champ d'Ayres

Route de la Brèze, 48150 Meyrueis (Lozère)

The road to Meyrueis is not for the faint-hearted, although we managed in quite a large motorhome with only a few stretches being a little on the narrow side. Le Champ d'Ayres is a traditionally French style site with a modern feel to it, set in the heart of the Cevennes. Very neat, tidy and well kept, it is run by a young family with young families in mind (teenagers might be bored). The site is slightly sloping with 70 grass pitches, the majority hedged with well trimmed bushes and most with some shade. All have electricity (6/10A) but may require long leads. The area is surrounded by mountains and gorges but the river Jonte is not a canoeing river (a trip to the Tarn would be needed). The Gorges de Jonte has an observatory from which vultures can be observed flying the thermals. Being very central there are many attractions in the area - wild horses have been introduced on the causses a few miles to the north, the observatory at the top of Mt Aigoual is well worth a visit and there are many caves in the region.

Facilities

The central toilet block, kept very clean, includes mainly British style WCs and some washbasins in cabins. Family sized shower room, room with facilities for disabled visitors and baby room. Laundry and dishwashing sinks. Washing machine and dryer. Reception incorporates a small bar (15/6-15/9) which also sells ices and bread. Takeaway (15/6-15/9). Swimming and paddling pools (20/5-15/9). Play area on grass (5-10 yrs), small games room, table tennis, basketball, netball and a boules pitch. In July/Aug activities are arranged for children, also paella evenings with music and activities such as walking and caving. Off site: The pretty small town of Meyrueis has many good shops and restaurants. Fishing 100 m. Riding 300 m. Bicycle hire 500 m.

At a glance

Welcome & Ambience	✓✓✓✓✓	Location	✓✓✓✓
Quality of Pitches	✓✓✓✓	Range of Facilities	✓✓✓✓

Directions

From N9 at Aquessac (5 km. north of Millau) take D907 signed Gorge du Tarn. At Rozier turn right on D996 signed Meyrueis and Gorges de la Jonte. In Meyrueis follow signs for Château d'Ayres and campsite signs. Site is 500 m east of the town.

Charges 2004

Per unit incl. 2 persons	€ 10,00 - € 15,00
extra person	€ 2,50 - € 3,50
child (under 7 yrs)	€ 1,60 - € 2,50
electricity (6A)	€ 2,50

Reservations

Contact site. Tel: 04 66 45 60 51.
E-mail: campinglechampdayres@wanadoo.fr

Open

9 April - 24 September.

FR48020 Camping de Capelan

48150 Meyrueis (Lozère)

The Lozère is one of France's least populated departements but offers some truly spectacular, rugged scenery, wonderful flora and fauna and many old towns and villages. The little town of Meyrueis, accessible from the campsite via a riverside walk, marks the start of the Gorges de la Jonte, with the better known Gorges du Tarn running a little to the north. Le Capelan is a friendly family site with English and Dutch spoken. It has 120 grassy pitches strung out alongside the river, most with some shade and all with electrical connections (6/10A). Around 40 pitches are used for mobile homes. The site has direct river access and trout fishing is popular. Although there are special facilities, the site is not ideal for disabled visitors. A 'Sites et Paysages' member.

Facilities

Two very good toilet blocks are of recent construction and well maintained. Facilities for disabled visitors (but see above). 3 bathrooms (bath, shower,, basin and WC) for rent. Small shop (from 1/6). Spacious bar (from 1/6) with satellite TV, internet access, pool table. Takeaway (from 1/7). Swimming and paddling pools with sunbathing terrace (from 1/6), accessible only via 60 steps. Multi-sports terrain. Play area. Range of leisure activities including supervised rock climbing. Fishing. Communal barbecue area; only gas and electric barbecues permitted on site. Off site: Town centre with shops, restaurants, banks, etc. 1 km. Bicycle hire 1 km. Riding 3 km. Canoeing. The Cévennes national park with innumerable walking and cycling opportunites. Several excellent caves. Vullture visitor centre.

At a glance

Welcome & Ambience	✓✓✓✓	Location	✓✓✓✓
Quality of Pitches	✓✓✓	Range of Facilities	✓✓✓✓

Directions

Site is 1 km. west of Meyruels on the D996, the road to La Jonte. It is well signed from the centre of the town.

Charges 2004

Per pitch and 2 persons including electricity	€ 13,00 - € 18,00
extra person	€ 3,70
child (under 7 years)	€ 2,40

Camping Cheques accepted.

Reservations

Contact site. Tel: 04 66 45 60 50.
E-mail: camping.le.capelan@wanadoo.fr

Open

30 April - 19 September.

FR48060 Camping Les Terrasses du Lac de Naussac

Lac de Naussac, 48300 Langogne (Lozère)

The Lac de Naussac is the largest in the Lozère and this site has direct access to the lake. This family owned, very spacious campsite and hotel complex is set out on the side of a steep hill at nearly 1,000 m. altitude (nights can be cold). There are 180 good size grassy, gently sloping pitches, often with part hard-standing (165 for touring). All have 6A electricity and many have panoramic views over the lake and surrounding hills. There are many small trees on site offering some shade on a few of the pitches. There is a small pool and various other leisure amenities, with plenty of room for children to play, although the facilities are widely spaced around this hilly site. The lake offers a wide range of water based activities, notably sailing and fishing. This is superb walking and bike riding country and the long distance Stevenson trail passes close by at Langogne.

Facilities

The three toilet blocks are modern and well maintained. Very small shop (1/5-30/9). Bar, restaurant and takeaway in adjacent hotel (1/4-30/9). Small swimming pool (1/6-30/9). Lively 'animation' programme in peak season including children's club but no discos. Play area. Communal barbecue area. Bicycle hire. Gas and electric barbecues only. Off site: Disco 300 m. All kinds of water sports with equipment for hire on lake. Bike ride around lake of 30km. Langogne (shops, restaurants, Stevenson trail etc.) 2 km. 9 hole golf course 3 km. Riding 3 km.

Open

15 April - 30 September.

At a glance

Welcome & Ambience	✓✓✓	Location	✓✓✓✓
Quality of Pitches	✓✓✓	Range of Facilities	✓✓✓✓

Directions

Leave the N88 (Le Puy - Mende) road just southwest of Langogne. Turn on D26 towards Lac de Naussac, pass by the village of Naussac and follow signs to site. Stop in the parking area beside the lake and just before the hotel, reception inside the hotel.

Charges 2004

Per pitch incl. 2 persons	€ 12,50 - € 13,50
extra person	€ 3,50
child (2-6 yrs)	€ 1,50
electricity	€ 2,50
dog	€ 1,00

Camping Cheques accepted.

Reservations

Contact site. Tel: 04 66 69 29 62.
E-mail: naussac@club-internet.fr

FR63040 Château Camping La Grange Fort

Les Pradeaux, 63500 Issoire (Puy-de-Dôme)

This site has good, modern facilities, yet is oozing with character. It is very popular with the Dutch. The 15th century castle is impressive, more British in style than the usual French château. The new reception is well stocked with tourist information and an internet access point. The restaurant in the castle, originally the kitchen and dining hall, has great atmosphere and offers a simple daily menu. The cosy bar still has the old stable stalls and hay racks. The 120 pitches (90 for touring units) are of average size, mostly on grass but with some hardstandings, and connected by rather narrow roads and with limited play space for children. Some of the smaller pitches are in sunny fields around the castle, others in bays with hedges and trees. All have 6A electrical hook-ups. There are pleasant walks in the extensive grounds and beyond. You are assured a warm welcome at this Dutch owned site.

Facilities

The main toilet facilities in the old stable buildings are modern and heated but hot water is only available morning and early evening. Both ladies and men have baby rooms, the men's also has facilities for disabled visitors and a 'hydra shower'. Dog shower. Laundry room. Reception has a few groceries (bread to order). Restaurant (1/5-15/9), bar (15/6-15/9) and takeaway (1/5-15/9). Small indoor pool with sliding glass doors, sauna and massage table (15/4-15/10). Two outdoor pools (15/6-1/10) with grass sunbathing areas. Play area and games room. Tennis, minigolf, table tennis, volleyball, football field and boules. Organised activities in season include archery, canoeing, riding and cycling (horses and bikes provided). Off site: Fishing 250 m. Riding 8 km. Good touring area with magnificent scenery. The Parc des Volcans and the Vulcania exhibition are a must.

At a glance

Welcome & Ambience	✓✓✓✓✓	Location	✓✓✓✓
Quality of Pitches	✓✓✓	Range of Facilities	✓✓✓✓

Directions

From A75 autoroute take exit 13 at Issoire. Travel east on D996 to Parentignat and in village turn right (D999) and after 200 m. right again on D34 signed Nonette. Site is 3 km. up the D34.

Charges 2005

Per adult	€ 3,85 - € 5,25
child (under 7 yrs)	€ 2,60 - € 3,00
pitch	€ 4,90 - € 9,50
dog	€ 3,00

Camping Cheques accepted.

Reservations

Contact site for details. Tel: 04 73 71 02 43.
E-mail: chateau@grangefort.com

Open

10 April - 15 October.

FR63050 Camping La Ribeyre

Jassat, 63790 Murol (Puy-de-Dôme)

About a kilometre from the centre of Murol, La Ribeyre has a charm about it which is quite unique. The owners, Mme. Pommier and her two sons, originally farmers, have put much personal effort in constructing the site, its buildings and the pool. There is an extremely friendly atmosphere here. Many young trees have been planted to add to those already on site and a man-made lake at one end provides facilities for water sports. There is a picturesque reception area, with a fountain and tastefully laid-out floral decorations. The site now provides 400 level, grassy pitches, of which 300 have electricity (6A) and 110 have individual electricity, water and drainage. Although not normally advertised, there are 10A outlets for those who ask. The surrounding area is very much worth a visit. From mountains rising to over 6,000 ft, to lakes, cavernes and many local craft centres, this site is a superb centre. It is only five or six kilometres from St Nectaire, about ten kilometres from Besse and about twenty kilometres from Le Mont Dore, which is a starting point for the Puy de Sancy, the highest peak in the area. This is a wonderful walking and cycling area and the flowers in May and June are a joy to behold.

Facilities

Six excellent, clean modern toilet blocks provide British and Turkish style WCs and some washbasins in cubicles. Snack bar (20/6-1/9). Heated swimming pool 200 sq.m.(1/5-1/9). TV and games room. Tennis, volleyball and fishing. Play area. Small campsite lake for swimming, canoeing and surf boarding (lifeguard July/Aug). Off site: Riding 300 m. Bicycle hire 1 km. Further shops and restaurants at Murol, 1 km. Fishing, boating and sailing at Lac Chambon 3 km.

Open

1 May - 15 September.

At a glance

Welcome & Ambience	✓✓✓✓✓	Location	✓✓✓✓
Quality of Pitches	✓✓✓✓	Range of Facilities	✓✓✓✓

Directions

From A75 autoroute, take exit 6, signed St Nectaire and carry on to Murol. Several sites are signed as you go into the town. Turn left and then, opposite Syndicat d'Initiative, turn right. La Ribeyre is the second site on the left, just after the entrance to Jassat and is well marked on left.

Charges 2004

Per unit incl. 1 adults	€ 9,00 - € 12,50

Camping Cheques accepted.
No credit cards.

Reservations

Contact site. Tel: 04 73 88 64 29.
E-mail: laribeyre@free.fr

FR63060 Camping Le Clos Auroy

Rue de la Narse, 63670 Orcet (Puy-de-Dôme)

You will receive a friendly welcome at Le Clos Auroy, a well maintained and popular site, 300 metres from Orcet, a typical Auvergne village just south of Clermont Ferrand. Being close (3 km) to the A75, and open all year, it makes an excellent stopping off point on the journey south. The 90 good size pitches are on level grass, separated by high conifer hedges, offering lots of privacy. All have electricity and many are fully serviced. In winter only 20 pitches are available. Access is easy for large units.

Facilities

Two high quality sanitary units include washbasins in cubicles. Dishwashing and laundry sinks. Washing machine and dryer. A smaller, heated unit at reception is used mainly for the winter season, when it is heated. Chemical disposal is at the motorcaravan service point, close to the entrance (a long walk from some pitches). Small shop and takeaway (both 1/7-15/9). Bar (15/6-15/9). Heated pool with attractive terrace next to the bar (15/5-30/9). Playground. Tennis. Children's activities. Off site: Large playground nearby and riverside walk just outside gate. Village with shops and three wine 'caves' 300 m. Fishing and canoeing 500 m.

At a glance

Welcome & Ambience	✓✓✓✓✓	Location	✓✓✓✓
Quality of Pitches	✓✓✓✓	Range of Facilities	✓✓✓✓

Directions

From A75 take exit 4 or 5 towards Orcet and follow campsite signs. It is just before the village.

Charges 2004

Per unit incl. 2 persons	€ 15,00
extra person	€ 3,80
child (1-7 yrs)	€ 2,75
electricity (5/10A)	€ 2,90 - € 4,40

Less for longer stays in low season. No credit cards.

Reservations

Advised for July/August. Tel: 04 73 84 26 97.
E-mail: infocamping@wanadoo.fr

Open

All year.

FR63080 Camping Le Moulin de Serre

D73, vallée de la Burande, 63690 Singles (Puy-de-Dôme)

This very spacious, family run site is set in a beautiful wooded valley beside the Burande river where one can pan for gold. It offers a good base for those seeking a quiet relaxing holiday in this lesser known area of the Auvergne. The 90 good size pitches (55 for touring) are separated and shaded by a variety of trees and hedges. Some pitches have hardstanding and all have electricity. Access around the site is easy but the roads leading to it are twisting and some are steep which might prove difficult for larger units.

Facilities

Two well appointed very clean toilet blocks with one block heated in spring, the latter having excellent facilities for disabled people and babies. Swimming pool with terrace (8/6-;28/9). Takeaway and bar/restaurant (July/Aug). Bread (high season). Washing machine and dryer. Motorcaravan service point. Simple but very large play area. Football, table tennis. Canoe hire in high season. Daily programme of organised activities (July/Aug). Off site: Large play area on the adjacent banks of the river, ideal for paddling. Small lake for water sports 2 km. Château de Val 20 km. Spa town of la Bourboule 25 km. Barrage de Bort les Orgues offers watersports. Many marked walks and cycle tracks. Riding.

At a glance

Welcome & Ambience	✓✓✓✓	Location	✓✓✓
Quality of Pitches	✓✓✓✓✓	Range of Facilities	✓✓✓✓

Directions

Site is about 25 km. southwest of La Bourboule. Turn west off D922 near Tauves onto D29. Just before Singles turn left on D73 and follow signs, site is on right in just over 1 km.

Charges 2004

Per unit incl. 2 persons	€ 10,40 - € 13,90
extra adult	€ 2,85 - € 3,80
child (under 10 yrs)	€ 1,90 - € 2,55
electricity (3-10A)	€ 2,80 - € 4,50

Reservations

Advised in high season. Tel: 04 73 21 16 06. E-mail: moulin-de-serre@wanadoo.fr

Open

15 April - 18 September.

FR63070 Camping Le Pré Bas

Lac Chambon, 63790 Murol (Puy-de-Dôme)

In the heart of the Parc des Volcans d'Auvergne, beside Lac Chambon, Le Pre Bas is especially suitable for families with younger children and those seeking the watersports opportunities that the lake provides. Large, level, grassy pitches are divided up by mature hedging and trees and, with 63 mobile homes for rent, around 120 pitches are available for tourists, all with electricity (4A). A gate leads to the lakeside, where in the high season there is windsurfing, pedaloes, canoes or fishing, and 50 m. away is a beach with supervised bathing. The site has a new pool complex with heated swimming pools (one covered), a large slide and a paddling pool.

Facilities

There is one large, newly refurbished central toilet building with four smaller units spread around site. These include washbasins in cubicles, facilities for disabled guests and dishwashing sinks. Laundry with sinks, washing machines, dryers and ironing facilities, and baby room. Motorcaravan service point. Snack bar with a small terrace (10/6-10/9 and some weekends in low season). Well fenced, swimming pool complex (10/6-10/9) has three pools of different depths (lifeguard in July/Aug). Watersports and fishing in lake. Games room with table tennis, table football, pool, etc, large 'salle' with giant TV screen and library. Adventure style playground alongside a football/basketball pitch. Organised activities (late June-early Sept) include local visits, guided walks, riding, archery and climbing.

At a glance

Welcome & Ambience	✓✓✓✓✓	Location	✓✓✓✓
Quality of Pitches	✓✓✓✓	Range of Facilities	✓✓✓✓

Directions

Site is located on the D966, 3 km. west of Murol towards Le Mont Dore.

Charges 2004

Per pitch incl. 1 adult	€ 8,70 - € 13,65
extra person	€ 3,70 - € 4,75
child (1-5 yrs)	€ 2,40 - € 3,15
electricity (6A)	€ 4,00 - € 4,20
animal	free - € 2,00

Reservations

Essential for high season, made with € 39 p/week deposit. Tel: 04 73 88 63 04. E-mail: prebas@lac-chambon.com

Open

1 May - 30 September.

FR63120 Camping Indigo Royat

Route de Gravenoire, 63130 Royat (Puy-de-Dôme)

This is a spacious, well tended and attractive site sitting high on a hillside on the outskirts of Clermont Ferrand, but close to the beautiful Auvergne countryside. It has nearly 200 terraced pitches on part hard-standing. There are 150 available for touring units, all with 6/10A electricity (long leads may be needed). The pitches are informally arranged in groups, with each group widely separated by attractive trees and shrubs. The bar overlooks the irregularly shaped swimming pool, paddling pool, sunbathing area, tennis courts and play areas. Although very peaceful off season, it could be lively in July and August. This site would be ideal for who would like a taste of both the town and the countryside.

Facilities

Five well appointed toilet blocks are placed around the site, some heated off season. They have all the usual amenities but it could be a long walk from some pitches. Small shop. Bar and takeaway. Internet point. Attractive swimming and paddling pools with sunbathing area. Two tennis courts. Boules. Table tennis. Bicycle hire. Two grassy play areas. Organised entertainment in the high season. Off site: Royat 20 minutes walk but bus available every 30 minutes. Clermont Ferrand, Puy de Dôme, Parc des Volcans, Volcania exhibition.

Open

1 April - 31 October.

At a glance

Welcome & Ambience	✓✓✓✓	Location	✓✓✓
Quality of Pitches	✓✓✓✓	Range of Facilities	✓✓✓✓

Directions

From A75 exit 2, just south of Clermont Ferrand follow signs for Bordeaux (D799). At third roundabout take third exit (D3, Beaumont). In 800 m. turn left (D777, Beaumont). At T-junction turn left (N89, Ceyrat). Turn right up the hill (D767, Royat). At T-junction turn right (D941C) signed Royat and Puy de Dôme. At top of hill turn left (D5, Route de Gravenoire) signed Royat Indigo. Entrance is 800 m. on the right (mini roundabout).

Charges 2004

Per person	€ 4,00
child (2-7 yrs)	€ 2,30
pitch	€ 4,50 - € 9,50
electricity (6/10A)	€ 4,00 - € 5,50

Reservations

Made with deposit (€ 5 per day) plus fee of € 15 (high season). Tel: 04 73 35 97 05.
E-mail: royat@camping-indigo.com

FR63140 Camping Les Loges

63340 Nonette (Puy-de-Dôme)

This is a pleasant, spacious, rural site bordering the River Allier. There are 126 good sized, level, grassy pitches offering plenty of shade, 100 for touring and all with 6A electricity. This site would suit those seeking a quieter holiday without too much organised activity. The river is ideal for bathing and canoeing and there are many walks and bike rides in the area. It is also well placed to explore the beautiful Auvergne countryside, the extinct volcanoes and the many attractive old towns and villages.

Facilities

The two modern toilet blocks contain all the usual facilities. Heated swimming pool with Small shop (July/Aug). Bar (June- Aug). TV room. Simple takeaway menu (all season). Heated swimming pool with slide and paddling pool (June-Sept). Volleyball. Table tennis. Play areas and play room. River fishing and bathing. Sunday evening dances in high season. Canoe trips arranged from site.
Off site: Walking and cycling routes. Riding 10 km. Small village of Nonette 3 km. Small range of shops at Saint Germain 5 km. Parc des Volcans, Volcania Exhibition.

Open

Easter - 8 October.

At a glance

Welcome & Ambience	✓✓✓✓	Location	✓✓✓✓
Quality of Pitches	✓✓✓✓	Range of Facilities	✓✓✓✓

Directions

From A75 take exit 17 (south of Issoire) and turn left (D214) signed Le Breuil and Jumeaux. Bypass Le Breuil and turn left (D123) signed Nonette. Cross river and turn left and then immediately very hard left - take care (site signed). Entrance is 1 km. down this lane.

Charges 2004

Per person	€ 3,20 - € 4,20
child (0-7 yrs)	€ 2,10 - € 2,80
pitch	€ 4,10 - € 6,60
electricity	€ 3,20
dog	free - € 1,50

Reservations

Made with 30% deposit and € 8 fee.
Tel: 04 73 71 65 82.
E-mail: camping.les.loges.nonette@wanadoo.fr

FR63090 Camping Les Domes

Les Quatre Routes de Nébouzat, 63210 Nébouzat (Puy-de-Dôme)

A friendly welcome awaits at this attractive, compact, well cared for site which is run by a family of enthusiastic caravanners. It is ideally situated for exploring the beautiful region around the Puy de Dôme. The site has 65 small to medium sized pitches, 50 with 10A electricity, separated by trees and hedges and most are available for touring. Some pitches have a level, paved area ideal for caravans and motorcaravans. Rock pegs are advised. The attractive reception area comprising the office, a small shop for essentials (high season only) and a meeting room has lots of local information and interesting artefacts. An added attraction is a heated, covered swimming pool, which can be opened in good weather. There are many interesting old villages in the area (Orcival 8 km) and châteaux (Chateau de Corde 4 km).

Facilities

A well appointed central toilet block is kept very clean, but there are no special facilities for disabled visitors. Basic shop (baker calls). Breakfast, snacks and chips. Boules, pool table, table football, table tennis, giant chess and drafts. Small play area. TV and games room. Off site: Fishing 100 m. Restaurant 200 m. Nebouzat 1.3 km (shops etc). Riding 6 km. Hang gliding and parascending 8 km (Puy de Dôme). Lac Adyat 9 km. Golf 10 km. Clermond Ferrand with its interesting old town and hypermarkets (18 km). Many marked walks and cycle routes.

At a glance

Welcome & Ambience	✓✓✓✓✓	Location	✓✓✓✓
Quality of Pitches	✓✓✓✓	Range of Facilities	✓✓✓✓

Directions

Site is 18 km. southwest of Clermont Ferrand and is well signed from the roundabout at the junction of the N89 and the D941A. It is a few hundred metres from the roundabout along the D216 towards Orcival.

Charges 2004

Per unit incl. 1 person	€ 9,00
extra person	€ 5,50
child (under 5 yrs)	€ 3,00
electricity (10A)	€ 3,50

Reservations

Advised in high season. Tel: 04 73 87 14 06.

Open

15 May - 15 September.

FR87020 Castel Camping Le Château de Leychoisier

Domaine de Leychoisier, 1 Route de Leychoisier, 87270 Bonnac-la-Côte (Haute-Vienne)

You are assured of a warm welcome at this beautiful, family run 15th century château site. It offers peace and quiet in superb surroundings. Explore the grounds and walk down to the four hectare lake. It is ideally situated for short or log stays being only 2 km. from the A20/N20 and 10 km. north of Limoges. The large and grassy pitches are in a parkland setting with many magnificent mature trees offering a fair amount of shade. Of the 90 pitches, 85 are for touring, 80 have 10A electricity and many have a tap, although long leads and hoses may be necessary. The lake provides free fishing, boating, canoeing and a marked off area for swimming.

Facilities

The toilet block is in the outbuildings of the château. Very clean, but perhaps cramped at busy times. Some washbasins in private cabins with good provision for disabled visitors. Washing machine. Basic food provisions (all season). Attractive restaurant with good menu (from 20/6). Bar, TV room and snack bar. Small swimming pool with large grass sunbathing area (proper swimming trunks, no shorts). Lake. Play area. Bicycle hire, table tennis, tennis and boules courts (both in need of repair when we visited), volleyball and bar billiards. Torch useful. Winter caravan storage. Off site: Mini-market 2 km. supermarket 5 km. Riding 7 km. Golf 20 km. Limoges, noted for its pottery.

At a glance

Welcome & Ambience	✓✓✓✓✓	Location	✓✓✓✓
Quality of Pitches	✓✓✓✓	Range of Facilities	✓✓✓✓

Directions

From A20 take exit 27 (west) signed Bonnac-La-Côte. Site is well signed from the autoroute (2 km).

Charges 2004

Per person	€ 5,50 - € 7,00
child (under 7 yrs)	€ 3,80 - € 4,50
pitch	€ 8,00 - € 9,00
electricity	€ 3,70 - € 3,90
dog	€ 0,80 - € 1,00

No credit cards.

Reservations

Made with deposit (€ 15.24) and fee (€ 12.20), although short reservations accepted without charge in low season. Tel: 05 55 39 93 43.
E-mail: contact@leychoisier.com

Open

15 April - 20 September.

Rhône Valley

Map 13

With such a rich and varied landscape, the Rhône Valley offers a spectacular region of craggy gorges and scented hills, ideal for life at a leisurely pace - easy to do when there are so many stunning views to take in.

Départements: 01 Ain, 07 Ardèche, 26 Drôme, 42 Loire, 69 Rhône

Major city: Lyon

The region's 2,000 year history as a cultural crossroads has blessed the area with a rich blend of customs, architecture and sights of interest. The city of Lyon was developed by the Romans as a trading centre, and was once the capital. It is now the second largest city of France. The Place de la Terreur in the centre of the city is where the guillotine was placed during the French revolution – until it wore out through over-use. Not far from Lyon lies the Dombes, the land of a thousand lakes, and the medieval village of Pérouges and Roman ruins of Vienne.

The Rhône valley holds areas of great interest and natural beauty. From the sun-baked Drôme, with its ever-changing landscapes and the isolated mountains of the Vercors to the deep gorges and high plateaux of the Ardèche, studded with prehistoric caves and lush valleys filled with orchards; and encompassing the vine-yards of the Beaujolais and the Rhône Valley. For the energetic there are cycling, horse riding and even white water rafting opportunities, while for the more leisurely inclined, the remote areas are a haven for bird watching and walking.

Cuisine of the region

The poultry, cheese, freshwater fish and mushrooms are superb. Local wines include Beaujolais, Côte Rotie, St Julien, Condrieu, Tain-Hermitage, Chiroubles and Julienas.

Bresse (Poulet, Poularde, Volaille de): the best French poultry, fed on corn and when killed bathed in milk; flesh is white and delicate

Gras-double: ox tripe, served with onions

Poulet au vinaigre: chicken, shallots, tomatoes, white wine, wine vinegar and a cream sauce

Poulet demi-deuil (half-mourning): called this because of thin slices of truffle placed under the chicken breast

Rosette: a large pork sausage

Sabodet: Lyonnais sausage of pig's head, pork and beef, served hot

Places of interest

Beaujolais: vineyards and golden-stone villages

Bourg-en-Bresse: church of Notre-Dame, craft shops, museum of Ain

Dombes: lakes, ornithological park

Lyon: Gallo-Roman artifacts, Renaissance quarter, historical Fabric Museum, silk museum.

Pérouges: medieval village, Galette de Pérouges

St Etienne: museum of Modern Art

Vallon-Pont d'Arc: base from which to visit Gorges de l'Ardèche; canoe and rafting centre

Vienne: Gothic style cathedral, 6th century church St Pierre

Alan Rogers tip

IF YOU HAVE A SWEET TOOTH, TAKE A TRIP TO MONTÉLIMAR, THE NOUGAT CAPITAL OF FRANCE. JOIN ONE OF THE FACTORY TOURS AND ENJOY A SAMPLE OR TWO!

FR01010 Camping La Plaine Tonique

Base de Plein Air, 01340 Montrevel-en-Bresse (Ain)

This site belongs to a syndicate of several local villages. It is a very well maintained, large site with 560 marked and numbered pitches, all with 10A electricity. The majority are of a good size, hedged and on flat grass, with reasonable shade in most parts. Although large, the site is spacious and certainly does not feel so as it is broken up into smaller sections by trees and hedges. The site is on the edge of a large, 320-acre lake with its own beach and adjacent public beach. A variety of watersports is available, including sailing, windsurfing, swimming, canoeing and, on other parts of the lake, water-skiing and fishing. Campers may bring their own boats, but not motor boats. A separate area of the site is used by Dutch tour operators (100 pitches).

Facilities

Sanitary facilities are in eleven blocks, with most now renovated to a very high standard. They include some washbasins in cabins, baby rooms and washing machines. Motorcaravan service point. Restaurant, bar (all season) and shop (July/Aug) are next to the site. 'Aquatonic' centre with five pools (reduced charge for campers). Watersports and fishing. Minigolf and several tennis courts. Adventure play area on beach. Games and TV rooms. Archery, bicycle hire and roller skating area. Off site: Montrevel town 300 m. walk. Riding 2 km.

At a glance

Welcome & Ambience	✓✓✓	Location	✓✓✓✓
Quality of Pitches	✓✓✓✓	Range of Facilities	✓✓✓✓

Directions

Site is 20 km. north of Bourg-en-Bresse and 25 km. east of Macon. Montrevel is on the D975; site is signed in town centre towards Etrez on D28.

Charges guide

Per unit incl. electricity	€ 6,90 - € 10,60
person	€ 2,60 - € 4,30
child (3-7 yrs)	€ 1,40 - € 2,10
pet	€ 1,40 - € 1,70

Reservations

Required mid July - end Aug; write with 25% deposit. Tel: 04 74 30 80 52.
E-mail: plaine.tonique@wanadoo.fr

Open

14 April - 28 September.

FR01020 Camping de l'Ile Chambod

01250 Hautecourt (Ain)

This small site has recently been redeveloped by its enthusiastic English-speaking owners. It provides two modern toilet blocks, a swimming pool and small café. The 110 grassy pitches (about 100 sq m.) are separated by low hedges and most have some shade. They all have access to water points and electricity (5/10A) although some may need long leads. A lakeside beach is only 300 m. (charged for in high season), offering simple watersports and minigolf. There is plenty to see in the region and Bourg-en-Bresse offers a wealth of shops, restaurants, museums, etc.

Facilities

Two modern toilet blocks include some washbasins in cabins, dishwashing, laundry and vegetable preparation sinks. Washing machine and dryer. Both blocks have facilities suitable for disabled visitors and one has a baby room. Bread available to order. Small shop and takeaway (June, July and Aug). Small play area. Activities organised in high season for children up to 12 years.

Open

1 May - 30 September.

At a glance

Welcome & Ambience	✓✓✓✓	Location	✓✓✓✓
Quality of Pitches	✓✓✓	Range of Facilities	✓✓✓

Directions

Site is approx. 23 km. southeast of Bourg-en-Bresse via the D979. It is well signed from the crossroads in Hautecourt, and is a further 4 km. down the lane.

Charges 2005

Per person	€ 4,50
child (up to 12 yrs)	€ 3,00
pitch	€ 3,00
vehicle	€ 2,50
electricity 5-10A	€ 2,50 - € 3,50
animal	€ 1,00

No credit cards.

Reservations

Advised for July/Aug. Tel: 04 74 37 25 41.
E-mail: camping.chambod@free.fr

FR01030 Camping Les Ripettes

Chavannes sur Reyssouze, 01190 Pont de Vaux (Ain)

Recently taken over by an enthusiastic and hardworking English couple, this spacious site is situated in quiet, flat countryside near the pleasant small town of Pont-de-Vaux. It would make a useful stop on the way to or from the south of France, but would also serve as a centre to explore the interesting surrounding area. The historic towns of Macon and Tournus are each about 20 km. away, and Bourg-en-Bresse and the vineyards of Beaujolais, Maconnais and Chalonnais are all within 40 km. The 2.5 hectare (6 acre) site has 54 large (over 100 sq.m. to 400 sq.m.) level grassy pitches, 51 of which are available to tourists. Nearly all are separated by hedges and about half are shaded by the many trees on the site. All but two have electrical connections (10A), and there are ample water points.

Facilities

Two small sanitary blocks contain toilets, small showers, washbasins in cubicles and a suite for disabled visitors. Dishwashing sinks. Washing machine and double sink for washing clothes. If the site became full there could be queues for these facilities. No shop, but wine, ice cream and meat for barbecues can be bought at reception, where bread can be ordered. Two swimming pools (one 11 x 5 m, the other 7 m. diameter). Small play area and sandpit. Areas for ball games, volleyball, badminton, table tennis, boules (free loan of equipment). Free loan of board games and books. Bicycle hire. Off site: Riding 2 km. Fishing 4 km. Golf 15 km. Restaurant 1 km. Shops, etc., in Pont-de Vaux 4 km.

Open

1 April - 31 October.

At a glance

Welcome & Ambience	✓✓✓✓	Location	✓✓✓✓
Quality of Pitches	✓✓✓✓✓	Range of Facilities	✓✓✓

Directions

Leave N6 at Fleurville (18 km. north of Macon, 14 km. south of Tournus). Go east on the D933A to Pont-de-Vaux (5 km). Take D2 east towards St Trivier-de-Courtes. After about 3 km. look for a water tower on the right. Turn left just after this, and left again at next junction (100 m). Site entrance is 300 m. ahead on the left.

Charges 2004

Per person	€ 3,50
child (0-10 yrs)	€ 2,50
pitch	€ 5,50
electricity (10A)	€ 2,50

No credit cards.

Reservations

Can be made at any time, without fee or deposit.
Tel: 03 85 30 66 58.
E-mail: info@camping-les-ripettes.com

FR07130 Camping Les Coudoulets

Pradons, 07120 Ruoms (Ardèche)

For those who prefer a more intimate, peaceful campsite beside the river Ardèche, only a short distance away from the main centre, then this well cared for site is for you. It is run by a very enthusiastic and friendly family who have developed this site from their farm. They have a small vineyard and their wine is on sale in the bar, we fully recommend it. There are 125 good sized, grassy and well shaded pitches, separated by trees and shrubs. With 112 for touring, and all have 6A electricity. Organised events in July/August for all the family include the occasional evening event such as barbecues and musical evenings (no discos). There is an area for bathing in the river and it is an ideal spot for canoeists, etc.

Facilities

The very good, clean, recently refurbished toilet block has all the necessary facilities including excellent facilities for disabled people. Motorcaravan service point. Bar with TV and terrace (May - Sept) also selling bread, ices and drinks. Snacks in July/Aug. Butcher calls three times a week in high season. Small heated swimming pool and paddling pool (May - Sept). Fishing, football, volleyball and table tennis. Off site: Shop 300 m. Ruoms with a range of shops 4 km. Canyoning and rafting etc on the river Ardèche. Tennis or riding 2 km. Golf 7 km. Accompanied walks, canoe trips and visits to a wine cellar from site.

Open

1 May - 12 September.

At a glance

Welcome & Ambience	✓✓✓✓✓	Location	✓✓✓✓
Quality of Pitches	✓✓✓✓	Range of Facilities	✓✓✓✓

Directions

Leave Montélimar going west on N102 towards Aubenas. Shortly after passing Villeneuve de Berg turn left on D103 towards Vogüé for 5 km. Turn left on D579 towards Ruoms and site is on right in approx. 10 km. on entering the village of Pradons.

Charges 2004

Per unit incl. 2 persons	€ 13,00 - € 19,00
extra person	€ 3,50 - € 4,00
child (under 7 yrs)	€ 3,00 - € 3,50
electricity (6A)	€ 3,50
dog	free - € 2,00

Reservations

Made with deposit (€ 70) but no booking fee.
Max. 6 persons and 1 car per pitch.
Tel: 04 75 93 94 95.
E-mail: camping@coudoulets.com

FR07020 Camping Caravaning L'Ardéchois

Mobile homes ▶ page 401

Le Chambon, Gluiras, 07190 St Sauveur-de-Montagut (Ardèche)

This attractive site is quite a way off the beaten track and the approach road is winding and narrow in places. However, it is worth the effort, to find in such a spectacular setting, a hillside site offering a wide range of amenities. There are 106 pitches (83 for touring) laid out on steep terraces, of varying sizes and many separated by trees and plants. Some are alongside the small, fast-flowing stream, while the rest (60%) are on higher, sloping ground nearer the restaurant/bar and pool. All 83 touring pitches have electricity (10A). The main site access roads are tarmac but are quite steep and larger units may find access to some terraces difficult. The amenities have been created by the careful conversion of old buildings which provide modern facilities in an attractive style (all from Easter). The friendly Dutch owners have developed an extensive excursion programme for exploring this attractive area on foot or by car. There are two entrances to the site so, on arrival, park outside on the road and go to reception on foot. A 'Sites et Paysages' member.

Facilities

Two good sanitary blocks provide washbasins in private cabins, baths and showers for babies and facilities for people with disabilities. Dishwashing and laundry rooms. Motorcaravan service point. Shop, bar/restaurant and takeaway (1/5-25/9). New restaurant planned. Swimming pool (heated in low season; no Bermuda style shorts; 1/5-25/9) with adjacent bar, snack bar and terrace, plus a paddling pool for children. TV room. Table tennis. Volleyball. Bicycle hire, archery and fishing. Comprehensive entertainment programme. Off site: Canyoning, climbing, river walking and canoeing trips organised.

Open

Easter - 31 October.

At a glance

Welcome & Ambience	✓✓✓✓	Location	✓✓✓
Quality of Pitches	✓✓✓✓	Range of Facilities	✓✓✓✓

Directions

From Valence take N86 south for 12 km. At La Voulte-sur-Rhône turn right onto D120 to St Sauveur de Montagut (site well signed), then take D102 towards Mézilhac for 8 km. to site.

Charges 2005

Per unit incl. 2 persons	€ 19,00 - € 25,50
extra person	€ 4,00 - € 5,50
child (0-3 yrs)	free
animal	€ 3,00 - € 4,00

Camping Cheques accepted.
Low season price for over 55s.

Reservations

Write with deposit (€ 69) and fee (€ 23); min. 10 days 6/7-24/8. Tel: 04 75 66 61 87.
E-mail: ardechois.camping@wanadoo.fr

FR07050 Sunêlia Le Ranc Davaine

St Alban-Auriolles, 07120 Ruoms (Ardèche)

Le Ranc Davaine is a quite large, busy, family oriented site set in two areas separated by a reasonably quiet road. The larger area provides all the entertainment facilities and most of the 430 pitches. The 113 touring pitches are mostly scattered between static caravan and tour operator pitches and are on fairly flat, rather stony ground under a variety of trees giving much needed shade. All are supplied with electricity (6/10A), some needing very long leads which may cross tarmac roads. Rock pegs are advised. The lower part is beside the river (unfenced). Sunbathing areas surround the pool complex, overlooked by the terrace of the restaurant, providing very pleasant surroundings, especially attractive with evening floodlighting. A lively entertainment programme (July/Aug) is aimed at young children and teenagers. The site is popular with tour operators (113 pitches) and there are 170 mobile homes. It can get very busy for much of the season. A 'Sites et Paysages' member.

Facilities

Five fully equipped toilet blocks include full facilities for disabled visitors. Dishwashing and laundry sinks, washing machines, dryers and irons. Large shop catering for most needs. Cash point. Internet point in reception. Bar/restaurant serving good range of meals. Pizzeria and takeaway (all open all season). Attractive large, irregularly shaped swimming pool, covered pool (heated), supplemented by two small square pools and a large slide (all open all season, no shirts or Bermuda style shorts). Play area. Tennis, table tennis, basketball, football, archery and minigolf. Fishing. Extensive programme of sports in the pools, clubs for youngsters and teenagers, many other organised activities. Discos in closed, air-conditioned room (until 3 am four times a week in high season).
Off site: Canoe hire nearby for excursions down the River Ardèche. Rafting. Bicycle hire 2 km. Riding 6 km. Karting.

At a glance

Welcome & Ambience	✓✓✓✓	Location	✓✓✓✓
Quality of Pitches	✓✓✓	Range of Facilities	✓✓✓✓✓

Directions

From Ruoms go south on the D111. Just before Grospierres turn right onto D246, cross the river bridge (2.5 m. width restriction) and then left on D208 towards Chandolas and site.

Charges 2004

Per unit incl. 2 persons	€ 20,00 - € 34,00
with electricity	€ 24,00 - € 38,00
extra person	€ 6,00 - € 9,00
child (2-13 yrs)	€ 3,50 - € 9,00
animal	free - € 4,00

Camping Cheques accepted.

Reservations

Made with deposit (€ 100) and fee (€ 30).
Tel: 04 75 39 60 55.
E-mail: camping.ranc.davaine@wanadoo.fr

Open

23 March - 14 September.

FR07080 Domaine de la Bastide

RD111, route de Gros-Pierres, Sampzon, 07120 Ruoms (Ardèche)

Though more expensive than some, this site is maintained to a high standard and this is evident as soon as you drive in, with its neat and tidy appearance and flowers everywhere. On driving down to your pitch, it seems that there are many mobile homes. Actually there are only 46 mobile homes, 25 small chalets plus another 16 pitches used by a tour operator, which out of 300 pitches is really not many. Once past these, the site opens up to reveal pleasant, good sized pitches, all with some shade and bordered by flowering trees and bushes. All have electricity, the basic pitches with 3A, and 86 fully serviced ones with 5A. Security patrols ensure quiet nights. Canoe trips are arranged down the Gorge d'Ardèche and in mid-June each year a large section of the river bank next to the site is cleared of boulders and sand put down - just the job for children.

Facilities

Two toilet blocks, the newest with very high quality fittings including washbasins in cubicles, a baby room and facilities for disabled people. The older block is only open in high season and has mainly Turkish style WCs, plus showers, etc. Shop. Attractive restaurant, pizzeria and bar (mid June to end Aug). Heated swimming pool with pleasant sunbathing area. Free sauna and gym with a resident instructor. Play area. Table tennis, boules, volleyball, football, basketball and tennis courts. Fishing. Games and competitions are organised in July/Aug. plus discos in a soundproof cellar. Doctor calls daily (July/Aug) and hairdresser weekly (July/Aug). Only gas barbecues are permitted.
Off site: Riding and bicycle hire 3 km. Golf 6 km. Watersports on the nearby River Ardèche. The small town of Ruoms is 4 km. Vallon-Pont-d'Arc 7 km. The old villages of Balazuc, Labaume and Largentière.

At a glance

Welcome & Ambience	✓✓✓✓✓	Location	✓✓✓✓
Quality of Pitches	✓✓✓✓	Range of Facilities	✓✓✓✓✓

Directions

Going south from Ruoms on the D579, after 2.5 km. at roundabout, turn right on D111 signed Alès. Cross river bridge and site is 200 m. on the left.

Charges 2004

Per unit incl. 2 persons	
with electricity	€ 23,00 - € 34,00
with water and drainage	€ 28,00 - € 38,00
extra person over 3 yrs	€ 5,00 - € 7,00
dog	free - € 4,00

No credit cards.

Reservations

Made with deposit (€ 110) and booking fee (€ 40).
Tel: 04 75 39 64 72.
E-mail: camping.bastide@wanadoo.fr

Open

1 April - 30 September.

FR07070 Camping Les Ranchisses

Mobile homes page 402

Route de Rocher, Chassiers, 07110 Largentière (Ardèche)

Combining farming, wine-making, running an Auberge and a friendly family campsite is no simple task, but the Chevalier family seem to manage it quite effortlessly. Well run and with the emphasis on personal attention, this is a highly recommended site. In a somewhat lesser known area of the Ardèche, the site has developed from an original 'camping à la ferme' into a very well equipped modern campsite. There are 165 good-sized, level, grassy pitches, 88 for tourists with electricity (10A) which include 42 multi-serviced pitches (electricity, water, waste water). The pitches are in two distinct areas - the original site which is well shaded, and the lower part which is more open with less shade, serviced by tarmac and gravel access roads. The site runs parallel to the road and there may be background traffic noise in some areas. There is a small lake (unfenced) connected to the river, providing opportunities for bathing, fishing or canoeing (free life jackets) with one part of the bathing area quite safe for youngsters. The site's own Auberge is set in the original 1824 building that once used to house silk worms. It serves meals and takeaway food at lunch-time and evenings (all season) either inside the cave-like restaurant or outside on the attractive, shaded terrace.

Facilities

Two modern, comprehensively equipped toilet buildings include washbasins in cubicles, dishwashing and laundry sinks and facilities for babies and disabled persons. It is an excellent provision, kept immaculate. Laundry in separate building. Motorcaravan service point. Small shop, takeaway and bar with terrace (all 10/4-19/9). Excellent pool complex with two large pools (both heated all season) and paddling pool. Adventure style playground. Organised amusements for children in high season. Tennis court. Minigolf. Table tennis. Boules. Canoeing. Off site: Canoe and kayaking .arranged from the site each Monday and Wednesday (mid -June - end Aug). Medieval village of Largentière (1.5 km.) with Tuesday market and medieval festival in July. Take to the back roads to see the real Ardèche and don't miss the wonderful old villages of Balazuc and Labaume.

At a glance

Welcome & Ambience	✓✓✓✓	Location	✓✓✓✓
Quality of Pitches	✓✓✓✓	Range of Facilities	✓✓✓✓✓

Directions

Largentière is southwest of Aubenas and is best approached using the D104. After 16 km. just beyond Uzer at a roundabout turn northwest on the D5. After 5 km. at far end of Largentière, fork left downhill signed Valgorge. Site is on left in about 1.8 km.

Charges 2004

Per unit incl. 2 persons	€ 19,00 - € 25,00
serviced pitch	€ 25,50 - € 32,00
extra person	€ 4,50 - € 6,00
child (1-10 yrs)	€ 4,50 - € 6,00
electricity	€ 4,50

Camping Cheques accepted.

Reservations

Made with 30% deposit plus booking/insurance fee (€ 15). Tel: 04 75 88 31 97.
E-mail: reception@lesranchisses.fr

Open

10 April - 19 September.

TRAVEL SERVICE SITE

TO BOOK CALL 0870 405 4055 OR www.alanrogersdirect.com

FR07140 Camping Les Lavandes

Le Village, 07170 Darbres (Ardèche)

Although slightly less sophisticated than some others in the region, this site should appeal to those seeking the real France for a pleasant family holiday. Situated to the northeast of Aubenas, in a quieter part of this region, Les Lavandes is surrounded by magnificent countryside, vineyards and orchards. A ride along the panoramic road to Mirabel is a must. The enthusiastic French owners, who speak good English, run a site that appeals to all nationalities. The 70 pitches (58 for touring) are arranged on low terraces separated by a variety of trees and shrubs that give welcome shade in summer. Visit at the end of May to see the campsite trees laden with luscious cherries. There is no problem with electricity, most pitches having 6A but a few have 10A. Water taps are not so abundant. Traditional buildings house the reception (full of tourist information including a touch screen), shop, restaurant, takeaway and cosy bar offering excellent views over the swimming pool to the village (just a stroll away) and hillside beyond. Organised activities include wine tasting, shows, musical evenings and children's games.

Facilities

The recently refurbished facilities are comprehensive and well maintained. Excellent room with facilities for disabled people and a baby room. Washing machine. Small shop (1/7-31/8). Cosy bar and terrace (1/6-31/8). Restaurant (1/7-31/8). Takeaway (14.4-31.8). Swimming pool and paddling pool surrounded by paved sunbathing area with larger grass area adjacent, all with super views. Two small play areas for younger children. Table tennis, table football and pool table. Electric barbecues are not permitted. Off site: Fishing 1 km. Bicycle hire 3 km. Tennis 5 km. Canoeing, walking, cycling, riding and carting nearby. Caves, troglodyte villages, historical villages, interesting geological formations and museums. Wonderful area for birds (Golden Orioles and Bonellis eagle).

At a glance

Welcome & Ambience	✓✓✓✓	Location	✓✓✓✓
Quality of Pitches	✓✓✓✓	Range of Facilities	✓✓✓

Directions

You are advised to approach the site from the south. From Montélimar take the N102 towards Aubenas. After passing through Villeneuve, in Lavilledieu, turn right at traffic lights on D224 to Darbres (10 km). In the village of Darbres turn very sharp left by the post office (care needed) and follow signs to site.

Charges 2004

Per unit incl. 2 persons	€ 11,00 - € 16,00
extra person	€ 2,80 - € 3,50
child under 8 yrs	€ 1,00 - € 2,60
electricity	€ 3,50
dog	free - € 3,50

Reservations

Made with deposit (€ 85) and fee (€ 15).
Tel: 04 75 94 20 65. E-mail: sarl.leslavandes@online.fr

Open

Easter - 15 September.

FR07030 Yelloh! Village Soleil Vivarais

Sampzon, 07120 Ruoms (Ardèche)

A large, lively, high quality site bordering the River Ardèche, complete with beach, Soleil Vivarais offers much to visitors, particularly families with children. A popular feature is the 'barrage' with its canoe ramp, used by children with rubber boats more than canoeists, and providing an invigorating shower for bathers. Water is shallow in high season, but swimming is best in one of the pools. Of the 350 pitches, 88 generously sized, level pitches are for tourers, all with 10A electricity. Rock pegs are advised. Many are shaded and 30 have full services. During the day the proximity of the swimming pools to the terraces of the bar and restaurant make it a pleasantly social area. In the evening the purpose built stage, with professional lighting and sound system, provides an ideal platform for a regular family entertainment programme, mostly mimed musical shows. A new section beyond the beach houses good quality chalets, and a very attractive new pool complex, which all may use. Used by tour operators (52 pitches). A 'Sites et Paysages' and 'Yelloh Village' member.

TRAVEL SERVICE SITE

TO BOOK CALL 0870 405 4055 OR
www.alanrogersdirect.com

Facilities

Four modern, very clean and well equipped toilet blocks. Baby and child room. Facilities for people with disabilities. Washing machines and dryers. Motorcaravan service area. Small supermarket. Bright, modern bar/restaurant complex which in addition to takeaways and occasional pizzas (cooked in a wood burning oven), caters for a range of appetites and budgets (all open all season). Sound-proof disco next to the bar (capacity 100-120). Heated main pool and paddling pool (no Bermuda style shorts). Water polo, aqua-aerobics, pool games. Tennis (charged). Basketball, volleyball and football. Fishing. Boules, table tennis and archery. Bicycle hire. Extensive animation programme for all ages in June, July and August. Off site: Riding 2 km. Golf 10 km. Activities nearby, many with qualified instruction and supervision, include mountain biking, walking, canoeing, rafting, climbing and caving. Get off the beaten track and explore the many old towns and villages in magnificent surroundings.

At a glance

Welcome & Ambience	✓✓✓✓	Location	✓✓✓✓✓
Quality of Pitches	✓✓✓✓	Range of Facilities	✓✓✓✓✓

Directions

From Le Teil, just west of Montélimar, turn off the N86 and take the N102 westwards through Villeneuve-de-Berg. Disregard the first sign for Vallon-Pont-d'Arc and continue for about 5 km. on N102 before turning left on D103, toward Vogüé, then left on D579 and through Ruoms. Still on the D579, follow Vallon-Pont-d'Arc signs towards Sampzon. Turn right over river bridge controlled by lights.

Charges 2004

Per unit incl. 2 persons and electricity	€ 20,00 - € 38,00
extra person	€ 4,00 - € 7,00
child (1-10 yrs)	free - € 6,50
pet	free - € 3,00

Reservations

Made by fax and credit card or write to site with 25% deposit (and € 30 fee in July/August).
Tel: 04 75 39 67 56. E-mail: info@soleil-vivarais.com

Open

Week before Easter - 11 September.

FR07090 Castel Camping Le Domaine des Plantas

Mobile homes page 398

07360 Les Ollières-sur-Eyrieux (Ardèche)

A good quality site in a spectacular setting on the steep banks of the Eyrieux river, Domaine des Plantas offers an attractive alternative to those in the more popular southern parts of the Ardèche. The Eyrieux valley is less well known, but arguably just as attractive as those further south and a good deal less crowded, particularly in the main season. Perhaps the only drawback to this site is the narrow twisting three kilometre approach road which, although by no means frightening, may present something of a challenge to those with large outfits - however, the helpful owners have an ingenious convoy system designed to assist campers on departure. There is a sandy beach beside the quite fast-flowing, but fairly shallow, river (used for bathing) and a swimming pool and paddling pool with tiled surrounds for sunbathing. The old, original buildings house the reception, restaurant and bar. The terrace provides a stunning viewpoint. The 162 pitches (90 for touring) are steeply terraced and shaded. They have electricity connections (10A, long leads may be needed). Much up and down walking is required making this site unsuitable for those with walking difficulties.

Facilities

Two excellent toilet blocks (one can be heated) are very well equipped. There are some facilities which will certainly please the very young. Dishwashing and laundry sinks. Washing machine. Motorcaravan service point. Small shop (bread to order). Bar, restaurant and disco. Heated kidney shaped swimming pool and paddling pool. Adventure play area beside river. High season animation for children organised six days a week, and discos for 14-18 year olds held in cellar twice weekly (strictly no alcohol). Many activities and excursions are possible, arranged according to campers' motivations. Only gas and electric barbecues are allowed. Off site: Riding 15 km. Mountain biking, canoeing, canyoning, rifding and walking. A wonderful area for touring.

At a glance

Welcome & Ambience	✓✓✓✓	Location	✓✓✓✓
Quality of Pitches	✓✓✓✓	Range of Facilities	✓✓✓✓

Directions

From A7 take exit 15 (Valence Sud). Immediately after the péage turn right to Valence centre, then follow signs to Montélimar via the N7 for 7 km. Turn right towards Charmes sur Rhône, thence to Beauchastel. On leaving Beauchastel follow signs to Ollieres sur Eyrieux. In the village cross the river and follow campsite signs (3 km).

Charges 2004

Per unit incl. 2 persons and electricity	€ 18,00 - € 28,00
extra person over 4 yrs	€ 4,00 - € 7,00
animal	€ 2,00

Camping Cheques accepted.

Reservations

Made with deposit (€ 110) and fee (€ 20).
Tel: 04 75 66 21 53.
E-mail: plantas.ardeche@wanadoo.fr

Open

8 May - 18 September.

TRAVEL SERVICE SITE

TO BOOK CALL 0870 405 4055 OR www.alanrogersdirect.com

FR07120 Camping Nature Parc L'Ardéchois

Mobile homes ▶ page 399

Route touristique des Gorges, 07150 Vallon-Pont-d'Arc (Ardèche)

This very high quality, family run site is within walking distance of Vallon-Pont-d'Arc. It borders the River Ardèche and canoe trips are run, professionally, direct from the site. This campsite is ideal for families with younger children seeking an active holiday. The facilities are comprehensive and of an extremely high standard, particularly the central toilet block. Of the 244 pitches, there are 197 for tourers, separated by trees and individual shrubs. All have electrical connections (6/10A) and 125 have full services. The focal point of the site is the bar and restaurant (good menus), with terrace and stage overlooking the attractive heated pool, large paddling pool and sunbathing terrace. There is a well thought out play area plus plenty of other space for the youngsters to play on the site and along the river. Activities are organised throughout the season; these are family based - no discos. Patrols at night ensure a good night's sleep. Access to the site is easy and suitable for large outfits.

Facilities

Two well equipped toilet blocks, one superb with 'everything' working automatically. Facilities are of the highest standard, very clean and include good facilities for babies, those with disabilities, washing up and laundry. Four bathrooms to hire. Washing machines. Well stocked shop. Swimming pool and paddling pool (no Bermuda shorts). Football, volleyball, tennis and table tennis. Very good play area. Internet access. Organised activities, canoe trips. Only gas barbecues are permitted. Communal barbecue area. Off site: Canoeing, rafting, walking, riding, mountain biking, golf, rock climbing. Vallon-Pont-d'Arc 800 m.

At a glance

Welcome & Ambience	✓✓✓✓✓	Location	✓✓✓✓
Quality of Pitches	✓✓✓✓	Range of Facilities	✓✓✓✓✓

Directions

From Vallon-Pont-d'Arc (western end of the Ardèche Gorge) at a roundabout go east on the D290. Site entrance is shortly on the right.

Charges 2004

Per standard pitch incl. 2 persons	€ 23,00 - € 35,00
140 sq.m. pitch with water and drainage	€ 29,00 - € 42,50
extra person	€ 5,20 - € 7,50
electricity	€ 4,20

Reservations

Made with deposit (€ 95) and fee (€ 35).
Tel: 04 75 88 06 63. E-mail: ardecamp@bigfoot.com

Open

Easter - 30 September.

FR07190 Camping Le Chambourlas

07360 Les Ollières sur Eyrieux (Ardèche)

Tucked away up a steep and winding country road in a beautiful setting, in the hills above Privas this is a small, neat, family owned site. The 75 grassy, slightly sloping pitches (72 for touring) are set on low terraces and separated by an interesting variety of trees. All have 10A electricity and excellent views over the wooded hills. The reception, cosy bar/restaurant and shop are housed in one building accessed by 28 steps. There is a wide range of family orientated activities, especially in July and August, but these do not extend late into the night. Although there are special facilities, this is not an ideal site for those with walking difficulties. It is not ideal for very large units due to the narrow and steep roads in the area.

Facilities

One modern toilet block with all the necessary facilities including those for disabled visitors. Bar, restaurant and takeaway (all 15/5-30/8). Small shop (July/Aug). Swimming pool, paddling pool and sunbathing area (1/5-15/9). Play area. Volleyball. Table tennis. Boules. Good range of activities. River fishing. Off site: Many walks and bike rides. Les Ollières 6 km. Cévennes Regional Mountain Park.

Open

24 April - 15 September.

At a glance

Welcome & Ambience	✓✓✓	Location	✓✓✓
Quality of Pitches	✓✓✓✓	Range of Facilities	✓✓✓✓

Directions

At traffic lights in Privas take D2 road north, signed Le Cheylard. Follow road as it bears left and right, then over two river bridges. Site entrance is on the right 12 km after traffic lights. Take care – this is a fairly tortuous climb.

Charges 2004

Per unit incl. 2 persons	€ 12,00 - € 21,50
extra person	€ 4,50 - € 5,50
electricity (6A)	€ 3,00

Camping Cheques accepted.

Reservations

Made with deposit (€ 100) and fee (€ 15).
Tel: 04 75 66 24 31.

FR07110 Domaine Le Pommier

Route Nationale 102, 07170 Villeneuve-de-Berg (Ardèche)

Domaine Le Pommier is an extremely spacious Dutch owned site of 10 hectares in 32 hectares of wooded grounds. It has first class facilities, including the most up-to-date toilet blocks, a very good bar/restaurant and one of the best swimming and paddling pool complexes we have seen – ideal for all the family. The site is steeply terraced (a tractor is available for assistance) and has wonderful views over the Ardèche mountains and beyond. There are 400 pitches with 275 for tourists. They are grassy/stony, of good size and well spaced. Separated by young trees and hedges, some have little or no shade. All have access to electricity and water is close by. The site is not recommended for large units.

Facilities

Four excellent toilet blocks, one with under-floor heating, provide all the necessary facilities. Comprehensive shop. Bar/restaurant. Heated pool complex with water slides, a flowing 'river', several good, unusual paddling pools and a conventional pool for serious swimming. Large fitness room. Everything opens from the end of April. Boules, football, minigolf, badminton, games in the woods, table tennis, archery, water polo, tug of war, volleyball, tennis etc. Sound proof disco. Very extensive programme of events on and off site. Off season excursions to vineyards, wine tasting, museums, nougat factory and old villages. Also bridge classes and water colour classes. Off site: Villeneuve de Berg 1.5 km. River Ardèche 12 km. Potholing, rock climbing, canoeing, canyoning, mountain biking, walking or horse riding. Touring the many old villages and the superb scenery of the Ardèche Gorge and mountains.

At a glance

Welcome & Ambience	✓✓✓✓	Location	✓✓✓✓
Quality of Pitches	✓✓✓	Range of Facilities	✓✓✓✓✓

Directions

Site is west of Montélimar on the N102. The entrance is adjacent to the roundabout at the eastern end of the Villeneuve-de-Berg bypass.

Charges 2004

Per unit incl. 2 persons	€ 14,00 - € 29,00
extra person over 4 yrs	€ 4,00 - € 6,50
electricity	€ 4,00
dog	free - € 4,00

Max. 6 persons per pitch.
Special offers for longer stays in low season.

Reservations

Made with 30% deposit and fee (€ 23).
Tel: 04 75 94 82 81.
E-mail: info@campinglepommier.com

Open

1 May - 30 September.

FR07150 Camping Domaine de Gil

Mobile homes page 399

Route de Vals-les-Bains, Ucel, 07200 Aubenas (Ardèche)

This very attractive and well organised, smaller site in a less busy part of the Ardèche should appeal to couples and families with smaller children. The 80, good sized, level pitches, 43 for touring, are surrounded by a variety of trees offering plenty of shade. All have 5A electricity with European type connectors. The focal point of the site is formed by the very attractive swimming pool, paddling pool and large sunbathing area, with the bar, restaurant and well appointed children's play areas all adjacent. A spacious sports area and shady picnic/play area are alongside the river Ardèche - an ideal spot to cool off on a hot day. You will receive a warm welcome from the enthusiastic and friendly, new Dutch owners (who speak excellent English).

Facilities

All the excellent facilities are in a single, cheerful, modern block adjacent to the pool. Most washbasins are in cabins. Plenty of dishwashing and laundry sinks plus a washing machine and iron. Motorcaravan service point. Small shop for basics. Bar/restaurant and takeaway (from June). Swimming pool and paddling pool, heated all season (proper swimming trunks only). Two play areas. Volleyball, boules, minigolf, football, tennis court. Canoeing, boating and fishing in the river. Some organised activities in high season. In July/Aug. only gas and electric barbecues are permitted. Off site: Shops, etc. at Vals-les-Bain 1.5 km. Ineresting old town with larger range of shops, restaurants and bars 3 km. Organised canoe trips and canyoning on the river Ardèche. Bicycle hire and riding 4 km.

At a glance

Welcome & Ambience	✓✓✓✓✓	Location	✓✓✓✓
Quality of Pitches	✓✓✓✓	Range of Facilities	✓✓✓✓

Directions

Site is just north of Aubenas at Ucel. Coming from the southeast on N102, just after passing through a tunnel, turn right at roundabout (signed Privas)and cross the river Ardèche into Pont d'Ucel. Shortly bear right and at roundabout, take last exit (signed Ucel). Shortly turn left (narrow road, signed Ucel D18) and then right (Ucel D578B). Site is about 2 km on the left.

Charges 2004

Per unit incl. 2 persons	€ 13,00 - € 22,50
extra person	€ 3,20 - € 5,50
child under 10 yrs	free - € 3,50
electricity	€ 3,60
animal	€ 2,00 - € 2,50

Reservations

Made with deposit (€ 120) and fee (€ 15).
Tel: 04 75 94 63 63. E-mail: raf.garcia@wanadoo.fr

Open

15 April - 15 September.

FR07170 Ludocamping

07170 Lussas (Ardèche)

Ludocamping is set amongst the magnificent scenery of the Auzon valley, a delight for nature lovers particularly in early season when the many wild flowers and cherry trees are at their best. There are numerous birds including eagles and the elusive golden oriole, heard but seldom seen. A ride through Darbres and Mirabel has breathtaking views. This site, run by a very friendly Dutch family (excellent English is spoken) should appeal to couples of all ages and young families. The emphasis is on a quiet family campsite whilst offering a really wide range of activities. From mid-July – early August, only families with children under 14 yrs are accepted which allows the activities to be focussed on this age group – an unusual and interesting idea. The 160 grassy pitches, all for touring, are in two separate areas. Those in the upper section are large super pitches (approx 160 sq.m.) with wonderful views of the surrounding hills but little shade. Those in the lower area, closer to the small river, are well spaced, set naturally amongst the trees and have good shade. All have electricity, most 5A but some 10A. There is an attractive swimming pool (heated all season), good sized paddling pool and large sunbathing area.

Facilities

Four very clean, good quality toilet blocks, two in each area, offering all the necessary facilities. Bar (all season), takeaway (from 1/5) and terrace area overlooking the valley. Play area. Volleyball. Table tennis. Very large recreational area next to the river. Paddling area in river and separate deeper area. Fishing, Bike hire. Excellent club for over 6/7 yr olds offering a very wide range of activities such as biking, climbing, carting, canoeing and canyoning. Off season club for older children, same as for the younger children plus abseiling and bungee jumping etc. Off season club for seniors with large range of excursions in the campsite coach. Only gas and electric barbecues allowed. Off site: Small village of Lussas (a few shops, restaurant and bar) 600 m. Riding 6 km. Gliding, hang gliding, canoeing and speed boating arranged. Old villages, with their markets, museums etc, caves, mountains, river gorges, caves, wine tasting.

At a glance

Welcome & Ambience	✓✓✓✓✓	Location	✓✓✓✓
Quality of Pitches	✓✓✓✓	Range of Facilities	✓✓✓✓

Directions

From Montélimar take the N102 west towards Aubenas, pass around Villeneuve and at the traffic lights in Lavilledieu turn right onto the D224 towards Lussas. The site entrance is on the right just before the village (approx 4 km. from N102).

Charges 2004

Per unit incl. 2 persons	€ 11,00 - € 22,00
extra person	€ 2,00 - € 6,00
child (0-7 yrs)	free - € 3,00
electricity (6A)	€ 3,00
dog	free - € 3,00

Special long stay, low season offers.
No credit cards.

Reservations

Contact site. Note: from 13 July - 8 Aug. only children under 14 yrs allowed. Tel: 04 75 94 21 22.
E-mail: info@ludocamping.com

Open

1 April - 15 October.

FR07200 Camping L'Oasis

07370 Eclassan (Ardèche)

Recommended by one of our readers, we hope to include a full report on this wooded campsite in a future inspection programme. L'Oasis is a little campsite on the banks for the River Ay in the northern Ardèche. The site offers just 51 pitches, all with electricity, water and drainage, and a good range of leisure amenities. Mobile homes for rent.

Facilities

Sanitary building. Snack bar, small shop and takeaway meals (covered in low season). Swimming pool. Minigolf. Playground. Table tennis. Games room. Fishing. Bicycle hire. Entertainment programme in high season. Off site: Riding 4 km. Tennis - 10 minutes walk. Golf 15 km. Canoeing 25 km. Hot air ballooning. Steam railway.

Open

1 April - 15 October.

Directions

From the north - take Chanas exit from the A7 auto-route, then follow signs to St Vallier on the N7, and cross the Rhone to Sarras. Continue on the D6 towards Eclassan, from where site is clearly signed.

Charges year

Per pitch incl. 2 persons and electricity	€ 11.00 - € 17.50
extra person	€ 3.70
child (2-12 yrs)	€ 3.20
child (0-2 yrs)	€ 2.70
electricity (6A)	€ 3.50

Reservations

Contact site. Minimum 7 nights in high season.
Tel: .04 75 34 56 23.

FR26030 Sunêlia Le Grand Lierne

B.P. 8, 26120 Chabeuil (Drôme)

In addition to its obvious attraction as an overnight stop, fairly convenient for the A7 autoroute, this site provides a pleasant base to explore this little known area between the Ardèche and the Vercors mountains and the Côte du Rhône wine area. It has 161 marked, stony pitches, 76 for touring units, mainly separated by developing hedges or oak trees. Many have good shade, some are on flat ground and all have electricity (6/10A). A more open area exists for those who prefer less shade and a view of the mountains, but this area contains many mobile homes. English and Dutch are spoken. Used by tour operators (30%).

Facilities

Two sanitary blocks include washbasins in cabins, facilities for disabled people and a small WC for children. Dishwashing under cover. Washing machines (powder provided), dryers and outdoor lines by the blocks. Motorcaravan services. Shop/restaurant and terrace (20/5-31/8). Bar/takeaway (all season). Fridge rental. Excellent swimming pool complex with three pools, one very small open all season and covered and heated in low season (other pools 15/5-31/8; no Bermuda shorts). Paddling pool and 50 m. water slide. Playgrounds and trampoline. Mini-tennis, minigolf, table tennis, volleyball, archery and football field. Bicycle hire. Library. Extensive entertainment programme for all the family, including excursions (from end-May). Only gas and electric barbecues are permitted. Dogs and other pets are not accepted in high season (3/7-21/8). Caravan storage. Off site: Golf 3 km. Bicycle hire 4.5 km. Fishing 5 km. Riding 7 km. Canoe/kayak near. Vercors mountains. Chabeuil with shops, restaurants and bank 5 km.

At a glance

Welcome & Ambience	✓✓✓	Location	✓✓✓
Quality of Pitches	✓✓✓	Range of Facilities	✓✓✓

Directions

Site signed in Chabeuil about 11 km. east of Valence (18 km. from autoroute). It is best to approach Chabeuil from the south side of Valence via the Valence ring road, thence onto the D68 to Chabeuil itself. Site is off the D125 to Charpey, 5 km. from Chabeuil, but well signed.

Charges 2004

Per unit incl. 2 adults	€ 16,00 - € 27,80
extra person	€ 6,60 - € 7,80
child (2-7 yrs)	€ 3,40 - € 5,60
electricity (6/10A)	€ 4,00 - € 5,50
animal	€ 4,00

Camping Cheques accepted.

Reservations

Accepted with 25% deposit and fee (€ 30). Tel: 04 75 59 83 14. E-mail: contact@grandlierne.com

Open

23 April - 12 September, with all services.

FR26040 Camping Le Couspeau

26460 Le Poet Célard (Drôme)

The approach to this site is via a steep road, and with several hairpin bends to negotiate, care is required (underpowered units not advised). However, for others the views are reward enough as a magnificent landscape of mountains and valleys unfolds; the overall impression is of beauty and tranquillity. There are 127 pitches with 87 for touring. Access to the 62 touring pitches (all with 6A electricity) on the older section of the site is reasonably easy; levelling blocks may be handy as some of the terraced pitches are slightly sloping. Mature trees provide shade and there are adequate water points around the site. The 25 pitches on the new lower section of the site are very large (150 sq.m) and all have electricity, water and a drain. They are separated by small hedges and some small trees but have little shade. Access is via a steep road but tractor assistance is available. Rock pegs are advised. The site has a good restaurant/bar and a terrace with panoramic views. In July and August on one evening each week there is live music, on another a themed meal. Those seeking to unwind and relax should appreciate the delightful scenery and setting of this medium sized site.

Facilities

Three sanitary blocks, two in the old section and one in the new, are kept very clean. Laundry and dishwashing sinks, washing machines and dryer. Facilities for disabled campers (on the older section), but the site is not ideal due to steep roads and steps. Well stocked shop (15/6-30/9). Restaurant/bar and takeaway (15/6-30/9). Main pool (1/6-30/9) and smaller, covered one (1/5-30/9 and heated in low seasons) plus a toddlers' pool. Play area and organised activities for children in high season. Tennis, table tennis and volleyball. Guided hill walks and cycle trips. Manual and electric bicycle hire. Rafting, canoe trips (on the River Drôme), riding and paragliding arranged. Off site: Riding and fishing 5 km. Canoeing, rafting and paragliding. Ideal area for the serious cyclists, mountain bikers and hikers. Medieval towns and villages, markets and châteaux. Crest, Po't-Laval. Vercors mountains.

At a glance

Welcome & Ambience	✓✓✓	Location	✓✓✓✓
Quality of Pitches	✓✓✓✓	Range of Facilities	✓✓✓✓

Directions

From A7 autoroute exit 16 take D104 to Crest. At traffic lights, on the Crest bypass, turn hard right on D538 south towards Bourdeaux. Shortly before Bourdeaux turn right over small river bridge onto D328B, signed Le Po't Célard. After climbing for about 1.5 km, at T-junction, turn right on D328 and just before Le Po't Célard turn left onto D328A. Site is up the hill on the left, well signed.

Charges 2004

Per unit incl. 2 persons	€ 13,00 - € 23,00
extra person	€ 4,00 - € 6,00
child (under 7 yrs)	free - € 4,00
electricity (6A)	€ 3,00

Camping Cheques accepted.

Reservations

Advised for July/Aug. and made with deposit (€ 80) and fee (€ 20). Tel: 04 75 53 30 14. E-mail: info@couspeau.com

Open

1 May - 14 September.

FR26080 Camping Le Gallo Romain

Route du Col de Tourniol, 26300 Barbières (Drôme)

Surrounded by wooded hills and mountains, this spacious site with new, enthusiastic Dutch owners, makes a good base from which to unwind and explore the spectacular Vercors mountains. It is quiet and peaceful, in an attractive location with pitches set on terraces that descend to a babbling stream. The 80 level and grassy pitches, 66 for touring, are separated by mature trees and shrubs, most with some shade and 6A electricity (long leads may be needed). The area is ideal for walking or mountain biking with many tracks in the hills, or for wild flower, bird or butterfly enthusiasts. A good bar/restaurant has a terrace overlooking the pool and the mountains beyond. English and Dutch are spoken.

Facilities

Two toilet blocks, although not new, are kept very clean. Facilities including for disabled visitors. Small shop. Bar/restaurant. Swimming pools. Games room with large screen TV, pool table, table tennis. Volleyball. Play area. All facilities open all season. Off site: Riding and golf 6 km.

Open

1 April - 30 October.

At a glance

Welcome & Ambience	✓✓✓✓✓	Location	✓✓✓✓
Quality of Pitches	✓✓✓✓	Range of Facilities	✓✓✓✓

Directions

Leave A49/E713 at exit 7 (Romans-sur-Isère) and turn south on D149, following signs to Col de Tourniol. Barbières is 12 km. Drive through narrow streets in village; site is 1 km. beyond the village on the right.

Charges 2004

Per adult	€ 3,20 - € 4,00
pitch	€ 10,00 - € 12,50
electricity (6A)	€ 2,15 - € 2,65

Reservations

Made for exact dates with deposit and fee.
Tel: 04 75 47 44 07. E-mail: info@legalloromain.net

FR26090 Camping Les Truffières

Lieu-dit Nachony, 26230 Grignan (Drôme)

This is a delightful small site in a rural setting within walking distance of the picturesque ancient village of Grignan with wonderful views and providing peace and tranquillity. The 85 good sized pitches are level and fairly stony with 79 for touring units. Shaded by oak trees and separated by rosemary or laurel hedging, each pitch has electricity . The Croze family are most welcoming and achieve high standards of cleanliness and order while maintaining a friendly, relaxed atmosphere. Many old towns and villages, reading like a wine list, with their restaurants, shops, wine tasting and local markets, are close at hand.

Facilities

The good, main toilet block provides all the necessary facilities. Extra facilities by the pool are opened when needed. Washing machine. Snack bar and takeaway with limited menu at mid-day and evening in congenial atmosphere (June - Sept). Swimming pool and smaller pool for children (no Bermuda shorts). Volleyball, table tennis and boules. Little in the way of on site entertainment but many activities can be booked. Dogs are not accepted.

Open

20 April - 1 October.

At a glance

Welcome & Ambience	✓✓✓✓✓	Location	✓✓✓✓
Quality of Pitches	✓✓✓✓	Range of Facilities	✓✓✓

Directions

From N7 (or A7 autoroute exit 18) south of Montélimar, take D133 (changes to D541) signed Grignan. After 9 km, just before entering Grignan, take D71 towards Charamet and site is shortly on the left.

Charges 2004

Per unit incl. 2 adults	€ 13,00 - € 15,00
extra person	€ 4,50
child (under 7 yrs)	€ 3,00
electricity (10A)	€ 4,00

Reservations

Contact site. Tel: 04 75 46 93 62
E-mail: info@lestruffieres.com

FR26110 Les 4 Saisons Camping de Grâne

Route de Roche-sur-Grâne, 26400 Grâne (Drôme)

This small, terraced site, open all year, nestles in the hillsides of the lower Drôme valley. With its 80 pitches (73 for touring units), it provides mainly overnight accommodation but it is worth a longer stay. The modern main building houses reception on the top floor, with other facilities below, and provides commanding views across the valley towards Crest and the Vercors. The pitches are level and stony, of variable size, cut out of the hillside and reached by a one-way system on tarmac roads. All pitches have electricity (6/16A), some with water and drain. This is an excellent base for exploring the Drôme valley and the Vercors mountains.

Facilities

A short flight of steps to a lower level leads to good toilet facilities, heated in low season, with roomy showers and washbasins in cabins. Washing machines. Baby room. Facilities for disabled visitors (but site is very sloping). Bar and snacks (15/4-15/9). Swimming pool (1/6-15/9). Play area. Off site: Village nearby. Fishing 1 km. Riding 3 km.

Open

All year.

At a glance

Welcome & Ambience	✓✓✓✓	Location	✓✓✓✓
Quality of Pitches	✓✓✓✓	Range of Facilities	✓✓✓

Directions

From A7 exit 17, or the N7 at Loriol, take the D104 towards Crest. After 8 km. in Grâne take D113 south. Site is on left about 600 m. beyond the village.

Charges 2004

Per unit incl. 2 persons	€ 9,00 - € 11,00
child (0-10 yrs)	€ 2,00 - € 4,00
electricity	€ 4,00

Reservations

Advised for July/ Aug; contact site.
Tel: 04 75 62 64 17.
E-mail: camping.4saisons@wanadoo.fr

FR26120 Gervanne Camping

Mobile homes page 403

Bellevue, 26400 Mirabel et Blacons (Drôme)

This spacious, riverside family run site with 177 pitches, 167 for touring, is divided into two sections. The newer section is adjacent to the bar, restaurant, superb swimming pool, jacuzzi and the large sunbathing terrace from which there are mountain views. The newer pitches are of average size with some shade and are separated by a few small shrubs and trees. The older section is close to the river and on the other side of the road, but is connected to the newer section by an underpass. It is less formally laid out and mature trees offer plenty of shade. All pitches, in both sections, have easy access to electricity (4 or 6A) and there are water points around the site. This interesting historic area on the edge of the Vercors National Park offers opportunities for walking, cycling and other outdoor activities. The pretty hillside villages sit amongst vineyards and fields of lavender and sunflowers.

Facilities

Each section has a well appointed, very clean toilet block with the majority of washbasins in cabins, and a baby room in each with bath, shower and changing facilities and some cabins now with showers and washbasins. Washing machine, tumble dryer, sinks for laundry and dishwashing. Large en-suite unit for disabled people. Bar/restaurant (1/6-15/9) with simple menu, takeaway service and internet terminal. Swimming pool. Small play area, table tennis and boules. Bicycle hire. Only electric and gas barbecues are allowed. Motorcaravan service point. Off site: Supermarket next door. Fishing, canoeing and bathing in river Drôme adjacent. Riding 5 km. Golf 13 km.

Open

1 April - 31 October.

At a glance

Welcome & Ambience	✓✓✓✓	Location	✓✓✓✓
Quality of Pitches	✓✓✓✓	Range of Facilities	✓✓✓✓

Directions

Site is about 22 km. east of exit 16 (D104 to Crest) on the A7 autoroute. After Crest follow signs to Die for about 6 km. and then turn left (D164A) and cross the river into Mirabel et Blacons, turn left at roundabout and follow signs to campsite.

Charges 2005

Per unit incl. 2 adults	€ 11,90 - € 16,60
extra person	€ 3,30 - € 4,90
child (up to 7 yrs)	€ 1,60 - € 2,50
dog	€ 1,60 - € 2,00
electricity (4/6A)	€ 2,60 - € 3,20

Reservations

Required mid July - end August; write with deposit of € 60 and € 10 fee. Tel: 04 75 40 00 20.
E-mail: info@gervanne-camping.com

FR26130 Camping L'Hirondelle

Bois de St Ferreol, 26410 Menglon (Drôme)

This natural, spacious and peaceful site is run by a very friendly family and you are assured a good welcome. It lies in a beautiful valley, south of the Vercors mountains and the Vercors National Park, beside the River Bez, a tributary of the River Drôme which is also close by. It is close to the interesting and ancient small town of Die, the home of the famous Clairette de Die - a sparkling wine mentioned in dispatches by the Romans around 40 AD. In natural openings in woodland, the 100 large to very large pitches all have electricity (3/6A) and are stony and slightly bumpy (rock pegs advised). There are 64 for touring units. If you are lucky you may see red squirrels and beavers and, in June there is a wide variety of flowers including several types of orchids. Although this site is not manicured liked some others, the large pitches, separated from others by a wide variety of trees, the 1.5 km of river bank on one side and the large open campsite field on the other, give both privacy and plenty of space. It is a very good site for couples and young families, to explore this beautiful part of France, partake in the local sporting activities and yet completely unwind and enjoy the views and the beautiful sunset over the mountains.

Facilities

Two large toilet blocks offer all the necessary facilities. Very good bar/restaurant with good menus and takeaway (1/5-7/9). Small range of supplies, including bread, on sale from the bar. Traditional rectangular swimming pool, plus new excellent pool complex with small slide, paddling pool, jacuzzi and a section that flows like a river (1/5-7/9). Ample room to play and paddle in the river. Playground. Club/TV room. Internet access. Fishing. Football, boules, volleyball, archery. Organised events for young children and adults (animateurs speaking French, Dutch and English). Advice on sporting activities, etc, in the region and bookings made. Occasional evening events. Off site: Riding and bicycle hire 3 km. Canoeing, kayaking, climbing, rambling, mountain biking and cycling over the steep local passes.

At a glance

Welcome & Ambience	✓✓✓	Location	✓✓✓✓
Quality of Pitches	✓✓✓	Range of Facilities	✓✓✓✓

Directions

From Die follow D93 southwards and after 5 km, at Pont de Quart, turn left on D539 signed Châtillon. After approx. 4 km. turn right on D140, signed Menglon. Site entrance is shortly on the right just after crossing a small river.

Charges 2004

Per pitch incl. 2 persons	€ 15,70 - € 22,60
extra adult	€ 4,70 - € 6,30
child (2-10 yrs)	€ 3,20 - € 5,25
electricity (3-6A)	€ 3,00 - € 4,00

Camping Cheques accepted.

Reservations

Made with 30% deposit and fee (€ 18.50).
Tel: 04 75 21 82 08.
E-mail: contact@campinghirondelle.com

Open

3 April - 11 September.

FR42010 Camping Municipal de Charlieu

Rue Riottier, 42190 Charlieu (Loire)

Charlieu is a very attractive little town, well worth a visit, and the well cared for municipal site here would make a good base for exploring the area. The 100 pitches (30 occupied by seasonal units), all have electricity (6-10A). The pitches are reasonably large and well spaced, on level grass. Most are separated by trim hedges but with little shade. There are few facilities on the site as the small, historic town is within about five minutes walk. A card from reception gives free entry to the municipal swimming pool adjacent to the site, plus discounts for other activities in and around the town.

Facilities

The clean toilet block should be adequate, except perhaps in high season. It has British and Turkish style WCs, facilities for disabled visitors. Laundry facilities. Simple snacks and takeaways. Bicycle hire. Volleyball, boules. Playground. Fishing. Off site: Swimming pool adjacent.

Open

1 May - 30 September.

At a glance

Welcome & Ambience	✓✓✓✓	Location	✓✓✓
Quality of Pitches	✓✓✓	Range of Facilities	✓✓✓

Directions

Charlieu is 20 km. northeast of Roanne. From Pouilly, on the D482, take D487 to Charlieu (5.5 km). The campsite is southeast of the town next to a sports stadium and is signed from the town centre.

Charges 2004

Per person	€ 2,10 - € 2,60
pitch	€ 1,90 - € 3,10

Reservations

Made without fee; contact site. Tel: 04 77 69 01 70.
E-mail: camp-charlieu@voila.fr

FR69010 Camping International Porte de Lyon

Porte de Lyon, 69570 Dardilly (Rhône)

Camping International is a modern overnight site just off the A6 autoroute. Kept busy with overnight trade, reception and the café (in main season) open until quite late. There are 175 separate numbered plots with electricity (10A). Those for caravans are mostly on hardstandings on a slight slope, with another small grassy part, while those for tents are on a flatter area of grass. A very large commercial centre has been developed just outside the site, with eight hotels, restaurants, a supermarket, petrol station, etc. There is some road noise. A bus service for Lyon is nearby (timetables in reception).

Facilities

Three heated sanitary blocks have free hot water (solar heated) and washbasins in cabins. Dishwashing and laundry sinks. Baby changing facilities and washing machines. Bar/snacks and takeaway (15/6-15/9). Unheated swimming and paddling pools (charged for). Playground. TV room.

Open

All year.

At a glance

Welcome & Ambience	✓✓✓✓	Location	✓✓✓✓
Quality of Pitches	✓✓✓	Range of Facilities	✓✓✓✓

Directions

Travelling south, do not take new A46 around Lyon, but continue on A6 and take exit marked 'Limonest, Dardilly, Porte de Lyon' about 8 km. north of the Lyon tunnel; at once turn left for Porte de Lyon.

Charges 2004

Per person	€ 2,98
pitch	€ 6,30 - € 8,20
caravan, 2 axle	€ 16,80
electricity (higher in winter)	€ 3,00 - € 4,60

Reservations

Made if you write, but there is usually space.
Tel: 04 78 35 64 55.
E-mail: camping.lyon@mairie-lyon.fr

TRAVEL SERVICE SITE

TO BOOK CALL 0870 405 4055 OR www.alanrogersdirect.com

FR69020 Camping Municipal La Grappe Fleurie

La Lie, 69820 Fleurie (Rhône)

With easy access from both the A6 autoroute and the N6, this site is ideally situated for night stops or indeed for longer stays to explore the vineyards and historic attractions of the Beaujolais region. Virtually surrounded by vineyards, but within walking distance (less than one kilometre) of the pretty village of Fleurie, this is an immaculate small site, with 85 separated touring pitches. All are grassed and fairly level with the benefit of individual access to water, drainage and electrical connections (10A). Baker calls 07.30 hrs - 08.30 hrs. Wine tasting twice per week in high season. Only gas or electric barbecues are allowed. Restaurant and shopping facilities are available in the village.

Facilities

Sanitary facilities in two blocks have British and Turkish style toilets and very satisfactory shower and washing facilities (showers closed 22.00-07.00 hrs). Facilities for the disabled. Two cold showers are provided for those wishing to cool down in summer. Washing machine and tumble dryer. Outdoor swimming pool (15m by 7m). Small playground. Table tennis, tennis and volleyball Off site: Fishing 10 km. Fleurie 600 m.

Open

End of March - End of October.

At a glance

Welcome & Ambience	✓✓✓✓	Location	✓✓✓✓
Quality of Pitches	✓✓✓✓	Range of Facilities	✓✓✓✓

Directions

From N6 at Le Maison Blanche/Romanech-Thorins, take D32 to village of Fleurie from where site is signed.

Charges 2004

Pitch + caravan + 2 adults + electricity	€ 12,50
pitch + tent + 2 adults + electricity	€ 11,50
extra adult	€ 4,00
child (5-10 yrs)	€ 2,50

Reservations

Advised in high season. Tel: 04 74 69 80 07.
E-mail: camping@fleurie.org

This is a corner of France that evokes dreamy images of lazy afternoons amongst sleepy village squares, sunny vineyards and beautiful lavender fields basking under the dazzling blue of the sky.

Only the départements from the mountainous region of Provence have been included in this section:
04 Alpes-de-Haute-Provence, 05 Hautes-Alpes, 84 Vaucluse

Provence is a region of magical light, bleached landscapes, olive groves, herb-scented garrigue, vineyards and Roman and medieval antiquities. The river valleys provide natural routes through the mountain barrier. Roman monuments can be seen at Orange, and Vaison-la-Romaine, where a 2,000 year old bridge is still in use. Avignon was the site of the papal court and the Palais des Papes at Avignon is a spectacular construction.

The Hautes-Alpes will reward with stunning vistas, peace and quiet. Briançon is the highest town in Europe and many of the high passes are not for the faint-hearted. The Vaucluse, where in the late spring the southern slopes of the Montagne du Luberon are a mass of colour with glades of wild flowers. The extinct volcanic cone of Mont Ventoux, of Tour de France fame provides dramatic views. The scents, the colours and an amazing intensity of light have encouraged artists and writers to settle amidst the sleepy villages, with narrow streets and ancient dwellings topped with sun-baked terracotta tiles, where the air is fragrant with the smell of wild herbs and lavender.

Cuisine of the region

Influenced by the Savoie area to the north and the Côte d'Azur to the south, with emphasis on herbs and garlic, and fish. The wine region is mainly known for its dry, fruity rosé wines: Bandol, Bellet, Palette, Cassis. Red wines include Côtes du Rhône and Châteauneuf-du-Pape.

Aigo Bouido: garlic and sage soup with bread (or eggs and cheese)

Farcement (Farçon Savoyard): potatoes baked with cream, eggs, bacon, dried pears and prunes

Pissaladière: Provencal bread dough with onions, anchovies, olives

Ratatouille: aubergines, courgettes, onions, garlic, red peppers and tomatoes in olive oil

Tartiflette: potato, bacon, onions and Reblochon cheese

Places of interest

Avignon: ramparts, old city, Papal Palace, old palace, Calvet museum

Mont Ventoux: near Carpentras, one of the best known stages of the classic Tour de France annual cycle race

Orange: Roman city, gateway to the Midi, Colline St Europe

St Vaison la Romaine: Roman city, the French Pompei

Alan Rogers tip

VISIT THE HAUTE-PROVENCE GEOLOGICAL RESERVE, THE LARGEST IN EUROPE, WHICH HAS FOSSILS DATING BACK 300 MILLION YEARS. GUIDED DAY-TRIPS ARE AVAILABLE.

FR04030 Camping Lac du Moulin de Ventre

Niozelles, 04300 Forcalquier (Alpes-de Haute-Provence)

This is a friendly, English speaking, family run site in the heart of Haute-Provence, near Forcalquier, a bustling small French market town. Attractively located beside a small lake and 28 acres of wooded, hilly land, which is available for walking. Herbs of Provence can be found growing wild and flowers, birds and butterflies abound – a nature lovers delight. The 124 level, grassy pitches for tourists are separated by a variety of trees and small shrubs, 114 of them having electricity (6A; long leads may be necessary). Some pitches are particularly attractive, bordering a small stream. The site is well situated to visit Mont Ventoux, the Luberon National Park, the Gorges du Verdon and a wide range of ancient hill villages with their markets and museums etc.

Facilities

The toilet block, recently refurbished, provides very good, clean facilities including washbasins in cabins and facilities for disabled people. Baby bath. Washing machines. Fridge hire. Bread and a few essentials on sale. Bar/restaurant with waiter service, takeaway meals (all season) and themed evenings (high season). Pizzeria. Large and small swimming pools with large shallow area (15/5-15/9). Playground. Fishing and boules. Some activities organised in high season. No discos. Only electric or gas barbecues are permitted. Off site: Shops, local market, doctor, tennis 2 km. Supermarket, chemist, riding, bicycle hire 5 km. Golf 20 km. Walking, cycling.

Open

1 April - 30 September.

At a glance

Welcome & Ambience	✓✓✓✓	Location	✓✓✓✓✓
Quality of Pitches	✓✓✓✓	Range of Facilities	✓✓✓✓

Directions

From A51 motorway take exit 19 (Brillanne). Turn right on N96 then turn left on N100 (westwards signed Forcalquier) for about 3 km. Site is signed on left, just after a bridge 3 km. southeast of Niozelles.

Charges 2004

Per unit incl. 2 persons	€ 20,00
incl. electricity	€ 25,00
extra person	€ 5,50
child (0-4 yrs)	€ 3,00
dog	€ 3,00

Camping Cheques accepted.
No credit cards.

Reservations

Advisable for July/Aug with 30% deposit and fee (€ 23). Tel: 04 92 78 63 31.
E-mail: moulindeventre@free.fr

FR04020 Castel Camping Le Camp du Verdon

Mobile homes page 404

Domaine du Verdon, 04120 Castellane (Alpes-de Haute-Provence)

Close to the 'Route des Alpes' and the Gorges du Verdon, this is a very popular holiday area, the gorge, canoeing and rafting being the main attractions, ideal for active families. Two heated swimming pools and numerous on-site activities during high season help to keep non-canoeists here. Du Verdon is a large level site, part meadow, part wooded, with 500 partly shaded, rather stony pitches (350 for tourists). Numbered and separated by bushes, they vary in size, have 6A electricity, and 120 also have water and waste water. They are mostly separate from the mobile homes (63) and pitches used by tour operators (110). Some overlook the unfenced river Verdon, so watch the children. One can walk to Castellane without using the main road. Dances and discos in July and August suit all age groups - the latest finishing time is around 11 pm. (after that time patrols make sure that the site is quiet). The site is popular and very busy in July and August.

Facilities

The toilet blocks have been refurbished with British style WCs and up-to-date equipment. One block has facilities for disabled visitors. Washing machines and irons. Motorcaravan service and car wash points. Popular restaurant with terrace and bar including room with log fire for cooler evenings. Large well stocked shop. Pizzeria/crêperie. Takeaway (open twice daily). Two heated swimming pools and new paddling pool with 'mushroom' style fountain (all open all season). Entertainers provide games and competitions for all (July and August). Playgrounds. Minigolf, table tennis, archery, basketball and volleyball. Organised walks. Bicycle hire. Riding. Small fishing lake. ATM.
Off site: Castellane and the Verdon Gorge 1 km. Riding 2 km. Boat launching 4.5 km. Golf 20 km. River Verdon and many water sports.

At a glance

Welcome & Ambience	✓✓✓	Location	✓✓✓✓✓
Quality of Pitches	✓✓✓✓	Range of Facilities	✓✓✓✓

Directions

From Castellane take D952 westwards towards Gorges du Verdon and Moustiers. Site is 1 km. on left.

Charges 2004

Per unit with up to 4 persons	€ 15,00 - € 26,00
with 6A electricity	€ 19,00 - € 30,00
dog	€ 2,50

Camping Cheques accepted.

Reservations

Made for any length with deposit (€ 80 - € 110 depending on pitch) and fee (€ 20).
Tel: 04 92 83 61 29.
E-mail: contact@camp-du-verdon.com

Open

15 May - 15 September.

FR04100 Camping International

Mobile homes page 404

Route Napoleon, 04120 Castellane (Alpes-de Haute-Provence)

Camping International has very friendly, English speaking owners and is a reasonably priced, less commercialised site situated in some of the most dramatic scenery in France with good views. The 250 pitches, 130 good sized ones for touring, are clearly marked, separated by trees and small hedges, and all have electricity and water. The bar/restaurant overlooks the swimming pool with its sunbathing area set in a sunny location, and all have fantastic views. In high season English speaking young people entertain children (3-8 years) and teenagers. On some evenings the teenagers are taken to the woods for campfire 'sing-alongs' which can go on till the early hours without disturbing the rest of the site. There are guided walks into the surrounding hills in the nearby Gorges du Verdon – a very popular excursion, particularly in high season. The weather in the hills here is very pleasant without the excessive heat of the coast. Access is good for larger units.

Facilities

Several small toilet blocks are of an older design with small cubicles and, although they are quite basic, the showers are fully controllable (these blocks are due to be replaced soon). One newer block has modern facilities, including those for disabled visitors, but this is not open early and late in the season. Washing machines, dryer and irons and a baby room. Chemical disposal at motorcaravan service point. Fridge hire. Shop. Restaurant/takeaway. Swimming pool (all 1/5-30/9). Club/TV room. Children's animation and occasional evening entertainment in July/Aug. Children's play area. Volleyball, football and boules pitches. Internet access. Off site: Riding 800 m. Castellane (1.5 km) is a very attractive little town with a superb river, canyon and rapids, ideal for canoeing, rafting and canyoning etc. Good area for walking and biking. Boat launching 5 km.

At a glance

Welcome & Ambience	✓✓✓✓	Location	✓✓✓✓
Quality of Pitches	✓✓✓✓	Range of Facilities	✓✓✓✓

Directions

Site is 1 km. north of Castellane on the N85 Route Napoleon.

Charges 2004

Per unit incl. 2 persons	€ 12,00 - € 19,00
extra person	€ 3,00 - € 4,00
electricity (6A)	€ 3,00 - € 4,00
dog	€ 2,00

Camping Cheques accepted.

Reservations

Necessary for July/Aug. and made with deposit (€ 45), no booking fee. Tel: 04 92 83 66 67.
E-mail: info@campinginternational.fr

Open

1 April - 30 September.

FR04080 Camping Caravaning L'Etoile des Neiges

04140 Montclar (Alpes-de Haute-Provence)

This attractive, family run site near the mountain village and ski resort of St Jean Montclar is open most of the year so is suitable for both summer and winter holidays. This beautiful alpine region offers all the usual alpine activities. Being at an altitude of 1,300 m. the nights can get quite cold even in summer. The 121 shady pitches, with 80 for touring, are laid out in terraces and separated by small shrubs and alpine trees. All pitches are close to electricity and water points. An attractive bar and restaurant overlooks the two swimming pools, with the shallow pool having a water slide ideal for children. The site has no shop as the local shops are only a few minutes walk away. Although situated in the southern high Alps, the site can be reached without climbing any stiff gradients. A 'Sites et Paysages' member.

Facilities

The central toilet block, heated in winter, includes washbasins in cabins. Separate room containing facilities for disabled visitors. Two washing machines. Motorcaravan service point. Bar/restaurant (mid June - Sept). Swimming pool (from 1 June). Tennis, table tennis and boules. Two play areas. Rafting and walking organised in July/Aug.
Off site: Shops in village a few minutes walk. Bicycle hire and riding in village. Fishing 1.5 km. Watersports and beach at Lac Serre Pon≤on 7 km.

Open

1 January - 30 September and 22-31 December.

At a glance

Welcome & Ambience	✓✓✓✓✓	Location	✓✓✓✓
Quality of Pitches	✓✓✓✓	Range of Facilities	✓✓✓✓

Directions

Site is 35 km. south of Gap via the D900B. Beyond Serre Pon≤on, turn right onto D900 signed Selonnet and St Jean Montclar. On entering St Jean Montclar turn left, go past chalets and shops and fork right to the campsite on the left. The roads (at 1,300 m.) are steep and can be snowy and icy in winter.

Charges 2005

Per unit incl. 2 persons	€ 12,50 - € 21,00
extra adult	€ 4,00 - € 5,00
electricity (6A)	€ 3,00 - € 4,00

Camping Cheques accepted.

Reservations

Advised for July/Aug. Deposit of 30% plus € 15 fee.
Tel: 04 92 35 01 29.
E-mail: contact@etoile-des-neiges.com

FR04060 Camping Caravaning Le Haut-Verdon

RD 908, 04370 Villars-Colmars (Alpes-de Haute-Provence)

For those seeking a quiet, family site set in most spectacular scenery, Camping Le Haut-Verdon is ideal. It is on the banks of the Verdon, an excellent trout river, which then flows through the spectacular gorge. Surrounded by the majestic peaks of the Alpes-de-Haute-Provence, it is on the doorstep of the Mercantour National Park. Set amongst the pines, the 87 pitches are mostly on the large size but are rather stony. With 73 for touring units, all have electricity (6/10A) but some will require long leads. There is a small village near, and the town of St André is 23 km. English is spoken. A 'Sites et Paysages' member.

Facilities

The main toilet block, recently refurbished, is heated and includes bidets and washbasins in cabins. Most WCs are British style. Washing machines and irons. Freezer for ice packs and room for tenters when inclement weather strikes. Motorcaravan service point. Small shop. Bar/restaurant and takeaway. Barbecue areas (portable ones banned). Swimming and paddling pools. Small play area. Volleyball. Basketball. Giant chess. Boules. Skittle alley. Table tennis. Excellent tennis. TV room. Games and competitions. Fishing.
Off site: Bicycle hire and riding 10 km.

Open

1 May - 30 September.

At a glance

Welcome & Ambience	✓✓✓✓✓	Location	✓✓✓✓✓
Quality of Pitches	✓✓✓✓	Range of Facilities	✓✓✓✓✓

Directions

Follow D955 north from St André les Alpes towards Colmar. After 11 km. the road number changes to D908. Site is on right at the southern edge of Villars-Colmars. Caravans are not advised to use the D908 from Annot or the Col d'Allos from Barcelonnette.

Charges 2004

Per person over 6 yrs	€ 3,00 - € 4,00
child (2-6 yrs)	€ 1,50 - € 2,50
pitch	€ 6,00 - € 10,00
electriicty	€ 2,50 - € 3,00

Camping Cheques accepted.

Reservations

Made with deposit (30%) and fee (€ 15.24).
Tel: 04 92 83 40 09.
E-mail: campinglehautverdon@wanadoo.fr

FR04010 Sunêlia Hippocampe

Mobile homes ▶ page 403

Route de Napoléon, 04290 Volonne (Alpes-de Haute-Provence)

Hippocampe is a friendly, 'all action' lakeside site situated in a beautiful area of France. The perfumes of thyme, lavender and wild herbs are everywhere and the higher hills of Haute Provence are not too far away. There are 447 level, numbered pitches (243 for touring units), medium to very large (130 sq.m) in size. All have electricity (10A) and 220 have water and drainage, most are separated by bushes and cherry trees. Some of the best pitches border the lake. The restaurant, bar, takeaway and shop have all been completely renewed (2004). This is a family run site with families in mind, with games, aerobics, competitions, entertainment and shows, plus a daily club for younger family members in July/August. A sound-proof underground disco is set well away from the pitches and is very popular with teenage customers. Staff tour the site at night ensuring a good night's sleep. The site is, however, much quieter in low season and, with its good discounts, is the time for those who do not want or need entertaining. The Gorges du Verdon is a sight not to be missed and rafting, paragliding or canoe trips can be booked from the site's own tourist information office. Being on the lower slopes of the hills of Haute-Provence, the surrounding area is good for both walking and mountain biking. This is a very good site for an active or restful holiday and is suitable for outfits of all sizes. Used by tour operators (20 pitches). English is spoken.

Facilities

Toilet blocks vary from old to modern, all with good facilities that include washbasins in cabins. They are very clean. Washing machines. Motorcaravan service point. Fridge rental. Bread available from reception (from 28/4), shop (26/6-3/9). Bar (1/5-12/9). Restaurant, pizzeria and barbecue chicken shop (all 15/5-12/9). Large, attractive pool complex (from 1/5-30/9) with two pools of differing sizes and depths, heated in early and late seasons. Tennis (free outside 3/7- 21/8). Fishing, canoeing, boules. Large selection of sports facilities to choose from, some with free instruction, including archery (high season). Charcoal barbecues are not permitted. Off site: Bicycle hire 2 km. Riding 6 km. Village of Volonne 600 m. Rafting, canoeing, canyoning, torrent walking, mountain biking, paragliding and hang gliding.

At a glance

Welcome & Ambience	✓✓✓✓✓	Location	✓✓✓✓
Quality of Pitches	✓✓✓✓✓	Range of Facilities	✓✓✓✓✓

Directions

Approaching from the north turn off N85 across river bridge to Volonne, then right to site. From the south right on D4, 1 km. before Château Arnoux.

Charges 2004

Per simple pitch incl. 2 persons	€ 12,00 - € 26,00
with electricity	€ 15,00 - € 31,00
with water/drainage 100 sq.m.	€ 15,00 - € 33,00
with water/drainage 140 sq.m.	€ 19,00 - € 38,00
extra person (over 4 yrs)	€ 2,50 - € 6,00

Camping Cheques accepted.

Reservations

Made with deposit (varies with size of pitch from € 50 - € 95) and booking fee (€ 25).
Tel: 04 92 33 50 00.
E-mail: camping@l-hippocampe.com

Open

1 April - 30 September.

FR04120 Camping Indigo - Forcalquier

Route de Sigonce, 04300 Forcalquier (Alpes-de Haute-Provence)

Since this site has acquired new ownership a large modernisation programme has been put in effect. Camping Indigo offers an excellent base for visiting Forcalquier, a 15th century fortified hill town, with its ancient buildings and the Monday market (which has the reputation of being the best in Haute Provence). Although this is an urban site, there are extensive views over the surrounding countryside where there are some excellent walks. The new owners (part of the Indigo group) have arranged for local guides to lead tours of the historic town and areas. The site is secure, with an electronic barrier (card deposit required) and there is no entry between 22.30 and 07.00. The swimming pool is heated to 30°C! The pitches are on grass and are of good size, all with electricity. There are 10 pitches with private water and waste water disposal.

Facilities

The two toilet blocks are undergoing reconstruction - the reconstructed disabled block is excellent and sets the standard for the other two blocks. Showers and wash basins are in cubicles. They are all cleaned twice a day (and signed for). Bar, snack bar and takeaway (1/7-30/9). Play area and paddling pool. Off site: All shops, banks etc. available in town centre, some 200m walk.

Open

29 March - 1 November.

At a glance

Welcome & Ambience	✓✓✓✓✓	Location	✓✓✓✓✓
Quality of Pitches	✓✓✓✓	Range of Facilities	✓✓✓✓

Directions

From the town centre, follow 'Digne - Sisteron' for 400 metres, turning sharp left at the petrol station, then first right and the site is 200 metres on the right. It is well signed from town.

Charges 2004

Per person	€ 4,50
child (2-7 yrs)	€ 3,00
pitch	€ 7,50 - € 10,00
animal	€ 2,00

Reservations

Contact site. Tel: 04 92 75 27 94.
E-mail: forcalquier@camping-indigo.com

FR05030 Camping Les Six Stations

Pont du Fossé, 05260 St Jean-St Nicolas (Hautes-Alpes)

This is a small, rural, unsophisticated site, run by a very friendly family, lying in the beautiful Drac Noir valley in the Parc National d'Ecrins. Level, grassy pitches are set in wooded glades with views of the surrounding mountains but with good shade. The 70 pitches, 48 for touring, all have access to electricity (2-16A) but very long leads may be necessary. Although the roads to the site offer no problems, the trees and narrow roads around the site makes access to some pitches difficult for large outfits. Some activities are organised in July and August for all the family and walks are arranged to see the marmots and mountain goats. The family pets, a donkey, pony and goat, share the woodland with campers. The area is fine for walking, cycling and canoeing and, of course in winter, for skiing.

Facilities

One modern toilet block, heated in winter, with all the usual facilities. Bar (June - Aug), Takeaway food (June - Aug). Small new swimming pool (June - Aug). Table tennis. Volleyball. Badminton. Walks and children's activities. Off site: Bicycle hire 1 km. Ski du fond 3 km. Riding 5 km. Golf 20 km. Restaurant outside gate. Paragliding. Climbing. Village of Fossé, only a 15 minute walk, with a few shops, restaurant and a bank.

Open

All year.

At a glance

Welcome & Ambience	✓✓✓✓	Location	✓✓✓✓
Quality of Pitches	✓✓✓	Range of Facilities	✓✓✓✓

Directions

Site is northeast of Gap. From N85, Route Napoleon, take D944 east and continue to village of Pont du Fossé. Site is on right 1 km. beyond the village.

Charges 2004

Per pitch incl. 2 persons	€ 12,50
extra adult	€ 3,00
child (2-10 yrs)	€ 2,00
electricity (2/4A)	€ 2,50

Reservations

Advised in high season with 25% deposit.
Tel: 04 92 55 91 95.
E-mail: les.6.stations@wanadoo.fr

FR05000 Camping des Princes d'Orange

05700 Orpierre (Hautes-Alpes)

This attractive, terraced site, set on a hillside above the village, has been gradually and thoughtfully developed by its owners over 20 years. Their genuine, friendly welcome means many families return year upon year, bringing in turn new generations. Divided into five terraces, each with its own toilet block, all its 120 generously sized pitches (96 for tourists) enjoy good shade from trees and wicker canopies and have electricity connections (4A). In high season one terrace is reserved as a 1-star camping area for young people (reservation not required). Renowned as a serious rock climbing venue, Orpierre also has an enchanting maze of medieval streets and houses, a walk through is to be recommended - almost like a trip back through the centuries. Whether you choose to drive, climb, walk or cycle there is plenty of wonderful scenery to discover in the immediate vicinity, whilst not far away, some exhilarating hang gliding and parascending can be enjoyed. For those seeking to 'get away from it all' in an area of outstanding natural beauty, there can be few more tranquil sites.

Facilities

Six toilet blocks with mostly British style WCs and washbasins in cubicles are extremely clean and accessible from all levels. Baby bath. Laundry facilities. Bread available (other basics from village). Takeaway from the bar in high season. Swimming pool (20 x 10 m), paddling pool (15/6-15/9). Play area. Table tennis, boules and games room. Fridge hire. Only gas barbecues permitted. Off site: Orpierre with bicycle hire 500 m. Fishing 7 km. Riding 19 km.

Open

1 April - 25 October.

At a glance

Welcome & Ambience	✓✓✓✓✓	Location	✓✓✓✓✓
Quality of Pitches	✓✓✓✓	Range of Facilities	✓✓✓✓

Directions

Turn off N75 road at Eyguians onto D30 - site is signed on left at crossroads in centre Orpierre village.

Charges 2004

Per unit incl. 2 persons	€ 18,00
incl. 3 persons	€ 19,50
extra person	€ 4,00
child (under 7 yrs)	€ 3,00
electricity	€ 3,00

Less 25% in low season. No credit cards.

Reservations

Essential for 14-7-20/8 (min. 14 days) and made with deposit (€ 84) and fee (€ 9). Tel: 04 92 66 22 53.
E-mail: campingorpierre@wanadoo.fr

FR84110 Camping Les Verguettes

Route de Carpentras, 84570 Villes sur Auzon (Vaucluse)

Friendly and family run, this small campsite is surrounded by fields and vineyards and should appeal to those seeking a more relaxed holiday. It is probably not the ideal site for active youngsters. Of the 89 pitches 81 are for touring. They are on the small side and are arranged in groups of six either side of the campsite road and are attractively laid out, separated by a variety of trees and shrubs. They all have electricity but long leads may be necessary. Close to the attractive swimming pool are the bar and small outside restaurant which offers a simple menu - a pleasant place to relax after a day sightseeing.

Facilities

Two toilet blocks, one near the entrance and other at the far end of the site. The buildings are old but have been refurbished to a high standard. Motorcaravan service point. Bar (all season). Small outside restaurant (1/5-30/9) with simple menu and takeaway. Small swimming pool. Tennis. Minigolf. Boules. Table tennis, table football and small games/TV room. Internet point. Off site: Wine tasting, walking, cycling. Carpentras 10 km.

Open

1 April - 15 October.

At a glance

Welcome & Ambience	✓✓✓✓	Location	✓✓✓✓
Quality of Pitches	✓✓✓✓	Range of Facilities	✓✓✓✓

Directions

Leave A7 autoroute at exit 22 just south of Orange and take D950 to Carpentras. Then take D942 east, signed Sault and Mazan. Site is about 10 km. on the right just after a roundabout on entering village.

Charges 2004

Per person	€ 4,50 - € 5,00
pitch	€ 6,50 - € 7,10
electricity	€ 2,50 - € 2,80
water and drainage	€ 2,30 - € 2,50

Camping Cheques accepted.

Reservations

Made with deposit (€ 16) and booking fee (€ 23). Tel: 04 90 61 88 18.
E-mail: info@provence-camping.com

FR84020 Domaine Naturiste de Bélézy

Mobile homes page 405

84410 Bédoin (Vaucluse)

At the foot of Mt Ventoux, Bélézy is an excellent naturist site with many amenities and activities and the ambience is essentially relaxed and comfortable. The site has two areas joined by a short pedestrian tunnel and the 238 marked and numbered pitches are set amongst many varieties of trees and shrubs. Electricity points (12A) are plentiful but you may need a long cable in places. The emphasis is on informality and concern for the environment and during high season cars are banned from the camping area to the supervised parking areas nearby. So far as naturism is concerned, the emphasis is on personal choice (and weather conditions!), the only stipulation being the requirement for complete nudity in the pools and pool area. The leisure park side of the site is an area of natural parkland with an orchard, fish-pond and woodland (complete with red squirrels), with a good range of sports facilities including tennis courts and swimming pools. The largest pool is for swimming and relaxation (you may enjoy a musical serenade), the smaller pool (heated 25/3-30/9) is also used for watersports and aquarobics. Near the pool area is the smart restaurant, with terrace, and the mellow old Mas (Provencal farmhouse) that houses many of the activities and amenities. Unusually there is a hydrotherapy centre to tone up and revitalise with qualified diagnosis. Member 'France 4 Naturisme'.

Facilities

Sanitary blocks are a little different. The newer ones are of a standard type and excellent quality, with free hot showers in cubicles with separators, and washbasins in cabins. One block, refurbished in 2003, has heating in low season. Another has an attractive children's section. In the same area the adult block has hot showers in the open air, separated by natural stone dividers and washing up areas again mostly in the open. Shop (1/4-30/9). Restaurant provides excellent food, waiter service, and takeaway meals at affordable prices. Three swimming pools. Sauna. Two tennis courts. Boules and table tennis. Adventure play area. Activities include painting and pottery courses and language lessons (not in July/Aug). Archery. Music (bring your own instrument). Guided walks. Children's clubs in holiday periods. Library and information centre. Disco. Hydrotherapy centre (1/4-30/9) - treatments include steam baths, massage and seaweed packs, osteopathy, Chinese medicine (including acupuncture) and Bach therapies. Barbecues are prohibited but there is a central barbecue area. Dogs and pets are not accepted. Off site: It is possible to walk into Bédoin (excellent street market - Monday mornings), Mount Ventoux (Tour de France), Carpentras, Avignon, Orange.

At a glance

Welcome & Ambience	✓✓✓✓	Location	✓✓✓✓
Quality of Pitches	✓✓✓✓	Range of Facilities	✓✓✓✓✓

Directions

From A7 autoroute or RN7 at Orange, take D950 southeast to Carpentras, then northeast via D974 to Bédoin. Site is signed in Bédoin, being about 1.5 km. northeast of the village

Charges 2005

Per unit incl. 1 adult	€ 13,00 - € 25,00
incl. 2 adults	€ 18,50 - € 31,50
incl. 3 adults	€ 24,50 - € 39,00
extra adult	€ 5,50 - € 10,50
child (3-8 yrs)	€ 4,00 - € 7,50
electricity (12A)	€ 4,20

Camping Cheques accepted.
Various offers and reductions outside high season.

Reservations

Write with deposit (25%) and fee (€ 30).
Tel: 04 90 65 60 18. E-mail: info@belezy.com

Open

21 March - 2 October.

FR84100 Camping Le Soleil de Provence

Route de Nyons, 84110 St Romain en Viennois (Vaucluse)

The views from this spacious, family run site must take some beating. The 360 degree panorama includes Mont Ventoux, the surrounding hills and the vineyards of northern Provence. It offers an excellent base from which to explore this very interesting area. Within a few kilometres one can find old towns such as Nyons, the olive capital of France, Orange and Avignon. The countryside is full of vineyards, lavender and sunflowers and the mountains offer a challenge to walkers and cyclists. The site has been developed to a high standard. The 140 pitches are of average size, most having only a little shade. They are all supplied with 10A electricity and there are a good number of water points. The excellent pool, surrounded by a sunbathing terrace, and overlooked by the bar, is an unusual shape with an island in the centre. Although there is no paddling pool one end of the pool is very shallow. This is a good family site with some organised entertainment in July and Aug.

Facilities

Two toilet blocks, heated early and late season, are very well appointed and include washbasins in cabins, facilities for disabled visitors and a baby changing room. Dishwashing and laundry sinks, washing machine, dryer and facilities for ironing. Motorcaravan service point. Small shop for bread, etc, open on demand. Bar and snack bar open all season. Swimming pool. Small play area. Off site: Tennis 1 km. Vaison la Romaine 4 km. Bicycle hire and riding 5 km. Fishing 15 km.

At a glance

Welcome & Ambience	✓✓✓✓✓	Location	✓✓✓✓✓
Quality of Pitches	✓✓✓✓	Range of Facilities	✓✓✓✓

Directions

Site is 4 km. north of Vaison la Romaine on the D938 road to Nyon. Entrance is on the right.

Charges 2005

Per person	€ 3,50 - € 5,50
pitch	€ 2,50 - € 3,00
electricity (10A)	€ 2,50

No credit cards.

Reservations

Advised for July/Aug. Tel: 04 90 46 46 00.
E-mail: info@camping-soleil-de-provence.fr

Open

15 March - 31 October.

FR84050 Camping Caravaning La Sorguette

Route d'Apt, 84800 L'Isle sur la Sorgue (Vaucluse)

This popular, well organised site is well placed, not too far (1.5 km.) from the small town of Isle sur la Sorgue. You will receive a warm welcome from the English speaking staff. Arranged in fairly close groups of four, the 164 level pitches (124 for touring) all have electricity (4/6A). Each group is separated by tall hedges and most pitches have a little shade at some part of the day. In high season a few competitions are organised (boule or volleyball), plus some children's entertainment, but this is quite low key. Running alongside a part of the site (fenced with a gate), the river Sorgue is only 6 km. from its source in the mountains at Fontaine de Vaucluse (a big tourist attraction). It is still very clear and used for canoeing, swimming or fishing. Isle sur la Sorgue is a very attractive small town, the river which forms small canals and waterways, interspersed with a number of water wheels. There are many bars and restaurants, some with seating overlooking the water which has a cooling effect in the height of summer. The markets on Thursday and Sunday (free shuttle bus) virtually fill the old streets of the town, and brightly coloured pottery, table covers, fruit and vegetable make it a photographer's paradise.

Facilities

Three well placed, clean and well maintained toilet blocks include some washbasins in cubicles for ladies, mainly British style WCs and dishwashing and laundry sinks. Two blocks have washing machines, dryer, ironing boards and clothes lines. Units for disabled people at all three. Baby room. Motorcaravan service point. Fridge hire. Shop and bar with snacks (1/7-25/8) set well away from the pitches, outside the entrance which ensures that the occasional entertainment in July/Aug does not disturb campers. Play area, volleyball, half-court tennis and basketball. Canoe and bicycle hire. Internet access. Off site: Indoor/outdoor swimming pools (preferential rates) 2 km. Fishing and riding 5 km. Walking and cycling circuits.

At a glance

Welcome & Ambience	✓✓✓✓✓	Location	✓✓✓✓
Quality of Pitches	✓✓✓	Range of Facilities	✓✓✓

Directions

Site is 1.5 km. east of L'Isle sur la Sorgue on the N100 towards Apt. It is well signed from the town.

Charges 2005

Per unit incl. 2 persons	€ 15,40 - € 19,20
extra person (over 7 yrs)	€ 5,20 - € 6,60
child (1-6 yrs)	€ 2,60 - € 3,30
electricity (4/10A)	€ 3,50 - € 4,60
animal	€ 2,10 - € 2,60

Reservations

Made with deposit and fee (€ 80).
Tel: 04 90 38 05 71. E-mail: sorguette@wanadoo.fr

Open

15 March - 15 October.

FR84070 Camping Club International Carpe Diem

Route de St Marcellin, B.P. 68, 84110 Vaison-la-Romaine (Vaucluse)

Perhaps Carpe Diem is a shade pretentious with its Greek statues and amphitheatre surround to its main pool. A developing site, it is only a few years old and will no doubt mellow as the trees and shrubs grow and old and new blend together. It is a good site for active families seeking all day entertainment and the situation is quite impressive with magnificent views over one of the most beautiful parts of France, yet only 800 m. from the village of Vaison la Romaine. There are 232 pitches with 100 small to medium sized, grass touring pitches all with electricity and many with some degree of shade. A new terraced area has mobile homes, chalets and unshaded touring pitches. One area is designated for pet owners, whilst another is for motorhomes. The main pool is impressive with its tiered seating, plants, etc. It is used as a theatre for evening entertainment. A simple square pool is near the play area with grass surrounds.

Facilities

The central toilet block – with fountain – provides mainly British and a few Turkish style toilets, washbasins in cabins and showers with an unusual cupboard for clothes. Dishwashing and laundry sinks. Small editions of everything are provided for children. Washing machine. Extra facilities are behind the main pool. Motorcaravan service point. Reception provides a small shop (20/3-6/11). Bar (10/5-30/9) near the main pool and pizzeria (5/4-30/9). TV room. Swimming pools (5/4-3/11). Play area. Minigolf, archery (cross-bow), volleyball, football and basketball. Mountain bike hire. Mini-club. Extensive entertainment programme, incl Roman extravagansas (which can be noisy) and off site activities in high season. There is a charge for participation in sports and entertainment. Barbecues for hire.
Off site: Fishing 1 km. Riding 2 km. Golf 20 km. Organised canoeing, riding, climbing, walking, mountain biking. Vaison la Romaine (800 m) with its magnificent Roman ruins, shops, restaurants, market and excellent wine.

At a glance

Welcome & Ambience	✓✓✓✓	Location	✓✓✓✓
Quality of Pitches	✓✓✓✓	Range of Facilities	✓✓✓✓✓

Directions

Leave Vaison la Romaine on D938 heading south towards Carpentras. 1 km. beyond the 'Super U' roundabout turn left on D151, signed St Marcellin. Site entrance is on the left immediately after the junction.

Charges 2004

Per pitch incl. 1-3 persons	€ 15,00 - € 29,00
extra person	€ 4,00 - € 5,50
child (2-10 yrs)	€ 2,50 - € 4,50
electricity (6/10A)	€ 3,20 - € 4,70
dog	free - € 2,50

Camping Cheques accepted.

Reservations

Made with deposit and fee (€ 77).
Tel: 04 90 36 02 02.
E-mail: contact@camping-carpe-diem.com

Open

20 March - 6 November.

FR84080 Camping Caravaning La Simioune

84500 Bollène (Vaucluse)

This unsophisticated, very basic, rural site is a reasonable base for those who love horses. Well off the beaten track and set amongst tall pines on sandy, undulating ground, it is bordered on one side by a vineyard. However, please don't go to La Simioune if you prefer a regimented site with neat lawns and flower beds or lots of entertainment. In fact, first impressions here are of it being untidy. This is actually a riding school with local children coming for lessons. Campers can also hire horses by the hour, although the favourite seems to be the day-long trek with a river crossing and picnic lunch (all at reasonable prices). The 80 unmarked and uneven pitches, 60 used for long stay caravans, are of varying size and shape, most with electricity (6A). The area has many lovely medieval villages and vineyards. Some (not all!) will visit the nearby crocodile farm down by the River Rhône. Not recommended for large units.

Facilities

The basic toilet block is quite old but adequately cleaned. Small room for babies with child's WC. Complete room for disabled people although the site itself will be difficult for wheelchairs due to the sandy and undulating terrain. Laundry and dishwashing sinks with two hot taps to draw from and an old washing machine. Small bar serves simple meals in July/Aug. Small swimming and paddling pool (June - Sept). Riding. Table tennis, boules, volleyball. Barbecues are not permitted. Off site: Tennis, fishing, walking and canoeing nearby.

Open

All year.

At a glance

Welcome & Ambience	✓✓	Location	✓✓
Quality of Pitches	✓✓	Range of Facilities	✓✓

Directions

From A7 take exit 19 (at Bollène). At first roundabout take third exit signed Carpentras (site signed). Just after traffic lights turn left, signed Lambisque (Rue Alphonse Daudet) and follow site signs for 5 km (the last section up a windy, narrow and bumpy road).

Charges guide

Per person	€ 3,40
child (under 7 yrs)	€ 1,50
pitch	€ 3,00 - € 3,10
electricity (6A)	€ 2,30
animal	€ 1,50

No credit cards.

Reservations

Contact site for details. Tel: 04 90 30 44 62.
E-mail: la-simioune@wanadoo.fr

FR84090 Camping du Pont d'Avignon

Ile dela Barthelasse, 84000 Avignon (Vaucluse)

This is a city site, yet it is in a quiet location and only a short walk or ferry ride from the town. With its island situation, some of the pitches are only yards away from the famous bridge, only the mighty Rhône separating them. A few pitches have views of the 'Pont' and also of the Pope's palace which is floodlit at night. There are 300 level pitches, some on grass and some with hardstanding. 118 with electricity. All have some shade but those with electricity are well shaded. A small play area, tennis courts and volley-ball pitch are in the centre of the site separating the tent pitches on one side and the electric pitches on the other. Many pitches are separated by hedges. The amenities are grouped around the new pool. The site, although close to the historic centre of Avignon, has a very rural feel, due no doubt to the many flowering trees and shrubs and the fact it is on an island. English is spoken at reception.

Facilities

Toilet blocks are placed around the periphery of the site and kept very clean and well maintained. Mainly British style toilets, roomy showers and all washbasins in cubicles. Dishwashing and laundry sinks. Three washing machines and a dryer. One block has full facilities for disabled visitors. Motorcaravan service point. Well stocked shop (1 April - end Sept). Bar/restaurant and takeaway (1 June - end Sept). Swimming pool and paddling pool (1 June - end Sept). Play area. Tennis (free). Volleyball. Bicycle hire (July/Aug). Internet access.

Open

24 March - 26 October.

At a glance

Welcome & Ambience	✓✓✓✓✓	Location	✓✓✓✓✓
Quality of Pitches	✓✓✓✓	Range of Facilities	✓✓✓✓

Directions

Site is on the Ile de la Barthelasse in the middle of the river Rhône, to the west of the city, almost opposite the famous bridge. It is well signed from the many roads into Avignon and accessed from Pont Daladier towards Villeneuve les Avignon on the west bank of the river.

Charges 2004

Per unit incl. 2 persons	€ 12,00 - € 32,50
extra person	€ 2,80 - € 4,10
child (3-12 yrs)	free - € 4,10
electricity	€ 2,50 - € 3,00

Camping Cheques accepted.

Reservations

Necessary for July/Aug. Tel: 04 90 80 63 50.
E-mail: info@camping-avignon.com

Midi-Pyrénées

Rolling fields of yellow sunflowers, the Armagnac vineyards and crumbling, ancient stone buildings amidst the sleepy villages make this colourful region popular with those who enjoy good food, good wine and a taste of the good life.

Départements: 09 Ariège, 31 Haute-Garonne, 32 Gers, 65 Hautes-Pyrénées, 81 Tarn, 82 Tarn-et Garonne. We have left out the départements of Aveyron (12) and Lot (46), which are in our Dordogne/Aveyron region

Still a relatively unknown region, the Midi-Pyrénées is the largest region of France, extending from the Dordogne in the north to the Spanish border. It is blessed by radiant sunshine and a fascinating range of scenery. High chalk plateaux, majestic peaks, tiny hidden valleys and small fortified sleepy villages, which seem to have changed little since the Middle Ages, contrast with the high-tech, industrial and vibrant university city of Toulouse.

Lourdes is one of the most visited pilgrimage sites in the world. Toulouse-Lautrec, the artist, was born at Albi the capital of the département of Tarn. Much of the town is built of pink brick which seems to glow when seen from the distance. In the east, the little town of Foix, with its maze of steep, winding streets, is a convenient centre from which to explore the prehistoric caves at Niaux and the Aladdin's Cave of duty-free gift shops in the independent state of Andorra. The Canal du Midi that links Bordeaux to the Mediterranean was commissioned by Louis XIV in 1666 and is still in working order today.

Cuisine of the region

Food is rich and strongly seasoned, making generous use of garlic and goose fat, and there are some excellent regional wines. Seafood such as oysters, salt-water fish, or piballes from the Adour river are popular

Cassoulet: stew of duck, sausages and beans

Confit de Canard (d'oie): preserved duck meat

Grattons (Graisserons): a mélange of small pieces of rendered down duck, goose and pork fat

Magret de canard: duck breast fillets

Poule au pot: chicken simmered with vegetables

Ouillat (Ouliat): Pyrénées soup: onions, tomatoes, goose fat and garlic

Tourtière Landaise: a sweet of Agen prunes, apples and Armagnac

Places of interest

Albi: birthplace and Museum of Toulouse-Lautrec, imposing Ste Cécile cathedral with 15th century fresco of 'The Last Judgement'

Auch: capital of ancient Gascony, boasts a fine statue of d'Artágnan

Collonges-la-Rouge: picturesque village of Medieval and Renaissance style mansions and manors

Conques: 11th century Ste Foy Romanesque church

Cordes: medieval walled hilltop village

Foix: 11th/12th century towers on rocky peak above town; 14th century cathedral.

Lourdes: famous pilgrimage site where Ste Bernadette is said to have spoken to the Virgin Mary in a grotto and known for the miracles said to have been performed there

Alan Rogers **tip**

IF YOU LIKE JAZZ MUSIC, HEAD TO MARCIAC FOR THE ANNUAL JAZZ FESTIVAL HELD IN EARLY AUGUST.

FR09020 Camping L'Arize

Mobile homes page 405

Lieu-dit Bourtol, 09240 La Bastide-de-Sérou (Ariège)

You will receive a warm welcome from Dominique and Brigitte at this friendly little family site and Brigitte speaks excellent English. The site sits in a delightful, tranquil valley among the foothills of the Pyrénées and is just east of the interesting village of La Bastide de Sérou beside the River Arize (good trout fishing). The river is fenced for the safety of children on the site, but may be accessed just outside the gate. Deer and wild boar are common in this area and may be sighted in quieter periods. The owners have built this site from ground level over the last few years and have put much love and care into its development. The 70 large pitches are neatly laid out on level grass within the spacious site. All have 3/6A electricity (French type sockets) and are separated into bays by hedges and young trees. Discounts have been negotiated for several of the local attractions (details are provided in the comprehensive pack provided on arrival - in your own language). This is a comfortable and relaxing base for touring this beautiful part of the Pyrénées with easy access to the medieval town of Foix and even Andorra for duty-free shopping.

Facilities

The central sanitary block (unheated) includes washbasins in cabins and good facilities for babies and disabled people. Laundry room with dryer. Dishwashing under cover. Chemical disposal (into a large holding tank - the organic sewage system is incompatible with chemicals). Small swimming pool with paved sunbathing area. Entertainment in high season, weekly barbecues and welcome drinks on Sundays. Fishing, riding and bicycle hire on site Off site: Golf 5 km. Several restaurants and shops are within a few minute's drive and the nearest restaurant, which is located at the national stud for the famous Merens horses just 200 m. away, will deliver takeaway meals to your pitch.

At a glance

Welcome & Ambience	✓✓✓✓✓	Location	✓✓✓✓✓
Quality of Pitches	✓✓✓✓	Range of Facilities	✓✓✓✓

Directions

Site is southeast of the village La Bastide-de-Sérou. Take the D15 towards Nescus and site is on right after approx. 1 km.

Charges 2005

Per pitch incl. 2 persons and electricity	€ 15,20 - € 22,60
extra adult	€ 4,00 - € 5,20
child (0-7 yrs)	€ 3,00 - € 3,60
dog	free - € 1,50

Discounts for longer stays in mid and low season.

Reservations

Made with 25% deposit and fee (€ 10).
Tel: 05 61 65 81 51. E-mail: camparize@aol.com

Open

28 March - 4 November.

FR09030 Camping Le Montagnou

Route de Guzet, 09140 Le Trein d'Ustou (Ariège)

The road going south out of St Girons appears to lead to nowhere other than Guzet, but it is well worth the short detour over easy roads to the little village of Le Trein d'Ustou, which is no more than 10 or 15 minutes short of the up and coming winter sports resort of Guzet. Just before Le Trein d'Ustou you will find Le Montagnou, a delightful small campsite nestling among the lush lower slopes of the mountains. Robert and Daniele created this charming site from the forest and opened for the first time in 1996. It is an attractive proposition either as a base for winter sports activities or for touring this lovely area, with 60 level pitches on grass, 30 with electricity (6, 10 or 16A). The site has been developed on modern lines with good quality installations. At a lower level there is an area of the river running alongside the site which the locals use for swimming, but really the attraction here is the surrounding mountains which offer excellent winter sports facilities which include a ski-lift (10 minutes drive) and no less than 24 pistes! There are also many places of interest which Robert, who doubles as the local Director of Tourism, will be pleased to tell you about and brief you on the local wildlife. The walks in this area are renowned - watch out for marmots and, yes, even bears!

Facilities

Two toilet blocks (one open in low season) can be heated and are kept clean. They include washbasins in cabins, covered dishwashing and laundry sinks, washing machine and dryers, and good facilities for disabled visitors. Snack bar with takeaway. Gas supplies. Baker calls every other day. Library (some English books) and TV. Fishing.
Off site: Restaurant 50 m. in the village. Shops at Seix. Riding 15 km.

Open

All year.

At a glance

Welcome & Ambience	✓✓✓✓	Location	✓✓✓✓✓
Quality of Pitches	✓✓✓	Range of Facilities	✓✓✓

Directions

Approaching from A64 from St Girons follow signs for Guzet; take first right at roundabout (Guzet), second right at next roundabout (Guzet, Seix) and second right at third roundabout to Seix. From Foix take third right at first roundabout and follow good signs for Guzet and Seix. Go through Seix (the river is on the right) and at Pont de la Taule turn left towards Trein d'Ustou. Site is on left before village.

Charges 2004

Per unit incl. 2 persons and electricity	€ 14,50 - € 15,50
tent pitch	€ 4,00
extra person	€ 4,00
child (2-7 yrs)	€ 2,50

No credit cards.

Reservations

Contact site by letter. Tel: 05 61 66 94 97.
E-mail: campinglemontagnou@wanadoo.fr

FR09080 Camping du Lac

RN 20, 09000 Foix (Ariège)

Du Lac is a new, large and sprawling lakeside site with many facilities. It is just three kilometres north of the very pretty town of Foix. There is some road noise as the site is alongside the old N20 but there is lots of room to manoeuvre at the entrance and a smart, air conditioned reception building. The site is informally divided into four areas, one for parking vehicles. The other areas are generally flat and some shade can be found under mature trees. There are 135 pitches, most with electricity, but the site is so big there appear to be more - there is lots of room. Access to the lake is through a gate which is locked at night and the fence is secure. Children will need supervision in this area. The lake is owned by a separate company but campers have free use of the attractive area. Here you will find canoeing and pedaloes, along with fishing, or just picnics and barbecues with a small bar operating. The lake is not for swimming as there is a fair amount of forbidding green weed but there is a clear area for canoes. The site is ideal for visiting Foix and exploring the local area.

Facilities

Four unisex sanitary blocks of different designs are all new, some of brick and others resembling pretty 'wendy houses' made of wood. The facilities are modern, clean and well equipped. One of the little blocks contains a washing machine, excellent facilities for disabled campers and a well equipped baby room. Reception sells basic goods but no fresh food. Pizza hut and bar/drinks stall close to the pool (a restaurant is planned). Swimming pool and separate paddling pool. Play areas around the site and another by the lake. Watersports, fishing and canoe instruction (hire charges apply). TV room, electronic games. Tennis court and boules pitch. Some animation in high season. Torches are necessary. Off site: Cycling and walking tours, riding, golf or even white water rafting.

At a glance

Welcome & Ambience	✓✓✓✓✓	Location	✓✓✓✓
Quality of Pitches	✓✓✓✓	Range of Facilities	✓✓✓✓

Directions

From Foix stay on the old N20 north for 3 km. (avoid the new bypass and tunnel). Site is signed on the left.

Charges 2004

Per unit incl. 2 persons	€ 14,00 - € 20,00
electricity	€ 3,00 - € 4,50
extra person	€ 3,50 - € 5,50
dog	€ 1,00 - € 2,00

Camping Cheques accepted.

Reservations

Advised for July/Aug. Tel: 05 61 65 11 58.
E-mail: camping-du-lac@wanadoo.fr

Open

All year.

FR09090 Naturist Camping Millfleurs

Le Tuilier Gudas, 09120 Varilhes (Ariège)

Millfleurs is a peaceful naturist site in a superb location for mature naturists. Owned by a Dutch couple, Gert and Annie Kos who provide a warm welcome and speak excellent English, it really is camping at a relaxed and sublime level. It is so peaceful with some 70 acres of woods and meadows to explore providing guided naturist walks in total privacy. Annie has found 16 different types of orchids and keeps a picture record in the 'salle de reunion'. The long drive leads to a traditional farmhouse housing the campsite office. The site has 40 large flat pitches (26 with 4/6A electricity) on well spaced terraces, but there are also very secluded pitches in wooded areas with shade, or you can pitch a tent in the meadows if you prefer. Long leads are required if you decide to pitch off the terraces. There are few of the normal camping leisure facilities here and the site is definitely aimed at the more mature naturist camper. Transport is required as there is no bus service. Explore the nearby mediaeval town of Foix with its stunning castle towering over the busy centre, and investigate the history of the Cathares and the region with its underground rivers and caves. With its temperate climate, the Foix valley is a prime area for growing the grapes for the white wine used in the production of the famous Cava, and the vineyards are worth a visit.

Facilities

An excellent central unisex toilet block, well thought out, includes great facilities for disabled campers, inside and outside showers and cheerful flowers and potted plants. Bread available to order in high season. Guests dine together in the 'salle de reunion' within the farmhouse two nights a week (Sat/Wed) or you just relax and meet friends for a drink. Refrigerator with drinks operated on an honesty system. Petanque court and guide book for walks and cycle rides in local area. Torches essential at night. Pick ups from airports and stations can be arranged. Off site: The coast is approximately 1.5 hours.

Open

1 April - 15 October.

At a glance

Welcome & Ambience	✓✓✓✓✓	Location	✓✓✓✓✓
Quality of Pitches	✓✓✓✓✓	Range of Facilities	✓✓✓

Directions

One can find the site very easily from the village of Varilhes which is 8 km. south of Pamiers on D624 (parallel to N20). Take D13 for Dalou and Gudas cross railway and N20. The site is 2 km. past Gudas, pass small road to left and site drive is further on right.

Charges 2004

Per person (all ages)	€ 4,15 - € 4,95
pitch	€ 4,15 - € 4,95
dog	€ 1,75
electricity	€ 2,50

No credit cards.

Reservations

Not necessary. Tel: 05 61 60 77 56.
E-mail: ag.kos@wanadoo.fr

FR09060 Camping Le Pré Lombard

09400 Tarascon-sur-Ariege (Ariège)

Didier Mioni, the manager here follows the town motto S'y passos, y demoros - 'if you wish to come here, you will stay here' in his aim to ensure your satisfaction on his site. This busy, good value site is located beside the attractive river Ariége on the outskirts of the town. There are around 180 level, grassy, numbered pitches with shade provided by a variety of trees. At the rear of the site are 60 site-owned chalets and mobile homes. Electricity is available to all. A gate in the fence provides access to the river bank for fishing (licences required). Open all year, it is an excellent choice for early or late breaks, or as a stop-over en-route to the winter sun destinations in Spain. This region of Ariége is in the foothills of the Pyrénées and 45 km. from Andorra. At Tarascon itself you can go underground at the Parc Pyrénéen de l'Art Préhistorique to view prehistoric rock paintings, or the really adventurous can take to the air for paragliding, hangliding, or microlighting.

Facilities

Five sanitary units of varying age, design and size (not all open in low season). Mostly British WCs, open and cubicled washbasins. Facilities for disabled people. Laundry. Excellent motorcaravan service point. Bar and takeaway (open according to demand). Bread, gas, papers and daily requirements sold in the bar. Good restaurant with entertainment and dancing (1/5-30/9). Fenced, unsupervised swimming pool (15/5-30/9, a new covered pool is planned). Separate playgrounds for toddlers and older children. Video games machines, table tennis, table football, boules and volleyball. Fishing. Full programme of entertainment for families in main season. Off site: Supermarket 300 m. Town 800 m.

At a glance

Welcome & Ambience	✓✓✓✓	Location	✓✓✓✓
Quality of Pitches	✓✓✓✓	Range of Facilities	✓✓✓✓

Directions

Site is 800 m. south of the town centre by the river. From north, turn off main N20 into town centre and there are prominent signs. From south (Andorra) site signed at roundabout on town approach.

Charges 2004

Per unit incl. 2 adults and 6A electricity	€ 15,00 - € 23,00
extra person	€ 4,00 - € 9,00

Camping Cheques accepted.

Reservations

Advised for high season and made with 25% deposit and € 15,24 booking fee. Tel: 05 61 05 61 94. E-mail: info@prelombard.com

Open

All year.

FR09050 Camping Municipal La Prade

09110 Sorgeat (Ariège)

Superbly situated high up on the mountainside overlooking the valley this site has magnificent views, with the river 300 m distant and a lake at two kilometres. A small site, it provides just 40 pitches on terraces. About two-thirds are occupied by long stay units. Well supervised, with the warden present at varying times, the site is kept very clean. Electrical connections (5/10A) are available. A small stream tinkles through the edge of the site and the attractive hills towering above it reverberate with the pleasant sounds of goat bells. A most reasonably priced campsite.

Facilities

The rather small sanitary block has only two showers and two WCs in each half. However, standards are very high and a further block is under construction. Facilities for the disabled are also very good. Chemical disposal point under construction. Small play area. Off site: Fishing 0.5 km. Riding and bicycle hire 5 km.

At a glance

Welcome & Ambience	✓✓✓	Location	✓✓✓✓
Quality of Pitches	✓✓✓	Range of Facilities	✓✓✓

Directions

From N20 (Foix - Andorra) through Ax-les-Thermes, in the centre of village take D613 to left, signed Quillan (hairpin bends) for 5 km. Site is signed on the right. The last kilometre is a narrow two way winding road (large units may find some difficulty). There are several sites as you climb.

Charges 2004

Per adult	€ 2,90
pitch	€ 1,60 - € 1,80
electricity (5/10A)	€ 2,70 - € 5,20

Reservations

Advised for high season - contact site. Tel: 05 61 64 36 34. E-mail: sorgeat@free.fr

FR32010 Le Camp de Florence

Mobile homes page 406

Route Astaffort, 32480 La Romieu (Gers)

Camp de Florence is an attractive site on the edge of an historic village in pleasantly undulating Gers countryside. It is run by the Mynsbergen family who are Dutch (although Susan is English) and they have sympathetically converted the old farmhouse buildings to provide facilities for the site. The 183 pitches (95 for tourers) are all over 100 sq.m. plus. Terraced where necessary, all have electricity, 10 with hard-standing and 25 fully serviced. They are arranged around a large field (full of sunflowers when we visited) with rural views, giving a feeling of spaciousness. The 13th century village of La Romieu is on the Santiago de Compostela pilgrim route and the collegiate church, visible from the site, is well worth a visit (the views are magnificent from the top of the tower), as is the local arboretum, the biggest collection of trees in the Midi-Pyrénées. The Pyrénées are a two hour drive, the Atlantic coast a similar distance. There are 20 tour operator pitches.

Facilities

Two unisex toilet blocks include some washbasins in cabins. Washing machine and dryer. Motorcaravan services. Water points are limited. Good upstairs, air-conditioned restaurant, open to the public as well as campers, serves a range of food, including local specialities and an à la carte menu (1/5-30/9, closed Weds, with a barbecue instead). Takeaway. Bread on site in season. Swimming pool area with jacuzzi, central island and protected children's pool (all open to the public in the afternoons). Adventure play area, games area and pets area. Games room, tennis, table tennis, volleyball and petanque. Bicycle hire. Video shows, discos, picnics, animation and musical evenings and excursions organised. Internet access.

Open

1 April - 10 October.

At a glance

Welcome & Ambience	✓✓✓✓✓	Location	✓✓✓✓
Quality of Pitches	✓✓✓✓	Range of Facilities	✓✓✓✓✓

Directions

Site is signed from D931 Agen - Condom road. Small units can turn left at Ligardes (signed) and follow D36 for 1 km. and take right turn for La Romieu (signed). Otherwise continue until outskirts of Condom and take D41 left to La Romieu and pass through village to site.

Charges 2004

Per unit incl. 2 persons and electricity	€ 13,50 - € 27,50
extra person	€ 3,50 - € 6,50
child (4-9 yrs)	€ 2,60 - € 4,50
water and drainage	free - € 3,00
dog (max 2)	€ 1,50 - € 2,00

Camping Cheques accepted.
Special prices for groups, rallies, etc.

Reservations

Write or phone for information (English spoken).
Tel: 05 62 28 15 58.
E-mail: info@campdeflorence.com

TRAVEL SERVICE SITE
TO BOOK CALL 0870 405 4055 OR www.alanrogersdirect.com

FR32030 Camping La Plage de Verduzan

Rue du Lac, 32410 Castera Verduzan (Gers)

This is a pleasant site situated 500 metres from the small village of Castera-Verduzan where there are restaurants, bars, shops, a casino and thermal baths. The site is on the shores of a small lake and access to its sandy beach is free for site customers. Here there is a water slide, pedaloes and a small sailing school. The 56 touring pitches at the site are on level grass, hedged with bushes and ornamental trees and all have electricity hook-up (3/10A). There are also a few mobile homes to rent.

Facilities

The two toilet blocks are mainly unisex with washbasins in cabins, adjustable, roomy showers and mixed laundry and dishwashing sinks with one hot tap to draw from. Washing machine and ironing board. Chemical disposal. Facilities for disabled people. New play area and motorcaravan service point planned for 2005. Small bar which also serves snacks and provides low key entertainment, games and competitions (open July/Aug). Table tennis. Fishing from the far side of the lake. Off site: Village shops and restaurants. Golf 25 km. Riding 5 km.

Open

10 April - 30 September.

At a glance

Welcome & Ambience	✓✓✓✓	Location	✓✓✓✓
Quality of Pitches	✓✓✓✓	Range of Facilities	✓✓✓

Directions

Castera-Verduzen is on the D930, 20 km. south of Condom. Site is on south side of village and well signed.

Charges 2004

Per unit incl. 2 persons	€ 12,00 - € 18,50
extra person	€ 3,00 - € 4,50
child (3-7 yrs)	€ 2,20 - € 3,20
electricity (6A)	€ 1,50

Reservations

Contact site. Tel: 05 62 68 12 23.
E-mail: la-plage-de-verduzan@wanadoo.fr

FR32080 Camping Le Talouch

32810 Roquelaure (Gers)

Although enjoying an 'away-from-it-all' location Auch, the region's capital, is within a ten kilometre drive from this family run site, which takes its name from the small Talouch river. The entrance, off the D148 road, is fronted by a parking area with reception to the right and the bar and restaurant facing. Beyond this point lies the top half of the touring area with generous pitches of at least 120 sq.m. located between mature trees and divided by hedges, some with chalets. There are 118 pitches, with electricity (4A). The rear half of the site has unshaded pitches in a more open aspect, and chalets have been built on the hillside to one side of the site.

Facilities

There are two immaculate toilet blocks, the larger refurbished building offering modern units with a clean appearance. The smaller block is of a more modern and unusual style, situated to rear of site. Baby bathroom and shower which can be used by people with disabilities. Small shop selling basic foodstuffs and snacks (1/5-30/9). Two swimming pools and new pool with 'jetstream'. Bicycle hire. Two play areas, volleyball, tennis, basketball and 9 hole swin golf course. Organised entertainment in high season.

Open

1 April - 30 September.

At a glance

Welcome & Ambience	✓✓✓✓	Location	✓✓✓✓
Quality of Pitches	✓✓✓✓	Range of Facilities	✓✓✓✓

Directions

From Auch take N21 for 8.5 km. north and turn west onto D272 to village of Roquelaure. Then follow signs to site 2 km. south of village on D148.

Charges 2004

Per unit incl. 2 adults	€ 12,90 - € 20,40
with electricity	€ 15,00 - € 24,00
extra person	€ 3,90 - € 6,10
child (3-7 yrs)	€ 3,15 - € 5,00
animal	€ 1,25 - € 2,00

Camping Cheques accepted.
Discounts for longer stays.

Reservations

Advisable for July/Aug. Tel: 05 62 65 52 43.
E-mail: info@camping-talouch.com

FR65010 Domaine Naturiste L'Eglantière

Aries-Espenan, 65230 Castelnau-Magnoac (Haute-Pyrénées)

This pretty site is situated in the valley between the Pyrénees and the plain, within easy reach of Lourdes and the mountains. Alongside a small, fast flowing river, in wooded surroundings it comprises 12 hectares for camping and caravanning, with a further 32 for walking and relaxing in the woods and fields. The river is said to be suitable for swimming and canoeing, with fishing nearby. The 83 traditional pitches are of mixed size on fairly level grass, the older ones secluded and separated by a variety of tall trees and bushes, the newer ones more open, with a natural tenting area across the river (28+ pitches). The traditional pitches have 10A electrical connections (long lead for some). The site has is an attractive, central, medium sized swimming pool with sunbathing areas both on paving and grass, and a children's pool, overlooked by the attractive style clubhouse and terrace. A small health centre (massage, sauna) is being developed in the old farmhouse. A range of studios, mobile homes, chalets and tents is on site. Used by a tour operator (six pitches). Member of France 4 Naturisme.

Facilities

Two main sanitary blocks at each end of the site are in typically naturist style, providing under cover, open plan, controllable hot showers, and sinks for washing up. A small centrally located sanitary block has individual cubicles. Shop (July-Aug). Clubhouse with bar (all season), small restaurant (June-Sept), pizzeria and takeaway (July-Aug), internet access and indoor soundproofed activities/disco area, play room for younger children and table tennis for older ones. Swimming pool (all season). Play area and children's animation in season. Volleyball, badminton, table tennis, petanque and archery. Activities on the river. Canoe and mountain bike hire. Trekking and cross country cycling. Barbecues are officially forbidden. Torches useful.
Off site: Restaurants in the nearby village.

At a glance

Welcome & Ambience	✓✓✓✓	Location	✓✓✓✓
Quality of Pitches	✓✓✓✓	Range of Facilities	✓✓✓✓

Directions

From Auch take D929 south towards Lannemezan. Just after Castelnau-Magnoac watch for signs to hamlet of Ariès-Espénan on left and follow site signs.

Charges 2004

Per pitch incl. 2 persons	€ 12,00 - € 29,00
extra person	€ 2,00 - € 5,50
child (3-8 yrs)	free - € 4,20
animal	€ 2,20 - € 3,50
electricity (10A)	€ 4,50

Camping Cheques accepted.

Reservations

Made with deposit (25%) and fee (€ 27.44).
Tel: 05 62 39 88 00. E-mail: info@leglantiere.com

Open

Easter - October.

FR65020 Sunêlia Les Trois Vallées

Ave des Pyrénées, 65400 Argelès-Gazost (Haute-Pyrénées)

This is a large and ever-expanding site on the valley road from Lourdes into the Pyrénées. It has a rather unprepossessing entrance and pitches near the road suffer from noise (this should reduce a little with the opening of a new by-pass) but at the back, open fields allow views of surrounding mountains on all sides. Recent additions include an indoor pool, two jacuzzis and an enormous play area that seems to have everything! The site now has 500 flat, grassy pitches of which 200 are for tourers; they are marked out and of reasonable size, all with electricity. The proximity to the road is at least advantageous for touring the area, being by a roundabout with Lourdes one way, Luz-St-Sauveur and mountains another way, and the dramatic Pyrénées Corniche Col d'Aubisque going off to the west. Argelès-Gazost is an attractive town with excellent restaurants and cultural interests. The site is popular with young people and could be quite lively at times.

Facilities

The two unisex toilet blocks are fairly modern and include facilities for disabled people and a laundry room. Cleaning can be variable and facilities could be under pressure at peak times. Bread available on site. Bar/disco. Café and takeaway. Swimming pool complex (from 1/6) with paddling pool and two water slides. TV room. Good playground. Volleyball, football, boules and archery.
Off site: Supermarket across the road. Bicycle hire 50 m. Fishing 500 m. Riding 3 km.

Open

1 April - 30 September.

At a glance

Welcome & Ambience	✓✓✓✓	Location	✓✓✓
Quality of Pitches	✓✓✓✓	Range of Facilities	✓✓✓✓✓

Directions

Take N21 from Lourdes to Argelès-Gazost. Approachong Argelès, pass a Champion supermarket on your right, and then a roundabout - take the furthest left exit and the site entrance is 100 m. or so on the left. A new express way is planned.

Charges 2004

Per pitch incl. 2 persons	€ 10,50 - € 21,50
incl. 3A electricity	€ 13,50 - € 24,50
incl. 6A electricity	€ 16,00 - € 27,00
extra person	€ 3,80 - € 7,00
child (under 7 yrs)	€ 2,00 - € 6,00

Camping Cheques accepted.

Reservations

Advised for July/Aug. and made with deposit (€ 70) and fee (€ 30). Tel: 05 62 90 35 47.
E-mail: info@camping-les-3-vallees.fr

FR65070 Camping Caravaning Le Rioumajou

Bousrisp, 65170 St Lary Soulan (Haute-Pyrénées)

Located in the heart of the Aure valley, adjacent to a fast flowing unfenced river, and with views to the surrounding mountains and countryside, Le Rioumajou is a good base from which to explore this part of the Hautes-Pyrénées. There are 240 pitches, with 48 mobile homes, leaving around 190 pitches for tourists. They are generally separated, varying in size, some shady and some more open, and all with electricity hook-ups (2-10A), and ten are all weather pitches. A good cycle track runs alongside the main road in both directions from the site and one can walk to the town along the river bank. Nearby is the Réserve Naturel du Néouvielle National Park, and the Spanish border via the Aragnouet - Bielsa tunnel, and the tourist village of Saint-Lary Soulan is 2 km.

Facilities

Three attractive, modern toilet blocks (only one open and heated in low season and facilities can be stretched). Some washbasins in cabins, controllable hot showers including some spacious twin units. Lights are on a time delay switch. Laundry with large drying room. One block (not open in winter) has a room for children with toilets, baby bath and shower, changing surfaces and basins. Facilities for disabled visitors (access by key). Small shop for essentials (July/Aug). Well fenced, outdoor heated swimming pool (10 x 25m; June-Sept). Sauna and jacuzzi. Good adventure style playground.

At a glance

Welcome & Ambience	✓✓✓	Location	✓✓✓✓✓
Quality of Pitches	✓✓✓✓	Range of Facilities	✓✓✓✓

Directions

From Lannemezan take the D929 south, pass through Arreau, and continue for about 10 km. After passing through Guchen and Guchan, site is on right before Bourisp.

Charges 2004

Per person	€ 4,45 - € 6,95
child (4-10 yrs)	€ 2,00 - € 3,45
electricity (2-10A)	€ 3,00 - € 6,00

Reservations

Advisable for high season. Tel: 05 62 39 48 32.
E-mail: lerioumajou@wanadoo.fr

Open

All year.

FR65030 Airotel Pyrénées

65120 Esquieze-Sere (Haute-Pyrénées)

Airotel Pyrénées is a small site in the heart of the Pyrénées. It is located on the main road into the mountains, south from Argelès-Gazost and surrounded by the high peaks (some pitches will have daytime road noise). There are 163 level pitches, with 85 for touring units, all with electricity and 45 fully serviced. They are on terraced ground and separated by bushes. The layout of the pitches with the mobile homes can give a rather crowded feel. In high season a programme of activities and tournaments is arranged, from walking and mountain bike trips to rafting. There are tour operator pitches.

TRAVEL SERVICE SITE

TO BOOK CALL 0870 405 4055 OR www.alanrogersdirect.com

Facilities

Two toilet blocks, both fairly modern and well appointed, include washbasins in cubicles, mixed British and Turkish style WCs and can be heated. The block adjoining the indoor pool and sauna has full facilities for disabled people, also doubling as a baby room. Indoor dishwashing and laundry sinks. Bottled water is advised for drinking and cooking. Motorcaravan service point. Small, quite limited shop (1/7-31/8) but bread available 15/5-15/9. Outdoor pool (15/6-15/9). Indoor pool, sauna and fitness room (1/12-30/9). A third pool has water slides. Practice climbing wall, half court tennis, boule and table tennis.
Off site: Skiing 10 km.

Open

All year, except 1 October - 30 November.

At a glance

Welcome & Ambience	✓✓✓	Location	✓✓✓✓
Quality of Pitches	✓✓✓	Range of Facilities	✓✓✓✓

Directions

Take N21 from Lourdes through Argelès-Gazost towards Luz-St-Sauveur. The site is on left at Esquièze-Sere, just before Luz-St-Sauveur. Site is on left immediately after Camping International.

Charges 2004

Per unit incl. 2 persons	€ 15,50 - € 18,00
extra person	€ 4,50
child (2-7 yrs)	€ 3,00
electricity (3/10A)	€ 3,00 - € 6,20
dog	€ 1,50

Reservations

Advised for most periods and made with deposit (€ 50) and fee (€ 25). Tel: 05 62 92 89 18.
E-mail: airotel.pyrenees@wanadoo.fr

FR65080 Camping Le Lavedan

Lau-Balagnas, 65400 Argelès-Gazost (Haute-Pyrénées)

Reasonably priced, Camping du Lavedan is an old established and very French site set in the Argelès Gazost valley south of the Lourdes. It is beside the road so there is some daytime road noise. The 105 touring pitches are set on grass with some shade. All have electricity (2-10A), water and waste water point. The area is fine for walking, biking, rafting and of course in winter skiing. There is a swimming pool which can be covered in inclement weather and a twice weekly event is organised in July/Aug and weekly in June.

Facilities

The toilet block, though quite old with some Turkish style toilets and also bidets, has recently been refurbished. Showers are quite small, but some washbasins are in cabins. Baby shower and bath. Facilities for disabled visitors. Dishwashing sinks under cover with hot tap to draw from. Washing machines and dryer in separate small block which is heated in winter. Restaurant/takeaway (1/5-15/9). Bar (all year). No shop but bread delivery daily (1/5-15/9). Swimming pool (with cover), paddling pool and sunbeds. Good play area. Off site: Fishing or bicycle hire 1 km. Supermarket or rafting 2 km. Riding 5 km. Golf 15 km.

Open

All year.

At a glance

Welcome & Ambience	✓✓✓✓	Location	✓✓✓
Quality of Pitches	✓✓✓	Range of Facilities	✓✓✓✓

Directions

Site is on the right side of the N21 (Lourdes - Cauterets), south of Argelès and just past the village of Lau Balagnas, which is 15 km. south of Lourdes.

Charges 2004

Per unit incl. 2 persons	€ 13,00 - € 17,00
incl. 3 persons	€ 17,00 - € 20,00
extra person	€ 4,50 - € 5,50
child (under 7 yrs)	€ 3,50 - € 4,00
electricity (2-6A)	€ 2,00 - € 6,00
dog	€ 2,00

Camping Cheques accepted.

Reservations

Contact site. Tel: 05 62 97 18 84.
E-mail: contact@lavedan.com

FR65060 Castel Camping Pyrénées Natura

Route du Lac, 65400 Estaing (Haute-Pyrénées)

Pyrénées Natura, at an altitude of 1,000 metres, on the edge of the National Park. is the perfect site for lovers of nature. Eagles and vultures soar above the site and a small open air observatory with seats and binoculars is provided. The Ruysschaert family's aim is that you go home from a holiday here feeling at peace with the world, having hopefully learned something about the flora and fauna of the High Pyrénées. Groups are taken walking in the mountains to see the varied flora and fauna (there are even a few bears but they are seen very rarely). The 60 pitches, all with electricity, are in a large, level, open and sunny field. Around 75 varieties of trees and shrubs have been planted – not too many to spoil the view though, which can only be described as fantastic. The reception and bar are in a traditional style stone building with tiled floors and an open staircase. The small shop in the old water mill is quite unique. Stocking a variety of produce, including wine, it is left unmanned and open all day and you pay at reception - very trusting, but they have not been let down yet. The last weekend in May is when the local shepherds take their flocks up to the high pastures. Campers help by walking up with them and then helping to separate the different flocks. Returning to the site by bus, with a good old sing-song with the shepherds, the site provides food for everyone. That sounds like a trip worth making.

Facilities

First class toilet facilities with high quality fittings include a cubicle for children, full facilities for disabled visitors and, in the same large room, baby bath, shower and changing mat. Dishwashing and laundry sinks. Washing machine and airers (no lines allowed). Motorcaravan service point. Small shop. Small takeaway (15/5-15/9). Small bar (15/5-15/9) and lounge area. Lounge, library and TV (mainly used for videos of the National Park). Sauna and solarium. Auditorium. Play area for the very young. Table tennis, boule and giant chess. Weekly evening meal in May, June and Sept.
Off site: Village has two restaurants.

Open

1 May - 20 September.

At a glance

Welcome & Ambience	✓✓✓✓✓	Location	✓✓✓✓✓
Quality of Pitches	✓✓✓✓✓	Range of Facilities	✓✓✓✓

Directions

From Lourdes take N21 to Argelès-Gazost. At roundabout at Argelès, take D918 signed Aucun, turning left after 8 km. on D13 to Bun. After Bun cross the river and right on D103 to site (5.5 km). Some parts are narrow but with passing places.

Charges 2005

Per unit incl. 2 persons and electricity (3A)	€ 14,50 - € 22,00
extra person	€ 4,00
child (under 8 yrs)	€ 2,50

Less in low season.

Reservations

Made with deposit (€55). Tel: 05 62 97 45 44.
E-mail: info@camping-pyrenees-natura.com

FR65090 Camping Soleil du Pibeste

Mobile homes page 406

16 Avnue du Lavedan, 65400 Agos Vidalos (Haute-Pyrénées)

Soleil du Pibeste is a quiet rural site with well tended grass and flower beds. It has 23 mobile homes to rent and 67 pitches for tourers. All pitches have electricity (3-15A) and there is some shade. The Dusserm family welcomes all arrivals with a drink and are clearly determined to ensure you have a good stay. They are particularly keen on developing eco-toursim in the Pyrenees. At times some domestic matters could perhaps have a little more attention. It is a perfect site for the active as many activities are organised from the site - from gentle ones like painting and Chinese dancing to walking, rafting, parasailing, climbing, riding and of course in the winter skiing. There is no shop but the supermarket is only 5 km. and ordered bread is delivered to your door daily. The swimming pool is on a terrace above the pitches with sunbeds, a paddling pool and waterfall and the most magnificent view of the mountains. The same wonderful view can be enjoyed whilst doing the washing up. A new by-pass should eliminate most of the road noise.

Facilities

Two heated toilet blocks have washbasins in cabins and large showers. Cleaning can be variable. Baby room. Facilities for disabled visitors (key). Washing machine and dryer. Motorcaravan service point. Bar with piano and internet access, which also servers snacks. Adjoining room for playing cards or reading. Swimming and paddling pools. Small play area. Boule, archery, basketball and volleyball. Table tennis. Bicycle hire. Off site: Fishing 800 m. Golf 10 km. Rafting 2 km. Skiing 2 km.

Open

All year.

At a glance

Welcome & Ambience	✓✓✓✓✓	Location	✓✓✓✓
Quality of Pitches	✓✓✓	Range of Facilities	✓✓✓✓

Directions

Agos Vidalos is on the N21, 5 km. south of Lourdes. Leave express-way at second exit, signed Agos Vidalos and continue to site on the right in a short distance.

Charges 2004

Per unit incl. 2 persons and 3A electricity	€ 15,00 - € 19,00
extra person	€ 3,00 - € 4,00
6A electricity	€ 3,00
animal	€ 2,00

Reservations

Made with 25% deposit and €26 fee.
Tel: 05 62 97 53 23.
E-mail: info@campingpibeste.com

FR81040 Camp Municipal des Auzerals

81800 Rabastens (Tarn)

Camping des Auzerals is a small, reasonably priced site with 38 pitches. These are arranged near the lake where fishing is possible and there are walks from the site (leaflets from the tourist information office in the town). This is a perfect site for couples seeking peace and quiet, especially in May, June and Sept. All the pitches are on grass, hedged with neat bushes and all with water, drainage and electricity (10A). The local swimming pool is adjacent and the village is only 2.5 km. away. There is no shop (ices from the reception) but a baker calls in July/Aug. All provisions can be found in the village – gas, food and restaurants. This is an unspoilt region of the Tarn within easy reach of Albi and Montauben.

Facilities

The sanitary block is basic but very clean, with mainly Turkish style WCs, good adjustable showers and some washbasins in cubicles. Dishwashing and laundry sinks with hot water. Washing machine. Freezer available in the telephone room. Baker calls. Off site: Village 2.5 km.

Open

1 May - 15 September.

At a glance

Welcome & Ambience	✓✓✓✓	Location	✓✓✓✓
Quality of Pitches	✓✓✓✓	Range of Facilities	✓✓✓

Directions

Site is northeast of Toulouse. Heading south leave A20 at exit 66 and take D930 south. This road changes to the D630 in 23 km. Follow until sign for Albi on D988. Rabastens is 8 km. and site is signed to left on entry to village.

Charges 2004

Per unit incl. 2 persons	€ 7,00 - € 8,00
incl. electricity	€ 8,40 - € 9,50
extra person	€ 2,50 - € 3,00
child (2-10 yrs)	€ 1,50 - € 2,00

Reservations

Contact site. Tel: 05 63 33 70 36.

FR81070 Camping Indigo Rieu Montagné

81320 Nages (Tarn)

Rieu Montagné is a delightful site in the heart of the Haut Languedoc Regional park, and at the corner of the départements of the Tarn, Aveyron and Hérault. The site is a member of the Indigo group and lies close to the Lac du Laouzas where a wide range of sporting activities can be enjoyed. There are 147 touring pitches, mostly on broad terraces with reasonable shade, all with 6A electrical connections. A heated swimming pool overlooks the lake and is used for occasional aqua gym. In high season there is a varied entertainment programme and a number of guided walks. Most of the leisure facilities are available at the lakeside complex, a five minute walk from the site, and these include tennis, a play area, sailing and other water activities.

Facilities

The two toilet blocks operate on a unisex basis, and are kept clean although both are quite old. Toilets are mainly Turkish style, but with a reasonable number of British style. Washing and drying machines. Site shop with basic provisions. Bar and snack bar with takeaway. Swimming pool. Entertainment programme (high season). Chalets and mobile homes to let. Off site: Lakeside leisure complex.

Open

18 June - 18 September.

At a glance

Welcome & Ambience	✓✓✓	Location	✓✓✓✓
Quality of Pitches	✓✓✓	Range of Facilities	✓✓✓✓

Directions

Site is on north side of the Lac de Laouzas on D162, well signed from village of Nages, which is roughly halfway between Lacaune and Murat-sur-Vebre.

Charges 2004

Per unit incl. 2 persons	€ 7,00 - € 17,00
extra person	€ 4,50
child (2-7 yrs)	€ 3,00
electricity (6/10A)	€ 3,50 - € 5,50

Reduced prices in low season.

Reservations

Advised for high season -; made with deposit.
Tel: 05 63 37 24 71.
E-mail: rieumontagne@camping-indigo.com

FR81030 Camping Municipal de Gourjade

Route de Roquecourbe, 81100 Castres (Tarn)

Camping de Gourjade is set in a country park belonging to the town of Castres. It has the river running along one side and the country park on the other. There are 100 level pitches, all with 6A electricity and separated by well trimmed hedges, and some with shade. There is a barrier at the entrance and a night watchman for security. A small play area caters for children of 3-12 yrs but the adjoining country park has everything – large indoor and outdoor swimming pools with slides etc, minigolf, table tennis, a miniature railway and a 9-hole golf course. In July and August competitions are organised. A boat makes regular trips for the 2 km. journey into the centre of Castres for markets and museums.

Facilities

The unisex toilet blocks are very clean with good adjustable showers, facilities for disabled visitors and baby changing. Washing machine and dryer. Drive over motorcaravan emptying point. Very limited shop, with bread daily. Attractive restaurant (all season). Bicycles kept at reception (in good condition) for the free use of campers. Country park with reduced charges for campers.
Off site: Supermarket 1 km.

At a glance

Welcome & Ambience	✓✓✓✓	Location	✓✓✓✓
Quality of Pitches	✓✓✓✓	Range of Facilities	✓✓✓✓

Directions

From Castres follow signs to Roquecourbe until roundabout with supermarket, then signs to 'Rive droite', Castres and camping. Site is 1 km. on left.

Charges 2005

Per person	€ 2,00 - € 3,00
pitch and vehicle	€ 7,50 - € 12,50
electricity	€ 2,50

Reservations

Made with 20% deposit. Tel: 05 63 59 33 51.
E-mail: camping.gourjade@cegetel.net

Open

1 April - 30 October.

FR81020 Camping Le Moulin de Julien

81170 Cordes-sur-Ciel (Tarn)

Close to the picturesque fortified old town of Cordes-sur-Ciel, in a secluded valley location in the heart of the Tarn region, this traditional style site has 130 spacious pitches. The grass pitches are arranged around a fishing lake with good shade in some areas and all with electricity hook-ups (5A). The area has magnificent scenery to enjoy and the fortified towns of the region to discover, including medieval Cordes (1 km). This site is full of character with a charming, friendly owner.

Facilities

Two rather elegant, well maintained sanitary buildings provide open and curtained washbasins. Washing machine, plus facilities for disabled people. Well fenced swimming pool (1/6-30/9) and splash pool with water slide (July/Aug). Minigolf, table tennis, TV room and boules. Fishing. Off site: Shops, bars and restaurants within 1 km. Bicycle hire 3 km.

Open

1 May - 30 September.

At a glance

Welcome & Ambience	✓✓✓✓	Location	✓✓✓✓✓
Quality of Pitches	✓✓✓✓	Range of Facilities	✓✓✓✓

Directions

Cordes is 25 km. northwest of Albi. From D600 just east of Cordes take D922 south, and within 0.5 km. the site is signed at a minor road junction to your left.

Charges 2004

Per unit incl. 2 persons	€ 13,60 - € 17,00
incl. 3 persons	€ 16,80 - € 21,00
extra person	€ 4,80 - € 6,00
electricity (5A)	€ 3,50

Reservations

Contact site for details. Tel: 05 63 56 11 10.

FR81060 Camping Les Clots

Mobile homes page 407

81190 Mirandol-Bourgnounac (Tarn)

Les Clots is a very rural, simple site in the heart of the countryside with 48 touring pitches and 15 used for chalets and caravans for rent. The 2.5 km. road from the nearest village of Mirandol is quite narrow but if you make sure that you arrive after 1 pm there should be no problem. Set around an old farmhouse, the outbuildings have been sympathetically converted into reception, the toilet facilities and a laundry room, all giving the site lots of character. The site has been carved out of a steep hillside giving variously sized terraces taking from 1 to 10 units. Nearly all pitches have electricity (6A). A few pitches, mainly for tents, are set well away the others giving lots of seclusion. Being amongst the trees there is some sunshine in places. A quiet site with no entertainment at all – the noisiest things we heard were the owls. A river borders the site but it is quite a long walk down the hillside to it.

Facilities

Toilet blocks are quite basic but have everything needed and are kept very clean. Baby bath. Facilities for disabled visitors. Washing machines. Bar (July/Aug). Shop with basic provisions incl. bread (July/Aug). Simple swimming and paddling pools (1/7-30/9). Table tennis. Minigolf. In July/Aug an evening meal is prepared (to order). Fishing. Leaflets for walks in the area. Site is not suitable for American style motorhomes. Off site: Riding 15 km.

Open

1 May - 1 October.

At a glance

Welcome & Ambience	✓✓✓✓	Location	✓✓✓✓
Quality of Pitches	✓✓✓✓	Range of Facilities	✓✓✓

Directions

Heading south on N88 from Rodez, take D911 at Baraqueville towards Villefranche. In 19 km. at Rieupeyrove take D905 south to La Salvetat, then on to Mirandol (approx. 22 km). On the outskirts of Mirandol, site is signed to the right.

Charges 2004

Per unit incl. 3 persons	€ 19,00
child (under 8 yrs)	€ 2,80
electricity (6A)	€ 2,70

Low season reductions.

Reservations

Contact site. Tel: 05 63 76 92 78.
E-mail: campclots@wanadoo.fr

FR82010 Camping Les Trois Cantons

82140 St Antonin-Noble-Val (Tarn-et-Garonne)

With only 100 pitches, Les Trois Cantons is a very friendly site with level pitches, all with electricity connections and set among trees that give dappled shade. The swimming pool is covered and heated in early and late season, with activities organised there in July/Aug. There are also walks, archery and boules, plus wine tastings and a weekly dance. It is however, primarily a site for nature lovers with peaceful evenings and nights. There are walks and mountain bike rides from the site. There is some road noise.

Facilities

The two toilet blocks, both refurbished, include British and Turkish style WCs, quite large showers, and facilities for disabled visitors. Lmited shop (bread daily). Bar with snacks and takeaways (all season). Games room. Play area. Tennis. Volleyball. Boules. Off site: Riding 4 km, fishing 7 km.

Open

15 April - 30 September.

At a glance

Welcome & Ambience	✓✓✓✓	Location	✓✓✓
Quality of Pitches	✓✓✓	Range of Facilities	✓✓✓✓

Directions

From N20 at Caussade, take D296 signed Caylus and Septfonds. In 13 km. site is signed to right (7 km. after Septfonds). Avoid the D5 towards St Antonin-Noble-Val (5 km. of narrow road).

Charges 2004

Per person	€ 4,10 - € 5,35
pitch	€ 4,80 - € 6,70
electricity (2/5A)	€ 2,00 - € 3,65

Camping Cheques accepted.

Reservations

Contact site. Tel: 05 63 31 98 57.
E-mail: info@3cantons.fr

Maps 15 & 16

Languedoc and Roussillon form part of the Massif Central. With its huge sandy beaches the mountainous Languedoc region is renowned for its long sunshine records, and the pretty coastal villages of Roussillon are at their most beautiful at sunset erupting in a riot of colour.

This section covers the south west coastal region of the Mediterranean, départements: 11 Aude, 30 Gard, 34 Hérault, 66 Pyrénées-Orientales.

Once an independent duchy, the ancient land of Languedoc combines two distinct regions: the vineyards of the Corbières and Minervois and the coastal plain stretching from the Rhône to the Spanish border. Much of the region is rugged and unspoilt, offering opportunities for walking and climbing.

There is ample evidence of the dramatic past. Ruins of the former Cathar castles can be seen throughout the region. The walled city of Carcassonne with its towers, dungeons, moats and drawbridges is one of the most impressive examples of medieval France.

Today, Languedoc and Roussillon are wine and agricultural regions. Languedoc, with considerable success, is now a producer of much of the nation's better value wines. But above all, vast hot sandy beaches and long hours of sunshine make this a paradise for sun worshippers and beach enthusiasts. La Grande Motte, Cap d'Agde and Canet, are all being promoted as an alternative to the more famous Mediterranean stretches of the Côte d'Azur.

Cuisine of the region

Cooking is Provençal, characterised by garlic and olive oil with sausages and smoked hams. Fish is popular along the coast. Wines include Corbières, Minervois, Banyuls and Muscat

Aïgo Bouido: garlic soup

Boles de picoulat: small balls of chopped-up beef and pork, garlic and eggs

Bouillinade: a type of *bouillabaisse* with potatoes, oil, garlic and onions

Boutifare: a sausage-shaped pudding of bacon and herbs

Cargolade: snails, stewed in wine

Ouillade: heavy soup of *boutifare* leeks, carrots, and potatoes

Touron: a pastry of almonds, pistachio nuts and fruit

Places of interest

Aigues-Mortes: medieval city

Béziers: wine capital of the region, St Nazaire cathedral, Canal du Midi

Carcassonne: largest medieval walled city in Europe

Limoux: medieval town, Notre Dame de Marseilla Basilica, St Martin church

Montpellier: universities, Roman sites; Gothic cathedral

Nîmes: Roman remains, Pont du Gard

Perpignan: Kings Palace; Catalan characteristics, old fortress

Pézenas: Molière's home

Villeneuve-lès-Avignon: Royal City and residence of popes in 14th century

Alan Rogers tip

TO ESCAPE THE HEAT OF THE DAY, TAKE A TRIP UP INTO THE PYRÉNÉES AND VISIT THE NATIONAL PARKS WHERE YOU'LL FIND BIRDS OF PREY AND BEARS.

FR11040 Camping Le Martinet Rouge

11390 Brousses et Villaret (Aude)

Le Martinet Rouge provides a peaceful retreat in the Aude countryside to the north of Carcassonne. It is a small site where the owners have been working hard to improve the facilities. The most striking features of the site are the massive granite boulders (outcrops of smooth rock from the last ice age). The site offers 55 pitches, all with electricity (6A), in two contrasting areas - one is well secluded with irregularly shaped, fairly level, large pitches amongst a variety of trees and shrubs, while the other is on a landscaped gentle hill with mature trees. The pool is attractively landscaped using the original boulders. This is a useful situation from which to visit Carcassonne or to follow the Cathare trail, or visit the Canal du Midi.

Facilities

Four sanitary blocks, including an excellent new one, have washbasins and showers in cabins, facilities for disabled visitors, baby bathroom and dishwashing and laundry facilities. Swimming pool (1/7-15/9, no bermuda style shorts). Small shop (no others locally). Small 'pub' bar with terrace serving snacks (both 15/6-15/9). Barbecue area. Fitness room. Croquet, volleyball, half court tennis, table tennis and a small play area. Off site: Tennis, riding and fishing quite close.

Open

1 April - 31 October.

At a glance

Welcome & Ambience	✓✓✓✓	Location	✓✓✓✓
Quality of Pitches	✓✓✓	Range of Facilities	✓✓✓✓

Directions

Site is just south of Brousses-et-Villaret, approx. 20 km. northwest of Carcassonne. It is best approached from the D118 Carcassonne - Mazamet road. Turn onto D103 15 km. north of Carcassonne to Brousses-et-Villaret. On western outskirts of village turn south to site (signed) in 50 m.

Charges guide

Per standard pitch incl. 2 persons	€ 11,50
with electricity	€ 14,00
extra person	€ 3,50
child (under 7 yrs)	€ 2,00
animal	€ 1,00

No credit cards.

sMade with deposit of € 30. Tel: 04 68 26 51 98.

FR11110 Camping Val d'Aleth

11580 Alet les Bains (Aude)

In the gateway to the upper Aude valley and open all year round, this popular small site is run by Christopher and Christine Cranmer who offer a warm welcome and personal service. The mellow medieval walls of Alet les Bains form one boundary of the site, while on the other and popular with anglers, is the River Aude (fenced for safety). Beyond this is the D118 and a railway which produces noise at times. The 37 mainly small, numbered pitches with electricity hook-ups (4A or more) are separated by hedges and mature trees which give shade. Recent works include improvements to the pitches and some hardstandings for winter use. Medieval Alet is a spa town with a thermal pool where the French take 'the cure'. The past life of the old city can be traced through its narrow streets, interesting buildings and the remains of an abbey and cathedral. The town has all services, including three restaurants and a Casino (a remnant of old aristocratic days). The site owners are keen to assist, with books, guides and walking maps available on loan along with brochures (in English) of attractions in the area. Bed and breakfast is also available.

Facilities

There are plans (in 2005) to replace the unsophisticated toilet block which is just adequate, with mostly British type WCs and high pressure hot showers. Laundry sinks and washing machine under cover, very basic dishwashing in the open. Reception has small stocks of essential goods, drinks, wine and beer, and the use of a freezer. Small play area. Mountain bike hire. Off site: White water sports nearby. The area is a Mecca for walkers and mountain-bikers. Bus and train services to Carcassonne and Quillan. Some shops and restaurants in town, full range at Limoux (10 km. north).

At a glance

Welcome & Ambience	✓✓✓	Location	✓✓✓✓
Quality of Pitches	✓✓✓	Range of Facilities	✓✓

Directions

From Carcassonne take D118 south for 32 km. Ignore first sign to Alet (to avoid narrow stone bridge) and after crossing the river, turn into town. Site is 800 m. on the left (signed).

Charges 2004

Per unit incl. 2 persons	€ 10,00
extra person	€ 2,75
child (under 8 yrs)	€ 1,60
dog	€ 1,10
electricity (4A)	€ 2,50

No credit cards.

Reservations

Contact site. Tel: 04 68 69 90 40.
E-mail: camping@valdaleth.com

Open

All year.

FR11060 Yelloh! Village Domaine d'Arnauteille

Mobile homes page 407

11250 Montclar (Aude)

Enjoying some beautiful and varied views, this rather unusual site is ideally situated for exploring, by foot or car, the little known Aude Département, the area of the Cathars and for visiting the walled city of Carcassonne (10 minutes drive). However, access could be difficult for large, twin axle vans. The site itself is set in 115 hectares of farmland and is on hilly ground with the original pitches on gently sloping, lightly wooded land and newer ones of good size with water, drainage and electricity (5/10A), semi-terraced and partly hedged. The facilities are quite spread out with the swimming pool set in a hollow basin surrounded by green fields and some newly developed pitches. The reception building is vast; originally a farm building, with a newer top floor being converted to apartments. This is a developing site with enthusiastic owners. Some up and down walking between the pitches and facilities is unavoidable. A 'Sites et Paysages' member.

Facilities

The main, heated sanitary block is now a distinctive feature, rebuilt to a very high specification with a Roman theme. Three other smaller blocks (one rebuilt) are located at various points. They include washbasins in cabins, dishwashing under cover (hot water), laundry, facilities for disabled people and a baby bath. Motorcaravan service point and gas. Small shop (15/5-30/9 - the site is a little out of the way). Restaurant in converted stable block offers plat du jour, grills, takeaway (15/5-30/9). Swimming pool (25 x 10 m.) with children's pool. Games court. Boules. Play area. Table tennis and volleyball. Riding (1/7-31/8). Day trips organised. Off site: Fishing 3 km. Bicycle hire 8 km. Golf 10 km. Rafting and canoeing near, plus many walks with marked paths.

At a glance

Welcome & Ambience	✓✓✓✓✓	Location	✓✓✓✓
Quality of Pitches	✓✓✓✓	Range of Facilities	✓✓✓✓✓

Directions

Using D118 from Carcassonne, after bypassing the small village of Rouffiac d'Aude, there is a small section of dual carriageway. Before the end of this, turn right to Montclar up a rather narrow road (with passing places) for 2.5 km. Site is signed very sharp left and up hill before the village.

Charges 2005

Per pitch incl. 2 persons	€ 13,50 - € 25,00
with 6A electricity	€ 17,00 - € 29,00
electricity, water and drainage	€ 20,00 - € 33,00
extra person	€ 4,00 - € 6,80

Camping Cheques accepted.

Reservations

Made with deposit (25%) and fee (€ 23).
Tel: 04 68 26 84 53. E-mail: Arnauteille@mnet.fr

Open

1 April - 30 September.

FR11030 Camping Municipal La Pinède

Avenue Gaston Bonheur, 11200 Lézignan-Corbières (Aude)

Within walking distance of the little town and only 35 km. from Narbonne Plage, La Pinède is laid out in terraces on a hillside, with good internal access on made-up roads. The 86 individual, level pitches vary in size and are divided up mainly by various trees and shrubs with 6A electricity (some 17 for mobile homes and chalets). The guardian sometimes organises local wine tasting. Outside the gates are the municipal swimming pool (July/Aug), a disco, restaurant and tennis courts. Generally better than many municipal sites in season – it is uncomplicated and peaceful.

Facilities

Three sanitary blocks of good quality are fully equipped and recently refurbished. Washing machine. Small shop with gas. Pleasant bar also providing hot food that can be eaten on the terrace (all July/Aug). Torches are necessary. Off site: Bicycle hire or riding 2 km. Fishing 4 km.

Open

1 March - 30 October.

At a glance

Welcome & Ambience	✓✓✓✓	Location	✓✓✓✓
Quality of Pitches	✓✓✓✓	Range of Facilities	✓✓✓

Directions

Access is directly off the main N113 on west side of Lézignan-Corbières. From A61 (to avoid low bridge) exit at Carcassonne or Narbonne on N113 to site.

Charges 2004

Per adult	€ 3,00 - € 4,20
child	€ 1,90 - € 3,10
pitch	€ 5,50 - € 7,30

No credit cards.

Reservations

Advisable in season. Tel: 04 68 27 05 08.

FR11070 Camping Les Mimosas

Mobile homes page 408

Chaussée de Mandirac, 11100 Narbonne (Aude)

Being some six kilometres inland from the beaches of Narbonne and Gruissan, this site benefits from a somewhat less hectic situation than others in the popular seaside environs of Narbonne. The site itself is, however, quite lively with plenty to amuse and entertain the younger generation while, at the same time, offering facilities for the whole family. A purchase of a club card is required in July/Aug. to use the children's club, gym, sauna, tennis, minigolf, billiards etc. (€ 26 per family for your entire stay). A very large, purpose built entertainment centre is under construction. The 150 pitches are mainly of good size, most with electricity (6A), including a few 'grand confort', and they benefit from a reasonable amount of shade, mostly from 2 m. high hedges. This could be a very useful site offering many possibilities to meet a variety of needs, on-site entertainment (including an evening on Cathare history), and easy access to popular beaches, interesting towns such as Narbonne itself, Béziers or the 'Cité de Carcassonne', the Canal du Midi and Cathare castles.

Facilities

Four sanitary buildings, all refurbished to high standards, include washbasins in cabins, some British WCs, baby baths, laundry and dishwashing sinks, and washing machines. Shop (1/4-31/10). Bar. Small lounge, amusements. Auberge with takeaway (1/4-30/9). Heated pool complex including new, landscaped pool with slides and islands, the original pool and a children's pool (open 1/5-31/8 when weather is suitable). Adventure play area. Minigolf. Mountain bike hire. Off site: Riding near. Windsurfing/sailing school 300 m. Gruissan's beach 10 minutes by car. Lagoon for boating and fishing can be reached via footpath (about 200 m).

Open

24 March - 31 October.

At a glance

Welcome & Ambience	✓✓✓✓	Location	✓✓✓✓
Quality of Pitches	✓✓✓✓	Range of Facilities	✓✓✓✓✓

Directions

From A9 take exit 38 (Narbonne Sud) and go round roundabout to last exit taking you back over the autoroute (site signed from here). Follow signs to La Nautique and then Mandirac and site (total 6 km. from autoroute). Also signed from Narbonne centre.

Charges 2004

Per basic pitch incl. 1 or 2 persons	€ 12,70 - € 19,00
pitch with electricity	€ 15,50 - € 24,00
with electricity, water and waste water	€ 20,00 - € 28,00
extra person	€ 3,70 - € 5,10
child (2-7 yrs)	€ 2,15 - € 3,30
animal	€ 1,45 - € 2,40

Camping Cheques accepted.

Reservations

Made with deposit (€ 100) and fee (€ 22).
Tel: 04 68 49 03 72. E-mail: info@lesmimosas.com

FR11080 Camping La Nautique

La Nautique, 11100 Narbonne (Aude)

This extremely spacious site is situated on the Etang de Bages, where flat water combined with strong winds make it one of the best windsurfing areas in France and is owned and run by a very welcoming Dutch family. The site is fenced off from the water for the protection of children and windsurfers can have a key for the gate (with deposit) that leads to launching points on the lake. La Nautique has 390 huge, level pitches (a small one is 130 sq.m), including a good number used for site owned mobile homes and chalets and 30 tour operator pitches. There are also six or seven overnight pitches with electricity in a separate area. The wide range of evergreens, flowering shrubs and trees on site give a pleasant feel and each pitch is separated by hedges making some quite private and providing shade. All have electricity (10A) and water. The difference between this and other sites is that each pitch has an individual toilet cabin. Various entertainment is organised for adults and children in July/Aug, plus a sports club for supervised surfing, sailing, rafting, walking and canoeing (some activities are charged for). The unspoilt surrounding countryside is excellent for walking or cycling and locally there is horse riding and fishing. English is spoken in reception by the very welcoming Schutjes family. This site caters for families with children including teenagers (in fact they say 8 months to 86 years!)

Facilities

Each individual cabin has a toilet, shower and washbasin (key deposit) and, as each pitch empties, the facilities are cleaned in readiness for the next. Special pitches for disabled people. Two fully equipped laundry areas. Shop at entrance. Bar/restaurant with splendid new terrace (evenings only May and Sept) plus large TV. Takeaway. All 1/5 - 15/9. Snack bar 1/7 - 31/8. Swimming pools (solar heated), slide and paddling pool with fountain and slide, and poolside bar (1/7-31/8). New play areas and active children's club. Tennis, table tennis, basketball, volleyball, football, minigolf and boules. Teenagers' disco in high season. Recreation area with TV for youngsters. Internet connection. Only electric barbecues are permitted.
Off site: Large sandy beaches at Gruissan (10 km) and Narbonne Plage (15 km). Narbonne 4 km. Walking and cycling. Canoeing, sailing and windsurfing on the Etang.

At a glance

Welcome & Ambience	✓✓✓✓✓	Location	✓✓✓✓
Quality of Pitches	✓✓✓✓	Range of Facilities	✓✓✓✓✓

Directions

From A9 take exit 38 (Narbonne Sud). Go round roundabout to last exit and follow signs for La Nautique and site, then further site signs to site on right in 3 km.

Charges 2004

Per unit incl. electricity, water and sanitary unit	€ 7,40 - € 17,50
person	€ 4,00 - € 5,20
child (1-7 yrs)	€ 2,00 - € 3,60
dog or cat	€ 1,35 - € 2,35

Reservations

Made with deposit (€ 130) and fee (€ 20).
Tel: 04 68 90 48 19.
E-mail: info@campinglanautique.com

Open

1 February - 25 November.

TRAVEL SERVICE SITE

TO BOOK CALL 0870 405 4055 OR www.alanrogersdirect.com

FR11140 Domaine La Royale

11600 Villardonnel (Aude)

Not a typical French campsite, Domaine La Royale can only be described as small. There are only 10 touring pitches, all slightly sloping and 6 with electricity connections (10A). From most pitches there are fantastic views south to the Aude valley and the distant, snow-capped Pyrenees. There is plenty of room here to spread out on the well kept grass with some shade available. The entrance porch of thehouse acts as reception and John and his Portuguese wife will help choose places to visit. This place would be ideal for complete relaxation, although for some it could be a little remote. There is no shop, although the baker calls in high season and a small village shop is 2.5 km. They hope to open a bistro, planning consents permitting, as John is a trained chef.

Facilities

Toilets and showers are in the farm buildings. Here also, dishwashing sinks, washing machine and free use of a freezer. Play area for very young children and field for ball games, although older children may soon get bored. Patio area for drinks. Bicycle hire. Gite for rent.
Off site: Carcassonne 17 km. Fishing 11 km. Golf 17 km.

Open

May - September.

At a glance

Welcome & Ambience	✓✓✓✓	Location	✓✓✓✓✓
Quality of Pitches	✓✓✓✓	Range of Facilities	✓✓✓

Directions

Site is between villages of Villardonnel (15 km. north of Carcassonne) and Salsigne. From north on D118 Castres - Caracassonne road turn left onto D73 signed Salsigne (about 22 km. south of Castres). After 3.6 km. turn right (opposite farm) and site is 2 km. From the south the route on the D111 is very narrow Villardonnel. Site is 2 km. to the left in about 6 km.

Charges 2004

Per person	€ 7,00
electricity	€ 3,00
dog	€ 2,00

Reservations

Contact owners. Tel: 04 68 77 51 13.
E-mail: info@laroyale.net

FR30000 Camping Domaine de Gaujac

Boisset et Gaujac, 30140 Anduze/ Boisset et Eaujac (Gard)

This large, woodland holiday site is enthusiastically run by the energetic and friendly Holley family (English is spoken). The 293 level pitches are well shaded and include 175 for touring and 70 for tour operators. All have electricity (4-10A) and 22 also have water and a drain. Access to some areas can be difficult for larger units due to narrow winding access roads, trees and hedges. Larger units should ask for lower numbered pitches (1-148) where access is a little easier. In high season this region is dry and hot, thus grass quickly wears off many pitches leaving just a sandy base. There are 12 special hard-standing pitches for motorcaravans. The site has a new covered animation area and courtyard terrace. The extensive and lively programme of activities in the main season includes a children's club, plus cabaret, karaoke, disco, buffet parties and even cinema shows. Just across the lane is the river with a small beach where one can swim, boat or fish.

Facilities

New heated toilet blocks include washbasins in cubicles, special children's low level equipment and good facilities for disabled visitors. Dishwashing and laundry sinks, washing machines, dryer and ironing facilities. Motorcaravan service point. Well stocked shop (15/6-30/8). Newsagent. Takeaway/crêperie (7/5-15/9). Bar and restaurant (7/5-15/9, on demand at other times). Fenced swimming and paddling pool complex (1/5-15/9 with lifeguard 5/7-15/8). Playground plus sports field for football, volleyball etc. Two tennis courts (free off season). Minigolf. Only gas and electric barbecues are permitted. Off site: Bicycle hire 5 km. Riding 4 km. Golf 10 km. Mining museum at Alès, steam trains run between Anduze and St Jean-du-Gard, a music museum at Anduze, and a number of spectacular caverns and grottoes. Beach 70 km.

At a glance

Welcome & Ambience	✓✓✓✓	Location	✓✓✓
Quality of Pitches	✓✓✓	Range of Facilities	✓✓✓✓

Directions

From Alès take N110 towards Montpellier. At St Christol-les-Alès fork right on D910 towards Anduze and in Bagard turn left on D246 to Boisset et Gaujac. Site is signed from village.

Charges 2005

Per unit incl. 2 adults	€ 13,00 - € 18,00
extra person	€ 3,50 - € 4,50
child (2-7 yrs)	€ 2,00 - € 3,50
dog	free - € 2,50
electricity (4/6A)	€ 3,00 - € 3,50

Camping Cheques accepted.
Credit cards accepted in high season only.

Reservations

Necessary in high season and made with deposit (€ 107) and fee (€ 12.20). Tel: 04 66 61 80 65.
E-mail: gravieres@club-internet.fr

Open

1 April - 30 September.

FR30060 Camping Domaine des Fumades

Les Fumades, 30500 Allègre (Gard)

Domaine des Fumades is a pleasant, busy site with a friendly atmosphere near the thermal springs at Allègre. Reception at the site is a joy to behold. Set in an attractive courtyard, within the farmhouse, it has a central fountain and masses of tubs and baskets of colourful flowers. The entrance as a whole has a very tropical feel with its banana plants and palm trees. The 230 pitches are large and level, all with 4A electricity. A variety of trees add privacy and welcome shade. Three pleasantly landscaped swimming pools have ample sunbathing space and bridges and new jacuzzis. This is a good area for walking, cycling, riding, climbing and fishing. Used by tour operators (80 pitches). A 'Sites et Paysages' member.

Facilities

Two well appointed sanitary blocks and one new one seem to cope well in high season. Some washbasins in cabins, baby baths and facilities for disabled people. Laundry and dishwashing sinks. These facilities are both clean and well maintained. Well stocked shop. Bar, enlarged restaurant, snack bar and takeaway (all with reasonable prices). Two designated barbecue areas. Swimming pools with ample sunbathing space. Large, well equipped and fenced playground. Games room, tennis, volleyball, table tennis and boules. Well planned animation and entertainment programme, designed to appeal to families. Barbecues are not permitted. Off site: Riding 2 km.

At a glance

Welcome & Ambience	✓✓✓✓	Location	✓✓✓✓
Quality of Pitches	✓✓✓	Range of Facilities	✓✓✓✓✓

Directions

From Alès take D16 through Salindres, continue towards Allègre, until signs for Fumades (and thermal springs) on the right.

Charges 2004

Per pitch incl. 2 persons	€ 13,50 - € 24,00
with electricity (4A)	€ 16,00 - € 30,00
extra person	€ 2,70 - € 7,00
child (2-7 yrs)	€ 1,60 - € 3,50
pet	€ 2,00

Reservations

Made with deposit (€ 121) and fee € 22.87).
Tel: 04 66 24 80 78.
E-mail: domaine.des.fumades@wanadoo.fr

Open

15 May - 5 September (with all services).

FR30030 Camping Abri de Camargue

320 route du Phare de l'Espiguette, Port Camargue, 30240 Le Grau-du-Roi (Gard)

This pleasant site has an attractive pool area overlooked by the bar and its outdoor tables on a pleasant sheltered terrace. The larger outdoor pool has surrounds for sunbathing and the smaller indoor one is heated. With 277 level pitches, there are 139 for touring units, mainly of 100 sq.m (there are also smaller ones). Electricity and water are available on most, and the pitches are well maintained and shaded, with trees and flowering shrubs quite luxuriant in parts. Recent additions include an air-conditioned cinema room and a club for children in high season. A summer fair is within walking distance which can be noisy until quite late. English is spoken.

Facilities

Two well appointed toilet blocks, include washbasins in cubicles, dishwashing and laundry sinks. Facilities for handicapped. Convenient motorcaravan service point. Shop. Bar with TV, restaurant and takeaway with reasonably priced food (all open when site is open). Heated indoor pool and outdoor pool. New cinema room. Play area of the highest quality (one of few with a rubber EU standard safety base). Children's club. Petanque. Off site: Tennis 800 m. Fishing, riding, golf and bicycle hire within 2 km. The nearest beach at Port Camargue is 900 m. and the one at L'Espiguette is 4 km. (in high season a free bus passes the gate to L'Espiguette).

Open

1 April - 30 September.

At a glance

Welcome & Ambience	✓✓✓✓	Location	✓✓✓✓
Quality of Pitches	✓✓✓✓✓	Range of Facilities	✓✓✓✓✓

Directions

From the A9 autoroute, 38 km. from Montelimar and 44 km. from Nimes take exit for Monpellier Est (Palavas) or for Gallargues. From Le Grau-du-Roi bypass follow signs for 'Port Camargue' and 'Campings' just northeast of Grau-du-Roi then 'Rive gauche' signs towards Phare l'Espiguette over roundabout and site is on right opposite Toboggan Park.

Charges 2004

Per unit incl. 1 or 2 persons	
and electricity	€ 23,00 - € 45,00
incl. 3-5 persons	€ 27,00 - € 47,00
extra person or extra car	€ 6,00 - € 9,00
pet	€ 6,00

Reservations

Advised for high season (1/7-31/8) when made for min. 1 week with € 33 fee. Tel: 04 66 51 54 83.
E-mail: contact@abridecamargue.com

FR30100 Camping Naturiste de la Sablière

Mobile homes ▶ page 408

Domaine de la Sablière, St Privat de Champclos, 30430 Barjac (Gard)

Spectacularly situated in the Cèze Gorges, this naturist site with a surprising 604 pitches tucked away within its wild terrain offers a wide variety of facilities, all within a really peaceful, wooded and dramatic setting. Pitches are grouped in areas - 'Mesange' (mainly for tents with cars parked 200 m. away) and 'Fauvette' at the bottom of the gorge alongside the river at some points close to the main access road, which is well surfaced but steep and winding. A newer area, 'Pinson', is near the top of the hill. The pitches themselves are mainly flat on terraces, attractively situated among a variety of trees and shrubs (some with low overhang). Many are of a good size and have electricity (6/10A). A pool complex (dynamited out of the hill and built in local style) provides a new children's pool area and two large pools, one of which can be covered by a sliding dome, sunbathing terraces, saunas and a bar. This is a family run and orientated site and the owner, Gaby Cespedes, provides a personal touch that is unusual in a large site. This no doubt contributes to the relaxed, informal atmosphere and first time naturists would find this a gentle introduction to naturism. You must expect some fairly steep walking between pitches and facilities, although there is a minibus shuttle service in high season. Member France 4 Naturisme.

Facilities

Six good unisex sanitary blocks (most refurbished 2003) have excellent free hot showers in typical open plan, naturist style, washbasins (cold water), baby baths and facilities for people with disabilities. Dishwashing and laundry sinks. Laundry. Supermarket. Open air, covered restaurant (all season) with good value waiter service meals and a takeaway. Swimming pool complex. Bar with TV room and disco. Small café/crêperie. Varied activities include walking, climbing, swimming, canoeing, fitness trail, fishing (permit required), archery, tennis, minigolf and volleyball, book binding, pottery, yoga etc. Entertainment for adults and children (mid June - end Aug). Mobile homes, caravans, chalet and tents to rent. Torch useful. Off site: Barjac with its Antiques Fair at Easter and mid-August. Alès, Chemin de Fer des Cevennes.

At a glance

Welcome & Ambience	✓✓✓✓	Location	✓✓✓✓
Quality of Pitches	✓✓✓	Range of Facilities	✓✓✓✓✓

Directions

From Barjac take D901 east for 3 km. Site is signed just before St Privat-de-Champclos and is approx. 3 km. on narrow roads following camp signs.

Charges 2004

Per pitch incl. 2 persons	€ 11,40 - € 28,40
extra person	€ 3,42 - € 6,34
child (under 8 yrs)	free - € 5,82
electricity	€ 3,55
dog	€ 1,00 - € 2,50

Camping Cheques accepted.

Reservations

Made with deposit (25%) and fee (€ 30)- contact site. Tel: 04 66 24 51 16. E-mail: sabliere@club-internet.fr

Open

27 March - 3 October.

FR30070 Castel Camping Le Château de Boisson

Boisson, 30500 Allegre-Les Fumades (Gard)

Château de Boisson is a quiet family site within easy reach of the Cévennes, Ardèche or Provence. It is set in the grounds of the château, beside the small medieval village of Boisson. Reception at the entrance is new, light and cool, built from the local stone in the local style so it blends beautifully with the rest of the buildings. The site is hilly so the pitches are on three levels, but they are level and have 5A electricity connections. A few have personal cabins that provide a WC, washbasin and shower. Trees provide some shade. The large swimming pool with a toboggan and paddling pool is at the castle in a sunny location and there is also an indoor pool (all season) of excellent quality. The restaurant in the castle is cool and elegant with tables also available outside.

Facilities

The two toilet blocks are quite old, but very clean and well maintained with washbasins in cabins – refurbishment is planned for 2003. Washing machines at both blocks, baby bath and shower, facilities for disabled visitors. Small shop. Restaurant, bar and snacks. Internet point. Play area. Indoor pool (all season). Outdoor pool (1/4-30/9). Bridge tournaments in low season. Painting classes. Tennis, boule, volleyball and basketball. Animation in July and Aug for 4-12 yr olds and outdoor competitions for adults. Dogs are not accepted. Barbecues are not allowed. Apartments to rent in the castle.

At a glance

Welcome & Ambience	✓✓✓✓	Location	✓✓✓✓
Quality of Pitches	✓✓✓✓	Range of Facilities	✓✓✓✓✓

Directions

From Alès take D16 northeast towards Salindres and Auzon. Just after Auzon turn right on D37 signed Boisson and site is signed from there.

Charges 2004

Per unit incl. 2 persons	
and electricity	€ 15,00 - € 31,00
with water and drainage	€ 17,00 - € 34,00
extra person	€ 5,40 - € 6,50
child (under 5 yrs)	€ 2,00 - € 3,20

Reservations

Made with deposit and €15 fee; contact site.
Tel: 04 66 24 82 21.
E-mail: reception@chateaudeboisson.com

Open

30 March - 3 November.

FR30080 Camping Le Mas de Reilhe

Crespian, 30260 Quissac (Gard)

This spacious family site has only 90 pitches (70 for tourers). All but the highest pitches have electricity (6/10A) and some of the upper ones may require long leads. The large lower ptiches are separated by tall poplar trees and hedges, close to the main facilities and may experience some road noise. The large terraced pitches in the upper section are scattered under mature pine trees, some with good views, and are more suited to tents and trailer tents. The organised entertainment in July and August is for the children with just the occasional competition for adults. A newly tiled, heated swimming pool is in a sunny position with sunbeds and a paddling pool. There are no shops in the village, the nearest being at the medieval city of Sommières ten kilometres away (and well worth a visit).

Facilities

The toilet blocks, one new, are clean and functional, with washbasins in cabins and pre-set showers. Dishwashing and laundry sinks. Washing machine. Reception doubles as a bar. Limited shop. Takeaway and restaurant. Small play area on grass. Table tennis. Heated swimming pool (14/5-25/9). Off site: Tennis 0.5 km. Fishing 3 km. Riding 5 km. Bicycle hire 25 km. The sea, the gorges and Nimes are all approx 40 km.

Open

2 April - 25 September.

At a glance

Welcome & Ambience	✓✓✓✓	Location	✓✓✓
Quality of Pitches	✓✓✓✓	Range of Facilities	✓✓✓✓

Directions

From the A9 take exit 'Nimes ouest' signed Alès, then onto the D999 towards Le Vigan. The site is on the N110 just north of the junction with the D999 at the southern end of the village of Crespian.

Charges 2004

Per unit incl. 2 persons	€ 12,50 - € 19,00
extra person	€ 3,10 - € 5,20
child (2-7 yrs)	€ 1,50 - € 2,60
electricity (6/10A)	€ 3,30 - € 4,00

Camping Cheques accepted.

Reservations

Made with deposit (€ 45.73 per week booked) and booking fee (€ 12.20). Tel: 04 66 77 82 12. E-mail: info@camping-mas-de-reilhe.fr

FR30120 Camping Campeole TCS Ile des Papes

Barrage de Villeneuve, 30400 Villeneuve-lez-Avignon (Gard)

Now ten years old, Camping Ile des Papes is a large, open and very well equipped site near Avignon with an extensive swimming pool area and a fishing lake with beautiful mature gardens. The railway is quite near but noise is not too intrusive. The 450 pitches are of a good size on level grass and all have electricity, 150 taken by mobile homes or chalets. Avignon and its Palace and museums is 8 km. away.

Facilities

Toilet blocks of very good quality include baby rooms. Dishwashing and laundry sinks. Washing machines. Motorcaravan services. Well stocked shop (limited hours in low seasons). Bar and restaurant. Two large swimming pools and one for children. Play area. Lake for fishing. Archery, tennis, table tennis, volleyball, minigolf and basketball (all free). Bicycle hire. Games and competitions for all ages in high season. Off site: Riding 3 km.

Open

25 March - 20 October.

At a glance

Welcome & Ambience	✓✓✓✓	Location	✓✓✓
Quality of Pitches	✓✓✓	Range of Facilities	✓✓✓✓

Directions

Take N100 Nîmes road out of Avignon towards Bagnoles-sur-Cèze and turn right after crossing the Rhône. Turn left along the river bank and follow signs for Roquemaure (D980). After 6 km. turn right on D228 signed Barrage de Villeneuve and site is 1 km.

Charges 2004

Per unit incl. 2 persons	€ 16,00 - € 25,00
extra person	€ 4,00 - € 6,00
child (2-6 yrs)	€ 2,60 - € 3,00
dog	€ 1,60 - € 3,00
electricity (6A)	€ 3,10 - € 3,20

Various special offers.

Reservations

Made with deposit (25%) and fee (€ 23). Tel: 04 90 15 15 90. E-mail: ile.papes@wanadoo.fr

FR30190 Camping International des Gorges du Gardon

Chemin de la Barque Vieille, 30210 Vers-Pont-du-Gard (Gard)

Probably the main attraction in the Gardon area of France is the Pont du Gard, an amazing Roman aqueduct built around 50AD. There are, however, other attractions worthy of a visit, such as the medieval village of Castillon-du-Gard perched on a rocky peak with narrow cobbled streets, and Collias at the bottom of the gorge from where you can hire canoes. Camping International is within easy (walking or cycling) distance of these attractions. It provides 200 level, good-sized pitches with electricity (6-16A); some are open while others are shaded. There is direct access to the river where swimming is permitted, although in summer the water level may be a little low. Unsupervised heated pools provide an alternative. The owners, Joseph and Sylvie Gonzales speak a little English, and visitors will always receive a warm and friendly welcome from them. Tourist information is in the reception (open all day) and Sylvie will share her local knowledge if you need any additional help.

Facilities

Two toilet blocks provide unisex facilities: showers, washbasins (some in cabins), and toilets. Facilities for disabled visitors in building nearest reception. Baby room. Washing machine, dishwashing and laundry sinks. Bar and restaurant (table service and takeaway). Swimming and paddling pools (unsupervised). Play areas. Table tennis. Games room and TV. Organised family entertainment during July/Aug. Off site: Pont du Gard approx 4 km. Collias 5 km. Canoeing arranged from site. Good area for walking and cycling.

Open

15 March - 30 October.

At a glance

Welcome & Ambience	✓✓✓✓✓	Location	✓✓✓✓✓
Quality of Pitches	✓✓✓✓	Range of Facilities	✓✓✓✓

Directions

Exit A9 at Remoulins, then take D981 towards Uzès. Follow campsite signs from this road – about 2 miles from the town.

Charges 2004

Per unit incl. 2 persons	€ 12,00 - € 16,00
extra adult	€ 3,50 - € 6,00
child (under 7 yrs)	€ 2,50 - € 3,00
electricity	€ 3,00
dog	€ 2,00

Reservations

Advisable during July and August.
Tel: 04 66 22 81 81.
E-mail: camping.international@wanadoo.fr

Mobile homes page 409

FR30140 Camping La Soubeyranne

Route de Beaucaire, 30210 Remoulins (Gard)

This site is well positioned for visiting the Pont du Gard, Nîmes and Uzès, famed for their Roman connections. It is approached by a short tree-lined avenue which leads to reception. The 200 pitches offer extremely generous amounts of shade and keeping the 4.5 hectares watered involves over five kilometres of hose pipe. Pitches are large, level, numbered and separated, with 170 having electricity connections. An animation programme (July/Aug) is aimed mainly at young children (teenagers may find the site rather quiet). Whilst quiet in some respects, train noise both by day and night can be an irritant.

Facilities

Two well appointed, unisex toilet blocks are basic but clean give more than adequate facilities and include washbasins in cubicles. Motorcaravan service point. Fridges for hire. Small shop selling basics. Restaurant, bar and takeaway (all from 5/5) - menu not extensive but adequate and moderately priced. Swimming pool complex with pool of 20 x 10 m. and smaller paddling pool (unsupervised), and partly shaded. Play area, including trampoline, table tennis, boules, tennis and volleyball. Bicycle hire. Off site: Fishing 1 km. Remoulins 1.5 km.

At a glance

Welcome & Ambience	✓✓✓	Location	✓✓✓
Quality of Pitches	✓✓✓	Range of Facilities	✓✓✓✓

Directions

From Uzès take D981 to Remoulins, turn right at lights over river bridge, left at roundabout, then left (D986 Beaucaire). Site is 1.5 km. further on left.

Charges 2004

Per unit incl. 2 persons	€ 12,00 - € 16,00
with electricity	€ 14,00 - € 19,00
extra person	€ 3,00 - € 4,20

Reservations

Contact site for details. Tel: 04 66 37 03 21.
E-mail: soubeyranne@wanadoo.fr

Open

3 April - 13 September.

FR30160 Camping Caravaning Le Boucanet

Mobile homes ▶ page 409

B.P. 206, 30240 Le Grau-du-Roi (Gard)

On the beach between Grande Motte and Le Grau-du-Roi, this is a sunny site with only a little shade. Many trees have been planted but as yet most are not tall enough to give much shade. As to be expected, the 458 pitches are sandy and level. The 343 for touring units are separated by small bushes, most with electricity (6A). Plenty of flowers decorate the site and the pleasant restaurant overlooks the large heated pool (open lunchtimes and evenings). An excellent shopping arcade provides groceries, fruit, newspapers, a butcher and cooked meats, rotisserie and pizzas. In July and August organised activities include games, competitions, gymnastics, water polo, jogging and volleyball for adults. There is access to the river for paddling and swimming and horse riding on the white horses of the Camargue is to be found within a few kilometres.

Facilities

The toilet blocks are convenient for the pitches providing washbasins in cubicles and some British style toilets in two blocks, the remainder Turkish style (about 70%). Some washbasins in cabins. Facilities for disabled people at two blocks. Baby rooms. Dishwashing and laundry sinks have warm water. Washing machines, dryers, irons and fridge hire. Motorcaravan service point. Range of shops. Restaurant. Bar with snacks. Large swimming pool and paddling pool. Play area on sand and miniclub in July/Aug. Table tennis, tennis. Bicycle hire. Dogs are not accepted. Off site: Riding 500 m. Bicycle hire 15 km. Golf 40 km. Shops, restaurants and bars within 3 km.

At a glance

Welcome & Ambience	✓✓✓	Location	✓✓✓✓
Quality of Pitches	✓✓✓	Range of Facilities	✓✓✓✓✓

Directions

Site is between La Grand Motte and Le Grau-du-Roi on the D255 coastal road, on the seaward side of the road.

Charges 2005

Per unit incl. 2 persons	€ 17,00 - € 31,00
with electricity	€ 20,50 - € 34,50
pitch on first row of beach, plus	€ 5,00 - € 6,00
extra adult	€ 6,00 - € 9,00
child (under 7 yrs)	€ 4,50 - € 7,50

Camping Cheques accepted.

Reservations

Necessary for July/Aug. and made with 25% deposit and booking fee (€ 25); by money order or credit card only. Tel: 04 66 51 41 48.
E-mail: contact@campingboucanet.fr

Open

16 April - 25 September.

FR30170 Camping La Sousta

Avenue du Pont du Gard, 30210 Remoulins (Gard)

With a long season, La Sousta is a former municipal site set under tall trees and with a ten minute walk of the famous Pont du Gard, a World Heritage site. The 300 pitches (including 60 mobile homes to rent) are mainly level and numbered, but are not very clearly defined. The reception office provides plenty of tourist information and coach trips are organised in high season to various places of interest. A large swimming pool set in a sunny location has surrounding grassy areas for sunbathing. A footpath leads to a private beach on the river.

Facilities

The four toilet blocks are quite basic but give clean facilities with mainly British style WCs, baby bath and showers, and facilities for disabled people. Washing machines and dryer. Bar. Snack bar and takeaway. Swimming and paddling pools. Various play area. Volleyball, tennis and football field. Bicycle hire. Weekly disco in July/Aug. Entertainment and canoes trips organised. Communal barbecue areas.

Open

1 March - 31 October

At a glance

Welcome & Ambience	✓✓✓	Location	✓✓✓✓
Quality of Pitches	✓✓✓	Range of Facilities	✓✓✓

Directions

Site is signed from the centre of Remoulins. From N100 follow signs for Beaucaire and Nimes, then site signs. Site is beside the D981, just before Pont du Gard.

Charges 2004

Per unit incl. 2 persons	€ 11,00 - € 18,00
incl. electricity	€ 15,00 - € 21,00
dog	free - € 2,00

Reservations

Contact site. Tel: 04 66 37 12 80.
E-mail: info@lasousta.com

FR30180 Camping Mas de la Cam

Route de St Andre de Valborgne, 30270 St Jean-du-Gard (Gard)

Camping Mas de la Cam is rather an unusual site for France in that all the pitches are used for touring units (no mobile home for rent). It is a very pleasant site with well trimmed grass and hedges and a profusion of flowers at the entrance. Lying alongside the Gardon river, the banks have been left free of pitches giving neat grass for sunbathing and some trees for shade, whilst children can amuse themselves in the water (no good for canoes). Slightly sloping, the pitches are on level terraces, some with shade and all with electricity (6A). A quiet, family site, there is no evening entertainment and just a few, low key daytime competitions in July and August.

Facilities

Good quality toilet blocks provide washbasins on cabins, adjustable showers in quite large cubicles, a baby bath and facilities for disabled visitors. Washing machines. Bar/restaurant and terrrace. Small shop with bread daily (to order). Attractive swimming and paddling pools. Play area. Club room. Fishing. Off site: St. Jean-de-Gard (3 km.) is a very attractive village. Riding 5 km.

Open

20 April - 22 September.

At a glance

Welcome & Ambience	✓✓✓✓	Location	✓✓✓✓
Quality of Pitches	✓✓✓✓	Range of Facilities	✓✓✓✓

Directions

Site is 3 km. northwest of St Jean-du-Gard in the direction of St André de Valborgne on the D9.

Charges 2004

Per unit incl. 2 persons	€ 12,20 - € 18,50
with electricity	€ 15,50 - € 21,50
extra person	€ 3,00 - € 4,35
child (under 7 yrs)	€ 2,30 - € 3,30
dog	€ 1,50 - € 2,00

Reservations

Made with deposit (€ 100) and fee (€ 15).
Tel: 04 66 85 12 02. E-mail: camping@masdelacam.fr

FR34020 Camping Le Garden

44, Place des Tamaris, 34280 La Grande Motte (Hérault)

Le Garden is a mature site, situated 300 m. back from a fine sandy beach and with all the choice of sports, entertainment and other facilities of the popular holiday resort of La Grand Motte. With space for 108 caravans and 101 mobile homes, the 100 sq.m. pitches are hedged with good shade on sandy/grass base. All have electricity (6A), water and waste water drains. The fine sandy beach and port are only 300 m. away, with a shopping complex, bar and restaurant next to site.

Facilities

Three well situated toilet blocks, 2 smartly refurbished in Mediterrarean colours, include washbasins in cabins and baby bath. Washing machines. Unit for disabled people. Shop to one side of the site with groceries, cigarettes, newspapers, boutique, etc., restaurant, bar and takeaway service (from 15/5). Swimming pool and paddling pool (from 15/5). Off site: Tennis courts, a riding club, a casino and a nightclub nearby.

Open

1 March - 31 October.

At a glance

Welcome & Ambience	✓✓✓✓	Location	✓✓✓✓
Quality of Pitches	✓✓✓✓	Range of Facilities	✓✓✓✓

Directions

Entering La Grand Motte from D62 dual-carriageway, keep right following signs for 'campings'. Turn right at traffic lights by the Office de Tourism and right again by the Bar Le Garden and site immediately on right.

Charges 2004

Per unit incl. 1-3 persons	€ 24,00
incl. 4 persons	€ 31,00
with electricity, water and drainage	€ 32,00
extra person	€ 7,00

Reservations

Not made. Tel: 04 67 56 50 09.

FR34130 Camping Le Neptune

Route du Grau, 34300 Agde (Hérault)

Camping Neptune is a rare find in this area of 'all singing, all dancing' campsites. This small, family run site with only 165 pitches makes a delightful change. There are also a few mobile homes. The Fray family are very welcoming and, even though it is in a busy area, it is a little oasis of calm, very suited to couples and young families. Placed along the D32 to Grau d'Agde which is beside the river Herault, there may be a little daytime road noise. The pitches are mostly separated by flowering bushes, with some shade and most have 6A electricity. The swimming pool is in a sunny position with sunbeds and overlooked by the bar. The only entertainment is in high season and is a twice weekly mini-club for children. The beach and the small resort of Grau d'Agde are 1.5 km. and Aqualand 5 km.

Facilities

The large toilet block provides roomy pre-set showers, washbasins in cabins and mainly British style WCs, plus three cold showers for really hot weather. An extra new small block is at the top of the site. Laundry and dishwashing sinks. Two washing machines and dryer. Small shop. Bar (both 15/5-30/9). Swimming pool heated in cool weather, bracelets required (€ 8 deposit). Table tennis and field for sports. Boat mooring facility on the River Herault across the road. Not all breeds of dog are accepted and only one is allowed. Off site: Golf and riding 1.5 km. Beach 1.5 km.

Open

1 April - 30 September.

At a glance

Welcome & Ambience	✓✓✓✓	Location	✓✓✓✓✓
Quality of Pitches	✓✓✓✓✓	Range of Facilities	✓✓✓✓

Directions

From A9 autoroute exit 34, follow N312 for Agde which joins the N112. After crossing bridge follow signs for Grau d'Agde then at triangle turn left at Grau d'Agde and turn left almost immediately at roundabout towards the river and left again at next roundabout signed Grau d'Agde/Les Berges de l'Herault on D32 which runs parallel to the River Herault. Site signed on left.

Charges 2004

Per unit incl. 2 persons	€ 16,00 - € 23,00
with electricity	€ 17,00 - € 25,90
extra person	€ 4,50 - € 5,30
child (under 7 yrs)	€ 2,25 - € 2,65

Camping Cheques accepted.

Reservations

Necessary for July and August. Tel: 04 67 94 23 94. E-mail: info@campingleneptune.com

FR34190 Camping Caravaning Les Champs Blancs

Route de Rochelongue, 34300 Agde (Hérault)

Les Champs Blancs is set in high trees, two kilometres from Agde and two kilometres from the sea. The 169 touring pitches, on level, sandy grass, are bordered with bushes with plenty of shade and greenery. All have 10A electricity and 58 have private sanitary cabins. Separate area for mobile homes. The pool area has now been augmented by a super new irregular pool, with tobogans, cascade, jacuzzi, bridges and palms with plenty of space for sunbeds but retaining the original pool and paddling pool. Games, shows and competitions are arranged in July and August. There are tennis courts and other leisure facilities in the area nearest the road, bordered by trees to deaden possible road noise.

Facilities

Two toilet blocks have been refurbished to provide showers and washbasins together, plus British style WCs. Unit for disabled visitors. Dishwashing and laundry sinks. Washing machines and dryers. Also 58 en-suite private cabins containing WC, shower and washbasin with an outside sink for dishes. Well stocked shop in high season; only bread available in low season. Bar (all season). Restaurant and bakery at busy times. Swimming complex. Good play area, minigolf, table tennis, tennis, basketball and volleyball. Bicycle hire. Off site: Horse riding 1 km. Golf 1.5 km.

Open

1 April - 30 September.

At a glance

Welcome & Ambience	✓✓✓✓	Location	✓✓✓
Quality of Pitches	✓✓✓✓✓	Range of Facilities	✓✓✓✓✓

Directions

From A9 autoroute exit 34, follow N312 for Adge which joins the N112 Beziers - Sete road, after crossing high river bridge take first turning signed Rochelongue and turn right, next left and next left (signed Adge) i.e. round 3 sides of a square. Site on left before you cross the bridge back over the N112.

Charges 2004

Per pitch incl. 2 persons	€ 18,00 - € 37,00
with individual sanitary facilities	€ 20,00 - € 44,00
incl. 4 persons	€ 24,00 - € 46,00
with individual sanitary facilities	€ 25,00 - € 52,00
extra person	€ 5,00 - € 10,00
dog	€ 2,00

Camping Cheques accepted.

Reservations

Necessary for July and August. Tel: 04 67 94 23 42. E-mail: champs.blancs@wanadoo.fr

FR34170 Camping Caravaning Les Mimosas

Port Cassafières, 34420 Portiragnes Plage (Hérault)

Les Mimosas is quite a large site with 400 pitches – 200 for touring units, the remainder for mobile homes – in a rural situation. The level, grassy pitches are of average size, separated and numbered, all with 6A electricity (long leads may be required). Some are in the shade, the choice is yours. The pool area, a real feature of the site, includes an impressive wave pool, various toboggans, a large swimming pool and a paddling pool (six pools in all) with lots of free sun beds. Many day trips and excursions are arranged all season, from canoeing to visiting castles. Portiragnes Plage is about 1 km. and it can be reached by cycle tracks. The Canal du Midi runs along the edge of the site (no access), providing another easy cycle ride. This is a friendly, family run site with families in mind.

Facilities

One large new toilet block has family sized, en-suite facilities, washbasins both open and in cabins, baby rooms, children's toilets and very good facilities for disabled people (the whole site is wheelchair friendly). The other two older blocks, with some Turkish style toilets, are to be refurbished in the future. Dishwashing and laundry sinks. Washing machines and dryers. Motorcaravan service point. Fridge hire. Large well-stocked shop (bread baked daily all season). Bar with snacks all season, restaurant (from 1/6). Swimming pool complex (early June) with lifeguards in July/Aug. Play area. Boules. Gym with instructor and sauna (charged). Supervised multi-sports court. Barbecues are not permitted. Off site: Portiragnes Plage with beach bars and restaurants 2 km.

At a glance

Welcome & Ambience	✓✓✓✓	Location	✓✓✓✓
Quality of Pitches	✓✓✓✓	Range of Facilities	✓✓✓✓✓

Directions

From A9 autoroute exit 35 (Bezieres Est) take N112 south towards Serignan (1 km). At large roundabout follow signs for Cap d'Agde but watch carefully for D37 Portiragnes (1-2 km) and follow signs for Portiragnes Plage. Site is well signed before Portiragnes Plage (5 km).

Charges 2004

Per unit incl. 2 persons	€ 21,00 - € 28,00
with electricity	€ 24,00 - € 32,00
extra person	€ 4,50 - € 7,00
child (under 4 yrs)	free - € 3,50
animal	free - € 5,00
private sanitary unit	€ 7,50 - € 8,50

Reservations

Necessary for July/Aug. Tel: 04 67 90 92 92.
E-mail: les.mimosas.portiragnes@wanadoo.fr

Open

1 May - 15 September.

FR34210 Camping Les Berges du Canal

promenade les Vernets, 34420 Villeneuve-les-Béziers (Hérault)

Although most campers or caravanners will be aware of the Canal du Midi, there are surprisingly few campsites which provide an opportunity to enjoy the rather special ambience for which this famous waterway is renowned, so we were really pleased to discover this delightful campsite right alongside the canal at Villeneuve-les-Beziers. Its situation is such that not only can one savour the ambience of the canal, but it is within a few minutes drive of the beaches at Serignan Plage, Vias or Valras, the old city of Beziers, the famous resort of Cap d'Agde, or you can even cycle along the tow-path to the beach at Portiragnes-Plage (10 km). The village of Villeneuve-les-Beziers itself, with shops, restaurants and market is just a few minutes walk along the 'towpath'/access road and over the canal bridge. The campsite has 75 level pitches on sandy grass of average size, mostly with 10A electrical connections (some occupied by mobile homes) in a peaceful and shady situation, separated from the canal only by an access road. There is a pleasant swimming pool complex, one of the two pools being fitted with a jacuzzi-style facility, but there are no big slides or toboggans thereby ensuring that it is relatively peaceful.

Facilities

A fully equipped toilet block has mainly British-style WCs and some Turkish style, and some washbasins in cabins. Facilities for disabled visitors (with key) and children. Beauty therapist visits weekly. Washing machine, laundry and dishwashing sinks, etc. Motorcaravan service point. Two swimming pools. Bar/snack-bar (serving breakfast too). Small restaurant attached to site. Evening entertainment during high season. Off site: Attractive old village centre of Villeneuve-les-Beziers. Beach at Portiragnes Plage. Horse riding 5km. Canal du Midi.

Open

15 April - 15 September.

At a glance

Welcome & Ambience	✓✓✓✓✓	Location	✓✓✓✓✓
Quality of Pitches	✓✓✓✓	Range of Facilities	✓✓✓✓

Directions

From A9 take exit 35, follow signs for Agde and at first roundabout take N112 (direction Beziers) turning. Then take first left onto D37 signed Villeneve-les-Beziers and Valras Plage. Pass traffic lights, then left at roundabout and follow site signs (take care at junction beside bridge).

Charges 2004

Per unit incl. 2 persons	€ 14,00 - € 18,00
with electricity	€ 16,00 - € 22,00
extra person	€ 2,50 - € 3,50
animal	€ 2,00

Reservations

Contact site. Tel: 04 67 39 36 09.
E-mail: contact@lesbergesducanal.com

FR34150 Yelloh! Village Nouvelle Floride

34340 Marseillan Plage (Hérault)

Marseillan Plage is a small, busy resort just east of Cap d'Adge and La Nouvelle Floride enjoys a super position immediately beside a long gently shelving sandy beach. It is a good quality site, very traditional in style and set under tall trees with neat hedges to separate the 520 pitches (370 for tourers). These are on sandy soil and all have water and electricity (6A). Some of the pitches in the newer area (across a small lane) and the hardstanding pitches near the beach have little shade as yet. There are a number of mobile homes but the site is mainly for tourers. Amenities and facilities are generally of excellent quality and include a strikingly attractive bar area overlooking the beach with a raised stage for entertainment. Alongside the play area is a multi-purpose ball court and fitness centre, also on sand with robust machines with the idea of keeping Mum and Dad fit whilst still keeping an eye on the children. Essentially a 'holiday site', there is an extensive programme of entertainment and activities catering for all ages, and a good heated pool complex. However, the main attraction for most will almost certainly be the direct access to a fine beach. The gates on the beach entrance are locked at 9 pm. for security. This is a well run, family run site aimed at families.

Facilities

The four toilet blocks are impressive, including two with a number of en-suite showers and washbasins, otherwise washbasins all in cabins. Baby rooms, excellent facilities for disabled visitors and even a dog shower. The showers and washing up areas are closed between 23.00-07.00 hrs. Motorcaravan service point. Bar and restaurant. Shop all season, plus a range of shops at Charlemagne across the road. Pool complex with slides, jacuzzi, paddling pools, etc (all season). Play area, fitness centre and multi-purpose ball court. Table tennis. Weekly films (DVD) and variety of organised games, competitions, dances and discos. Mini-club in school holidays. Bicycle hire. Off site: Riding and bicycle hire 500 m. Golf 5 km.

At a glance

Welcome & Ambience	✓✓✓✓	Location	✓✓✓✓✓
Quality of Pitches	✓✓✓✓	Range of Facilities	✓✓✓✓✓

Directions

From A9 autoroute exit 34, follow N312 to Agde then take N112 towards Sete. Watch for signs to Marseillan Plage from where site is well signed.

Charges 2005

Per unit incl. 1 or 2 persons, water and electricity	€ 15,00 - € 43,00
extra person (over 1 yr)	€ 5,00 - € 8,50
animal	€ 3,00 - € 3,50

Reservations

Contact site. Tel: 04 67 21 94 49.
E-mail: info@nouvelle-floride.com

Open

19 March - 24 September.

FR34160 Yelloh! Village Charlemagne

34340 Marseillan Plage (Hérault)

Charlemagne is under the same family ownership as Nouvelle Floride and situated across the road from it, 200 metres from the beach. It boasts a large range of amenities, consisting of a large supermarket, bakery, takeaway/fast food, bar, restaurant and disco. Facing the main street, these facilities are open to the public and are consequently well stocked, well equipped and open for the whole season. The site is traditionally laid out under the shade of tall trees providing 480 level pitches. Of these 270 are available for touring units, neatly hedged and all with electricity (6A) and water. Access to the beach is by a foot-path past Nouvelle Floride but the site also has a super new pool complex complete with 'Niagara Falls'. This is a site which caters for all ages with a wide range of activities.

Facilities

Four toilet blocks, two of the same modern design and quality as at Nouvelle Floride, with washbasins in cabins, dishwashing under cover, laundry sinks and washing machine. The two more traditional blocks have some Turkish style toilets. Motorcaravan service point. Fridge hire. Full range of shops, bar/cafe, restaurant, takeaway and disco, all open all season. Pool complex (all season). Good fenced play area. Mini-club (May-Sept). Range of evening entertainment covering concerts, cabarets, dances and discos. Off site: Nearby tennis, golf, karting, riding, bicycle hire and range of water sports.

At a glance

Welcome & Ambience	✓✓✓✓	Location	✓✓✓✓✓
Quality of Pitches	✓✓✓✓	Range of Facilities	✓✓✓✓✓

Directions

From A9 exit 34, follow N314 to Agde then take the N112 towards Sete and watch for signs to Marseillan Plage from where site is well signed.

Charges guide

Per unit incl. up to 2 persons, water and electricity	€ 15,00 - € 38,00
extra person (over 1 yr)	€ 5,00 - € 8,00
pet	€ 3,00 - € 3,50

Camping Cheques accepted.

Reservations

Necessary for July and August. Tel: 04 67 21 92 49.
E-mail: info@charlemagne-camping.com

Open

5 April - 27 September.

FR34200 Camping Club Californie Plage

Côte Ouest, 34450 Vias-Plage (Hérault)

With the benefit of direct access to a sandy cove, with a few, much sought-after pitches overlooking the sea, this is a fairly typical holiday-style campsite with a range of good quality facilities. These include a covered pool on the site (1/4-30/10) and a superb tropical swimming pool complex with the inevitable toboggans, etc., and even a naturist swimming pool (1/7-31/8) situated across the road from the Californie Plage site in the grounds of its sister site. Both sites are located away from Vias Plage, on the Côte Ouest and thereby enjoy a degree of tranquillity in this bustling resort area. The site is traditionally laid out, with mobile homes to one side of the central road and touring pitches to the other. Pitches are mostly of 100 sq.m with shade from tall trees, although those close to the beach are slightly smaller with less shade. All are mainly on level sandy ground, separated by low hedging with electricity connections (3-10A) and in most parts there is a fair amount of shade from tall poplars.

Facilities

Sanitary facilities are of a generally good standard, in three traditional blocks which have been fully refurbished in recent years. Washbasins in cabins, baby rooms, facilities for disabled visitors. Laundry with washing machines and dryer. Shop. Bars. Traditional comfortable restaurant with takeaway. Beach café serving Tapas and fish dishes. Covered pool on site (1/4-30/10). Range of pools on sister site across the road (1/7-31/8; code supplied). Tennis court. Bicycle hire. Games room. Children's play area. Sports nets. Archery. Extensive entertainment programme and children's activities in July/Aug. Off site: Crazy golf 2km. Horse riding 3km. Golf 9km.

At a glance

Welcome & Ambience	✓✓✓✓✓	Location	✓✓✓✓
Quality of Pitches	✓✓✓✓	Range of Facilities	✓✓✓✓✓

Directions

From N112 Beziers-Agde road take D137 Vias Plage turn. Watch for signs to 'Cote Ouest' and follow campsite signs thereafter.

Charges 2004

Per unit incl. 1 or 2 persons and 6A electricity	€ 16,00 - € 35,00
extra person (4 yrs and over)	€ 3,00 - € 5,00
extra tent	€ 2,50 - € 4,00
10A electricity	€ 3,50 - € 4,50
animal	€ 2,00 - € 4,50

Reservations

Made with deposit (€ 102) and fee (€ 23). Before 30 March reservation fee. Tel: 04 67 21 64 69. E-mail: californie.plage@wanadoo.fr

Open

Easter - 30 October.

FR34110 Yelloh! Village Le Club Farret

34450 Vias-Plage (Hérault)

This superb site of excellent quality has been developed by the Giner family with love and care over the last 40 years. Well maintained and with welcoming, helpful staff (English spoken), everywhere is neat and tidy - quite outstanding and impressive. It is a large site but even though it was very busy when we visited, the atmosphere seemed very relaxed and not too frantic. There are 756 pitches, with 370 for touring units and only 14% for tour operators, which do not overwhelm at all. The good-sized, level pitches are on grass and sand, with 6A electricity. There is some shade and many trees and shrubs provide a green environment. The mobile home areas are very smart, and some have been attractively landscaped, with an African theme. The large heated pool has lots of sunbathing room. The safe beach is alongside the site so some pitches have sea views. There is a wide range of evening entertainment and the extensive list of activities includes an unusual art programme offering pottery, silk painting, mosaics and water colours. The restaurant is high above the pool with views of the sea. Everything is open all season, so a visit in the quiet months of May, June or September doesn't mean less facilities (especially the heated pool). There is a policy of no advance booking for the touring pitches - they say that they rarely turn anyone away and will accept a phone call the day before arrival to give details of availability. A Yelloh Village member.

Facilities

Seven very clean toilet blocks provide excellent facilities, especially the new blocks, with British style toilets (one or two Turkish in the older blocks). Large showers, many with washbasin. Children's toilets, baby rooms and showers in the guise of a clown. Full facilities in large rooms for disabled customers. Washing machines. Dog shower at the block nearest the beach. The toilets are open all night but the showers are closed. Well stocked supermarket. Hairdresser. Bars with pizzas and snacks to takeaway. Restaurant. Swimming pool complex with lifeguard all season. Play areas. Mini-club (5-10 yrs). Teenagers' club (11-15 yrs). Tennis, table tennis, archery, volleyball, football and a full programme of games. Bicycle hire. Off site: Riding 1 km. Golf 5 km. Windsurfing on beach.

At a glance

Welcome & Ambience	✓✓✓✓✓	Location	✓✓✓✓✓
Quality of Pitches	✓✓✓✓	Range of Facilities	✓✓✓✓✓

Directions

Site is south of Vias at Vias Plage. From N112 (Beziers - Agde) take D137 signed Vias Plage. Site signed on left.

Charges 2005

Per unit incl. 1 or 2 persons	€ 15,00 - € 39,00
extra person	€ 6,00
pet	€ 3,00

Reservations

Not accepted. Tel: 04 67 21 64 45. E-mail: farret@wanadoo.fr

Open

Easter - end of September.

FR34030 Camping International Le Napoléon

Avenue de la Méditérranée, 34450 Vias-Plage (Hérault)

Le Napoléon is a smaller, family run site situated in the village of Vias Plage bordering the Mediterranean. The town of Vias itself is set further back from the sea, in the wine-growing area of the Midi, an area which includes the Camargue, Béziers and popular modern resorts such as Cap d'Agde. The single street that leads to Vias Plage is hectic to say the least in season, but once through the security barrier and entrance to Le Napoléon, the contrast is marked - tranquillity, yet still only a few yards from the beach and other attractions. Not that the site itself lacks vibrancy, with its Californian style pool, amphitheatre for entertainment and other new facilities, but thoughtful planning and design ensure that the camping area is quiet. With good shade from many tall trees, the 250 mainly hedged pitches (105 with hire units) vary in size from 80-100 sq.m. and most have electricity connections. No British tour operators.

Facilities

Three sanitary blocks are of a reasonable standard and were well maintained when seen in peak season. They include washbasins in cabins, baby bath, laundry and facilities for disabled people. Motorcaravan services. Fridges for hire. Well stocked supermarket. Bar. Restaurant/pizzeria. Heated swimming pool with lively piped music. Gym/fitness room. Sauna (on payment) and sun room. Bicycle hire. Tennis, archery, volleyball, basketball, boules. New TV and young people rooms. Children's club. New amphitheatre and wide range of free entertainment until midnight. Site-owned disco outside campsite (Easter-Sept). Off site: Shops, restaurants, and laundry etc. immediately adjacent. Fishing nearby. Riding 1 km. Golf 5 km.

At a glance

Welcome & Ambience	✓✓✓✓	Location	✓✓✓✓
Quality of Pitches	✓✓✓✓	Range of Facilities	✓✓✓✓✓

Directions

From autoroute take exit for Vias. From town, take D137 towards Vias Plage. Site is on the right near the beach; watch carefully for turning between restaurant and shops.

Charges 2005

Per unit incl. 2 persons and electricity	€ 14,00 - € 37,00
extra person (over 4 yrs)	€ 5,00 - € 6,00
dog	€ 3,00 - € 4,00
10A electricity	€ 1,50 - € 2,00

Reservations

Taken from 1 Jan. with 30% deposit and fee incl. cancellation insurance. Tel: 04 67 01 07 80. E-mail: reception@camping-napoleon.fr

Open

25 March - 26 September.

CAMPSITE INSPECTIONS

Every campsite in this guide has been inspected and selected by one our seasonal campsite inspection teams.

Our teams are required to visit typically between 30 and 50 sites and submit detailed reports on each site visited.

We now have a number of vacancies for campsite Inspectors and would be interested to hear from candidates with a good knowledge of camping and caravanning. A fee is paid for each inspection, as well as travel expenses.

For applications for these posts and further information, please contact:

Rod Wheat
Alan Rogers Guides Ltd, Spelmonden Old Oast, Goudhurst TN17 1HE
Fax: 01580 214001 Email: contact@alanrogers.com

INSPECTED & SELECTED CAMPSITES

FR34070 Yelloh! Village Le Sérignan Plage

Mobile homes page 410

Le Sérignan Plage, 34410 Sérignan (Hérault)

A large, friendly, family-orientated site with direct access to superb sandy beaches, including a naturist beach, Serignan Plage exudes a strongly individualistic style which we find very attractive. However, those who look for 'manicured' sites may be less impressed, as its situation on 'the littoral' and proximity to the beach makes it difficult to keep things neat and tidy. With some 450 mainly good sized, level touring pitches, including some (with little shade) actually alongside the beach, coupled with perhaps the most comprehensive range of amenities we've come across, the hugely enthusiastic owners, Jean-Guy and Katy Amat continually surprise us with new ideas and developments. New for 2004 was a superb 1,800 sq.m. 'Spa Water Fitness centre' with more new pools, a fitness centre and jacuzzi. The amenities are just too extensive to describe in detail, but they include a pool complex, with slides surrounded by large grassy sunbathing areas with sun loungers, and another indoor pool. Perhaps the most remarkable aspect is the cluster of attractive buildings which form the 'heart' of this site with courtyards housing attractive bars, a smart restaurant, shops, takeaway, a stage for entertainment, disco, etc. – all very attractive and with a very special ambience.

Facilities

Nine unisex toilet blocks. The older circular ones with a mixture of British and Turkish style WCs are nearest the sea and central 'village' area, seasonal units and mobile homes, etc. and thus take most of the wear and tear. The touring area, furthest from the sea has three modern blocks of individual design. Well planned with good facilities, these include large controllable hot showers with washbasin and WC en-suite, well equipped baby rooms, facilities for disabled people. Dishwashing and laundry facilities in all blocks and washing machines. At peak times maintenance can be a little variable. Well stocked supermarket, bakery, tabac, ATM and market stalls. Poissonnerie and boucherie (7/6-8/9). Central launderette. Hairdresser. Bars, restaurant and takeaway (all 7/4-10/9). Much animation for children and a range of evening entertainment. Secluded roof-top bar (9 pm - 1 am). - ask for a 'Cucaracha'! Soundproof disco. Heated indoor pool and outdoor pool complex (also heated) with lifeguards in the main season and an ID card system (April - Sept). Sporting activities organised. Bicycle hire. Off site: Riding 2 km. Golf 10 km. Bicycle hire. Sailing and windsurfing school on beach (lifeguard in high season).

At a glance

Welcome & Ambience	✓✓✓✓	Location	✓✓✓✓✓
Quality of Pitches	✓✓✓✓	Range of Facilities	✓✓✓✓✓

Directions

From A9 exit 35 (Béziers Est) follow signs for Sérignan on D64 (9 km). Don't go into Sérignan, but take sign for Sérignan Plage for 4 km. At small multi sign (blue) turn right on single carriageway. At T-junction turn left over small road bridge and after left hand bend, site is 100 m. after Sérignan Plage Nature.

Charges 2004

Per unit incl. 1 or 2 persons and 5A electricity	€ 15,00 - € 36,00
extra person	€ 6,00 - € 6,50
pet	€ 3,00

Camping Cheques accepted.
Low season offers.
Discounts in low season for children under 7 yrs.

Reservations

Made from 1 Feb. with deposit (25%) and fee (€ 30).
Tel: 04 67 32 35 33.
E-mail: info@leserignanplage.com

Open

10 April - 22 September.

FR34080 Camping Le Sérignan Plage Nature

34410 Sérignan (Hérault)

Benefiting from many improvements over the past few years, Serigan Plage Nature is a distinctly characterful family-orientated site right beside a superb sandy naturist beach. At present it has some 260 good sized touring pitches, on level grass and with plenty of shade except on those right beside the beach. A friendly bar and restaurant are housed in the Romanesque style buildings which form the 'heart' of the site, including the setting for evening entertainment. In recent years the site has been developed by Jean-Guy and Katy Amat, but was originally owned by Jean-Guy's father, who retains an interest and who was behind the award-winning environmentally friendly irrigation system which serves both this site and Camping Serignan Plage, the adjoining 'textile' site whose extensive range of facilities are also available to visitors here. Jean-Guy and Katy have some very ambitious plans for both their sites, which will involve significant developments on Serignan Plage Nature in particular, including a new 'aqua-village' with pools, fitness centre, jacuzzi, etc. Member 'France 4 Naturisme'.

Facilities

The toilet blocks of differing design have all been refurbished, and all offer modern facilities with some washbasins in cabins and both British and Turkish style WCs. All is clean and well maintained. Dishwashing under cover. Washing machines. Supermarket, market for fresh fruit and vegetables, newsagent/souvenir shop and ice cream kiosk. Small bar-café. Evening entertainment. Children's disco. Off site: Riding 2 km.

Open

1 April - 30 September.

At a glance

Welcome & Ambience	✓✓✓✓	Location	✓✓✓✓✓
Quality of Pitches	✓✓✓✓	Range of Facilities	✓✓✓✓

Directions

Follow directions given for Sérignan Plage above.

Charges 2004

Per unit incl. 1 or 2 persons and electricity	€ 17,00 - € 34,00
extra person	€ 6,00 - € 6,50
child (under 7 yrs)	free - € 6,50

Camping Cheques accepted.
Special discounts in low season.

Reservations

Made from 1 Feb. with deposit (€ 61), fee (€ 15.24) and cancellation insurance (€ 70).
Tel: 04 67 32 09 61.
E-mail: info@serignannaturisme.com

Le Sérignan Plage

The magic of the Mediterranean

Imagine – hot sunshine, blue sea, vineyards, olive and eucalyptus trees, alongside a sandy beach – what a setting for a campsite – not just any campsite either !

With three pool areas, one with four toboggans surrounded by sun bathing areas, an indoor pool for baby swimmers plus a magnificent landscaped, Romanesque spa-complex with half Olympic size pool and a superb range of hydro-massage baths to let you unwind and re-charge after the stresses of work.

And that's not all – two attractive restaurants, including the atmospheric "Villa" in its romantic Roman setting beside the spa, three bars, a mini-club and entertainment for all ages, all add up to a fantastic opportunity to enjoy a genuinely unique holiday experience.

Le Sérignan-Plage - F-34410 SERIGNAN
Tel: 00 33 467 32 35 33 - Fax: 00 33 467 32 26 36
info@leserignanplage.com - www.leserignanplage.com

Camping Villages yelloh! Village

FR34140 Haven Camping La Carabasse

Route de Farinette, 34450 Vias-sur-Mer (Hérault)

La Carabasse, a Haven Europe holiday park, is on the outskirts of Vias Plage, a popular place with lots of shops and restaurants. The site has everything you could need with two good pools, and its own bars and a restaurant. Very much orientated to British visitors. There are lots of activities for young families and teenagers. The bars and restaurant provide live music in the evenings and entertainment. There are 950 pitches in total, 400 for touring, with many mobile homes. The touring pitches are set amongst tall poplar and birch trees on level hard ground, all have electricity and partial shade. Some have private sanitary facilities. The wonderful Mediterranean beaches are close and La Carabasse has its own beach club. It is a lively busy site in high season, and Vias Plage itself can also be quite hectic. Haven Europe are continuing to develop and improve the site with a wide range of facilities for children and teenagers. Football coaching from U.F.A. qualified staff, for two hours a day, five days a week, can be booked from 40 or you can learn snorkelling, life saving or body-boarding and become a 'wave rider'!

Facilities

Two of the toilet blocks are modern and fully equipped. With an older block used in high season. Some pitches have their own private sanitary cabin providing a WC and shower (extra charge). Bars, restaurant and swimming pools. Beach club for windsurfing and pedaloes. Wealth of daytime activities (some charged for) from golf lessons to aqua-aerobics and tennis tournaments. Children's clubs and multi-sports unit. Evening entertainment. Off site: Vias town with twice weekly market. Modern resort of Cap d'Adge nearby with Aqualand and golf course (18 holes).

At a glance

Welcome & Ambience	✓✓✓✓	Location	✓✓✓✓
Quality of Pitches	✓✓✓	Range of Facilities	✓✓✓✓✓

Directions

Site is south of Vias. From N112 (Agde - Beziers) road turn right for Vias-Plage (D137) and site (on the left).

Charges 2004

Per pitch incl. up to 6 persons and electricity	€ 11,00 - € 37,00
with private sanitary cabin	€ 12,00 - € 43,00

Reservations

Accepted at any time for min. 4 days; no booking fee. Tel: 04 67 21 64 01.
E-mail: europe.website@bourne-leisure.co.uk

Open

16 April - 13 September.

FR34230 Sunêlia Le Plein Air des Chênes

Route de Castelnau, RD 112, 34830 Clapiers (Hérault)

Situated just outside the village of Clapiers, only about 5 km. from the exciting and interesting city of Montpellier, yet merely 15 km. from the beach, this is one of those few campsites which really does seem to try to provide something for everyone. There are 130 touring pitches (some large with their own individual toilet cabin), plus chalets, bungalows and mobile homes to rent; all in a shaded terraced setting – in fact you name it and Des Chênes seems to have it. The site boasts an amazing landscaped pool complex, with multi-lane toboggan, four pools and surrounding facilities such as bars, restaurants, etc., which is very impressive. It is also open to the public and obviously very popular and noisy.

Facilities

Three well equipped modern toilet blocks of circular design provide washbasins in cabins and facilities for disabled people. Laundry and dishwashing sinks. Three washing machines. Shop (07-08). Restaurant (all year), bar and pool side bar and café (06-09). Takeaway (06-09). Swimming pools (1/6-12/9). 4 tennis courts. Multi-sports court. Play area. Mini club and evening entertainment in main season. Off site: Golf 10 km. Beaches 15 km. Fishing 15 km.

Open

All year.

At a glance

Welcome & Ambience	✓✓✓✓	Location	✓✓✓✓
Quality of Pitches	✓✓✓✓	Range of Facilities	✓✓✓✓✓

Directions

Site is north of Montpellier, 8 km. from the A9. Take exit 28 on N113 toward Montpellier passing village of Vendargues. Leave N113 and cross the N110 (which joins the N113) to follow D65 for Clapiers circling north of Montpellier. Follow signs for village then site.

Charges 2004

Per unit incl. 2 persons, electricity	€ 22,00 - € 35,00
with water and drainage	€ 17,00 - € 43,00
extra person	€ 3,00 - € 6,00

Camping Cheques accepted.

Reservations

Made with booking fee (€ 28); contact site.
Tel: 04 67 02 02 53. E-mail: pleinairdeschenes@free.fr

FR34220 Camping La Creole

74 avenue des Campings, 34340 Marseillan-Plage (Hérault)

This is a surprisingly tranquil, well cared for small campsite almost in the middle of this bustling resort that will appeal especially to those seeking a rather less frenetic ambience than that which typifies many sites in this area. Essentially a family orientated site, it offers around 110 good-sized, level grass pitches, all with 6A electricity connections, and mostly with shade from tall poplars and other trees and shrubs. It also benefits from direct access to an extensive sandy beach and the fact that there is no swimming pool or bar actually contributes to the tranquillity and may even be seen as an advantage for families with younger children. The beach will be the main attraction here no doubt, and the town's extensive range of bars, restaurants and shops are all within a couple of minutes walk.

Facilities

Toilet facilities are housed in a traditional building, modernised inside to provide perfectly adequate, if not particularly luxurious, facilities including some washbasins in private cabins, a baby room and dog shower. Small play area. Table tennis. In high season beach games, dances, sangria evenings etc, are organised, all aimed particularly towards families. Barbecue area. Bicycle hire. Off site: Local market day Tuesday. Riding 1 km.

Open

6 April - 8 October.

At a glance

Welcome & Ambience	✓✓✓✓	Location	✓✓✓✓✓
Quality of Pitches	✓✓✓✓✓	Range of Facilities	✓✓✓

Directions

From autoroute A9 take exit 34 on N312 towards Agde, then N112 towards Sete keeping a look-out for signs to Marseillan Plage off this road. Site is well signed in Marseillan Plage.

Charges 2004

extra person	€ 2,50 - € 4,00
electricity	€ 2,50
dog	€ 2,00

Reservations

Made with deposit (€ 84) and fee (€ 16). Essential for high season. Tel: 04 67 21 92 69. E-mail: campinglacreole@wanadoo.fr

FR34060 Hotel de Plein Air L'Oliveraie

Chemin de Bedarieux, 34480 Laurens (Hérault)

Situated at the foot of the Cevennes, L'Oliveraie has many attractive features and is open all year. Don't assume that the extensive range of sport and recreation available here means that it is all hectic activity - in fact it is surprisingly peaceful. Most of the 116 pitches are large (up to 150 sq.m. in some parts) and all have electrical connections (6/10A). Arranged in rows on two levels, those on the higher level are older and have more shade from mature trees (mainly olives). The ground is stony. The large leisure area is slightly apart from the pitches on the lower area, overlooked by the bar. The old village of Laurens is well worth visiting and is walkable through the vineyards. A 'Sites et Paysages' member.

Facilities

The main modern toilet block on the higher terrace includes washbasins in cabins, baby bathroom, and covered dishwashing and washing machine. A good clean provision. The second block on lower level is open for high season. All perfectly adequate and clean when seen in high season. Small, well stocked shop (1/7-31/8). Bar/restaurant serving pizzas, salads, etc. Indoor bar, also used for films and activities for younger children. Good sized pool and children's pool (1/6-30/9). Tennis court and tennis practice wall. Volleyball, basketball, minigolf. Bicycle hire. Play area. Barbecue area. Adjoining riding stables (1/7-30/8). Good facilities for archery - quite a feature of the site. Off site: Local shops at Laurens 1 km.

At a glance

Welcome & Ambience	✓✓✓✓	Location	✓✓✓✓
Quality of Pitches	✓✓✓✓	Range of Facilities	✓✓✓✓

Directions

Site is signed 2 km. north of Laurens off the D909 (Béziers-Bédarieux) road.

Charges 2004

Per unit incl. 1 or 2 persons	€ 9,00 - € 23,60
extra person	€ 5,00
electricity (6-10A)	€ 3,20 - € 4,60
dog	free - € 2,00

Special rates for longer stays.

Reservations

Contact site. Tel: 04 67 90 24 36. E-mail: oliveraie@free.fr

Open

All year.

FR34040 Camping Lou Village

B.P. 30, Chemin des Montilles, 34350 Valras-Plage (Hérault)

Valras is perhaps smarter and is certainly larger than nearby Vias and it has a good number of campsites. Lou Village is a well kept, family owned site with direct access to a sandy beach. A busy site with lots of facilities and quite competitive prices, it does becomes crowded in high season as this is a popular area. The central 'village' area is a veritable hive of holiday activity, with several attractively designed pools and water slides, bars, pizzeria, restaurant and a purpose built stage for the site's extensive entertainment programme. With straw parasols and palm trees, it is an attractive, clean area with a pleasant ambience. There are 600 pitches (200 with mobile homes), all with electricity (10A) and 100 also with water and waste water facilities. Pitches further inland are of grass, partly separated by tall trees that provide good shade; nearer the beach the pitches are smaller, sandy and separated by bushes and bamboo hedges. There is lots to do off the site and the history of the Languedoc to discover. English is spoken.

Facilities

Four modern, well sited toilet blocks, all recently refurbished, have reasonable facilities. Mixture of Turkish and British style WCs, showers with no separator and half the washbasins in cabins. Facilities for disabled visitors and babies. Dishwashing and laundry sinks at each block. For a beach site, maintenance seems quite satisfactory. Supermarket, bakery, bazaar and, in high season, a boutique for gifts. Bar and restaurant with ample seating. Takeaway. Swimming pools (some heated), water slides and paddling pool. Playground, children's club and football field. Tennis. Volleyball. Minigolf. Bicycle hire. Sailing and windsurfing. Off site: Riding 500 m. Canoe kayaking, river fishing 1 km. Golf 12 km.

At a glance

Welcome & Ambience	✓✓✓✓	Location	✓✓✓✓✓
Quality of Pitches	✓✓✓✓	Range of Facilities	✓✓✓✓✓

Directions

Site is south of Béziers. From autoroute, take Béziers-Ouest exit for Valras Plage and continue for about 14 km. Follow 'Casino' signs and site is 1 km. south of centre of Valras Plage in the direction of Vendres. Site is signed to the left at the end of Valras Plage and the start of Vendres Plage.

Charges 2004

Per unit incl. 2 persons and electricity	€ 19,40 - € 34,50
extra person	€ 4,00 - € 5,80
child (under 7 yrs)	free - € 3,20
dog	€ 3,00 - € 4,00

Pool complex bracelet € 5.50 (once only payment).

Reservations

Made with deposit (€ 183) and fee (€ 30).
Tel: 04 67 37 33 79. E-mail: info@louvillage.com

Open

End April - mid September.

FR34100 Camping Le Mas du Padre

4 chemin du Mas du Padre, 34540 Balaruc les Bains (Hérault)

The Durant family took over this site a few years ago and have made many alterations and improvements. Madame Durant speaks excellent English. It is a small site, just 2.5 km. from Balaruc-Les-Bains, near the Lake of Thau and unusually is part of an estate that has obviously been built around it over the years. Its 116 secluded pitches of varying sizes are enclosed by hedges and mature trees, some on a very gentle slope and 98 have electricity (6/10A). The site is peaceful and popular with the French who love its simplicity, although a large commercial centre is just 500 m. Beaches and many local attractions are close, but if you decide to stay here it would be advisable to have transport. The road from the site to Sete passes some rather unsightly factory works – don't be put off.

Facilities

Two neat, fully equipped toilet blocks include baby changing area, facilities for disabled campers, dishwashing and laundry sinks, and washing machines. Reception sells basic provisions, gas and bread (to order in low season). Two small circular pools including one for children (20/5-16/9). Tennis half-court, table tennis, boules courts, mini-adventure playground. Sports programme including tournaments, aqua-aerobics, animation for children, along with a weekly dance when a temporary bar is organised (all in high season). Torch useful. Off site: Fishing or riding 2 km. Golf 20 km. Bus service to the historic city of Balaruc-Les-Bains from just outside the site.

Open

2 April - 9 October.

At a glance

Welcome & Ambience	✓✓✓✓	Location	✓✓✓
Quality of Pitches	✓✓✓✓	Range of Facilities	✓✓✓✓

Directions

From A9 take exit for Sete and follow N800 to Balaruc le Vieux, at the first roundabout follow Sete/Balaruc les Bains. Pass the centre commercial (Carrefour on the left). At second roundabout again follow Balaruc les Bains/Sete. After 50 m take right for Balaruc les Bains and immediately left across the road you have just left and back down it (50 m) to go immediately right, and follow Chemin du Mas du Padre site on left well hidden.

Charges 2004

Per unit incl. 2 persons and electricity	€ 13,45 - € 31,95
extra person (over 14 years)	€ 2,70 - € 4,00
child	€ 1,05 - € 3,30
1 person, 60 sq.m. pitch	€ 7,60 - € 15,80
dog	€ 0,85 - € 1,85

Reservations

Advised for high season only.
Tel: 04 67 48 53 41.
E-mail: contact@mas-du-padre.com

FR34180 Camping La Borio de Roque

Route de la Salvetat, 34220 St Pons de Thomières (Hérault)

A small peaceful site, La Borio de Roque is set in a very rural location on a quiet hillside four kilometres from St Pons. It lies at the end of a 1.5 km. track (rough in places) but it is well worth the effort and is set around a typical farmhouse with the outbuildings made into four very attractive gites. The 25 large, level, terraced pitches have 10A electricity and some shade. Some are very private which Ted the owner will escort you to. Children are encouraged to help with feeding and grooming the goats, sheep, donkeys and horses. Riding is possible on a daily, half daily or lessons basis and the rides into the forest with a picnic are very popular. There are numerous walks and tracks for mountain bikes from the site. Marit and Ted, your Dutch hosts, are only too happy to advise on routes. St Pons (4 km.) is an attractive small town with bars, restaurants and a museum. La Borio is especially suited to couples and young families - not a site for teenagers who like lots of entertainment.

Facilities

The modernised toilet blocks provide adjustable, roomy showers and washbasins en-suite. Baby bath. Dishwashing and laundry sinks. Adequate chemical disposal. Free use of large freezer. Bread is available all season and ices. Local wine and home produced goat's cheese, honey and cherry jam are for sale. A set menu is cooked four times weekly (to order) in high season and eaten with the family in the bar/barn. This is a very popular event and well subscribed. Swimming pool (from 1/6) and small lake for fishing. Small play area on grass. Barbecue areas. The site is not suitable for American motorhomes. Off site: Bicycle hire 5 km. Golf and riding 20 km. Beach 50 km.

Open

1 May - 30 September.

At a glance

Welcome & Ambience	✓✓✓✓✓	Location	✓✓✓✓
Quality of Pitches	✓✓✓✓✓	Range of Facilities	✓✓✓✓

Directions

St Pons de Thomières is on the N112 northwest of Bezieres. Site is 4.5 km. north of the town on the D907 signed Salvatat, on the right on a bend; then 1.5 km. on a rough track (signed).

Charges 2005

Per adult	€ 4,00
child (under 7 yrs)	€ 3,00
pitch	€ 8,50
electricity	€ 3,00
vehicle	€ 2,00
extra tent	€ 4,00

No credit cards.

Reservations

Necessary for the main season and made with booking fee (€ 15.25). Tel: 04 67 97 10 97. E-mail: info@borioderoque.com

FR34090 Camping Caravaning Domaine de la Yole

B.P. 23, 34350 Valras-Plage (Hérault)

A busy happy holiday village with over 1,100 pitches could seem a little daunting. We expected things to be a little hectic when we arrived on a busy day in mid-August. However, the multi-lingual reception was calm and people were enjoying themselves. There are 590 pitches for touring units, the remainder taken by mobile homes and a few tour operator pitches. Most pitches are of a good size, all are level, hedged and have electricity, water and waste water points and, very importantly for this area, they all have shade. The extensive pool area is attractive with lots of sunbathing areas and the impressive activities are located in a central area. A shopping area provides a supermarket, outdoor vegetable stall, butchers, wine shop (take your own bottles for really good wines on draught), boutique and a takeaway, very much like a village market. The beach, a long stretch of beautiful sand, is 500 m. and here is trampolining, paragliding and jet-skis. This is a busy site with something for all the family English is spoken.

Facilities

Eight well maintained toilet blocks include some showers and washbasins en-suite, mostly British style WCs and many washbasins in cubicles. One/two blocks have extra large cubicles with everything including a baby bath can be used by families or disabled visitors. All have dishwashing and laundry sinks. Central laundry with washing machines and dryers. Motorcaravan service point (the only chemical disposal point is here, a long walk from many pitches). Refrigerators for hire. Shops. Good restaurant with huge terrace and amphitheatre for daily entertainment (in season). Two large pools and paddling pool, all supervised by lifeguard in July/Aug. All facilities open when site open. Two half size tennis courts (free) and two full size (charged July/Aug). Multi-sports court. Large play areas with amusements such as moto-track and daily children's club, minigolf, table tennis, boules, volleyball and basketball. Doctor calls daily in high season. Internet access. Off site: Fishing or riding 1 km. Beach 500m, path from site.

At a glance

Welcome & Ambience	✓✓✓✓	Location	✓✓✓✓
Quality of Pitches	✓✓✓✓	Range of Facilities	✓✓✓✓✓

Directions

From A9 autoroute take Beziers Ouest exit for Valras Plage (13-14 km) and follow Casino signs. Site is on left, just after sign for Vendres Plage.

Charges 2004

Per unit incl. 2 adults	€ 16,85 - € 32,75
extra adult	€ 5,35
child 7-16 yrs	free - € 3,30
child under 7 yrs	free - € 1,70
dog	free - € 3,10

Reservations

Made with deposit (€ 90 or € 130) and, in high season, a fee (€ 25); contact site for form. Tel: 04 67 37 33 87. E-mail: layole34@aol.com

Open

30 April - 17 September.

FR34050 Camping Naturiste Le Mas de Lignières

Cesseras-en-Minervois, 34210 Olonzac (Hérault)

A naturist site hidden in the hills of the Minervois, this is a delightful find, only three kilometres from the medieval town of Minerve with its Cathar connections. Parts of this site enjoy some marvellous views to the Pyrénées, the Corbières and the coast at Narbonne. We recommend that you watch at least one wonderful sunrise over the Pyrénées. The owners Jeanne and Gilles, offer a warm welcome and promote a most enjoyable family atmosphere. The site provides 50 large (200 sq.m.) pitches, all with electricity (6A), and 25 with water and waste water connections. Mainly level grass, they are separated by mature hedges that give considerable privacy. Some smaller pitches (100 sq.m.) are available for tents, with cars parked elsewhere. There is natural shade and a variety of fauna and flora including four types of orchid. Within the confines of the seven hectare site there are some good walks with superb views and, although the camping area is actually quite small, the very large pitches create a very relaxing ambience and a nice introduction to naturist camping. If you ask nicely, Gilles may take you out in his Landrover (he's a bit of an expert on all things natural) to places you would never find otherwise. The owners are proud that the site has recently been awarded the coveted 'Clef Vert' award for environmental awareness (similar to the Blue Flag award for beaches).

Facilities

The pleasant, clean toilet block has open washbasins and semi-open showers. Dishwashing and laundry sinks. En-suite facilities for disabled people. Washing machine. Simple shop for essentials and local specialities. Bread can be ordered (15/06 -15/09). Bar and snack bar (15/7-15/8). Swimming pool with sliding cover for use in early and late season. Paddling pool. Comfortable room for general use with TV, library and tourist information and separate provision for young people. Playground. Tennis, volleyball and boules (all free). Torch useful. Only gas barbecues are permitted. Off site: Sailing, riding and canoeing nearby - Lac de Jouarres. Canal du Midi.

Open

1 April - 31 October.

At a glance

Welcome & Ambience	✓✓✓✓✓	Location	✓✓✓✓✓
Quality of Pitches	✓✓✓✓	Range of Facilities	✓✓✓✓

Directions

From A61 autoroute take Lézignan-Corbières exit, through town via the D611 to Homps, then on D910 to Olonzac. Go through village following the signs to Minerve (D10). Follow road for approx. 4 km. taking left hand turn to Cesseras (D168). At Cesseras follow signs to Fauzan for approx another 4 km. Site is signed to the right where there is a climb up a winding road, which is a little narrow in places.

Charges 2004

Per pitch incl. 2 persons and electricity (6A), water and drainage	€ 23,00
smaller pitch excl. electricity	€ 16,50
extra person	€ 3,80
child (2-7 yrs)	€ 2,60
dog	€ 1,50
electricity 10A	€ 1,50 - € 3,00

Less for longer booked stays.

Reservations

Made until 25/6 with deposit (25%) and fee (€ 10). Tel: 04 68 91 24 86. E-mail: lemas1@tiscali.fr

FR34240 Camping Le Castellas

Route Nationale 112, 34200 Sète (Hérault)

You would expect a campsite situated beside the main road which runs alongside the beach and with a railway line behind to be noisy, whereas in fact once you are within the confines of this site it is surprisingly peaceful offering everything you could want. It is conveniently situated directly across the road from a superb sandy beach, with the Etang du Thau behind, yet it's within a short drive of Sète, Marseillan Plage or Agde. It is a large site but is very well organised. In total there are 994 pitches with 307 used for mobile homes or chalets. The pitches are mainly large and hedged on sandy ground with 6A electricity with some smaller ones at the far end without electricity. All are accessed by hard roads with a variety of shade - the sorts of shrubs that will grow by the sea. A large pool, without noisy toboggans and a sports area have been developed at the back of the site under pine trees, along with a restaurant and bar, all of which appear to be very well managed. Because of its situation security has to be tight, and so it is. There is an obvious emphasis on entertainment with all ages being provided for, although families with younger children are likely to be the most appreciative.

Facilities

Nine toilet blocks of a standard design, fully equipped, some with en-suite showers and basins mainly operate on a unisex basis. Dishwashing sinks. Laundry. Provision for disabled people. Fridge hire. Large supermarket and range of smaller shops and café open to public as well. Restaurant, bars and snack bars. Swimming pool with lifeguards. All open when site is open. Tennis. Multi-sports court. Sports field. Play area and bouncy castles. Hairdresser. Masseurs. Internet bus. ATM. Wide range of entertainment. Site Paper in English for high season. Off site: Bus for Sete daily in July/Aug.

At a glance

Welcome & Ambience	✓✓✓✓	Location	✓✓✓✓
Quality of Pitches	✓✓✓✓	Range of Facilities	✓✓✓✓✓

Directions

Site is beside the RN112 which links Marseillan Plage and Sete (nearer to Marseillian Plage). This road can get very busy indeed in main season.

Charges 2004

Per unit incl. electricity (6A)	€ 19,00 - € 34,00
extra person	€ 4,00 - € 7,00
extra car	€ 2,00 - € 5,00
dog	€ 4,00

Reservations

Advised for July and August and made with booking fee (€ 25) and 30% deposit. Tel: 04 67 51 63 00. E-mail: camping.lecastellas@wanadoo.fr

Open

1 May - 20 September.

FR34250 Camping des Sources

34700 Soubes (Hérault)

This is a 'real' campsite tucked into the side of a small valley with views of the mountains, yet very easily accessed from the A75 autoroute. It has a rural feel with some up and down walking but all your needs will be met. The pitches vary in size and are tucked into bays catering for small or large tents, motorhomes and caravans. All are level with some grass (metal tent pegs could be useful) and with 6A electricity provided. A natural spring water pool is large enough for children to splash around in, whilst another is ideal to cool your drinks if you are travelling light (the water is drinkable). You can also clamber down to the river and cool off there or simply relax. For children it is a marvellous natural playground, although there is also a play area on site. The owner is very proud of his site and happy to provide information and advice on the wide range of activities available, ranging from walking, climbing, riding, sailing, trout fishing and potholing to bird watching and botanic walks. Yet the site is less than an hours drive from the Mediterranean coast.

Facilities

The central traditionally built toilet block is fully equipped including some washbasins in cabins and a washing machine. Simple snack bar. Small pool fed by spring water. Play area. Table tennis. Communal barbecues. Dogs are not accepted. Off site: Village of Soubes 10 minute walk across the river with shop, bar/restaurant etc. Lodeve 5 km. Montpellier and Mediterranean within one hours drive. On route of the Cirque de Navacelles.

Open

15 May - 15 September.

At a glance

Welcome & Ambience	✓✓✓✓	Location	✓✓✓✓
Quality of Pitches	✓✓✓✓	Range of Facilities	✓✓✓

Directions

Site is 3 km. north ol Lodeve. Soubes is signed from A75. Take first right towards Fozieres and follow site signs (approx. 1 km).

Charges 2004

Per unit incl. 2 persons	€ 14,00
extra person	€ 4,50
child (under 7 yrs)	€ 3,00
electricity	€ 2,50

Reservations

Contact site. Tel: 04 67 44 32 02.
E-mail: jlsources@wanadoo.fr

FR66170 Camping Mar I Sol

Route de la Plage, 66440 Torreilles (Pyrénées-Orientales)

Good quality sites with direct access to the beach are hard to find and Mar i Sol is a useful addition. It is a fairly large site with 377 pitches with a significant number of mobile homes but with 170 available for touring units. These are sandy grass pitches of good size with some shade and connected by hard-core roads. All have electricity (10A). The new owners have renovated the pool area and continue with other improvements. This is essentially a 'holiday' site with all the popular facilities and an extensive entertainment programme and children's club throughout the main season.

Facilities

Three fully equipped toilet blocks of the same design include mixed British and Turkish toilets, some washbasins in cabins and covered dishwashing and laundry sinks. Washing machine in each block. Small supermarket. Bar (1/6-15/9) TV. Restaurant and takeaway. Swimming pool, water slide and children's pool. All facilities are open in the main season. Play area. Tennis court (charged). Table tennis. Archery. Fitness room. Football and volleyball. Side gate with access to path across semi-sand dunes to sandy beach (lifeguards in main season). Watersport activities possible.

Open

1 April - 30 September.

At a glance

Welcome & Ambience	✓✓✓✓✓	Location	✓✓✓✓✓
Quality of Pitches	✓✓✓✓	Range of Facilities	✓✓✓✓✓

Directions

From A9 take exit 41(Perpignan Nord) towards Le Barcarès for 9 km then south on D81 towards Canet for 3 km. before turning to Torreilles Plage. Site is signed.

Charges 2004

Per unit incl. 2 persons	€ 16,40 - € 26,40
extra person (over 6 yrs)	€ 3,60 - € 6,60
child (under 6 yrs)	free - € 3,50
electricity (10A)	€ 4,20
dog	€ 5,15

Reservations

Necessary for July/Aug. and made with deposit (€ 150.45) and booking fee (€ 22.87).
Tel: 04 68 28 04 07.
E-mail: marisol@camping-marisol.com

FR66210 Chadotel Camping Le Roussillon

Chemin de la Mer, 66750 St Cyprien (Pyrénées-Orientales)

This a comfortable site, although perhaps somewhat lacking in character. It is part of the Chadotel Group and has a quiet situation on the edge of St Cyprien village, some two kilometres from the beach. A bus service runs in the main season. The site benefits from having a good sized, traditionally shaped swimming pool, with the added attraction for children of a water slide, and plenty of sunbathing areas for adults. There are 166 pitches in total with a number taken by our tour operators and the rest for mobile homes available to rent but there are 25 well-kept, grassy and level touring pitches. Of a good size, they all have 16A electrical connections.

Facilities

Two toilet blocks (one older but refurbished, one more modern) provide modern facilities including a baby bath, laundry and facilities for disabled visitors. Bar/snack-bar with entertainment in season. Play area on grass.

Open

30 March - 30 September.

At a glance

Welcome & Ambience	✓✓✓✓	Location	✓✓✓
Quality of Pitches	✓✓✓✓	Range of Facilities	✓✓✓✓

Directions

Via the D81 southwards, don't go into St Cyprien Plage, but follow signs towards Argelès. At roundabout ('Aqualand' signed left) turn right towards St Cyprien village. Bear right and site is on the right hand side of this road.

Charges 2004

incl. electricity	€ 18,00 - € 26,50
extra person	€ 5,50
child (under 5 yrs)	€ 3,50

Reservations

Contact Chadotel Central Reservations, B.P. 12 85520 Jard-sur-Mer. Tel: 02 51 33 05 05.
Tel: 04 68 21 06 45. E-mail: info@chadotel.com

FR66220 Camping du Stade

Avenue du 8 Mai 1945, 66702 Argelès-sur-Mer (Pyrénées-Orientales)

Quieter and more peaceful family orientated sites are about as rare as hens' teeth in this immediate area, so we were pleasantly surprised to discover one in a pleasant shady setting midway between the village and the beach resort – less than one kilometre from both. The 180 good sized pitches, (most with electricity) are in green surroundings with plenty of shade. This traditionally French campsite, could be a quiet haven for those who want to relax at the end of the day without the distraction of a noisy pool and bar, but who want to be close to all the various attractions offered by this resort.

Facilities

With so much within easy walking distance the site itself has few facilities, but it does have two good quality, part modern, part traditional, well-maintained toilet blocks with good sized showers, washbasins in cabins, etc. Unit for disabled people, facilities for babies and washing machine. Snack bar and takeaway (high season only). Adventure-style play area. Table tennis.

Open

1 April - 30 September.

At a glance

Welcome & Ambience	✓✓✓✓	Location	✓✓✓✓
Quality of Pitches	✓✓✓✓	Range of Facilities	✓✓✓

Directions

From A9 exit 42 (Perpignan Sud) take N114 towards Argelès. Take exit 10 for Pujols and Argles, then follow signs towards Centre Plage. At first roundabout go straight on (Ave Molliere). At next (small) roundabout turn left and site is on left.

Charges 2004

Per unit incl. 2 adults	€ 12,90 - € 18,00
with electricity	€ 16,00 - € 21,60
extra person	€ 2,15 - € 4,80

Reservations

Contact site. Tel: 04 68 81 04 40.
E-mail:info@campingdustade.com

FR66240 Chadotel Camping Le Trivoly

Route des Plages, 66440 Torreilles-Plage (Pyrénées-Orientales)

The popularity of Torreilles derives mainly from its huge sandy beach and for off-site nightlife, shopping, etc. but for smarter resorts one really needs to visit Le Barcares or Canet a few kilometres distance in either direction. Le Trivoly (a member of the French Chadotel Group) is about 500 m. gentle stroll from the beach, in a fairly tranquil setting. It has 170 good size, shaded and hedged pitches with electricity and 100 mobile homes. It perhaps offers a rather more peaceful situation than do the other sites here.

Facilities

Four toilet blocks, although not new, provide modern facilities, including washbasins in (rather small) cabins, and were all clean and well cared for. Small shop (June- mid Sept). Snack-restaurant and takeaway (June-mid Sept). Reasonably sized pool with water slide and paddling pool. Play area. Bicycle hire. Basketball. Entertainment programme in high season. Off site: Centre Commercial 300 m.

Open

1 April - last week of September.

At a glance

Welcome & Ambience	✓✓✓✓	Location	✓✓✓✓
Quality of Pitches	✓✓✓✓	Range of Facilities	✓✓✓✓

Directions

From A9 take exit 42 (Perpignan Nord) towards Le Barcarès for 9 km, then turn south ont D81 towards Canet. After 3 km. turn left at roundabout, signed Torreilles Plage. Site is on left, after about 500 m.

Charges 2004

Per unit incl. 2 persons	
with electricity	€ 18,00 - € 26,50
extra person	€ 5,50
child (under 5 yrs)	€ 3,50

Reservations

Contact Chadotel Central Reservations, BP 12, 85520 Jard-sur-Mer. Tel: 02 51 33 05 05.
Tel: 04 68 28 20 28. E-mail: info@chadotel.com

FR66190 Sunêlia Les Tropiques

Mobile homes page 410

Bvd de la Méditerranée, 66440 Torreilles-Plage (Pyrénées-Orientales)

Les Tropiques makes a pleasant holiday venue, only 400 metres from a sandy beach and also boasting two pools. There are 450 pitches with 200 given over to mobile homes and chalets. Pleasant pine and palm trees with other Mediterranean vegetation give shade and provides an attractive environment. Activities are provided for all including a large range of sports, caberets and shows but an identity bracelet for entry to the site is obligatory in high season (small payment required).

Facilities

Modern, fully equipped sanitary facilities include provision for disabled visitors. Launderette. Bar, restaurant with takeaway meals and pizzeria (all 14/6–15/9). Shop. Two outdoor swimming pools (1/6–30/9) Tennis, table tennis, football, volleyball and pétanque. Archery (1/7-31/8). TV and billards room. Play area. Disco (every evening and club for 6-12 yr old children in July/Aug. New car-wash installed. Off site: Minigolf 300 m. Windsurf board hire and sea fishing 400 m. Riding 400 m. Bicycle hire 5 km. Golf 15 km.

Open

9 April - 7 October.

At a glance

Welcome & Ambience	✓✓✓✓	Location	✓✓✓✓
Quality of Pitches	✓✓✓✓	Range of Facilities	✓✓✓✓✓

Directions

From autroute A9 take exit for Perpignan Nord and follow D83 towards Le Barcarès for 9 km. Take D81 suth towards Canet for 3 km. before turning left at roundabout for Torreilles Plage. Site is the last but one on the left.

Charges 2005

Per unit incl. 2 persons with electricity	€ 17,00 - € 33,00
extra person	€ 3,60 - € 6,00
child (0-13 yrs)	€ 2,70 - € 4,50
animal	€ 4,00

Camping Cheques accepted.

Reservations

Contact site. Tel: 04 68 28 05 09.
E-mail: camping.tropiques@wanadoo.fr

TO BOOK CALL 0870 405 4055 OR www.alanrogersdirect.com

TRAVEL SERVICE SITE

FR66020 Camping Caravaning Ma Prairie

Route de St Nazaire, 66140 Canet-en-Roussillon (Pyrénées-Orientales)

The Gil family provide a warm welcome immediately as you arrive at the very pretty ivy covered reception area, which boasts an impressive international collection of hats/helmets and uniform caps. Ma Prairie is an excellent site set three kilometres back from the sandy Canet beaches. It has an excellent pool complex over looked by a large air conditioned bar situated across a small road from the camping area. There are 260 pitches of around 100 sq.m. on flat grassy ground, separated by various trees and bushes which provide shade (possible road noise). Most have electricity, with water and drainage on 35. The Gils have produced another superb touch in their restaurant which is very much a family affair down to mother's cushion designs and grandfather's paintings on the wall. The area of the old restaurant is now used for children's entertainment. Organised wine tastings are held once a week in high season. Used by tour operators (40 pitches). There is a lively family atmosphere. A 'Sites et Paysages' member.

Facilities

Three toilet blocks, fully equipped, include washbasins in cabins with dividers. Baby bath. Washing machines and dryers. Dishwashing and laundry sinks. Extra provision near reception. Shop for basics only, covered snack bar and takeaway. Large air-conditioned bar and restaurant. Large adult pool (10 x 22 m), splendid children's pool. Play area. Tennis. Bicycle hire. Volleyball. Satellite TV, table tennis, billiards and amusement machines. Dancing about three times weekly and busy daily animation programme in season. Caravan storage. Off site: Riding 600 m. Golf 6 km. Canet Village within walking distance with all amenities. Bus/tram services to the busy modern resort of Canet Plage.

Open

5 May - 25 September.

At a glance

Welcome & Ambience	✓✓✓✓	Location	✓✓✓
Quality of Pitches	✓✓✓✓	Range of Facilities	✓✓✓✓

Directions

Leave autoroute A9 at Perpignan North towards Barcares. Site access is from the D11 Perpignan road (exit 5) close to the junction with D617 in Canet-Village. Go under bridge, right at roundabout the left to site.

Charges 2005

Per unit with 2 persons	€ 17,00 - € 28,00
extra person	€ 3,00 - € 6,00
child 4-10 yrs	€ 2,30 - € 4,00
child under 4 yrs	free - € 3,00
electricity (10A)	€ 4,00
water and drainage	€ 5,00

Camping Cheques accepted.

Reservations

Made for any length with deposit (€ 61) and fee (€ 12.20). Tel: 04 68 73 26 17.
E-mail: ma.prairie@wanadoo.fr

TO BOOK CALL 0870 405 4055 OR www.alanrogersdirect.com

TRAVEL SERVICE SITE

FR66030 Camping Cala Gogo

La Vigie, 66750 St Cyprien-Plage (Pyrénées-Orientales)

This is an excellent large and well organised site (sister site to 6604, Le Soleil) and it is agreeably situated by a superb sandy beach where there is a beach bar and boats can be launched. The 450 pitches for touring units are on flat ground and around 100 sq.m. with some 50 odd chalets or mobile homes to let. They are fully marked out on level grass with easy access, electrical connections (6A) everywhere and some shade. The site has a most impressive pool complex carefully laid out with palm trees in ample sunbathing areas. The large bar complex becomes very busy in season and dancing or entertainment is arranged on some evenings on a large stage recently built alongside the bar. A large Aquapark, reputed to be amongst the best in southern France, is nearby. Used by tour operators (148 pitches). An interesting feature of the site is the provision of special beach buggies for the handicapped.

Facilities

All four toilet blocks are of a high standard, fully equipped including British and Turkish style toilets and washbasins in cabins. Good supermarket, small shopping mall and wine boutique. Sophisticated restaurant with excellent cuisine and service, plus a self-service restaurant with simple menu and takeaway. Bar and small bar by the beach in high season. Disco. TV. Three adult pools plus one for children, water-jets, jacuzzi and waterfall. Children's play area and remote control cars for children. Tennis, table tennis and a playground. Programme of events and sports organised in season. Torches useful. Off site: Fishing, riding, bicycle hire and golf within 5 km. Boat excursions and courses in skin-diving, windsurfing or sailing nearby.

At a glance

Welcome & Ambience	✓✓✓✓✓	Location	✓✓✓✓✓
Quality of Pitches	✓✓✓✓✓	Range of Facilities	✓✓✓✓✓

Directions

Using D81 (southward) avoid St Cyprien Plage and continue towards Argeles. Turn right at roundabout signed Le Port and Aquapark and pick up site signs. Site is just past the Aquapark.

Charges 2004

Per person (over 5 yrs)	€ 7,50
pitch	€ 10,50
electricity (6A)	€ 3,00
dog	€ 3,50

Reservations

Made for Sat. to Sat. and necessary for Jul/Aug, with deposit (€ 81.70) and fee (€ 18.30).
Tel: 04 68 21 07 12. E-mail: calagogo@campmed.com

Open

14 May - 24 September.

FR66040 Camping Le Soleil

Route du Littoral, 66702 Argelès-sur-Mer (Pyrénées-Orientales)

Le Soleil (sister site to Cala Gogo, no. FR66030), with direct access to the sandy beach, is a busy, popular, family owned site which has grown in the last few years. A large site, more like a small village, it has over 800 individual numbered pitches of ample size, with over 200 used by tour operators, over 70 occupied by mobile homes and around 550 used for touring units. On sandy/grassy ground and with a mixture of trees and shrubs providing some shade, electricity connections (6A) are provided in all areas. Access for caravans sometimes needs care on the narrow access roads. The site has a wide range of amenities, including an impressive pool complex. Spain and the Pyrénées are near enough for excursions. English is spoken and there is a comprehensive reservation system (advised for most of July/Aug) with all facilities open when the site is open.

Facilities

Seven toilet blocks of the type with external access to individual units should give good coverage with showers in four of them. Some now offer family cabins with washbasins and showers with unusually two additional pressure water outlets at waist level in each. Washing machines. Supermarket, general shop, press, tabac and restaurant for sit down or takeaway food is centrally situated. ATM machine. Internet connection. Bar with disco (July/Aug) and beach bar. California type swimming pool complex and entertainment area. Adventure playground. TV room. Tennis. Riding in high season (charge). Dogs are not accepted. Off site: Fishing and mooring boats on the adjacent river. Golf 5 km.

At a glance

Welcome & Ambience	✓✓✓✓	Location	✓✓✓✓✓
Quality of Pitches	✓✓✓✓	Range of Facilities	✓✓✓✓✓

Directions

Site is at north end of the beach about 1 km. from Argelès-Plage village.

Charges 2005

Per person (over 5 yrs)	€ 7,80
pitch	€ 11,90
electricity (6A)	€ 3,10

Less 20% outside July/Aug.
Swimming pool deposit € 15.24 per pitch.

Reservations

Made from Sat or Wed (min. 1 week) with deposit (30%) and booking fee (€ 18.30).
Tel: 04 68 81 14 48.
E-mail: camping.lesoleil@wanadoo.fr

Open

14 May - 25 September.

2 Campsites DIRECT ON THE BEACH !
- 20 % in may, june and september on the pitchprices.
Cala-Gogo
La Vigie • F-66750 SAINT CYPRIEN
Tél. +33 4 68 21 07 12
Fax +33 4 68 21 02 19
www.campmed.com
e-mail : calagogo@campmed.com
le Soleil
Route du Littoral
66702 Argelès sur Mer
✆ 04 68 95 94 62 • Fax 04 68 95 92 81
www.campmed.com
e-mail : lesoleil@campmed.com

FR66050 Camping Le Haras

Domaine Sant Galdric, 66690 Palau del Vidre (Pyrénées-Orientales)

A distinctly 'French' site, Le Haras is situated midway between the coast (about eight kilometres) and the Pyrénées on the edge of a village, in quiet countryside removed from the bustle of the coastal resorts. Under the same family management as Ma Prairie at Canet Village (nr. 66020), they are dedicated to many improvements. Le Haras has some 75 individual pitches all with electricity and drainage, arranged informally in bays of four, in the grounds of an old hunting lodge (designed by Gustave Violet on the lines of a small Italianate palace). A marvellous mixture of trees, shrubs and flowers provides colour and shade. There is an attractive pool complex and courtyard area beside the restaurant (developed in the old stables, with an excellent chef) and large function room, often used for weddings, with a distinctly Italian feel. Rail noise is possible from the line that runs beside the site, although this is screened by large trees.

Facilities

The unusually designed toilet block, fully equipped with mixed British and Turkish toilets, has been supplemented by a smart new block decorated in greens and terracotta in keeping with the site. It is planned that the smaller block near the pool will be renovated and heated. Covered dishwashing and laundry sinks. Washing machines. Fridge hire. Bar. Restaurant, also open to the public (all year, but not every day). Takeaway. Swimming and paddling pools (1/5-15/9). Play area. Charcoal barbecues are no permitted. Off site: Three bakers in the village, two butchers and a general stores. Beaches 10 minutes drive. Fishing 500 m. Riding 2 km. Bicycle hire 6 km. Golf 7 km.

Open

20 March - 20 October.

At a glance

Welcome & Ambience	✓✓✓✓	Location	✓✓✓✓
Quality of Pitches	✓✓✓✓	Range of Facilities	✓✓✓✓✓

Directions

To avoid possible heavy traffic around Perpignan leave autoroute at exit 43 (Le Boulou) and follow D618 in the direction of Argelés for approx. 13 km. Take left turn for Palau-del-Vidre (D11) as you bypass St André. Bear right through village still on D11 in direction of Elne. As you leave village, site is on right, entrance just before railway bridge.

Charges 2004

Per pitch incl. two persons	€ 14,00 - € 22,00
extra person	€ 3,00 - € 5,00
child (under 7 yrs)	free - € 3,50
electricity (5A)	€ 3,80
dog	€ 3,00

Camping Cheques accepted.

Reservations

Necessary for July and August. Made with € 100 deposit and € 16 booking fee. Tel: 04 68 22 14 50. E-mail: haras8@wanadoo.fr

FR66000 Camping Caravaning De Pujol

Route du Tamariguer, 66700 Argelès-sur-Mer (Pyrénées-Orientales)

Le Pujol is a very attractive, pretty and well cared for site which has been thoughtfully designed. Argelès is a busy tourist area and in high season it doesn't matter which of the 50 or so sites you are on, there are various loud open air discos and activities which may impinge on the wrong side of midnight for a while. It is however possible to avoid the standard hectic seaside sites in otherwise attractive Argelès, and Pujol may represent the best chance of doing so. There are 310 numbered pitches, all larger than 100 sq.m. on flat grass, nearly all with electrical connections (6A). They include some 90 privately owned British mobile homes and 10 site owned for letting. The site's pride and joy is a delightful pool complex with semi-tropical shrubs and fountains. Care is taken to ensure that the bar is a family bar rather than one overrun by youngsters, who are catered for in an attractively covered meeting area opposite which also houses animation and dances. The site is very close to an interesting fortress and only two kilometres from the fast N114, via which the pretty ports of Collioure and Port-Vendres are a short distance to the south. There is some road noise near the entrance to the site.

Facilities

Well kept fully equipped toilet blocks include a smart shower block. Baby bath. Washing machines. Small supermarket (1/6-15/9). Good terraced restaurant and friendly family bar (1/6-15/9). Fairly large L-shaped swimming pool, children's pool, and spa pool (1/6-15/9). Table tennis, small multi-gym, volleyball, boules and minigolf. Playground. Games room. Only gas or electric barbecues are permitted. Off site: Riding 500 m. Fishing, bicycle hire 1 km. Argelès Plage and quiet resort of Racou short distance.

Open

1 June - 15 September.

At a glance

Welcome & Ambience	✓✓✓✓	Location	✓✓✓✓
Quality of Pitches	✓✓✓✓✓	Range of Facilities	✓✓✓✓

Directions

Perpignan-Nord exit from autoroute, follow N114 from Perpignan and use exit 10 for Argelès, Cross first roundabout onto Chemin de Neguebous (avoiding town). Turn left at second roundabout and site is 200 m. on right opposite Tour de Pujol.

Charges 2004

Per pitch incl. 2 adults	€ 21,00
with electricity	€ 24,00
extra person	€ 5,00
child (under 3 yrs)	€ 2,50

Less 20% in June and Sept. No credit cards.

Reservations

Made with € 100 deposit. Tel: 04 68 81 00 25.

FR66110 Camping Le Dauphin

Route de Taxo-d'Avall, 66701 Argelès-sur-Mer (Pyrénées-Orientales)

Near Taxo in the quieter, northern part of Argelès (a somewhat frenzied resort in season), this family owned site on flat, grassy parkland with plenty of tall trees enjoys good views of the Pyrénées from the terrace area surrounding its excellent complex of swimming pools. There are 310 level, grassy well shaded pitches, all with 10A electricity and some with individual sanitary units; however some 150 pitches are taken by mobile homes and chalets either privately owned or for rent. Tour operators use 70 of the pitches. Although located some 1.5 km. from the town and beach, there is a regular connecting 'road train' service to and fro throughout the day and evening up to midnight.

Facilities

A central sanitary block, although mature, provides all essential facilities including washbasins en-suite. One third of the pitches have their own fully equipped individual sanitary unit. Shops, bar/restaurant, pizzeria with takeaway (all 1/6-15/9). Pool complex (small charge). Children's play area. Tennis courts, minigolf, table tennis, multi-sport court, sports ground and games room. Entertainment programme in high season. Torches useful in some areas.
Off site: Riding 1 km. Fishing 2 km.

Open

1 June - 30 September.

At a glance

Welcome & Ambience	✓✓✓✓	Location	✓✓✓✓
Quality of Pitches	✓✓✓✓✓	Range of Facilities	✓✓✓✓

Directions

Site is on north side of Argelès. From autoroute take exit Perpignan-Nord for Argelès and follow directions for Plage-Nord and Taxo d'Avall (similarly from the N114).

Charges 2004

Per unit incl. 2 adults	€ 19,00 - € 24,50
with electricity	€ 21,50 - € 28,50
extra person	€ 4,00 - € 6,00
child (under 5 yrs)	€ 2,50 - € 3,50
water and drainage	€ 2,50 - € 4,00
Individual sanitation	€ 6,00 - € 8,00

Reservations

Made with deposit (€ 77) and booking fee (€ 16).
Tel: 04 68 81 17 54.
E-mail: camping.ledauphin66@wanadoo.fr

FR66200 Camping Les Marsouins

Avenue de la Retirada, 66702 Argelès-sur-Mer (Pyrénées-Orientales)

Les Marsouins is a large site situated on the beach road out of Argelès. About 103 of the 587 pitches are taken by mobile homes, with those for tourers of a good size on level, mown grass divided by hedging. There is a degree of shade from some tall trees and electricity (5A) is available to all. An outdoor entertainment area is located at the entrance beside the bar and restaurant (for high season entertainment) but the lagoon style heated pool and paddling pool (no water slides) are tucked away to one side of the site with ample space for sunbathing on the lawns surrounding it. The site is well situated for easy access to the good sandy beach, with windsurfing and sea kayaking possible (free from 15/5 to 30/9).

Facilities

Four fully equipped toilet blocks provide facilities for the handicapped and there are dishwashing and laundry sinks, washing machine and iron. Motorcaravan service point. Shop (26/5-8/9). Bar (7/6-5/9) and self-service restaurant (16/6-5/9) near entrance. Takeaway (1/4-30/9). Mini-market (8/6–7/9). Heated swimming pool (identity bracelet required; 15/04 – 29/9). Large play area. Children's club with free organised activities (24/6–1/9). Tennis, volleyball, table tennis. Range of evening entertainment (30/5–30/8).
Off site: Beach 800 m. Riding next door. Boat launching 2 km. Golf 7 km.

At a glance

Welcome & Ambience	✓✓✓✓✓	Location	✓✓✓✓
Quality of Pitches	✓✓✓✓	Range of Facilities	✓✓✓✓✓

Directions

Take the Perpignan sud exit from A9 autoroute. Follow signs for Argelès (RN114) exit junction 10 and follow Pujols at roundabout then Plage Nord at next roundabout. Site is 1.5 km. on left.

Charges 2005

Per unit incl. 2 persons	
and 5A electricity	€ 12,00 - € 24,50
with water and drainage	€ 13,50 - € 26,00
extra person (over 5 yrs)	€ 4,00 - € 5,50

Reservations

Made with booking fee (€ 15). Tel: 04 68 81 14 81.
E-mail: marsouin@campmed.com

Open

9 April - 30 September.

FR66070 Yelloh! Village Le Brasilia

B.P. 204, 66141 Canet-en-Roussillon (Pyrénées-Orientales)

An impressive family site beside the beach, well managed. It is pretty, neat and well kept with an amazingly wide range of facilities and activities, and though it is a large site it does not seem so. There are 826 neatly hedged pitches all with electricity varying in size from 100 to 150 sq.m. Some of the longer pitches are suitable for two families together. With a range of shade from mature pines and flowering shrubs, less on pitches near the beach, there are neat access roads (sometimes narrow for large units) and many flowering shrubs. Over 100 of the pitches have mobile homes or chalets to rent. The sandy beach here is busy, with a beach club (you can hire windsurfing boards) and a naturist section is on the beach to the west of the site. There is also a large California type pool, with sunbathing areas bounded by an attractive mosaic wall and bar. The village area of the site provides bars, a busy restaurant, entertainment (including a night club) and a range of shops. In fact you do not need to stir from the site which is almost a resort in itself also providing a cash dispenser, exchange facilities, telephone, post office, gas supplies and even weather forecasts. It does have a nice, lively atmosphere but is orderly and well run - very good for a site with beach access. They seem to have thought of everything, including an escort to your pitch and advice on the best way to site your unit. A 'Yelloh Village' member.

Facilities

Ten modern sanitary blocks are very well equipped and maintained, with British style WCs (some Turkish) and washbasins in cabins. Some very modern and impressive with good facilities for children and for disabled people. All have dishwashing and laundry sinks. Laundry room with washing machines and dryers. Special refuse areas. Hairdressing salon. Bars and restaurant. Swimming pool with life guards (heated and free). Children's play areas. Sports field for football and a smaller games pitch (with 'Astroturf'). Tennis courts. Sporting activities such as aqua gym, aerobics, football, etc. Library, games and video room. Internet café. Daily entertainment programme for young and old. Bicycle hire. Fishing. Special dog walking area, cleaned daily. Torches useful. English is spoken.
Off site: Riding 5 km. Golf 12 km. Canet Plage with its long esplanade edging the beach.

At a glance

Welcome & Ambience	✓✓✓✓✓	Location	✓✓✓✓✓
Quality of Pitches	✓✓✓✓✓	Range of Facilities	✓✓✓✓✓

Directions

From A9 motorway take exit 41 (Perpignan Centre/Rivesalts) follow signs for Le Barcarès/Canet on D83 for 10 km, then signs for Canet (D81). Arriving at first Canet roundabout, make a full turn back on yourself (direction Sainte-Marie) and watch for Brasila sign almost immediately on right and follow.

Charges 2004

Per unit incl. 2 persons and electricity (6A)	€ 15,00 - € 38,00
extra person	€ 4,50 - € 7,50
child (1-4 yrs)	free - € 4,00
extra electricity (10A)	€ 1,50
dog	€ 2,00 - € 3,50

Reservations

Advised for July/Aug. Tel: 04 68 80 23 82.
E-mail: camping-le-brasilia@wanadoo.fr

Open

30 April - 24 September.

FR66180 Mas Llinas Camping

66160 Le Boulou (Pyrénées-Orientales)

The highest terraces on this campsite have commanding views over the valley and to the surrounding mountains. On the nearby slopes are vineyards and lower in the valley large quantities of geraniums are grown professionally. The roads up to the level, terraced, hillside pitches (100) are paved to make access easy, with good places to choose from. Some are larger, some grassy and a few hedged for privacy, many with outstanding views and lovely trees (electricity is available 5/10A). The ground is stony and may be difficult for tents. This is a simple, peaceful and well maintained site with a relaxed feel and helpful, friendly owners. The beautiful original old farmhouse is situated near the top of the property. The reception is near the bar/café that serves a very limited range of snacks and some local produce, including the wine of the region. Explore the region of the Roussillon wines, historic sites including the military fortress as it would have been in the time of Louis XV1, or just enjoy the peace and quiet.

Facilities

Two unisex toilet blocks, one clean and modern, the other rather small, basic and cramped. Full range of facilities for disabled campers. Washing machine. Motorcaravan services. Limited bar/café. Bread and croissants (July/Aug). Small swimming pool (mid-May - Oct. depending on weather). Volleyball. Table tennis. Games room. Electronic games. Torches necessary. Riding. Bicycle hire. Only gas barbecues are permitted. Off site: VTT with guide. Fishing 5 km. Golf 25 km. The site is close to the border and its associated shopping opportunities.

Open

1 February - 30 November.

At a glance

Welcome & Ambience	✓✓✓✓✓	Location	✓✓✓✓
Quality of Pitches	✓✓✓✓	Range of Facilities	✓✓✓✓

Directions

Le Boulou is about 26 km. from the eastern side of the Spanish border. Travel south from Perpignan on the A9/E15 or N9 to Le Boulou (approx. 30 km). Site is well signed from town and is on the northern outskirts, approached through a light commercial area of town. Follow road uphill through countryside for about 2 km. If crossing the Spanish border at Le Perthus expect long delays as the road travels through the extremely busy and narrow main street.

Charges 2004

Per person	€ 4,00 - € 4,50
child (under 10 yrs)	€ 2,50 - € 2,60
pitch	€ 4,50 - € 5,70
electricity (5/10A)	€ 3,00 - € 4,00

Less 10% for 7 days, 20% for 14 days, in low season.

Reservations

Contact site. Tel: 04 68 83 25 46.
E-mail: info@camping-mas-llinas.com

FR66130 Hotel de Plein Air L'Eau Vive

Chemin de St Saturnin, 66820 Vernet-les-Bains (Pyrénées-Orientales)

Enjoying dramatic views of the towering Pic du Canigou (3,000 m.), this small site is 1.5 km. from the centre of the spa town of Vernet-les-Bains in the Pyrénées. It is approached via a twisting road through a residential area. The 77 tourist pitches, all with electricity (4/10A) and 45 with water and drain, are on a slight slope, part hedged and some terraced, with a separate tent field. Most pitches have some shade. Although there is no swimming pool as such, the site has a very attractive, more or less natural pool (created by pumping and circulating running water from the nearby stream) that even provides a small beach with water slide (high season only). There is a central floating safety line across the pool but parents should keep an eye on children around the pool as there is no supervision or safety fence. Access to the bubbling mountain stream is now possible. Well situated for touring this area of the Pyrénées and with very comfortable amenities, this small site quickly becomes fully booked in season and advance reservation is essential. English is spoken by the welcoming Dutch owners, Ria and Gertjan, who will arrange walks, canoe and rafting trips or even 4x4 excursions up Mont Canigou.

Facilities

First class toilet facilities in two modern blocks include washbasins in cabins, dishwashing under cover and facilities for disabled people. Washing machine in each block. Bread can be ordered in main season. Bar/reception with pool table, amusement machine, library, etc. Attractive open air (but under cover) snack bar with simple food and takeaway (1/6-30/9). A 'meal of the day' can be ordered in advance (good value) Play area. Natural pool for children. Sports field. Basketball. Bicycle hire. Off site: Fishing 200 m. Swimming pool and thermal centre in village 1 km. The nearby medieval, walled town of Ville Franche de Conflent, the Grottes des Canalettes and Fort Libena with its many steps are well worth visiting. Organised rafting, canoeing, and hydrospeed trips.

Open

All year except 12 Nov - 15 Dec.

At a glance

Welcome & Ambience	✓✓✓✓✓	Location	✓✓✓✓✓
Quality of Pitches	✓✓✓✓	Range of Facilities	✓✓✓✓

Directions

Following the N116 to Andorra, 6 km. after Prades, take turning at Villefranche de Conflent for Vernet-les-Bains. Continue up hill for 5 km. and keep right avoiding town centre. Turn right over bridge towards Sahorre. Immediately, at one end of small block of shops, turn right into Ave de Saturnin and follow for about 1 km. past houses to more open area and site is signed.

Charges 2004

Per unit incl. up to 3 persons	€ 11,00 - € 19,00
incl. electricity	€ 13,00 - € 22,00
extra person (over 4 yrs)	€ 1,50 - € 2,50
animal	€ 2,50

Camping Cheques accepted.
Discounts for weekly stays.
Credit cards accepted 15/6-15/9 only.

Reservations

Made with deposit (20%), € 15 fee (high season only) and cancellation insurance (details from site).
Tel: 04 68 05 54 14. E-mail: leauv@club-internet.fr

FR66230 Camping Caravaning Le Romarin

Route de Sorède, Chemin des Vignes, 66702 Argelès-sur-Mer (Pyrénées-Orientales)

In an area dominated by 'all-singing, all-dancing' holiday sites, we were pleased to discover almost by accident this charming little gem of a site tucked away some two kilometres behind the busy resort of Argelès. Essentially a site for families with younger children, or for adults seeking peace and quiet, it provides some 110 good sized touring pitches, all with electricity (6-10A) set among pine, eucalyptus, oak and mimosas. Ideal for exploring this area, especially the Albères range of Pyreneen mountains and the ancient city of Perpignan, it is nevertheless within easy reach of shops, supermarket (two kilometres) and all the attractions of Argelès, both village and Plage.

Facilities

One good large toilet block (half traditional style, half modern) provides a mix of British and Turkish WCs, showers, washbasins in cabins, dishwashing and laundry sinks and washing machine. Snack bar (mid June - end Sept). Swimming pool (mid June - mid Sept). Play area. Table tennis. Some traditional (local) family entertainment in high season. Off site: Riding and bicycle hire 2 km. Fishing 4 km. Golf 8 km.

Open

15 May - 30 September.

At a glance

Welcome & Ambience	✓✓✓✓	Location	✓✓✓✓
Quality of Pitches	✓✓✓✓	Range of Facilities	✓✓✓✓

Directions

From autoroute A9 take exit 42 (Perpignan Sud) on N114 towards Argelès for 25 km. to exit 11a. At roundabout follow directions to St Andre for 300 m. Watch carefully for left turn (with site sign), almost back on youself. Road is narrowish and unnumber. After aprrox 2km at 'T' junction turn left on to D11. After short distance take third left (site signed) and follow lane to site.

Charges 2005

extra person	€ 3,00 - € 4,00
child (2-5 yrs)	free - € 2,00
electricity	€ 2,00 - € 3,50
dog	€ 2,00 - € 3,00

Reservations

Made with 25% deposit. Tel: 04 68 81 02 63.
E-mail: camping.romarin@libertysurf.fr

Bathed in sunshine from early spring to late autumn, surrounded by stunning scenery, cosmopolitan towns and superb sandy beaches, no wonder this is one of France's most sought-after destinations.

This section covers the eastern coastal region of the Mediterranean. We include two départements from the official region of Provence and the region of Côte d'Azur:
13 Bouches-du-Rhône, 83 Var,
06 Alpes-Maritime

The glittering Côte d'Azur, perhaps better known as the French Riviera, is a beautiful stretch of coast studded with sophisticated towns such as the famous Monte Carlo, Nice, and Cannes, not forgetting the other famous and arguably the most glamorous resort of St Tropez. With its vast expanses of golden sandy beaches and long lazy hours of sunshine, this is a paradise for sun worshippers and beach enthusiasts. It's a spectacular coast of rugged coves, sweeping beaches and warm seas.

The quaint harbours and fishing villages have become chic destinations, now full of pleasure yachts, harbour-side cafes and crowded summertime beaches. Further up in the hills are quieter tiny medieval villages with winding streets and white-walled houses with terracotta roofs, which have attracted artists and visitors for many years. In St Paul-de-Vence visitors can browse through shops and galleries set on narrow winding cobblestone streets and inland Grasse is the perfume capital of the world, surrounded by the provencal lavender fields and shady olive groves which pervade the air with a magical scent at certain times of the year.

Cuisine of the region

Aigo Bouido: garlic and sage soup

Bouillabaisse: fish soup

Rouille: an orange coloured sauce with peppers, garlic and saffron

Bourride: a creamy fish soup

Pissaladière: Provençal bread dough with onions, anchovies and olives

Pistou (Soupe au): vegetable soup bound with *pommade*

Pommade: a thick paste of garlic, basil, cheese and olive oil

Ratatouille: aubergines, courgettes, onions, garlic, *red peppers and tomatoes in olive oil*

Salade Niçoise: tomatoes, beans, potatoes, black olives, anchovy, lettuce, olive oil and tuna fish

Places of interest

Aix-en-Provence: old town with 17th-18th century character, Paul Cézanne and Tapestry museums

Cannes: popular for conventions and festivals, Cannes Film Festival, la Croisette, old city

Monte Carlo: main city of Monaco, casinos, gardens, Napoleon Museum. motorsport circuit

Alan Rogers tip

THE PHOENIX FLORAL PARK IN NICE, HAS BOTANICAL GARDENS, A BIRD AND INSECT ZOO PLUS A THEME PARK - A GREAT DAY OUT FOR THE WHOLE FAMILY

FR06030 Camping Caravaning Domaine de la Bergerie

Route de la Sine, 06140 Vence (Alpes-Maritimes)

La Bergerie is a quiet, family owned site, situated in the hills about three kilometres from Vence and ten kilometres from the sea at Cagnes-sur-Mer. This extensive, lightly wooded site has been left very natural and is in a secluded position about 300 m. above sea level. Because of the trees most of the pitches are shaded and all are of a good size. It is a large site but because it is so extensive it does not give that impression. There are 450 pitches, 300 with electricity (2/5A) and 65 also with water and drainage. Because of the nature of this site, some pitches are a little distance from the toilet blocks. There are no organised activities and definitely no groups allowed.

Facilities

Both toilet blocks have been refurbished and include washbasins in cabins and excellent provision for disabled people (pitches near the block are reserved for disabled people). Very good shop, small bar/restaurant with takeaway (all 1/5-30/9). Large swimming pool, paddling pool and spacious sunbathing area (5/6-30/9). Playground. Bicycle hire. Table tennis, tennis courts and 10 shaded boules pitches with competitions in season. Barbecues are not permitted. Off site: Riding 6 km. Fishing 10 km. Golf 12 km. Hourly bus service (excl. Sundays) to Vence.

Open

25 March - 15 October.

At a glance

Welcome & Ambience	✓✓✓✓	Location	✓✓✓✓
Quality of Pitches	✓✓✓	Range of Facilities	✓✓✓✓

Directions

From A8 exit 47 take Cagnes-sur-Mer road towards Vence. Site is west of Vence; follow 'toutes directions' signs around the town to join the D2210 (Grasse). Follow this to roundabout (2 km), turn left and follow site signs for 1 km. Site is on right in light woodland.

Charges 2004

Per unit incl. 2 persons	€ 13,50 - € 19,00
with electricity (2A)	€ 17,23 - € 23,00
water, drainage, electricity (5A)	€ 22,00 - € 29,00
extra person	€ 4,60

Camping Cheques accepted.
Less 10-15% for longer stays.

Reservations

Necessary only in July/Aug. for the special pitches and made with 25% deposit and € 12.96 fee.
Tel: 04 93 58 09 36.

FR06070 Domaine Naturiste Club Origan

06260 Puget-Theniers (Alpes-Maritimes)

Origan is a naturist site set in the mountains behind Nice. Despite its rather spectacular location, it is easily accessible from the coast and you only discover that you are at a height of 500 m. when you arrive! The access road is single track and winding with a few passing places for about a mile, so arrival is not recommended until late afternoon. The terrain within the the site is fairly wild and the roads distinctly stony. The site is not suitable for caravans longer than 6 metres due to the steep slopes, although the site will assist with a 4x4 vehicle. The scenery is impressive and footpaths around the site offer good, if fairly strenuous, walks. The 100 touring pitches, in three different areas are of irregular size and shape and all have views. Electricity is possible on most pitches (by long cable). Member 'France 4 Naturisme'

Facilities

Sanitary facilities, exceptionally clean when we visited, are of a standard and type associated with most good naturist sites - mainly British type WCs, mostly open plan hot showers and ample washbasins with hot and cold water. Laundry facilities. Shop (1/5-21/8). Bar/restaurant (all season). Takeaway. Heated pools, one for children (1/5-31/8). Jacuzzi and sauna. Disco in cellars. Tennis. Fishing. Bicycle hire. Organised activities (high season). Only gas or electric barbecues are permitted. Torches advised. Off site: Puget-Theniers offers choice of bars, cafés, shops.

At a glance

Welcome & Ambience	✓✓✓✓	Location	✓✓✓✓
Quality of Pitches	✓✓✓✓	Range of Facilities	✓✓✓✓

Directions

Heading west on the N202, just past the town of Puget-Theniers, turn right at camp sign at level crossing; site is 1.5 km.

Charges 2004

Per person	€ 5,00 - € 9,00
pitch	€ 14,00 - € 22,00
electricity (5/6A)	€ 4,00

Camping Cheques accepted.

Reservations

Made with 25% deposit and fee (€ 30) - contact site.
Tel: 04 93 05 06 00. E-mail: info@club-origan.com

Open

12 April - 30 September.

FR06100 Camping Les Pinèdes

Route du Pont de Pierre, 06480 La Colle-sur-Loup (Alpes-Maritimes)

Les Pinèdes is seven kilometres inland from the busy coast, located at the centre of all the attractions of the Côte d'Azur, yet far enough away to be peaceful retreat at the end of a busy day sightseeing. In a terraced situation on a wooded hillside where olives and vines used to grow the site, has been in the hands of the welcoming Dugauguez family for the past 30 years. All the level pitches have electricity (3-10A), most also with water and are separated by low bushes. Due to the nature of the terrain there are no facilities for wheelchair users. The owners are keen to attract wildlife to the site and there are many varieties of birds and the odd fox to be seen. Two donkeys are an added attraction. For three weeks from the end of May into June, the evenings are alive with fireflies lighting up the site. The restaurant at the site entrance has an excellent reputation. The owner is very interested in all the local art galleries and will advise on where all the famous painters have paintings hung. There are many typical Provencal villages in close proximity not to mention the towns of Grasse, Menton, Monaco and Antibes, and all are well worth a visit - the family will be only too pleased to give advice. A 'Sites et Paysages' member.

Facilities

Two clean and well maintained toilet blocks have mainly British and a few Turkish style toilets and large shower cubicles. One block has been refurbished, the other is due to be soon. All the usual facilities for dishwashing and laundry etc and a baby room. Shop and bakery. Bar, restaurant and takeaway. Swimming pool. Two small play areas. Field for volleyball, basketball, football and archery. Boule pitch. Entertainment is organised for young and old in July/Aug. Weekly walks in the surrounding hills June - September (with light breakfast carried by the donkeys). Off site: Fishing in Loup river (50 m). Village 1 km with tennis court, riding school, leisure park with keep fit course and antiques quarter.

At a glance

Welcome & Ambience	✓✓✓✓✓	Location	✓✓✓✓✓
Quality of Pitches	✓✓✓✓✓	Range of Facilities	✓✓✓✓✓

Directions

From A8 take D2 towards Vence. At Colle sur Loup roundabout take D6 signed Grasse, site on right in approx. 3 km. at large sign after the restaurant entrance.

Charges 2004

Per tent incl. 2 persons	€ 13,50 - € 17,50
caravan or motorcaravan	€ 14,80 - € 22,50
extra person	€ 3,70 - € 4,60
child (under 5 yrs)	€ 1,90 - € 2,90
dog	€ 1,50 - € 2,00
electricity (3-10A)	€ 2,90 - € 4,20

Reservations

Necessary for July/Aug. and made with 25% deposit and fee (€ 18.29). Tel: 04 93 32 98 94.
E-mail: camplespinedes06@aol.com

Open

15 March - 1 October.

FR06050 Camping La Vieille Ferme

296 boulevard des Groules, 06270 Villeneuve-Loubet-Plage (Alpes-Maritimes)

Open all year, in a popular resort area, La Vieille Ferme is a family owned site with good facilities. It provides 131 level gravel-based pitches, 106 with electricity, water and waste water connections and the majority separated by hedges. Some are only small, simple pitches for little tents. There is also a fully serviced pitch on tarmac for motorhomes. There are special winter rates for long stays with quite a few long stay units on site. The entrance to the site is very colourful with well tended flower beds. English is spoken at reception and the whole place has a very friendly feel to it. A one kilometre walk beside the road towards Antibes brings you to the railway station, giving access to all the towns along the coast and to the beach.

Facilities

Three modern, well kept toilet blocks (two heated in winter) provide washbasins all in cabins, children's toilets, baby room and two units for disabled people. Motorcaravan service point. Dishwashing and laundry sinks. Three washing machines and dryer. Shop (Easter - Sept). Drinks, sweets and ices machine in the TV room for all year use. Gas, bread and milk to order when shop closed. Refrigerator hire. Swimming pool (20 x 10 m.) and children's pool, heated and covered for winter use (closed mid Nov-mid Dec) with jacuzzi. Internet point. Table tennis, basketball and boule pitch. Games and competitions organised in July/Aug. Off site: Fishing 1 km, golf 2 km.

Open

All year.

At a glance

Welcome & Ambience	✓✓✓✓✓	Location	✓✓✓✓
Quality of Pitches	✓✓✓✓	Range of Facilities	✓✓✓✓✓

Directions

From west take Antibes exit from Esterel autoroute and turn left towards Nice when joining the N7 outside Antibes. After 3.5 km. on N7 turn left for site. From east take N7 towards Antibes and turn right after Villeneuve Loubet Plage. The turning off the N7, though signed, is not easy to see particularly at busy times but, coming from Antibes, it is on the left, more or less between the Marine Land and the Parc de Vaugrenier. Site is 150 m. on right. Avoid N98 Route du Bord de Mer. Site has prepared its own small, yellow site signs.

Charges 2004

Per tent incl. 2 persons and car	€ 14,00 - € 23,00
caravan incl. 2 persons and car	€ 17,00 - € 27,00
extra person	€ 3,50 - € 4,50
child (under 5 yrs)	€ 2,30 - € 3,00
electricity 2-10A	€ 2,30 - € 5,00

Reservations

Advised over a long season and made with 25% deposit and € 20 fee; Sat.-Sat. only in July/Aug. and at Easter. Tel: 04 93 33 41 44
E-mail: vieilleferme@bigfoot.com

FR06080 Camping Caravaning Les Cigales

Mobile homes page 411

505 ave. de la Mer, 06210 Mandelieu-la-Napoule (Alpes-Maritimes)

It is hard to imagine that such a quiet, peaceful site could be in the middle of such a busy town and so near to Cannes - we were delighted with it. The entrance (easily missed) with reception and parking has large electronic gates that ensure that the site is very secure. There are only 115 pitches (40 used for mobile homes) so this is really quite a small, personal site. There are three pitch sizes, from small ones for tents to pitches for larger units. All are level with much needed shade in summer, although the sun will get through in winter when it is needed, and all have electricity (6A), some also with water and waste water. The site is alongside the Canal de Siagne and for a fee, small boats can be launched at La Napoule, then moored outside the campsite's side gate. Les Cigales is open all year so it is useful for the Monte Carlo Rally, the Cannes Film Festival and the Mimosa Festival, all held out of the main season.

Facilities

Two well appointed unisex toilet blocks are kept very clean, one heated for the winter months. Washbasins in cabins and facilities for babies and disabled visitors. Dishwashing and laundry sinks. Washing machine. Motorcaravan service point. Restaurant at entrance also serves takeaways (April - 30 Sept). Swimming pool, quite new with large sunbathing area (March - Oct, heated mid-March - mid-Oct). Small play area. Table tennis. Fishing possible in the canal (but not many fish!). Off site: Beach 800 m. The town is an easy walk. Two golf courses within 1 km. Railway station 1 km. for trains to Cannes, Nice, Antibes and Monte Carlo. Centre commercial (supermarket and 40 shops) 2 km.

At a glance

Welcome & Ambience	✓✓✓✓✓	Location	✓✓✓✓✓
Quality of Pitches	✓✓✓✓✓	Range of Facilities	✓✓✓✓

Directions

From A8 take exit 40 and bear right. Remain in right hand lane and continue right signed Plages-Ports and Creche-Campings. New supermarket is on the right. Continue under motorway to T-junction. Turn left and site is 60 m. on left opposite Chinese restaurant.

Charges 2004

Per person	€ 5,00
child (under 5 yrs)	€ 2,50
pitch	€ 13,50 - € 27,00

Reservations

Made with deposit (€ 77). Tel: 04 93 49 23 53.
E-mail: campingcigales@wanadoo.fr

Open

All year.

FR06010 Camping Domaine Sainte Madeleine

Route de Moulinet, 06380 Sospel (Alpes-Maritimes)

Sainte Madeleine is an attractive, peaceful site in spectacular mountain scenery. It is about 28 kilometres inland from Menton, and very near the Italian border. The approach to this site is not for the faint-hearted although having said that, when we visited in late July, the site was very busy with touring caravans so it cannot be too bad. The site itself makes the effort worthwhile - situated on a terraced hillside with mountain views towards Italy. On a fairly steep hillside, manoeuvring within the site presents no problem and the pitches are on level, well drained grass. The lower ones have shade but those higher up on the hill have none. There are way-marked walks for serious walkers in the surrounding hills.

Facilities

The single toilet block is good, including washbasins in cabins and showers on payment. Hot water (often only warm) for dishwashing and laundry sinks drawn from single tap. Washing machines. Motorcaravan services. Gas supplies. Bread can be ordered. Swimming pool (140 sq.m. and heated in spring and autumn). Off site: Sospel 4 km. Tennis, riding and mountain biking. Fishing 1 km.

Open

1 April - 30 September.

At a glance

Welcome & Ambience	✓✓✓✓	Location	✓✓✓✓
Quality of Pitches	✓✓✓	Range of Facilities	✓✓✓

Directions

Site is on D2566, 4 km. north of Sospel. The D2566 can be reached from either the A8 autoroute via Menton exit, or from the N7 at Menton.

Charges 2004

Per unit incl. 2 adults	€ 17,00
extra person	€ 2,10 - € 3,70
electricity (10A)	€ 2,90

Less 15% outside July/Aug. No credit cards.

Reservations

Necessary for July/Aug. and made with € 50 deposit.
Tel: 04 93 04 10 48.
E-mail: camp@camping-sainte-madeleine.com

TRAVEL SERVICE SITE
TO BOOK CALL 0870 405 4055 OR www.alanrogersdirect.com

FR06120 Camping Green Park

Mobile homes page 411

159, Vallon des Vaux, 06800 Cagnes-sur-Mer (Alpes-Maritimes)

Green Park has had a very extensive renewal programme over the past 18 months with many of the facilities having been rebuilt to a high standard of which the owning family are justifiably proud. Situated just over 4 km from the beaches at Cagnes-sur-Mer, Green Park is at the centre of the Cote d'Azur. There are two parts to Green Park, one newly constructed and very active site to keep every member of the family occupied for most of the day and evening, with club activites for children, teenagers and even adults, while on the other side of the apporach road there is a quieter and more traditional site, with limited facilities. Activities and facilities are interchangeable. There are 78 touring pitches mostly on the left or west side of the site, mainly on grass, all with electricity of which 24 are the 'Grand Comfort' style, plus 67 mobile homes and chalets. The site has two swimming pools (one on each side of the road-this road is not busy and goes 'nowhere' further up the valley). Green Park is situated in an area which benefits from a 'micro climate'. Hot during the day but pleasantly cooler at night.

Facilities

All the toilets are modern and mostly British, with facilities for children and disabled visitors (the disabled facilities are superb). Showers and washbasins are modern and kept very clean. Dishwashing and laundry sinks and three washing machines. Bar, restaurant and takeaway. Two swimming pools - one heated. Internet point. Games room. Green Park is secure - with an electronic barrier (€ 5 card deposit) and a gate keeper on duty all night. Off site: Golf 12 km. Riding 10 km.

Open

29 March - 17 October.

At a glance

Welcome & Ambience	✓✓✓✓✓	Location	✓✓✓✓
Quality of Pitches	✓✓✓✓	Range of Facilities	✓✓✓✓✓

Directions

Coming from Aix on the A8, take exit 47 onto the N7 towards Nice. Go straight on at traffic lights by the racecourse for 2 km. then turn left towards Val Fleuri on Av. du Val Fleuri. Go over roundabouts onto Chemin Vallon des Vaux to site on right in 2 km. From Nice on N98 coast road, turn right at Le Port du Cros de Cagnes and follow camping signs. It is important to avoid the town centre.

Charges 2004

Per unit incl. 2 persons	€ 12,00 - € 30,60
extra person	€ 3,50 - € 3,90
child (2-7 yrs)	free - € 2,80
electricity	€ 3,60 - € 4,80
dog	€ 2,00 - € 2,50

Camping Cheques accepted.

Reservations

Contact site. Tel: 04 93 07 09 96.
E-mail: info@greenpark.fr

FR06140 Ranch Camping

06110 Le Cannet (Alpes-Maritimes)

Recommended by our agent, we hope to include a full report on this wooded Riviera campsite in a future inspection programme. Le Ranch is just 2 km. from the beaches and the glistening resort of Cannes. The site offers 130 shady pitches of varying sizes, priced according to size, and an attractive range of amenities. Mobile homes for rent.

Facilities

Sanitary building. Swimming pool (covered in low season). Playground. Small shop. Table tennis. Games room.
Off site: Tennis 200 m. Regular bus service to Cannes, Cannes centre 2 km, nearest beach 2 km.

Open

1 April - 30 October.

Directions

Take the Le Cannet exit from the A8 autoroute, then follow signs to La Bocca on the D809 , to L'Aubarede, from where the site is clearly signposted.

Charges year

Per unit incl. 1 person	€ 10,00 - € 16,00
extra person	€ 5,00
child (5-10 yrs)	€ 2,00
electricity (6A)	€ 3,00

Reservations

Contact site; minimum 7 nights. Tel: 04 93 46 00 11.

FR13010 Camping Municipal Les Romarins

13520 Maussane (Bouches du Rhône)

A well kept, neat municipal site, Les Romarins has been in the guide for several years and remains popular with readers. Tarmac access roads lead to 145 good sized grassy pitches separated by hedges and bushes, all with electrical connections (4A). The municipal swimming pool (with discounts) is near and shops and restaurants are in the pleasant little town. Les Baux and St Remy-de-Provence are tourist attractions not to be missed, especially St Remy's Roman ruins. Les Romarins is popular and becomes very busy from 1 July - late August.

Facilities

There are three good toilet blocks, especially the newly refurbished one which provides British style toilets, adjustable, roomy showers and washbasins in cubicles. Baby room, washing machine, laundry and dishwashing sinks and facilities for disabled visitors. The two older blocks have some Turkish style WCs and are of an older design, but still kept very clean and well maintained. Children's play area. Free tennis courts. Pleasant reading room for cooler days.
Off site: Bicycle hire or golf 1 km. Fishing or riding 3 km.

At a glance

Welcome & Ambience	✓✓✓✓	Location	✓✓✓
Quality of Pitches	✓✓✓✓	Range of Facilities	✓✓✓

Directions

Site is within the little town of Maussane on the eastern edge.

Charges 2004

Per unit incl. 1 or 2 adults + 1 child	€ 14,00
extra person	€ 3,20
child	€ 1,80
dog	€ 2,10
electricity	€ 2,50 - € 3,20

Less 10-20% for longer stays.

Reservations

Made for any length with fee. Tel: 04 90 54 33 60.

Open

15 March - 15 October.

FR06090 Camping Caravaning Les Gorges du Loup

965 chemin des Vergers, 06620 Le Bar sur Loup (Alpes-Maritimes)

In the hills above Grasse, Les Gorges du Loup is situated on a steep hillside. Some pitches are only suitable for tents and the site roads are quite steep. The one kilometre lane which leads to the site is narrow but there are many passing places. The 70 pitches are on level terrace areas, all with electricity, and many have quite stupendous views. A quiet family site, there is no organised entertainment. Bar-de-Loup with its few shops and restaurants is only a 500 m. walk. Grasse (9 km.) is surrounded by fields of lavender, mimosa and jasmine and has been famous for the manufacture of perfume since the 16th century. The Musée International de la Perfume has a garden of fragrant plants and the cathedral in the old town has three paintings by Reubens. The very friendly and enthusiastic owners will site your caravan with their 4x4 free of charge if required. They also speak a little English.

Facilities

Two tiled toilet blocks are kept very clean and include washbasins mostly in cubicles. More than half the WCs are British style. Dishwashing and laundry sinks have a single hot tap to draw from. Washing machine and iron. Reception has small shop with bread daily. Small bar/restaurant and takeaway (July/Aug). Swimming pool (no Bermuda style shorts), small slide and diving board, but no pool for small children. Boules pitches, table tennis, basketball, volleyball and skittles. TV room with tables and chairs for board games, plus a library. Children's climbing frame and slide. Charcoal barbecues are not allowed. Chalets and mobile homes for hire.

Open

1 April - 30 September.

At a glance

Welcome & Ambience	✓✓✓✓✓	Location	✓✓✓✓✓
Quality of Pitches	✓✓✓✓	Range of Facilities	✓✓✓✓

Directions

From Grasse take D2085 Nice road. Take D3 briefly and then at Châteauneuf Pré du Lac take D2210 to Pont-de-Loup and Vence. Site is signed on right. Pass village of Bar-sur-Loup on left and then, after a very tight right turn, take 0.75 km. narrow access road (a few passing places). From direction of Vence, site is well signed and straightforward.

Charges 2004

Per unit incl. 2 persons	€ 13,50 - € 23,70
extra person	€ 3,80
child (under 5 yrs)	€ 3,10
dog	€ 2,00
electricity (4/10A)	€ 2,50 - € 4,00

No credit cards.

Reservations

Advised in high season. Tel: 04 93 42 45 06.
E-mail: info@lesgorgesduloup.com

FR83600 Holiday Green – Camping Caravaning

Route de Bagnols, 83600 Fréjus (Var)

Holiday Green is seven kilometres inland from the busy resort of Fréjus. It is a large, modern campsite with a fantastic view of the red massif of Esterelle – very impressive as you arrive. The site has been developed on a hillside and by reception at the top of hill is a large Californian style heated swimming pool and a wide range of other facilities. This is where everything happens and it is said there are activities and entertainment from morning until closing. The rest of the site is terraced into the hillside and almost completely hidden in the 15 hectares of pine woods which absorbs about 500 large touring pitches and some 200 mobile homes. Sloping in parts, there is plenty of shade and electricity connections (6A) available. The site provides a free daily bus (16/6-14/9) to go to the beach and to Aquatica, the biggest aqua park in the region with Europe's largest wave pool (open 7/6-14/9).

Facilities

Modern toilet facilities include good hot showers. Dishwashing and laundry sinks. Laundry. Shopping centre. Bar, restaurant and fast food. Sound proof disco. Swimming pool. Three tennis courts. Archery. Petanque. All facilities open all season. Excursions are organised on foot, on horse-back and on mountain bikes (to hire) offering the chance to explore the countryside. Entertainment programme of dances, concerts and festivals. Playground. Children's club (July/Aug). Charcoal barbecues are not permitted.
Off site: Beach 7 km. Golf 8 km.

At a glance

Welcome & Ambience	✓✓✓✓	Location	✓✓✓✓
Quality of Pitches	✓✓✓✓	Range of Facilities	✓✓✓✓✓

Directions

From A8 autoroute exit 38 follow signs for Bagnols-en-Forêt about 2 km. back over the autoroute, and the site is clearly signed at roundabout.

Charges 2004

Per unit incl. 2 persons	€ 21,00 - € 38,00
extra person	€ 6,00 - € 9,00
child (under 6 yrs)	€ 4,00 - € 6,00
animal	€ 2,00 - € 3,00

Reservations

Advanced booking necessary for high season.
Tel: 04 94 19 88 30. E-mail: info@holiday-green.com

Open

30 March - 30 September.

FR13050 Camping Mas de Nicolas

Avenue Plaisance du Touch, 13210 Saint Rémy-de-Provence (Bouches du Rhône)

Saint Rémy de Provence is a very popular town and this reflects on Mas de Nicolas, as this too is very popular and always reasonably busy. The site has a very spacious feel to it, due mainly to the central area of gently sloping grass, dotted with shrubs, that is kept clear of pitches and used for leisure and sunbathing. The 140 pitches are separated by hedges, 120 with electricity, water and drainage, and access roads are wide. Some pitches are an irregular shape and some are sloping, but many have views and they are mostly organised into groups of two and four.

Facilities

Two toilet blocks have been refurbished to give excellent facilities including British style toilets, washbasins in cabins, a baby bathroom and even a dog shower. The other blocks are of an older design with mainly Turkish style WCs. Washing machines and drying lines. Swimming pool (15/5-15/9). Off site: Adjacent municipal gym, tennis and volley-ball. Bicycle hire or riding 1 km. Fishing 2 km. Golf 15 km.

Open

1 March - 31 October.

At a glance

Welcome & Ambience	✓✓✓✓	Location	✓✓✓✓
Quality of Pitches	✓✓✓✓	Range of Facilities	✓✓✓✓

Directions

St Rémy de Provence is located where the D571 from Avignon connects with the D99 Tarascon - Cavaillon road. Site is signed from the village centre on the north side. Leave autoroute A7 at Cavaillon or Avignon-Sud.

Charges 2005

Per unit incl. 2 persons	€ 13,50 - € 15,10
extra adult	€ 4,30 - € 4,60
electricity (6A)	€ 3,00

Reservations

Necessary for main season and made with € 16.77 fee (non returnable). Tel: 04 90 92 27 05.
E-mail: camping-masdenicolas@nerim.fr

FR83230 Camping Domaine du Colombier

Mobile homes ▶ page 415

Route de Bagnols-en-Forêt, 83600 Fréjus (Var)

Domaine du Colombier is a busy site alongside a main road, so a few of the pitches will have some road noise. The majority however are down a hillside and pine trees help to deaden the noise. The pitches (326 for touring units out of 470) vary in size from smallish ones to quite large ones, of which 40 are fully serviced. The hillside is terraced, with all pitches level and with electricity. The pool area with palm trees, a tiled surround and free sunbeds is in a sunny location. There are also three slides and water polo nets for competitions. A disco is underground to deaden the noise. Like the cabarets and competitions all these facilities operate in high season. This is a family site and no groups are accepted. The only down-side is that the swimming pool is at the bottom of the site, giving a long pull back up to the majority of pitches, although there is now a new snack bar beside the pool. Much new planting of attractive trees and shrubs has taken place after the fires of 2003.

Facilities

Well maintained and positioned toilet blocks are fully equipped, including baby rooms. Three blocks have en-suite units for people in wheelchairs. Two can be heated on cooler days. Well equipped laundry. Well stocked shop. Bar/restaurant with takeaway. Snack bar (from 1/6). Disco. Large heated swimming pool (30 x 20 m) and paddling pool (all season). Communal barbecue areas for July/Aug. Internet terminal. Two play areas of excellent quality on safety bases. Games room, mini club room. Half court tennis, volleyball, basketball and boule. Tourist office with bookings to major attractions possible. Only gas or electric barbecues are permitted. Off site: Bus passes the gate.

At a glance

Welcome & Ambience	✓✓✓✓	Location	✓✓✓✓
Quality of Pitches	✓✓✓✓	Range of Facilities	✓✓✓✓✓

Directions

From A8 autoroute take 38 and follow D4 for Frejus. Site is on left, well signed.

Charges 2005

Per unit incl. 2 or 3 persons	€ 19,00 - € 43,00
extra person	€ 6,00 - € 7,50
child (under 10 yrs)	€ 4,00 - € 5,50

Camping Cheques accepted.
Special low season offers.

Reservations

Made with 25% deposit plus booking fee (€ 25).
Tel: 04 94 51 56 01.
E-mail: info@domaine-du-colombier.com

Open

19 March - 1 October.

FR83020 Camping Caravaning Esterel

Mobile homes page 412

Avenue des Golf, 83700 St Raphaël (Var)

For caravans only, Esterel is a quality site east of St Raphaël, set among the hills at the back of Agay. Developed by the Laroche family over the last 27 years, the site has an attractive quiet situation with good views of the Esterel mountains. The site is 3.5 km. from the sandy beach at Agay where parking is perhaps a little easier than at most places on this coast. In addition to a section for permanent caravans, it has some 250 pitches for tourists, on which caravans of any type are taken but not tents. Pitches are on shallow terraces, attractively landscaped with good shade and a variety of flowering plants, giving a feeling of spaciousness. Each pitch has an electricity connection and tap, and 18 special ones have their own individual en-suite washroom adjoining. Some maxi pitches from 110 to 160 sq.m. are now available. A pleasant courtyard area contains the shop and bar, with a terrace overlooking the attractively landscaped (floodlit at night) pool complex, which has recently been extended. Wild boar come to the perimeter fence each evening to be fed by visitors. This is a very good site, well run and organised in a deservedly popular area. A member of 'Les Castels' group.

Facilities

Toilet facilities in three blocks have been refurbished and are excellent. They can be heated and include washbasins mostly in cabins. Individual toilet units on 18 pitches. Facilities for disabled people. Laundry room. Motorcaravan service point. Shop. Takeaway. Bar/restaurant. Five circular swimming pools (two heated), one large for adults, one smaller for children and three arranged as a waterfall (1/4-30/9). Disco. Archery, volleyball, minigolf, two tennis courts, pony rides, petanque and squash court. Playground. Bicycle hire. Events and entertainment are organised in season. Barbecues of any type are forbidden. A new nursery and restaurant have been built. Off site: Good golf courses very close. Trekking by foot, bicycle or by pony in the surrounding natural environment of L'Esterel forest park. Beach 3 km.

Open

19 March - 1 October.

At a glance

Welcome & Ambience	✓✓✓✓	Location	✓✓✓✓✓
Quality of Pitches	✓✓✓✓	Range of Facilities	✓✓✓✓✓

Directions

You can approach from St Raphaël via Valescure but easiest way is to turn off the coast road at Agay where there are good signs. From Fréjus exit from autoroute A8, follow signs for Valescure throughout, then for Agay, and site is on left. (Reader's comment: If in doubt, follow golf complex signs, or Leclerc). The road from Agay is the easiest to follow.

Charges 2004

Per unit incl. 2 persons,	
standard pitch	€ 22,00 - € 40,00
de-luxe pitch	€ 30,00 - € 52,00
extra person	€ 8,00
child (1-7 yrs)	€ 6,00
animal	€ 2,00

Reservations

Necessary for high season and made for min. 1 week with deposit (€ 80) and fee (€ 30). CD brochure available from site. Tel: 04 94 82 03 28. E-mail: contact@esterel-caravaning.fr

FR83250 Sunêlia Douce Quiétude

Mobile homes page 415

3435 boulevard Jacques Baudino, 83700 St Raphaël (Var)

Douce Quiétude is only seven kilometres from the beaches at Saint Raphaël and Agay but is quietly situated at the foot of the Estérel massif. There are 400 pitches, but only 70 of these are for touring units (around half are used for mobile homes) set in pleasant pine woodland or shaded, green areas. The pitches are of a comfortable size, separated by bushes and trees with electricity (6A), water, drainage and telephone/TV points provided. This mature site offers a wide range of services and facilities complete with a pool complex. It can be busy in the main season yet is relaxed and spacious. Security is good with the wearing of identity bracelets mandatory throughout your stay.

TRAVEL SERVICE SITE

TO BOOK CALL 0870 405 4055 OR www.alanrogersdirect.com

Facilities

Fully equipped modern toilet blocks have changing facilities for babies and provision for disabled visitors. Launderette. Bar and restaurant with takeaway and pizzeria (1/6-3/9). Shop. Three outdoor swimming pools (two heated), water slide and jacuzzi. Play area. Children's club and activities for teenagers (all July/Aug). Sports area for volleyball, basketball and petanque. Games room (July/Aug). Tennis. Table tennis and billards. Minigolf. Archery. Fitness centre and sauna (July/Aug). Evening entertainment with shows, karaoke and discos. Mountain bike hire. Only gas barbecues are permitted. Off site: Golf and riding 5 km. Windsurf hire and sea fishing 7 km.

At a glance

Welcome & Ambience	✓✓✓✓	Location	✓✓✓✓
Quality of Pitches	✓✓✓✓	Range of Facilities	✓✓✓✓✓

Directions

Take exit 38 from A8 autoroute signed Fréjus/St Rapha'l. Follow directions for Valescure then Agay on the D100, then site signs (takes you round the back of Frejus/St Raphael). Site can also be reached from the N98 coast road turning north at Agay on D100; continue past Esterel Camping to pick up site signs.

Charges 2004

extra person	€ 6,00 - € 8,00
child (3-12 yrs)	€ 5,00 - € 6,00
animal	€ 2,00 - € 4,00

Camping Cheques accepted.

Reservations

Contact site. Tel: 04 94 44 30 00. E-mail: info@douce-quietude.com

Open

3 April - 2 October.

LES CASTELS
LUXURY CAMPSITE WITH OUTSTANDING FACILITIES
ON THE CÔTE D'AZUR, BETWEEN CANNES AND SAINT-TROPEZ
IN THE HEART OF THE ESTEREL MASSIF, 3 KM AWAY FROM THE SANDY BEACHES OF AGAY
All services are open from 19.03 to 01.10.2005
Esterel
CARAVANING
www.esterel-caravaning.fr
uxury mobil homes for rent
nd maxi pitches for touring
aravans and camping cars !
range of high quality services !
Heated Swimming pools !
ON-STOP lively activities !
A Paradise for children !
Avenue des Golfs
3530 Saint-Raphaël
FRANCE
el : +33 4.94.82.03.28
x : +33 4.94.82.87.37

FR83060 Camping Caravaning de la Baume

Mobile homes page 412

Route de Bagnols, 83618 Fréjus (Var)

La Baume is large, busy site that has been well developed with much investment. It is about 5.5 km. from the long sandy beach of Fréjus-Plage, but it has such a fine and varied selection of swimming pools on site that many people do not bother to make the trip. The pools with their palm trees are a feature of this site and are remarkable for their size and variety (water slides, etc.) – the very large 'feature' pool a highlight. The site has nearly 500 pitches of varying but quite adequate size with electricity, water and drainage, with another 200 larger ones with mains sewerage to take mobile homes. Separators are being installed to divide the pitches and shade is available over most of the terrain. Although tents are accepted, the site concentrates mainly on caravanning. It is likely to become full in season, but one section with unmarked pitches is not reserved, and there is plenty of space off-peak. La Baume's convenient location has its 'downside' as there is some traffic noise from the nearby autoroute - somewhat obtrusive at first but we soon failed to notice it. A popular site with tour operators. Adjoining La Baume is its sister site La Palmeraie, containing self-catering accommodation, its own landscaped pool and providing some entertainment to supplement that at La Baume.

Facilities

The seven toilet blocks should be a satisfactory supply. Two have been enlarged recently, the others refurbished to provide mainly British style toilets with a few Turkish; washbasins in cabins and sinks for clothes and dishes with hot water. Supermarket and several other shops. Bar with external terrace overlooking pools and TV. Restaurant and takeaway. Five swimming pools (heated all season). Fitness centre. Tennis courts. Archery (July/Aug). Oganised events - sports, competitions, etc. in daytime and some evening entertainment partly in English. Amphitheatre for shows. Discos daily in season. Off site: Bus to Fréjus passes the gate.

Open

26 March - 30 September, with full services

At a glance

Welcome & Ambience	✓✓✓	Location	✓✓✓✓
Quality of Pitches	✓✓✓✓	Range of Facilities	✓✓✓✓✓

Directions

Site is 3 km. up the D4 road, which leads north from N7 just west of Fréjus. From west on autoroute A8 take exit for Fréjus/St Raphaël (junction 37), turn towards them and after 4 km., turn left on D4. From east take exit for Fréjus/St Raphaël (junction 38); after exit turn right immediately on small road marked 'Musée' etc. which leads you to D4 where right again.

Charges 2005

Per unit incl. 2 persons,	
6A electricity, water and drainage	€ 18,00 - € 37,00
extra person	€ 4,00 - € 8,00
child (under 7 yrs)	free - € 5,00
car	€ 3,50 - € 4,00

Min. stay for motorhomes 3 nights.
Large units should book.

Reservations

Essential for high season, and made for exact dates with substantial deposit and fee (€ 31.25), from 1 Jan. Tel: 04 94 15 88 88.
E-mail: reception@labaume-lapalmeraie.com

FR83240 Camping Caravaning Moulin des Iscles

83520 Roquebrune-sur-Argens (Var)

A haven of peace and tranquillity, Moulin des Iscles is hidden down 0.5 km. of private, unmade road - an unusual find in this often quite hectic part of Provence. Based around a former mill, it is a small, pretty site beside the river Argens with access to the river in places for fishing, canoeing and swimming, with a concrete bank and fenced where deemed necessary (some sought after pitches overlook the river). The 90 grassy, level pitches with electricity (6A) and water to all, radiate out from M. Dumarcet's attractive, centrally situated home which is where the restaurant and shop are situated. A nice mixture of deciduous trees provide natural shade and colour and the old mill house rests comfortably near the entrance which has a security barrier closed at night. This is a quiet site with little on site entertainment, but with a nice little restaurant. A good effort has been made to welcome handicapped visitors. It is a real campsite not a 'camping village'.

Facilities

The toilet block is fully equipped, including ramped access for disabled visitors. Some Turkish style toilets. Washbasins have cold water, some in cubicles. Baby bath and changing facilities en-suite. Covered laundry and dishwashing sinks. Small separate unisex provision for pitches near the entrance. Washing machine. Restaurant with home cooked dish-of-the-day on a weekly rotation. Surprisingly well stocked shop. Library - some English books. TV room incl. satellite, Pool table, table tennis. Play area, minigolf and boules all outside the barrier for more peace and quiet on site. Internet terminal. Canoeing possible. Off site: Riding and golf 6 km. Bicycle hire 2 km. (new bicycle way to St Aygulf). Beach 7 km.

At a glance

Welcome & Ambience	✓✓✓✓	Location	✓✓✓✓
Quality of Pitches	✓✓✓✓	Range of Facilities	✓✓✓

Directions

Follow as for site no. 8320, Les Pecheurs, but continue past it through the village of Roquebrune towards St Aygulf for 1 km. Site signed on left. Follow private unmade road for approx. 500 m. to site entrance in front of you.

Charges 2005

Per unit incl. 2 or 3 persons	€ 19,00
extra adult	€ 3,20
child (over 10 yrs)	€ 2,20
electricity	€ 2,70

Camping Cheques accepted.
Prices are lower out of high season.

Reservations

Contact site. Tel: 04 94 45 70 74.
E-mail: moulin.iscles@wanadoo.fr

Open

1 April - 30 September.

FR83070 Caravaning L'Etoile d'Argens

Mobile homes page 413

83370 St Aygulf (Var)

First impressions of L'Etoile d'Argens are of space, cleanliness and calm. Reception staff are very friendly and English is spoken (open 24 hrs). This is a site run with families in mind and many of the activities are free, making for a good value holiday. There are 493 level grass pitches (265 for touring units) laid out in typical French style, separated by hedges. There are five sizes of pitch, ranging from 50 sq.m. (for small tents) to 250 sq.m. These are exceptionally large and two families could easily fit two caravans and cars or one family could have a very spacious plot with a garden like atmosphere. All pitches are fully serviced with fresh and waste water and 10A electricity, with mainly good shade although the site is not overpowered by trees which leads to a spacious feeling. The pool and bar area is attractively landscaped with old olive and palm trees on beautifully kept grass. Two heated pools (one for adults, one for children) have been added recently – both very much with families in mind, not teenagers as there are no big slides. The river runs along one side of the site and a free boat service (15/6-15/9) runs every 40 minutes to the beach. It is also possible to moor a boat or fish. This is a good family site for the summer but also good in low season for a quiet stay in a superb location with excellent pitches. Tour operators take 85 pitches and there are 175 mobile homes but for a large site it is unusually calm and peaceful even in July.

Facilities

Two new toilet blocks were added in 2000, whilst all but 4 of the 20 original small unisex blocks have been renovated. All are well kept and include some washbasins in cubicles. Dishwashing sinks and laundry with outside clothes line. Supermarket and gas supplies. Bar, restaurant, pizzeria, takeaway. Two adult pools (one heated), paddling pool, jacuzzi and solarium. Tennis (two of the four courts are floodlit) with coaching and minigolf (both free in low season), aerobics, archery (July/Aug), football and swimming lessons. Volleyball, basketball, table tennis and boule. Play area with rubber base. Children's entertainer in July/Aug. Activity programme includes games, dances for adults and escorted walking trips to the surrounding hills. within 3 km. Off site: Golf 2 km. Riding 3 km. Beach 3.5 km.

Open

Easter - 30 September, with all services.

At a glance

Welcome & Ambience	✓✓✓✓	Location	✓✓✓✓
Quality of Pitches	✓✓✓✓✓	Range of Facilities	✓✓✓✓✓

Directions

Leave A8 at exit 36 and take N7 to Le Muy and Fréjus. After about 8 km. at roundabout take D7 signed Roquebrune and St Aygulf. In 9.5 km. (after roundabout) turn left signed Fréjus. Watch for site sign and ignore width and height limit signs as site is 500 m. to right.

Charges 2004

Per tent pitch (100 sq.m.) with electricity and 2 persons	€ 20,00 - € 37,00
'comfort' pitch (100 sq.m.) incl. 3 persons, water and drainage	€ 27,00 - € 46,00
'luxury' pitch incl. 4 persons 180 sq.m	€ 39,00 - € 62,00
extra person	€ 5,50 - € 8,00
child (under 7 yrs)	€ 3,50 - € 6,00
car and dog	€ 4,00

Reservations

Made for any period with substantial deposit and fee. Tel: 04 94 81 01 41. E-mail: info@etoiledargens.com

FR83160 Parc Camping Les Cigales

721 chemin du Jas de la Paro, 83490 Le Muy (Var)

Parc Les Cigales is a pleasant site benefiting from the shady environment of cork umbrella pines, further enhanced by olives, palm trees, sweet smelling mimosa and colourful shrubs. It has now undergone major rejuvenation. The entrance has been completely resited which, in fact, turns the site round utilising the top of the site around the pretty pool area more. The entrance is wide and smart with a new reception, shop and all facilities but the 'piece de resistance' is the new 'survival area' with courses forall ages and a wide range of equipment including arial runways. All the necessary safety equipment is in evidence and it is open to the public with costs varying according to the type of course used. A riding school, a vegetable garden and a small animal farm complete this unusual but environmentally thought out development. The terrain is typical of the area with rough, sloped and stony, dry ground but the pitches are of a good size, terraced where necessary and nestling amongst the trees. There are 163 pitches in total with 35 mobile homes to rent, nicely landscaped. Convenient for the autoroute, this is a spacious family site away from the hectic coast, to be enjoyed.

Facilities

Six modern sanitary blocks of varying size more than serve the site and include washbasins in cabins and facilities for disabled people. Laundry area with washing machines and ironing boards. Shop (1/5-30/8). Restaurant/bar with patio. Heated pool complex. Adventure play area. Survival courses. Multi-sport area (basketball, volleyball, etc). Trampoline. Riding. Canoeing and hang-gliding are organised. Entertainment each evening in season, with a disco twice weekly and daytime activities for children and senior citizens. Internet terminal. Charcoal barbecues are not permitted. Off site: Le Muy 2 km. Fishing 2 km. Riding 7 km. Golf 10 km.

At a glance

Welcome & Ambience	✓✓✓✓✓	Location	✓✓✓✓
Quality of Pitches	✓✓✓✓	Range of Facilities	✓✓✓✓✓

Directions

Site is signed off approach to autoroute péage on A8 at Le Muy exit and is 2 km. west of Le Muy on N7. It is necessary to cross the dual-carriageway as you approach the toll from Le Muy. Site well signed.

Charges 2005

Per unit incl. 2 persons	€ 12,00 - € 22,00
extra person	€ 3,00 - € 5,50
electricity (6-10A)	€ 3,00 - € 5,00

Less 5% for stays over 3 weeks.

Reservations

Advised for July/Aug. Tel: 04 94 45 12 08. E-mail: contact@les cigales.com

Open

2 April - 5 November.

L'Etoile d'Argens

2005

" 36 years experience with you "

ESE Communication - draguignan - tél : 04.94.67.06.00

www.etoiledargens.com

E-mail : info@etoiledargens.com

3370 St Aygulf - Tél. +33 4 94 81 01 41

FR83010 Camping Caravaning Les Pins Parasols

Route de Bagnols, 83600 Fréjus (Var)

Not everyone likes very big sites and Les Pins Parasols with its 189 pitches is of a size which is quite easy to walk around. It is family owned and run. Although on very slightly undulating ground, virtually all the pitches are levelled or terraced and separated by hedges or bushes with pine trees for shade. They are around 100 sq.m. and all have electricity. What is particularly interesting is that 48 of the pitches are equipped with their own fully enclosed, tiled sanitary unit, consisting of WC, washbasin, hot shower and dishwashing sink, all quite close together. These pitches naturally cost more but may well be of interest to those seeking extra comfort. The nearest beach is the once very long Fréjus-Plage (5.5 km) now reduced a little by the new marina, and adjoins St Raphaël. (See note on La Baume entry concerning traffic delays at the D4/N7 road junction.) Used by tour operators (10%).

Facilities

Besides the individual units there are three toilet blocks of good average quality providing washbasins in cabins and facilities for disabled people. One block can be heated when necessary. Small shop with reasonable stocks and restaurant with takeaway (both 1/5-20/9). General room with TV. Swimming pool (200 sq.m) with attractive rock backdrop and separate long slide with landing pool and small paddling pool (heated). Half-court tennis.
Off site: Bicycle hire or riding 2 km. Fishing 6 km. Golf 10 km. Bus from the gate into Fréjus 5 km. Beach 6 km.

Open

Easter - 30 September.

At a glance

Welcome & Ambience	✓✓✓✓	Location	✓✓✓✓
Quality of Pitches	✓✓✓✓	Range of Facilities	✓✓✓✓

Directions

From A8 take exit 38 for Fréjus Est. Turn right on leaving pay booths on a small road which leads across to D4, where right again and under 1 km. to site.

Charges 2004

Per normal pitch with electricity incl. 2 persons	€ 17,40 - € 24,90
pitch with sanitary unit	€ 22,00 - € 31,00
extra person	€ 4,40 - € 6,00
child (under 7 yrs)	€ 2,90 - € 3,65

Reservations

Necessary for July/Aug. only and made for min. 10 days for exact dates with deposit (€ 100) but no fee. Tel: 04 94 40 88 43.
E-mail: lespinsparasols@wanadoo.fr

FR83030 Camping Caravaning Leï Suves

Quartier du Blavet, 83520 Roquebrune-sur-Argens (Var)

This quiet, pretty site is a few kilometres inland from the coast, two kilometres north of the N7. Close to the unusual Roquebrune rock, it is within easy reach of resorts such as St Tropez, Ste Maxime, St Raphaël and Cannes. The site entrance is appealing - wide and spacious, with a large bank of well tended flowers. Mainly on a gently sloping hillside, the 310 pitches are terraced with shade provided by the many cork trees which give the site its name. All pitches have electricity and access to water, with a good number taken by mobile homes. A pleasant pool area is beside the bar/restaurant and entertainment area. It is possible to walk in the surrounding woods as long as there is no fire alert.

Facilities

Two modern, well kept toilet blocks include washbasins in cabins, external dishwashing sinks, laundry room with washing machines and ironing boards and facilities for disabled visitors. Shop. Good sized swimming pool and paddling pool. Bar and terrace, snack bar and takeaway (all 15/5-30/9). Outdoor stage near the bar for evening entertainment in high season. Excellent play area for all ages. Table tennis, tennis and sports area. Internet terminal. Only gas barbecues are permitted. Off site: Riding 1 km. Fishing 3 km. Bicycle hire 5 km. Golf 7 km. Beach 15 km.

At a glance

Welcome & Ambience	✓✓✓✓	Location	✓✓✓✓
Quality of Pitches	✓✓✓✓	Range of Facilities	✓✓✓✓✓

Directions

Leave autoroute at Le Muy and take N7 towards St Raphaël. Turn left at roundabout on D7 heading north signed La Boverie. Site on right in 2 km.

Charges 2005

Per unit incl. 2 persons	€ 19,00 - € 30,00
extra person	€ 4,20 - € 5,25
electricity	€ 6,00

Camping Cheques accepted.

Reservations

Contact site. Tel: 04 94 45 43 95.
E-mail: camping.lei.suves@wanadoo.fr

Open

26 March - 15 October.

FR83200 Camping Caravaning Les Pêcheurs

Mobile homes page 414

83520 Roquebrune-sur-Argens (Var)

Developed over three generations by the Simoncini family, this peaceful, friendly site is set in more than four hectares of mature, well shaded countryside at the foot of the Roquebrune Rock. It will appeal to families who appreciate natural surroundings together with many activities, cultural and sporting. Interspersed with a number of mobile homes, the 130 touring pitches are all of a good size with electricity (6/10A) and separated by trees or flowering bushes (there are 24 mobile homes and 75 pitches used by tour operators). The Provencal style buildings are delightful, especially the bar, restaurant and games room, with its terrace down to the river and the site's own canoe station (locked gate). Adjacent to the site, across the road, is a lake used exclusively for water skiing with a sandy beach, a restaurant and minigolf. Activities include climbing the 'Rock' with a guide. We became more and more intrigued with stories about the Rock, as unfolded by Sabine Simoncini. The Holy Hole, the Three Crosses and the Hermit all call for further exploration which Sabine is happy to arrange, likewise trips to Monte Carlo, Ventiniglia (Italy) and the Gorges du Verdon, etc. The medieval village of Roquebrune is within walking distance.

Facilities

Modern, well designed toilet facilities are in three blocks, one new and attractively designed in the local style, the other two refurbished. Overall, it is a good provision, open as required, with washbasins in cabins (warm water only), baby baths and facilities for disabled visitors. Dishwashing and laundry sinks (H&C). Washing machines. Sheltered swimming pool (heated in low season) with separate paddling pool (child-proof gates, lifeguard in high season; closed lunch times in July/Aug.) with ice cream bar. Shop. Bar, restaurant and games room (all open all season). New play field with nets and play equipment. Fishing. Canoeing (free) and water skiing. Animation arranged in main season for children and adults, visits to local wine caves and sessions at rafting and diving schools. Only gas or electric barbecues are permitted. Only one dog per pitch is accepted. Off site: Bicycle hire 1 km. Riding and golf 6 km (reduced fees).

At a glance

Welcome & Ambience	✓✓✓✓✓	Location	✓✓✓✓
Quality of Pitches	✓✓✓✓	Range of Facilities	✓✓✓✓✓

Directions

From A8 autoroute take Le Muy exit and follow N7 towards Frèjus for approx. 13 km. bypassing Le Muy. After crossing over the A8, turn right at roundabout towards Roquebrune sur Argens. Site is on left after 2 km. just before bridge over river (watch carefully for fairly narrow entrance).

Charges 2005

Per unit incl. 2 persons	€ 18,00 - € 31,00
extra person	€ 4,00 - € 6,00
child (under 7 yrs)	€ 3,00 - € 5,00
electricity (6/10A)	€ 4,00 - € 5,00
dog (max 1)	€ 3,00

Camping Cheques accepted.

Reservations

Made for touring pitches with deposit and fee.
Tel: 04 94 45 71 25.
E-mail: info@camping-les-pecheurs.com

Open

23 March - 30 September.

TO BOOK CALL 0870 405 4055 OR www.alanrogersdirect.com

TRAVEL SERVICE SITE

FR83170 Camping Domaine de la Bergerie

Mobile homes page 413

Vallée du Fournel, 83520 Roquebrune-sur-Argens (Var)

This excellent site near the Côte d'Azur will take you away from all the bustle of the Mediterranean to total relaxation amongst the cork, oak, pine and mimosa. The 60 hectare site is quite spread out over terrain that varies from natural, rocky, semi-landscaped areas for mobile homes to flat, grassy avenues of 200 separated pitches for touring caravans and tents. All pitches average over 80 sq.m. and have electricity, with those in one area also having water and drainage. The restaurant/bar, a converted farm building, is surrounded by shady patios, whilst inside it oozes character with high beams and archways leading to intimate corners. Activities are organised daily and, in the evening, shows, cabarets, discos, cinema, karaoke and dancing at the amphitheatre prove popular (possibly until midnight). A superb new pool complex supplements the orginal pool adding more outdoor pools with slides and a river feature, an indoor pool and a fitness centre with jacuzzi, sauna, massage and gym.

Facilities

Four toilet blocks are kept clean and include washbasins in cubicles, facilities for disabled people and babies, plus dishwashing and laundry areas with washing machines. Well stocked supermarket. Bar/restaurant. Takeaway. New pool complex (1/4-30/9) with indoor pool and fitness centre (body building, sauna, gym, etc). Five tennis courts and two half courts. Archery, roller skating and minigolf. Volleyball and mini football. Mini-farm for children. Fishing. Only gas barbecues are permitted. Off site: Riding or golf 4 km. Bicycle hire 7 km. Beach, St Aygulf or Ste Maxime 7 km. Water skiing and rock climbing nearby.

Open

Touring: 1 June - 15 September; mobile homes: 15 March - 15 October.

At a glance

Welcome & Ambience	✓✓✓✓✓	Location	✓✓✓✓✓
Quality of Pitches	✓✓✓✓	Range of Facilities	✓✓✓✓✓

Directions

Leave A8 at Le Muy exit on N7 towards Fréjus. Proceed for 9 km. then right onto D7 signed St Aygulf. Continue for 8 km. and then right at roundabout on D8; site is on the right.

Charges 2004

Per unit incl. 2 adults and electricity (5A)	€ 17,00 - € 28,00
3 persons and electricity, water and drainage	€ 24,50 - € 40,00
extra person	€ 3,00 - € 5,40
child (under 7 yrs)	€ 4,00 - € 6,80
electricity (10A)	€ 1,80 - € 2,70
dog	free - € 3,00

Reservations

Made with deposit (€ 200) and fee (€ 20). Touring: 1 June - 15 September; mobile homes: 15 March - 15 October. Tel: 04 98 11 45 45. E-mail: info@domainelabergerie.com

FR83080 Au Paradis des Campeurs

La Gaillarde-Plage, 83380 Les Issambres (Var)

Having direct access to a sandy beach (via an underpass) and being so well maintained are just two of the reasons which make Au Paradis so popular. Family owned and run, it now has 180 pitches, all with 6A electricity and 132 with water tap and drainaway. The original pitches vary in size and shape but all are satisfactory and most have some shade. The newer pitches are all large but at present have little shade although trees and bushes have been planted and shade is developing. There is no entertainment which gives peaceful nights. The gates are surveyed by TV (especially the beach gate) and a security man patrols all day. The site has become popular and it is essential to book for June, July and August.

Facilities

Two toilet blocks, refurbished to an excellent standard with high quality fittings and well maintained, include the majority of washbasins in cabins. Facilities for children are very good with baby baths and a shower at suitable height. En-suite unit for disabled visitors. Dishwashing, laundry sinks, two washing machines and dryer. Motorcaravan service point. Shop and restaurant (with takeaway service) front onto main road and open all season. TV room. Two excellent play areas, catering for the under and over 5s, both with top quality safety bases. Boules. Car wash area. Off site: Bicycle hire 2.5 km. Riding 3 km. Golf 6 km.

At a glance

Welcome & Ambience	✓✓✓✓	Location	✓✓✓✓
Quality of Pitches	✓✓✓✓	Range of Facilities	✓✓✓✓

Directions

Site is signed from N98 coast road at La Gaillarde, 2 km. south of St Aygulf.

Charges 2005

Per unit incl. 2 persons	€ 12,60 - € 19,50
with water and drainage	€ 14,50 - € 23,50
extra person	€ 5,00
child (under 4 yrs)	€ 2,80
electricity (6A)	€ 3,40

Reservations

Advised for main season. Tel: 04 94 96 93 55.

Open

20 March - 15 October.

FR83100 Camping de la Plage

Route National 98, 83310 Grimaud (Var)

A site actually on the beach is always in great demand, and Camping de la Plage is no exception and consequently it becomes very crowded. The site is divided into two parts by the N98 although a dangerous crossing is avoided by an underpass. All pitches are numbered and can be reserved - the pitches away from the beach will be the more peaceful. They are mostly of a decent size, with the ones over the road having more grass and more shade. All pitches have electricity (2-10A) but long leads may be required. Ste Maxime is six kilometres and it is not very far to all the familiar names of the south of France - St Tropez, Port Grimaud, Fréjus and St Aygulf.

Facilities

There are three toilet blocks on each side of the site. Of varying quality, but clean when we visited and, according to regulars, cleaned regularly. They are fully equipped, the majority of WCs of the British type. Baby bath. Large, well stocked supermarket (all season). Bar, restaurant and takeaway (from May). Beach volleyball. Tennis. Small play area. Off site: Bicycle hire 2 km. Golf and riding 3 km. Boat hire nearby.

Open

Two weeks before Easter - 21 October.

At a glance

Welcome & Ambience	✓✓✓	Location	✓✓✓✓✓
Quality of Pitches	✓✓✓	Range of Facilities	✓✓✓

Directions

Site is on N98 main coast road about 6 km. southwest of Ste Maxime. Take care - this road is very busy in main season.

Charges 2004

Per unit with 2 persons	€ 19,00 - € 23,00
extra person	€ 5,00 - € 6,00
child (under 7 yrs)	€ 2,50 - € 3,00
electricity (2-10A)	€ 3,50 - € 8,00
animal	€ 1,50

Reservations

Bookings taken for exact dates with booking fee from Oct.- March only. Tel: 04 94 56 31 15. E-mail: campingplagegrimaud@wanadoo.fr

FR83220 Camping Caravaning Cros de Mouton

Mobile homes page 414

B.P. 116, 83240 Cavalaire-sur-Mer (Var)

Cros de Mouton is a reasonably priced campsite in a popular area. High in the hills on a steep hillside, 1.5 km. from Cavalaire and its popular beaches, the site is a calm oasis away from the hectic coast. There are stunning views of the bay but, unfortunately, due to the nature of the terrain, some of the site roads are very steep - the higher pitches with the best views are especially so. However, Olivier and Andre are happy to take your caravan up with their 4x4 Jeep if you are worried. There are 199 terraced pitches under cork trees which include 46 for mobile homes, 73 suitable only for tents with parking close by, and 80 for touring caravans. These are large and have electricity (10A), some also with water. The restaurant terrace and the pools share the wonderful view of Cavalaire and the bay. English is spoken by the welcoming and helpful owners.

Facilities

Two clean and well maintained toilet blocks have all the usual facilities including washbasins in cubicles. Washing machine at each and a fully fitted facility for disabled customers (although site is perhaps a little steep in places for wheelchairs). Bar/restaurant serving reasonably priced meals, plus takeaways. Swimming and paddling pools with lots of sunbeds on the terrace and small bar for snacks and cold drinks. Small play area and games room.
Off site: Beach 1.5 km. Bicycle hire 1.5 km. Riding 16 km. Golf 20 km.

Open

15 March - 1 November.

At a glance

Welcome & Ambience	✓✓✓✓✓	Location	✓✓✓✓
Quality of Pitches	✓✓✓✓	Range of Facilities	✓✓✓✓

Directions

Take the D559 to Cavalaire-su-Mer (not Cavalière 4 km. away). Site is about 1.5 km. north of the town, very well signed from the centre.

Charges 2004

Per person	€ 5,80 - € 7,10
child (under 7 yrs)	€ 4,00
pitch	€ 5,80 - € 7,10
electricity (10A)	€ 4,00
dog	free - € 2,00

Camping Cheques accepted.

Reservations

Made with deposit (€ 80) and fee (€ 20).
Tel: 04 94 64 10 87.
E-mail: campingcrosdemouton@wanadoo.fr

FR83120 Camp du Domaine

La Favière B.P. 207, 83230 Bormes-les-Mimosas (Var)

Camp du Domaine, three kilometres south of Le Lavandou, is a large, attractive beach-side site with 1,200 pitches set in 45 hectares of pine woods, although surprisingly it does not give the impression of being so big. Most pitches are reasonably level and 800 have 10A electricity. The most popular pitches are at the beach, but the ones furthest away are, on the whole, larger and have more shade amongst the trees, although many of them are more suitable for tents. The beach is the attraction, however, and everyone tries to get as near to it as they can. Despite its size, the site does not give the feeling of being busy, except perhaps around the supermarket. This is mainly because many pitches are hidden in the trees, the access roads are quite wide and it all covers quite a large area (some of the beach pitches are 600 m. from the entrance). Its popularity makes early reservation necessary over a long season (about mid June to mid Sept.) as regular clients book from season to season. English is spoken.

Facilities

Ten modern toilet blocks are kept clean but, due to high usage because of the popularity of the site, parts soon begin to show wear and tear. WCs are mostly of the Turkish type (management policy). All facilities have pre-mixed hot water with many washbasins in cabins (some with showers). Facilities for disabled visitors (but steep steps). Block for children and baby room. Washing machines in most blocks. Fridges to hire. Well stocked supermarket. Bars and a pizzeria. Excellent play area. Boats and pedaloes for hire. Wide range of watersports. Games and competitions arranged in July/Aug. Children's club. Six tennis courts, table tennis and minigolf. Multi-sports courts. American motorhomes not accepted. Barbecues are strictly forbidden. Off site: Bicycle hire 500 m. Riding or golf 15 km.

At a glance

Welcome & Ambience	✓✓✓✓✓	Location	✓✓✓✓✓
Quality of Pitches	✓✓✓✓	Range of Facilities	✓✓✓✓✓

Directions

Just outside and to west of Le Lavandou, at roundabout, turn off D559 towards the sea on road signed Favière. After some 2 km. turn left at camp signs.

Charges 2005

Per unit incl. 2 persons	€ 17,00 - € 24,00
with electricity and water	€ 25,00 - € 30,50
extra person	€ 5,00 - € 6,50
child (under 7 yrs)	€ 2,80 - € 3,40

Reservations

Made with 30% deposit and fee (€ 22.87).
Tel: 04 94 71 03 12.
E-mail: mail@campdudomaine.com

Open

18 March - 31 October.

FR83140 Camping Les Lacs du Verdon

Domaine de Roquelande, 83630 Régusse (Var)

In beautiful countryside and within easy reach of the Grand Canyon du Verdon and its nearby lakes (20 minutes drive), this site is only 90 minutes from Cannes. This bustling and possible noisy campsite is suitable for active families and teenagers. The 30 acre wooded park is divided in two by a minor road. The 480 very stony, but level pitches (rock pegs advised) are marked and separated by lines of stones and trees (watch for overhang). There are 130 pitches for tourists which are scattered amongst the trees and often have an irregular shape, although all are of average size. There are plenty of electricity boxes but long leads may be necessary. Water taps are few. The part across the road is used mainly for mobile homes but has some pitches for tourers, mostly at the far end. There are toilet blocks close by but the pitches are a long way from all the other site facilities. The main site is closer to all the activities. Tour operators and mobile homes, for hire and privately owned, take up nearly three quarters of this site.

Facilities

The toilet blocks are old and much of the equipment is looking very jaded, but they are just about acceptable. They mainly have British style WCs and some washbasins in cubicles with warm water only. The block we tried had fairly hot water but campers complained they were not so lucky. All blocks have sinks for laundry and dishes. Washing machines and dryers. At the end of May very little was open and the level of cleanliness was barely adequate. Motorcaravan service point (with charge). Shop. Bar. Restaurant and pizzeria (all 18/5-13/9). TV and teenage games. Discos, dances and theme nights. Excellent swimming pool/paddling pool complex (all season) and new artificial grass tennis courts - the highlight of this campsite. Volleyball, table tennis, archery and boules. Bicycle hire. Playground. Daily entertainment for all the family in May and June, with a more extensive programme in high season. Only electric barbecues are permitted. Off site: The village of Regusse is about 2.5 km. and the small town of Aups is 7 km. Fishing, beach, sailing and windsurfing at the site's club at Saint Croix (15 km). Riding 10 km.

At a glance

Welcome & Ambience	✓✓✓✓	Location	✓✓✓
Quality of Pitches	✓✓	Range of Facilities	✓✓✓✓

Directions

Leave the A8 motorway at St Maximin and take the D560 northeast to Barjols. At Barjols turn left on D71 to Montmeyan, turn right on D30 to Regusse and follow site signs.

Charges 2004

Per pitch incl. 1 or 2 persons	€ 18,00 - € 27,00
extra person	€ 5,00 - € 7,50
child (3-7 yrs)	€ 4,00 - € 6,00
electricity (10A)	€ 4,00
dog	€ 3,00

Camping Cheques accepted.

Reservations

Made with 25% deposit and fee (€ 20).
Tel: 04 94 70 17 95. E-mail: info@lacs-verdon.com

Open

27 April - 28 September.

FR83210 Camping Les Tournels

Route de Camarat, 83350 Ramatuelle (Var)

Les Tournels is a large site set on a hillside and some of the pitches have wonderful panoramic views of the Gulf of St Tropez and Pampelonne beach. The whole hill is covered in parasol pines and old olive trees, so all pitches have some shade. Reasonably level, but varying in size, there is electricity on the majority (long electricity leads may be required). The rest are reserved for tents. Clean and well equipped sanitary blocks are within reasonable distance of the pitches, but the swimming pool, play area, shop and bar could turn out to be quite some distance away. The large swimming pool is of an unusual shape, the circular paddling pool has a mushroom shaped fountain, and both are surrounded by sunbathing areas with sun-beds. Competitions and shows are produced for adults and children in July/Aug. A shuttle bus runs the 500 m. to the local shopping centre and also to Pampelonne beach. Reception opens for long hours and English is spoken. The beaches are a big draw, but also who can resist a visit to St Tropez where perhaps you will see someone famous as they parade along the famous waterfront, and the floating 'gin palaces' are a sight to behold.

Facilities

Two of the toilet blocks are of older design, the other six being very good. These include some washbasins in cubicles, mainly British style WCs (paper required), baby baths, children's WCs and facilities for disabled visitors. Three blocks are heated in low season. Washing and drying machines at five blocks, with refrigerators to rent outside all of them. Dishwashing and laundry sinks. Bar/restaurant (1/4-15/10). Takeaway. Another bar with disco at the furthest end of the site, well away from most pitches. Large swimming pool (600 sq.m, open 1/4-20/10 and heated in low season). Large fenced play area with good quality equipment. Table tennis, volleyball, basketball and boules pitches. Archery. Mini-club for children over 5 years for sporting activities. Safety deposit boxes to rent. Only gas barbecues are permitted. Off site: Shopping centre 500 m. from the site entrance (owned by the family) contains supermarket, tobacconist, launderette, rotisserie and a snack bar. Beach 1.5 km.

At a glance

Welcome & Ambience	✓✓✓✓	Location	✓✓✓✓
Quality of Pitches	✓✓✓✓	Range of Facilities	✓✓✓✓

Directions

From A8 exit 36 take D25 to Ste Maxime, then D98 towards St Tropez. On outskirts of St Tropez, take D93 to Ramatuelle. Site is signed on left in 9 km.

Charges 2005

Per unit incl. 2 persons with electricity and water	€ 23,00 - € 34,00
extra person	€ 5,50 - € 7,60
child (2-7 yrs)	€ 2,90 - € 3,80

Reservations

Contact site for details. Tel: 04 94 55 90 90.
E-mail: info@tournels.com

Open

All year except 11 January - 28 February.

FR83260 Camping Château de l'Eouvière

Route de Tavernes, 83670 Montmeyan (Var)

This spacious new site is in the grounds of an 18th century château, close to the magnificent hill village of Montmeyan. There are 30 hectares of grounds to explore and the swimming pool, bar, restaurant which are in front of the château, have lovely views over the valley and mountains beyond. The toilet block and children's play area are to one side. The 80 large pitches (all for tourers) are well marked and separated on terraces, mostly behind the château and many have magnificent views. The pitches are part grassy, part stony with varying amounts of shade from mostly mature trees. The majority have water and all have electricity points at the edge of the pitch. A log cabin toilet block is installed in the upper reaches for the high season. The owner will assist with his 4x4 vehicle any visitor experiencing difficulty in siting their unit on the higher pitches. This is a quieter site for those seeking the 'real' France.

Facilities

The main, refurbished toilet block includes all the necessary facilities. Facilities for disabled visitors are available with access from the lower pitches. Laundry and dishwashing sinks, washing machine and iron. Bar, restaurant and small shop (June - Sept). Swimming pool with large tiled sunbathing area. Small play area and paddling pool (some distance from the pool). Some entertainment and children's activities in high season. Virtually soundproof disco room in the cellars of the château. Off site: Montmeyan 1 km. Beach at Lake Quinson (7 km) and other lakes with a range of watersports. Gorges du Verdon. Many interesting towns with their markets and museums.

At a glance

Welcome & Ambience	✓✓✓✓✓	Location	✓✓✓✓✓
Quality of Pitches	✓✓✓✓	Range of Facilities	✓✓✓✓

Directions

Leave A8 autoroute at St Maximin and take D560 to Barjols and then D71 to Montmeyan. At roundabout on entering village, take D13 southeast signed Cotignac and site entrance is very shortly on the right.

Charges 2004

Per person	€ 5,50 - € 7,00
child (under 7 yrs)	€ 3,80 - € 4,50
pitch	€ 8,00 - € 10,00

Reservations

Contact site. Tel: 04 94 80 75 54.
E-mail: leouviere@wanadoo.fr

Open

15 April - 15 October.

FR83270 Camping La Cigale

83350 Ramatuelle (Var)

One of those delightful 'little gems' in a pretty setting yet close (about ten minutes by car) to the trendy resort of St Tropez, this is a family-run site with 115 pitches. Of these 75 are for tourers, all with 6A electricity. The pitches, with some terracing, vary in size but are mostly pretty level, with varying amounts of shade. Mainly on hard sandy earth, they are nothing to write home about, but are generally quite adequate. Although only around 800 m. from the well known, sandy Plage d'Escalet, the site nevertheless has its own quietly situated small pool (no noisy slides) and its own attractive restaurant.

Facilities

Sanitary facilities, in two blocks, include large showers, mainly British style WCs, washbasins in cabins and a washing machine – all clean and well cared for when we visited. Shop, Bar/restaurant. Takeaway. Swimming pool. Bicycle hire. Off site: Beach and boat launching 800 m. Riding 5 km. Golf 7 km.

Open

1 April - 15 October.

At a glance

Welcome & Ambience	✓✓✓✓✓	Location	✓✓✓✓✓
Quality of Pitches	✓✓✓	Range of Facilities	✓✓✓✓

Directions

From N98 coast road just east of St.Tropez take D93 towards Ramatuelle. After around 10 km. fork left towards L'Escalet (site is signed).

Charges 2005

Per person	€ 5,50 - € 7,50
pitch	€ 15,00 - € 32,00
electricity (6A)	€ 5,00

Camping Cheques accepted.

Reservations

Contact site. Tel: 04 94 79 22 53.
E-mail: campinglacigale@wanadoo.fr

FR83130 Camping Le Beau Vezé

Route de la Moutonne, 83320 Carqueiranne (Var)

Le Beau Vezé is a quiet site, some way inland from the busy resort of Hyères. The owner tries to keep it as a family site with its quiet position, although the superb beaches and hectic coastal areas are within easy reach. On a steep hillside it has terraced pitches and a plateau with more pitches on the top. The 150 pitches are well shaded but due to over-hanging trees some could be difficult for motorcaravans. There is some road noise on the lower pitches. The lovely old town of Hyères is only 8 km.

Facilities

Three sanitary blocks of a reasonable standard, two quite modern with heating, although maintenance may be variable in high season. All have hot showers and some cubicles have a washbasin also, making them more roomy. Both British and Turkish style WCs. Baby room. Two washing machines. Bar/restaurant and takeaway. Bread to order. Medium sized pool and paddling pool. Play area. Bicycle hire. Minigolf, table tennis, volleyball, boule and tennis court. Off site: Riding and golf 2 km.

Open

1 May - 15 September.

At a glance

Welcome & Ambience	✓✓✓✓	Location	✓✓✓✓
Quality of Pitches	✓✓✓✓	Range of Facilities	✓✓✓✓

Directions

From D559 between Carqueiranne and Le Pradet, take D76 northwards signed La Moutonne and site is signed on right of D76.

Charges guide

Per unit incl. 2 persons	€ 26,00
extra person	€ 6,20
child (under 10 yrs)	€ 4,57
electricity (6A)	€ 3,81

Camping Cheques accepted.

Reservations

Made with deposit (€ 46) and fee (€ 15.24).
Tel: 04 94 57 65 30.
E-mail: info@camping-beauveze.com

FR83280 Campasun Mas de Pierredon

652, chemin Paoul Coletta, 83110 Sanary-sur-Mer (Var)

Situated on the outskirts of the pretty resort of Sanary, this small site is open from Easter through to October. Terraced under the traditional pines of the area, it provides 120 pitches of which many are taken by mobile homes. The ground is fairly rocky but some sand and grass exists and trees and shrubs help to divide the pitches making it an attractive environment. All pitches have 10A electricity. The bar and restaurant overlook the heated pool at the entrance to the site and provide a comfortable family environment, all are open all season. Close to a fairly busy main road, the access is quite sharp and uphill.

Facilities

Two toilet blocks with modern facilities include washbasins in cabins. 16 en-suite individual units on pitches. Unit for disabled visitors. Washing machines. Motorcaravan service point. Bar/restaurant with pizza oven. Bread to order. Oudoor pool and paddling pool. Play equipment. Table tennis, minigolf, boules and tennis court. Entertainment in July/Aug. Barbecues not permitted. Off site: Shop 800 m. Beach 3 km. Golf, bicycle hire and riding 10 km.

Open

15 March - 30 October.

At a glance

Welcome & Ambience	✓✓✓✓✓	Location	✓✓✓✓
Quality of Pitches	✓✓✓✓	Range of Facilities	✓✓✓✓✓

Directions

From A50 take exit for Bandol and follow directions for 'Jardin Exotique'. After Mercedes garage take first right and follow straight on for 5 km. (narrow road with lots of roads off) until a T-junction with a stop sign. Turn right and site is almost immediately on left.

Charges 2005

Per person	€ 4,50 - € 5,90
pitch	€ 5,90 - € 10,55
electricity (10A)	€ 4,70

Camping Cheques accepted.

Reservations

Made with deposit (€ 80) and booking fee (€ 23).
Tel: 04 94 74 25 02. E-mail: campasun@free.fr

FR83290 Camping de Saint Aygulf Plage

270, avenue Salvarelli, 83370 St Aygulf-Plage (Var)

This is a large, well run and self-sufficient campsite with a range of good facilities including a small supermarket and private bakery, two restaurants with takeaways and a long bar with an extensive patio and stage for discos and entertainment. It has direct access to the beach which is part of a long sandy bay which shelves gradually into the sea, suitable for children of all ages. The site is situated in Saint Aygulf which is a lively town with bars, restaurants and a popular market on Tuesdays. The theme parks of Aqatica and Luna Park are less than 2 km. away. The pitches here are well marked, flat and arranged in long rows, many with good shade from the pine trees. There are 1,100 in total, with 700 for touring units and the remainder used for mobile homes and chalets. Electricity is available on 500 touring pitches. Perhaps the only disappointment is the lack of a swimming pool on the site, but this is definitely offset by the direct access to the beach and overall this is a fine family holidaying campsite.

Facilities

Four large toilet blocks provide good, clean facilities in traditional style with British and Turkish style WCs, washbasins with warm water and free, pre-set showers. No facilities for disabled visitors. Washing machines in two blocks. Supermarket. Bakery. Two restaurants. Bar, pizzeria and takeaways. Play areas. Boules. First aid. Caravan storage. Entertainment. Beach. Only gas and electric barbecues are permitted. Off site: Bicycle hire 100 m. Riding 1 km. Golf 6 km. Restaurants, shops and bars nearby.

Open

1 May - 19 September

At a glance

Welcome & Ambience	✓✓✓✓✓	Location	✓✓✓✓✓
Quality of Pitches	✓✓✓✓	Range of Facilities	✓✓✓✓

Directions

From A8 autoroute take exits for Puget or Fréjus and take RN7 to Fréjus town. Follow signs to seas front and join RN98. Saint Aygulf is 2 km. in direction of St Tropez and site is signed.

Charges 2004

Per unit incl. 2 persons	€ 11,50 - € 25,50
Incl. electricity	€ 15,00 - € 29,50
extra person	€ 3,00 - € 7,50
child (0-7 yrs)	€ 2,00 - € 3,50
dog	€ 1,50 - € 3,50

Reservations

Made with deposit and fee; contact site.
Directions: Tel: 04 94 17 62 49.
E-mail: info@camping-cote-azur.com

FR83300 Camping Clos Sainte Thérèse

Route de Bandol, 83270 St Cyr-sur-Mer (Var)

This is a very attractive, family run campsite set in hilly terrain four kilometres from the beaches of Saint Cyr. The terraced pitches are level, some with sea views, the friendly owners offering a tractor service to visitors who have difficulties in reaching their pitch. There is a good shade cover from pines, olives, almonds and evergreen oaks and all pitches have electricity (6/10A). There are 86 pitches for touring units and 26 used for chalets or mobile homes. The landscaped pool complex is pretty and well kept, with a small slide, jacuzzi and a separate paddling pool. Activities are organised in high season, for example, pool games, boules tournaments, bingo and karaoke. This is a friendly, small site, ideal for couples of families with younger children.

Facilities

Toilet facilities are clean and well maintained in two modern and two older blocks. British style WCs, open washbasins and controllable free showers. Fridge hire. Shop (from 1/5). Bar and restaurant (15/6-15/9). Swimming pools (one heated) and children's pool. Games room. Table tennis. TV room and library. Boules. Play area. Activities in high season. Off site: Golf course (9 and 18 holes, driving range) and tennis courts opposite site entrance. Bicycle hire 2 km. Fishing 4 km. Riding 8 km. Beach 4 km.

At a glance

Welcome & Ambience	✓✓✓✓	Location	✓✓✓✓
Quality of Pitches	✓✓✓✓	Range of Facilities	✓✓✓✓

Directions

From A50 motorway take D559 to Saint Cyr. Continue towards Bandol and site is 3 km. on the left.

Charges 2004

Per unit incl. 2 persons	€ 12,30 - € 19,00
extra person	€ 3,10 - € 4,60
child (3-7 yrs)	€ 2,10 - € 3,10
electricity	€ 2,60 - € 4,70
dog	€ 1,60 - € 2,00

Camping Cheques accepted.

Reservations

Contact site. Tel: 00 33 4 94 32 1.
E-mail: camping@clos-therese.com

Open

1 April - 1 October.

Map 16

The island of Corsica is both dramatic and beautiful. The scenery is spectacular with bays of white sand lapped by the clear blue waters of the Mediterranean. At certain times of the year the entire island is ablaze with exotic flowers, aided by Corsica's excellent sunshine record.

Départements: 2A Corse-Sud; 2B Haute-Corse

Major Cities: Ajaccio and Bastia

Corsica is regarded by some as the jewel of the Mediterranean islands and is made up of two départements: Haute Corse (upper Corsica) and Corse du Sud (southern Corsica). The island has endured a bloody history, having being much disputed the Greeks, Romans and Lombards. Five hundred years of Italian rule has influenced the look of the island with Italian-style hilltop hamlets and villages developed alongside mountain springs. Many of the villages feature rustic, unadorned churches and also a few Romanesque examples too.

The variety of scenery is spectacular. Across much of the island one can discover dramatic gorges, glacial lakes, gushing mountain torrents and magnificent pine and chestnut forests.You'll also experience the celebrated perfume of the Corsican maquis: a tangled undergrowth of fragrant herbs, flowers and bushes that fills the warm spring and summer air. The highest mountains lie to the west, while the gentler ranges, weathered to strange and often bizarre shapes, lie to the south and a continuous barrier forms the island's backbone.

Cuisine of the region

Brocchui: sheeps' milk cheese is used much in cooking in both its soft form (savoury or sweet) or more mature and ripened.

Capone: local eels, cut up and grilled on a spit over a charcoal fire

Dziminu: fish soup, like bouillabaise but much hotter. Made with peppers and pimentos

Figatelli: a sausage made of dried and spiced pork with liver. Favourite between-meal snack

Pibronata: a highly spiced local sauce

Prizzutu: a peppered smoked ham; resembles the Italian prosciutto, but with chestnut flavour added

Places of interest

Ajaccio: a dazzling white city full of Napoleonic memorabilia

Bastia: historic citadel towering over the headland. The old town has preserved its streets in the form of steps connected by vaulted passages, converging on the Vieux port (the old port). The new port is the real commercial port of the island

Alan Rogers tip

TO ESCAPE THE CROWDS AND APPRECIATE THE SCENERY CLOSE-UP, HEAD INLAND AND TAKE ADVANTAGE OF THE NETWORK OF TRAILS AND FOREST TRACKS.

FR20010 Camping Arinella Bianca

Route de la Mer, 20240 Ghisonaccia (Haute-Corse)

Arinella is a lively, family oriented site situated on Corsica's east coast. It is a tribute to its owner's design and development skills as it appears to be in entirely natural glades where, in fact, these have been created from former marshland with a fresh water lake. The 429 marked pitches (182 for touring units) are on flat grass among a variety of trees and shrubs providing ample shade. They are irregularly arranged but are all of a good size with 6A electricity (long leads may be necessary). The site is right beside a beach of soft sand that extends a long way either side of the attractive central complex which, together with the swimming pool, forms the hub of this site. A large range of sport and leisure facilities is available at or adjacent to the site. Evening entertainment starts at 10 pm. and continues until midnight and unfortunately a local disco nearby can go on until the early hours. Used by tour operators (76 pitches).

Facilities

Four open plan sanitary blocks provide showers in larger than average cubicles (some with dressing area), washbasins in cabins and mainly British, some Turkish style WCs. Open air dishwashing areas. Laundry with washing machines and ironing boards. Motorcaravan service point. Shop, bar, terraced restaurant, amphitheatre and snack bar (all 10/5-15/9). Swimming pool (from 1/5) free. Windsurfing, canoeing, fishing, volleyball, bicycle hire, tennis, riding. Children's mini-club and play area. Disco. Entertainment programme in the main season.

Open

Easter - 30 September.

At a glance

Welcome & Ambience	✓✓✓✓	Location	✓✓✓✓✓
Quality of Pitches	✓✓✓✓	Range of Facilities	✓✓✓✓✓

Directions

Site is 4 km. east of Ghisonaccia. From N198 after entering Ghisonaccia look for sign 'La Plage / Li Mare' (this road is easy to miss coming from south and difficullt for caravans to turn into, so go further through town and turn in garage forecourt to approach from north). Turn east on to D144 and continue for 3.5 km. to roundabout. Turn right and site is on left in approx. 500 m.

Charges 2005

Per unit incl. 2 adults	€ 19,00 - € 33,00
extra person	€ 6,50 - € 9,00
child (up to 7 yrs)	free - € 5,00
electricity (6A)	€ 3,50
animal	€ 2,50

Camping Cheques accepted.

Reservations

Contact site. Made with € 155 deposit and € 30.50 fee. Tel: 04 95 56 04 78.
E-mail: arinella@arinellabianca.com

FR20000 Camping Pertamina U. Farniente

Pertamina Village, 20169 Bonifacio (Corse-du-Sud)

Irrespective of whether or not you are using the ferry to Sardinia, Bonifacio deserves a visit and it would be difficult to find a more attractive or convenient site than this one at which to pitch for a night stop or longer stay. The 120 pitches, many with electricity, are partially terraced and are hedged with trees and bushes, providing reasonable shade. They are reasonably flat and vary in size, many being well over 100 sq.m. A central feature is the large pool, surrounded by terraces, a bar and a good pizzeria/grill.

Facilities

Two toilet blocks include washbasins in semi-private cubicles, British and Turkish style WCs, dishwashing and washing machines plus drying and ironing facilities. Shop. Takeaway. Pizzeria/grill serving set meals and à la carte at reasonable prices (shorter opening hours in May, June and Oct). Swimming pool. Tennis, table tennis. Play area. TV room. Off site: Bonifacio 4 km.

Open

Easter - 15 October.

At a glance

Welcome & Ambience	✓✓✓✓	Location	✓✓✓✓
Quality of Pitches	✓✓✓✓	Range of Facilities	✓✓✓✓

Directions

Site is on RN198, 4 km. north of Bonifacio to the east. Watch for the sign - you come on it quite suddenly.

Charges 2004

Per unit incl. 2 persons with electricity (3A)	€ 14,00 - € 23,00
extra person	€ 6,00 - € 7,00

Camping Cheques accepted.

Reservations

Contact site. Made with € 15.25 fee and 30% deposit. Tel: 04 95 73 05 47.
E-mail: pertamina@wanadoo.fr

FR20070 Camping Caravaning Santa Lucia

Lieudit Mulindinu, 20144 St Lucie-de Porto-Vecchio (Corse-du-Sud)

Camping Santa Lucia is a friendly, family run site in a delightful southern Corscian setting. It is a well appointed site set in a cork oak forest just off the main road, the entrance enhanced by a huge palm tree which characterises the approach to reception. At this point you also find the restaurant and bar which overlook the swimming pool - particularly pleasant in the evening when ornamental lamps light up the patio area. There are 160 pitches, 40 with 6A electrical connections. Pitches are numbered and some are in little enclosed bays which offer privacy. Chalets and bungalow tents blend unobtrusively with the setting. You are only minutes by car from Porto Vecchio which is surrounded by lovely beaches.

Facilities

Two toilet blocks include some washbasins in cubicles, dishwashing and laundry sinks, and a washing machine. Bread to order. Bar (15/6-15/9). Restaurant and takeaway (1/7-31/8). Children's play area. Table tennis, volleyball, and minigolf. Barbecues are only permitted in specific area. Off site: Fishing 5 km. Supermarket opposite site entrance and services in village

Open

15 May - 10 October.

At a glance

Welcome & Ambience	✓✓✓	Location	✓✓✓✓
Quality of Pitches	✓✓✓✓	Range of Facilities	✓✓✓✓

Directions

Site is at south end of Sainte-Lucie-de-Porto-Vecchio village, off N198 and well signed.

Charges guide

Per adult	€ 4,00 - € 6,00
child (2-10 yrs)	free - € 3,00
pitch	€ 1,80 - € 3,50
with electricity	€ 5,00 - € 6,00
car	€ 1,50 - € 2,50
motorcycle	€ 0,80 - € 1,50

Reservations

Contact site. Made with deposit and € 15 fee.
Tel: 04 95 71 45 28. E-mail: santalucia@wanadoo.fr

FR20050 Camping Naturiste Club La Chiappa

Mobile homes page 416

20137 Porto-Vecchio (Corse-du-Sud)

This holiday paradise stands in a magnificent setting on the Chiappa peninsula, which juts out into the bluest of seas. It is an extensive naturist site with three kilometres of private beach. There are 220 pitches for caravans and tents, plus 250 bungalows to rent. The quality of the pitches varies, as does the size (75-125 sq.m.) and many are on sloping ground. Very long electricity leads are necessary of some places. Some pitches have sea views. There are three beaches where you are sure to find a quiet spot and where it is safe to swim, or alternatively enjoy the pool. There are also extensive grounds and gardens.

Facilities

There are more than enough sanitary blocks and open plan facilities, which are clean and modern. Washing machines. Motorcaravan service point. Well stocked shop. Three bars, restaurant and snacks. Baby sitting. Swimming pool. Play area and club for children. Riding, tennis, minigolf, fishing, diving, windsurfing, sailing, sauna and much more (some at extra cost). Disco (almost soundproof). Torches useful.

Open

14 May - 1 October.

At a glance

Welcome & Ambience	✓✓✓	Location	✓✓✓✓✓
Quality of Pitches	✓✓✓	Range of Facilities	✓✓✓✓✓

Directions

From Bastia on N198 south, take Porto-Vecchio bypass (signed Bonofaccio). At southern end, after last roundabout, take first left signed 'Pont de la Chiappa' onto unclassified road. After 8 km. site sign is on left of road. Turn left for 2 km. to site.

Charges 2005

Per adult	€ 7,50 - € 9,50
child (5-13 yrs)	€ 3,50 - € 4,50
pitch incl. electricity	€ 10,50 - € 13,00

Less for longer stays in low season.

Reservations

Contact site. Tel: 04 95 70 00 31.
E-mail: chiappa@wanadoo.fr

FR20060 Camping La Vetta

Route de Bastia, La Trinité, 20137 Porto-Vecchio (Corse-du-Sud)

In a pleasing country park setting to the north of La Trinité village, La Vetta is only three kilometres from Porto-Vecchio and its magnificent sandy beaches. This 8.5 hectare campsite enjoys a tranquil setting and is a part sloping, part terraced site, that seems to stretch endlessly. It is well maintained and has an abundance of tree varieties including cork oaks. Giving the impression of being off the beaten track, many of the delights of Corsica are only a short drive away. If you want to do no more than relax there is much on offer - a pool for hot days, plenty of trees for shade and a patio area for cool drinks. The site has 100 pitches, most with 16A electrical connections. The entrance is directly off the main road with security gates closed midnight - 7 am.

Facilities

Clean, modern, fully equipped toilet facilities are more than adequate and include dishwashing, laundry sinks and washing machine. Shop (July/Aug) with gas supplies. Patio bar (July/Aug). Swimming pool (all season), table tennis, table football, snooker table, a play area, TV and entertainment in high season. Barbecues are not permitted in certain weather conditions. Off site: Fishing 3 km. Riding 4 km. Bicycle hire 5 km. Golf 7 km.

Open

1 June - 1 October.

At a glance

Welcome & Ambience	✓✓✓✓✓	Location	✓✓✓✓
Quality of Pitches	✓✓✓	Range of Facilities	✓✓✓✓

Directions

Site is in La Trinité village, off the RN198 (east side), north of Porto-Vecchio.

Charges 2004

Per adult	€ 6,00 - € 7,00
child (under 7 yrs)	€ 3,00 - € 4,00
tent or caravan	€ 2,50 - € 3,00
car	€ 2,00
motorcaravan	€ 4,50 - € 5,00
electricity	€ 3,00

No credit cards.

Reservations

Made with 30% deposit. Tel: 04 95 70 09 86.
E-mail: info@campinglavetta.com

FR20030 Camping Merendella

Moriani-Plage, 20230 San-Nicolao (Haute-Corse)

This attractive smaller, family run site has the advantage of direct access to a pleasant beach. It is peacefully situated on level grass with many trees and shrubs providing shade and colour. There are 133 pitches of a min. 100 sq.m. with electricity available on practically all (although long cables may be needed). The site is about 800 m. from the village but also has its own well stocked shop.

Facilities

Modern toilet facilities are in two main blocks, apart from a couple of individual cabin units near beach. Washbasins in private cubicles and some British style WCs plus further Turkish style ones. Washing up and laundry areas. Two washing machines. Shop. Restaurant/Pizzeria. TV and games room. No dogs or cats are accepted. Off site: Tennis, riding and various watersports including a diving centre nearby.

Open

15 May - 15 October.

At a glance

Welcome & Ambience	✓✓✓✓	Location	✓✓✓✓
Quality of Pitches	✓✓✓✓	Range of Facilities	✓✓✓✓

Directions

Site is to seaward side of the RN198, 800 m. south of Moriani Plage.

Charges 2004

Per person	€ 5,80 - € 6,90
caravan	€ 3,10 - € 3,65
tent	€ 2,45 - € 2,85
car	€ 2,55 - € 2,80
motorcaravan	€ 5,45 - € 6,65

Camping Cheques accepted.

Reservations

Are advisable; write to site. Tel: 04 95 38 53 47.
E-mail: merendel@club-internet.fr

FR20130 Camping San Damiano

Lido de la Marana-Pineto, 20620 Biguglia-Bastia (Haute-Corse)

What we found pleasing about this site was the friendly reception we received and also its convenient situation only nine kilometres from the port of Bastia. It makes an excellent night halt, or alternatively a suitable base for visiting Bastia, the northeast of the island or its mountainous interior. Despite being on the outskirts of a city, it enjoys an ideal location off the busy N193, situated between the Etang de Biguglia and the golden sands of Corsica's east coast. It is divided in two by a public access road to the beach and is a sprawling site with 280 pitches, all separated by shrubs and shaded by trees. There are 180 electricity connections (10A). A security guard patrols in high season.

Facilities

Two basic toilet blocks, but clean when we visited, include washing cabins and good provision for disabled visitors. Motorcaravan service point. Well-stocked shop (1/6-20/9). Bar and restaurant (from 1/5). Launderette. TV room. Minigolf. Play area for children. Fishing. Riding. Jet-ski and quad-bike hire. Off site: Golf 15 km.

Open

1 April - 15 October.

At a glance

Welcome & Ambience	✓✓✓✓	Location	✓✓✓✓
Quality of Pitches	✓✓✓✓	Range of Facilities	✓✓✓✓

Directions

From port of Bastia travel 5 km. on N193 then take D107 towards Lido de la Marana for 4 km. Site is signed on the left.

Charges 2004

Per person	€ 5,50 - € 6,50
child (under 8 yrs)	€ 3,50 - € 4,50
pitch	€ 4,50 - € 6,50
electricity (6A)	€ 3,00

Reservations

Possible by phone. Tel: 04 95 33 68 02.
E-mail: l.pradier@wanadoo.fr

FR20120 Camping Le Panoramic

Route de Lavatoggio, Lumio, 20260 Calvi (Haute-Corse)

On the scenic route that winds inland and upwards from the coast between Calvi and L'Ile Rousse, Le Panoramic, as its name suggests, enjoys magnificent views across the Golfe d'Ambroggio. It is a simple family run site with 120 pitches laid out in named avenues (Rue Josephine, etc) and the marked places are shaded by many trees and vegetation, with quite a number having 15A electricity connections. Whilst the ground is level, the site is terraced and hard going if climbing from the bottom towards reception. It is probably best suited for small motorcaravans or tents. A recommended scenic drive is the five kilometre climb to St Antonino, a mountain village piled upon a rock face.

Facilities

Four sanitary blocks are housed in typical rough-cast buildings with basic decor, but appear well maintained and fully equipped. Sinks for dishwashing and two washing machines. Chemical disposal can be arranged through reception. Small shop, takeaway and bar. Swimming pool. Table football, pool table. Children's play area. Caravan storage. Off site: Riding 3 km. Bicycle hire 4 km. Golf 5 km.

Open

1 June - 15 September.

At a glance

Welcome & Ambience	✓✓✓	Location	✓✓✓✓
Quality of Pitches	✓✓✓✓	Range of Facilities	✓✓✓✓

Directions

From Calvi take N197 towards L'Ile Rousse. Proceed for 10 km. to village of Lumio, then east on D71 and site is 2 km. on the left.

Charges 2004

Per adult	€ 5,80
child (2-7 yrs)	€ 2,90
caravan	€ 4,20
tent	€ 2,20
car	€ 1,70

No credit cards.

Reservations

Phone or write. Tel: 04 95 60 73 13.
E-mail: panoramic@web-office.fr

FR20220 Camping Les Oliviers

20150 Porto (Corse-du-Sud)

Because of its location on this difficult to access west coast of Corsica and the steepness of the site itself, Les Oliviers is best suited for tents and small motorhomes. An attractive, family run site on the edge of this busy coastal resort, it has direct access to the river. The 190 pitches are mainly small and terraced, with 64 having electricity. An outdoor pool has been added recently, with a sauna and gym. There is also access to the river for swimming. The site has an attractive restaurant/pizzeria and bar.

Facilities

Toilet facilities are in four blocks spread throughout the site. Some washbasins in cubicles, British style WCs. Dishwashing and laundry areas. Four washing machines. Fridge hire. Bread supplies. Restaurant, pizzeria and bar. Swimming pool, gym, sauna and Turkish bath. Play area. Internet access. Off site: Supermarket 50 m. Corsican Trek organises a variety of active sports. Visits to Scandola nature reserve.

Open

28 March - 30 October.

At a glance

Welcome & Ambience	✓✓✓✓	Location	✓✓✓✓
Quality of Pitches	✓✓✓✓	Range of Facilities	✓✓✓✓

Directions

When approaching Porto the road crosses a river bridge. Les Oliviers is on the right after the bridge.

Charges 2004

Per adult	€ 6,00 - € 8,50
caravan	€ 5,00 - € 6,50
tent	€ 2,50 - € 3,50
car	€ 2,50 - € 3,50
electricity (10A)	€ 3,50

Reservations

Essential for caravans and motorcaravans at all times, advised for tents in July/Aug; contact site.
Tel: 04 95 26 14 49. E-mail: guy.lannoy@wanadoo.fr

FR20230 Camping Le Sagone

Route de Vico, 20118 Sagone (Corse-du-Sud)

Situated just outside the bustling seaside resort of Sagone, this campsite is in a superb location for exploring Corsica's wild and rocky west coast or its mountainous interior. Adjacent to a mixed farm with orchards, there are 300 pitches which are all marked out, the majority with electrical connections (6A). The restaurant/bar and games room overlooking the pool are a focal point of this well managed site.

Facilities

Four clean, fully equipped toilet blocks include two with internal courtyard gardens. Washbasins in cubicles, washing up and laundry area. Facilities for disabled people. Four washing machines, one dryer. Motorcaravan service point. Coccinelle supermarket at entrance. Restaurant, pizzeria, bar and games room. Swimming pool. Half court tennis, volleyball, table tennis, basketball. Children's play area. Off site: Riding 500m. Diving, wind surfing, mountain biking and climbing nearby.

Open

1 May - 30 September.

At a glance

Welcome & Ambience	✓✓✓✓	Location	✓✓✓✓
Quality of Pitches	✓✓✓✓	Range of Facilities	✓✓✓✓✓

Directions

From Ajaccio take the RD81 in direction of Cergése and Calvilby (by coast road). In Sagone take RD70 in direction of Vico, Sagone camping can be found on left after 1.5 km. next to Coccinelle supermarket.

Charges 2005

Per unit incl. 2 persons	€ 14,50 - € 23,00
extra person	€ 4,50 - € 7,70
child (under 12 yrs)	€ 2,25 - € 3,90
electricity	€ 3,00

Camping Cheques accepted.

Reservations

Made with 30% deposit and € 18.50 booking fee; write to site. Tel: 04 95 28 04 15.
E-mail: sagone.camping@wanadoo.fr

FR20100 Camping Caravaning Santa Barbara

RN 200 route d'Aleria, Aerodrome de Corte, 20250 Corte (Haute-Corse)

Santa Barbara is a developing campsite in Corsica's mountainous interior. Corte, the historical capital of the island, stands at 396 m. altitude in the central mountains where you get a feel of the real Corsica and the site is three kilometres east of the town. Already established as a restaurant/bar, the campsite is an ongoing project with, at present, 50 level touring pitches and 10 mobile holiday homes. The pitches are separated by young shrubs and there are 32 electricity connections (12A). An excellent swimming pool is an established focal point and very welcome in this hot, mountainous region. The patio area, which overlooks the pool, is popular and the restaurant is outside near the pool. The owners of the site are friendly and helpful. There could be some noise from the road or small local airport.

Facilities

The toilet facilities are modern and spotlessly clean units including facilities for the disabled, dishwashing, laundry sinks and washing machine. Restaurant/bar offers varied menu also pizza style hut. Swimming pool. Children's play area, table tennis and pool table. Off site: Corte has a full range of shops.

Open

April - 31 October.

At a glance

Welcome & Ambience	✓✓✓✓✓	Location	✓✓✓
Quality of Pitches	✓✓✓✓	Range of Facilities	✓✓✓✓

Directions

Site is 3 km. southeast of Corte by the N200 Aléria road.

Charges guide

Per adult	€ 4,50
child (under 10 yrs)	€ 2,60
caravan	€ 3,70
car	€ 2,50
motorcaravan	€ 5,40
electricity	€ 3,70

Reservations

Write to site. Tel: 04 95 46 20 22.

FR20040 Domaine Naturiste Riva Bella

Mobile homes page 416

B.P. 21, 20270 Alèria (Haute-Corse)

A relaxed, informal naturist site beside a glorious beach, Riva Bella is arguably camping and caravanning at its very best. Although offering a large number and variety of pitches, they are situated in such a huge area of varied and beautiful countryside and seaside that it is difficult to believe it could ever become overcrowded. The site is divided into several distinct areas - pitches and bungalows, alongside the sandy beach, in a wooded glade with ample shade, behind the beach, or beside the lake/lagoon which is a feature of this site. The ground is undulating, so getting an absolutely level pitch could be a problem in the main season. Although electric hook-ups are available in most parts, a long cable is probably a necessity. There is an interesting evening entertainment programme. A recent addition is a therapy centre with treatments and massages based on marine products. Noël Pasqual is fully proud of his site and the fairly unobtrusive rules are designed to ensure that everyone is able to relax, whilst preserving the natural beauty of the environment. There is, for example, a restriction on the movement of cars in certain areas (but ample free parking). Generally the ambience is relaxed and informal with nudity only obligatory on the beach itself. Member 'France 4 Naturisme'.

Facilities

Toilet facilities in several blocks have been completely refurbished. Whilst fairly typical in design for naturist sites, they are fitted and decorated to the highest standards facilities for disabled people and babies. Large well stocked shop (15/5-30/9). Fridge hire. Excellent restaurant (all season) with reasonable prices overlooks the lagoon. Snack bar beside the beach during the main season (1/6-30/9). Watersports including sailing school, fishing, sub-aqua etc. Therapy centre. Sauna. Volleyball, aerobics, table tennis, giant draughts and archery. Fishing. Mountain bike hire. Half-court tennis. Herd of llamas to watch. The police/fire service ban barbecues during the summer as a safety precaution Off site: Riding 5 km.

At a glance

Welcome & Ambience	✓✓✓✓✓	Location	✓✓✓✓✓
Quality of Pitches	✓✓✓✓	Range of Facilities	✓✓✓✓✓

Directions

Site is approx. 8 km. north of Aleria on N198 (Bastia) road. Watch for signs and unmade road to it and follow for 4 km

Charges 2004

Per unit incl. 2 persons	€ 17,00 - € 30,00
extra person	€ 4,00 - € 8,50
child (3-8 yrs)	€ 2,00 - € 5,00
electricity	€ 3,50
dog	€ 3,00 - € 3,00

Camping Cheques accepted.
Special offers and half-board arrangements available.

Reservations

Made with deposit and fee/cancellation insurance.
Tel: 04 95 38 81 10. E-mail: riva-bella@wanadoo.fr

Open

12 April - 11 October.

home from home

Over recent years many of the campsites featured in this guide have added large numbers of high quality mobile homes and chalets. Many site owners believe that some former caravanners and motorcaravanners have been enticed by the extra comfort they can now provide, and that maybe this is the ideal solution to combine the freedom of camping with all the comforts of home.

Quality is consistently high and, although the exact size and inventory may vary from site to site, if you choose any of the sites detailed here, you can be sure that you're staying in some of the best quality and best value mobile homes available.

Home comforts are provided and typically these include a fridge with freezer compartment, gas hob, proper shower - often a microwave and radio/cassette hi-fi too but do check for details. All mobile homes and chalets come fully equipped with a good range of kitchen utensils, pots and pans, crockery, cutlery and outdoor furniture. Some even have an attractive wooden sundeck or paved terrace - a perfect spot for outdoors eating or relaxing with a book and watching the world go by.

Regardless of model, colourful soft furnishings are the norm and a generally breezy décor helps to provide a real holiday feel.

For your convenience and as a result of feedback from many of our readers, we have now included a distinct section on mobile homes and chalets.

Although some sites may have a large number of different accommodation types, we have restricted our choice to one or two of the most popular accommodation units (either mobile homes or chalets) for each of the sites listed.

The mobile homes here will be of modern design, and recent innovations, for example, often include pitched roofs which substantially improve their appearance.

Design will invariably include clever use of space and fittings/furniture to provide for comfortable holidays - usually light and airy, with big windows and patio-style doors, fully equipped kitchen areas, a shower room with shower, washbasin and WC, cleverly designed bedrooms and a comfortable lounge/dining area (often incorporating a sofa bed).

In general, modern campsite chalets incorporate all the best features of mobile homes in a more traditional structure, sometimes with the advantage of an upper mezzanine floor for an additional bedroom.

Our selected campsites offer a massive range of different types of mobile home and chalet, and it would be impractical to inspect every single accommodation unit. Our selection criteria, therefore, primarily takes account of the quality standards of the campsite itself. However, there are a couple of important ground rules

- ☑ Featured mobile homes must be no more than 5 years old, and chalets no more than 10 years old.
- ☑ All listed accommodation must, of course, fully conform with all applicable local, national and European safety legislation.

For each campsite we given details of the type, or types, of accommodation available to rent, but these details are necessarily quite brief. Sometimes internal layouts can differ quite substantially, particularly with regard to sleeping arrangements, where these include the flexible provision for 'extra persons' on sofa beds located in the living area. These arrangements may vary from accommodation to accommodation, and if you're planning a holiday which includes more people than are catered for by the main bedrooms you should check exactly how the extra sleeping arrangements are to be provided!

INSPECTED CAMPSITES & SELECTED

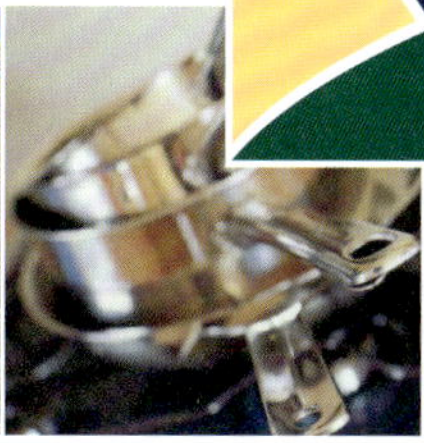

Charges

An indication of the tariff for each type of accommodation featured is also included, indicating the variance between the low and high season tariffs. However, given that many campsites have a large and often complex range of pricing options, incorporating special deals and various discounts, the charges we mention should be taken to be just an indication. We strongly recommend therefore that you confirm the actual cost when making a booking.

We also strongly recommend that you check with the campsite, when booking, what (if anything) will be provided by way of bed linen, blankets, pillows etc. Again, in our experience, this can vary widely from site to site.

On every campsite a fully refundable deposit (usually between 150 and 300 euros) is payable on arrival. There may also be an optional cleaning service for which a further charge is made. Other options may include sheet hire (typically 30 euros per unit) or baby pack hire (cot and high chair).

FR29000 Yelloh! Village Les Mouettes

La Grande Grève, 29660 Carantec

For our full description of this campsite see page 26

The site-owned mobile homes are located together at the top of the site.

AR1 – LOFT 75 – Mobile Home

Sleeping:
2 bedrooms, sleeps 6: 1 double, 1 twin with 2 single beds, 1 double sofa bed; pillows & blankets provided

Living:
living / kitchen area, heating, shower & WC

Eating:
fitted kitchen with cooking hobs, microwave & fridge

Outside:
table & chairs, parasol

Pets:
not accepted

Weekly Charges

	AR1
Low Season *(from)*	€ 210
High Season *(from)*	€ 770

FR29010 Castel Camping Le Ty-Nadan

Route d'Arzano, 29310 Locunolé

For our full description of this campsite see page 37

The chalets are set amongst trees on a slope overlooking the river and woods beyond.

AR1 – BLUE BIRD – Mobile Home

Sleeping:
2 bedrooms, sleeps 6: 1 double, 1 twin with 2 single beds, 1 double sofa bed. pillows & blankets provided

Living:
living / kitchen area, heating, shower & WC

Eating:
fitted kitchen with cooking hobs, oven & fridge

Outside:
table & chairs, sun loungers and parasol

Pets:
accepted

AR2 – Accommodation – Wooden Chalet

Sleeping:
2 bedrooms, sleeps 6: 1 double, 1 twin with 2 single beds, 1 double sofa bed. pillows & blankets provided

Living:
living / kitchen area, heating, shower & WC

Eating:
fitted kitchen with cooking hobs & fridge

Outside:
table & chairs, sun loungers and parasol

Pets:
accepted

Weekly Charges

	AR1	AR2
Low Season *(from)*	€ 312	€ 372
High Season *(from)*	€ 840	€ 980

FR29050 Castel Camping L'Orangerie de Lanniron

Château de Lanniron, 29336 Quimper

For our full description of this campsite see page 29

The mobile homes are situated together on large (150m²) pitches at the top of the site in a peaceful area, all are fitted with wooden terraces.

AR1 – O'HARA – Mobile Home

Sleeping:
2 bedrooms, sleeps 4-6: 1 double, 1 twin with 2 single beds, 1 double sofa bed. pillows & blankets provided

Living:
living / kitchen area, heating, shower & WC

Eating:
fitted kitchen with cooking hobs, microwave & fridge/freezer

Outside:
table & chairs, sun loungers, parasol and BBQ

Pets:
not accepted

AR2 – SUPER MERCURE – Mobile Home

Sleeping:
2 bedrooms, sleeps 4-6: 1 double, 1 twin with 2 single beds, 1 double sofa bed.

Living:
living / kitchen area, heating, shower & WC

Eating:
fitted kitchen with cooking hobs, microwave & fridge/freezer

Outside:
table & chairs, sun loungers, parasol and BBQ

Pets:
not accepted

Weekly Charges

	AR1	AR2
Low Season *(from)*	€ 371	€ 350
High Season *(from)*	€ 798	€ 763

FR29060 Camping Caravaning Le Pil-Koad

Route de Douarnenez, Poullan-sur-Mer, 29100 Douarnenez

For our full description of this campsite see page 28

Most of the chalets are situated together in a 'village' style complex - well landscaped but no adjacent parking. The mobile homes are spread out throughout the site with attractive plants and shrubs.

AR1 – IRM – Mobile Home

Sleeping:
2 bedrooms, sleeps 6: 1 double, 1 twin with 2 single beds, 1 sofa bed in living area. pillows & blankets provided

Living:
living / kitchen area, heating, shower & WC

Eating:
fitted kitchen with cooking hobs, & fridge

Outside:
table & chairs, parasol

Pets:
accepted

AR2 – FABRE – Chalet

Sleeping:
2 bedrooms, sleeps 6: 1 double, 1 twin with 2 single beds, 1 bunk bed, 1 sofa bed in living area. pillows & blankets provided

Living:
living / kitchen area, TV (supplement payable), heating, shower & WC

Eating:
fitted kitchen with cooking hobs microwave & fridge/freezer

Outside:
table & chairs, parasol

Pets:
accepted

Weekly Charges

	AR1	AR2
Low Season *(from)*	€ 250	€ 290
High Season *(from)*	€ 550	€ 630

FR29090 Camping Le Raguénès-Plage

19 rue des Iles, Raguénéz, 29920 Névez

For our full description of this campsite see page 38

The accommodation is located in the north part of the site in small groups, each mobile home is divided by hedges and trees to provide privacy.

AR1 – WILLERBY 2 – Mobile Home

Sleeping:
2 bedrooms, sleeps 5: 1 double, 1 twin with 2 single beds, 1 sofa bed; pillows & blankets provided

Living:
living / kitchen area, fan, heating, shower & WC

Eating:
fitted kitchen with cooking hobs, microwave & fridge/freezer

Outside:
table & chairs, sun loungers, parasol & BBQ

Pets:
accepted

AR2 – WILLERBY 3 – Mobile Home

Sleeping:
2 bedrooms, sleeps 4: 1 double, 1 twin with 2 single beds; pillows & blankets provided

Living:
living / kitchen area, heating, fan, shower & WC

Eating:
fitted kitchen with cooking hobs microwave & fridge/freezer

Outside:
table & chairs, sun loungers, parasol & BBQ

Pets:
accepted

Weekly Charges

	AR1	AR2
Low Season *(from)*	€ 275	€ 340
High Season *(from)*	€ 660	€ 720

FR29130 Camping des Abers

Dunes de Sainte Marguerite, 29870 Landéda

For our full description of this campsite see page 25

The accommodation is located in a quiet, high part of the site, each one is separated by hedges and some have sea views.

AR1 – IRM CONFORT – Mobile Home

Sleeping:
2 bedrooms, sleeps 4-5: 1 double, 1 twin with 2 single beds, 1 single sofa bed; pillows & blankets provided

Living:
living / kitchen area, heating, shower & WC

Eating:
fitted kitchen with cooking hobs & fridge

Outside:
table & chairs, sun loungers, parasol & BBQ

Pets:
accepted

AR2 – GRAND CONFORT – Mobile Home

Sleeping:
2 bedrooms, sleeps 4-6: 1 double, 1 twin with 2 single beds, 1 double sofa bed; pillows & blankets provided

Living:
living / kitchen area, heating, shower & WC

Eating:
fitted kitchen with cooking hobs & fridge

Outside:
table & chairs, sun loungers, parasol & BBQ

Pets:
accepted

Weekly Charges

	AR1	AR2
Low Season *(from)*	€ 250	€ 270
High Season *(from)*	€ 460	€ 520

FR35040 Camping Le P'tit Bois

35430 St Jouan des Guerets

For our full description of this campsite see page 39

The accommodation is dispersed throughout this attractive site.

AR1 – RÉSIDENCE – Mobile Home

Sleeping:
2 bedrooms, sleeps 6: 1 double, 2 twin with 2 single beds

Living:
living / kitchen area, heating, shower & WC

Eating:
fitted kitchen with cooking hobs, microwave & fridge

Outside:
table & chairs, sun loungers, parasol & BBQ

Pets:
one small dog accepted

AR2 – COLORADO – Mobile Home

Sleeping:
2 bedrooms, sleeps 6: 1 double, 1 twin with 2 single beds, 1 sofa bed.

Living:
living / kitchen area, heating, shower & WC

Eating:
fitted kitchen with cooking hobs, microwave & fridge

Outside:
table & chairs, sun loungers, parasol & BBQ

Pets:
one small dog accepted

Weekly Charges

	AR1	AR2
Low Season *(from)*	€ 500	€ 370
High Season *(from)*	€ 900	€ 650

FR44090 Camping Château du Deffay

B.P. 18 Le Deffay, Ste Reine de Bretagne, 44160 Pontchâteau

For our full description of this campsite see page 45

The mobile homes are in areas surrounded with flowers and vegetation. Some of the chalets overlook the lake.

AR1 – Accommodation – Mobile Home

Sleeping:
2 bedrooms, sleeps 5: 1 double, 1 single bed, 2 bunk beds in living area; pillows & blankets provided

Living:
living / kitchen area, heating, shower & WC

Eating:
fitted kitchen with cooking hobs, microwave & fridge/freezer

Outside:
table & chairs, sun loungers, parasol & BBQ

Pets:
accepted (1 per mobile home)

AR2 – Accommodation – Chalet

Sleeping:
2 bedrooms, sleeps 6: 1 double, 2 bunk beds, 1 double sofa bed; pillows & blankets provided

Living:
living / kitchen area, heating, shower & WC

Eating:
fitted kitchen with cooking hobs, dishwasher, microwave & fridge/freezer

Outside:
table & chairs, sun loungers, parasol & BBQ

Pets:
accepted (1 per chalet)

Weekly Charges

	AR1	AR2
Low Season *(from)*	€ 205	€ 225
High Season *(from)*	€ 569	€ 629

FR44100 Sunêlia Le Patisseau

29 rue du Patisseau, 44210 Pornic

For our full description of this campsite see page 42

Comfortable mobile homes and chalets on this site with superb amenities, including an all year heated swimming pool.

AR1 – CHALET 6

Sleeping:
2 bedrooms, sleeps 6: 1 double, 1 twin with 2 single beds, 1 double sofa bed; pillows & blankets provided

Living:
living / kitchen area, heating, shower & WC

Eating:
fitted kitchen with cooking hobs, microwave, pressure cooker & fridge

Outside:
table & chairs, parasol & BBQ

Pets:
not accepted

AR2 – MOBILE HOME 6

Sleeping:
2 bedrooms, sleeps 6: 1 double, 2 single beds, 1 double sofa bed; pillows & blankets provided

Living:
living / kitchen area, heating, shower & WC

Eating:
fitted kitchen with cooking hobs, pressure cooker & fridge

Outside:
table & chairs, parasol & BBQ

Pets:
not accepted

Weekly Charges

	AR1	AR2
Low Season *(from)*	€ 332	€ 297
High Season *(from)*	€ 869	€ 816

FR44190 Camping Le Fief

57, chemin du Fief, 44250 St Brévin-les-Pins

For our full description of this campsite see page 47

AR1 – Accommodation – Cottages

Sleeping:
3 bedrooms, sleeps 6: 1 double, 2 bedrooms with 2 twin beds

Living:
living / kitchen area, shower & W/C, sofa bed

Eating:
fitted kitchen with cooking hobs & fridge & microwave

Outside:
table & chairs

Pets:
accepted

AR2 – Accommodation – Cottages

Sleeping:
2 bedrooms, sleeps 6: 1 double, 1 twin with 2 single beds

Living:
living / kitchen area, shower & WC, sofabed

Eating:
fitted kitchen with cooking hobs, microwave & fridge

Outside:
table & chairs

Pets:
accepted

Weekly Charges

	AR1	AR2
Low Season *(from)*	€ 315	€ 315
High Season *(from)*	€ 750	€ 700

FR76130 Camping de la Forêt

Rue Mainberthe, 76480 Jumieges

For our full description of this campsite see page 70

AR1 – CHATAIGNER – Chalet

Sleeping:
2 bedrooms, sleeps 5: 1 double, 1 twin with 2 single beds, 1 sofa bed; pillows & blankets provided

Living:
living / kitchen area, heating, shower & WC

Eating:
fitted kitchen with cooking hobs, microwave & fridge

Outside:
table & chairs, parasol

Pets:
accepted

AR2 – CONFORT – Mobile Home

Sleeping:
2 bedrooms, sleeps 6: 1 double, 1 twin with 2 beds, 1 double sofa bed; pillows & blankets provided

Living:
living / kitchen area, heating, shower & WC

Eating:
fitted kitchen with cooking hobs, microwave & fridge

Outside:
table & chairs, parasol

Pets:
accepted

Weekly Charges

	AR1	AR2
Low Season *(from)*	€ 260	€ 260
High Season *(from)*	€ 450	€ 450

FR02030 Caravaning La Croix du Vieux Pont

02290 Berny-Riviere

For our full description of this campsite page 73

AR1 – APARTMENT – Apartment

Sleeping:
Sleeps 6 Mezzanine with 2 singles beds (or 1 double), bedroom with 2 single beds (or 1 double)

Living:
living with 2 single sofa beds, tv, shower & WC

Eating:
fitted kitchen with dishwasher, oven & microwave

Outside:
terrace with garden furniture, balacony & BBQ

Pets:
AR1pets

Weekly Charges

	AR1
Low Season *(from)*	€ 460
High Season *(from)*	€ 860

FR62060 Caravaning L'Orée du Bois

Chemin Blanc, 62180 Rang-du-Fliers

For our full description of this campsite see page 75

Attractively sited accommodation on this beautiful site

AR1 – EVASION – Chalet

Sleeping:
1 bedrooms, sleeps 2 - 4: 1 double, 1 sofa bed

Living:
living / kitchen area, shower & WC

Eating:
fitted kitchen with cooking hobs & fridge (oven on request)

Outside:
table & chairs

Pets:
accepted

AR2 – REVE – Chalet

Sleeping:
2 bedrooms, sleeps 4-6: 1 double, 1 twin with 2 single beds

Living:
living / kitchen area, shower & WC

Eating:
fitted kitchen with cooking hobs & fridge (oven on request)

Outside:
table & chairs

Pets:
accepted

Weekly Charges

	AR1	AR2
Low Season *(from)*	€ 231	€ 290
High Season *(from)*	€ 476	€ 616

FR80060 Camping Le Val de Trie

Bouillancourt-sous-Miannay, 80870 Moyenneville

For our full description of this campsite see page 80

The mobile homes are all grouped together in a dedicated area of the site, each one separated by hedges and flowers to provide privacy.

AR1 – MORÉVA – Mobile Home

Sleeping:
2 bedrooms, sleeps 6: 1 double, 1 twin with 2 single beds, 1 double sofa bed; pillows & blankets provided

Living:
living / kitchen area, heating, shower & WC

Eating:
fitted kitchen with cooking hobs, microwave & fridge/freezer

Outside:
table & chairs, parasol & BBQ

Pets:
not accepted

AR2 – ZEN – Mobile Home

Sleeping:
3 bedrooms, sleeps 6: 1 double, 2 twin with 2 single beds

Living:
living / kitchen area, shower & WC

Eating:
fitted kitchen with cooking hobs, microwave, fridge/freezer

Outside:
table & chairs, sun loungers, parasol & BBQ

Pets:
not accepted

Weekly Charges

	AR1	AR2
Low Season *(from)*	€ 195	€ 305
High Season *(from)*	€ 400	€ 500

FR80070 Camping La Ferme des Aulnes

1 rue du Marais, Fresne-sur-Authie, 80120 Nampont-St Martin

For our full description of this campsite see page 77

Attractive locations within this beautiful site, with all amenities (swimming pool etc.) operating for the full season.

AR1 – CONFORT – Mobile Home

Sleeping:
2 bedrooms, sleeps 5: 1 double, 1 twin with 2 single beds, 1 sofa bed

Living:
living / kitchen area, heating, shower & WC, TV

Eating:
fitted kitchen with cooking hobs, microwave & fridge/freezer

Outside:
table & chairs, sun loungers, parasol & BBQ

Pets:
accepted (supp. €50. per stay)

AR2 – PRIVILEGE – Mobile home

Sleeping:
3 bedrooms, sleeps 6: 1 double, 2 twin with 2 single beds

Living:
living / kitchen area, heating, shower & WC. TV

Eating:
fitted kitchen with cooking hobs, microwave, fridge/freezer, dishwasher

Outside:
table & chairs, sun loungers, parasol & BBQ

Pets:
accepted (supp. €50. per stay)

Weekly Charges

	AR1	AR2
Low Season *(from)*	€ 460	€ 560
High Season *(from)*	€ 660	€ 770

FR08040 Camping La Samaritaine

08240 Buzancy

For our full description of this campsite see page 90

Attractive locations around this calm and beautiful site.

AR1 – SYMPA 26 – Mobile Home

Sleeping:
2 bedrooms, sleeps 5: 1 double, 1 twin with 2 single beds, 1 sofa bed

Living:
living / kitchen area, shower & WC

Eating:
fitted kitchen with cooking hobs & fridge

Outside:
table & chairs, sun loungers & parasol

Pets:
accepted (supplement payable)

AR2 – CASALIVE – Chalet

Sleeping:
2 bedrooms, sleeps 6: 1 double, 1 twin with 2 single beds, 1 sofa bed.

Living:
living / kitchen area, shower & WC

Eating:
fitted kitchen with cooking hobs, microwave & fridge

Outside:
table & chairs, sun loungers & parasol

Pets:
accepted (supplement payable)

Weekly Charges

	AR1	AR2
Low Season *(from)*	€ 275	€ 350
High Season *(from)*	€ 470	€ 550

FR77060 Le Parc de la Colline

Route de Lagny, 77200 Torcy

Pitches at this campsite are exclusively for mobile homes & chalets

Set in the heart of Marne-la-Vallée, with easy access to Paris and Disneyland, Parc de la Colline is in a relatively green area on the outskirts of the capital, situated on a fairly steep slope. There is a childrens' play area and a shop on site, with a supermarket and water park nearby. The site runs a minibus service to the nearest métro station at Torcy, for easy access to Paris or Disneyland, plus trips to Parc Asterix and group visits to central Paris. Reception will advise on the best value travel cards and these can be purchased on site. Reception staff speak good English. Note - you are close to a major city environment. Petty crime can be a problem and we recommend the use of the safety deposit boxes.

Facilities

Shop (all year). Snack bar (high season). Several children's play areas, minigolf, basketball and table tennis. Bus service (every 15 minutes between 0800 and 2400 with a pause at lunchtime). Off site: Disneyland 10 mins. (métro), central Paris 20 mins (métro), Parc Asterix 30 mins (car). Supermarket and restaurants nearby.

Open

All year.

Directions

From A104 (La Francilienne) take exit 10, turn left (westwards) and the site entrance is approx. 1km (well signposted).

Reservations

Contact site. Tel: 01 60 05 42 32

E-mail: camping.parc.de.la.colline@wanadoo.fr

AR1 – O'HARA – Mobile Home

Sleeping:

2 bedrooms, sleeps 6: 1 double, 1 twin with 2 single beds, 1 double sofa bed; pillows & blankets provided

Living:

living / kitchen area, heating, shower & WC

Eating:

fitted kitchen with cooking hobs & fridge

Outside:

table & chairs

Pets:

accepted (€4.50 per night)

AR2 – NEVA – Chalet

Sleeping:

2 bedrooms, sleeps 4: 1 double, 1 twin with 2 bunk beds; pillows & blankets provided

Living:

living / kitchen area, heating, shower & WC

Eating:

fitted kitchen with cooking hobs & fridge

Outside:

table & chairs

Pets:

accepted (€4.50 per night)

Weekly Charges

	AR1	AR2
Low Season *(from)*	€ 666	€ 652
High Season *(from)*	€ 666	€ 652

FR52030 Camping Lac de la Liez

Peigney, 52200 Langres

For our full description of this campsite see page 92

The 23 chalets are situated between 100-200 m. from the swimming pool, restaurant, etc. They are on large, terraced pitches, separated by hedges and bushes, most have views of the lake.

AR1 – COUNTRY LODGE – Chalet

Sleeping:
2 bedrooms, sleeps 6: 1 double, 1 twin with 2 bunk beds, 1 single bed; pillows & blankets provided

Living:
lounge, american kitchen, bathroom & WC

Eating:
fitted kitchen with cooking hobs, microwave & fridge/freezer

Outside:
table & chairs, sun loungers & parasol

Pets:
accepted with supplement

AR2 – ZEN – Mobile Home

Sleeping:
3 bedrooms, sleeps 6: 1 double, 2 twin with 2 single beds

Living:
AR2living

Eating:
fitted kitchen with oven, microwave, fridge/freezer, cooking hobs

Outside:
table & chairs, sun loungers, parasol

Pets:
accepted with supplement

Weekly Charges

	AR1	AR2
Low Season *(from)*	€ 336	€ 336
High Season *(from)*	€ 670	€ 670

FR88040 Camping Club Lac du Bouzey

19 rue du lac, 88390 Sanchey (Vosges)

For our full description of this campsite see page 98

AR1 – ADI – Mobile Home

Sleeping:
2 bedrooms, sleeps 6: 1 double, 1 twin with 2 single beds, 1 double sofa bed; pillows & blankets provided

Living:
living / kitchen area, heating, shower & WC

Eating:
fitted kitchen with cooking hobs, microwave & fridge

Outside:
table & chairs, sun loungers, parasol & BBQ

Pets:
accepted

AR2 – ZEN – Mobile Home

Sleeping:
3 bedrooms, sleeps 6: 1 double, 2 twin; pillows & blankets provided

Living:
living / kitchen area, heating, shower & WC

Eating:
fitted kitchen with cooking hobs, microwave & fridge

Outside:
table & chairs, sun loungers, parasol

Pets:
not accepted

Weekly Charges

	AR1	AR2
Low Season *(from)*	€ 300	€ 450
High Season *(from)*	€ 600	€ 800

FR17010 Camping Bois Soleil

2 avenue de Suzac, 17110 St Georges-de-Didonne

For our full description of this campsite see page 102

The area of the site where mobile homes are situated is beside the sea and has direct access to the beach by steps.

AR1 – O'HARA COTTAGE CHARME – Mobile Home

Sleeping:
2 bedrooms, sleeps 6: 1 double, 1 twin with 2 single beds, 1 double sofa bed; pillows & blankets provided

Living:
living / kitchen area, heating, shower & WC

Eating:
fitted kitchen with cooking hobs, microwave & fridge

Outside:
table & chairs, parasol

Pets:
not accepted (July and August)

AR2 – BURSTNER COTTAGE – Mobile Home

Sleeping:
2 bedrooms, sleeps 5: 1 double, 1 twin with 2 single beds, 1 single sofa bed; pillows & blankets provided

Living:
living / kitchen area, heating, hair dryer, shower & WC

Eating:
fitted kitchen with cooking hobs, microwave & fridge

Outside:
table & chairs, parasol

Pets:
not accepted (July and August)

Weekly Charges

	AR1	AR2
Low Season *(from)*	€ 358	€ 218
High Season *(from)*	€ 860	€ 520

FR17140 Castel Camping Sequoia Parc

La Josephtrie, 17320 St Just-Luzac

For our full description of this campsite see page 104

The chalets are situated near the swimming pool or the tennis courts and the mobile homes are near to the château.

AR1 – GITOTEL – Chalet

Sleeping:
2 bedrooms, sleeps 6: 2 double, 1 twin with 2 bunk beds; pillows & blankets provided

Living:
living / kitchen area, heating, shower & WC

Eating:
fitted kitchen with cooking hobs, microwave & fridge

Outside:
table & chairs, sun loungers

Pets:
not accepted

AR2 – COTTAGE 6 – Mobile Home

Sleeping:
2 bedrooms, sleeps 6: 1 double, 1 twin with 2 single beds, 1 double sofa bed; pillows & blankets provided

Living:
living / kitchen area, heating, shower & WC

Eating:
fitted kitchen with cooking hobs, microwave & fridge

Outside:
table & chairs, sun loungers

Pets:
not accepted

Weekly Charges

	AR1	AR2
Low Season *(from)*	€ 231	€ 210
High Season *(from)*	€ 882	€ 826

Bois Soleil

Camping ★★★★
Charente-Maritime

Surrounded by pine trees and a sandy beach on the Atlantic Coast, with one direct access to the beach, Bois Soleil proposes to you many attractions like tennis, tabletennis, children playgrounds and entertainment.
Shops, take-away and snack-bar with big TV screen.

Camping-Caravaning Les pieds dans l'eau
www.lespiedsdansleau.com

Camping Cheque

Camping Qualité

Spring and Summer 2005

2, avenue de Suzac - 17110 ST GEORGES DE DIDONNE
Tel: 0033 546 05 05 94 - Fax: 0033 546 06 27 43
www.bois-soleil.com / e-mail: camping.bois.soleil@wanadoo.fr

FR17230 Camping de L'Océan

La Passe, La Couarde sur Mer, 17670 Ile de Ré

For our full description of this campsite see page 110

AR1 – SAVANAH – Mobile Home

Sleeping:
2 bedrooms, sleeps 6: 1 double, 1 twin with 1 single bed, 1 bunk bed, 1 double sofa bed; pillows & blankets provided

Living:
huge rooms

Eating:
fitted kitchen

Outside:
table & chairs, parasol

Pets:
accepted

AR2 – CRL – Residence Mobile

Sleeping:
Sleeps 4 - 7

Living:
huge rooms

Eating:
fitted kitchen

Outside:
Terrace, table, chairs, parasol & 2 sun loungers

Pets:
accepted

Weekly Charges

	AR1	AR2
Low Season *(from)*	€ 314	€ 350
High Season *(from)*	€ 650	€ 700

FR85040 Castel Camping Caravaning La Garangeoire

St Julien-des-Landes, 85150 La Mothe-Achard

For our full description of this campsite see page 122

The featured accommodation is situated in a discreet area among oak trees but close to the main facilities, within a 200 hectare estate.

AR1 – O'HARA – Mobile Home

Sleeping:
2 bedrooms, sleeps 5: 1 double, 1 twin with 2 single beds, 1 sofa bed; pillows & blankets provided

Living:
living / kitchen area, fan, heating, shower & WC

Eating:
fitted kitchen with cooking hobs, oven & fridge

Outside:
table & chairs, sun loungers, parasol & BBQ

Pets:
accepted (€4.20 per night)

AR2 – 3 SEASONS ELITE – Chalet

Sleeping:
2 bedrooms, sleeps 4-6: 1 double, 1 twin with 2 single beds, 1 double sofa bed; pillows & blankets provided

Living:
living / kitchen area, heating, shower & WC

Eating:
fitted kitchen with cooking hobs, oven, fridge freezer & dishwasher

Outside:
table & chairs, sun loungers, parasol & BBQ

Pets:
accepted (€4.20 per night)

Weekly Charges

	AR1	AR2
Low Season *(from)*	€ 260	€ 350
High Season *(from)*	€ 715	€ 900

FR85070 Camping Les Biches

Route de Notre-Dame-de-Riez, 85270 St Hilaire-de-Riez

For our full description of this campsite see page 125

The featured accommodation are situated amongst the touring area, all divided by hedges.

AR1 – O'HARA – Mobile Home

Sleeping:
2 bedrooms, sleeps 6: 1 double, 1 twin with 2 single beds

Living:
living / kitchen area, heating, shower & WC

Eating:
fitted kitchen with cooking hobs, microwave & fridge

Outside:
table & chairs, sun loungers

Pets:
small dogs accepted

AR2 – GITOTEL – Chalet

Sleeping:
3 bedrooms, sleeps 6: 1 double, 1 twin with 2 single beds, 2 bunk beds; pillows & blankets provided

Living:
living / kitchen area, heating, shower & WC

Eating:
fitted kitchen with cooking hobs, microwave & fridge

Outside:
table & chairs, sun loungers

Pets:
small dogs accepted

Weekly Charges

	AR1	AR2
Low Season *(from)*	€ 364	€ 441
High Season *(from)*	€ 630	€ 735

FR85150 Camping La Yole

Chemin des Bosses, Orouet, 85160 St Jean-de-Monts

For our full description of this campsite see page 129

The featured accommodation are situated in a wooded area within the campsite.

AR1 – LOUISIANE FLORES 2 – Mobile Home

Sleeping:
2 bedrooms, sleeps 6: 1 double, 2 twin with 2 single beds; pillows & blankets provided

Living:
living / kitchen area, heating, shower & WC

Eating:
fitted kitchen with cooking hobs, microwave & fridge/freezer

Outside:
table & chairs, sun loungers & parasol

Pets:
not accepted

AR2 – LOUISIANE FLORES 3 – Mobile Home

Sleeping:
3 bedrooms, sleeps 6: 1 double, 2 twin with 2 single beds; pillows & blankets provided

Living:
living / kitchen area, heating, safe, shower & WC

Eating:
fitted kitchen with cooking hobs, microwave & fridge/freezer

Outside:
table & chairs, sun loungers & parasol

Pets:
not accepted

Weekly Charges

	AR1	AR2
Low Season *(from)*	€ 392	€ 420
High Season *(from)*	€ 740	€ 775

FR85300 Camping La Grand' Métairie

8 rue de la Vineuse en Plaine, 85440 St Hilaire-la-Forêt

For our full description of this campsite see page 125

The mobile homes are situated in their own dedicated area close to the centre of the site, about 5 minutes from the swimming pool and main facilities. The chalets are on the edge of the site a little further away from the facilities.

AR1 – ABI – Mobile Home

Sleeping:
2 bedrooms, sleeps 7: 1 double, 1 twin with 2 single beds, 2 bunk beds, 1 sofa bed; pillows & blankets provided

Living:
living / kitchen area, heating, shower & WC

Eating:
fitted kitchen with cooking hobs, microwave & fridge/freezer

Outside:
table & chairs, parasol

Pets:
accepted

AR2 – GITOTEL – Chalet

Sleeping:
2 bedrooms, sleeps 6: 1 double, 1 twin with 2 single beds, 1 double sofa bed.

Living:
living / kitchen area, heating, shower & WC

Eating:
fitted kitchen with cooking hobs, microwave & fridge/freezer

Outside:
table & chairs, parasol

Pets:
accepted

Weekly Charges

	AR1	AR2
Low Season *(from)*	€ 190	€ 230
High Season *(from)*	€ 670	€ 710

FR85330 Camping Naturiste Cap Natur'

151 ave de la Faye, 85270 St Hilaire-de-Riez

For our full description of this campsite see page 126

Attractive locations within this pretty naturist site

AR1 – MOBILE HOME 4

Sleeping:
2 bedrooms, sleeps 4: 1 double, 1 twin with 2 single beds. All bed linen provided

Living:
living / kitchen area, heating, shower & WC

Eating:
fitted kitchen with cooking hobs & fridge

Outside:
table & chairs, parasol

Pets:
accepted

AR2 – CONVIVES – Appartment

Sleeping:
2 bedrooms, sleeps 4: 1 double, 1 twin with 2 single beds. All bed linen provided

Living:
living / kitchen area, heating, shower & WC

Eating:
fitted kitchen with cooking hobs, oven microwave & fridge

Outside:
table & chairs, sun loungers & parasol

Pets:
accepted

Weekly Charges

	AR1	AR2
Low Season *(from)*	€ 388	€ 240
High Season *(from)*	€ 675	€ 703

FR37060 Camping L'Arada Parc

Rue de la Baratière, 37360 Sonzay

For our full description of this campsite see page 137

Chalets and mobile homes are separated by maturing trees, shrubs and flowers that provide some shade.

AR1 – SAMEBOIS – Chalet

Sleeping:
3 bedrooms, sleeps 6: 2 double, 2 bunk beds; pillows & blankets provided

Living:
living / kitchen area, heating, shower & WC

Eating:
fitted kitchen with cooking hobs, microwave & fridge

Outside:
table & chairs, parasol & BBQ

Pets:
accepted

AR2 – BÜRSTNER – Mobile Home

Sleeping:
2 bedrooms, sleeps 5: 1 double, 1 single bed, 1 bunk bed, 1 sofa bed; pillows & blankets provided

Living:
living / kitchen area, heating, shower & WC

Eating:
fitted kitchen with cooking hobs, microwave & fridge/freezer

Outside:
table & chairs, sun loungers, parasol & BBQ

Pets:
accepted

Weekly Charges

	AR1	AR2
Low Season *(from)*	€ 200	€ 235
High Season *(from)*	€ 525	€ 590

FR45010 Sunêlia Les Bois du Bardelet

Route de Bourges, Poilly, 45500 Gien

For our full description of this campsite see page 145

The mobile homes are situated in a group with paved terraces and the chalets are in a rural landscaped setting on the edge of the woods and fields.

AR1 – LOUISIANE – Mobile Home

Sleeping:
3 bedrooms, sleeps 6: 1 double, 1 twin with 2 single beds, 2 bunk beds; pillows & blankets provided (must be reserved)

Living:
living / kitchen area, heating, shower & WC

Eating:
fitted kitchen with cooking hobs, oven & fridge/freezer

Outside:
table & chairs, parasol & BBQ

Pets:
not accepted

AR2 – TITOM – Chalet

Sleeping:
2 bedrooms, sleeps 4: 1 double, 1 twin with 2 single beds; pillows & blankets provided (must be reserved)

Living:
living / kitchen area, heating, shower & WC

Eating:
fitted kitchen with cooking hobs, oven & fridge

Outside:
table & chairs, parasol & BBQ

Pets:
accepted

Weekly Charges

	AR1	AR2
Low Season *(from)*	€ 371	€ 322
High Season *(from)*	€ 875	€ 707

FR41010 Le Parc du Val de Loire

Route de Fleuray, 41150 Mesland

For our full description of this campsite see page 142

AR1 – FABRE – Chalet

Sleeping:
2 bedrooms, sleeps 7: 1 double, 1 twin with 2 single beds, 1 bunk bed, 1 double sofa bed; pillows & blankets provided

Living:
living / kitchen area, shower & WC

Eating:
fitted kitchen with cooking hobs, microwave & fridge

Outside:
table & chairs, sun loungers & parasol

Pets:
accepted

AR2 – O'HARA – Chalet

Sleeping:
2 bedrooms, sleeps 7: 1 double, 1 twin with 2 single beds, 1 bunk bed, 1 double sofa bed; pillows & blankets provided

Living:
living / kitchen area, shower & WC

Eating:
fitted kitchen with cooking hobs, microwave & fridge

Outside:
table & chairs, sun loungers & parasol

Pets:
accepted

Weekly Charges

	AR1	AR2
Low Season *(from)*	€ 209	€ 176
High Season *(from)*	€ 657	€ 591

FR41020 Castel Camping Château de la Grenouillière

41500 Suèvres

For our full description of this campsite see page 140

AR1 – WILLERBY – Mobile Home

Sleeping:
2 bedrooms, sleeps 6: 2 double, 2 bunk beds; pillows & blankets provided

Living:
living / kitchen area' heating, shower & WC

Eating:
fitted kitchen with cooking hobs & fridge

Outside:
table & chairs, parasol

Pets:
accepted

Weekly Charges

	AR1
Low Season *(from)*	€ 290
High Season *(from)*	€ 507

FR41070 Camping Caravanning La Grande Tortue

3 route de Pontlevoy, 41120 Candé-sur-Beuvron

For our full description of this campsite see page 143

The featured accommodation are situated amongst trees which provide welcome shade as well as some sunshine.

AR1 – IRM – Mobile Home

Sleeping:
2 bedrooms, sleeps 6 1 double, 1 twin with 2 single beds, 1 double sofa bed; pillows & blankets provided

Living:
living / kitchen area, heating, shower & WC

Eating:
fitted kitchen with cooking hobs & fridge

Outside:
table & chairs, sun loungers and parasol

Pets:
accepted

AR2 – SHELBOX – Chalet

Sleeping:
2 bedrooms, sleeps 6: 1 double, 1 twin with 2 single beds, 1 double sofa bed; pillows & blankets provided

Living:
living / kitchen area, heating, shower & WC

Eating:
fitted kitchen with cooking hobs, microwave & fridge

Outside:
table & chairs, sun loungers and parasol

Pets:
accepted

Weekly Charges

	AR1	AR2
Low Season *(from)*	€ 257	€ 317
High Season *(from)*	€ 600	€ 650

FR49040 Camping de l'Etang

Route de St Mathurin, 49320 Brissac

For our full description of this campsite see page 146

Large pitches with gravel terraces. Free access to adjacent leisure park.

AR1 – WILLERBY – Mobile Home

Sleeping:
2 bedrooms, sleeps 6: 1 double, 1 twin with 2 single beds, 1 double sofa bed. Disposable sheets for sale. Blankets provided

Living:
living / kitchen area, heating, shower & WC

Eating:
fitted kitchen with cooking hobs & fridge

Outside:
table & chairs, sun loungers, BBQ

Pets:
accepted €2 per night

AR2 – CONCORDE – Mobile Home

Sleeping:
2 bedrooms, sleeps 6: 1 double, 1 twin with 2 single beds, 1 double sofa bed; blankets provided. Disposable sheets for sale

Living:
living / kitchen area, heating, shower & WC

Eating:
fitted kitchen with cooking hobs & fridge

Outside:
table & chairs, BBQ

Pets:
accepted (€2 per night)

Weekly Charges

	AR1	AR2
Low Season *(from)*	€ 370	€ 370
High Season *(from)*	€ 560	€ 560

FR86030 Camping Le Relais du Miel

Route d'Antran, 86100 Châtellerault

For our full description of this campsite see page 151

Attractive appartments in an old French house.

AR1 – FURNISHED FLAT

Sleeping:
1 bedroom, sleeps 2

Living:
living / kitchen area, shower & W/C

Eating:
fitted kitchen with cooking hobs, microwave & fridge

Outside:
table & chairs

Pets:
not accepted

AR2 – FURNISHED FLAT

Sleeping:
1 bedroom sleeps 4. 1 double, 1 sofa bed

Living:
living / kitchen area, shower & WC

Eating:
fitted kitchen with cooking hobs, microwave & fridge

Outside:
table & chairs

Pets:
not accepted

Weekly Charges

	AR1	AR2
Low Season *(from)*	€ 250	€ 350
High Season *(from)*	€ 295	€ 395

FR58010 Camping des Bains

15 avenue Jean Mermoz, 58360 St Honoré-les-Bains

For our full description of this campsite see page 160

Gîtes are situated on the edge of the site in groups of two, three or four, separated from each other by hedges.

AR1 – Accommodation – Gîte

Sleeping:
2 bedrooms, sleeps 4: 1 double, 1 twin with 2 bunk beds; pillows & blankets provided

Living:
living / kitchen area, fan, heating, shower & WC

Eating:
fitted kitchen with cooking hobs, oven & fridge

Outside:
table & chairs, parasol

Pets:
accepted

Weekly Charges

	AR1
Low Season *(from)*	€ 110
High Season *(from)*	€ 460

FR71020 Le Village des Meuniers

71520 Dompierre-les-Ormes

For our full description of this campsite see page 161

Most of the 12 chalets / gîtes enjoy stunning views of the surrounding countryside - the Beaujolais, the Maconnais, the Charollais and the Clunysois.

AR1 – FRENE – Chalet

Sleeping:
3 bedrooms, sleeps 8: 1 double, 2 twin with 2 single beds, 1 double sofa bed; pillows & blankets provided

Living:
living / kitchen area, heating, shower & WC

Eating:
fitted kitchen with cooking hobs, microwave & fridge

Outside:
table & chairs

Pets:
accepted

AR2 – VERONA – Mobile Home

Sleeping:
2 bedrooms, sleeps 5: 1 double, 1 with 3 single beds

Living:
living / kitchen area, TV, heating, shower & WC

Eating:
fitted kitchen with cooking hobs, oven, microwave & fridge/freezer, washing machine & dishwasher

Outside:
table & chairs

Pets:
accepted

Weekly Charges

	AR1	AR2
Low Season *(from)*	€ 250	€ 170
High Season *(from)*	€ 510	€ 460

FR39040 Sunêlia La Pergola

339130 Marigny

For our full description of this campsite see page 168

Mobile homes are situated in an area away from the activities, on the edge of the lake but not too far from the facilities.

AR1 – CONFORT – Mobile Home

Sleeping:
2 bedrooms, sleeps 6: 1 double, 1 twin with 2 single beds, 1 double sofa bed; pillows & blankets provided

Living:
living / kitchen area, fan, heating, shower & WC

Eating:
fitted kitchen with cooking hobs, oven & fridge/freezer

Outside:
table & chairs, sun loungers, parasol & BBQ

Pets:
accepted (€4 per night)

AR2 – CLASSIC – Mobile Home

Sleeping:
2 bedrooms, sleeps 6: 1 double, 1 twin with 2 single beds, 1 double sofa bed; pillows & blankets provided

Living:
living / kitchen area, fan, heating, shower & WC

Eating:
fitted kitchen with cooking hobs & fridge/freezer

Outside:
table & chairs, sun loungers, parasol & BBQ

Pets:
accepted (€4 per night)

Weekly Charges

	AR1	AR2
Low Season *(from)*	€ 336	€ 300
High Season *(from)*	€ 805	€ 721

FR86040 Camping Le Futuriste

86130 St Georges-les-Baillargeaux

For our full description of this campsite see page 154

All chalets are situated in the centre of the site and are accessed via neat, level and firmly rolled gravel roads.

AR1 – FABRE – Chalet

Sleeping:
2 bedrooms, sleeps 6: 1 double, 1 twin with 2 single beds, 1 double sofa bed; pillows & blankets provided

Living:
living / kitchen area, TV, heating, shower & WC

Eating:
fitted kitchen with cooking hobs, microwave & fridge/freezer

Outside:
table & chairs

Pets:
not accepted

AR2 – Accommodation – Chalet

Sleeping:
Sleeps 4

Living:
living / kitchen area, TV, heating, shower & WC

Eating:
fitted kitchen with cooking hobs, microwave & fridge/freezer

Outside:
table & chairs

Pets:
not accepted

Weekly Charges

	AR1	AR2
Low Season *(from)*	€ 334	€ 267
High Season *(from)*	€ 480	€ 343

FR86090 Camping du Parc de Saint Cyr

86130 Saint Cyr

For our full description of this campsite see page 153

A good modern site and a good place to relax.

AR1 – IRM – Mobile Home

Sleeping:
sleeps 4/6

Living:
living room

Eating:
fitted kitchen with oven

Outside:
table & chairs

Pets:
accepted

AR2 – WILLERBY – Mobile Home

Sleeping:
sleeps 4/6

Living:
living room

Eating:
fitted kitchen with oven

Outside:
table & chairs

Pets:
accepted

Weekly Charges

	AR1	AR2
Low Season *(from)*	€ 290	€ 290
High Season *(from)*	€ 510	€ 510

FR21000 Camping Lac de Panthier

21320 Vandenesse-en-Auxois

For our full description of this campsite see page 159

The mobile homes and chalets are situated near to the swimming pool and have some shade.

AR1 – CLUB – Chalet

Sleeping:
2 bedrooms, sleeps 5: 1 double, 1 twin with 2 single beds, 1 single bed; pillows & blankets provided

Living:
living / kitchen area, fan, heating, shower & WC

Eating:
fitted kitchen with cooking hobs, microwave & fridge

Outside:
table & chairs, sun loungers, parasol & BBQ

Pets:
accepted

AR2 – COTTAGE GRAND CONFORT – Mobile Home

Sleeping:
2 bedrooms, sleeps 5: 1 double, 1 twin with 2 single beds, 1 bunk bed; pillows & blankets provided

Living:
living / kitchen area, fan, heating, shower & WC

Eating:
fitted kitchen with cooking hobs, microwave & fridge/freezer

Outside:
table & chairs, sun loungers, parasol & BBQ

Pets:
accepted

Weekly Charges

	AR1	AR2
Low Season *(from)*	€ 266	€ 210
High Season *(from)*	€ 616	€ 588

FR21040 Camping de l'Etang de Fouche

Rue du 8 Mai 1945, 21230 Arnay le Duc

For our full description of this campsite see page 157

AR1 – GRAND CONFORT – Chalet

Sleeping:
2 bedrooms, sleeps 4: sofa

Living:
living / kitchen area, bathroom

Eating:
fitted kitchen with cooking hobs & fridge

Outside:
covered terrace, garden furniture & parasol

Pets:
accepted

AR2 – CONFORT – Chalet

Sleeping:
2 bedrooms, sleeps 4

Living:
living / kitchen area, bathroom

Eating:
fitted kitchen with cooking hobs, oven & fridge

Outside:
covered terrace, garden furniture & parasol

Pets:
accepted

Weekly Charges

	AR1	AR2
Low Season *(from)*	€ 240	€ 210
High Season *(from)*	€ 490	€ 460

FR38010 Le Coin Tranquille

38490 Les Abrets

For our full description of this campsite see page 172

The Shelbox chalets are across the road from the main section of the campsite, but still close to the bar, restaurant and swimming pool. The Fabre chalets are at the far end of the site with magnificent views.

AR1 – SHELBOX – Chalet

Sleeping:
2 bedrooms, sleeps 7: 1 double, 1 twin with 2 single beds, 1 bunk bed, 1 double sofa bed; pillows & blankets provided

Living:
living / kitchen area, heating, shower & WC

Eating:
fitted kitchen with cooking hobs, oven & fridge/freezer

Outside:
table & chairs, sun loungers, parasol & BBQ

Pets:
accepted

AR2 – FABRE 2012 – Chalet

Sleeping:
2 bedrooms, sleeps 7: 1 double, 1 twin with 2 single beds, 1 bunk bed, 1 double sofa bed; pillows & blankets provided

Living:
living / kitchen area, heating, shower & WC

Eating:
fitted kitchen with cooking hobs, microwave & fridge

Outside:
table & chairs, sun loungers, parasol & BBQ

Pets:
accepted

Weekly Charges

	AR1	AR2
Low Season *(from)*	€ 350	€ 290
High Season *(from)*	€ 760	€ 660

FR73030 Camping Les Lanchettes

73210 Peisey-Nancroix

For our full description of this campsite see page 177

AR1 – Accommodation – Chalet

Sleeping:
sleeps 4/5, 1double bed, 3 single beds

Living:
living / kitchen area, shower & WC

Eating:
dishwasher, oven, fridge/freezer, cooking hobs

Outside:
table & chairs, parasol

Pets:
not accepted

AR2 – CHARLAY-BALLARIO – Chalet

Sleeping:
Sleeps 4 to 6, 1double bed, 4 single beds

Living:
living / kitchen area, shower & WC

Eating:
fitted kitchen with dishwasher,oven fridge, freezer & cooking hobs

Outside:
table & chairs, parasol

Pets:
not accepted

Weekly Charges

	AR1	AR2
Low Season *(from)*	€ 250	€ 300
High Season *(from)*	€ 550	€ 600

FR33110 Airotel Camping de la Côte d'Argent

33990 Hourtin-Plage

For our full description of this campsite see page 188

Mobile homes are situated in the centre of the site, amongst the pine trees.

AR1 – LOUISIANE – Mobile Home

Sleeping:
2 bedrooms, sleeps 6: 1 double, 1 twin with 2 single beds, 1 double sofa bed; pillows & blankets provided

Living:
living / kitchen area, shower & WC

Eating:
fitted kitchen with cooking hobs & fridge

Outside:
table & chairs, parasol

Pets:
not accepted

AR2 – O'HARA – Mobile Home

Sleeping:
2 bedrooms, sleeps 6: 1 double, 1 twin with 2 single beds, 1 double sofa bed; pillows & blankets provided

Living:
living / kitchen area, shower & WC

Eating:
fitted kitchen with cooking hobs & fridge

Outside:
table & chairs, parasol

Pets:
not accepted

Weekly Charges

	AR1	AR2
Low Season *(from)*	€ 490	€ 490
High Season *(from)*	€ 791	€ 791

FR33130 Camping Caravaning Les Grands Pins

33680 Lacanau-Océan

For our full description of this campsite see page 191

AR1 – PREMIER – Mobile Home

Sleeping:
2 bedrooms, sleeps 4: 1 double, 1 twin with 2 single beds

Living:
living / kitchen area, heating, shower & WC

Eating:
fitted kitchen with cooking hobs, microwave & fridge

Outside:
table & chairs, sun loungers & parasol

Pets:
accepted

AR2 – SUNSET – Mobile Home

Sleeping:
3 bedrooms, sleeps 6: 1 double, 1 twin with 2 single beds, 1 bunk bed

Living:
living / kitchen area, TV, heating, shower & WC

Eating:
fitted kitchen with cooking hobs, microwave & fridge

Outside:
table & chairs, sun loungers & parasol

Pets:
accepted

Weekly Charges

	AR1	AR2
Low Season *(from)*	€ 196	€ 245
High Season *(from)*	€ 742	€ 1015

FR33300 Parc Residentiel de Loisirs La Jenny

33680 Le Porge

Pitches at this campsite are exclusively for mobile homes & chalets

Situated at the heart of Europe's largest forest, yet within walking distance - through the forest - to the Atlantic beaches, La Jenny naturist site provides an ideal spot for a quiet and peaceful holiday, yet with a great deal on offer for those seeking a more lively holiday. With four pools covering an area of 1000 sq m, a wide range of sports amenities, including golf, tennis and archery, there is always something to do. There are many children's activities, including a special club in high season, as well as an extensive programme of evening entertainment.

Facilities

Shop. Restaurant, pizzeria and bar. Golf clubhouse. Hairdressers. Newsagent. Body care centre. Bicycle hire. Launderette. Heated pool complex. Tennis, archery, yoga, aqua gym, pony club. Golf and tennis lessons. Fitness centre. Sauna. Diving. Off site: Fishing and watersports 300m, riding 4km.

Open

28 May - 17 September.

Directions

Take exit 7 from the Bordeaux ring road signposted Lacanau. Follow the D107 to Lacanau via Le Temple and La Porge, then towards Lege/Cap Ferret on the D3 to La Jenny (on the right).

Reservations

Contact site. Tel: 05 56 26 59 90
E-mail: info@lajenny.fr

AR1 – LOUISIANE – Chalet

Sleeping:
3 bedrooms, sleeps 8: 2 double, 2 bunk beds, 1 double sofa bed

Living:
living / kitchen area, shower & WC

Eating:
fitted kitchen with cooking hobs, oven, dishwasher & fridge

Outside:
table & chairs

Pets:
accepted (€28 per week)

AR2 – TOURTERELLE – Chalet

Sleeping:
1 bedroom, sleeps 6: 1 double, 2 single beds on mezzanine, 1 double sofa bed

Living:
living / kitchen area, shower & WC

Eating:
fitted kitchen with cooking hobs & fridge

Outside:
table & chairs

Pets:
accepted (€28 per week)

Weekly Charges

	AR1	AR2
Low Season *(from)*	€ 787	€ 525
High Season *(from)*	€ 1260	€ 780

FR40100 Camping du Domaine de la Rive

Route de Bordeaux, 40600 Biscarosse

For our full description of this campsite see page 198

AR1 – SAVANAH – Mobile Home

Sleeping:
2 bedrooms, sleeps 6: 1 double, 1 twin with 2 single beds, 1 double sofa bed; pillows & blankets provided

Living:
dining corner convertible into double bed, shower & WC

Eating:
fitted kitchen with cooking hobs & fridge, microwave

Outside:
table & chairs, parasol

Pets:
not accepted

AR2 – COTTAGE 3 – Mobile Home

Sleeping:
3 bedrooms, sleeps 6: 1 doulbe, 4 single beds

Living:
living / kitchen area, shower & WC

Eating:
fitted kitchen with cooking hobs & fridge, microwave

Outside:
table & chairs

Pets:
not accepted

Weekly Charges

	AR1	AR2
Low Season *(from)*	€ 315	€ 329
High Season *(from)*	€ 861	€ 875

FR40140 Camping Caravaning Lou P'tit Poun

110 avenue du Quartier Neuf, 40390 St Martin de Seignanx

For our full description of this campsite see page 200

Excellent locations within this beautiful, quiet campsite, ideal for a quiet holiday and close to Biarritz and the ocean.

AR1 – FABRE REVE – Chalet

Sleeping:
2 bedrooms, sleeps 5: 1 double, 1 twin with 2 single beds, 1 single bed

Living:
living / kitchen area, shower & WC

Eating:
fitted kitchen with cooking hobs, & fridge

Outside:
table & chairs, sun loungers

Pets:
not accepted

AR2 – IRM MERCURE – Mobile Home

Sleeping:
2 bedrooms, sleeps 5: 1 double, 1 twin with 2 single beds, 1 single sofa bed

Living:
living / kitchen area, shower & WC

Eating:
fitted kitchen with cooking hobs & fridge

Outside:
table & chairs, sun loungers

Pets:
not accepted

Weekly Charges

	AR1	AR2
Low Season *(from)*	€ 270	€ 260
High Season *(from)*	€ 680	€ 660

FR40160 Camping Les Vignes

Route de la Plage du Cap de L'Homy, 40170 Lit-et-Mixe

For our full description of this campsite see page 197

The mobile homes and chalets have been arranged around the edge of the site.

AR1 – GITOTEL S3 – Chalet

Sleeping:
3 bedrooms, sleeps 5: 1 double, 1 single bed, 2 sofa beds

Living:
living / kitchen area, heating, shower & WC

Eating:
fitted kitchen with cooking hobs, microwave & fridge

Outside:
table & chairs, sun loungers

Pets:
not accepted

AR2 – SELECTION – Mobile Home

Sleeping:
2 bedrooms, sleeps 4: 1 double, 1 twin with 2 single beds

Living:
living / kitchen area, shower & WC

Eating:
fitted kitchen with cooking hobs, microwave & fridge

Outside:
table & chairs, sun loungers

Pets:
not accepted

Weekly Charges

	AR1	AR2
Low Season *(from)*	€ 235	€ 235
High Season *(from)*	€ 798	€ 798

FR40180 Camping Le Vieux Port

Plage sud, 40660 Messanges

For our full description of this campsite see page 202

Mobile homes and chalets are dispersed around this site on large, shady pitches.

AR1 – Accommodation – Mobile Home

Sleeping:
2 bedrooms, sleeps 4: 1 double, 1 twin with 2 single beds; pillows & blankets provided

Living:
living / kitchen area, heating, shower & WC

Eating:
fitted kitchen with cooking hobs, oven, grill & fridge

Outside:
table & chairs, parasol

Pets:
not accepted

AR2 – Accommodation – Chalet

Sleeping:
3 bedrooms, sleeps 6: 2 double rooms, 1 twin with 2 single beds; pillows & blankets provided

Living:
living / kitchen area, heating, shower & WC

Eating:
fitted kitchen with cooking hobs, oven, toaster, grill & fridge/freezer

Outside:
table & chairs, sun loungers & parasol. Covered terrace.

Pets:
not accepted

Weekly Charges

	AR1	AR2
Low Season *(from)*	€ 265	€ 385
High Season *(from)*	€ 600	€ 900

FR40190 Camping Airotel Saint Martin

Avenue de l'Océan, 40660 Moliets-Plage

For our full description of this campsite see page 203

The chalets are attractively grouped on pitches separated by hedges, and surrounded by a variety of plane, pine and mulberry trees

AR1 – Accommodation – Chalet

Sleeping:
3 bedrooms, sleeps 6; sheets provided

Living:
living / kitchen area, Tables & chairs

Eating:
fitted kitchen with cooking hobs & fridge, dishwasher

Outside:
table & chairs

Pets:
not accepted

AR2 – CLUB – Chalet

Sleeping:
2 bedrooms, sleeps 5; sheets provided

Living:
living / kitchen area, Tables & chairs

Eating:
fitted kitchen with cooking hobs & fridge, microwave, electric coffee pot

Outside:
table & chairs

Pets:
accepted

Weekly Charges

	AR1	AR2
Low Season *(from)*	€ 450	€ 320
High Season *(from)*	€ 1000	€ 860

FR64110 Camping du Col d'Ibardin

64122 Urrugne

For our full description of this campsite see page 207

AR1 – O'HARA – Mobile Home

Sleeping:
2 bedrooms, sleeps 5: 1 double, 1 twin with 2 single beds, 1 single sofa bed; pillows & blankets provided

Living:
living / kitchen area, heating, shower & WC

Eating:
fitted kitchen with cooking hobs, microwave & fridge

Outside:
table & chairs, parasol

Pets:
not accepted

AR2 – WILLERBY – Mobile Home

Sleeping:
2 bedrooms, sleeps 5: 1 double, 1 twin with 2 single beds, 1 single sofa bed; pillows & blankets provided

Living:
living / kitchen area, heating, shower & WC

Eating:
fitted kitchen with cooking hobs & fridge

Outside:
table & chairs, parasol

Pets:
not accepted

Weekly Charges

	AR1	AR2
Low Season *(from)*	€ 215	€ 195
High Season *(from)*	€ 550	€ 520

FR64140 Sunêlia Bérrua

Rue Berrua, 64210 Bidart

For our full description of this campsite see page 208

Excellent locations within this beautiful family campsite, close to the beach and Pyrénées, and with a new swimming pool complex for 2005.

AR1 – CONFORT – Mobile Home

Sleeping:
2 bedrooms, sleeps 6: 1 double, 1 twin with 2 single beds, 1 double sofa bed.

Living:
living / kitchen area, heating, shower & WC

Eating:
fitted kitchen with cooking hobs & fridge

Outside:
table & chairs, parasol

Pets:
accepted (max. 6 kg)

AR2 – CHALET

Sleeping:
2 bedrooms, sleeps 6: 1 double, 1 twin with 2 single beds, 1 sofa bed.

Living:
living / kitchen area, shower & WC

Eating:
fitted kitchen with cooking hobs & fridge

Outside:
table & chairs, sun loungers

Pets:
accepted (max 6kg.)

Weekly Charges

	AR1	AR2
Low Season *(from)*	€ 324	€ 342
High Season *(from)*	€ 805	€ 847

FR12010 Castel Camping Le Val de Cantobre

112230 Nant-d'Aveyron

For our full description of this campsite see page 215

AR1 – ABI – Mobile Home

Sleeping:
2 bedrooms, sleeps 4: 1 double, 1 twin with 2 single beds

Living:
living / kitchen area, shower & WC

Eating:
fitted kitchen with cooking hobs

Outside:
table & chairs, sun loungers, parasol & BBQ

Pets:
accepted

AR2 – FABRE 2012 CHALET

Sleeping:
2 bedrooms, sleeps 5: 1 double 1 single with 1 bunk bed, blankets & pillows provided

Living:
living / kitchen area, shower & WC

Eating:
fitted kitchen with cooking hobs, fridge

Outside:
table & chairs, sun loungers, parasol & BBQ

Pets:
accepted

Weekly Charges

	AR1	AR2
Low Season *(from)*	€ 245	€ 315
High Season *(from)*	€ 595	€ 763

FR12020 Camping Caravaning Les Rivages

Avenue de l'Aigoual, Route de Nant, 12100 Millau

For our full description of this campsite see page 216

The IRM mobile homes are situated in a spacious area on the edge of the site and the O'Hara mobile homes are situated in a central area of the site. Both enjoy views of the cliffs and hills.

AR1 – IRM – Mobile Home

Sleeping:
2 bedrooms, sleeps 4: 1 double, 1 twin with 2 single beds; pillows & blankets provided

Living:
living / kitchen area, heating, shower & WC

Eating:
fitted kitchen with cooking hobs & fridge

Outside:
table & chairs, sun loungers & parasol

Pets:
accepted

AR2 – O'HARA – Mobile Home

Sleeping:
2 bedrooms, sleeps 4: 1 double, 1 twin with 2 single beds; pillows & blankets provided

Living:
living / kitchen area, heating, shower & WC

Eating:
fitted kitchen with cooking hobs, microwave & fridge

Outside:
table & chairs, sun loungers & parasol

Pets:
accepted

Weekly Charges

	AR1	AR2
Low Season *(from)*	€ 318	€ 336
High Season *(from)*	€ 550	€ 580

FR12070 Camping La Grange de Monteillac

112310 Séverac-l'Eglise

For our full description of this campsite see page 213

Located on grassy sites separated by flowering shrubs in contary to the area of animations and playground.

AR1 – EPICEA – Chalet

Sleeping:
sleeps 4, 1single bed under 10 years

Living:
table, chairs

Eating:
fitted kitchen with cooking hobs, fridge & microwave

Outside:
table & chairs, parasol

Pets:
accepted

AR2 – O'HARA – Mobile Home

Sleeping:
2 bedrooms, sleeps 6: 1 double, 1 twin with 2 single beds, 1 double sofa bed; pillows & blankets provided

Living:
living / kitchen area, heating, shower & WC

Eating:
fitted kitchen with cooking hobs, microwave & fridge/freezer

Outside:
table & chairs, parasol

Pets:
accepted

Weekly Charges

	AR1	AR2
Low Season *(from)*	€ 308	€ 334
High Season *(from)*	€ 416	€ 486

FR12180 Le Hameau Saint Martial

Rue de la Calquière, 12240 Rieupeyroux

Pitches at this campsite are exclusively for mobile homes & chalets

Le Hameau St Martial is a chalet development lying on the edge of the pretty village of Rieupeyroux, capital of the Haut Ségala region. Originally the village was developed around a Benedictine monastery, but is now at the heart of a popular area for walking and cycling. St Martial is a new site, offering 37 Fabre chalets, but is a 'parc residentiel de loisirs' and does not therefore offer any traditional camping pitches. The chalets are attractively situated on large grassy pitches and each can accommodate up to 5 people. Parking is away from the chalets, ensuring a pleasant, relaxed ambience. St Martial offers a number of good leisure facilities including a swimming pool, children's play ground and volleyball court, and is situated alongside a small lake, suitable for fishing.

Facilities

Swimming pool and children's pool, volleyball and badminton, laundry. Off site: Riding, bike hire, Rieupeyroux (various shops and restaurants).

Open

All year

Directions

Rieupeyroux can be found on the D911 between Villefranche de Rouergue and Baraqueville. The site is clearly signposted within the village.

Reservations

Contact site. Tel: 05 65 65 81 81
Email: info@les-hameaux.fr

AR1 – CHALET REVE

Sleeping:
2 bedrooms, sleeps 5: 1 double, 3 single beds

Living:
living / kitchen area, heating, shower & WC

Eating:
fitted kitchen with cooking hobs, microwave & fridge/freezer

Outside:
table & chairs

Pets:
accepted (€25 per week, I per unit)

AR2 – CHALET DÉTENTE

Sleeping:
2 bedrooms, sleeps 5: 1 double, 3 single beds.

Living:
living / kitchen area, heating, shower & WC

Eating:
fitted kitchen with cooking hobs, microwave & fridge / freezer

Outside:
table & chairs

Pets:
accepted (€25 per week, I per unit)

Weekly Charges

	AR1	AR2
Low Season *(from)*	€ 195	€ 195
High Season *(from)*	€ 530	€ 540

FR12080 Camping Club Les Genêts

Lac de Pareloup, 12410 Salles Curan

For our full description of this campsite see page 217

Mobile homes are situated in the centre of the site, not far from the lake.

AR1 – IRM TITANIA – Mobile Home

Sleeping:
2 bedrooms, sleeps 6: 1 double, 1 twin with 2 single beds, 1 double sofa bed; pillows & blankets provided

Living:
living / kitchen area, heating, shower & WC

Eating:
fitted kitchen with cooking hobs, oven & fridge/freezer

Outside:
table & chairs, parasol

Pets:
accepted (small charge)

AR2 – O'HARA – Mobile Home

Sleeping:
2 bedrooms, sleeps 6: 1 double, 1 twin with 2 single beds, 1 double sofa bed; pillows & blankets provided

Living:
living / kitchen area, heating, shower & WC

Eating:
fitted kitchen with cooking hobs, microwave & fridge/freezer

Outside:
table & chairs, parasol

Pets:
accepted (small charge)

Weekly Charges

	AR1	AR2
Low Season *(from)*	€ 220	€ 220
High Season *(from)*	€ 620	€ 620

FR12150 Camping Marmotel

12130 St Geniez-d'Olt

For our full description of this campsite see page 212

AR1 – LOUISIANE – Mobile Home

Sleeping:
2 bedrooms, sleeps 6-7: 1 double, 1 twin with 2 single beds, 1 single bunk (for under 6 years), 1 double sofa bed; pillows & blankets provided

Living:
living / kitchen area, TV, heating, shower & WC

Eating:
fitted kitchen with cooking hobs, microwave & fridge

Outside:
table & chairs, sun loungers, parasol & BBQ

Pets:
accepted (low season only)

AR2 – FABRE – Chalet

Sleeping:
2 bedrooms, sleeps 5: 1 twin with 2 single beds, 1 single bunk (for under 6 years), 1 double sofa bed; pillows & blankets provided

Living:
living / kitchen area, TV, heating, shower & WC

Eating:
fitted kitchen with cooking hobs, microwave & fridge

Outside:
table & chairs, sun loungers, parasol & BBQ

Pets:
accepted (low season only)

Weekly Charges

	AR1	AR2
Low Season *(from)*	€ 230	€ 214
High Season *(from)*	€ 624	€ 587

FR12160 Camping Caravaning Les Peupliers

Route des Gorges du Tarn, 12640 Rivière-sur-Tarn

For our full description of this campsite see page 219

AR1 – Mobile Home

Sleeping:
2 bedrooms, sleeps 4: 1 double, 1 twin with 2 single beds

Living:
living / kitchen area shower & WC

Eating:
fitted kitchen with microwave, fridge

Outside:
wood terrace, table & chairs

Pets:
accepted

Weekly Charges

	AR1
Low Season *(from)*	€ 250
High Season *(from)*	€ 550

FR24010 Castel Camping Château Le Verdoyer

Champs Romain, 24470 St Pardoux

For our full description of this campsite see page 223

AR1 – ATLAS – Mobile Home

Sleeping:
2 bedrooms, sleeps 6: 1 double, 1 twin with 2 single beds, 1 double sofa bed; pillows & blankets provided

Living:
living / kitchen area, heating, shower & WC

Eating:
fitted kitchen with cooking hobs, microwave & fridge

Outside:
table & chairs, sun loungers & parasol

Pets:
not accepted

AR2 – BÜRSTNER – Mobile Home

Sleeping:
2 bedrooms, sleeps 7: 1 double, 1 twin with 2 single beds, 1 bunk bed, 1 double sofa bed; pillows & blankets provided

Living:
living / kitchen area, heating, shower & WC

Eating:
fitted kitchen with cooking hobs, microwave & fridge

Outside:
table & chairs, sun loungers & parasol

Pets:
not accepted

Weekly Charges

	AR1	AR2
Low Season *(from)*	€ 295	€ 295
High Season *(from)*	€ 650	€ 650

FR24080 Camping Caravaning Le Moulin de David

Gaugeac, 24540 Monpazier

For our full description of this campsite see page 230

AR1 – BLUE BIRD – Mobile Home

Sleeping:
2 bedrooms, sleeps 6: 1 double, 1 twin with 2 single beds, 1 double sofa bed; pillows & blankets provided

Living:
living / kitchen area, heating, shower & WC

Eating:
fitted kitchen with cooking hobs, microwave & fridge

Outside:
table & chairs, sun loungers & parasol

Pets:
accepted

AR2 – PARADIS – Mobile Home

Sleeping:
2 bedrooms, sleeps 6: 1 double, 1 twin with 2 single beds, 1 double sofa bed; pillows & blankets provided

Living:
living / kitchen area, heating, shower & WC

Eating:
fitted kitchen with cooking hobs, microwave & fridge/freezer

Outside:
sun loungers & parasol

Pets:
accepted

Weekly Charges

	AR1	AR2
Low Season *(from)*	€ 273	€ 301
High Season *(from)*	€ 634.2	€ 692.3

FR24090 Camping Soleil Plage

Vitrac, 24200 Sarlat

For our full description of this campsite see page 233

AR1 – RÊVE – Chalet

Sleeping:
2 bedrooms, sleeps 5/7: 1 double & 3 single beds, 1 double sofa bed, blankets

Living:
living / kitchen area, shower & WC

Eating:
fitted kitchen with cooking hobs & fridge

Outside:
table & chairs, sun loungers, parasol & BBQ

Pets:
accepted (vaccinated)

AR2 – SUPER MERCURE – Mobile Home

Sleeping:
2 bedrooms, sleeps 4/6: 1 double, 2 single beds, 1 sofa bed, blankets & pillows provided

Living:
living / kitchen area, shower & WC

Eating:
fitted kitchen with cooking hobs & fridge

Outside:
table & chairs, sun loungers, parasol & BBQ

Pets:
accepted (vaccinated)

Weekly Charges

	AR1	AR2
Low Season *(from)*	€ 280	€ 250
High Season *(from)*	€ 680	€ 620

FR24310 Camping Caravaning La Bouquerie

24590 St Geniès-en-Périgord

For our full description of this campsite see page 234

The mobile homes and chalets are settled on individually marked off pitches, in the shade or sun.

AR1 – MOREA – Chalet

Sleeping:
2 bderooms, sleeps 5: 1 double, 1 single with bunk bed, blankets & pillows provided

Living:
living / kitchen area, heating, shower & WC

Eating:
fitted kitchen with cooking hobs & fridge

Outside:
table & chairs, sun loungers & BBQ

Pets:
accepted

AR2 – O'HARA – Mobile Home

Sleeping:
2 bedrooms, sleeps 4/5: 1 double, 1 twin, 1 sofa bed, blankets & pillows provided

Living:
living / kitchen area, heating, shower & WC

Eating:
fitted kitchen with hobs & fridge

Outside:
table & chairs, sun lounger, BBQ

Pets:
accepted

Weekly Charges

	AR1	AR2
Low Season *(from)*	€ 260	€ 250
High Season *(from)*	€ 690	€ 680

FR24320 Camping Les Peneyrals

Le Poujol, 24590 St Crépin-Carlucet

For our full description of this campsite see page 235

AR1 – ENEA – Mobile Home

Sleeping:
2 bedrooms, sleeps 6: 1 double, 1 twin with 2 single beds, sofa

Living:
living / kitchen area, shower & W/C

Eating:
fitted kitchen with cooking hobs, fridge

Outside:
table & chairs, 2 sun loungers

Pets:
accepted

AR2 – RÊVE CONFORT – Chalet

Sleeping:
2 bedrooms, sleeps 7: 1 double, bedroom with 3 single beds

Living:
living / kitchen area, shower & WC

Eating:
fitted kitchen with cooking hobs and fridge

Outside:
garden furniture, table, 7 chairs and 2 sun loungers

Pets:
accepted

Weekly Charges

	AR1	AR2
Low Season *(from)*	€ 230	€ 330
High Season *(from)*	€ 690	€ 750

FR46010 Castel Camping Le Domaine de la Paille Basse

46200 Souillac-sur-Dordogne

For our full description of this campsite see page 238

The mobile homes are situated in calm surroundings 300 m. from the centre of the site.

AR1 – OAKLEY LOUISIANE – Mobile Home

Sleeping:
2 bedrooms, sleeps 4: 1 double, 1 twin with 2 single beds and 3rd child bed

Living:
living / kitchen area. shower & WC

Eating:
fitted kitchen with cooking hobs, microwave & fridge

Outside:
table & chairs, BBQ

Pets:
not accepted

AR2 – ZEN LOUISIANE – Mobile Home

Sleeping:
3 bedrooms, sleeps 6: 1 double, 2 single beds, 2 bunk beds. Bed linen provided

Living:
living / kitchen area. heating, cd player, shower & WC

Eating:
fitted kitchen with cooking hobs and fridge

Outside:
table & chairs, BBQ

Pets:
not accepted

Weekly Charges

	AR1	AR2
Low Season *(from)*	€ 265	€ 285
High Season *(from)*	€ 695	€ 795

FR46050 Camping Le Rêve

46300 Le Vigan

For our full description of this campsite see page 237

AR1 – FABRE – Chalet

Sleeping:
2 bedrooms, sleeps 4: 1 double, 1 twin with 2 single beds

Living:
living / kitchen area. heating, shower & WC

Eating:
fitted kitchen with cooking hobs & fridge

Outside:
table & chairs, parasol

Pets:
accepted

AR2 – FABRE – Chalet

Sleeping:
2 bedrooms, sleeps 5: 1 double, 1 twin with 2 single beds

Living:
living / kitchen area. heating, shower & WC

Eating:
fitted kitchen with cooking hobs & fridge

Outside:
table & chairs, parasol

Pets:
accepted

Weekly Charges

	AR1	AR2
Low Season *(from)*	€ 231	€ 247
High Season *(from)*	€ 430	€ 445

FR47010 Camping Caravaning Moulin du Périé

47500 Sauveterre-la-Lemance

For our full description of this campsite see page 241

The mobile homes are situated in a quiet area on the edge of the site and the chalets are on the edge of a stream in a private and sunny setting.

AR1 – IRM – Mobile Home

Sleeping: 2 bedrooms, sleeps 6: 2 double, 1 twin with 2 single beds; pillows & blankets provided

Living: living / kitchen area, heating, shower & WC

Eating: fitted kitchen with cooking hobs & fridge

Outside: table & chairs, parasol

Pets: not accepted

AR2 – HAVITAT RÊVE – Chalet

Sleeping: 2 bedrooms, sleeps 7: 2 double, 1 twin with 2 single beds, 1 bunk bed; pillows & blankets provided

Living: living / kitchen area, heating, shower & WC

Eating: fitted kitchen with cooking hobs & fridge

Outside: table & chairs, parasol

Pets: not accepted

Weekly Charges

	AR1	AR2
Low Season *(from)*	€ 325	€ 360
High Season *(from)*	€ 630	€ 690

FR07090 Castel Camping Le Domaine des Plantas

07360 Les Ollières-sur-Eyrieux

For our full description of this campsite see page 265

The mobile homes are situated at the highest point of the site in a calm area, yet close to the facilities.

AR1 – SHELBOX – Mobile Home

Sleeping: 2 bedrooms, sleeps 5: 1 double, 2 bunk beds, 1 single bed; pillows & blankets provided

Living: living / kitchen area, heating, shower & WC

Eating: fitted kitchen with cooking hobs, microwave & fridge/freezer

Outside: table & chairs, sun loungers & parasol

Pets: accepted

Weekly Charges

	AR1
Low Season *(from)*	€ 270
High Season *(from)*	€ 650

FR07120 Camping Nature Parc L'Ardéchois

Route touristique des Gorges, 07150 Vallon-Pont-d'Arc

For our full description of this campsite see page 266

The mobile homes are located between the swimming pool and the river, about 150 m. from the shop, bar and restaurant, in a particularly quiet part of the site. Each mobile home has a large, private pitch, and all are equipped with shaded terraces.

AR1 – LOUISIANE OAKLEY – Mobile Home

Sleeping:
2 bedrooms, sleeps 5: 1 double, 1 twin with 2 single beds, 1 bunk bed; pillows & blankets provided

Living:
living / kitchen area, heating, shower & WC

Eating:
fitted kitchen with cooking hobs & fridge

Outside:
table & chairs, sun loungers, parasol

Pets:
accepted (low season only)

AR2 – LOUISIANE PACIFIQUE – Mobile Home

Sleeping:
2 bedrooms, sleeps 5: 1 double, 1 twin with 2 single beds, 1 bunk bed; pillows & blankets provided

Living:
living / kitchen area, heating, shower & WC

Eating:
fitted kitchen with cooking hobs & fridge/freezer

Outside:
table & chairs, sun loungers & parasol

Pets:
accepted (low season only)

Weekly Charges

	AR1	AR2
Low Season *(from)*	€ 360	€ 360
High Season *(from)*	€ 790	€ 790

FR07150 Camping Domaine de Gil

Route de Vals-les-Bains, Ucel, 07200 Aubenas

For our full description of this campsite see page 268

AR1 – O'HARA – Mobile Home

Sleeping:
2 bedrooms, sleeps 4/5: blankets & pillows provided

Living:
living / kitchen area, shower & WC

Eating:
fitted kitchen with cooking hobs & fridge

Outside:
terrace & garden furniture

Pets:
accepted

AR2 – O' HARA – Mobile Home

Sleeping:
2 bedrooms, sleeps 4 to 7: blankets & pillows provided

Living:
living / kitchen area, shower & WC

Eating:
fitted kitchen with cooking hobs & fridge

Outside:
terrace, garden furniture, 2 sun loungers

Pets:
accepted

Weekly Charges

	AR1	AR2
Low Season *(from)*	€ 210	€ 260
High Season *(from)*	€ 585	€ 685

FR63030 Hotel de Plein Air L'Europe

Route de Jassal, 63790 Murol

Pitches at this campsite are exclusively for mobile homes & chalets

L'Europe is a pleasant site on the edge of the little town of Murol, best known perhaps for its fine 13th century castle. The site is 800m from the Lac de Chambon which boasts a sandy beach and range of water sports. There are 219 pitches at L'Europe, many of which are occupied by mobile homes. Pitches are generally of a good size and offer reasonable shade. This is quite a lively site in peak season with a busy animation programme including evening entertainment. The bar / restaurant overlooks the pool and is the site's focal point and entertainment centre. The surrounding area offers very many superb walking and cycling opportunites, and the site organises a number of popular excursions.

Facilities

Swimming pool and paddling pool. Waterslide. Bar, restaurant, take away food, Tennis, archery, Children's play area. Organised activities and entertainment.
Off site: Lakeside beach 800m, Murol centre 600m, riding, watersports.

Open

29 May - 1 September.

Directions

Leave the A75 autoroute at the St Nectair exit (No. 6) and follow signs to Murol. The site is clearly signposted upon arrival at Murol.

Reservations

Contact site. Tel: 04 73 39 76 66
E-mail: europe.camping@wanadoo.fr

AR1 – IRM – Mobile Home

Sleeping:
2 bedrooms, sleeps 5: 1 double, 1 twin with 2 single beds, sofa bed

Living:
living / kitchen area, heating, shower & WC

Eating:
fitted kitchen with cooking hobs & fridge, microwave

Outside:
table & chairs, parasol

Pets:
accepted (under 10kg)

AR2 – IRM – Mobile Home

Sleeping:
2 bedrooms, sleeps 4: 1 double, 1 twin with 2 single beds.

Living:
living / kitchen area, heating, shower & WC

Eating:
fitted kitchen with cooking hobs & fridge, microwave

Outside:
table & chairs, parasol

Pets:
accepted (max 10kg.)

Weekly Charges

	AR1	AR2
Low Season *(from)*	€ 240	€ 220
High Season *(from)*	€ 710	€ 690

FR23010 Castel Camping Le Château de Poinsouze

Route de la Châtre, B.P. 12, 23600 Boussac-Bourg

For our full description of this campsite see page 250

The mobile homes and chalets are grouped together in a quiet area of the campsite on the edge of the touring area, some facing the lake and Château. Very large pitches.

AR1 – BURSTNER NATUR'HOME – Mobile Home

Sleeping:
2 bedrooms, sleeps 5: 1 double, 1 twin with 2 single beds, 1 sofa bed; pillows & blankets provided

Living:
living / kitchen area, heating, shower & WC

Eating:
fitted kitchen with cooking hobs, microwave & fridge/freezer

Outside:
table & chairs, sun loungers, parasol & BBQ

Pets:
not accepted

AR2 – SHELBOX COUNTRY LODGE – Chalet

Sleeping:
2 bedrooms, sleeps 5: 1 double, 2 twin with 2 single beds, sofa bed; pillows & blankets provided

Living:
living / kitchen area, heating, shower & WC

Eating:
fitted kitchen with cooking hobs, microwave & fridge/freezer

Outside:
table & chairs, sun loungers, parasol & BBQ

Pets:
not accepted

Weekly Charges

	AR1	AR2
Low Season *(from)*	€ 220	€ 285
High Season *(from)*	€ 520	€ 630

FR07020 Camping Caravaning L'Ardéchois

Le Chambon, Gluiras, 07190 St Sauveur-de-Montagut

For our full description of this campsite see page 261

AR1 – WILLERBY – Mobile Home

Sleeping:
2 bedrooms, sleeps 4 / 5: 1 double, 1 twin with 2 single beds, 1 sofa bed; pillows & blankets provided

Living:
living / kitchen area, heating, shower & WC

Eating:
fitted kitchen with cooking hobs & fridge/freezer

Outside:
table & chairs, sun loungers, parasol

Pets:
accepted

AR2 – ARTISANAT DU PAYS – Chalet

Sleeping:
2 bedrooms, sleeps 4 / 5: 1 double, 1 twin with 2 single beds, sofa bed; pillows provided

Living:
living / kitchen area, heating, shower & WC

Eating:
fitted kitchen with cooking hobs & fridge/freezer

Outside:
table & chairs, sun loungers & parasol

Pets:
accepted

Weekly Charges

	AR1	AR2
Low Season *(from)*	€ 285	€ 295
High Season *(from)*	€ 595	€ 595

FR07070 Camping Les Ranchisses

Route de Rocher, Chassiers, 07110 Largentière

For our full description of this campsite see page 263

Attractive locations around this beautiful family campsite.

AR1 – SHELBOX PARADIS – Mobile Home

Sleeping:
2 bedrooms, sleeps 6: 1 double, 2 bunk beds, 1 single bed, 1 double sofa bed; pillows & blankets provided

Living:
living / kitchen area, heating, shower & WC

Eating:
fitted kitchen with cooking hobs, microwave & fridge/freezer

Outside:
table & chairs, sun loungers & parasol

Pets:
not accepted

AR2 – LOUISIANE FAMILY – Mobile Home

Sleeping:
3 bedrooms, sleeps 6: 1 double, 2 twin with 2 single beds; pillows & blankets provided

Living:
living / kitchen area, heating, shower & WC

Eating:
fitted kitchen with cooking hobs, microwave & fridge/freezer

Outside:
table & chairs, sun loungers & parasol

Pets:
not accepted

Weekly Charges

	AR1	AR2
Low Season *(from)*	€ 336	€ 350
High Season *(from)*	€ 826	€ 868

FR26030 Sunêlia Le Grand Lierne

B.P. 8, 26120 Chabeuil

For our full description of this campsite see page 270

Accommodation is located in a quiet oak wood, with easy access to the leisure and entertainment facilities.

AR1 – LOUISIANE SUNÊLIA CONFORT – Mobile Home

Sleeping:
2 bedrooms, sleeps 6: 1 double, 2 bunk beds, 1 single bed, 1 single sofa bed; pillows & blankets provided

Living:
living / kitchen area, heating, shower & WC

Eating:
fitted kitchen with cooking hobs, oven & fridge

Outside:
table & chairs, sun loungers & parasol

Pets:
not accepted

AR2 – FAMILY SUNÊLIA

Sleeping:
3 bedrooms, sleeps 6: 1 double, 2 single rooms each with 2 twin beds

Living:
living / kitchen area, heating, shower & WC

Eating:
fitted kitchen with cooking hobs & fridge freezer

Outside:
table & chairs, sun loungers & parasol

Pets:
not accepted

Weekly Charges

	AR1	AR2
Low Season *(from)*	€ 315	€ 371
High Season *(from)*	€ 819	€ 903

FR26120 Gervanne Camping

Bellevue, 26400 Mirabel et Blacons

For our full description of this campsite see page 272

AR1 – O'HARA – Mobile Home

Sleeping:
2 bedrooms, sleeps 4: 1 double, 1 twin with 2 single beds; pillows & blankets provided

Living:
living / kitchen area, heating, shower & WC

Eating:
fitted kitchen with cooking hobs, oven & fridge

Outside:
table & chairs, parasol

Pets:
not accepted

AR2 – RÊVE – Chalet

Sleeping:
2 bedrooms, sleeps 6: 1 double, 1 twin with 2 single beds, 1 double sofa bed; pillows & blankets provided

Living:
living / kitchen area, heating, shower & WC

Eating:
fitted kitchen with cooking hobs, oven & fridge

Outside:
table & chairs, parasol

Pets:
not accepted

Weekly Charges

	AR1	AR2
Low Season *(from)*	€ 240	€ 260
High Season *(from)*	€ 520	€ 590

FR04010 Sunêlia Hippocampe

Route de Napoléon, 04290 Volonne

For our full description of this campsite see page 279

Most mobile homes are situated away from the entrance and activities, though not far from the swimming pool. Some are attractively located near to the lake with good views.

AR1 – WATIPI COTTAGE – Mobile Home

Sleeping:
3 bedrooms, sleeps 6: 1 double, 2 twin with 2 single beds; pillows & blankets provided

Living:
living / kitchen area, heating, shower & WC (air conditioning on request)

Eating:
fitted kitchen with cooking hobs, microwave & fridge/freezer

Outside:
table & chairs, sun loungers & parasol

Pets:
accepted

AR2 – IRM – Mobile Home

Sleeping:
2 bedrooms, sleeps 4: 1 double, 1 twin with 2 single beds; pillows & blankets provided

Living:
living / kitchen area, heating, shower & WC

Eating:
fitted kitchen with cooking hobs & fridge

Outside:
table & chairs, parasol

Pets:
accepted

Weekly Charges

	AR1	AR2
Low Season *(from)*	€ 273	€ 203
High Season *(from)*	€ 889	€ 735

FR04020 Castel Camping Le Camp du Verdon

Domaine du Verdon, 04120 Castellane

For our full description of this campsite see page 276

AR1 – WATIPI – Mobile Home

Sleeping:
2 bedrooms, sleeps 4: 1 double, 1 twin with 2 single beds; pillows & blankets provided

Living:
living / kitchen area, heating, shower & WC

Eating:
fitted kitchen with cooking hobs & fridge

Outside:
table & chairs, sun loungers

Pets:
accepted

AR2 – TITOM – Chalet

Sleeping:
2 bedrooms, sleeps 6: 1 double, 1 twin with 2 single beds, 2 bunk beds; pillows & blankets provided

Living:
living / kitchen area, heating, shower & WC

Eating:
fitted kitchen with cooking hobs & fridge

Outside:
table & chairs, sun loungers

Pets:
accepted

Weekly Charges

	AR1	AR2
Low Season *(from)*	€ 336	€ 364
High Season *(from)*	€ 630	€ 665

FR04100 Camping International

Route Napoléon, 04120 Castellane

For our full description of this campsite see page 276

AR1 – SHELBOX – Mobile Home

Sleeping:
2 bedrooms, sleeps 5: 1 double, 2 bunk beds, 1 single bed; pillows & blankets provided

Living:
living / kitchen area, heating, shower & WC

Eating:
fitted kitchen with cooking hobs, microwave & fridge/freezer

Outside:
table & chairs, sun loungers

Pets:
accepted

Weekly Charges

	AR1
Low Season *(from)*	€ 190
High Season *(from)*	€ 620

FR84020 Domaine Naturiste de Bélézy

84410 Bédoin

For our full description of this campsite see page 282

The mobile homes have large, quiet pitches and each have a terrace and pergola. The wooden chalets are close to the swimming pool and the childrens' activity zone.

AR1 – IRM – Mobile Home

Sleeping:
2 bedrooms, sleeps 5: 1 double, 1 twin with 2 single beds, 1 single sofa bed.

Living:
large living / kitchen area, shower & WC

Eating:
fitted kitchen with cooking hobs, microwave & fridge/freezer

Outside:
teak table & chairs, sun loungers

Pets:
not accepted

AR2 – FABRE – Chalet

Sleeping:
2 bedrooms, sleeps 5: 1 double, 2 single beds, 1 bunk bed.

Living:
living / kitchen area, shower & WC

Eating:
fitted kitchen with cooking hobs & fridge/freezer

Outside:
teak table & chairs, sun loungers

Pets:
not accepted

Weekly Charges

	AR1	AR2
Low Season *(from)*	€ 343	€ 329
High Season *(from)*	€ 805	€ 693

FR09020 Camping L'Arize

Lieu-dit Bourtol, 09240 La Bastide-de-Sérou

For our full description of this campsite see page 286

AR1 – WILLERBY – Mobile Home

Sleeping:
2 bedrooms, sleeps 6: 1 double, 1 twin with 2 single beds, 1 double sofa bed; pillows & blankets provided

Living:
living / kitchen area, heating, shower & WC

Eating:
fitted kitchen with cooking hobs & fridge

Outside:
table & chairs, parasol & BBQ

Pets:
accepted

AR2 – Accommodation – Chalet

Sleeping:
2 bedrooms, sleeps 7: 1 double, 2 single beds, 1 bunk bed, 1 double sofa bed; pillows & blankets provided

Living:
living / kitchen area, heating, shower & WC

Eating:
fitted kitchen with cooking hobs, microwave & fridge/freezer

Outside:
table & chairs, parasol & BBQ

Pets:
accepted

Weekly Charges

	AR1	AR2
Low Season *(from)*	€ 266	€ 288
High Season *(from)*	€ 598	€ 622

FR32010 Le Camp de Florence

Route Astaffort, 32480 La Romieu

For our full description of this campsite see page 289

Type 1: spacious village of 10 cottages, Type 2: very large pitches on edge of campsite with magnificent views.

AR1 – WILLERBY/IRM – Mobile Home

Sleeping:
2 bedrooms, sleeps 6: 1 double, 1 twin with 2 single beds, sofabed

Living:
sitting area

Eating:
sitting/dining area

Outside:
table & chairs, covered terrace

Pets:
accepted

AR2 – IRM – Mobile Home

Sleeping:
2 bedrooms, sleeps 6: 1 double, 1 twin with 2 single beds,sofabed

Living:
sitting area

Eating:
separate dining room

Outside:
table & chairs, covered terrace

Pets:
accepted

Weekly Charges

	AR1	AR2
Low Season *(from)*	€ 241	€ 265
High Season *(from)*	€ 670	€ 715

FR65090 Camping Soleil du Pibeste

16 Avenue du Lavedan, 65400 Agos Vidalos

For our full description of this campsite see page 294

AR1 – Mobile Home

Sleeping:
2 bedrooms, sleeps 5: 1 double, 1 twin with 2 single beds, 1 bunk bed; pillows & blankets provided

Living:
living / kitchen area, TV, heating, shower & WC

Eating:
fitted kitchen with cooking hobs, microwave & fridge/freezer

Outside:
table & chairs, sun loungers, parasol & BBQ

Pets:
accepted

AR2 – RONDINS DE BOIS – Chalet

Sleeping:
2 bedrooms, sleeps 4-5: 1 double, 2 single beds, 1 bunk bed; pillows & blankets provided

Living:
living / kitchen area, TV, heating, shower & WC

Eating:
fitted kitchen with cooking hobs, oven, microwave & fridge/freezer

Outside:
table & chairs, sun loungers, parasol & BBQ

Pets:
accepted

Weekly Charges

	AR1	AR2
Low Season *(from)*	€ 280	€ 300
High Season *(from)*	€ 496	€ 638

FR81060 Camping Les Clots

81190 Mirandol-Bourgnounac

For our full description of this campsite see page 296

AR1 – G44 – Gîte

Sleeping:
sleeps 4 to 6

Living:
living / kitchen area, sofabed.

Eating:
fitted kitchen with cooking hobs, fridge, microwave & dishwasher

Outside:
2 tables & chairs, parasol, seat

Pets:
accepted

AR2 – H15 – Chalet

Sleeping:
sleeps 4

Living:
living / kitchen area

Eating:
fitted kitchen with cooking hobs & fridge

Outside:
table & chairs

Pets:
accepted

Weekly Charges

	AR1	AR2
Low Season *(from)*	€ 440	€ 390
High Season *(from)*	€ 550	€ 490

FR11060 Yelloh! Village Domaine d'Arnauteille

11250 Montclar

For our full description of this campsite see page 299

Chalets are located in the southeast part of the site on top of a hill and the mobile homes are on a terrace above the swimming pool with good views.

AR1 – GRAND CONFORT – Chalet

Sleeping:
2 bedrooms, sleeps 6: 1 double, 1 bedroom with 3 single beds, 1 sofa bed; pillows & blankets provided

Living:
living / kitchen area, heating, shower & WC

Eating:
fitted kitchen with cooking hobs, microwave & fridge/freezer

Outside:
table & chairs, sun loungers & parasol

Pets:
accepted

AR2 – LOUISIANE – Mobile Home

Sleeping:
3 bedrooms, sleeps 6: 1 double, 2 twin with 2 single beds, 1 sofa bed. all bedding provided

Living:
living / kitchen area, heating, shower & WC

Eating:
fitted kitchen with cooking hobs, microwave & fridge/freezer

Outside:
table & chairs, sun loungers & parasol

Pets:
accepted

Weekly Charges

	AR1	AR2
Low Season *(from)*	€ 299	€ 350
High Season *(from)*	€ 725	€ 819

FR11070 Camping Les Mimosas

Chaussée de Mandirac, 11100 Narbonne

For our full description of this campsite see page 300

AR1 – Mobile Home

Sleeping:
2 bedrooms, sleeps 4: 1 double, 2 single beds, blankets & pillows provided

Living:
living / kitchen area, shower & WC

Eating:
fitted kitchen with cooking hob, coffee maker & fridge

Outside:
table & charis, 2 sun loungers

Pets:
accepted

AR2 – Mobile Home

Sleeping:
2 bedrooms, sleeps 6: 1 double, 2 single beds, sofa bed, blankets & pillows provided

Living:
living / kitchen area, shower & WC

Eating:
fitted kitchen with cooking hob, coffee maker & fridge

Outside:
table & charis, 2 sun loungers

Pets:
accepted

Weekly Charges

	AR1	AR2
Low Season *(from)*	€ 251	€ 265
High Season *(from)*	€ 533	€ 601

FR30100 Camping Naturiste de la Sablière

Domaine de la Sablière, St Privat de Champclos, 30430 Barjac

For our full description of this campsite see page 304

Mobile homes and chalets are mainly on terraces amongst natural woodland and wild flower species.

AR1 – MAS – Chalet

Sleeping:
2 bedrooms, sleeps 6/7: 1 double, 1 room with 3 bunk beds, sofa bed

Living:
living / kitchen area, heating, shower & WC

Eating:
fitted kitchen with cooking hobs, pressure cooker, microwave, dishwasher & fridge

Outside:
table & chairs, sun loungers & parasol

Pets:
accepted

AR2 – AMANDIERS & OLIVIERS – Mobile Home

Sleeping:
2 bedrooms, sleeps 6: 1 double, 2 single beds, 1 sofa bed.

Living:
living / kitchen area, heating, shower & WC

Eating:
fitted kitchen with cooking hobs, pressure cooker, dishwasher & fridge

Outside:
table & chairs, sun loungers & parasol

Pets:
accepted

Weekly Charges

	AR1	AR2
Low Season *(from)*	€ 339	€ 219
High Season *(from)*	€ 799	€ 619

FR30160 Camping Caravaning Le Boucanet

B.P. 206, 30240 Le Grau-du-Roi

For our full description of this campsite see page 307

AR1 – O'HARA – Mobile Home

Sleeping:
2 bedrooms, sleeps 6: 1 double, 1 twin with 2 single beds, 1 double sofa bed; pillows & blankets provided

Living:
living / kitchen area, shower & WC

Eating:
fitted kitchen with cooking hobs & fridge

Outside:
table & chairs

Pets:
not accepted

AR2 – LUXE – Mobile Home

Sleeping:
2 bedrooms, sleeps 6: 1 double, 1 twin with 2 single beds, 1 double sofa bed. pillows & blankets provided

Living:
living / kitchen area, shower & WC

Eating:
fitted kitchen with cooking hobs & fridge

Outside:
table & chairs, sun loungers

Pets:
not accepted

Weekly Charges

	AR1	AR2
Low Season *(from)*	€ 280	€ 343
High Season *(from)*	€ 665	€ 756

FR30190 Camping International des Gorges du Gardon

Chemin de la Barque Vieille, 30210 Vers-Pont-du-Gard

For our full description of this campsite see page 306

AR1 – Accommodation – Mobile Home

Sleeping:
2 bedrooms, sleeps 6: 1 double, 1 twin with 2 single beds, 1 double sofa bed; pillows & blankets provided

Living:
living / kitchen area, heating, shower & WC

Eating:
fitted kitchen with cooking hobs & fridge/freezer

Outside:
table & chairs, parasol

Pets:
accepted

AR2 – Accommodation – Chalet

Sleeping:
2 bedrooms, sleeps 5: 1 double, 1 twin with 2 single beds, 1 bunk bed; pillows & blankets provided

Living:
living / kitchen area, heating, shower & WC

Eating:
fitted kitchen with cooking hobs & fridge/freezer

Outside:
table & chairs, parasol & BBQ

Pets:
accepted

Weekly Charges

	AR1	AR2
Low Season *(from)*	€ 240	€ 210
High Season *(from)*	€ 540	€ 520

FR34070 Yelloh! Village Le Sérignan Plage

Le Sérignan Plage, 34410 Sérignan

For our full description of this campsite see page 314

Chalets and mobile homes are located beside the beach or in shady areas. All accommodation is separated by hedges to provide privacy.

AR1 – COTTAGE – Mobile home

Sleeping:
2 bedrooms, sleeps 6: 1 double, 1 twin with 2 single beds, 1 sofa bed.

Living:
living / kitchen area, heating, shower & WC

Eating:
fitted kitchen with cooking hobs & fridge

Outside:
table & chairs, sun loungers

Pets:
not accepted

AR2 – VIP – Mobile Home

Sleeping:
2 bedrooms, sleeps 5: 1 double, 1 twin with 2 single beds, 1 single sofa bed.

Living:
living / kitchen area, fan, heating, shower & WC

Eating:
fitted kitchen with cooking hobs & fridge

Outside:
table & chairs, sun loungers

Pets:
not accepted

Weekly Charges

	AR1	AR2
Low Season *(from)*	€ 210	€ 210
High Season *(from)*	€ 770	€ 868

FR66190 Sunêlia Les Tropiques

Bvd de la Méditerranée, 66440 Torreilles-Plage

For our full description of this campsite see page 323

Attractive locations amongst pines, palm trees and oleanders on this friendly site just 400 m. from the beach.

AR1 – CAMPITEL – Chalet

Sleeping:
2 bedrooms, sleeps 5: 1 double, 1 room with 1 single bed & 2 bunks

Living:
living / kitchen area, shower & WC

Eating:
fitted kitchen with cooking hobs & fridge

Outside:
table & chairs

Pets:
accepted (€4 per night)

AR2 – MOBILE HOME 4/6 – Mobile Home

Sleeping:
2 bedrooms, sleeps 6: 1 double, 1 twin with 2 single beds, 1 double sofa bed.

Living:
living / kitchen area, shower & WC

Eating:
fitted kitchen with cooking hobs & fridge

Outside:
table & chairs

Pets:
accepted (€4 per night)

Weekly Charges

	AR1	AR2
Low Season *(from)*	€ 259	€ 329
High Season *(from)*	€ 567	€ 637

FR06080 Camping Caravaning Les Cigales

505 avenue de la Mer, 06210 Mandelieu-la-Napoule

For our full description of this campsite see page 333

AR1 – O'HARA – Mobile Home

Sleeping:
2 bedrooms, sleeps 6: 1 double, 1 twin with 2 single beds, 1 double sofa bed; pillows & blankets provided

Living:
living / kitchen area, heating, shower & WC

Eating:
fitted kitchen with cooking hobs & fridge/freezer

Outside:
table & chairs, parasol

Pets:
accepted (max 10kg)

AR2 – ROLLER – Mobile Home

Sleeping:
2 bedrooms, sleeps 6: 1 double, 1 twin with 2 single beds. pillows & blankets provided

Living:
living / kitchen area, heating, shower & WC

Eating:
fitted kitchen with cooking hobs & fridge/freezer

Outside:
table & chairs, parasol

Pets:
accepted

Weekly Charges

	AR1	AR2
Low Season *(from)*	€ 385	€ 340
High Season *(from)*	€ 680	€ 635

FR06120 Camping Green Park

159, Vallon des Vaux, 06800 Cagnes-sur-Mer

For our full description of this campsite see page 334

All pets must be on leads (dangerous breeds not accepted).

AR1 – LE LOFT – Mobile Home

Sleeping:
2 bedrooms, sleeps 6: 1 double, 1 twin with 2 single beds, sofabed

Living:
living / kitchen area, shower & WC

Eating:
fitted kitchen with cooking hobs, microwave, fridge/freezer

Outside:
garden furniture

Pets:
not accepted

AR2 – CLUB 5 – Chalet

Sleeping:
2 bedrooms, sleeps 4/5 1 double, 3 single beds including bunk bed

Living:
living / kitchen area, shower & WC

Eating:
fitted kitchen with cooking hobs, microwave & fridge

Outside:
covered terrace, garden furniture

Pets:
accepted, vaccine obligatory

Weekly Charges

	AR1	AR2
Low Season *(from)*	€ 315	€ 308
High Season *(from)*	€ 581	€ 581

FR83020 Castel Caravaning Esterel

Avenue des Golf, 83700 St Raphael

For our full description of this campsite see page 338

The mobile homes have terraces and panoramic views of the Estérel.

AR1 – LA SUITE – Mobile Home

Sleeping:
2 bedrooms, sleeps 6: 1 double, 1 twin with 2 single beds, 1 double sofa bed

Living:
living / kitchen area, heating, shower & WC

Eating:
fitted kitchen with cooking hobs, oven & fridge/freezer

Outside:
table & chairs, sun loungers & parasol

Pets:
accepted

AR2 – MINI LUXE – Mobile Home

Sleeping:
1 bedroom, sleeps 4: 1 twin with 2 single beds, sofa bed

Living:
living / kitchen area, shower & WC

Eating:
fitted kitchen with cooking hobs & fridge

Outside:
table & chairs, sun loungers & parasol

Pets:
accepted

Weekly Charges

	AR1	AR2
Low Season *(from)*	€ 360	€ 220
High Season *(from)*	€ 810	€ 650

FR83060 Camping Caravaning de La Baume/La Palmeraie

Route de Bagnols, 83618 Fréjus

For our full description of this campsite see page 340

AR1 – BASTIDON – Chalet

Sleeping:
1 bedroom, sleeps 4-6: 1 double, sofa bed

Living:
living / kitchen area, WC

Eating:
fitted kitchen with cooking hob & fridge

Outside:
covered terrace, table & chairs

Pets:
accepted

AR2 – PHOENIX – Mobile Home

Sleeping:
2 or 3 bedrooms, sleeps 6: 1 double, 2 (or 4) single beds, sofa bed

Living:
living / kitchen area, WC

Eating:
fitted kitchen with cooking hob & fridge

Outside:
table & chairs

Pets:
accepted

Weekly Charges

	AR1	AR2
Low Season *(from)*	€ 280	€ 294
High Season *(from)*	€ 875	€ 890

FR83070 Caravaning L'Etoile d'Argens

83370 St Aygulf

For our full description of this campsite see page 342

Both types of mobile homes are in several different areas throughout the site.

AR1 – WATIPI – Mobile Home

Sleeping:
2 bedrooms, sleeps 6: 1 double, 1 twin with 2 single beds, 1 double sofa bed; pillows & blankets provided

Living:
living / kitchen area, heating, shower & WC

Eating:
fitted kitchen with cooking hobs, oven & fridge

Outside:
table & chairs, sun loungers & parasol

Pets:
accepted

AR2 – IRM – Mobile Home

Sleeping:
2 bedrooms, sleeps 6: 1 double, 1 twin with 2 single beds, 1 double sofa bed; pillows & blankets provided

Living:
living / kitchen area, heating, shower & WC

Eating:
fitted kitchen with cooking hobs, oven & fridge/freezer

Outside:
table & chairs, sun loungers & parasol

Pets:
accepted

Weekly Charges

	AR1	AR2
Low Season *(from)*	€ 280	€ 250
High Season *(from)*	€ 820	€ 640

FR83170 Camping Domaine de la Bergerie

Vallée du Fournel, 83520 Roquebrune-sur-Argens

For our full description of this campsite see page 346

All featured accommodation is situated in a natural, wooded park - 10 minutes from the coast. Large 200 sq.m; pitches with terraces and parking space.

AR1 – IRM – Mobile Home

Sleeping:
2 bedrooms, sleeps 4: 1 double, 1 twin with 2 single beds

Living:
living / kitchen area, heating, shower & WC

Eating:
fitted kitchen with cooking hobs, microwave & fridge/freezer

Outside:
table & chairs, sun loungers

Pets:
accepted (supplement payable)

AR2 – RAPIDHOME LOFT – Mobile Home

Sleeping:
2 bedrooms, sleeps 5: 1 double, 1 twin with 2 single beds, 1 single sofa bed

Living:
living / kitchen area, heating, shower & WC

Eating:
fitted kitchen with cooking hobs, microwave & fridge/freezer

Outside:
table & chairs, sun loungers

Pets:
accepted (supplement payable)

Weekly Charges

	AR1	AR2
Low Season *(from)*	€ 308	€ 350
High Season *(from)*	€ 763	€ 889

FR83200 Camping Caravaning Les Pêcheurs

83520 Roquebrune-sur-Argens

For our full description of this campsite see page 345

The mobile homes can be found on large pitches (100 m²) in the quiet lower part of the site.

AR1 – SHELBOX PARADIS'HOME – Mobile Home

Sleeping:
2 bedrooms, sleeps 6: 1 double, 1 twin with 2 single beds, 1 double sofa bed; pillows & blankets provided

Living:
living / kitchen area, fan, heating, shower & WC

Eating:
fitted kitchen with cooking hobs, oven, microwave & fridge/freezer

Outside:
table & chairs, sun loungers & parasol

Pets:
accepted (supplement payable)

Weekly Charges

	AR1
Low Season *(from)*	€ 330
High Season *(from)*	€ 680

FR83220 Camping Caravaning Cros de Mouton

B.P. 116, 83240 Cavalaire-sur-Mer

For our full description of this campsite see page 348

Mobile homes are located at the lowest part of the site, each divided by hedges with plenty of shade provided by trees. The chalets are situated at the highest point of the site and some have panoramic views across the bay of Cavalaire.

AR1 – IRM – Mobile Home

Sleeping:
2 bedrooms, sleeps 6: 1 double, 1 twin with 2 single beds, 1 double sofa bed; pillows & blankets provided

Living:
living / kitchen area, heating, shower & WC

Eating:
fitted kitchen with cooking hobs, microwave & fridge

Outside:
table & chairs, parasol

Pets:
accepted

AR2 – GITOTEL – Chalet

Sleeping:
2 bedrooms, sleeps 6: 2 double, 1 twin with 2 bunk beds; pillows & blankets provided

Living:
living / kitchen area, heating, shower & WC

Eating:
fitted kitchen with cooking hobs, microwave & fridge

Outside:
table & chairs, parasol

Pets:
accepted

Weekly Charges

	AR1	AR2
Low Season *(from)*	€ 350	€ 350
High Season *(from)*	€ 655	€ 655

FR83230 Camping Caravaning Domaine du Colombier

Route de Bagnols en Forêt, 83600 Fréjus

For our full description of this campsite see page 337

AR1 – LOUISIANE – Mobile Home

Sleeping:
2 bedrooms, sleeps 4: 1 double, 1 twin with 2 single beds

Living:
living/l Kitchen area.

Eating:
fitted kitchen with cooking hobs & fridge

Outside:
table & chairs, sun loungers, parasaol

Pets:
accepted

AR2 – LOUISIANE MILLENIUM – Mobile Home

Sleeping:
2 bedrooms, sleeps 4/6: 1 double, 2 single beds, 1 sofa bed

Living:
living with tv satellite, air conditioning

Eating:
fitted kitchen with cooking hobs, microwave & fridge/freezer

Outside:
table & chairs, sun loungers, parasol

Pets:
accepted

Weekly Charges

	AR1	AR2
Low Season *(from)*	€ 343	€ 552
High Season *(from)*	€ 714	€ 980

FR83250 Sunêlia Douce Quiétude

3435 boulevard Jacques Baudino, 83700 St Raphaël

For our full description of this campsite see page 338

AR1 – SUNÊLIA GRAND CONFORT – Mobile Home

Sleeping:
2 bedrooms, sleeps 6: 1 double, 1 twin with 2 single beds, 1 bunk bed pillows & blankets provided

Living:
living / kitchen area, TV, heating, air conditioning, shower & WC

Eating:
fitted kitchen with cooking hobs, oven, dish washer & fridge/freezer

Outside:
table & chairs, sun loungers & parasol

Pets:
accepted

AR2 – LOUISIANE FAMILY – Mobile Home

Sleeping:
3 bedrooms, sleeps 6: 1 double, 2 twin with 2 single beds; pillows & blankets provided

Living:
living / kitchen area, TV, heating, air conditioning, shower & WC

Eating:
fitted kitchen with cooking hobs, oven, dish washer & fridge/freezer

Outside:
table & chairs, sun loungers & parasol

Pets:
accepted

Weekly Charges

	AR1	AR2
Low Season *(from)*	€ 518	€ 595
High Season *(from)*	€ 1050	€ 1120

FR20040 Domaine Naturiste Riva Bella

B.P. 21, 20270 Alèria

For our full description of this campsite see page 358

AR1 – CHALET 4

Sleeping:
2 bedrooms, sleeps 5: 1 double, 1 single bed, 2 bunk beds; all bed linen provided

Living:
living / kitchen area, heating, shower & WC

Eating:
fitted kitchen with cooking hobs & fridge

Outside:
table & chairs, sun loungers & parasol

Pets:
accepted

AR2 – CHALET 2

Sleeping:
2 bedrooms, sleeps 4: 1 double, 2 bunk beds; all bed linen provided

Living:
living / kitchen area, heating, shower & WC

Eating:
fitted kitchen with cooking hobs & fridge

Outside:
table & chairs, sun loungers & parasol

Pets:
accepted

Weekly Charges

	AR1	AR2
Low Season *(from)*	€ 329	€ 322
High Season *(from)*	€ 749	€ 728

FR20050 Camping Naturiste Club La Chiappa

20137 Porto-Vecchio

For our full description of this campsite see page 355

AR1 – TYPE C – Bungalow

Sleeping:
2 bedrooms, sleeps 4: 2 twin with 2 single beds; pillows & blankets provided

Living:
living / kitchen area, shower & WC

Eating:
fitted kitchen with fridge

Outside:
table & chairs

Pets:
accepted

AR2 – TYPE B – Bungalow

Sleeping:
1 bedroom, sleeps 2: 1 twin with 2 single beds; pillows & blankets provided

Living:
living / kitchen area, shower & WC

Eating:
fitted kitchen with fridge

Outside:
table & chairs

Pets:
accepted

Weekly Charges

	AR1	AR2
Low Season *(from)*	€ 582	€ 396
High Season *(from)*	€ 994	€ 679

MER MONTAGNE VACANCES

www.mmv.fr

With more than 20 years experience of providing quality holidays, Mer Montagne Vacances again welcomed thousands of holidaymakers to their campsites this year. Our aim is always to offer top quality holidays which are exceed all your expectations!

We have just launched a new programme of very special luxury mobile home holidays at some top-class campsites on both the Atlantic Coast and the Western Mediterranean Coast.

Our four commitments to you:

1

The very best sites:
Everything you need to know about the region
We only use 4 star campsites (French Camping Federation classification)
Always with direct access to the beach
Sound environmental policy
All campsite amenities must be available for the full season and all top quality

2

The best suppliers:
Our mobile homes are specially designed by the top French manufacturer O'Hara.
All our campsite owners have fully committed to all our quality standards.

3

Quality guaranteed:
On our sites, reception is open from 7.00 am to midnight
Outstanding restaurant facilities (set menus, good value takeaways, etc.)
Free children's club in peak season
Entertainment programme for everyone
Top class pool complexes - always free of charge

4

Comfort guaranteed:
The pitches on our sites are at least 120 m^2
Our mobile homes are fully equipped to a high standard
and have two fully fitted bath rooms.
Our mobile homes are at least 33 m^2.
They also have a private terrace of 18 m^2 (with garden furniture)
Easy parking on your pitch

Our campsites

We have a top quality 4 star campsite near the attractive seaside town of Biscarosse in the Landes region. This great site has direct access and a massive pool complex with 2 main pools, 4 waterslides, a jacuzzi and a separate spa with sauna, jacuzzi and many more amenities. It is very close to Europe's biggest sand dune, the Dune de Pyla.

Our 4 star campsite on the Western Mediterranean coast is right on the popular beach at Sète with all its super, top quality amenities - such as tennis, football and a range of water sports. What's more, there are a couple of great restaurants on-site.

Interested?

Our holiday prices range from as little as £175 (all inclusive) in low season to £629 (all inclusive) in high season. For more details of our prices, our 4 star campsites and our luxury mobile homes please visit our website http://www.mmv.fr/anglais/index-ang.htm

Or. for a free brochure: MER MONTAGNE VACANCES, 51 Avenue France d'Outremer. BP 39, 06701 Saint Laurent du Var CEDEX, France. Telephone Call Centre : 00 33 (4) 92 12 62 12 (English is spoken).

OPEN ALL YEAR

The following sites are understood to accept caravanners and campers all year round, although the list also includes some sites that are open for at least ten months. For sites marked with a star (*) – please refer to the site's individual entry for dates and other restrictions. In any case, it is always wise to phone as the facilities available, for example, may be reduced.

Normandy
FR76090 Etennemare

Northern France
FR02030 Croix du Vieux Pont
FR59050 Mauberge

Paris & Ile de France
FR75020 Bois de Boulogne
FR94000 Tremblay

Eastern France
FR88040 Lac de Bouzey
FR88090 Lac de la Moselotte
FR88130 Vanne de Pierre

Vendée & Charente
FR85540 Eden

Loire Valley
FR36050 Vieux Chênes
FR41060 De Dugny
FR86040 Le Futuriste

Burgundy
FR21060 Les Bouleaux

Savoy & Dauphiny Alps
FR73020 Le Versoyen*
FR73030 Les Lanchettes*
FR74010 Deux Glaciers
FR74070 Escale*
FR74130 La Plage*

Atlantic Coast
FR64040 Les Gaves

Dordogne & Aveyron
FR24150 Deux Vallées
FR24280 Barnabé

Limousin & Auvergne
FR63060 Le Clos Auroy

Rhône Valley
FR26110 Les 4 Saisons
FR69010 Porte de Lyon

Provence
FR05030 Les Six Stations
FR84080 La Simioune

Midi-Pyrénées
FR09030 Le Montagnou
FR09050 La Prade
FR09060 Le Pré Lombard
FR09080 Du Lac
FR65030 Pyrénées*
FR65070 Le Rioumajou
FR65080 Le Lavedan
FR65090 Soleil du Pibeste

Mediterranean West
FR11110 Val d`Aleth
FR34060 Oliveraie
FR34230 De Chênes
FR66130 Eau Vive*
FR66180 Mas Llinas*

Mediterranean East
FR06050 La Vieille Ferme
FR06080 Les Cigales
FR83210 Les Tournels*

DOGS

Since the introduction in 2000 of the Passports for Pets scheme many British campers and caravanners have been encouraged to take their pets with them on holiday. However, Pet Travel conditions are understandbly strict, the procedure is quite lengthy and complicated so we would advise you to check the current situation before travelling. The Passports for Pets website is: http://www.freespace.virgin.net/passports.forpets

For the benefit of those who want to take their dogs to France, we list here the sites which have indicated to us that they do not accept dogs or have certain restrictions. If you are planning to take your dog we do advise you to phone the park first to check – there my be limits on numbers, breeds, or times of the year when they are excluded.

FR06140 Ranch
FR07200 Oasis
FR14090 Brévedent
FR14150 Le Port'land
FR16020 Gorges du Chambon
FR17010 Bois Soleil
FR17020 Puits de L`Auture
FR17040 Bonne Anse Plage
FR17180 La Pignade
FR17260 Le Cormoran (Ré)
FR17270 L`Anse des Pins
FR20030 Merendella
FR22010 Les Capucines
FR24040 Moulin du Roch
FR29140 Kerlann
FR30070 Boisson
FR30160 Le Boucanet
FR34140 La Carabasse
FR34250 Des Sources (Soubes
FR40040 La Paillotte
FR40170 La Réserve
FR40220 Les Acacias
FR46040 Moulin de Laborde
FR64060 Pavillon Royal
FR66040 Le Soleil
FR74170 Moulin de Dollay
FR77020 Le Chêne Gris
FR84020 Bélézy
FR85050 Village de Florine
FR85210 Les Ecureuils
FR85420 Bel
FR85690 Moncalm

Sites that accept dogs but with certain restrictions:
FR17190 Logis du Breuil
FR17210 Interlude
FR23010 Château de Poinsouze
FR24290 Moulin du Bleufond
FR25000 Val de Bonnal
FR26030 Grand Lierne
FR32010 Florence
FR34130 Le Neptune
FR40050 Le Col-Vert
FR40120 Arnaoutchot
FR49060 Montsabert
FR50030 Lez-Eaux
FR62030 Château de Gandspette
FR66170 Mar I Sol
FR66210 Le Roussillon
FR68080 Clair Vacances
FR76110 Les Boucaniers
FR81070 Rieu Montagné
FR83120 Domaine
FR83200 Les Pêcheurs
FR85310 La Trévillière
FR85430 Bolée D`Air
FR85520 Renardieres

BICYCLE HIRE

We understand that the following campsites have bicycles to hire on site. Where bicycle hire facilities are within an easy distance (and we have been given details) we include this information in the individual reports. However, we would recommend that you contact the site to check as the situation can change.

FR01020	l'Ile Chambod
FR01030	Les Ripettes
FR02000	Vivier aux Carpes
FR02030	Croix du Vieux Pont
FR03010	La Filature
FR03050	La Petite Valette
FR03170	Dompierre
FR04010	Hippocampe
FR04020	Verdon
FR04120	Indigo - Forcalquier
FR06030	La Bergerie
FR06120	Green Park
FR07020	Ardéchois
FR07030	Soleil Vivarais
FR07090	Des Plantas
FR07110	Le Pommier
FR07130	Les Coudoulets
FR07170	Ludocamping
FR09020	Arize
FR09060	Le Pré Lombard
FR11070	Les Mimosas
FR11080	La Nautique
FR11110	Val d'Aleth
FR11140	La Royale
FR12070	Grange de Monteillac
FR12080	Les Genêts
FR12120	Rouergue
FR12150	Marmotel
FR12170	Le Caussanel
FR14030	Martragny
FR14060	Hautes Coutures
FR14070	La Vallée
FR14090	Brévedent
FR15030	Le Val Saint Jean
FR16020	Gorges du Chambon
FR16030	Le Champion
FR17010	Bois Soleil
FR17020	Puits de L'Auture
FR17040	Bonne Anse Plage
FR17050	Orée du Bois
FR17060	Airotel Oléron
FR17110	Monplaisir
FR17140	Sequoia Parc
FR17170	Les Charmilles
FR17190	Logis du Breuil
FR17210	Interlude
FR17220	La Brande
FR17230	L'Océan
FR19050	La Rivière
FR19060	Le Mialaret
FR19070	Chateau de Gibanel
FR19100	Au Soleil d'Oc
FR20040	Riva Bella
FR21000	Lac de Panthier
FR21040	De Fouché
FR21050	Grappe d'Or
FR22050	Le Vieux Moulin
FR22130	Port l'Epine
FR22160	Le Neptune
FR22200	Le Bocage
FR23010	Château de Poinsouze
FR24010	Le Verdoyer
FR24060	Le Paradis
FR24080	Moulin de David
FR24100	Le Moulinal
FR24110	Aqua Viva
FR24150	Deux Vallées
FR24170	Port de Limeuil
FR24180	Saint Avit Loisirs
FR24230	Moulin de Paulhiac
FR24240	Les Bo-Bains
FR24310	La Bouquerie
FR24320	Les Peneyrals
FR24350	Moulin de la Pique
FR24360	Le Mondou
FR25000	Val de Bonnal
FR25030	Bois de Reveuge
FR26040	Le Couspeau
FR26110	Les 4 Saisons
FR26120	Gervanne
FR28110	Bonneval
FR29010	Ty-Nadan
FR29050	Orangerie de Lanniron
FR29080	Le Panoramic
FR29090	Raguénès-Plage
FR29110	La Plage
FR29120	Manoir de Kerlut
FR29130	Des Abers
FR29140	Kerlann
FR29160	Genets d'Or
FR29250	Bois des Ecureuils
FR29290	Grand Large
FR29310	Roche Percée
FR30120	Ile des Papes
FR30140	Soubeyranne
FR30160	Le Boucanet
FR30170	La Sousta
FR32010	Florence
FR32080	Le Talouch
FR33010	La Dune
FR33080	Barbanne
FR33110	Côte d'Argent
FR33130	Les Grands Pins
FR33210	Pointe du Medoc
FR33220	Petit Nice
FR33240	L'Océan
FR33310	Panorama
FR33320	Talaris
FR34030	Le Napoléon
FR34040	Lou Village
FR34060	Oliveraie
FR34070	Sérignan Plage
FR34080	Sérignan Plage Nature
FR34090	La Yole
FR34110	Le Club Farret
FR34130	Le Neptune
FR34170	Les Mimosas
FR34200	Californie Plage
FR34210	Berges du Canal
FR34240	Le Castellas
FR35020	Des Ormes
FR37010	Mignardière
FR37030	Moulin Fort
FR37050	La Citadelle
FR37060	Arada Parc
FR37090	La Rolandière
FR37120	Fierbois
FR38010	Coin Tranquille
FR39030	Chalain
FR40020	Les Chênes
FR40030	Pins du Soleil
FR40040	La Paillotte
FR40050	Le Col-Vert
FR40070	Lous Seurrots
FR40100	La Rive
FR40110	Sen Yan
FR40120	Arnaoutchot
FR40140	Lou P'tit Poun
FR40160	Les Vignes
FR40170	La Réserve
FR40180	Le Vieux Port
FR40200	Sylvamar
FR41010	Val de Loire
FR41020	Grenouillière
FR41030	Alicourts
FR41040	Des Marais
FR41060	De Dugny
FR41070	Grande Tortue
FR41090	de la Varenne
FR41100	Les Saules
FR42010	Charlieu
FR43030	Vaubarlet
FR44040	Sainte-Brigitte
FR44090	Deffay
FR44100	Le Patisseau
FR44130	Hermitage
FR44170	Ajoncs d'Or
FR45010	Bois du Bardelet
FR46040	Moulin de Laborde
FR46050	Le Rêve
FR46110	Du Port
FR46150	La Truffière
FR47010	Moulin du Périé
FR47030	Fonrives
FR48060	Lac de Naussac
FR49000	Lac de Maine
FR49010	Etang de la Brèche
FR49020	Chantepie
FR49040	Etang
FR49060	Montsabert
FR49080	Ile d'Offard
FR49090	Isle Verte
FR50000	Etang des Haizes
FR50030	Lez-Eaux
FR50050	Le Cormoran
FR50070	Anse du Brick
FR52020	Forge de Ste Marie
FR56010	Grande Métairie
FR56020	La Plage
FR56050	Kervilor
FR56120	Les Iles
FR56130	Mané Guernehué
FR56200	Lann Hoedic
FR62010	La Bien-Assise
FR63040	La Grange Fort
FR63060	Le Clos Auroy

BICYCLE HIRE continued

FR63080	Le Moulin de Serre
FR63120	Indigo Royat
FR64070	Le Ruisseau
FR64110	Col d`Ibardin
FR64140	Bérrua
FR64150	Residence des Pins
FR65010	Eglantière
FR65090	Soleil du Pibeste
FR66020	Ma Prairie
FR66070	Le Brasilia
FR66130	Eau Vive
FR66180	Mas Llinas
FR66190	Les Tropiques
FR66200	Les Marsouins
FR66210	Le Roussillon
FR66240	Le Trivoly
FR68070	Les Sources
FR71050	Moulin de Collonge
FR71060	Montrouant
FR71070	Epervière
FR71090	Lac de St-Point
FR71110	Du Lac
FR71120	Heronniere
FR72030	Chanteloup
FR74030	Belvédère
FR74060	La Colombière
FR74100	Europa
FR74110	Le Taillefer
FR76040	La Source
FR76130	La Forêt
FR77030	Jablines
FR77070	Belle Etoile
FR78050	Le Val de Seine
FR79040	la Venise Verte
FR80010	Drancourt
FR80040	Le Royon
FR80060	Val de Trie
FR80080	Bois des Pêcheurs
FR80090	Val d`Authie
FR80100	des Cygnes
FR80120	les Aubépines
FR81030	Gourjade
FR82010	Trois Cantons
FR83020	Esterel
FR83060	La Baume
FR83070	Etoile d`Argens
FR83130	Le Beau Vezé
FR83140	Lacs du Verdon
FR83160	Les Cigales
FR83170	La Bergerie
FR83210	Les Tournels
FR83250	Douce Quiétude
FR83260	Eouvière
FR83270	La Cigale
FR83600	Holiday Green
FR84050	La Sorguette
FR84070	Carpe Diem
FR84090	Pont d`Avignon
FR85020	Du Jard
FR85040	La Garangeoire
FR85070	Les Biches
FR85080	Puerta del Sol
FR85090	Abri des Pins
FR85120	Le Bois Masson
FR85130	Pong
FR85200	Petite Boulogne
FR85210	Les Ecureuils
FR85240	Jarny-Ocean
FR85260	Guyonnière
FR85270	Oceano d`Or
FR85280	Places Dorées
FR85300	Grand` Métairie
FR85310	La Trévillière
FR85320	Val de Vie
FR85330	Cap Natur`
FR85360	La Forêt
FR85400	Bois Soleil
FR85430	Bolée D`Air
FR85440	Les Brunelles
FR85450	Les Roses
FR85470	Les Pirons
FR85510	Le Bois Joli
FR85530	Parée Préneau
FR85540	Eden
FR85550	Port de Moricq
FR85570	Le Pomme de Pin
FR85580	Les Blancs Chenes
FR85590	Plein Sud
FR85610	Calypso
FR85630	Maison Blanche
FR85660	Le Pont Rouge
FR86010	Petit Trianon
FR86030	Relais du Miel
FR86090	Saint Cyr
FR87020	Leychoisier
FR88040	Lac de Bouzey
FR88080	Des Bans
FR88090	Lac de la Moselotte
FR88130	Vanne de Pierre
FR89060	Les Ceriselles

FISHING

We are pleased to include details of sites which provide facilities for fishing on site. Many others are near rivers or in popular fishing areas and have facilites within easy reach Where we have been given details, we have included this information in our reports. It is always best to contact sites to check that they provide for your individual requirements.

FR01010	La Plaine Tonique
FR02000	Vivier aux Carpes
FR02030	Croix du Vieux Pont
FR02060	Guignicourt
FR03010	La Filature
FR03050	La Petite Valette
FR03170	Dompierre
FR04010	Hippocampe
FR04020	Verdon
FR04030	Moulin de Ventre
FR04060	Haut-Verdon
FR05030	Les Six Stations
FR06070	Origan
FR06080	Les Cigales
FR06100	Les Pinèdes
FR07020	Ardéchois
FR07030	Soleil Vivarais
FR07050	Le Ranc Davaine
FR07070	Les Ranchisses
FR07080	La Bastide
FR07090	Des Plantas
FR07110	Le Pommier
FR07120	Ardéchois
FR07130	Les Coudoulets
FR07150	Domaine de Gil
FR07170	Ludocamping
FR09020	Arize
FR09030	Le Montagnou
FR09060	Le Pré Lombard
FR09080	Du Lac
FR11110	Val d`Aleth
FR12000	Peyrelade
FR12020	Les Rivages
FR12040	Les Tours
FR12050	Terrasses du Lac
FR12080	Les Genêts
FR12150	Marmotel
FR12160	Les Peupliers
FR12170	Le Caussanel
FR12190	Les Calquières
FR14030	Martragny
FR14060	Hautes Coutures
FR14080	Le Puits
FR14090	Brévedent
FR14100	Du Château
FR14130	Fanal
FR15030	Le Val Saint Jean
FR16030	Le Champion
FR16050	Cognac
FR16060	Marco de Bignac
FR17060	Airotel Oléron
FR17110	Monplaisir
FR17200	Au Fil de l`Eau
FR17220	La Brande
FR17230	L`Océan
FR19050	La Rivière
FR19060	Le Mialaret
FR19070	Chateau de Gibanel
FR19080	Le Vianon
FR19090	Le Vaurette
FR19100	Au Soleil d`Oc
FR20010	Arinella Bianca
FR20030	Merendella

FR20040 Riva Bella
FR20050 La Chiappa
FR20220 Les Oliviers
FR21000 Lac de Panthier
FR21030 Savigny-les-Beaune
FR21040 De Fouché
FR21070 Les Grèbes
FR22030 Nautic International
FR22040 Le Châtelet
FR22060 La Hallerais
FR22090 Galinée
FR22130 Port l'Epine
FR22140 Port La Chaine
FR22200 Le Bocage
FR23010 Château de Poinsouze
FR24000 La Tuilière
FR24010 Le Verdoyer
FR24040 Moulin du Roch
FR24060 Le Paradis
FR24070 Lestaubière
FR24090 Soleil Plage
FR24100 Le Moulinal
FR24110 Aqua Viva
FR24150 Deux Vallées
FR24170 Port de Limeuil
FR24230 Moulin de Paulhiac
FR24240 Les Bo-Bains
FR24280 Barnabé
FR24290 Moulin du Bleufond
FR24310 La Bouquerie
FR24320 Les Peneyrals
FR24330 Etang Bleu
FR24340 Val de la Marquise
FR24350 Moulin de la Pique
FR25000 Val de Bonnal
FR25030 Bois de Reveuge
FR25050 Saint Point-Lac
FR26120 Gervanne
FR27020 Catinière
FR28110 Bonneval
FR29010 Ty-Nadan
FR29020 Saint-Laurent
FR29030 Du Letty
FR29050 Orangerie de Lanniron
FR29060 Le Pil-Koad
FR29090 Raguénès-Plage
FR29110 La Plage
FR29130 Des Abers
FR30000 Gaujac
FR30060 Fumades
FR30070 Boisson
FR30100 La Sablière
FR30120 Ile des Papes
FR30160 Le Boucanet
FR30170 La Sousta
FR30180 Mas de la Cam
FR32030 Verduzan
FR33020 Fontaine-Vieille
FR33080 Barbanne
FR33310 Panorama
FR33320 Talaris
FR34110 Le Club Farret
FR34130 Le Neptune
FR34150 Nouvelle Floride
FR34160 Charlemagne
FR34170 Les Mimosas
FR34180 Borio de Roque
FR34200 Californie Plage
FR34240 Le Castellas
FR34250 Des Sources (Soubes)
FR35000 Vieux Chêne
FR35020 Des Ormes
FR36050 Vieux Chênes
FR37030 Moulin Fort
FR37050 La Citadelle
FR37070 L'Ile Auger
FR37110 Bord du Cher
FR37120 Fierbois
FR38050 Temps Libre
FR38110 Champ du Moulin
FR38120 Bontemps
FR39010 Plage Blanche
FR39030 Chalain
FR39040 La Pergola
FR39050 Fayolan
FR39080 Domaine de l'Epinette
FR40040 La Paillotte
FR40050 Le Col-Vert
FR40070 Lous Seurrots
FR40100 La Rive
FR40120 Arnaoutchot
FR40170 La Réserve
FR40190 Saint Martin
FR41020 Grenouillière
FR41030 Alicourts
FR41040 Des Marais
FR41060 De Dugny
FR41090 de la Varenne
FR41100 Les Saules
FR42010 Charlieu
FR43030 Vaubarlet
FR44020 Du Moulin
FR44040 Sainte-Brigitte
FR44090 Deffay
FR45010 Bois du Bardelet
FR46040 Moulin de Laborde
FR46110 Du Port
FR47030 Fonrives
FR47050 Moulin de Campech
FR48020 Capelan
FR48060 Lac de Naussac
FR49010 Etang de la Brèche
FR49020 Chantepie
FR49040 Etang
FR49070 Vallée des Vignes
FR49090 Isle Verte
FR50000 Etang des Haizes
FR50030 Lez-Eaux
FR50050 Le Cormoran
FR50060 Le Grand Large
FR50080 Haliotis
FR50090 La Gerfleur
FR51020 Châlons-sur-Marne
FR52020 Forge de Ste Marie
FR52030 Lac de la Liez
FR55010 Les Breuils
FR56010 Grande Métairie
FR56080 Le Pâtis
FR56120 Les Iles
FR56130 Mané Guernehué
FR56160 Vallée du Ninian
FR56180 Le Cénic
FR58030 Bezolle
FR59010 La Chaumière
FR59050 Mauberge
FR61010 La Campière
FR62060 Orée du Bois
FR63040 La Grange Fort
FR63070 Le Pré Bas
FR63080 Le Moulin de Serre
FR63140 Les Loges
FR64040 Les Gaves
FR64060 Pavillon Royal
FR64070 Le Ruisseau
FR64090 La Chêneraie
FR65060 Pyrenees Natura
FR66030 Cala Gogo
FR66040 Le Soleil
FR66070 Le Brasilia
FR67030 Du Ried
FR68030 Masevaux
FR70020 Lac Vesoul
FR71050 Moulin de Collonge
FR71060 Montrouant
FR71070 Epervière
FR71080 Etang Neuf
FR71090 Lac de St-Point
FR71110 Du Lac
FR72030 Chanteloup
FR72060 Val de Sarthe
FR73030 Les Lanchettes
FR74070 Escale
FR76040 La Source
FR77030 Jablines
FR77070 Belle Etoile
FR77080 Les Prés
FR77090 Etangs Fleuris
FR78010 International
FR78050 Le Val de Seine
FR80010 Drancourt
FR80030 Port de Plaisance
FR80060 Val de Trie
FR80070 Ferme des Aulnes
FR80100 des Cygnes
FR81020 Moulin de Julien
FR81030 Gourjade
FR81040 Auzerals
FR81060 Les Clots
FR83070 Etoile d'Argens
FR83080 Au Paradis
FR83100 La Plage
FR83120 Domaine
FR83170 La Bergerie
FR83200 Les Pêcheurs
FR83240 Moulin des Iscles
FR83290 Saint Aygulf
FR84050 La Sorguette
FR85040 La Garangeoire
FR85130 Pong
FR85260 Guyonnière
FR85350 La Ningle
FR85510 Le Bois Joli
FR85540 Eden
FR85550 Port de Moricq
FR86030 Relais du Miel
FR86040 Le Futuriste
FR86080 Les Peupliers
FR86090 Saint Cyr
FR87020 Leychoisier
FR88040 Lac de Bouzey
FR88080 Des Bans
FR88090 Lac de la Moselotte
FR89060 Les Ceriselles
FR94000 Tremblay
FR95000 Séjours Etang

HORSE RIDING

We understand that the following sites offer riding on site for at least part of the year. However, we recommend that you contact the site to check that the facility meet your requirements. It is worth bearing in mind that French attitudes to safety may differ from your own (for example, you may be required to take your own hard hat).

Brittany
FR29010 Ty-Nadan
FR35000 Vieux Chêne
FR35020 Des Ormes
FR44090 Deffay
FR56120 Les Iles

Normandy
FR50050 Le Cormoran

Northern France
FR80010 Drancourt

Paris & Ile de France
FR77030 Jablines
FR78050 Le Val de Seine

Eastern France
FR68070 Les Sources
FR88040 Lac de Bouzey
FR88080 Des Bans

Vendée & Charente
FR17060 Airotel Oléron
FR17140 Sequoia Parc
FR17230 L'Océan
FR85040 La Garangeoire
FR85540 Eden

Loire Valley
FR49020 Chantepie

Burgundy
FR58030 Bezolle

Franche-Comté
FR25030 Bois de Reveuge

Savoy & Dauphiny Alps
FR38120 Bontemps

Atlantic Coast
FR33110 Côte d'Argent
FR40050 Le Col-Vert
FR40180 Le Vieux Port

Dordogne & Aveyron
FR24240 Les Bo-Bains
FR24250 Tourterelles
FR46110 Du Port

Limousin & Auvergne
FR03010 La Filature
FR63050 La Ribeyre

Rhône Valley
FR07030 Soleil Vivarais
FR07050 Le Ranc Davaine

Provence
FR04020 Verdon
FR04100 International
FR84080 La Simioune

Midi-Pyrénées
FR09020 Arize

Mediterranean West
FR11060 Arnauteille
FR34060 Oliveraie
FR34170 Les Mimosas
FR34180 Borio de Roque
FR34190 Champs Blancs
FR34200 Californie Plage
FR34210 Berges du Canal
FR66040 Le Soleil
FR66180 Mas Llinas
FR66200 Les Marsouins

Mediterranean East
FR83020 Esterel
FR83160 Les Cigales

Corsica
FR20010 Arinella Bianca
FR20050 La Chiappa

GOLF

We understand that the following sites have facilities for playing golf. However, we would recommend that you contact the site to check that the facility meets your requirements.

Brittany
FR35020 Des Ormes

Northern France
FR80010 Drancourt

Loire Valley
FR41030 Alicourts
FR49010 Etang de la Brèche

Burgundy
FR71110 Du Lac

Atlantic Coast
FR40120 Arnaoutchot

Limousin & Auvergne
FR15030 Le Val Saint Jean

Rhône Valley
FR07120 Ardéchois

Midi-Pyrénées
FR81030 Gourjade

Mediterranean West
FR34190 Champs Blancs
FR34200 Californie Plage
FR34210 Berges du Canal

Mediterranean East
FR83300 Clos Sainte Thérèse

We have had very favourable feedback from readers concerning our choice of naturist sites, which we first introduced in our 1992 edition. Over the last few years we have gradually added a few more, including two in Corsica.

Apart from the need to have a 'Naturist Licence' (see below), there is no need to be a practising naturist before visiting these sites. In fact, at least as far as British visitors are concerned, many are what might be described as 'holiday naturists' as distinct from the practice of naturism at other times. The emphasis in all the sites featured in this guide at least, is on naturism as 'life in harmony with nature', and respect for oneself and others and for the environment, rather than simply on nudity. In fact nudity is really only obligatory in the area of the swimming pools.

There are a number of rules, which amount to sensible and considerate guidelines designed to ensure that no-one invades someone else's privacy, creates any nuisance, or damages the environment. Whether as a result of these rules, the naturist philosophy generally, or the attitude of site owners and campers alike, we have been very impressed by all the naturist sites we have selected. Without exception they had a friendly and welcoming ambience, were all extremely clean and tidy and, in most cases, provided much larger than average pitches, with a wide range of activities.

The purpose of our including a number of naturist sites in our guide is to provide an introduction to naturist camping in France for British holidaymakers; we were actually surprised by the number of British campers we met on naturist sites, many of whom had 'stumbled across naturism almost by accident' but had found, like us, that these sites were amongst the nicest they had encountered. You may still be required to have a Naturist Licence. These can be obtained in advance from either the British or French national naturist associations, but are also available on arrival at any recognised naturist site (a passport sized photograph is required).

The Law

You must be aged 18 or over to drive a car in France, but a UK national driving licence is sufficient – only non-EU nationals require an International Driving Permit. You should carry your Registration Document, and your Insurance (valid for use in Europe) and you must display a GB plate. You must carry a warning triangle, and a spare set of light bulbs and your headlights must be adjusted to dip to the right. A first-aid kit and fire extinguisher are recommended but not compulsory.

Drive on the right-hand-side of the road, and remember to look left when turning onto a another road.

Conditions and Conventions

'A' roads are Autoroutes, usually toll roads
'N' roads are Routes Nationale, the equivalent of our A roads
'D' roads are Routes Departemental, the equivalent of our B roads
'C' roads are Routes Communale, unclassified minor roads
'*Prioité à Droite*' means 'Give way to traffic coming from your right' (even if you think you are on a more main road and have the right of way – you don't, so give way.

On roundabouts (rounded anti-clockwise of course) traffic already IN the roundabout has priority.

Traffic Lights

Lights in France turn from Red to Green without going through an amber period. Flashing amber means you can proceed with caution

Most traffic lights have small repeater lights at shoulder height adjacent to the line where you must stop – these are very useful as many traffic lights don't have a set of lights on the far side of the junction.

Watch for 'right filters' – a slowly flashing amber light/arrow which allows you to filter right, with care.

Pedestrian Crossings

There are lots of pedestrian crossings, even more than in the UK, but they are more often than not ignored by motorists (except those from abroad). Don't be surprised if you're honked at for stopping for pedestrians!

Autoroutes

Mostly these are toll roads, and you must pay to use them. You will either have to pay at the toll (*Péage*) where you join, or you must take a ticket from the machine at the Péage and surrender this, with your money or credit card, at the *Péage* where you leave the Autoroute. There are service areas (*Aires de Service*) with full facilities every 40 km. on Autoroutes, and rest areas (*Aires de Repos*) also at regular intervals. Both have warning signs well in advance, indicating the facilities and even the price of fuel.

Signposting

Is better than in the past but the positioning and angling of signposts is something one just gets used to.

Navigating

Michelin Maps are the most popular, particularly the Michelin 1: 200,000 scale Atlas, but for more detailed maps you can buy IGN Maps, which are the French equivalent of our Ordnance Survey maps, but often even more expensive.

Breakdowns

You should have breakdown insurance; towing in France can involve long distances and hefty charges. If you do break down you are required to display your warning triangle 30 m. behind your car (or car and caravan) and it should be visible for at least 100 m. if possible. Don't forget to turn on hazard lights as well. There are emergency phones every two kilometres on Autoroutes.

Security

Take sensible precautions against theft of, or from, your vehicle and/or caravan – be vigilant in car parks and Aires de Service where thieves are often active.

Before you set off for a holiday abroad it's worth making yourself a checklist of things to do, and what to pack. It's not always best to rely on our memory for this, so here is a shortlist of essentials to start you off:

- ☐ Passports
- ☐ Tickets
- ☐ Motor Insurance Certificate, Green Card or Continental Cover clause
- ☐ V5 Registration Document and/or (if not your vehicle) the owners authority
- ☐ Breakdown Insurance Certificate
- ☐ Driving Licence
- ☐ Form E1-11 (to extend NHS Insurance to European destinations)
- ☐ Foreign Currency (euros) and/or Travellers Cheques
- ☐ Credit Card(s)
- ☐ Campsite and Tourist Guide(s)
- ☐ Maps/Road Atlas
- ☐ GB Stickers on car & caravan/trailer
- ☐ Beam deflectors to ensure headlights dip towards the right hand side
- ☐ Red Warning Triangle
- ☐ Spare vehicle/caravan driving light bulbs
- ☐ Torch
- ☐ First-Aid Kit (incl. mosquito repellent)
- ☐ Fire extinguisher
- ☐ Basic tool kit (eg screwdriver, pliers)
- ☐ Continental mains connector/ adaptor, and long cable
- ☐ Polarity tester
- ☐ Spare fuses for car and caravan
- ☐ Spare fan/alternator belt

Remember: it is well worth having your car and caravan serviced before you go, and do check that your outfit is properly 'trimmed'.

Speed

Most of Europe has a bewildering range of speed limits, but in France it is simple and logical. One set of limits covers motor caravans, solo cars and cars towing trailers or caravans. These are the limits:

In built-up areas 50 kph (31 mph)
Outside built-up areas 90 kph (56 mph)
Motorways 130 kph (81 mph)

There is also a requirement that no vehicle may use a French motorway unless it can cruise at 80 kph (50 mph).

When it is raining the maximum speed outside built-up areas is automatically reduced to 80 kph (50 mph) and on motorways to 110 kph (68 mph). The definition of rain is any time you have to put wipers on, so reduce speed even if it has stopped raining but roads are wet.

On non-charged sections of motorway, speed limits may be reduced to 110 kph (68 mph) and there may be signs on any road reducing the maximum speed allowed because of road conditions or other factors.

The French do not tend to use a sign on the outskirts of a town or village to tell you a speed limit applies. A name post is sufficient to indicate that built-up area limits apply. On the exit from the town you will see the name post again, but with the name crossed out. That means the built-up area speed limits no longer apply.

Speed limits are rigidly enforced: 110 kph means exactly that, not 111 kph. The French have adopted the Gatso automatic speed recording and photographing machine and holidaymakers have returned home to find a speeding summons waiting.

Under French Law the summons for speeding cannot be enforced unless the driver of the vehicle is clearly identifiable in the photograph. However the majority of speeding motorists are caught by a following Police vehicle or Police speed camera. French Police don't wear reflective jackets and do hide behind hedges.

During the summer months French magistrates escape from stuffy court rooms and set up court in a tent by the road. Motorists caught speeding are escorted there and given on-the-spot fines. In some circumstances the Police can themselves impose an on-the-spot fine. On-the spot means just that. If you can't pay there and then they'll escort you to a cash machine or bank to draw out money.

Since 2001 laws have come into effect so that anyone caught exceeding the speed limit by more than 40kph will LOSE THEIR LICENCE ON THE SPOT – this means you won't be able to complete your journey without a substitute driver, to say nothing of the standard £900 fine! If you really cannot pay, magistrates have the power to confiscate your vehicle until you do. Anyone caught for a second offence faces a three month jail sentence plus a £2,200 fine. So although French speed limits are more generous than ours, exceeding the limit can be a seriously expensive pastime.

INSURANCE

There is probably no subject which causes campers, caravanners and motor-caravanners venturing abroad more worries than insurance. The problem is that there is an overlap, so that sometimes one problem is apparently covered on two insurance policies. To avoid confusion let's cut through the hype and take a clear look at insurance and what you will need.

Road traffic insurance

Under European Law your ordinary car or motorcaravan road insurance will cover you anywhere in the EU. But many policies only provide minimum cover. So if you have an accident your insurance may only cover the cost of damage to the other person's property.

To maintain the same level of cover abroad as you enjoy at home you need to tell your vehicle insurer. Some will automatically cover you abroad with no extra cost and no extra paperwork. Some will say you need a Green Card – which is neither green nor on card – but won't charge for it. Some will charge extra for the green card.

Ideally you should contact your vehicle insurer 3-4 weeks before you set off, and confirm your conversation with them in writing.

A good insurance company will provide a European recognised accident report form. On this you mark details of damage to yours and the other party's property and draw a little diagram showing where the vehicles were in relation to each other. You give a copy of your form to the other motorist, he gives you a copy of his. It prevents all the shouting which often accompanies accidents in this country.

Holiday insurance

This is a multi-part insurance. One part covers your vehicles. If they breakdown or are involved in an accident they can be repaired or returned to this country. The best will even arrange to bring your vehicle home if the driver is unable to proceed.

Many new vehicles come with a free breakdown and recovery insurance which extends into Europe. Some professional motoring journalists have reported that the actual service this provides can be patchy and may not cover the recovery of a caravan or trailer. Our advice is to buy the motoring section of your holiday insurance.

The second section of holiday insurance covers people. It will include the cost of doctor, ambulance and hospital treatment if needed. If needed the better companies will even pay for English language speaking doctors and nurses and will bring a sick or injured holidaymaker home by air ambulance.

The third part of a good holiday insurance policy covers belongings. If someone breaks in to your motorhome and steals your passports and money, one phone call to the insurance company will have everything sorted out. If you manage to drive over your camera, it's covered.

One part of the insurance which is often ignored is the cancellation section. Few things are as heartbreaking as having to cancel a holiday because a member of the family falls ill. Cancellation insurance cannot take away the disappointment, but it makes sure you don't suffer financially as well.

Ideally you should arrange travel insurance when you book your ferry. If you are using the Alan Rogers' Travel Service they will be able to take care of all your travel insurance requirements.

For those travelling independently, we have arranged special terms with Insure4Europe run in association with Green Flag (and which imposes no restriction on the age of your vehicle). Full details are shown overleaf.

Form E111

By arrangement between the British Government and rest of the European Community Governments, British holiday-makers can enjoy similar health care as that Government offers its own citizens. The form which shows you are entitled to take advantage of this arrangement is called E111.

E111 doesn't replace holiday insurance, but is in addition to. The form is available from all main UK Post Offices. Fill out one for every adult member of your family (children under 16 should be marked as dependents on your form). Get it stamped by the counter staff and take it on holiday with you.

Form E111 is valid indefinitely (unless you change your address).

And that is all you need to know about insurance. You know what they say about insurance, don't you? You'll only need it if you haven't got it.

Mike Cazalet

PUBLIC HOLIDAYS IN FRANCE 2005

1 January (Sat)	New Year
25 March	Good Friday (Moselle and Alsace)
27 March (Sun)	Easter
28 March	Easter Monday
1 May (Sun)	Labour Day
8 May (Sun)	Victory Day 1945
20 May (Fri)	Ascension
29 May (Sun)	Whitsun
30 May	Whit Monday
14 July (Thur)	Bastille Day
15 August (Mon)	Assumption
1 November (Tues)	All Saint's Day
11 November (Fri)	Armistice Day
25 December (Sun)	Christmas
26 December (Mon)	Boxing Day (Alsace and Moselle)

Come and get active at Urban Escapes

URBAN escapes™

LEE VALLEY SHOWGROUND
17 - 19 JUNE 2005
M25 JUNCTION 26
LONDON IN 30 MINS

Walking   Camping & Caravanning   Cycling
Angling   Boating   Canoeing
Adventure/Extreme Sports   Gardening & Conservation

- a great weekend and/or days out for everyone
- situated in a beautiful countryside setting, next to the meandering River Lee
- with surrounding attractions including Historic Waltham Abbey, Myddelton House Gardens and the majestic Epping Forest

Your active leisure show

Retail therapy + interaction =

More activities, more choices in one show

- Camping and caravanning showcase
- Outdoor equipment and leisure wear sales
- Have-a-go at different outdoor activities
- Selection of talks from leading speakers
- Meet The Camping & Caravanning Club sessions
- Tent pitching competitions
- Stay on site at our 400 pitch camping and caravanning site
- Free visitor parking

Send original or photocopy of this advertisement by 30 April 2005 for a chance to win two free weekend tickets.

Title (Mr, Mrs, Miss, Ms) Initials . . . . Surname . . . .

Home Address . . . .

. . . . Postcode . . . .

If you **wish** to receive more information, please tick these boxes:

☐ by post   ☐ by email   ☐ from selected third parties

Email address . . . .

Presented by
Lee Valley Park
Open spaces and sporting places

Support Partners
The Camping and Caravanning Club — The friendly Club
British Canoe Union
enjoyEngland
British Waterways London

Register at www.urban-escapes.co.uk for latest updates and special offers.
For more details about camping on site call The Camping & Caravanning Club line 02476 475442

ESCAPADES
Terre Océane
TAKE A GOOD
BREATH IN !
The campsites to feel good
A good idea for a holiday in a campsite
in the most beautiful regions of France :
Alsace • Auvergne • Brittany • Dordogne • Landes • Lot
Normandy • Savoy • Loire Valley
Booking centre
B.P. 53 132 (PO Box) - F -17 033 LA ROCHELLE - FRANCE
Phone : +33 (0) 546 551 001
Online booking
www.campingterreoceane.com

LES CASTELS

41 superb 4-star touring sites in exceptional settings across France

Photos © P. Allan : kura-images.com

Welcome to Les Castels where the grounds of stunning castles, beautiful manors and charming country houses provide unique natural settings for some of the finest touring sites in France.

LES CASTELS
★ ★ ★ ★

Enjoy the different pace of life, discover authentic French 'art de vivre' and experience the hospitality of site owners who all share a passion for the good and simple things life has to offer.

CAMPING & CARAVANING

Choice, comfort & 4-star quality

Each Castels site has it's own distinctive character and flavour. From the small and exquisitely tranquil to the larger, more lively sites the choice is large. All Castels sites are 4-star rated and you'll find good-sized pitches and a wide range of facilities and services to make your stay a truly enjoyable experience.

So whether you wish to explore a new region, walk the local hills, fish for carp, play some golf, take a dip in the pool or simply do nothing we're sure that you'll find a Castels site that matches your idea of the perfect holiday destination. Contact us for a brochure and discover what Les Castels can offer you.

Discover a 'different France'...

LES CASTELS - CP 3751 - 56037 VANNES CEDEX, FRANCE
Tel : +33 297 425 712 / Fax : +33 297 425 767
Visit our web site at : www.les-castels.com

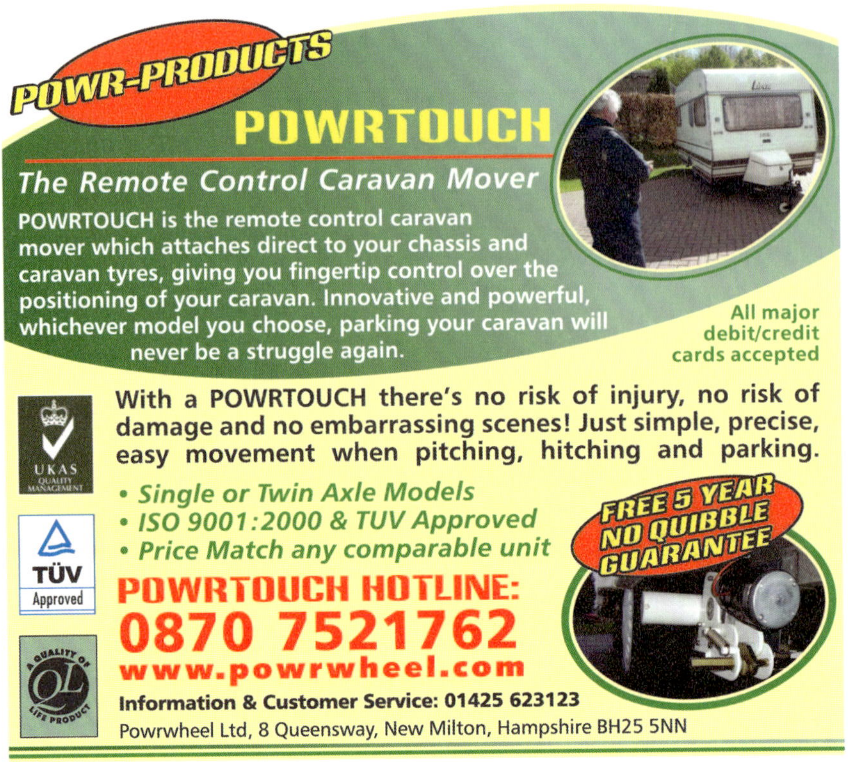
POWR-PRODUCTS
POWRTOUCH
The Remote Control Caravan Mover
POWRTOUCH is the remote control caravan mover which attaches direct to your chassis and caravan tyres, giving you fingertip control over the positioning of your caravan. Innovative and powerful, whichever model you choose, parking your caravan will never be a struggle again.
All major debit/credit cards accepted
With a POWRTOUCH there's no risk of injury, no risk of damage and no embarrassing scenes! Just simple, precise, easy movement when pitching, hitching and parking.
• Single or Twin Axle Models
• ISO 9001:2000 & TUV Approved
• Price Match any comparable unit
FREE 5 YEAR NO QUIBBLE GUARANTEE
UKAS QUALITY MANAGEMENT
TÜV Approved
A QUALITY OF LIFE PRODUCT
POWRTOUCH HOTLINE:
0870 7521762
www.powrwheel.com
Information & Customer Service: 01425 623123
Powrwheel Ltd, 8 Queensway, New Milton, Hampshire BH25 5NN

WIN A Caravan...
A holiday...and lots more
Alan Rogers
Prize Draw Bonanza
Alan Rogers Guides, in association with Towsure, providers of everything for the outdoors, are running a unique new prize draw for 2005. This is your chance to win a fantastic set of prizes, never before offered in the UK.
YOU COULD WIN ALL THESE!
WIN A brand new Avondale caravan
WIN A Camping Cheque holiday, including return ferry
WIN £500 of Towsure products
WIN A complete set of Alan Rogers 2005 guides
To enter, simply visit www.towsure.com
Towsure

Brittany Map 1

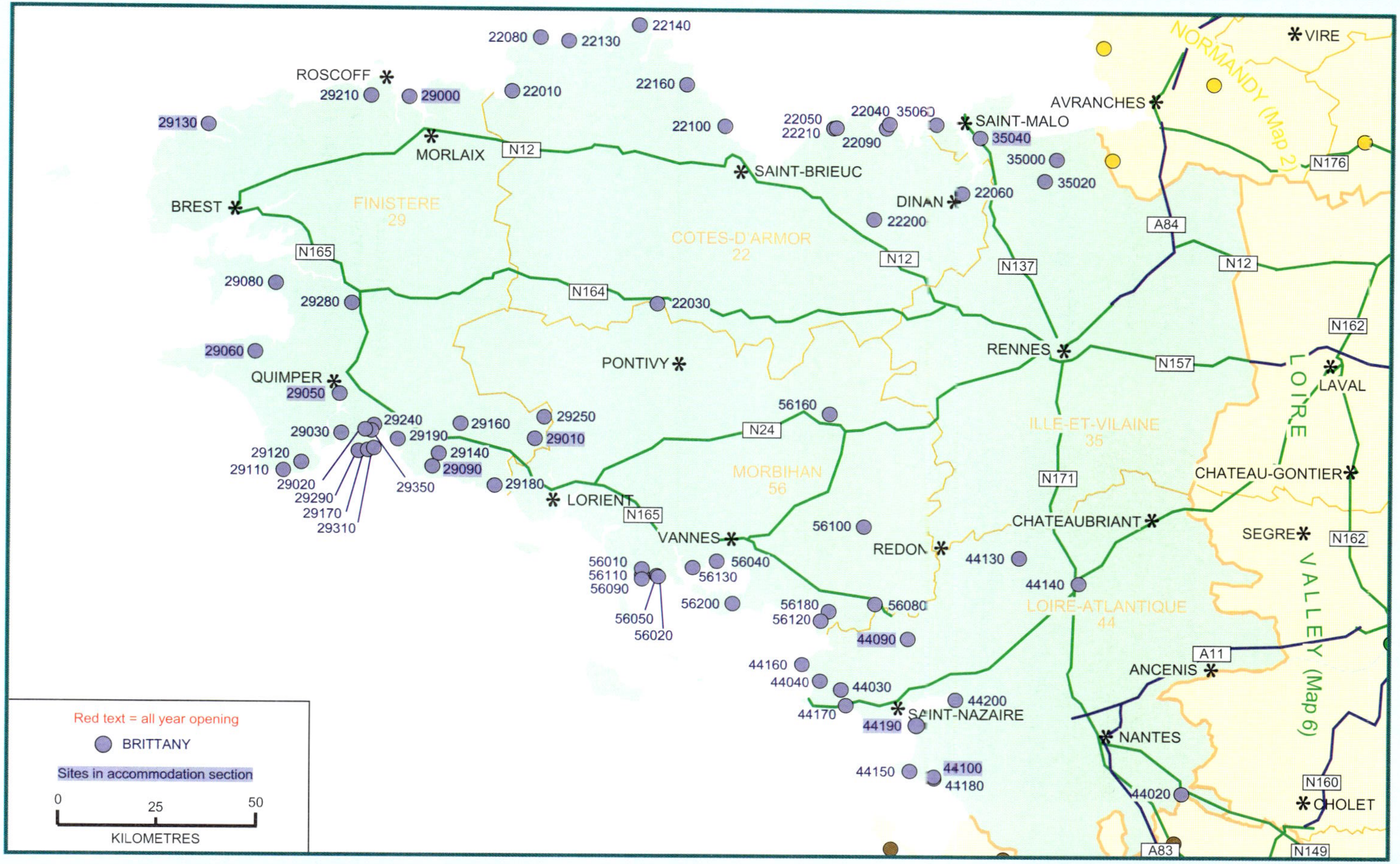

Please refer to the numerical index for campsite page reference

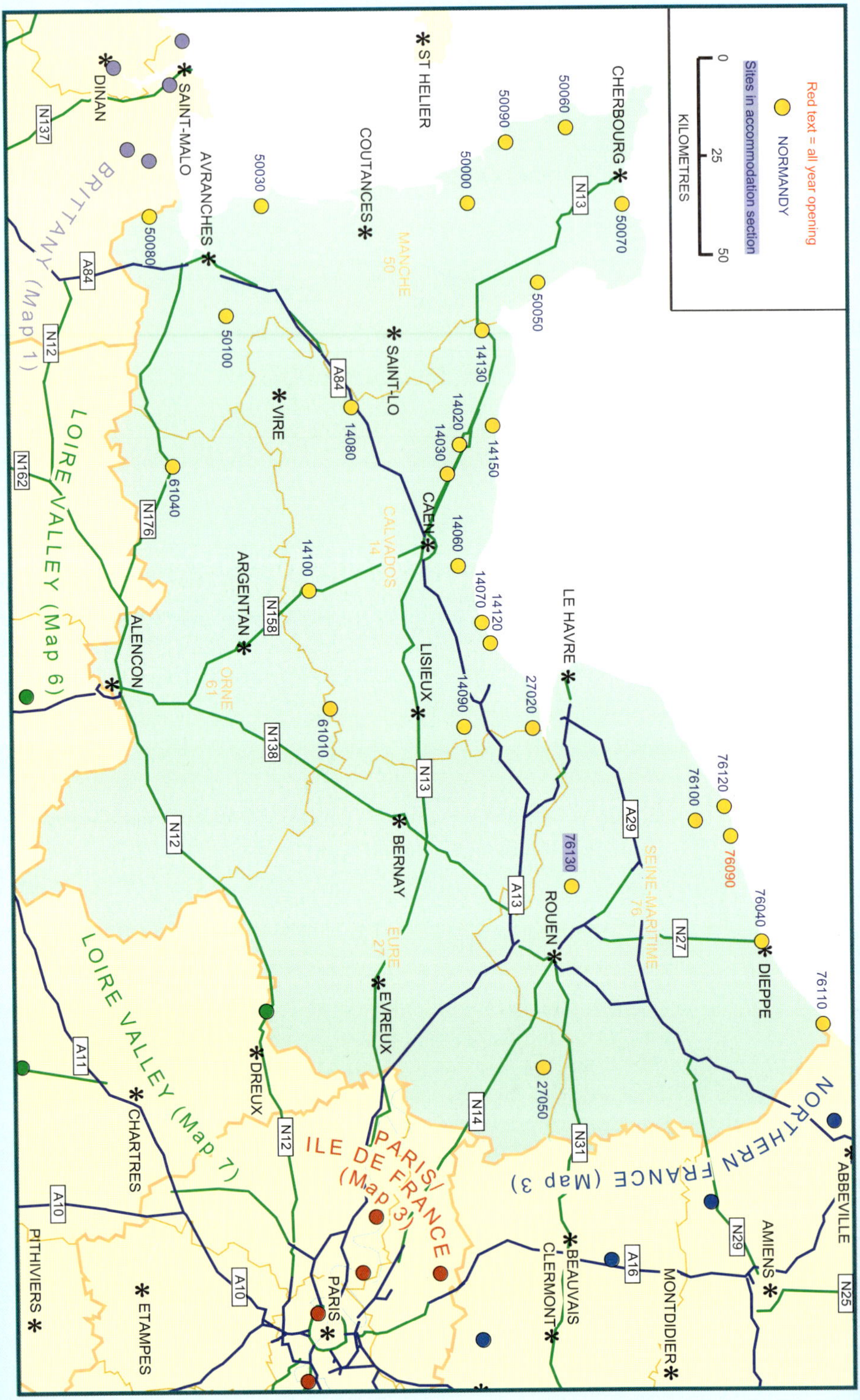
Red text = all year opening
NORMANDY
Sites in accommodation section
0 25 50
KILOMETRES
CHERBOURG
ST HELIER
COUTANCES
SAINT-MALO
DINAN
AVRANCHES
BRITTANY (Map 1)
MANCHE 50
SAINT-LO
VIRE
CAEN
CALVADOS 14
ARGENTAN
ORNE 61
ALENCON
LOIRE VALLEY (Map 6)
LISIEUX
LE HAVRE
BERNAY
EURE 27
EVREUX
DREUX
ROUEN
SEINE-MARITIME 76
DIEPPE
ABBEVILLE
AMIENS
MONTDIDIER
BEAUVAIS
CLERMONT
NORTHERN FRANCE (Map 3)
PARIS/ ILE DE FRANCE (Map 3)
PARIS
CHARTRES
LOIRE VALLEY (Map 7)
ETAMPES
PITHIVIERS
50070
50060
50090
50000
50050
50030
50080
50100
14130
14150
14020
14030
14080
14060
14070
14120
14100
14090
61040
61010
27020
27050
76120
76100
76090
76130
76040
76110
N13
A84
N12
N137
N162
N176
N158
N138
A29
A13
N27
N14
N31
A16
N29
N25
A11
A10

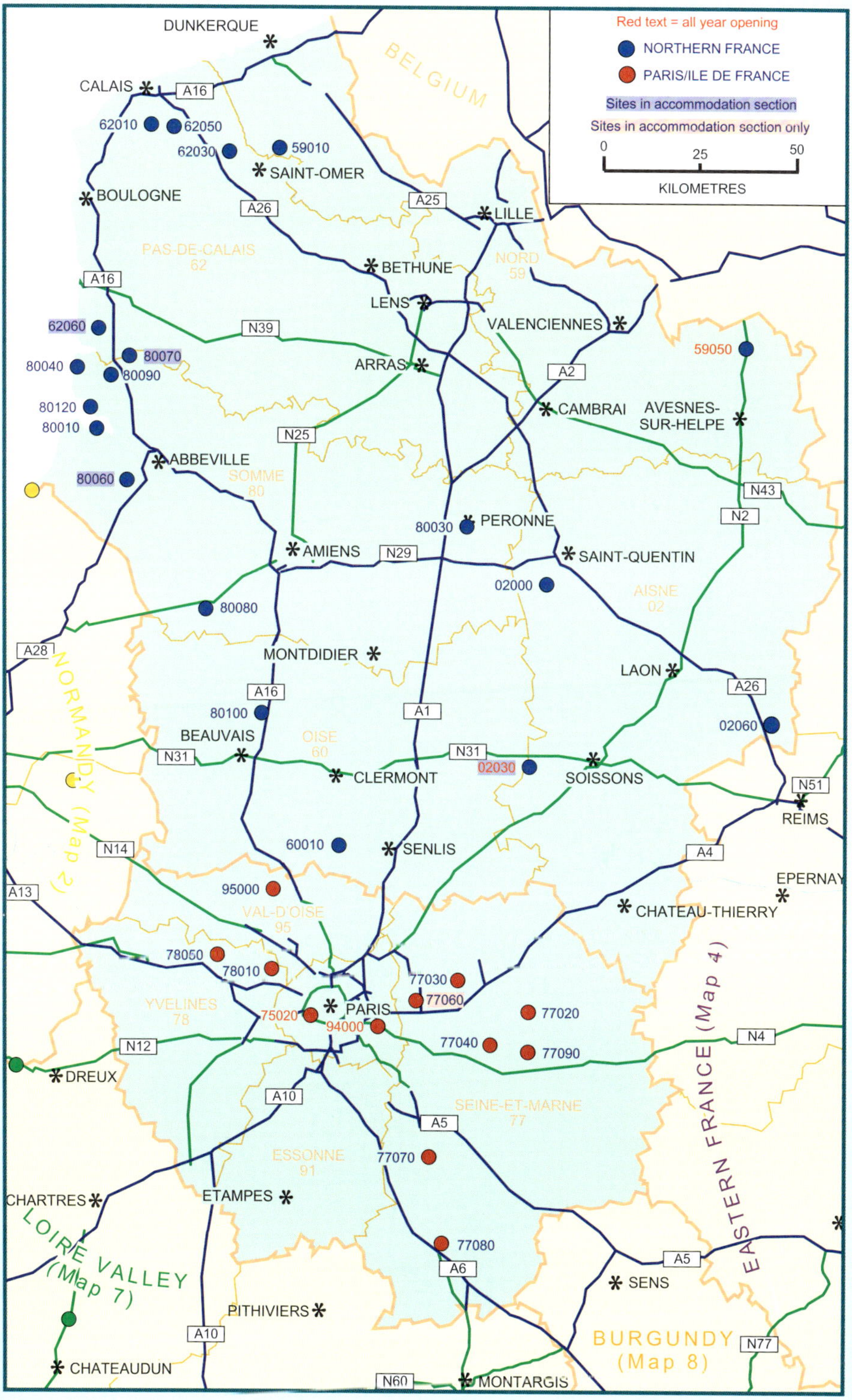

Please refer to the numerical index for campsite page reference

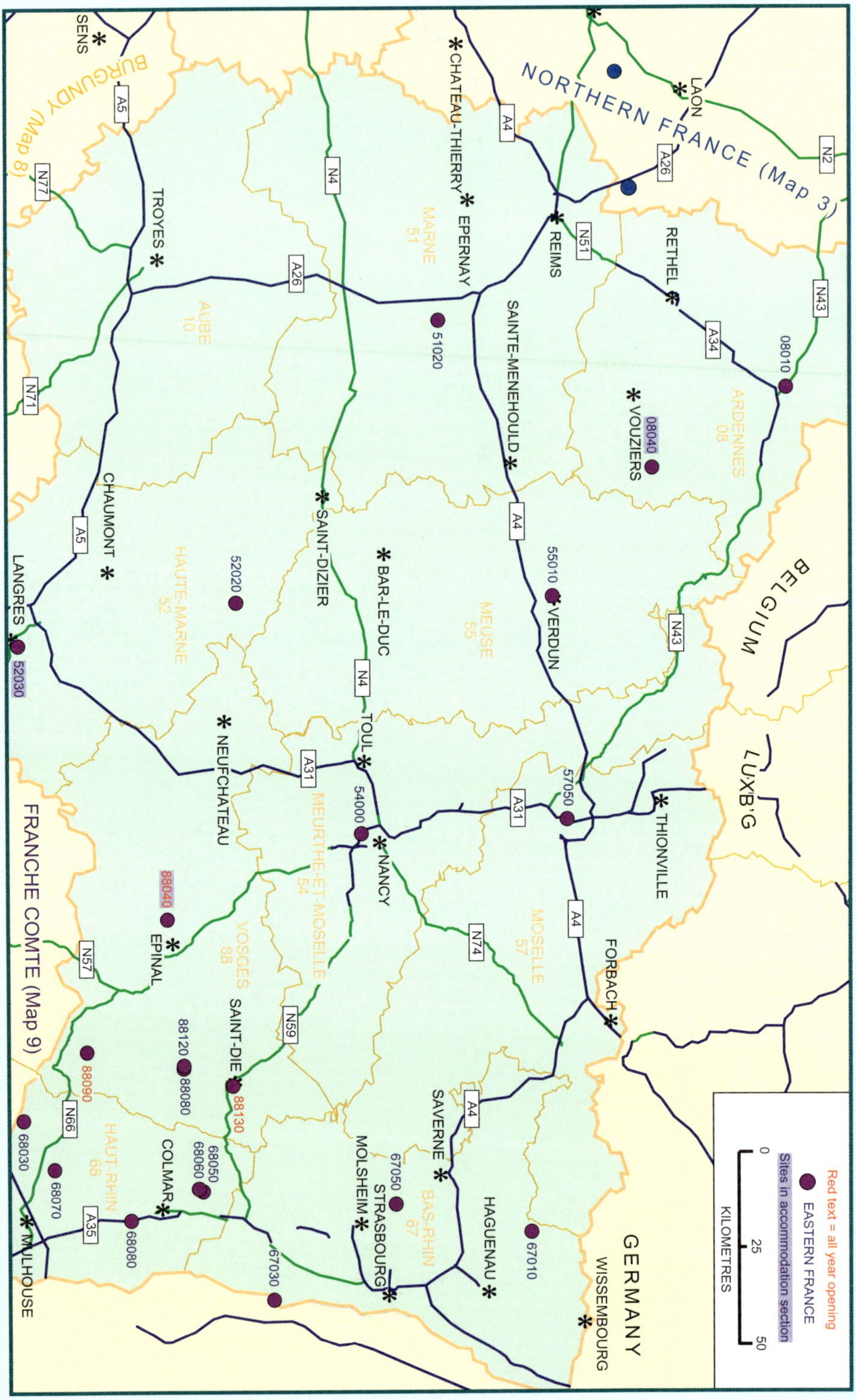

Please refer to the numerical index for campsite page reference

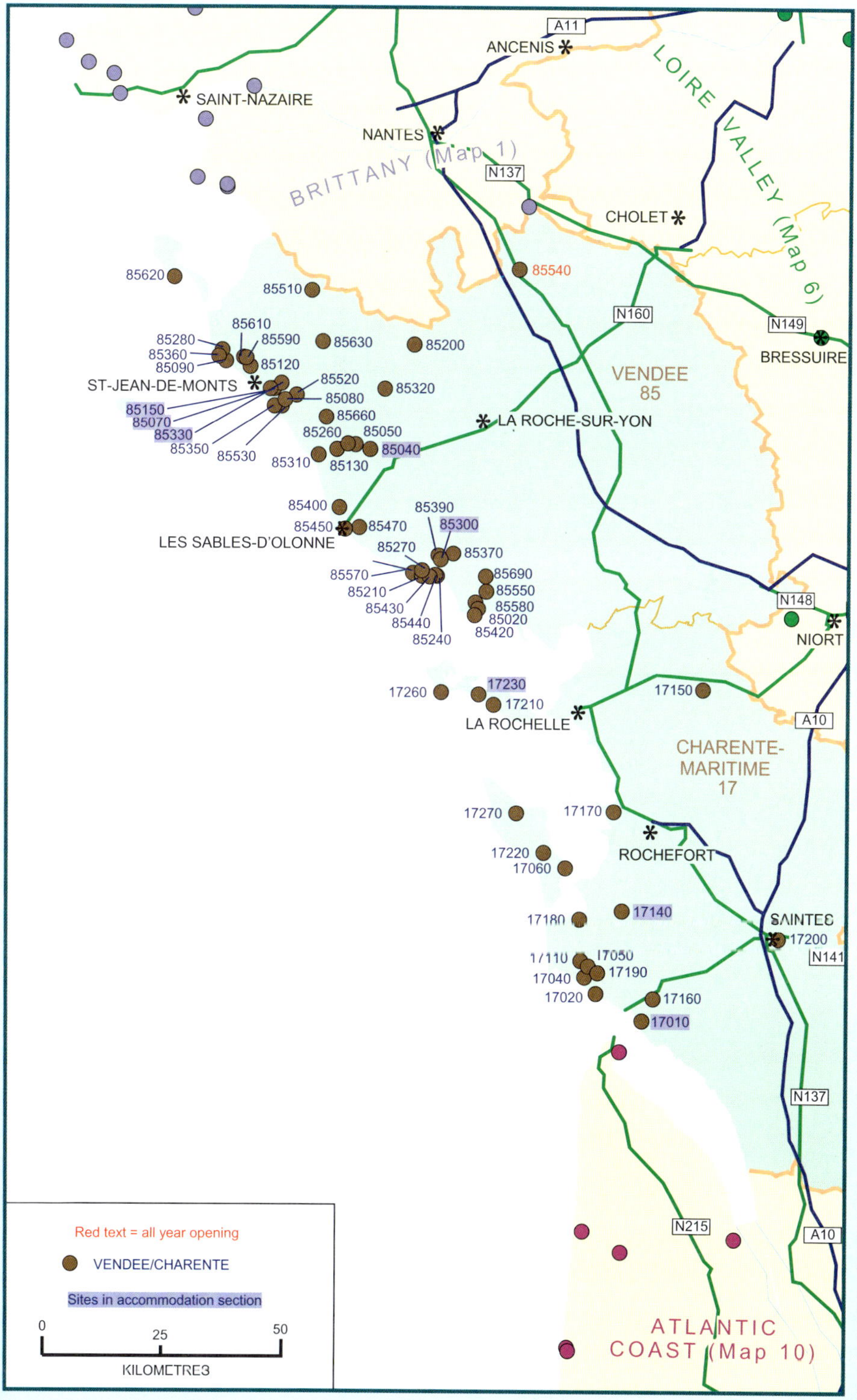

Please refer to the numerical index for campsite page reference

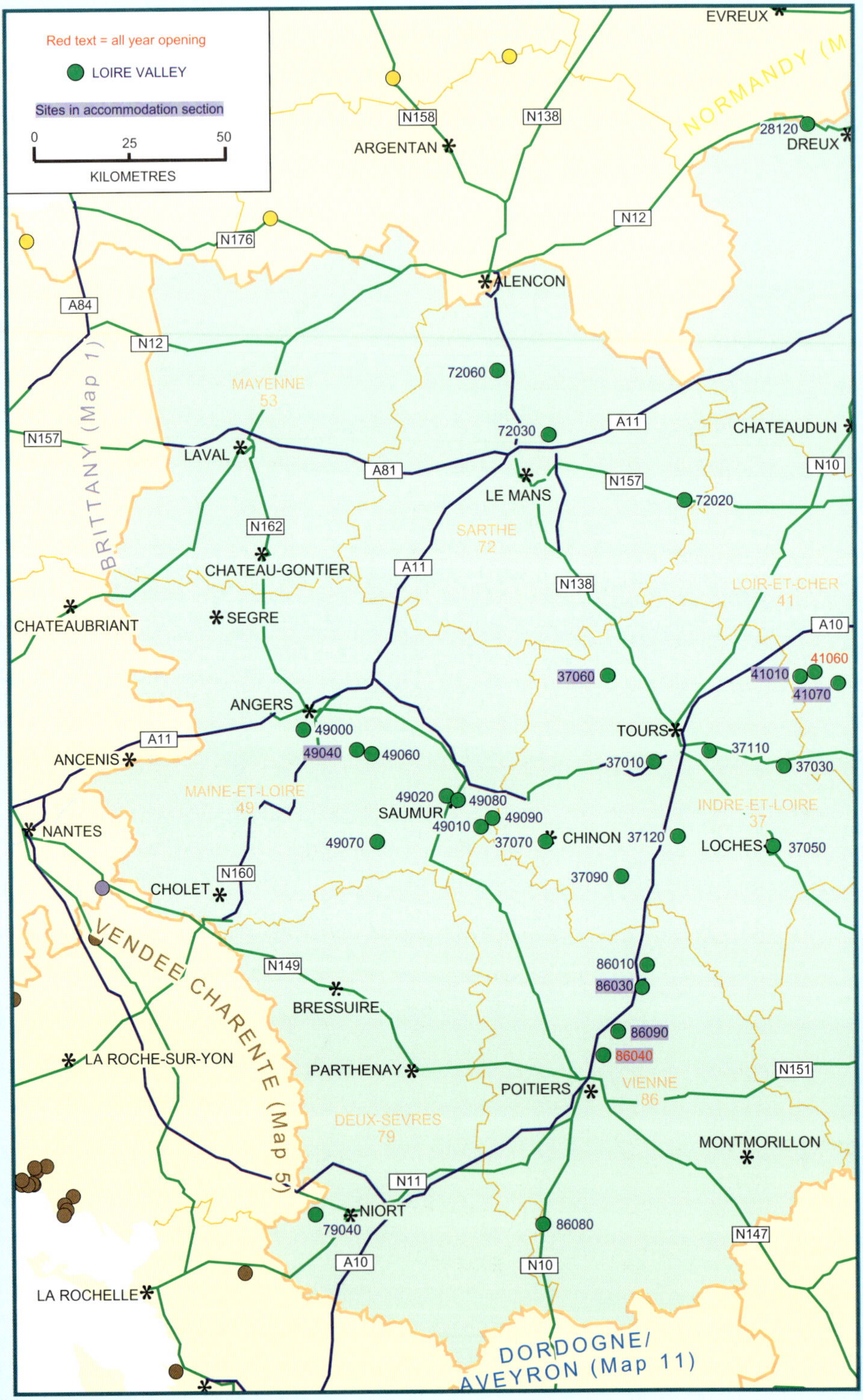

Please refer to the numerical index for campsite page reference

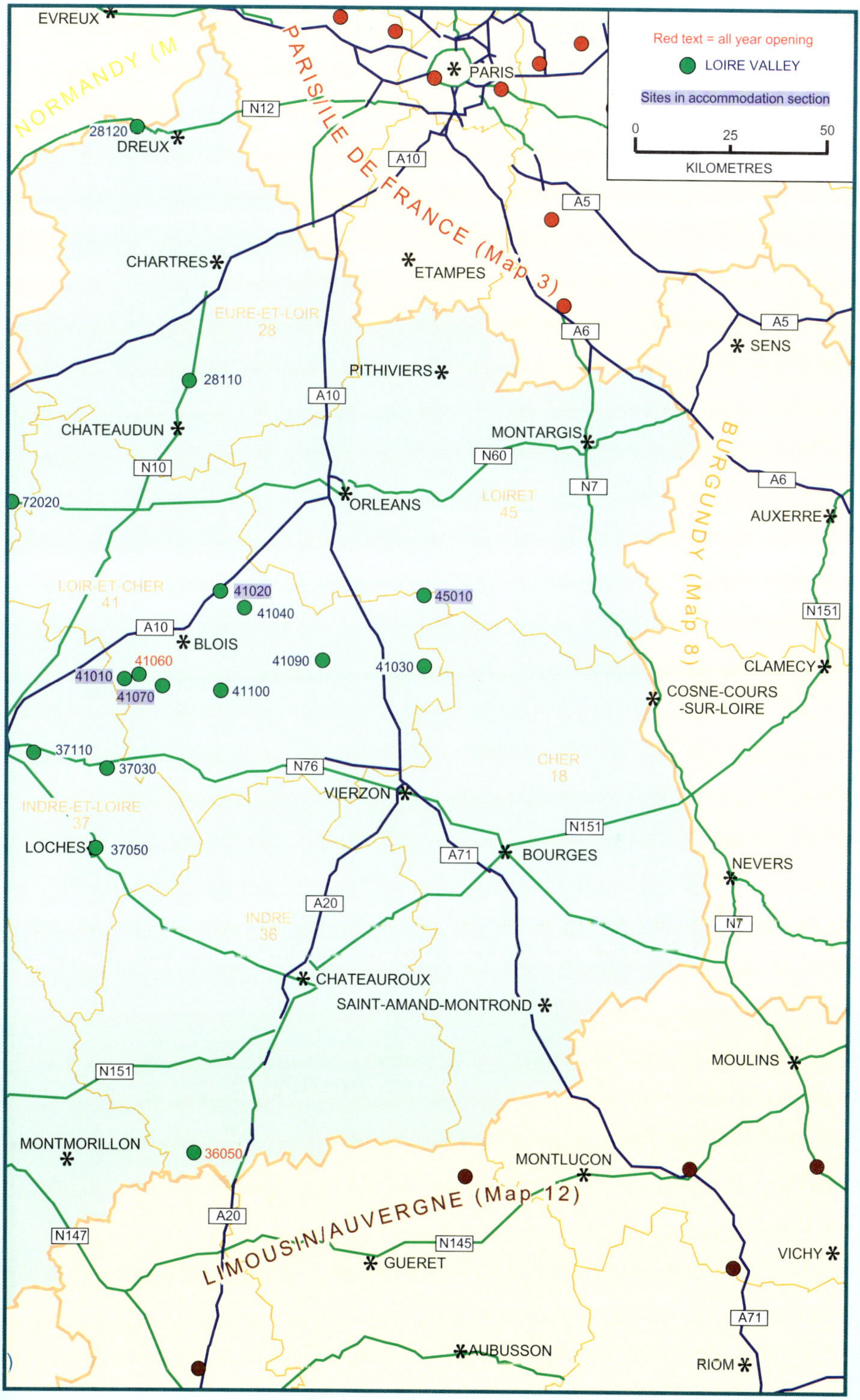

Please refer to the numerical index for campsite page reference

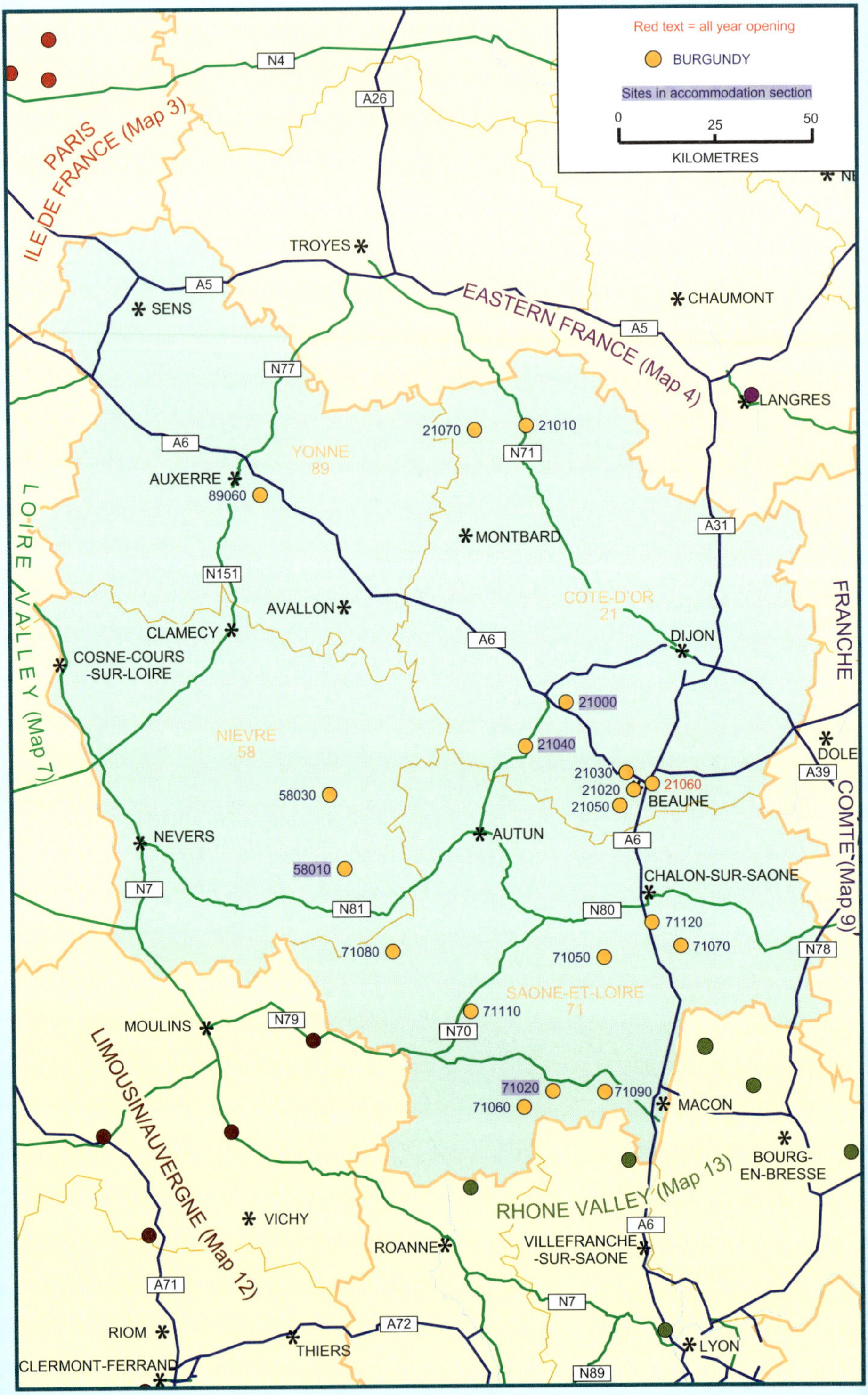

Please refer to the numerical index for campsite page reference

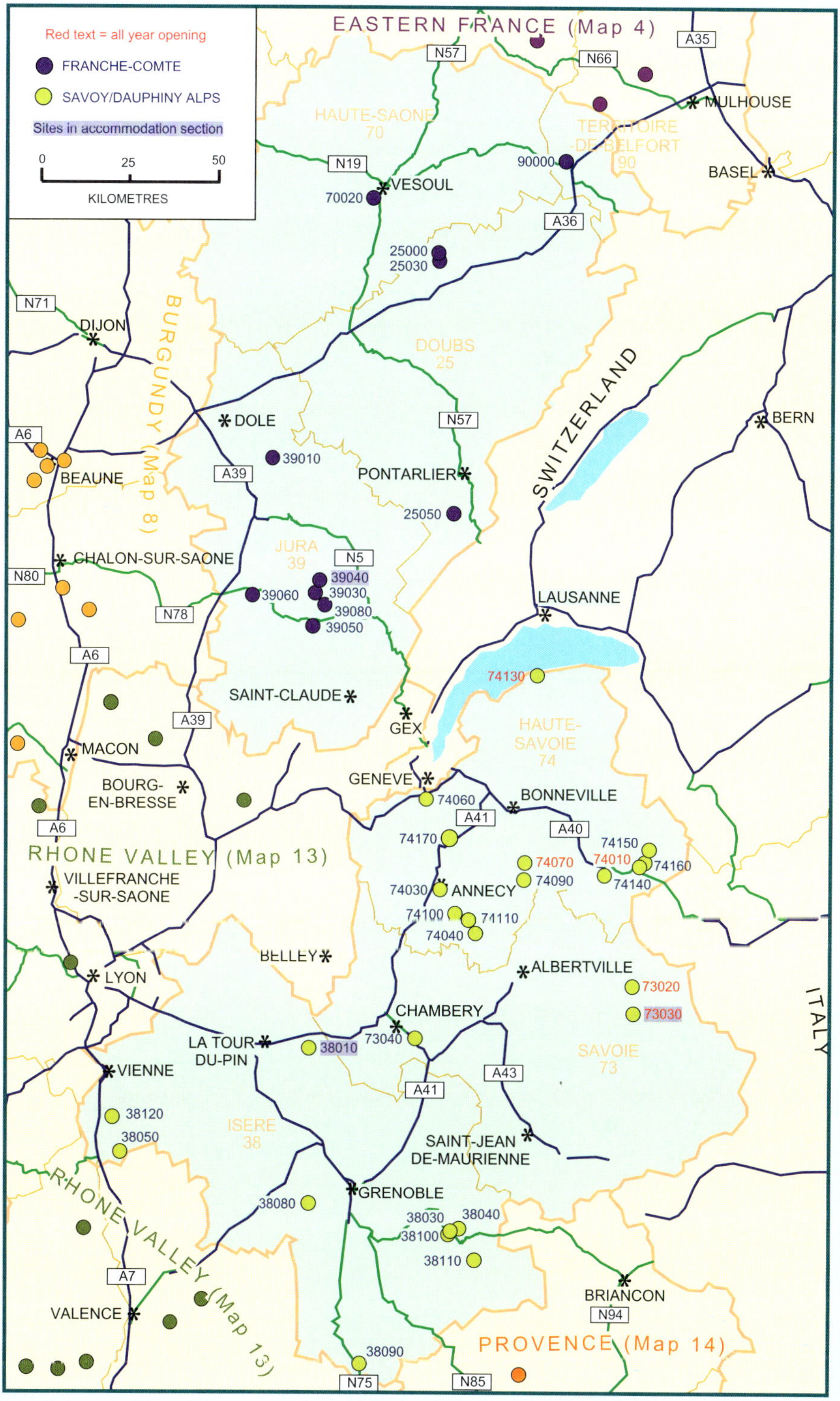

Please refer to the numerical index for campsite page reference

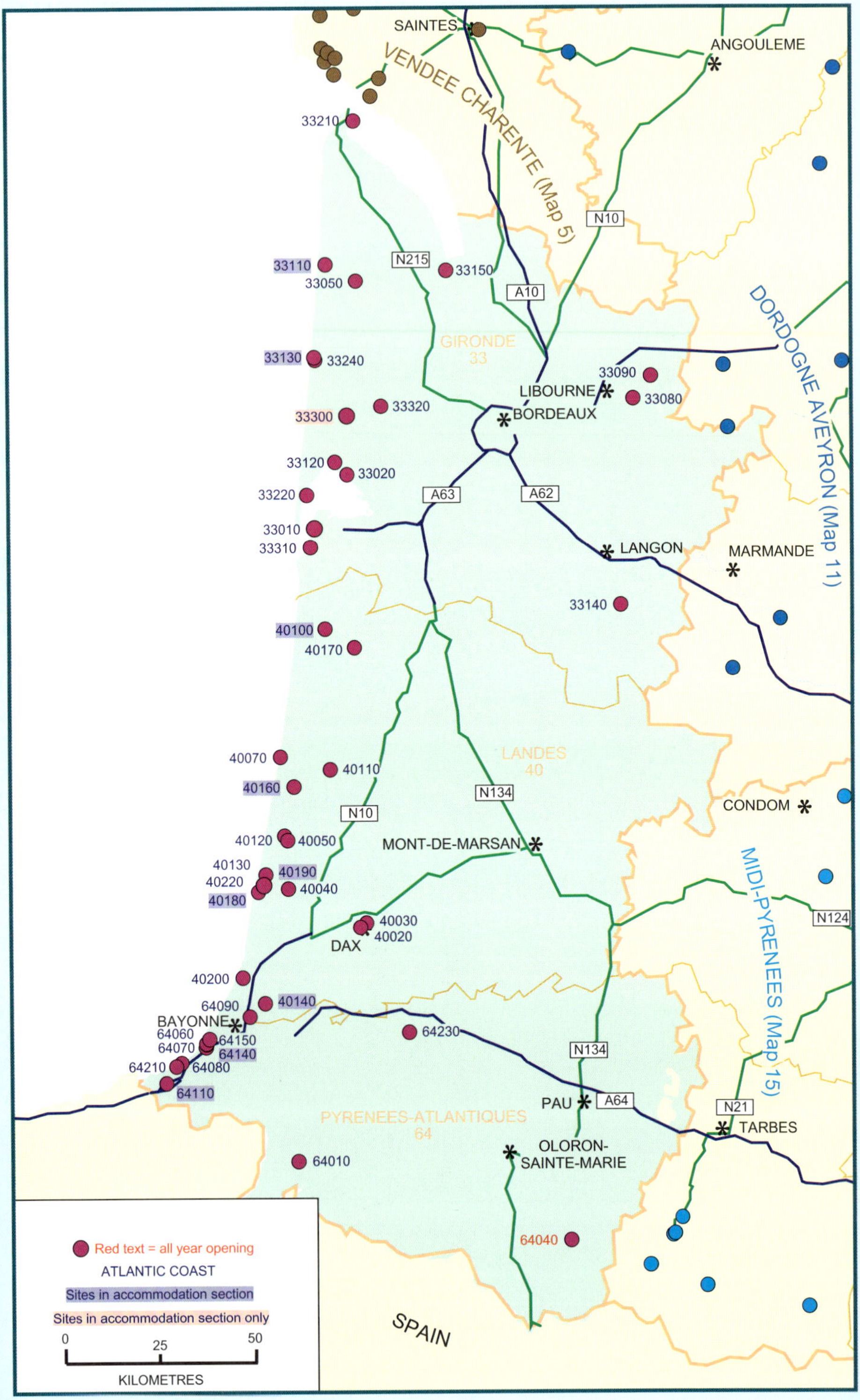

Please refer to the numerical index for campsite page reference

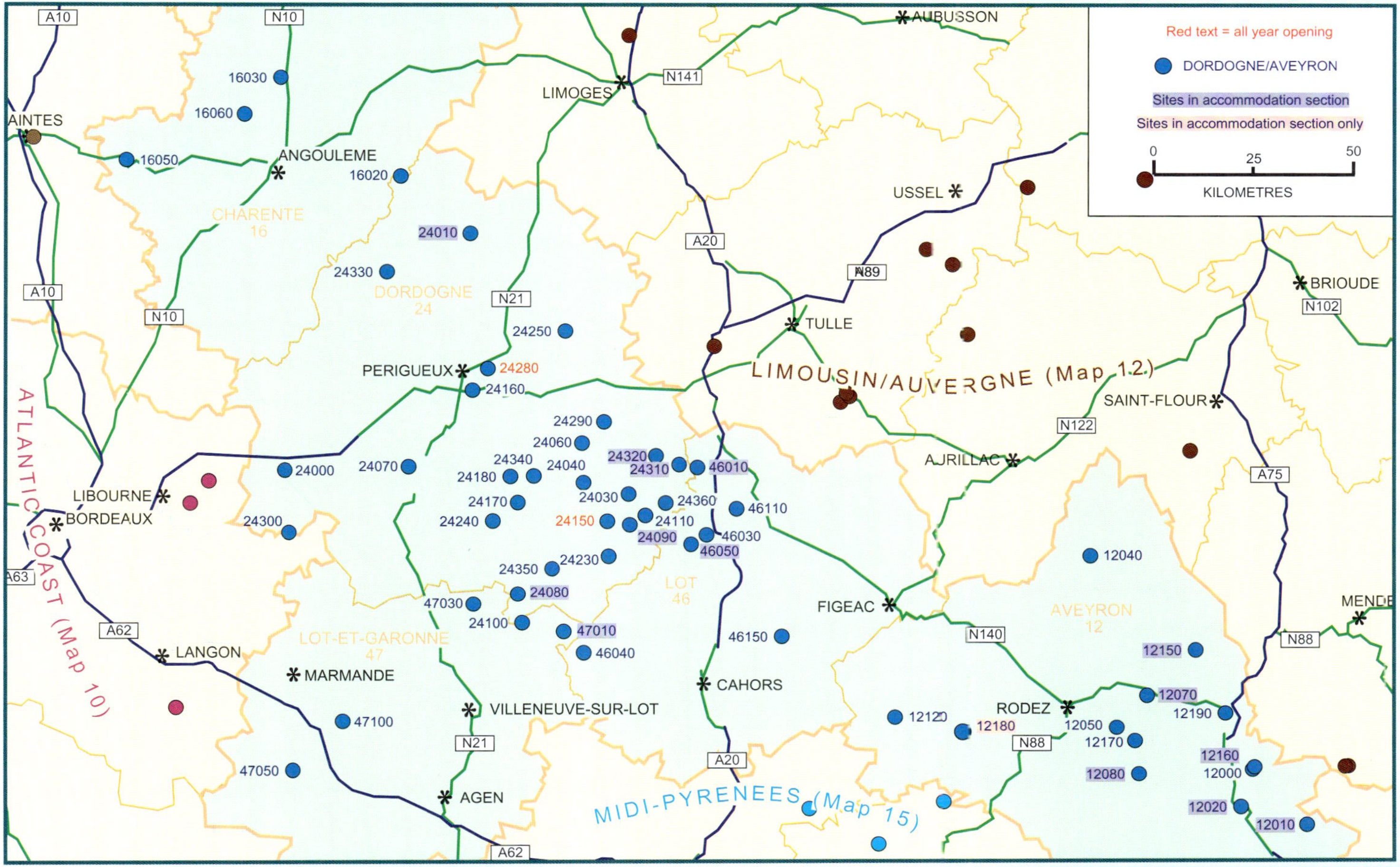

Please refer to the numerical index for campsite page reference

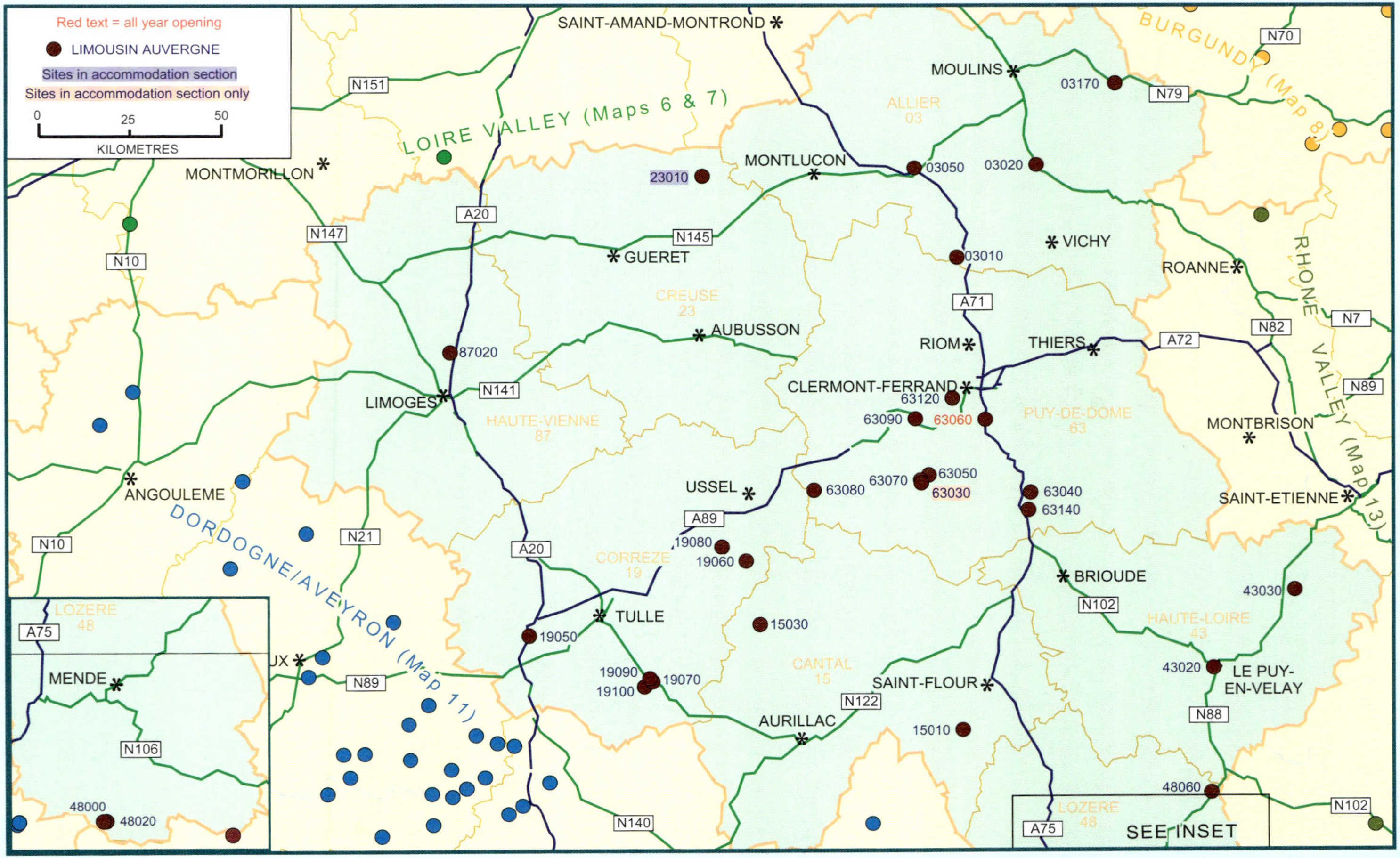

Please refer to the numerical index for campsite page reference

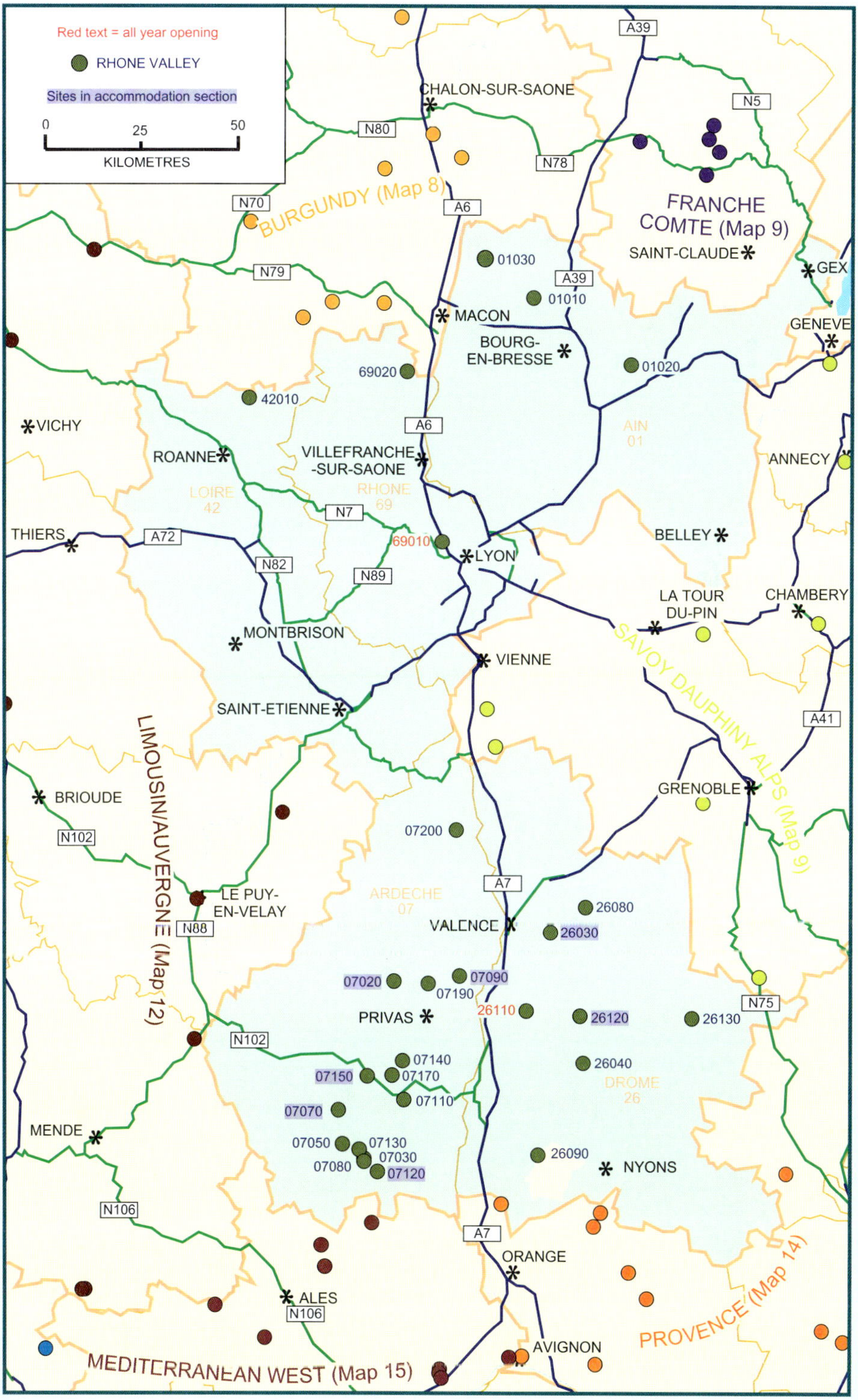

Please refer to the numerical index for campsite page reference

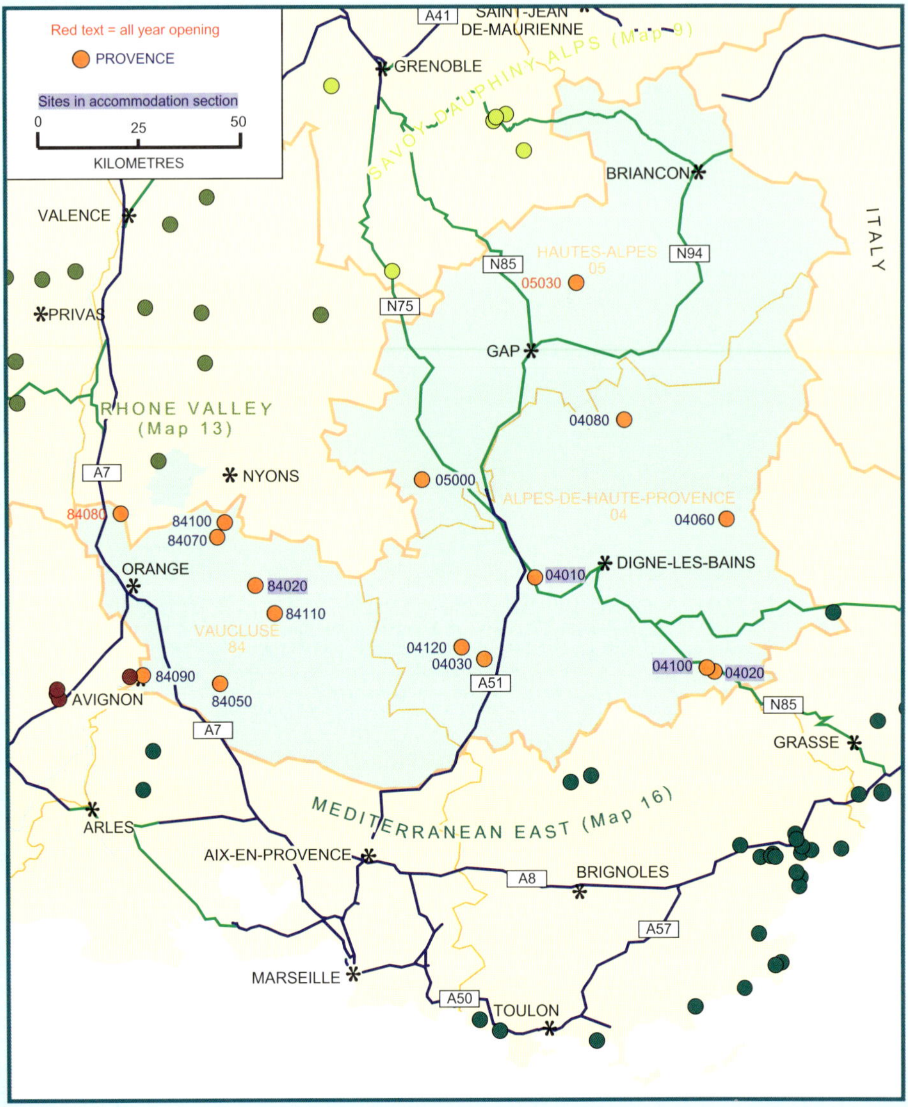

Please refer to the numerical index for campsite page reference

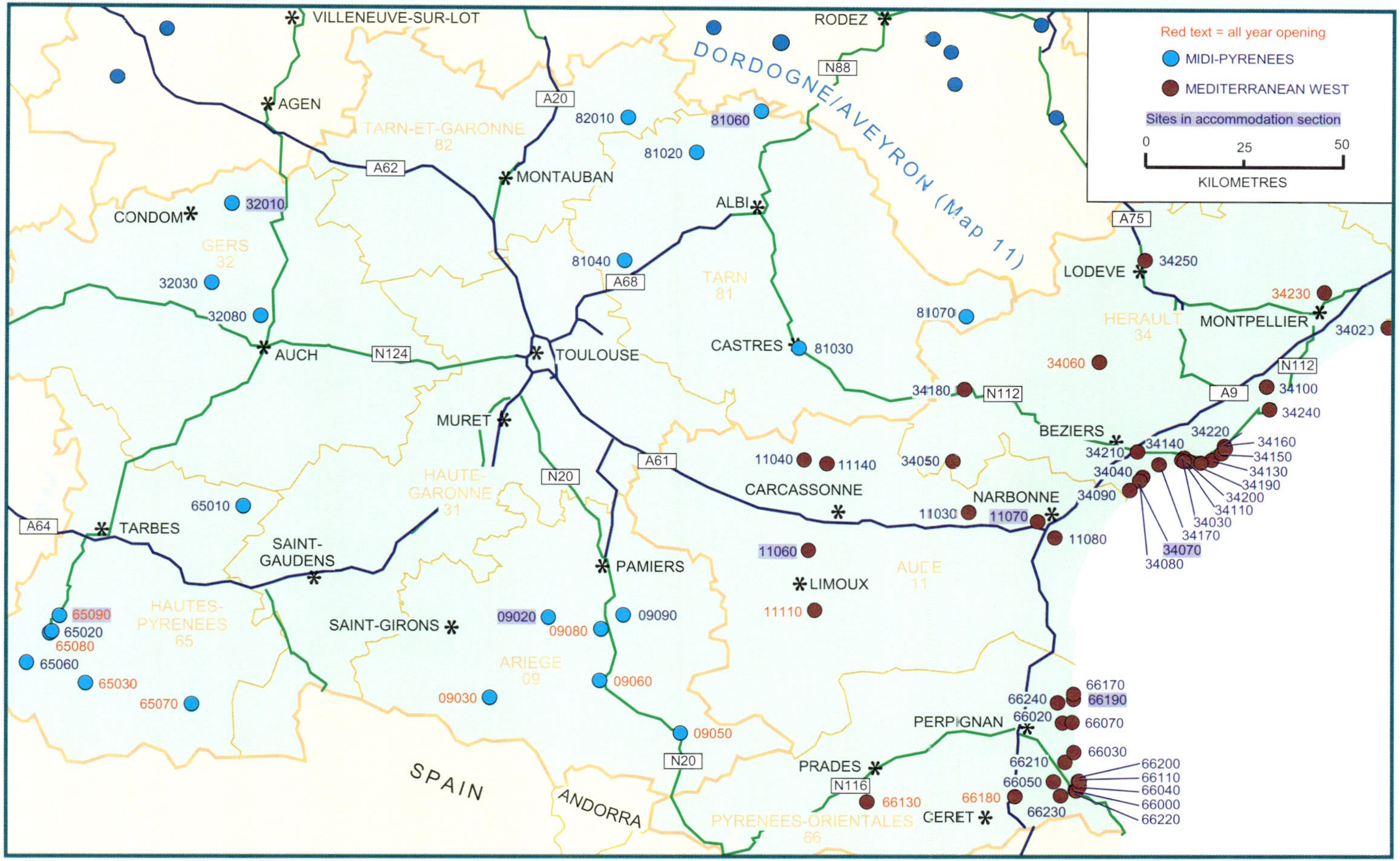

Please refer to the numerical index for campsite page reference

Mediterranean & Corsica Map 16

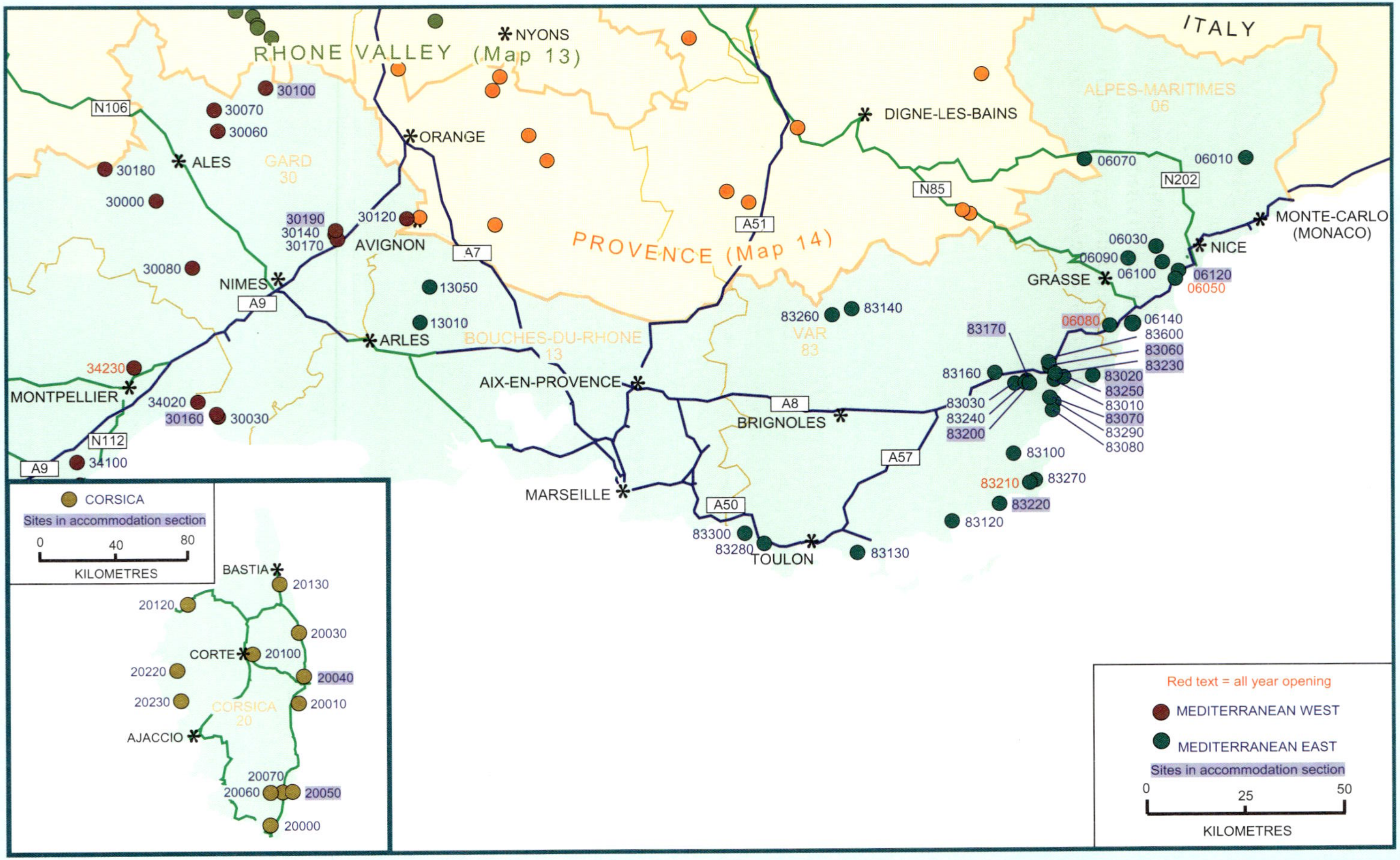

Please refer to the numerical index for campsite page reference

For administrative purposes France is actually divided into 23 official Regions covering the 95 départements (similar to our counties).

However, theses do not always coincide with the needs of tourists (for example, the area we think of as the 'Dordogne' is split between two official regions. We have, therefore, opted to feature our campsites within unofficial 'tourist' regions.

We use the departement numbers as the first two digits of our campsite numbers so, for example, any site in the Manche departement will start with the number 50.

TOWN AND VILLAGE INDEX

INDEX OF ADVERTISERS

MOBILE HOMES & CHALETS INDEX

Tell Us About the Alan Rogers Guides!

We're keen to constantly improve our service to you and the key to this is information. If we don't know what makes our readers 'tick' then it's difficult to offer you more of what you want.

WIN A COMPLETE SET OF ALAN ROGERS GUIDES

Return this completed questionnaire and you could win a complete set of 2006 Alan Rogers Guides. Why not complete an on-line version of this? Go to www.alanrogers.com/feedback

About the Alan Rogers Guides

1 **For how many years have you used the Alan Rogers Guides?**

Never 1-2 yrs 3-6 yrs 7-10 yrs Over 10 yrs

2 **How frequently do you refer to it?**

Never Each year Every 2 yrs Every 3 yrs

3 **How frequently do you buy a new copy?**

Never Each year Every 2 yrs Every 3 yrs

4 **If you lend it to friends, how many others might refer to it?**

1 2 3 4 Over 4

5 **Please rate the Alan Rogers Guides on a scale of 1–10 where 10 is excellent and 1 is extremely poor**

1 2 3 4 5 6 7 8 9 10

6 **Do you have any comments about the Alan Rogers Guides?**

....

....

7 **What do you consider to be the best thing about the guides?**

Independent reviews Honest descriptions Accurate information Range of sites Depth of information

Other ....

8 **What do you consider to be the worst thing about the guides?**

....

9 **How many sites featured in the guides have you visited in the past?** *(best estimate)* ....

10 **Can you comment on any other campsite guides?**

Title .... Your opinion ....

About Your Holidays

11 **a) Do you own any of the following?**

Caravan Motorhome Trailer Tent Tent

Other *(please specify)* ....

b) How many times a year do you use it?

1 2-3 4-6 7-10 More than 10

12 **When on holiday, do you participate in any of the following?**

Fishing Golf Cycling Sailing/Boating Walking Bird Watching

Other *(please specify)* ....

13 **How many years have you been camping / caravanning?**

3 yrs or less 4 – 7 yrs 8 – 12 yrs 13 – 15 yrs 16 – 20 yrs Over 20 yrs

WIN A COMPLETE SET OF ALAN ROGERS GUIDES

WIN A COMPLETE SET OF ALAN ROGERS GUIDES

About You

Mr/Mrs/Ms, etc. Initial Surname

Address

Post code

e-mail address @ Telephone

14 **Your age** 30 and under 31-50 51-65 Over 65

15 **Do you have children – if so, how old is the youngest?**
6 and under 7-12 Over 12

16 **Do you work (full or part time)?** Yes No

17 **Are you retired?** Yes No

About Your Leisure Time

18 **Are you a member of any caravan/motorhome clubs?**
The Caravan Club The Camping & Caravanning Club The Motor Caravanners Club

Other *(please specify)*

19 **Are you a member of the following?**
National Trust English Heritage RSPB CSMA Ramblers

20 **Which (if any) camping/caravanning magazines do you read regularly?**
MMM Practical Motorhome Practical Caravan Caravan Life Which Motorcaravan Motor-caravan Caravan

21 **Which other magazines do you read regularly?**

22 **Which newspapers do you read regularly?**
Express Mail Telegraph Times Guardian Observer Sun

Other (please specify)

23 **Do you enjoy any particular hobbies?** *(please specify)*

24 **Do you have regular access to the internet?** Yes No

If yes, which camping/caravanning websites do you visit regularly?

And Finally

25 **Do you have any useful camping/caravanning tips?**

26 **If you could change one thing about camping/caravanning holidays what would it be?**

We may wish to publish your comments, please tick this box if you would prefer us not to.

Might you be interested in becoming an Alan Rogers site inspector?
If so, please tick the box and we will send you further information

Camping Cheque and Alan Rogers may use this data to send you information and Special Offers. Please tick here if you do not wish to receive such information

Thank you very much for your time and trouble in completing this questionnaire

Please return to: Alan Rogers Travel Service, FREEPOST NAT17734, Cranbrook, TN17 1BR